Death in Jewish Life

Studia Judaica

Forschungen zur Wissenschaft des Judentums

Begründet von
Ernst Ludwig Ehrlich

Herausgegeben von
Günter Stemberger, Charlotte Fonrobert
und Alexander Samely

Band 78

Rethinking Diaspora

Edited by
Stefan C. Reif, Simha Goldin and Andreas Lehnardt

Volume 1

Death in Jewish Life

Burial and Mourning Customs Among Jews
of Europe and Nearby Communities

Edited by
Stefan C. Reif, Andreas Lehnardt and
Avriel Bar-Levav

DE GRUYTER

The subseries Rethinking Diaspora is published on behalf of the Goldstein-Goren Diaspora Research Center, Tel Aviv University.

ISBN 978-3-11-055216-4
e-ISBN 978-3-11-033918-5
ISSN 0585-5306

Library of Congress Cataloging-in-Publication Data
A CIP catalog record for this book has been applied for at the Library of Congress.

Bibliographic information published by the Deutsche Nationalbibliothek
The Deutsche Nationalbibliothek lists this publication in the Deutsche Nationalbibliografie; detailed bibliographic data are available in the Internet at http://dnb.dnb.de.

This volume is text- and page-identical with the hardback published in 2014.
Typesetting: Meta Systems Publishing & Printservices GmbH, Wustermark
Printing and binding: CPI books GmbH, Leck
♾ Printed on acid-free paper
Printed in Germany

www.degruyter.com

Dedicated to the cherished memory of
Shulie Reif (1945–2010)
who left a treasured legacy to those
among whom she lived, loved and laboured

לזכר נשמתה של מרת
שולמית דבורה בת מאיר ואסתר
עזר כנגד אישה
טוב טעם ודעת לימדתנו

Editors' Foreword

The need to enhance the study of Jewish attitudes towards death in their broadest aspects was recognized and discussed in 2007 by Simha Goldin and Stefan Reif. They decided to organize a conference, and set up an international steering committee composed of Andreas Lehnardt, Avriel Bar-Levav and Uri Ehrlich, as well as themselves, chaired by Stefan Reif.

The conference was held at the Cymbalista Jewish Heritage Center and the Lester and Sally Entin Faculty of Humanities of Tel Aviv University on 10–12 May 2010, with the aid of the Johannes Gutenberg University, Mainz, and under the auspices of the Goldstein-Goren Diaspora Research Center at Tel Aviv University. A total of twenty-two papers were delivered, in English and in Hebrew, the latter in the context of a Workshop devoted to 'Reading Gravestones as Texts', directed by Avriel Bar-Levav. The present volume represents the outcome of that conference, with some minor omissions and significant additions.

Frederick Paxton, whose keynote address provided the necessary background in the medieval Christian world for the whole topic of the conference, was also kind enough to respond favourably to the editors' request to append to his paper some comments on the texts of all the other presentations that are included here. This was greatly appreciated.

The editors wish to thank all those individuals and institutions who contributed to the success of the conference and the preparation of the volume, especially Sara Appel, Ora Azta and other staff at the Goldstein-Goren Diaspora Research Center. They are also grateful to Dvora Bregman and Menahem Schmelzer for reviewing the manuscript and to the Johannes Gutenberg University, Mainz, and to the Harry and Gertrude Landy Charitable Trust for their support. They would also like to express their thanks to Albrecht Döhnert for establishing the Rethinking Diaspora Sub-Series at De Gruyter Publishing House, and to the editors of the Studia Judaica Series – Charlotte Fonrobert, Alexander Samely, and Günther Stemberger – for kindly accepting the volume as the first in the new Sub-Series.

SCR
AL
ABL

List of Acknowledgements

1. To the Jewish Theological Seminary in New York for permission to reproduce figures 1 and 9 in the article by Mauro Perani.

2. To the work *Eletta dei monumenti più illustri e classici*, published in Bologna in 1840, volume II, for figure 20 in the article by Mauro Perani.

3. To Brooklyn Museum, Gift of the Ernest Erickson Foundation, Inc., for permission to reproduce figure 6 in the article by Minna Rozen.

4. To Christie's Inc for permission to reproduce figure 9 in the article by Minna Rozen.

5. To the William Gross Collection, Tel Aviv, for permission to reproduce figure 16 in the article by Minna Rozen.

6. To the Walters Art Museum, Baltimore, for permission to reproduce figure 17 in the article by Minna Rozen.

7. To the Beinecke Rare Book and Manuscript Library, Yale University, for permission to reproduce figure 18 in the article by Minna Rozen.

8. To Professor Yaakov Bentolila and Professor Dvora Bregman for their kind assistance with the preparation of the article by Mauro Perani.

The rights to all the other figures reproduced in the volume belong to the authors of the articles in which they appear.

Contents

Editors' Foreword — vii

List of Acknowledgements — ix

The Contributors and Summaries of their Essays — xiii

Section 1: **Death in Life — 1**

Avriel Bar-Levav
Jewish Attitudes towards Death: A Society between Time, Space and Texts — 3

Frederick S. Paxton
The Early Growth of the Medieval Economy of Salvation in Latin Christianity — 17

Stefan C. Reif
A Response to Professor Paxton's Paper — 43

Shmuel Shepkaru
From Here to the Hereafter: The Ashkenazi Concept of the Afterlife in a Crusading Milieu — 51

Section 2: **Texts in Society — 63**

Andreas Lehnardt
Christian Influences on the *Yahrzeit Qaddish* — 65

Ruth Langer
Investigation into the Early European Forms of the *Ṣidduq ha-Din* — 79

Peter Sh. Lehnardt
***Ha-Ṣur Tamim be-khol Po'al*: On some Italian roots of the Poetic *Ṣidduq Ha-Din* in the Early Ashkenazi rite — 99**

Joseph Isaac Lifshitz
***Av ha-raḥamim*: On the 'Father of Mercy' Prayer — 141**

Abraham Gross
Liturgy as Personal Memorial for the Victims in 1096 — 155

Yechiel Y. Schur
'When the Grave was Searched, the Bones of the Deceased were not found': Corporeal Revenants in Medieval Ashkenaz — 171

Nati Barak
The Early Ashkenazi Practice of Burial wih Religious Paraphernalia — 187

Section 3: **Re-Placing the Dead — 197**

Avraham (Rami) Reiner
The Dead as Living History: On the Publication of *Die Grabsteine vom jüdischen Friedhof in Würzburg 1147–1346* — 199

Nathanja Hüttenmeister and Andreas Lehnardt
Newly Found Medieval Gravestones from Magenza — 213

David Malkiel
The Structures of Hebrew Epitaph Poetry in Padua — 225

Mauro Perani
The *Corpus Epitaphiorum Hebraicorum Italiae* (CEHI): A Project to Publish a Complete Corpus of the Epitaphs Preserved in Italian Jewish Cemeteries — 241

Minna Rozen
Romans in Istanbul. Part 1: Historical and Literary Introduction — 289

Minna Rozen
Romans in Istanbul. Part 2: Texts and Photographs — 327

Indexes — 359
- Primary Sources — **359**
- Names — **367**
- Subjects — **373**

Details of the Contributors, with Summaries of their Essays

Avriel Bar-Levav is Senior Lecturer in Judaic Studies in the Department of History, Philosophy and Judaic Studies at the Open University of Israel, and editor of *Pe'amim: Studies in Oriental Jewry*, published by the Ben-Zvi Institute, Jerusalem, Israel.

Bar-Levav offers a framework for depicting and understanding the varied Jewish attitudes towards death, particularly in the medieval period. The author differentiates between death as an idea and death as a reality, and between the presence and absence of death. He suggests that, by and large, death is marginal in the framework of Jewish culture. Jewish attitudes towards death can be anchored between time, space and texts. There is a time of mourning and remembrance, there is a place for the dead (the cemetery), and there are distinct texts that are used in the contexts of dying and mourning. The paper describes various axes along which ideas about death may be perceived: death as punishment or desideratum; the amalgamation of the personality during life and its disintegration in death; the relationship between this world and the world to come; the connection of the soul and the body; and the burial society as a social and religious organization. Death offers a moral perspective on life, and this is also connected with the comprehension of dying as a life passage, and with the construction of the idea of the proper death.

Frederick S. Paxton is the Brigida Pacchiani Ardenghi Professor of History at Connecticut College, in New London, Connecticut, U.S.A.

Paxton's paper attempts to gather together the myriad social and religious behaviours around death, dying and commemoration of the dead in the Latin Christian Middle Ages within a common conceptual framework: the medieval economy of salvation. He argues that the medieval economy of salvation grew out of the patristic notion of the divine economy, whereby God's gift of his son's life opened up a path to eternal salvation for humankind, to eventually encompass the transfer of people, goods, lands and incomes from private hands to religious communities in exchange for masses, psalms, prayers and alms for the poor, which were then offered to God in return for the salvation of the souls of the donors and their families. Paxton's particular focus is on the early growth of the economy of salvation, which culminated in the extraordinary success of the Benedictine Abbey of Cluny in the eleventh century and twelfth centuries.

Stefan C. Reif is Emeritus Professor of Medieval Hebrew Studies and Fellow of St John's College at the University of Cambridge, U.K.

Reif began his response to Paxton's keynote address by stressing the need for Jewish scholars clinically to investigate the reasons, both theological and more general, for the revolutionary developments in death liturgy, especially among the Ashkenazi communities of the high Middle Ages. He stressed the major contribution made by pre-medieval and medieval Jewish teachers to liturgical development, how closely related Jewish trends were to their Christian counterparts, and the link made in the rabbinic sources, especially in liturgical custom, between prayers for the dead and charitable gifts. Reif also pointed to the tensions between halakhists and philosophers on one side of the religious spectrum and mystics on the other with regard to customs appertaining to burial and cemeteries. His concluding remarks drew parallels between Christian and Jewish periods of mourning, trends towards standardization and the composition of special benedictions for those who performed special communal tasks.

Shmuel Shepkaru is Associate Professor of Judaic History at the University of Oklahoma, U.S.A.

This article points out that the three Hebrew accounts pertaining to the massacres of the Ashkenazi Jews during the First Crusade do not mention resurrection when discussing the afterlife of the Jewish victims. Given the centrality of the doctrine of resurrection in rabbinic Judaism and the high probability that the authors of these Ashkenazi accounts were rabbis themselves, the absence of resurrection in these accounts is intriguing. As the references to talmudic, midrashic, and biblical texts (Daniel 12) that do mention resurrection suggest, the Ashkenazi accounts intentionally avoided resurrection. This article proposes several reasons for this absence. By ascribing to the victims an immediate reward in heaven, the accounts vindicated God and the victims, thus addressing the question of theodicy. Other factors were the role resurrection played in the attempts to impose forced conversion on the Jews, and in the Christian propaganda of the First Crusade in general.

Andreas Lehnardt is Professor of Jewish Studies at the Faculty of Protestant Theology, Johannes Gutenberg-University, Mainz, Germany.

This article deals with the late custom of reciting an additional *qaddish* to commemorate the anniversary of a parent's death. As often noted, Ya'aqov ben Moshe Moellin ('Maharil') was apparently the first to mention the custom. The term *yahrzeit* already occurs in the responsa of the Austrian, Rabbi Shalom of Wiener Neustadt, a teacher of the Maharil. Significantly, at the very time when *yahrzeit* customs were being adopted by Ashkenazi Jews in the thirteenth-fourteenth centuries, comparable developments were occurring in Catholic Christianity. The paper therefore goes on to deal with Christian sources that provide insights into the development of similar liturgical usages relating to the *Paternoster* or Lord's Prayer in the fourteenth century. While there may not exist a direct and demonstrable Christian influence on the Jewish liturgical practice, the evolution of a similar custom in the same region and under similar circumstances may indicate how a dominant Christian environment could have left its imprint on a smaller religious group operating within it.

Ruth Langer is Professor of Jewish Studies in the Theology Department at Boston College and Associate Director of its Center for Christian-Jewish Learning, U.S.A.

Although the prayer's origins remain unknown, European Jews, by the time of the Rishonim, expected that recitation of the liturgical composition known as *Ṣidduq ha-Din* would be a central element of burial rituals. Its conclusion with biblical verses provided the liturgical context for the recitation of *qaddish* at the burial itself. After discussing the evidence for the prayer in early and high medieval rabbinic literature, this paper presents critical studies of the manuscript evidence for the prayer's specific forms in the various high medieval rites of Ashkenaz, France, and Spain. This data in turn allows identification of the core literary and ideational features of the text and an understanding of how various communities elaborated upon it and transformed its meaning. The prayer moves from simply accepting God's justice in the face of death, to meditating on divine justice and mercy more broadly, and to petitioning for divine mercy for the living community.

Peter Sh. Lehnardt is Senior Lecturer in Medieval Hebrew Literature in the Department of Hebrew Literature at Ben-Gurion University of the Negev, Beersheba, Israel.

This paper intends to illuminate the use in Ashkenaz of the poetic *Ṣidduq Ha-Din*, namely, *Ha-Ṣur Tamim Be-Khol Po'al*, in the context of its forming a part of the composite burial ceremony in the rite of Rome. To that end, it includes an annotated, critical edition of the textual part of the burial ceremony that goes back to Apulia in the eighth and ninth centuries and that was used and transmitted in Italy throughout the Middle Ages and up to the seventeenth century under the heading of *Ṣidduq Ha-Din*. The different textual elements of this *agenda mortuorum* are then considered and evaluated according to the relevant literary history of liturgical poetry and as parts of the burial ceremony as a *rite de passage* for the dead and *mutatis mutandis* for the mourning community.

Joseph Isaac Lifshitz is Senior Fellow at the Shalem Center, Jerusalem, and a Fellow at the Goldstein-Goren Diaspora Research Center, Tel Aviv University, Israel.

The prayer, *Av ha-raḥamim* ('Father of Mercy'), recited to this day in Ashkenazi communities during the Sabbath morning prayers, is mentioned in the Worms community records as a prayer that was composed in memory of those killed in the riots that took place during the First Crusade. This paper demonstrates how *Av ha-raḥamim*, which may initially have been composed as a memorial prayer, had much deeper theological meanings ascribed to it in later periods. It was these theological meanings that gave *Av ha-raḥamim* the importance that it has carried into our own day. The first was the idea of revenge as a proof of the existence of a just God. The second perceived the martyrs as holy figures – not mere mortals who required mercy – and their memory became a source of strength for the Jews, not only when facing their Christian neighbours, but primarily when facing the Creator Himself.

Abraham Gross is Professor in the Department of Jewish History at Ben-Gurion University of the Negev, Beersheba, Israel.

The massacres of the Jewish communities in Germany at the hands of the Crusaders, and the collective suicides arising out of that persecution, during the spring of 1096, have been recorded in Jewish and Christian sources, mainly in the form of chronicles. This article deals with another type of literature composed in the wake of those tragic events, namely, Jewish liturgical verse [*piyyuṭ*]. The author highlights aspects of memory and memorialization embedded in that essentially religious poetry. It is claimed that the significant corpus of 1096 liturgy, which describes graphically the bloody events, and hints at specific facts and individual martyrs, reflects the social and emotional needs of the first and second generation of survivors for memorialization of the events and of the victims. Those needs, it is claimed, are not so different from those with which we are familiar in our own day, although the medieval medium of expression discussed here is characteristically a more religious one.

Yechiel Y. Schur teaches at the University of Pennsylvania and is Klatt Family Director for Public Programs at its Herbert D. Katz Center for Advanced Judaic Studies, Philadelphia, U.S.A.

While Jews in medieval Ashkenaz clearly believed in the bodily resurrection of the dead in the days to come, certain Jews – like their Christian counterparts – also believed in revenants, that is, in dead bodies coming alive in the immediate period after death. Moreover, like Christians, some Ashkenazi Jews, including leading rabbis, believed that revenants are composed of actual corporeal elements of the deceased and are not merely spiritual entities (like ghosts), lacking tangible, corporeal elements. Following a brief survey of the topic in rabbinic texts, this paper considers references to revenants in exegetic texts, halakhic works, and paradigmatic stories, primarily from the thirteenth and fourteenth centuries. The overall aim of the paper is to demonstrate the novelty of these Ashkenazi views and the degree to which Jews and Christians held common views on revenants.

Nati Barak lectures in the Overseas Students Program at Tel Aviv University, Israel. He spent a year at the Hochschule fur Jüdische Studien in Heidelberg, and is currently a high school principal.

The article discusses the burial of the deceased together with items of spiritual value and covers the two centuries following the Black Death. Attention is centred on the changes in ritual and in the perception of death in the Ashkenazi communities of Germany and northern France, as reported in halakhic and historical sources deriving from Austria. While in generations preceding the Black Death requests for the burial of items of special value were fulfilled at the time of interment, a subsequent custom was also to permit this at a later date by opening the grave and placing the item inside it, while adhering to explicit rabbinical instructions. Through such an act, the surviving family could remain in a form of physical contact with the deceased, as well as striving for a spiritual connection with them by praying or giving charity for their souls. The sealing of the grave was not then necessarily final.

Avraham (Rami) Reiner lectures in the Department of Jewish Thought at Ben-Gurion University of the Negev, Beersheba, Israel.

This article begins by describing the major discovery of some 1,500 Jewish tombstones from 1147–1346 in Würzburg, Germany, in 1988. In spite of the size of this collection and the existence of lists of those killed in the Second Crusade (1147) and in the pogroms of 1298, there are difficulties about drawing conclusions, especially demographic, from this collection. Three women's tombstones are then considered. Two are of daughters of noted rabbinic families, one of whom, the grand-daughter of Rabbi Eli'ezer ben Nathan ('Raban') of Mainz, died during childbirth. Most surprising is that of a convert who died in the mid-thirteenth century, and whose tombstone's wording reflects the cultural world of her earlier faith. The article concludes with details of tombstones of Jews who died at the hands of Christians 'in sanctifying the Name' (of God). Although other tombstones have the usual blessings or wishes for the deceased as they enter into their eternal rest, these do not. The author offers a possible explanation for this phenomenon.

Nathanja Hüttenmeister M.A. is a research assistant at the Salomon Ludwig Steinheim-Institute for German-Jewish History at the University of Duisburg-Essen, Germany.

The Jewish cemetery of Mainz is one of the oldest Jewish cemeteries of medieval Ashkenaz. When the Jews were expelled from Mainz in 1438, the gravestones were spoilt and used for building purposes. In 1449, the premises were partly returned to the Jewish community that had returned to Mainz, and they served that community until 1880. Over 200 medieval Jewish gravestones have been found in Mainz in the last two hundred years, dating from the years 1049 to 1421, among them a stone from the year 1049, which is the oldest Jewish gravestone ever found in Germany. Most of the gravestones have been returned to their places of origin and assembled in a field adjacent to the Jewish cemetery, constituting a 'memorial cemetery'. In 2008, additional gravestones from the end of the eleventh to the middle of the thirteenth century were discovered, together with some fragments. These stones are discussed in this paper.

David Malkiel is Professor in the Israel and Golda Koschitzky Department of Jewish History at Bar-Ilan University, Ramat Gan, Israel, and has recently completed a study of the tombstones of Paduan Jewry, 1529–1862.

Hebrew epitaph poetry becomes the norm in sixteenth-century Italy and remains popular for nearly three centuries. This study focuses on its appearance in Padua in the mid-cinquecento, as the reception of the epitaph poem reflects the acculturation to the Italian environment of the largely Ashkenazi constituency. The sixteenth and seventeenth centuries are the heyday of the epitaph poem in Padua, in quantity and quality, and this article surveys the form and content of this body of literature in the various phases of its development. This period is followed by one of stagnation and enervation in the eighteenth century, when the epitaph poem is ubiquitous but no longer creative. The epitaph is radically redesigned in the early nineteenth century, from approximately 1820. Prose inscriptions replace the poems, and these are more personalized, underlining the new importance of the individual in the modern era.

Mauro Gabriele Perani is Professor of Hebrew at the University of Bologna, Italy, and a former President of the European Association for Jewish Studies.

Perani introduces the Corpus Epitaphiorum Hebraicorum Italiae (CEHI), a project founded by him to publish a complete corpus of the epitaphs preserved in Italian Jewish cemeteries of the sixteenth–nineteenth centuries. In the Barocco period and later, the art of writing Hebrew epitaphs, true or fictitious, commissioned by relatives or written for himself as a personal after-death-memory, became a discrete literary genre, formulated in rhyme and rhythm by rabbis and learned scholars. This poetical feature is typically Italian, and the epitaphs often constitute a true *diwan* of poetry, as well as an important source for historical and genealogical study. Perani also illustrates the evolution, language and style of Italian Jewish epitaphs as well as their palaeographical development and stylistic characteristics. This source, testifying to the concept of the death in the Italian Jewish communities, may be integrated with other manuscript evidence such as personal records or the statutes of charitable fraternities charged with burying the dead.

Minna Rozen is Professor in the Department of Jewish History at the University of Haifa, Israel, and specializes in the history of the early modern and modern Mediterranean.

Rozen pursues several avenues of research arising from the systematic study of large cemeteries, and combines her findings with knowledge derived from other sources. The material used here was assembled and processed from four cemeteries in Istanbul where Jews were buried during the Ottoman era: Hasköy, Ortaköy, Kuzguncuk, and the Italian cemetery in Şişli, all in all some 40,000 tombstones. The case selected to demonstrate the research potential concerns a specific group from the Jewish community of Istanbul, with the surname of 'Romano', and one of its branches in particular, whose members were buried in the Hasköy cemetery and were known by the name 'Roman.' The research reveals how this family, which apparently originated in the city of Rome, weaved family connections with Romaniot and Sefardi Jews of its own class. The varied material also exemplifies the intellectual and cultural connections of family members with seventeenth-century Muslim and Christian cultures.

Section 1: **On Death in Life**

Avriel Bar-Levav

Jewish Attitudes towards Death: A Society between Time, Space and Texts

The aim of this paper is to present a framework for depicting and understanding the varied Jewish attitudes towards death, mainly (but not only) since the medieval period; or, in other words, to suggest an initial map and coordinates for this topic. The basic map for western attitudes towards death was supplied by Philipes Ariès, who, as Frederick Paxton wrote in the *Macmillian Encyclopedia of Death and Dying*, almost single-handedly established attitude to death as a field of historical study.[1] Ariès proposed a model of four attitudes: 'tamed death', in which death is perceived as a natural part of life; 'death of the self', in which final judgement motifs emerge; 'wild death', in which death is seen as terrifying; and the 'forbidden death', in which death is considered to be a failure, with the dead removed from society.[2] Ariès suggested that the interaction between four factors causes the transitions between the different attitudes: human awareness of the self, social defences against wild nature, belief in an afterlife, and belief in the existence of evil. It is a wonderful story, said Robert Darnton, but is it true? Darnton, along with other critics, called Ariès's system 'historical impressionism'.[3] In any case, it seems that, as beautiful as this model is and as fruitful as it was for the historical study of attitudes to death, it is of little if any relevance for the Jewish approaches to this topic. Moreover, no attempt has yet been made to present an overview of the Jewish attitudes to death, and I would now like to rectify this. I am not, however, aiming at presenting here a comprehensive bibliography of the topic.[4]

What I am offering, as an initial proposal, are the coordinates for what, some fifty years ago, Joseph Weiss termed 'the evolutions of the death-sensa-

---

1 Frederick S. Paxton. Art. 'Ariès, Philippe'. *Macmillan Encyclopedia of Death and Dying* (2003). Encyclopedia.com. (June 1, 2011). http://www.encyclopedia.com/doc/1G2-3407200020.html. See also John McManners, 'Death and the French Historians', in *Mirrors of Mortality: Studies in the Social History of Death*, ed. by Joachim Whaley (London: Europa Publications, 1981), pp. 106–30.

2 The major works of Ariès in English are: *Western Attitudes towards Death*, Eng. trans. Patricia M. Ranum (Baltimore: Johns Hopkins University Press, 1974); *The Hour of Our Death*, Eng. trans. Helen Weaver (New York: A. A. Knopf, 1981); and *Images of Man and Death*, Eng. trans. Janet Lloyd (Cambridge, Mass: Harvard University Press, 1985).

3 Robert Darnton, *The Kiss of the Lamourtette: Reflections in Cultural History* (New York: Norton, 1990), p. 279.

4 See the most useful and comprehensive bibliography of Falk Wiesemann, *Sepulcra Judaica: Jewish Cemeteries, Death, Burial and Mourning from the Period of Hellenism to the Present: a Bibliography* (Essen: Klartext, 2005).

tion in the Jewish spirit and religion'.[5] The imagery of coordinates is especially apt for this topic, since it reflects a broad view of a map with different regions, and not of rigid and one-dimensional focal points or definitions. The rich and diverse Jewish culture, which has existed in some sort of continuity for many centuries, contains a broad diversity of approaches to death.[6] As I will show, the coordinates that I will suggest function as axes at different points along which the phenomena are to be examined. The conception of axes is necessary because of the great diversity of sources, regions, and periods that this culture encompasses, and because of its links with neighbouring cultures, primarily the pagan, Christian, and Muslim. These ties are expressed in the conceptions of death and accompanying customs. I will present several conceptions, some theoretical, and others anchored in the historical context.

1 Death as a reality and as an idea

The main distinction that we should make is the one between death as an idea and death as a reality. Needless to say, reading about death and related issues such as the afterlife, is something totally different than experiencing the death of someone near or dear. This distinction is relevant also for Jewish literature about death. Death as an idea appears almost everywhere. The following are the main types of sources in which shared or singular conceptions of death can be characterized: the Bible, rabbinic literature (while noting the distinction between the Land of Israel and Babylonia),[7] geonic literature, ethical teaching and homiletic literature (philosophical, rabbinical, kabbalistic, and that of the Ashkenazi pietists), Jewish philosophy, kabbala,[8] *halakha*, custom, *piyyuṭ*

---

5 Joseph Weiss, *Studies in Braslav Hasidism*, ed. by Mendel Piekarz (Hebrew; Jerusalem: Mosad Bialik, 1975), p. 173.

6 See for example Simcha Paull Raphael, *Jewish Views of the Afterlife* (Northvale, NJ: Jason Aronson, 1994); Chaim Z. Rozwasky, *Jewish Meditations on the Meaning of Death* (Northvale, NJ: Jason Aronson, 1994); Michael Swirsky (ed.), *At the Threshold: Jewish Meditations on Death* (Northvale, NJ: Jason Aronson, 1996); Shmuel Glick, *Light and Consolation: The Development of Jewish Consolation Practices*, Eng. trans. Fern Seckbach (Jerusalem: Ori Foundation, 2004); Maurice Lamm, *The Jewish Way in Death and Mourning* (Middle Village, NY: J. David Publishers, 2000); Yechezkel Shraga Lichtenstein, *Consecrating and Profane: Rituals Preformed and Prayers Recited at Cemeteries and Burial Cites of the Pious Midrash* (Hebrew; Tel Aviv: Hakibutz Hameuhad, 2007); and the various citations in this paper.

7 Nissan Rubin, *The End of Life: Rites of Mourning in the Talmud and Midrash*, (Hebrew; Tel Aviv: Hakibutz Hameuhad, 1977).

8 See Moshe Idel, 'The Light of Life: Kabbalistic Eschatology', *Sanctity of Life and Martyrdom: Studies in Memory of Amir Yekutiel*, ed. by Isaiah Gafni and Aviezer Ravitzky (Hebrew; Jerusalem: Shazar Center, 1992), pp. 191–211; Yehuda Liebes, 'Two Young Roes of a Doe: The Secret

(liturgical hymns) and poetry,[9] popular literature in Jewish languages,[10] and material culture.[11] Wherever Jews lived we find texts on death, the most prominent among these being the specific conceptions of death found in the Land of Israel and Babylonia, Philo, Byzantium, Ashkenaz in the period of the Ashkenaz pietists, Spain, Italy, Poland, and the Islamic lands. Most of these belong to the realm of death as an idea. Yet there are also texts that belong to the realm of death as a reality, or combining both aspects. These are mainly the genre that comprises books for the sick and the dying which I will discuss below.

2 Presence and absence

There is an occupation with death in all the centres just listed, which include almost all the spheres of Jewish culture and its literary corpus (possibly similar to the standing of this topic in human culture as a whole). Notwithstanding this, such an occupation co-exists with a significant Jewish cultural choice, concerning the marginality of death. This marginality finds expression in the fact that in almost every realm of Jewish creativity the occupation with death is partial and generally brief. As well phrased by Meir Benayahu, in his important study of death customs, 'everyone is present in times of joy and no one is present in times of sorrow or grief'.[12] This is not necessarily true for some of the public Jewish mourning customs, such as the *shiv'a*, which is sometimes crowded,[13] but it is certainly true for the study of death in Judaism, which is still in its initial stages, especially in comparison with the study of death in other cultures, mainly western.

Sermon of Isaac Luria Before his Death', *Lurianic Kabbala*, ed. by Rachel Elioar and Yehuda Liebes (Hebrew: Jerusalem Studies in Jewish Thought X) 1992, pp. 113–69.

9 See Raymond P. Scheindlin, *Wine Women and Death: Medieval Hebrew Poems on the Good Life* (New York et al.: Oxford University Press, 1999).

10 See Eli Yassif, *Jewish Folklore: An Annotated Bibliography* (New York: Gerland, 1986).

11 See Michael Brocke and Christiane E. Müller, *Haus des Lebens: Jüdische Friedhöfe in Deutschland* (Leipzig: Reclam, 2001).

12 Meir Benayahu, *Ma'amadot u-Moshavot* (Hebrew; Jerusalem: Yad Harav Nissim, 1985), p. 8.

13 See for example Samuel C. Heilman, *When a Jew Dies: The Ethnography of a Bereaved Son* (Berkeley: University of California Press, 2001).

3 A society between time, space and texts

Jewish attitudes towards death are delineated by four parameters: society, time, space and texts. In Jewish culture (as well as in other cultures) death is a social phenomenon.[14] It is forbidden, for example, to leave a dying person alone. Moreover, the ritual of saying the *qaddish*, which is central among the Jewish mourning rituals, can be said only in a *minyan*, that is a group of ten men. One needs to have a community in order to mourn properly or to mark properly days of remembrance (by reciting the *qaddish*), such as the yearly *yahrzeit*. Time is another factor – mourning rituals being timed for seven days (*shiv'a*), thirty days, a year and then the annual day of remembrance. The dead are mentioned (by saying texts in synagogue) at certain times of the year – Yom Kippur and the three festivals. Again this can be done, according to the Jewish law, only when there is a *minyan*. The space of the dead is the cemetery, which is the most minor factor of the four. The space of the mourners is the home (during the *shiv'a*) and then the synagogue, where the *qaddish* is recited.

4 Marginality and centrality

Jewish culture's basic position regarding death and the dead is in various respects to accord them a marginal standing. The occupation with death is marginal, and in some ways so are the dead themselves. Using the four parameters given above, death is marginal in time – mourning is structured and restricted to certain times and therefore is not supposed to be expressed in other times; regarding space – the dead are put in the cemetery which is almost always isolated and marginal; and, in the matter of society, death is also socially marginal, and has only a limited place in the Jewish community. These are different categories, but they share this marginality.

In the Garden of Eden narrative, death is presented as a punishment for the primordial sin. The central expression of this marginality is the impurity of the corpse, which is the deepest form of impurity: the corpse is the progenitor of impurity, from which all ritual impurity is derived. And (since the time of the talmudic rabbis) cemeteries have been located on the outskirts of settle-

14 See Richard Huntington and Peter Metcalf, *Celebrations of Death: The Anthropology of Mortuary Ritual* (Cambridge: Cambridge University Press, 1979).

ments, as a marginal quarter whose inhabitants are marginal.[15] The Bible mentions other burial possibilities, including family burial, in which the situation is different, but beginning in the talmudic period, and especially since the medieval period, Jewish cemeteries acquired a nature similar to what we now know.

Jewish mourning practices restrict the possibility of expressing any connection with the dead, and they are limited to fixed and delineated times and modes. Nonetheless, there are periods and places in which death has a more noticeable presence. The main (and almost sole) day in which the presence of death is palpable is Yom Kippur (Day of Atonement), in the liturgical context and ancillary philosophical conceptions of which much attention is paid to death. This is because of its perception as a day of judgement, and because the prayer includes the *Yizkor* ceremony of mentioning the dead. The Yom Kippur prayer service is perceived as encompassing both the living and the dead, in which the living pray and can be of avail to the dead, and the dead, too, come to the synagogue. R. Moshe Isserles cites R. Ya'aqov Weil: 'Therefore Yom Ha-Kippurim is in the plural – for the living and for the dead.'[16]

The High Holy Days, of which Yom Kippur is part, are also the period in which the cemetery has a more central place than the rest of the year, and it is customary to visit the cemetery and conduct various rites, such as that of encompassing the cemetery with a string that is afterwards used as wicks for the Sabbath candles. Elsewhere I have set forth eight cultural functions of the Jewish cemetery: neighbourhood, gate or portal, communication centre, stage, setting or backdrop, refuge, trap, and centre of identity[17]. Each of these roles reflects a different aspect of the cemetery's cultural significance.[18] The cemetery is what Michel Foucalt called 'heterotopia', that is, 'another space', one that is beyond any place, but nevertheless possible, specifically because it is one that encompasses all places. As such, the cemetery reflects social values in a complex fashion.

---

15 On the cemetery in Jewish culture see Avriel Bar-Levav, 'We Are Where We Are Not: The Cemetery in Jewish Culture', *Jewish Studies*, 41 (2002), pp. 15*–46*.

16 See Avriel Bar-Levav, 'The Concept of Death in *Sefer ha-Ḥayyim* (The Book of Life) by Rabbi Shimon Frankfurt', doctoral dissertation (Hebrew; The Hebrew University of Jerusalem, 1997), p. 180.

17 See Bar-Levav, 'The Cemetery'.

18 See Elliot S. Horowitz, 'Speaking to the Dead: Cemetery Prayer in Medieval and Early Modern Jewry', *Journal of Jewish Thought & Philosophy*, 8 (1999), pp. 303–17.

5 Punishment or desideratum

Most Jewish conceptions view death as something daunting and disheartening, which is to be avoided or delayed, if possible. Thus, it is related that Moses and King David sought to defer their deaths, to the extent that the Angel of Death, who executes the divine sentence, had to outwit them in order to fulfill his mission. At the other end of this scale is the notion that death (to be precise, mystical death) can be the culmination of a theurgic or unio-mystical process. Such, for example, was the death of R. Simeon bar Yoḥai, as related in the *Zohar*. The death of Moses, too, at least according to some conceptions, possessed such a dimension, but more prominent in his case is the legitimization – rare in the Jewish sources – of expressing fear of one's own death.

A phenomenon of another sort, namely, choosing death, also exists in instances of *Qiddush ha-Shem* (martyrdom), both in practice – for example, during the time of the Crusades, as we learn from the important book by Shmuel Shepkaru[19] – and as a matter of principle, as in the spiritual aspiration to die a martyr's death for the 'Sanctification of the Name of God' that appears in the mystical diary of R. Joseph Caro, *Maggid Mesharim*.[20]

6 Disintegration and combination

Death is perceived as the disintegration of an integral wholeness: 'And the dust returns to the ground as it was, and the lifebreath returns to God who bestowed it' (Eccl 12:7). This dismantling is not total, and according to most understandings, a certain connection remains between the material part that is consumed after death and interred in the grave, and the spirit or soul, and this bond turns the grave into the address of the deceased's personality. When people desire to address a deceased person, they usually go to his or her grave. For example, the book *Ma'ane Lashon*, that was printed in scores of editions and with textual variations in Central Europe beginning in the middle of the sixteenth century, includes personal prayers to be recited at the grave of rela-

19 See Shmuel Shepkaru, *Jewish Martyrs in the Pagan and Christian World* (Cambridge: Cambridge University Press, 2006).

20 See R. J. Z. Werblowsky, *Joseph Karo: Lawyer and Mystic* (Philadelphia: Jewish Publication Society of America, 1977); Joseph R. Hacker, 'Was the Sanctification of the Name Transformed in the Early Modern Period Towards Spirituality?', *Sanctity of Life and Martyrdom: Studies in Memory of Amir Yekutiel*, ed. by Isaiah Gafni and Aviezer Ravitzky (Hebrew; Jerusalem: Shazar Center, 1992), pp. 221–32.

tives, teachers, rabbis, and the like. This is a point of connection between the dead and a certain space, their space, which becomes also a partial space for the people who come to visit them.

This disintegration is not only between the body and the soul, but also between the different parts of the soul. Thus, for example, *Sefer Ḥasidim* explains what enables the deceased to appear in a dream:

> 324. If two good people took an oath or pledged together during their lifetime, that if one were to die he would tell his fellow how it is in that world, whether in a dream or awake – if in a dream, the spirit will come and whisper in the ear of the living, or in his mind, as the angel of dreams does. And if they took an oath to speak with the other while awake, the dead will ask of the appointed angel to represent him as a garbed figure, and the dissipated spirit will come together, until he speaks with his fellow whom he promised to inform. How can he check that what appears to him is not a demon and a destructive agent? He is to adjure him, which would not be a case of uttering the name of Heaven in vain. Furthermore, the dead cannot mention [the name of God] *Yah*, because by it this world and the world to come were created, for he [the deceased] is beyond these worlds. And it is written [Ps 115:17]: 'The dead cannot praise the Lord' but rather [Ps 150:6]: 'Let all that breathes praise the Lord.'

A situation is depicted in which there is an obligation to communicate between the dead and the living. The friends took an oath to give each other information regarding 'that world' – the world to come, where one goes after death. The oath taken by the living person obligates him when dead, as well. Since, however, death is the dissolution of the components of the individual's identity, he must, in order to appear before the living and fulfil his obligation, ask the angel responsible for the dead (according to some conceptions this is the angel Duma, to whom the biblical phrase [Ps 115:17] 'who go down into silence [*dumah*]' refers) to represent him as a garbed figure, that is, an astral figure visible to the living, and bring together the dispersed parts of the soul that separated upon death. The dead of this type who return to the world of the living are similar in appearance to demons, hence the need to confirm that this emissary is indeed that deceased, and not a demon imposter. *Sefer Ḥasidim* suggests a technique for examining the origin of the astral entity with whom the living meets and who delivers this information.

The conception of disintegration and combination is one instance in which the Jewish conceptions resemble those in other cultures, as demonstrated by Metcalf and Huntington.

7 Vestibule and banquet hall: this world and the world to come

'R. Ya'aqov says: This world is like a vestibule before the world to come. Prepare yourself in the vestibule, that you may enter into the banquet hall' (*mAvot* 4.16). R. Ya'aqov's dictum distinguishes between this world, in which we live, and the world to come, where we will go after death. It is claimed that the next world is the more important, and therefore one should make efforts in this world to attain a suitable standing there. This world is one of action and building, while the next is the world in which recompense is given for the actions done in this world. According to some conceptions, the world to come is divided into Paradise, the region of reward, and Gehinnom, the zone of punishment. According to another understanding, the souls come to the Throne of Glory, and as Rami Reiner shows in a brilliant article, this conception is reflected on tombstones in Ashkenaz.[21]

R. Naḥman wrote of this world and the world to come in his book *Liqquṭei Maharan*:

> He spoke with us several times concerning the tribulations of this world, in which all are replete with sufferings; there is not a single person who possesses this world. And even the great wealthy ones, and even the mighty ones, do not possess this world at all, for all their days are anger and pains. All are filled with cares and sadness, woe and anguish always. Each one has his own tribulations, nor are there any among the worthies and the princes for whom everything is in order as he wishes always, but every single one is filled with suffering and cares, always [...] there is no advice and stratagem to save one from this toil and woe, save to flee to the Lord, may He be blessed, and to be occupied with the Torah [...]
>
> Our master, may his memory be for a blessing, answered:
>
> Behold, all say that there is both this world and the world to come. Concerning the world to come – all believe that there is a world to come. It is also possible that there is this world, too, as some sort of world, for here it seems to be Gehinnom, since all are filled with great sufferings, always. And he said, 'this world' does not seem to exist at all.
>
> (*Liqqutei Maharan* 2.119, http://breslev.eip.co.il/?key=296)

In his typical way, R. Naḥman presents a paradox, according to which the poles of human existence are Gehinnom in the here and now, while Paradise comes only after death.

---

21 See Abraham (Rami) Reiner, 'Blessings for the Dead in Ashkenzi Tombstones in the Medieval Period', *Zion*, 76 (Hebrew; 2011), pp. 5–28.

8 The souls are within the appearance of the bodies

Sefer Ḥasidim, which is an important source for conceptions and notions relating to death, contains the idea that the state of the corpse in the grave, the condition of the grave itself, its location relative to other graves and those interred, and the maintenance of the cemetery, all influence the souls of the dead. This principle is formulated thus: 'The souls are within the appearance of the bodies.' The state of the corpse impacts on that of the soul, and the condition of the soul influences the process undergone by the buried body. 'Appearance' here denotes the reflection of the soul in the body, and the reverse.[22]

> 331. A person washing a corpse must be careful not to leave any dirt on its flesh, and similarly, one who places the corpse in the grave and lays him down must take care that there not be dirt on his face, for this is shameful for him, because the souls are within the appearance of the bodies.

The principle 'the souls are within the appearance of the bodies' is reciprocal, and in certain matters the bodies, too, are within the appearance of the souls. The bodies of people at a high level of sanctity do not deteriorate and decompose. 'There were seven over whom the worms had no dominion' (*bB. Bat.* 17a).

The passage concerned with the attire of the righteous and of the wicked in the world to come refers to an examination of the corpse in the grave as confirming the words of the deceased in a dream. When the body is stripped of its shrouds, the soul, too, remains 'naked'.

> 335. Two disagreed: One said that the garments of the wicked, who are adorned with the choicest ornaments, are removed, and they are placed on the righteous, who do not wear fine shrouds because of their poverty. And his fellow said: Many righteous who were stripped of their clothing came in a dream to the people of the city where they were naked, and they asked to be dressed; and they checked, and found that they had been stripped. R. Yannai gave orders not to dress them – meaning that one should not be undressed and another dressed with the same garments.

According to one opinion, if the garments of the righteous are not fine enough according to his standing, then in the world of truth a wicked one must be stripped in order to clothe him. This undressing fulfills the goal of depriving the wicked of a standing of which he is undeserving, that of a dead person

---

22 See Avriel Bar-Levav, 'Death and the (Blurred) Boundaries of Magic: Strategies of Coexistence', *Kabbalah*, 7 (2002), pp. 51–64.

dressed 'with the choicest ornaments'. The garments of the dead here are seemingly limited in number, and they can be interchanged among themselves, but no new ones can be produced. Diametrically opposed to this are positions such as those held by Maimonides and other Jewish philosophers, that the immortality of the soul means adherence to the Active Intellect, with no trace of the preservation of the personal identity.

9 The burial society and the importance of burial

In Jewish society the main, and almost only, method of treatment of the corpse is burial. The Bible also mentions other possibilities (without directives for burial), such as embalming and cremation. In the time of the early talmudic rabbis the predominant practice consisted of the collection of the bones after the flesh had been consumed and their reinterment in secondary burial, while beginning in the early medieval period burials were conducted in a manner similar to the present practice. Burial in a Jewish cemetery is perceived as valuable and meritorious (related to the conception that the souls are 'within the appearance of the bodies').

Burial societies are mentioned in general terms in the Palestinian Talmud, but the first substantial testimonies to their existence are known to us from Spain. Until the sixteenth century Jewish burials were conducted, in an unorganized fashion, by members of the community. The sixteenth to the eighteenth centuries witnessed the development of the *ḥevra qaddisha*, the burial society, that attended to the burial of the dead, and became a central society among the many societies in this period.[23] Initially there were three classes within the burial society: (1) leaders or officers; (2) an interim class; (3) '*mlatch*' – apprentices. The burial society had verbal and practical tasks. Its verbal roles included prayers, the conducting of ceremonies, and the like. Its practical functions including bearing the corpse, the technical aspects of purification, the digging of the grave and the actual burial. The status of the practical roles was relatively low, and these were assigned to members of low standing, and at times to hired individuals who were not members of the society. It should be stressed that the process of the ritual fashioning of death in the early modern period paralleled the development of the burial society and its standing. The first books to appear in Italy of the type of *Sifrei Ḥolim u-Metim* ('Books for the Sick and Dying'), *Ṣari la-Nefesh u-Marpe la-Eṣem* ('Balm for the

23 See Sylvie-Anne Goldberg, *Crossing the Jabbok: Illness and Death in Ashkenazi Judaism in Sixteenth- through Nineteenth-Century Prague* (Berkeley: University of California Press, 1996).

Soul and a Cure for the Bone') by R. Leone (Yehuda Aryeh) Modena, and *Ma'avar Yabboq* by R. Aharon Berekhia of Modena, were written at the request of burial society members, who were desirous of infusing their task with religious and spiritual content.[24]

10 The importance of rites of passage: a proper death and books for the sick and the dying

The rise in the importance of the burial society led to the spread among the public at large of the idea, previously current among the circles of the elite, of the 'proper' or 'good' death – a ceremonial death, one accompanied by rites of passage conducted by those around the deceased and by the recitation of texts. In a broader sense, the significance of a proper death is that life is perceived as a preparation for death. The ceremonies conducted before death appeared in dozens of 'books for the sick and the dying', that were printed in hundreds of editions. When first fashioned, the conception of a proper death contained two components, one relating to the individual who passed away, and the other to those around him. The anchoring of the proper death in a social context is so strong that there could hardly be a proper death without the presence of additional people, and the books for the sick and the dying even prefer a *minyan* (quorum of ten) when the soul expires. The social participation in a proper death seemingly lessens, if only to some degree, a part of the dying person's loneliness, since he is not alone, but is the focal point of the group's attention. The group acts in an effective, defined, and structured manner, taking an active part in the process. By its actions it demonstrates the concern it feels for the sick one. It should be noted, however, that the group keeps the dying person's family at arm's length. The degree to which this distancing harms the individual and his family depends on the way in which the family functions during this event, and on the possibility of their taking their leave of the dying person in a meaningful manner.

---

24 See Avriel Bar-Levav, 'Leon Modena and the Invention of the Jewish Death Tradition', *The Lion Shall Roar: Leon Modena and his World*, ed. by David Malkiel (Hebrew; Jerusalem: Magnes Press and Ben-Zvi Inistiute, 2003), pp. 85–101; Bar-Levav, 'Games of Death in Jewish Books for the Sick and the Dying', *Kabbalah*, 5 (2000), pp. 11–33; Elliot S. Horowitz, 'The Jews of Europe and the Moment of Death in Medieval and Modern Times', *Judaism*, 44 (1995), pp. 271–281.

11 Death affording a moral perspective

Death affords an absolute point of reference for life and its accomplishments, with an inherent moral perspective. A prime example of this thought appears in *mAvot* (2.10), that advises: 'Repent one day before your death.' The Babylonian Talmud (*bŠab*. 123a) presents the lack of knowledge of the time of one's death as a motive for a perpetual state of repentance:

> R. Eli'ezer says: Repent one day before your death. His students asked R. Eli'ezer: But does a person know on which day he will die? He answered: All the more so – let him repent today lest he die tomorrow, hence throughout his life he will be in a state of repentance.

The concept that the time of death is the time of truth, a notion that is close to that of the moral perspective afforded by death, also influenced the laws of acquisition, for example, as in the cases of gifts given by one mortally ill, the last wills of those contemplating death. The moral perspective may also be understood in the sense that an improper life is like a living death. Thus, we find in the following poem, *Elegy*, by Pinḥas Sadeh:[25]

> There, at the edge of the vale, lies a dead lad.
> How beautiful is his face in its cold paleness.
> Only at moments does it quiver
> When the memory of his first love touches him.
> Sleep, precious lad. How good it is to sleep in the vale.
> How deep is the silence, how quiet the grass.
> I am that lad. Don't see that I am alive.
> Only for moments when I awaken will I know how dead I am.

The poem contrasts awareness (wakefulness) with death. Only by awakening can man sense the existence of death in his life.

I would like to conclude with a re-examination of the question of the centrality or marginality of death in Jewish life. A *midrash* in *Yalquṭ Shim'oni* portrays the journey in the wilderness of the Ark of the Covenant, alongside which is the coffin in which, at his request, the bones of Joseph are taken to the Land of Israel:

> Joseph's coffin [*aron*] went alongside the ark [*aron*] of the Eternal. The nations would say: What is the nature of these two chests [*aronot*]? They [the Israelites] would reply: This one is the coffin of a corpse, and that one is the ark of the Eternal. The nations would ask them: Why is this dead person important enough to accompany the ark of the Eternal? They replied: The one lying in this coffin fulfilled what is written in the other (*Yalquṭ Shim'oni*, Exodus 227).

25 Pinḥas Sadeh, *Collected Poems* (Hebrew; Jerusalem: Schocken), 2005, p. 206.

This passage contains an echo of the parallelism between Scripture and the body of a holy man, with the act linking them: 'The one lying in this coffin fulfilled what is written on that.'[26] The Torah is a Torah of life, and the Talmud states that the lips of a (deceased) Torah scholar in whose name a teaching is reported move gently in the grave. But there is also a sense in which the time when the teachings of previous generations are read and studied is also the time of the dead. I wish to suggest that this study, that is mainly of texts whose authors are deceased, and the rest, of texts by authors who will die in the future, also contains another dimension, namely, allotting places to the dead and their teachings. Thus, the question of the marginality and centrality of death becomes extremely complicated. The two arguments about the place of death are complementary and not contradictory, and together paint a complex picture. The cemetery is not only a heterotopia, but also the place of Jewish texts. If we view study, that is so central in Jewish culture, as a type of connection with the dead, then it may be possible to say that there is a deep structure in which death is not only not marginal, but that a certain aspect of it – the creative product of the dead – is at the centre of the Jewish experience.

26 On this topic see Adiel Kadari, 'This one fulfilled what is written in that one': On an Early Burial Practice in its Literary and Artistic Contexts', *Journal for the Study of Judaism in the Persian, Hellenistic and Roman Period*, 41.2 (2010), pp. 191–213.

Frederick S. Paxton

The Early Growth of the Medieval Economy of Salvation in Latin Christianity

The last thirty years have seen a wealth of research on death, dying and the dead in Latin Christianity. Some scholars have focused on liturgy, ritual and the cult of the saints. Others have studied cemeteries, graves and epitaphs; relics and relic translations; visions of the afterlife; grants to religious communities for the care of the dead; or the records created to ensure that such care would be delivered, ideally in perpetuity. While research on this body of material has opened up rich and fascinating fields in the cultural history of Europe, it has not been brought together within a unifying framework. That is the object of this essay, which argues that all this varied human activity was bound together through a system of exchanges among the living, the dead, and the court of the living God – a 'medieval economy of salvation'. The multiplicity of connections within this system, the complexity of the exchanges involved, and the fact that the currency included tangible assets, like labour, land, and treasure, add up to something like an economy as we understand it today. But it was also very different, especially in the early and central Middle Ages, before the mercantile culture of Europe took off. Whatever practitioners of the economics of religion might think, the early medieval Church bears only a superficial resemblance to a modern multinational corporation.[1] The medieval economy of salvation deserves to be understood on its own terms as a peculiarly distinctive and dynamic product of the religious and social practices of people who adopted Latin Christianity as their religion but also adapted it to the needs of their families and communities.

Three historical watersheds will frame our discussion. The first, on either side of the year 400, defines the border between Late Antiquity and the early Middle Ages. The second watershed more traditionally divides the early from the later Middle Ages, before and after the year 1100. The third is the late medieval/early modern watershed defined by the reformations of the sixteenth century. While working within the historical parameters established by these three models, we will focus on the period between the first and second water-

1 See Robert B. Ekelund, Robert D. Tollison, Gary Anderson, Robert F. Hébert, and Audrey B. Davidson, *Sacred Trust: The Medieval Church as an Economic Firm* (New York: Oxford University Press, 1996); and Ekelund, Hébert, and Tollison, *The Marketplace of Christianity* (Cambridge: MIT Press, 2006); see also Laurence R. Iannaccone, 'Introduction to the Economics of Religion', *Journal of Economic Literature*, 36 (1998), pp. 1465–96.

Three Watersheds in Latin Christianity

Late Antique	400	Early Medieval
Early Medieval	1100	Later Medieval
Late Medieval	1500	Early Modern

sheds, that is, the early and central Middle Ages, from the fifth century to the twelfth.

We will begin by defining the medieval economy of salvation more closely and briefly sketching its overall history. We will then turn to some recent findings in the history of late antique and early medieval Christianity that shed light on two important questions. First, when did the Latin Church begin to involve itself systematically in death, dying and the care of the dead? And second, when it came to such things, how different was the Church of, say, Alcuin of York from that of Ambrose of Milan? That should give some idea of the growth of the economy of salvation between the fourth and the ninth centuries. Finally, we will present the Benedictine Abbey of Cluny, at its height in the eleventh and twelfth centuries, as the culminating expression of the early medieval economy of salvation, even as changing social, theological and economic conditions were beginning to call into question some of the system's most characteristic features.

1 The medieval economy of salvation

The early Church Fathers called God's management of his creation an 'economy'. The defining act of the 'divine economy' was the sacrifice of Jesus, an exchange of suffering and death for reconciliation between the creator and his human creations.[2] Ever since, Christians have been replaying, and extending the benefits of that primal act of exchange through the mass and the other sacraments. The Catholic Church still refers to such secondary manifestations of God's plan of salvation as the 'sacramental economy'.[3] By 'the medieval economy of salvation', I mean an elaboration of such notions and behaviours, peculiar to the Latin Middle Ages, which encompassed the transfer of large numbers of people and large amounts of goods, lands and incomes to religious

2 M. R. E. Masterman, 'Economy, Divine', *New Catholic Encyclopedia* 2nd ed., 15 vols (Farmington Hills, MI: Gale, 2002), V, p. 58.

3 See paragraph 1076 of the official *Catechism of the Catholic Church*, on-line at http://www.vatican.va/archive/catechism/p2s1.htm. Accessed October 9, 2010.

communities in exchange for masses, psalms, prayers and alms for the poor. Those goods were then offered to God for the salvation of souls in the afterlife, the souls of the donor and his family in particular. In the early Middle Ages, these exchanges operated within a predominantly gift-based economy, which was less directed toward the accumulation of wealth than the creation of social bonds and thus helped knit individuals and families into larger communities with mutual responsibilities to one another. The medieval economy of salvation was a subset of the larger gift economy. Within a Christian framework, such habits of exchange were increasingly put to the service of acquiring the most important commodity of all, the eternal salvation of one's family, which the gift to mankind from God of his own son made possible.

The growth of the economy of salvation in the early Middle Ages was fuelled by ambiguity in Christian teaching about the state and place of the soul between death and the final resurrection. Scripture was clear about the Last Judgement, but vague about what happened after death. This fostered belief in an interim state, of punishment to be sure, but also of purgation and preparation for paradise. At the same time, Church leaders expressed only minor opposition to the notion that the living could affect the state of souls in the afterlife. To the contrary, they offered ever-more elaborate services for the dead and dying, advertising them through popular accounts of dreams and visions that highlighted the positive effects of post-mortem intercession. Given all this, it should not be surprising that the small-scale agricultural societies of the early Middle Ages, who tended to view their dead as just 'another age group', would be interested in caring for souls after death.[4] Indeed, their demand for services was at least as important a factor in the early growth of the medieval economy of salvation as the supply provided by the clergy. Nevertheless, the economy of salvation remained more or less a clerical phenomenon until the Carolingian Reforms of the eighth and ninth centuries. The three centuries that followed the reigns of Charlemagne and his son, Louis the Pious, however, saw continuous growth in both the number of dead being memorialized by the living and the number of the living whose job it was to see to the welfare of the dead. Among these, the practitioners of reformed Benedictine monasticism were considered the best, and the monks of Cluny the best of all. Founded in 910, the Abbey of Cluny was heir to all of the impulses of the Carolingian reforms. And the early medieval economy of

---

4 Bruce Gordon and Peter Marshall identify Natalie Zemon Davis as the ultimate source of this insight in recent scholarship; see *The Place of the Dead: Death and Remembrance in Late Medieval and Early Modern Europe* ed. by Bruce Gordon and Peter Marshall (Cambridge: Cambridge University Press, 2000), p. 6.

The Early to Later Medieval Watershed

950	1100	1250
Gift economy		Profit economy
Rural settings		Urban settings
Monks		Friars
Landlords		Merchants
Customary law		Codified law
Localized dissent		Organized dissent

salvation was the engine of Cluny's phenomenal growth, which peaked right at the watershed between the early and the later Middle Ages.

It is worth pausing to take a close look at that watershed. On the early medieval side, the economy of salvation was characterized by the circulation of wealth in the form of gifts made to rural monasteries. In the later Middle Ages, the increase in the number and size of towns and cities, and in trade and cash transactions, led to the disappearance of many features of the early medieval economy of salvation and the introduction of new ones. Grants of land and children to rural monasteries more or less disappeared, for example, as did the pre-eminence of monks in the exchange of spiritual goods. New agents, like the friars, brought the goods of the sacramental economy, including the new currency of indulgences, to the growing urban masses. Not everyone went along, though. Beginning around the year 1000, dissident voices questioned and even opposed some of the key features of the economy of salvation. In spite of being declared heretical, such complaints were regularly reiterated right up until the sixteenth century, when Protestants rejected almost every one of the essential features of the economy of salvation, from the miraculous nature of the Eucharist to the very notion that the living could do anything to affect the condition of souls in the afterlife.

2 Death, dying and the dead in late antiquity and the early Middle Ages

Turning back from the last of the three watersheds to the first, we can begin to investigate the early growth of the medieval economy in more detail. In a provocative study of Christian responses to death in Late Antiquity, published in 1994, Éric Rebillard argued that a strongly optimistic attitude toward death, which prevailed in the fourth century, was replaced in the fifth century by a

The Late Antique to Early Medieval Watershed

250	400	550
Baptismal theology		Penitential theology
Emphasis on salvation		Emphasis on sin
Death not to be feared		Death to be feared
Few if any death rituals		Increasing ritualization

profound pessimism.[5] Representative bishops of the earlier period, like Ambrose of Milan, urged their congregations to regard life as a kind of death and death as birth into real life. 'Death is not a terrible thing', Ambrose preached, 'only one's attitude toward death'.[6] Baptized Christians in good standing need have no fear of death, for their salvation was assured. According to Ambrose, only souls in despair would fear death. To Augustine, however, only the arrogant would fail to do so. Donatists, Manichees and Pelagians all believed that their purity or rigour guaranteed their salvation. So as not to fall into their errors, it was necessary to remember man's basic sinfulness and absolute dependence on God's inscrutable judgement and mercy, especially at death. According to Rebillard, clerical interest in the pastoral needs of the dying and the dead was a response to this fundamental shift in attitudes.[7]

Rebillard's work supports a growing consensus among scholars of Late Antiquity that the generations immediately before and after the year 400 mark a watershed in the history of Latin Christianity, which separates a religion centred on baptism and assured salvation from one centred on penance, sin and the uncertainty of heavenly grace.[8] Their conclusions are in accord with those of medievalists who have traced the surprisingly slow growth of Christian responses to death, dying and the dead over the course of the early Middle

---

5 Éric Rebillard, *'In hora mortis': Évolution de la pastorale chrétienne de la mort au IVe et Ve siècles*, Bibliothèque des Écoles Français de Athènes et Rome, 283 (Rome: École française de Rome, 1994).

6 Ambrose, *De bono mortis*: PL 14.555A: *Non mors ipsa terribilis est, sed opinio de morte.* Although Rebillard does not look back beyond Ambrose, the last great representative of this strain, Cyprian's words to the persecuted in the third century certainly laid the groundwork for Ambrose's imperial triumphalism in the fourth. See, for example, Cyprian's *Liber de laude martyrii* (PL 4.788–804).

7 Rebillard, '*In hora mortis*', pp. 169–224.

8 Robert Markus, *The End of Ancient Christianity* (Cambridge: Cambridge University Press, 1990) is the touchstone, but see also the works of Ramsay McMullen, Peter Brown, Philip Rousseau, Kate Cooper, and others.

Ages.[9] They remain, however, at odds with two long-standing assumptions about ancient Christianity: that the Church had its own cemeteries as early as the end of the second century and that the systematic burial of the poor was the motivating factor behind their creation.

3 Catacombs and cemeteries

Since the groundbreaking work of the Catholic archaeologist Giovanni-Battista De Rossi in the nineteenth century, the Roman Church has believed that the so-called Catacomb of Callixtus was an exclusively Christian cemetery and that the Roman catacombs in general were the graveyards of Roman Christians. Recent philological research by Éric Rebillard, however, has shown that neither the Greek word *koimeterion* nor its Latin equivalent *coemeterium* denoted a communal burial ground. To the contrary, they referred to individual tombs, and at most their immediate surroundings.[10] There was, in fact, no ancient term at all for a cemetery in the modern sense of the word. Nor were there any 'cities of the dead'. The only ancient occurrence of the Greek word *necropolis* is a reference in Strabo's *Geography* to a suburb of Alexandria, a place with 'many gardens and graves and halting-places fitted out for the embalming of corpses', whose tombs and gardens were no doubt, like those everywhere else in the Roman Empire, privately owned.[11] Under this reading, the famous text assigning the future pope Callixtus 'to the cemetery', the *locus classicus* for the argument that the Church had its own cemeteries by the end of the second century, must have meant simply that he was to oversee the initial outfitting

9 See, for example, Frederick S. Paxton, *Christianizing Death: The Creation of a Ritual Process in Early Medieval Europe* (Ithaca and London: Cornell University Press, 1990) and Bonnie Effros, *Caring for Body and Soul: Burial and the Afterlife in the Merovingian World* (University Park: Pennsylvania State University Press, 2002).

10 Éric Rebillard, '*Koimeterion* et *coemeterium*: Tombe, tombe sainte, nécropole', *Mélanges de l'École française de Rome, Antiquité*, 105 (1993), pp. 975–1001; 'Les *areae* carthaginoises (Tertullian, *Ad Scapulam* 3,1): cimetières communautaires ou enclos funéraires de chrétiens?', in *Mélanges de l'École française de Rome, Antiquité*, 108 (1996), pp. 175–89; 'L'Église de Rome et le développement des catacombes: à propos de l'origine des cimetières chrétiens', in *Mélanges de l'École française de Rome, Antiquité*, 109 (1997), pp. 741–63.

11 *The Geography of Strabo*, Eng. trans. by Horace Leonard Jones, 8 vols (Cambridge: Harvard University Press, 1917–32), 17. 1. 10. On private ownership of graves in ancient Rome, see J. M. C. Toynbee, *Death and Burial in the Roman World* (Ithaca: Cornell University Press, 1971), pp. 73–100.

of the so-called 'Crypt of the Popes', a single room owned by the Church in a rapidly growing catacomb on the Appian Way.[12]

This conclusion is supported by recent research on pre- and non-Christian burials in Rome by the archaeologist John Bodel, who argues that catacombs evolved out of late Republican and early Imperial *columbaria* and, like *columbaria*, served the whole population of the city. As inhumation replaced cremation as the dominant means of disposing of of dead bodies over the course of the second century, the characteristic niches of the *columbaria*, which had received the ashes of the dead, were enlarged to hold whole bodies, and the *columbaria* themselves, built both above and below ground, and sometimes both at once, were replaced by underground galleries carved directly into the easily-worked volcanic tufa around the city. Bodel's argument is based not just on archaeology, but also on demographics. If the catacombs were exclusively Christian, he asked, then where were non-Christians buried in the third and fourth centuries, when the catacombs were in regular use? There is no avoiding the conclusion. Since the catacombs comprise the largest repository of burial evidence for the period, they must have served the whole population of the city.[13] Except for 'the crypt of the popes', there were no places reserved exclusively for the burial of Christians overseen by the Roman Church. That is why we find Christians and pagans, and perhaps even Jews, sharing the same small catacomb on the Via Latina as late as the second half of the fourth century.[14] Families purchased individual rooms and had artists, no doubt supplied by the owner of the catacomb, decorate them with images from the appropriate religious tradition.

4 The poor and the dead

As mentioned above, the persistence of the assumptions that the early Church had its own cemeteries and that the catacombs were exclusively Christian has

12 Rebillard, '*Koimeterion* et *coemeterium*', and idem, *The Care of the Dead in Late Antiquity*, Eng. trans. Elizabeth Trapnell Rawlings and Jeanine Routier-Pucci, (Ithaca and London: Cornell University Press, 2009), pp. 2–7.

13 John Bodel, 'From *Columbaria* to Catacombs: Collective Burial in Pagan and Christian Rome', in *Commemorating the Dead: Texts and Artifacts in Context: Studies of Roman, Jewish and Christian Burials*, ed. by Laurie Brink, O. P. and Deborah Green (Berlin: de Gruyter, 2008), pp. 177–242.

14 On the Via Latina catacomb, see Fabrizio Mancinelli, *The Catacombs of Rome and the Origins of Christianity* (Florence: Scala, c. 1981), pp. 33–38; and J. Stevenson, *The Catacombs: Rediscovered Monuments of Early Christianity* (London: Thames and Hudson, 1978).

depended in part on the belief that the Church developed a commitment to burying the poor early on in its history. Once again, however, Rebillard has convincingly argued that, while churchmen encouraged individual Christians and even Christian congregations to bury and pray for indigents and strangers, it was not because of a general commitment to burying the poor, but because strangers and the indigent did not have families who could see to those duties themselves.[15] This distinction is clear even in the works of St. Augustine. Behind the pronouncements in his letters and his seminal treatise *On the Care to be Given to the Dead* lies the unstated assumption that individual families would see to the burial and commemoration of their dead, just as they saw to other intimate matters, like birth, marriage, illness and death itself, none of which were overseen by priests.[16] Augustine prohibited Christians from eating and drinking at the tombs of the martyrs, for example, but allowed them to do so at their ancestral tombs, as long as they did not get drunk and engage in immoral behaviour, although he famously recommended that the money spent on such commemorative feasts be redirected to the poor as a way of bringing solace to the dead.[17]

Augustine's adult life spanned the watershed between late antique and early medieval Christianity, however, and, while he may not have urged the general burial of the poor, he took up their cause, even if primarily as a strategic move in a struggle over who would direct the cultural forces of the later empire, as Peter Brown has argued.[18] In Brown's argument, championing the cause of the poor in a world of ever increasing distance between the humble and the mighty gave bishops of the later fourth and early fifth centuries both a populist base and an excuse for their own rapidly accumulating wealth. Augustine's suggestion, in a letter written around the year 392, that Christians give the food and drink traditionally offered to the dead as alms was thus

15 Éric Rebillard, 'Église et sépulture dans l'Antiquité tardive', *Annales HSS*, 54 (1999), pp. 1027–46; 'Les formes de l'assistance funéraire dans l'Empire romain et leur évolution dans l'Antiquité tardive', *Antiquité Tardive*, 7 (1999), pp. 269–82.

16 Frederick S. Paxton, 'Birth and Death', in *The Cambridge History of Christianity* vol. 3, *600–1100*, ed. by Thomas F. X. Noble and Julia M. H. Smith (Cambridge: Cambridge University Press, 2008), pp. 386–87, 390.

17 *S. Aureli Augustini Hipponiensis episcopi Epistulae*, ed. by Alois Goldbacher, 5 vols (Vienna: F. Temsky, 1895–1923), I, pp. 58–59; see also Rebillard, '*Nec deserere memorias suorum*: Augustine and the Family-based Commemoration of the Dead', *Augustinian Studies*, 36 (2005), pp. 99–111; and idem, 'The Cult of the Dead in Late Antiquity: Towards a New Definition of the Relation between the Living and the Dead', in *Acta ad Archaeologicum et Artium Historiam Perintentia*, 17 (2003), pp. 47–55.

18 Peter Brown, *Power and Persuasion in Late Antiquity: Towards a Christian Empire*, (Madison: University of Wisconsin Press, 1992).

easily assimilated to the notion that the Church was the natural broker for such charitable acts.

My own research has shown how, fifty years later, the connection between the poor and the Church had tightened to the point that a church council at Vaison, in southeastern Gaul, presided over by Bishop Hilary of Arles, excommunicated anyone refusing to turn over deathbed offerings to the church 'as if they were murderers of the poor'.[19] The canon of Vaison gives evidence of two important developments. On the one hand, the dying were regularly making offerings to the Church to distribute to the poor. On the other hand, survivors were not always making good on their dead relative's vows. Even bishops could be at fault. Hilary praised his predecessor Honoratus, who succeeded a bishop who clung too tightly to the offerings of the dead (*oblationes defunctorum*), for assigning 'at last to worthy uses that which had been for so long piled up uselessly', so that 'they once again experienced the refreshments of the offerings that they had given'.[20]

These texts reveal the initial construction of one of the core networks of the medieval economy of salvation. Links were forged between offerings made in the name of the dead and the ecclesiastical authorities who would see to it that they brought refreshment to the poor, and, by extension, to the dead themselves. A bad bishop could impede the flow of offerings and the solace they brought and a good one could restore the system to its proper functioning. But something else was going on as well. By the early sixth century, Bishop Caesarius of Arles was equating gifts to the church with alms to the poor by urging his congregations to direct their charity as much to monks and nuns as to their impoverished neighbours. Although the poverty of monks was voluntary, they could still claim need. Moreover, because they were 'dead to the world', they could receive both alms for the poor and offerings for the dead.

Together, these new findings on burial, cemeteries and the relationship between the poor and the dead sweep away the last vestiges of the notion that Christian leaders were quick to translate the Gospel into new responses to death, burial and commemoration. They also allow us to add two more lines to the chart on the watershed of the year 400.

In spite of the rhetoric of the imperial Church, there was no concerted push in Late Antiquity to bring all forms of social behaviour within a thor-

---

19 Frederick S. Paxton, '*Oblationes defunctorum*: The Poor and the Dead in Late Antiquity and the Early Medieval West', in *Proceedings of the Tenth International Conference of Medieval Canon Law*, ed. by Kenneth Pennington, Stanley Chodorow and Keith H. Kendall (Città del Vaticano: Bioblioteca Apostolica Vaticana, 2001), pp. 245–67.

20 *Sermo de uita s. Honorati*, PL 50:1265.

The Late Antique to Early Medieval Watershed Revisited

250	400	550
Baptismal theology		Penitential theology
Emphasis on salvation		Emphasis on sin
Death not to be feared		Death to be feared
Few if any death rituals		Increasing ritualization
No Christian cemeteries		Exclusively Christian cemeteries
Little attention to the poor		The poor linked ritually to the dead

oughly Christian framework. That was the goal of the medieval, not the ancient Church, as medievalists have long suspected. And scholars of Late Antiquity have done a real service in revealing why it took so long. That said, the divisions on the above chart may not be as clear-cut as they appear. In particular, if we extend the investigation beyond the centuries immediately before and after the watershed, and direct our attention to the top three pairs on the chart, the picture becomes more complicated. This is best seen by considering the issue of Christian attitudes toward death itself.

5 Triumphant death and timor mortis

Anyone coming to the history of death and dying in medieval Europe through the work of Philippe Ariès would expect to see little difference in Christian attitudes toward death between the years 200 and 1100. The attitude toward death among early medieval people was, in fact, as old as humanity itself. Death was 'tame' or 'familiar'.[21] People did not fear death, but accepted it as a natural part of life. The death of any particular person was subsumed into the larger contexts of family, community, even species, and death and dying were met with simple rituals and emotional restraint. Change came only in the twelfth century when clerics started to highlight the significance of each individual's death. Fear and tension grew around the deathbed only in the later Middle Ages, as God's judgement came to seem more personal and more immediate.

Subsequent research has shown how oversimplified this picture is. There was no primordial attitude toward death as familiar and tame in the early

21 Philippe Ariès, *Western Attitudes toward Death from the Middle Ages to the Present*, Eng. trans. by Patricia M. Ranum (Baltimore and London: Johns Hopkins University Press, 1974); idem, *The Hour of our Death*, Eng. trans. by Helen Weaver (New York: Knopf, 1981), pp. 5–92.

Middle Ages. This was implicit in my work on early medieval death rituals, but it is worth making more explicit when even as sensitive a scholar as Caroline Walker Bynum could write that 'As the great historian Philippe Ariès has taught us, the medieval stress on personal death, 'my death', developed within an attitude that was far older, even pre-Christian: a sense that death is familiar and near, an expected part of life, an experience of which persons are often forewarned.'[22] Ariès' literary exemplars of 'tame' death, like the hero of *The Song of Roland*, died as they did not because their authors were in touch with age-old rhythms of pre-Christian culture, but because they had inherited a complex of ritualized gestures and utterances assembled over the preceding thousand years by Christian clerics, monks and nuns. That is supported by the research on late ancient Christianity reviewed above. One question remains, though. Did a brooding sense of sin and fear of death dominate Latin Christianity from the fifth century onwards? Peter Brown has explicitly taken up where Rebillard left off. Comparing early medieval views on sin with those held by the ancient Church and by Greek Christianity and Islam, he found that, by the seventh century, the Latin West had gone its own way, towards what he has called a 'peccatization of the world', defined by 'the reduction of all experience, of history, politics and the social order quite as much as the destiny of individual souls, to two universal explanatory principles, sin and repentance'.[23] Such conclusions might lead us to think that early medieval Christians were doomed to 'a *longue durée* of terror' in the face of death and the afterlife.[24] Were they?

In part, the answer lies in directions already noted by both Rebillard and Brown. That is, for every turn toward fear and the awareness of sin, there was a corresponding turn toward their amelioration. As the hour of death became more frightening, the Church offered more rituals to reassure and comfort the dying. As recognition of sin and the need for penance grew, so did the availability, variety, and precision of forms of confession and satisfaction, both in this life and the next. In fact, one could regard the early growth of the medieval economy of salvation as a sustained reaction to the new attitudes introduced by Augustine in the early fifth century. But something else happened

---

22 'Death and Resurrection in the Middle Ages: Some Modern Implications', *Proceedings of the American Philosophical Society*, 142 (1998), pp. 589–96, at p. 590.

23 Peter Brown, 'Vers la naissance du purgatoire. Amnistie et pénitence dans le christianisme occidental de l'Antiquité tardive au haut Moyen Âge', *Annales HSS*, 52 (1997), pp. 1247–61, p. 1260. But cf. Brown's, *The Rise of Western Christendom* 1st edition (Oxford: Blackwell, 1996), 148–66; and 2nd edition (Oxford: Blackwell, 2003), pp. 248–66.

24 Caroline Walker Bynum, *The Resurrection of the Body in Western Christendom, 200–1336* (New York: Columbia University Press, 1995), p. 12.

as well. Remnants of ancient attitudes remained scattered about the textual and mental landscape. They had never really disappeared, and could be reintroduced into the discourse around death and dying when conditions changed. This occurred in two important ways in the ninth century.

The first was through the introduction of a death ritual known as the Roman *ordo in agenda defunctorum* into the growing body of rituals around death and burial in the Carolingian world. I have previously discussed the details of how this occurred, so will not go into them here, but I do want to make one argument.[25] I followed Damien Sicard in dating the Roman death ritual to the fifth century, if not earlier, but Rebillard rejected its antiquity on the grounds that any ritual with deathbed communion must postdate the changes he identified on the latter side of the late antique/early medieval watershed.[26] In so far as he meant communion as viaticum, the argument is strong. Rites of deathbed penance did become more regular and widespread between 500 and 700, as public penance diminished in use and private confession began to spread. Since the viaticum was always embedded in deathbed penance rituals, its use spread along with them. Such rituals may have emerged and spread because bishops saw it as their pastoral duty to extend aid to dying sinners, but ordinary Christians may have been equally responsible by demanding something to mitigate the fears that resulted from the new attitudes towards death being demonstrated by the clergy. Whatever the case, Rebillard is right that this sort of deathbed communion became more common in the early Middle Ages.

If we go along with him completely, however, we are faced with a dilemma. As Sicard first revealed, the Roman *ordo* is permeated with themes of optimism and confidence in salvation. It is a ritual of triumph over death and entry into the heavenly Jerusalem that is in perfect accord with Rebillard's description of the dominant attitude toward death before the fifth century. That is particularly true of its reference to deathbed communion, which is not referred to as a 'viaticum' but as an agent in the resurrection of the dead and an 'advocate and helper' at the court of the last judgement.[27]

Even if Rebillard is right – if the Roman *ordo* was written after the fifth century, at Rome or elsewhere – it would then attest to a counter-current to

---

25 Paxton, *Christianizing Death*, pp. 37–44.

26 Cf. Damien Sicard, *La liturgie de la mort dans l'église latine des origines à la réforme carolingienne*, Liturgiewissenschaftliche Quellen und Forschungen, 63 (Münster: Aschendorff, 1978), pp. 1–257; and Rebillard, *In hora mortis*, pp. 226–27.

27 I myself confused the issue by referring to the deathbed communion in the Roman *ordo* as 'viaticum' (*Christianizing Death*, pp. 38–46) and remain grateful to Rebillard for making me aware of my mistake.

the one that is supposed to distinguish the spirituality of the early-medieval Latin Church from its late-ancient predecessor. In either case, the frame seems too stiff. Whether or not it is an authentic product of the period before the watershed (and given the well-known conservatism of the Roman Church, it is possible that the *ordo* was preserved, even if not practised, from the fourth to the eighth century), once it arrived in Francia, it was positioned to contribute a triumphant strain to the fully articulated ritual process that became the medieval Latin Christian death ritual by the later ninth century.

This happened because the Carolingian Church, however much it focused on sin and the need for penance, had a place for optimism in the face of death. While Rebillard did not make the claim, I would be willing to argue that the tone of those late fourth-century sermons on death and dying arose in part from the triumphant mood of a Church that had gone from a persecuted sect to one of the central institutions of the Roman Empire in just three generations. The Carolingians were in a similar position. The Franks were a 'New Israel' and Charles was a new King David. The Frankish Church marched from victory to victory along with the Frankish empire. It should not surprise us that the return of imperial ideologies brought with it the return of triumphant attitudes towards death.

The other way such attitudes entered the discourse around death and dying under the Carolingians is through the same sort of literature that Rebillard used so compellingly in his analysis of the late antique/early medieval watershed: scriptural commentary and exegetical sermons. The Epistle of Paul to the Hebrews was not accepted as canonical in the West until the fifth century, so there are no Latin patristic commentaries on it. John Chrysostom, however, wrote a series of 34 Greek homilies on Hebrews, which were translated into Latin in the sixth century.[28] Because of its Greek origin and the late date of its translation, Rebillard did not discuss this text, but it represents the same attitude toward death apparent in the sermons of Chrysostom's north Italian contemporaries such as Ambrose of Milan.

No one seems to have done much with the Latin translation of Chrysostom's homilies until Alcuin of York (d. 804) used them as the basis for his own commentary on Paul's letter to the Hebrews.[29] Commenting on chapter 2, verses 14 and 15, where Paul discusses Jesus's deliverance of those whom the devil kept in bondage through fear of death, Chrysostom had asked his audi-

28 The original text of the 34 Homilies and its Latin translations is in the *Patrologia Graeca* 63.9–456; there is an English translation in *A Select Library of the Nicene and Post-Nicene Fathers* (New York, 1899; repr. Grand Rapids: Eerdmans, 1983), pp. XIV, 365–522.
29 *Vita Alcuini*, PL 100.103C; the commentary is in PL 100.1031–84.

ence: 'Why are you afraid when that which you fear has been already destroyed? Death is no longer terrible, but trodden underfoot ...' Alcuin departed from his model at just this point, writing instead:

> Death is no longer terrible, but desirable, like the end of labour and the beginning of rest. Why does Paul talk of 'those who through fear of death were subject to lifelong bondage'? Because they had been servants of death; because they feared death. They had not yet been released from fear of death, by whose laws they were held. Now, however, the saints, who have passed through the struggle and conquered death, laugh at it, as they pass into the kingdom.[30]

Alcuin's treatment goes well beyond Chrysostom's in its triumphant acclamation of Christ's salvation. He does not pretend that death itself is easy, it is still an *agon*, a struggle, but he assures his readers that death's power is laughable to those who have passed beyond it. When Alcuin's pupil, Hrabanus Maurus, made his own commentary on Hebrews, he retained more of Chrysostom's original text, at least in some places, but followed Alcuin exactly here.[31] Hrabanus' student Walafrid Strabo did not write a commentary on Hebrews, but there may be an echo of Alcuin in his gloss to the end of verse 3 of Psalm 131, 'I will not enter my house or get into my bed' when he notes that 'to the right of the Father, where the bed is, there is rest and the end of labours'.[32]

Alcuin also addressed the question raised by Christ's agony in the Garden, which had been so important to patristic discussions of the fear of death.[33] In his commentary on Hebrews 5, verse 7, 'In the days of his flesh, Jesus offered up prayers and supplications, with loud cries and tears, to him who was able to save him from death', Alcuin asserted that Paul did not mean that Christ feared death. His prayers and supplications were poured out not from fear of death but for our salvation.[34] Hrabanus once again followed Alcuin exactly, as did Sedulius Scottus, a little later in the ninth century.[35]

---

30 PL 100.1042BC (Alcuin's additions are in boldface): Quare tremitis, quare timetis eam quae jam condemnata est? Jam terribilis non est, sed optabilis, quasi laborum finis et requiei initium. Cur ait: *Timore mortis per totam vitam obnoxii erant servituti*? Servi quidem omnes fuerant mortis, quia mortem timebant; necdum erant soluti a timore mortis, cujus legibus tenebantur. Nunc itaque sancti derident eam, qui agone transacto et morte devicta ad regnum transituri sunt; cf. PG 63.265–66.

31 PL 112.711–752.

32 PL 113.1050D: ascendero etc., ad dexterum Patris, ubi lectus, id est requies et finis laborum. In the tenth century, Atto of Vercelli once again copied Alcuin: PL 134.727–834.

33 Rebillard, *In hora mortis*, pp. 70–78.

34 PL 100.1054D: Beatus Paulus hic dicit preces eum et supplicationes fundere, non timore mortis, sed nostrae causa salutis.

35 Cf. PL 112.743D–744A; and PL 103.258B: *Et lacrymis*. Pro nostra salute, non timore mortis profusis.

While Latin Christians may have emphasized sin or salvation at particular times and places, over the long term they avoided too much emphasis on the one, because it could lead to despair, or the other, because it could lessen the importance of divine judgement and individual responsibility. To argue that death was not feared for the first 400 or so years of Christian history is, in the end, as misleading as to the argument that fear of death dominated the medieval mind. On the one hand, the ancient Church hardly ignored sin or fear of judgement. The penitential system that emerged in the second and third centuries was so strict that it had to be scrapped once the majority of the population converted. On the other hand, while fifth-century clerics may have put the accent on sin in a way earlier Christians had not, they nevertheless joined in a chorus whose themes had already been laid down. The triumphant optimism of the imperial Church may indeed have been followed by a period where the stress shifted to pessimism. During the Carolingian period, however, a new balance was struck, which fostered the continued growth of the medieval economy of salvation.

6 The community of the living and the dead

The reception and spread of triumphant attitudes toward death is not the only example of a countervailing response to the heightened sense of sin and uncertainty identified by historians of the watershed between the late antique and early medieval Church in the Latin West. The most important was the rise of the cult of the saints, who acted as powerful, and powerfully present, patrons of individuals and families, both natural and monastic. The resistance of saints' relics to decomposition and their power to cure the sick acted both as proof of the resurrection and as a powerful antidote to the deeply human fear of disintegration in the face of death.[36] The cult of the saints was also responsible for the dissolution of the strict boundaries that had always divided the living and the dead in Mediterranean antiquity, and their eventual coming together as one community of the faithful both in heaven and on earth. In the ancient Mediterranean world, burials were prohibited within city walls, which led to a characteristic feature of the landscape, where graves and catacombs lined the roads to and from the city, a situation that persisted right to the end of the imperial period. In the newly Christianized and predominantly rural lands of the north, relics of saints and the desire for their patronage attracted

36 Peter Brown, *The Cult of the Saints: Its Rise and Function in Latin Christianity* (Chicago: University of Chicago Press, 1982); Bynum, *Resurrection of the Body*, pp. 59–114.

the bodies of the dead to the churches and churchyard cemeteries of the emerging parish system. First in the form of saints' relics, and then later in the form of the bodies of those who wished to be buried near them, the dead slowly but surely came to rest in the midst of villages, towns and cities. Essentially complete by the year 1100, this process caused a clean break with antiquity and reconfigured the landscape of Christendom. From that time on, the dead resided at the heart of even the most urban of communities.

The space of Christian society, however, only encompassed those who lived and died in good standing. Burials were organized according to a moral scale, with the holiest of the dead at the centre and others around them in proportion to their own claims to holiness: saints, bishops, abbots, monks, and pious (and wealthy) lay men and women.[37] Those not in good standing, like suicides, murderers, the excommunicated, and heretics, were relegated to unconsecrated ground away from both living and dead Christians. Research on Anglo-Saxon cemeteries, for example, has revealed the widespread presence of execution sites along parish boundaries, often in conjunction with ancient barrows.[38]

Once the dead were buried, attention turned to commemorative practices that were designed to usher their souls into the community of the blessed in paradise. From the seventh century onwards, under the influence of Gregory the Great's *Dialogues*, whose fourth book detailed the benefits of the mass to souls in the afterlife, monk-priests and clerics began to participate directly in the economy of salvation by offering private masses for the dead. They also developed more commemorative rituals for members of their religious *familiae*, lasting for seven and thirty days after a death, and yearly on anniversaries, which became characteristic features of medieval monastic commemorations.[39] Then, around 761, a group of Carolingian churchmen officially committed themselves to mutual commemoration after death, creating the first formal confraternity of prayer. Not long afterwards, monastic congregations began to make similar arrangements with other houses, and in 805, a Bavarian council included alms for the poor among their contractual obligations, a move that

---

37 Megan McLaughlin, *Consorting with Saints: Prayer for the Dead in Early Medieval France* (Ithaca: Cornell University Press, 1994), pp. 113–32.

38 Andrew Reynolds, 'The Definition and Ideology of Anglo-Saxon Execution Sites and Cemeteries', in *Death and Burial in Medieval Europe: Papers of the 'Medieval Europe Brugge 1997' Conference*, vol. 2, ed. by Guy de Boe and Frans Verhaege, IAP rapporten, 2 (Brugge: Zellik, 1997), pp. 33–41.

39 E. Freistedt, *Altchristliche Totengedächtnistage und ihre Beziehung zum Jenseitsglauben und Totenkultus der Antike*, Liturgiewissenschaftliche Quellen und Forschungen, 24 (Münster: Aschendorff, 1928). pp. 4–35; McLaughlin, *Consorting*, pp. 50–54.

brought the poor into the centre of the early medieval economy of salvation.[40] Over the course of the following three centuries, Benedictine houses of men and women made the commemoration of the dead, and the care of the poor in their name, central aspects of their communal lives. The poor remained as anonymous, ubiquitous, and oppressed as they had ever been, of course. They were unlikely to be remembered as individuals or prayed for after their own deaths, except in the most general way. But they were not entirely forgotten. And their inclusion in the economy of salvation had real results. Ulrich of Cluny reported that in the late eleventh century as many as 17,000 paupers received meals each year at the great Burgundian abbey in the name of the dead.[41] There is also good evidence that the standard of living of the men and women who worked the estates of the Cluniacs in the eleventh century was as high as that of the monks themselves.[42]

Carolingian monks also introduced the regular performance of the office of the dead and began to allow laymen and women to take vows at the end of life, so as to die in the monastic infirmary, be buried in the community's cemetery, and benefit from proximity to those who spent their days and night praying for the faithful departed. Finally, they set down the names of those for whom they owed masses, prayers and alms in new sorts of books, known as *libri vitae* or *libri memoriales*, some of which grew to include as many as 40,000 entries by the twelfth century.[43] They may have acted as much out of anxiety as out of confidence in the face of death, but, whatever their motivations, their actions, like the actions of the saints, bound together the community of the living and the dead in an increasingly complex exchange of material and spiritual goods.

7 Cluny and the early medieval economy of salvation

The Benedictine monastery of Cluny was the most perfect expression of the early medieval economy of salvation. This is apparent even in its foundation charter. Duke William I of Aquitaine (875–918), Cluny's founder, was the

40 MGH LL 3 *Concilia* 2.233.

41 PL 149.753.

42 Joachim Wollasch, *Cluny 'Licht der Welt': Aufstieg und Niedergang der klösterlichen Gemeinschaft* (Düsseldorf: Artemis & Winkler, 1996), pp. 113–19.

43 Nicholas Huyghebaert and Jean-Loup Lemaître, *Les documents nécrologiques*, Typologie des sources du Moyen Âge occidental, 4 (Turnhout: Brepols, 1972).

grandson of the extraordinary Dhuoda, whose famous manual for her eldest son (William's uncle) testifies to the importance of prayer for the dead among the Carolingian aristocracy in the mid-ninth century.[44] William may never have seen Dhuoda's book, but he certainly shared its central conceptions, the most important of which was the obligation to pray for those who gave life and land. William must also have shared in the conceptions behind the many visions of the afterlife that circulated in his lifetime. Not long before he founded Cluny, for example, the Carolingian emperor Charles the Fat was reported to have had a dream vision of the afterlife, where he met his father, Louis the German, standing in a boiling cask up to his thighs. Louis said to him, 'If you, and my faithful bishops and abbots, and the whole ecclesiastical order will quickly assist me with Masses, prayers and psalms, and alms and vigils, I will shortly be released from the punishment of the boiling water'.[45] William of Aquitaine's charter for Cluny was a hedge against a similar fate.[46]

As the charter tells us, after considering the biblical proverb that 'the riches of a man are the redemption of his soul', William decided both that he should 'reserve' some of his wealth for that purpose and that there was no better use for it than by 'making friends with God's poor' – by whom he meant reformed monks. Although the property being granted represented only 'a bit' (*aliquantulum*) of the duke's vast resources, it was enough to provide the new community with a solid foundation in the region's agricultural economy. With the means of life so provided, the monks were to fill the church at Cluny with 'prayers, petitions and exhortations' to help William obtain 'the reward of the righteous'. They were also directed to pray for William's king, parents, wife, family, faithful servants, and all right-believing Christians; and to engage daily in 'works of mercy toward the poor, the needy, strangers and pilgrims'.

The transactional character of the foundation charter of Cluny is no accident. The transfer of property and power in return for spiritual services it

---

44 Dhuoda, *Handbook for William: A Carolingian Woman's Counsel for Her Son*, translated and with an introduction by Carol Neel (Lincoln, Nebraska: The University of Nebraska Press, 1991); reprinted with an Afterword by Carol Neel (Washington: Catholic University of America Press, 1999).

45 Eileen Gardiner, *Medieval Visions of Heaven and Hell* (New York: Garland, 1993), pp. 131–32; cf. Paul Edward Dutton, *The Politics of Dreaming in the Carolingian Empire* (Lincoln: University of Nebraska Press, 1994), pp. 233–37.

46 The charter is in A. Bruel, *Recueil des chartes de l'abbaye de Cluny* (Paris, 1876; repr. Impr. Nationale, 1974), pp. 124–28 (no. 112); and H. Atsma and J. Vezin, with the collaboration of S. Barret, *Les plus anciens documents originaux de l'abbaye de Cluny*, vol. 1 (Turnhout: Brepols, 1997), pp. 33–42 (no. 4). There is an English translation in Patrick Geary, *Readings in Medieval History*, 2nd ed. (Peterborough: Broadview Press, 1997), pp. 304–6. Its dating clause is ambiguous, but it was signed on September 11 in either 909 or 910.

records derives from the combined dynamics of the early medieval gift economy and the economy of salvation. The first assured that most exchanges involved reciprocal obligations of a personal nature, and the second insisted that the transfer of wealth to the poor in this world (both monks, who chose their poverty, and the involuntary poor, to whom the monks were to provide food and other forms of care) was the primary means of bringing aid to souls in the afterlife.

For all its clarity over the importance of prayer and almsgiving for the dead at Cluny, the foundation charter makes no mention of rituals around death itself or when and how often the monks were to perform the intercessory activities they owed to William. Moreover, since no liturgical sources survive from the first century of Cluny's existence, there is no way to know. It is safe to assume, however, that members of the community were prepared for death through anointing with oil, deathbed confession and communion as viaticum, since those were standard features of later ninth- and tenth-century monastic death rituals in the Carolingian realms.[47] It is also likely that the early Cluniacs commemorated their dead brothers and lay benefactors with alms, prayers and psalms on the anniversary of their deaths and, in a more general way, at regular masses for the dead and at the offices of vespers, matins and lauds of the dead.[48]

The earliest specific information on death rituals at Cluny comes from the mid-eleventh-century *Liber tramitis*, an Italian version of the customs of Cluny under Abbot Odilo (994–1049). Comparison of the *Liber tramitis* with the later customaries of Ulrich and Bernard of Cluny suggests that, around the year 1000, the Cluniacs began a concentrated and long-term intensification of their commitment to the care of the dying and the dead, which produced their own highly distinctive death rituals and brought them to the height of their fame as intercessors for suffering souls.[49] Sometime in the 1020s, Odilo reconfirmed

47 Paxton, *Christianizing Death*, pp. 169–200.

48 For a continental example of a tenth-century monastic death ritual, see Julian Montgomery Hendrix, 'Liturgy for the Dead and the Confraternity of Reichenau and St. Gall, 800–950', doctoral dissertation, King's College Cambridge, 2007; for the British Isles, see *Regularis concordia Anglicae nationis*, ed. by Thomas Symons and Sigrid Spath, CCM 7.3 (Siegburg: Schmitt, 1984), pp. 69–14; and *Aelfric's Letter to the Monks of Eynsham*, ed. and trans. Christopher A. Jones, Cambridge Studies in Anglo-Saxon England, 24 (Cambridge: Cambridge University Press, 1998).

49 *Liber tramitis aevi Odilonis abbatis*, ed. Peter Dinter (Siegburg: Schmitt, 1980); Frederick S. Paxton, 'Death by Customary at Eleventh-Century Cluny', in *From Dead of Night to End of Day: The Medieval Customs of Cluny/Du cœur de la nuit à la fin du jour: Les coutumes clunisiennes au Moyen Âge*, ed. by Susan Boynton & Isabelle Cochelin, Disciplina monastica, 3 (Turnhout: Brepols, 2005), pp. 297–318; and Paxton, *The Death Ritual at Cluny in the Central Middle Ages, Disciplina monastica*, 9 (Turnhout: Brepols, 2013).

and extended Cluny's responsibility for the salvation of all Christians when he established the Feast of All Souls (November 2). After his death, hagiographical accounts advertised his responsibility for initiating the feast and the success of his monks in aiding suffering souls with their prayers, masses, and care of the poor.[50] A monastic chronicler of the period wrote how masses for the dead at Cluny could literally snatch souls from the jaws of the demons below.[51] Under Odilo and his three successors, the abbey of Cluny received the greatest number of gifts, and buried and commemorated the most monks and laity, of any church in Christendom.[52]

When the early growth of the medieval economy of salvation peaked, like Cluny itself, in the later eleventh and twelfth centuries, the social, institutional and cultural changes that mark the watershed between the early and later Middle Ages were already calling into question some of its essential features. Around the year 1000, just as the Cluniac movement was hitting its stride, voices began to be raised in the Latin West against the power of priests and the cult of the saints.[53] By the later eleventh and early twelfth century, critics had begun to reject the whole notion that the living could bring succour to the dead. Henry of Le Mans allegedly taught that 'No good work helps the dead, for as soon as men die they either are utterly damned or are saved,' and Peter of Bruys scorned 'the sacrificial offerings, prayers, charities, and the rest of the good works done by the faithful who live, on behalf of the faithful who are dead.'[54] The tide was even turning within the Benedictine tradition itself. The Cluniac abbot Peter the Venerable (1122–56) had to respond not just to the relentless internal logic of the medieval economy of salvation by limiting its growth, but also to Cistercian criticisms of the use of gold and other luxury objects around the deathbed. He also vigorously defended the importance of commemoration of the dead, both from the Cistercians, who thought it took

50 *Iotsald von Saint-Claude, Vita des Abtes Odilo von Cluny*, ed. Johannes Staub, MGH SRG 68 (Hannover: Hansche, 1999), pp. 218–20, 293–94.

51 Radulfus Glaber/Raoul Glaber, *Rudolfi Glabri historiarum libri quinque/ Rodulfus Glaber, The Five Books of the Histories*, V.13, ed. and trans. by John France (Oxford: Clarendon, 1989), pp. 234–37.

52 Dominique Iogna-Prat, 'Des morts très spéciaux aux morts ordinaires: la pastorale funéraire clunisienne (XIe–XIIe siècles)', *Médiévales*, 31 (1996), pp. 79–91; 'Les morts dans la comptabilité des Clunisiens de l'an Mil', in *Religion et culture autour de l'an mil: Royaume capétien et Lotharingie*, ed. by Dominique Iogna-Prat and Jean-Charles Picard (Paris: Picard, 1990), pp. 55–69; Dietrich Poeck, 'Laienbegräbnisse in Cluny', *Frühmittelalterliche Studien*, 14 (1980), pp. 68–179.

53 Walter L. Wakefield and Austin P. Evans, *Heresies of the High Middle Ages* (New York: Columbia University Press, 1969), pp. 76, 85.

54 Wakefield and Evans, *Heresies*, pp. 117, 121.

up to much time away from private prayer and contemplation, and from more radical critics like Peter of Bruys and Henry of Le Mans. Unfortunately, his defensive posture put Cluny at odds not just with Cistercians and heretics, but also with Muslims and Jews, who were being increasingly viewed as threats to the very existence of the Latin Church.[55] Moreover, as the gift economy of the early Middle Ages gave way to a growing profit economy, new ways to contract for care of the dead emerged, subtly but irrevocably changing the system at whose heart Cluny lay.[56] One of the most important, the granting of indulgences, helped spark the dismantling of the medieval economy of salvation in the Protestant Reformation. In spite of all this, the products of the early growth of the medieval economy of salvation were significant and lasting. By the twelfth century, Latin Christian death rituals had become standardized and most ordinary Christians sought confession and other sacraments before death, burial in consecrated ground, and liturgical commemoration by religious specialists afterwards. The Christian dead everywhere shared the same space as the living and the living believed that their dead family members expected and deserved their help in the afterlife. In spite of critics, changing economic realities and the fact that the Cluniacs had seen their day, the medieval economy of salvation was there to stay.

8 Later reflections on the conference papers (26 May 2011)

When Stefan Reif invited me to this conference I expected to learn more about medieval Ashkenazi responses to death than anyone would from my thoughts on the overall development of such things in Latin Christendom. I was not disappointed. Scholars of medieval Christianity have made impressive advances in this field, but in almost total ignorance of corresponding work in Jewish Studies. As the wide-ranging papers showed, closing that gap will be well worth the trouble.

---

55 Dominique Iogna-Prat, *Ordonner et exclure: Cluny et la société chrétienne face à l'hérésie, au judaïsme et à l'islam* (Paris: Aubier, 2000), pp. 103–52; Eng. trans. by Graham R. Edwards, *Order and Exclusion. Cluny and Christendom Face Heresy, Judaism, and Islam (1000–1150)* (Ithaca: Cornell University Press, 2002).

56 Jean-Claude Schmitt, *Ghosts in the Middle Ages: The Living and the Dead in Medieval Society*, Eng. trans. by Teresa Lavender Fagan, (Chicago: University of Chicago Press, 1998), pp. 123–38; Lester K. Little, *Religious Poverty and the Profit Economy in Medieval Europe* (Ithaca: Cornell University Press, 1978).

While the development of Christian death rituals was a slow process, barely under way as late as the fourth and fifth centuries CE, the corresponding development in Judaism was even slower, in large part because of the continuing power of the notion that death brought ritual impurity, a notion whose banishment was itself a major marker of Christianity's divergence from its Judaic roots. That said, the common stock of biblical texts that Christians and Jews shared, along with belief in the resurrection of the dead and doctrinal ambiguity about the state and location of the soul between death and final judgement, provided ample openings for cultural interchange over the long run. Once Ashkenazi communities had established themselves in north-western Europe in the central Middle Ages, these and other factors, such as the tension between popular religion and orthodoxy that is endemic in monotheism, and the common experience of the Black Death, led to a surprising amount of convergence. Thus, by the later Middle Ages, similarities may have come to outweigh differences, at least with regard to the importance of graves and cemeteries as markers of communal and individual identity, memorial practices and belief in ghosts. Not surprisingly, the cultural drift was toward Christian practice, but not at the expense of elements that marked Ashkenazi beliefs and practices as distinctively Jewish. They could always claim, if they thought about it at all, that whatever they appropriated from the dominant culture had been theirs to begin with, and their responses to death were too deeply marked by the memories of those murdered or forced into suicide by Christians to be mistaken as anything else.

In the first presentation of the day, Yitzhak Lifshitz argued that *Av ha-raḥamim*, a 'memory poem' about the Crusader massacres of 1096, became a lasting feature of Jewish death rituals, right down to the present, in part through the *loss of memory* of its original context, namely, remembering the names of the dead. Abraham Gross then situated *Av ha-raḥamim* within the genre of poems (*piyyuṭim*) commemorating the *Tatnu*, as the massacres came to be called, arguing that the *piyyuṭim* were themselves part of a larger 'memory system' that was 'unique to the event and to those killed'. In so doing, he helped explain the phenomenon observed by Dr Lifshitz. A poem or prayer could not become part of a liturgical ritual if it mentioned specific people, for that would obstruct the 'ritualization of emotion' that is at the heart of communal liturgies. Many *piyyuṭim* named names, for that was in part their point – to memorialize the martyrs of 1096. *Av ha-raḥamim*, which did not name names, was thus perfectly suited for general use.

The papers by Shmuel Shepkaru and Lucia Raspe were similarly revealing. Professor Shepkaru showed that another response to the *Tatnu* was a shift in notions of the afterlife. The belief that the martyrs of 1096 were already enjoying the fruits of resurrection in heaven may or may not have been influenced by the Christian cult of the saints, which originated in devotion to Christians martyred by the Roman state, but the emergence of a cult of martyrs among Ashkenazi Jews seems to have opened up space for ritual elaboration and cultural convergence that had not previously been possible. The long-term consequences are apparent in Raspe's work [not published in this volume], which reveals that reverence for the dead, as marked by visits to the graves of righteous men, both evoked controversy and bound together Jewish communities in Bavaria and the Rhineland in the fifteenth and sixteenth centuries. Her observation that the Jewish cemetery in Regensburg contained not only a mass grave for victims of the *Tatnu*, but also the grave of one Amran, whom the community believed to be Emmeran, the patron saint of the city, suggests either a bid for a place in a common culture or a kind of thumbing of the nose to the Christian community.

Avriel Bar-Levav's survey of changing attitudes towards death in medieval Ashkenaz highlighted the Jewish notion that, since death is a punishment for sin, the dead were seen as impure and marginal, to be kept separate from the living. Nevertheless, over time, the belief in a connection between physical remains and individual souls led to the practice of visiting graves and their placement in cemeteries according to the reputation for piety or learning of the person buried there. Dr Bar-Levav's own research suggests that the emergence of 'burial societies' in Spain in the thirteenth and fourteenth centuries, and the ritual books that they generated, reflects the influence of Christian confraternities and deathbed rituals. Andreas Lehnardt took the discussion further by focusing on the recitation of the *qaddish* on the anniversary (*yahrzeit*) of the death of one's parents. The development of the practice, from its origin in the rabbinic *yahrzeit* fast to its medieval development as part of the general reaction to the *Tatnu*, and to the burgeoning practice of memorial masses for the dead among Christians in the thirteenth and fourteenth centuries, shows how the later medieval economy of salvation appealed to urban populations of both faiths before and after the Black Death. Yechiel Schur returned to that theme in his survey of learned discussions of the resurrection of the dead in the thirteenth century, which reflects exactly the kinds of concerns about disintegration and ghosts that Caroline Walker Bynum and Jean Claude-Schmitt have uncovered in the works of contemporary Christian writers and theologians.

While these results display the convergence of practice across the religious divide, Jeffrey Woolf looked at a striking example of how they diverged. Woolf reported that, while ritual impurity of the dead was a minor concern among medieval Ashkenazim, they transferred the notion of impurity from the dead to the Christian land that surrounded their cemeteries, the sacred space they had carved out for the graves of the righteous. Similarly, Peter Lehnardt and Ruth Langer showed how one particular poem, the *ṣidduq ha-din*, a song of praise and faith in God's mercy and in the resurrection of the dead, spread from the Land of Israel to medieval Ashkenaz, where it was assimilated to emerging death rituals in different ways all over Europe. Chana Friedman argued that the mourning rite of 'turning the bed' developed out of a talmudic resistance to popular and persistent cultural practices; Adiel Kadari reported on the practice of placing Torah scrolls on the biers of the dead; and Nati Barak presented evidence of a growing tendency after the Black Death to ask for personal items to be included in one's grave.

The essays on epitaphs and tombstones, which I read during the preparation of this volume, deepened my sense of the similarities and differences of the two communities in a number of important ways. The matter-of-fact tone of Natanja Hüttenmeister, Andreas Lehnhardt and Avraham Reiner in their reports on the discovery of new gravestones from the medieval cemeteries of Mainz and Würzburg heightened, if anything, the emotional impact of the crimes perpetrated upon the Jewish communities of those cities from the eleventh through the fourteenth centuries that they record, especially the almost total obliteration of the Jews of Würzburg in the so-called Rindfleisch Massacres of 1298. The state of the evidence is in fact directly related to those disasters, for most of the gravestones had either been buried or reused in buildings erected after the destruction of the communal cemeteries. Epitaphs on tombstones from Mainz provide poignant testimonies of otherwise unrecorded pogroms. Others from Würzburg show how a convert could bring the biblical image of 'the bosom of Abraham' from a Christian back into a Jewish cultural context, how tombstones located the dead in relation to Jewish sages, and how the living struggled to remember properly those killed or driven to suicide by their Christian neighbours.

Epitaphs from the cemeteries of more fortunate communities in central and northern Italy and Istanbul during the early modern period (sixteenth–nineteenth centuries), on the other hand, reveal the depth of artistry that could be brought to bear on the ordinary facts of human mortality by drawing on the rich cultural heritage of Torah, Mishna, Kabbala and medieval Ashkenazi and Sefardi poetry. David Malkiel traces the literary history of the rhymed and metered epitaph from its introduction in the early sixteenth century, flowering between 1550 and 1650, decadence and decline between 1750 and 1830 and replacement thereafter by totally new forms that signaled the assimilation of the Jews of Padua into the emergent nation-state of Italy. Mauro Perani introduces the corpus of Italian Jewish epitaphs as a historical source base and makes an impassioned plea for its preservation. Minna Rozen, then, shows how the presence of a similar corpus, not just of epitaphs but of tombstones and their location, can be used to zero in on subsets of a wider population. Her detailed investigation of the tombstones of a group of seventeenth-century Istanbul Jews with the common surname 'Roman' reveals not only tombstone designs that drew on the model of Muslim prayer rugs, but also the Hebrew rhymed and metered epitaph at its height. In the hands of the Romani, who were as often as not poets themselves and composed the epitaphs on the tombs of their loved ones, the representation of grief at the loss of an only daughter, not yet married, or of a wife who died in childbirth, achieves, at times, in a 'truly original' Hebrew, a truly original expression of human loss.

The cumulative effect of all of these fascinating papers is to challenge the notion that there is any point in studying medieval and early modern Christians or Jews (or Muslims for that matter, as Minna Rozen's contribution shows) in isolation from one another. Investigating phenomena like death, dying and the presence of the dead is always a good subject for comparative history, but there is more at stake here. In this case, the objects of comparison are different religious communities that lived in the same cities for centuries. However troubled their relations, their shared descent from Abraham made cultural transmission and some measure of a common, trans-communal culture possible. Studying their responses to death and dying and their relations with the dead makes strikingly clear how much understanding the one more deeply can enhance our understanding of the other. Shedding light on the common culture that they shared from all sides will provide a richer sense of life and death, not just in Jewish, Christian and Muslim communities, but in medieval and early modern Europe and the Dar al-Islam as a whole.

Stefan C. Reif

A Response to Professor Paxton's Paper

1 Introduction

Tel Aviv may justifiably be proud not only, of course, of arranging this important international congress but also of staging, at the Tel Aviv Opera House this week, Sergei Prokoviev's rarely seen opera *Betrothal in a Monastery.* In this opera there is a scene in which the monks, as well as praising wine and pretty women (perhaps a nod in the direction of Soviet Russian ideology by the composer Prokoviev in the 1940s), welcome the death of the half-blind gravedigger who has left them 100 ducats to pray for his soul. They agree to do so, or at least to pray for him to be happy in hell! I mention this so that there can be no accusation that our efforts at this congress are not relevant to the wider world outside. In this case, it may confidently be stated that they even relate directly to the local world of musical culture.[1]

2 Thirty years of research in Latin Christianity

As has so often been the case with aspects of modern Jewish scholarship from its earliest manifestations, *wie es christelt sich, so es yudelt sich.* What modern Christian scholars choose to research also ultimately receives the attention of Jewish academics. I say ultimately because the problem is that it usually takes some little time for the influence to be felt. While what may be called the plastic aspects of such study, ie cemeteries, graves and epitaphs, have received considerable attention, the liturgical aspect has for unclear reasons lagged somewhat behind. I believe that in this case it may have an apotropaic element to it. I recall in my youth having a regular Talmud *shi'ur* (or seminar) in the home of a rabbi who was not only traditionally learned but also took a delight in demonstrating his adherence to at least some notions of *Wissenschaft des Judentums* (חכמת ישראל). His wife was seriously ill with cancer at the time and was bedridden in the next room. When we reached the beginning of the third chapter of the tractate *Berakhot* which begins מי שמתו מוטל לפניו and

1 Each of my headings relates to a consecutive section of Paxton's paper and introduces my thoughts on some of the comments that he makes in that section.

deals with the laws applicable to those who have lost a close relative but have not yet conducted the burial, he requested that we skip over that chapter and move on to the next one. Similarly, I am sure that many Jewish scholars, however *wissenschaftlich* their approach, have not cheerfuly relished the prospect of devoting their attention to such deathly topics. Whatever the rationale behind such hesitations, I have from time to time commented in the course of the past fifteen years or so that it was time that we Jewish scholars clinically investigated the reasons for the revolutionary developments in death liturgy, especially among the Ashkenazi communities of the high Middle Ages. And now I am delighted to say that we are doing so here at Tel Aviv University and that we shall, as a result, perhaps catch up with Christian scholarship.

3 Medieval economy of salvation

Here again the tendency of recent decades has been to pursue in many areas of Jewish studies Weberian notions of historical development and to neglect the theological, literary and cultural significance of revolutionary changes in favour of their social and economic motivations. I therefore welcome Professor Paxton's caution in this respect and hope that we can find the religious notions that underlie the creation of novel liturgy in the period under discussion at this congress, without of course in any way denying that there are always, as I have myself often argued, all manner of non-religious or a-religious inspirations for some of the developments.

4 Watersheds of the fifth and twelfth centuries

So often in Jewish literary and religious history, the assumption is made that the source of much evolution of thought, custom and practice is to be found in the talmudic period and that the innovative aspect is then subsequently lost until about the twelfth century. In the field of liturgy, Ismar Elbogen, who dictated the scholarly agenda for virtually a century was particularly guilty of this foible.[2] Whatever his protestations, the truth is that the geonic period and

---

2 See Elbogen's comments on the medieval period in I. Elbogen, German edition (= G), *Der jüdische Gottesdienst in seiner geschichtlichen Entwicklung* (Frankfurt am Main: Kaufmann, 1931; reprint, Hildesheim: Olms, 1962), pp. 271–72; Hebrew edition (= H), התפילה בישראל בהתפתחותה ההיסטורית (eds. J. Heinemann, I. Adler, A. Negev, J. Petuchowski and H. Schirmann, Tel Aviv: Dvir, 1972), pp. 203–4; English edition (= E), *Jewish Liturgy: A Comprehensive*

the century or two afterwards were highly productive periods. The difficulty facing the researcher is that many rabbinic authorities presenting fresh ideas and suggesting radical changes during those centuries did so under the guise of interpreting, summarizing and codifying the talmudic traditions, preferring to conceal the novel nature of much of what they were proposing, presumably in order to forestall any criticism from more strictly traditional circles. What we are therefore required to do is to uncover precisely what was genuinely talmudic and what amounted to a progression beyond the talmudic position.

5 Christian liturgical developments at Cluny

If I may be permitted to cite a sentence that I penned in a volume that I published in 1993: 'whether such prayers [linked with death] had their origins in earlier Jewish tradition or, as may be suspected, constituted a Jewish version of mourning practices performed in the more general Christian environment, as Petuchowski has briefly suggested, remains to be researched in a satisfactory way'.[3] This issue does indeed remain to be satisfactorily resolved – and I hope the required resolution will at least partly be achieved in this week's round of presentations – but it seems to me highly unlikely that the intense and important liturgical development in such a major Christian centre as Cluny in Burgundy and the novel, and indeed contemporary, Jewish concern with introducing liturgies of various sorts for the dead, sometimes accompanied by acts of charity, are to be viewed as unrelated. After all, we know of Jewish-Christian cultural contacts in France at that period and such contacts may well have inspired in Jewish worshippers the notion that their Christian counterparts had effected a system for, as Professor Paxton puts it, 'snatching souls from the jaws of the demons below'. In that case, would they not have felt themselves duty-bound to accord similar liturgical favours to their own deceased sisters and brothers?

6 Theology, economy and salvation

The Christian doctrinal definition of theology, economy and salvation, noted by Paxton, is somewhat reminiscent, *mutatis mutandis*, of the rabbinic division

History (ed. and trans. by Raymond P. Scheindlin, Philadelphia, Jerusalem and New York: Jewish Publication Society of America, 1993), p. 213.

3 S. C. Reif, *Judaism and Hebrew Prayer: New Perspectives on Jewish Liturgical History* (Cambridge: Cambridge University Press, 1993), p. 220.

of Judaism into *Torah*, *'Avoda* and *Gemillut Ḥasadim* (that is, 'Study and Practice, Worship and Ethics', if you like). Part of this third-listed rabbinic notion undoubtedly includes charitable donations to Torah institutions, as was much practised in the geonic period. What is particularly interesting is the link also made in the rabbinic sources, especially in liturgical custom, between prayers for the dead and charitable gifts. These latter are identified as the *matnat yad* that is pentateuchally ordained on the three pilgrim festivals (eg Deut 16:16–17), and those festivals became the occasions on which special memorial prayers were recited for close relatives who had gone to their heavenly repose.[4]

7 Memorialization of the dead for three centuries after Charlemagne

This was precisely the period – the ninth to the twelfth centuries – during which the Ashkenazi Jews developed their liturgies for memorializing the dead, especially by way of the *hazkarat neshamot* or *yizkor* prayers and of course the *qaddish yatom* (the orphan's *qaddish)*, as well as by the recitation of such memorials to martyrs as *Av ha-raḥamim.*[5]

8 Criticism of the living acting for the dead

In the Jewish arena, the ongoing tension between halakhic purists and enthusiasts of more mystical indulgences was often expressed in divergent attitudes to the liturgical treatment of the dead. The halakhists (including such major figures as the Ge'onim Sherira, Hai and Nissim) and, no less, the philosophers, were not of a mind to approve the notion that one's prayers could have any

4 See Elbogen G, pp. 201–4, H, pp. 150–51 and E, pp. 162–63; B. S. Jacobson, *Netiv Bina* (5 vols; Tel Aviv: Sinai, 1968–83), 2.230–40; S. B. Freehof, '*Hazkarath Neshamoth*', *Hebrew Union College Annual*, 36 (1965), pp. 179–89; A. Yaari, 'Miy Sheberakh Prayers: History and Texts', *Kiryat Sefer*, 33 (1957–58), pp. 118–30 and 233–50, and 36 (1960), pp. 103–18; D. de Sola Pool, *The Kaddish* (Leipzig: Haupt, 1909); J. J. Petuchowski, 'The History of the Synagogue. History, Structure and Contents', in *Approaches to Ancient Judaism*, vol. 4, ed. by W. S. Green (Chico: Scholars Press, 1983); I. Ta-Shma, 'Some Notes on the Origins of the "Kaddish Yathom"', *Tarbiz*, 53 (1984), pp. 559–68, and reprinted in his *Early Franco-German Ritual and Custom* (Hebrew; Jerusalem: Magnes, 1992), pp. 299–310; and Reif, *Hebrew Prayer*, p. 386, nn. 26–28.
5 Such prayers received the attention of Gross, A. Lehnardt, Lifshitz and Bar-Levav at the conference and their papers are published in this volume.

direct effect on the dead while those anxious to express more mystical or more popular forms of religiosity were not averse to making such a close connection between prayers or pious deeds and the fate of one's departed relatives.[6]

9 Exclusive plots for the burial of Christians

It is generally assumed that Jewish interment in the Land of Israel during the early Christian centuries was a private matter and that the physical disposal of the remains was done in a family plot or in a cave, sometimes to be followed by the collection of the bones (ליקוט עצמות) at a later date, and their storage in an ossuary. The place of a burial was marked so that those (such as priests) seeking to avoid ritual contamination by the dead could be made aware of areas to be avoided. The situation appears to have changed in the talmudic period, especially in Babylonia, when the communal aspect came to be more central. The location, status and maintenance of the communal cemetery was of concern to the rabbinic teachers and there were many superstitions attached to one's presence in such an area, especially in the hours of darkness. It would therefore seem that during the late talmudic and early geonic periods, the institution of the communal cemetery saw some significant developments.[7]

10 Augustine's prohibition of eating and drinking at martyrs' tombs

Taking his lead from the Yerushalmi (Palestinian Talmud) and not the Bavli (Babylonian Talmud), Maimonides (d. 1204) argues that the recitation of prayers in a cemetery is inappropriate because it is a place of ritual impurity,

6 *Oṣar Ha-Geonim*, ed. B. M. Lewin, vol. 4, *Ḥagiga* (Jerusalem: Hebrew University Press Association, 1931), p. 27; Aharon Ha-Kohen of Lunel, *Orḥot Ḥayyim* (Florence: de Pass, 1750), p. 107a; Avraham bar Ḥiyya, *Sefer Hegjon Ha-Nefesch oder Sitten-Buch*, ed. by E. Freimann (Leipzig: Vollrath, 1860), p. 32 (Eng. trans. by G. Wigoder, *The Meditation of the Sad Soul*, London: Schocken, 1969, p. 120).

7 For brief and general surveys of the history of Jewish burial, see *Encyclopaedia Judaica* 4, cols. 1515–23; 'Cemeteries: Antiquity' by Matthew Goff and 'Cemeteries: Medieval and Modern' by Alisa Gayle Mayor in *Reader's Guide to Judaism*, ed. by Michael Terry (Chicago: Fitzroy Dearborn, 200), pp. 102–4; and Nolan Menachemson, *A Practical Guide to Jewish Cemeteries* (Bergenfield, NJ: Avotaynu, 2007), pp. 1–7. See also the contributions of Barak, Huttenmeister and A. Lehnardt, Langer, P. Lehnardt, Perani, Reiner and Rozen to this volume.

not because of any effect it might have on the dead who are interred there. Worries about such an effect are tantamount to an indulgence in magical beliefs and practices, and consequently forbidden. Given that the best memorials to the departed are the good deeds they have performed in this world, there is no justification for buildings to be erected at their tombs. Visits to cemeteries should not be made for such religiously dubious purposes or in order to pray; if those are the motivations, the time would better be spent on Torah study. They should rather be an encouragement to contrition and humility.[8]

11 The control of social behaviour within a thoroughly Christian framework

The early geonic age saw much creativity and expansion in the liturgical arena, no less than in other spheres of rabbinic learning. The basic elements of prayer and lectionary having been designed earlier, every opportunity was taken to expand on these. There was of course a constant tension within the liturgy between spontaneity and rigidity, synagogue and home, law and mysticism, Hebrew and vernacular, and brevity and protraction, to name only a few. At times, a relaxed attitude to variation gave way to a strong stand about what represents the preferable textual or ritual alternative in each case. Many such developments appear to have occurred in the latter part of the geonic period and to have reached their peak in the century or two immediately afterwards. The theme then became one of standardization and conformity and all the authority of Jewish religious law (*halakha*) was employed to ensure that variation from the established norm was kept to a minimum. Behind so many of these trends lay emerging attitudes to the synagogue and the academy; the influences of Karaism, Christianity and Islam; the tightening of rabbinic authority, and the broad intellectual stimulation of the day. But no less significant was the impact made by the adoption of the codex for the recording of rabbinic traditions that had previously been generally transmitted in oral format.[9]

---

8 See Y. S. Lichtenstein, 'The Rambam's Approach regarding Prayer, Holy Objects and Visiting the Cemetery', *Hebrew Union College Annual*, 72 (2001), Hebrew section, pp. 1–34 and Reif, 'Maimonides on the Prayers' in *Traditions of Maimonideanism*, ed. C. Fraenkel (Leiden and Boston: Brill, 2009), pp. 73–100.
9 See Reif, *Hebrew Prayer*, pp. 122–52.

12 Ninth-century Christian standardization

In Jewish liturgical history too, what was thought to enjoy talmudic authority was in fact often the creation of rabbinic leaders and communities in the geonic and early medieval periods. I suspect that some of the papers being delivered during this congress will illuminate the matter of how far this is true in matters of death and burial. Should they fail to do so, researchers should make this a priority for future attention.

13 Christian rituals for seven and thirty days after a death, and annually thereafter

The periods one, three, seven and thirty days, and one year, appear in the Palestinian and Babylonian Talmudim and it is therefore unlikely that they are later than about the fifth or sixth centuries. The strictest degree of mourning applies to the first day, which the talmudic rabbis regard as of biblical origin and stringency, and this reduces progressively from time period to time period. The detailed rules of mourning that apply to each of these time periods developed from the talmudic through the geonic and early medieval period with close attention being given to the topic in the talmudic tractate *Mo'ed Qaṭan*, the post-talmudic tractate *Semaḥot* and the earliest codes, especially that of Maimonides in the twelfth century.[10] Unless there is evidence of such periods of time in the earliest Christian sources, it would seem that the Christian monastic tradition owes its origin in this respect to Jewish precedent. The matter would no doubt benefit from further investigation.

14 Obligation to pray for those who gave life and land

From about the twelfth century there is evidence, in Jewish prayer collections and in the halakhic discussion of liturgical topics, of special blessings, often beginning with the words מי שבירך ('May he who blessed our forefathers ...'), for particular groups and individuals. These benedictions are invoked on those

10 *Encyclopedia Talmudica*, vol. 1 (Hebrew: Jerusalem: Mosad Harav Kook, 1948), pp. 26–36; Eng. trans. (Jerusalem: Yad Harav Herzog, 1969), pp. 75–103.

who behave in an appropriately religious fashion, who devote themselves to the needs of the synagogue, or who perform generous acts of charity. It is fascinating that the community also offered its prayers for those who undertook communal tasks, especially with regard to burial, congregants who did not disturb the services with idle chatter, women who donated their handiwork for religious purposes, and those who abstained from drinking non-Jewish wine. Also documented from the eleventh and twelfth centuries are prayers on behalf of local non-Jewish rulers, sometimes justified on biblical or talmudic grounds but more probably innovative in many respects.[11]

11 See Genizah text, Cambridge University Library, T-S 110.26 published by P. B. Fenton, '*Tefilla be-'ad Ha-Rashut U-Reshut be'ad Ha-Tefilla*', *Mi-Mizraḥ Umi-Ma'arav* 4 (1984), pp. 7–21; Yaari, *Kiryat Sefer*, 33, p. 247, and 36, p. 115; B. Schwartz, '*Hanoten Teshu'a*: The Origin of the Traditional Jewish Prayer for the Government', *Hebrew Union College Annual*, 57 (1986), pp. 113–20; and Reif, *Hebrew Prayer*, p. 218.

Shmuel Shepkaru

From Here to the Hereafter: The Ashkenazi Concept of the Afterlife in a Crusading Milieu

A comparison of early rabbinic views on the afterlife with those presented in the three Hebrew narratives that pertain to the Crusader massacres of Ashkenazi Jews during the First Crusade reveals several significant changes in the views of the latter. The purpose of this article is to identify and explain these shifts in Ashkenazi thinking.[1]

Basing itself on several biblical verses and their elaborated commentary, rabbinic Judaism canonized the doctrine of the resurrection of the dead, or, in its own terminology, as *teḥiyyat ha-metim*. *Teḥiyyat ha-metim* is a stage in the eschatological drama that will usher in the new post-historical age of *'olam ha-ba* ('the world to come'). *'Olam ha-ba* has both spatial and temporal meanings. At the end of the messianic era, God will raise the physical bodies of the dead from the grave so that they can receive their punishment or reward in a restored physical world.

The Mishna in *Sanhedrin* 10.1 makes this point in an explicit fashion. Except for those who do not believe in resurrection, and that resurrection is from the Torah, and those who are 'Epicureans', all Israel have a share in the age to come, and 'they shall inherit the *land* (*areṣ*) forever' (emphasis mine).[2] Also telling is the association made (*yBer.* 5.2; *Genesis Rabba* 13.6) between rain or dew and resurrection. The dead will rise from the grave as the rain revives nature. The dead will break through the soil and rise up in their own clothes in Jerusalem 'like grass of the earth' (*bKetub.* 111b). The physical nature of resurrection in a terrestrial world is further demonstrated by the claim that those who die outside the Land of Israel will not live again, or by the counter claim (*Pesikta Rabbati* 1.6, *bKetub.* 111a–b) that God will create tunnels for the righteous, so that their bodies can roll all the way up to the Land of Israel from

1 The Hebrew narratives are in Eva Haverkamp, *Hebräische Berichte über die Judenverfolgungen während des Ersten Kreuzzugs*. Monumenta Germaniae Historica 1 (Hannover: Hahnsche Buchhandlung, 2005).

2 Attempts to support the rabbinic claim that resurrection is from the Torah can be found in *bSanh.* 90b–92a. See also Lieberman's article, 'Some Aspects of After Life in Rabbinic Literature', in Harry Austryn Wolfson and Saul Lieberman, *Harry Austryn Wolfson Jubilee Volume: On the Occasion of His Seventy-Fifth Birthday: English Section* (Jerusalem: American Academy for Jewish Research, 1965), 2:495–532.

wherever their graves are found, in order to be resurrected. These are recurrent motifs in numerous discussions, some of which will be discussed below.

Of course, rabbinic views must be approached with great caution. Contradicting opinions and concepts are common. But even when the neoplatonic concept of an existing dichotomy between the transitory body and the eternal soul does emerge in rabbinic texts, the physical resurrection of the dead in a terrestrial world stands its ground. Indeed, similarly to the neoplatonic notion of the 'world-soul' (ψυχή κόσμου; *anima mundi*) that is reunited with the νους or the 'One',[3] rabbinic texts maintain that the soul returns to the treasury of all souls after death.[4] But this is a temporary location for the soul.[5] In the time to come, God will restore the soul to the body because the two are not mutually exclusive. The body will rise from the earth, while the soul will descend from heaven in order to face divine judgement. Rabbi Yehuda Ha-Nasi is said to have explained this principle to Antoninus in the parable of the king and the watchman over his orchard: the body and soul are to face judgement before the King as one entity (*bSanh.* 91a–b).

Another attempt to explain this synthesis may be found in the teachings of R. Yehoshu'a b. Levi:

> At every word which went forth from the mouth of the Holy One, blessed be He, the souls of Israel departed, for it is said, My soul went forth when he spake [Cant 5:6]. But since **their souls** departed at the first word, how could they receive the second word? – He brought down the dew with which He will **resurrect the dead and revived them**, as it is said, 'Thou, **O God, didst send a plentiful rain**, Thou didst confirm thine inheritance, when it was weary' [Ps 68:10]' [b*Šabb*. 88b, according to the Soncino translation].

A conflation of the two views, with the emphasis on bodily resurrection, has lasted to this day in Orthodox and traditional texts. The early morning benediction praises God 'who restores souls to the dead'. The *gevurot*, the second blessing of the *'amida*, reads 'O Lord, You revive the dead' ..., 'cause salvation to sprout' ... and 'restore life to the dead', thus mentioning God's ability to restore life three times. These prayers further demonstrate the centrality in rabbinic teaching of physical resurrection taking place in a terrestrial environment.

This, however, does not seem to be the case in the Hebrew accounts of the First Crusade. Employing the language of the Bible, Talmud, and various

---

3 *Enneads*, III.4.2; IV.1.21; IV.7.2; IV.8.6 in the Loeb edition of Plotinus translated by A. H. Armstrong (Cambridge, Harvard University Press; London, Heinemann, 1966–1988).

4 On other signs of pagan influence see again Lieberman, 'Some Aspects of After Life in Rabbinic Literature', especially pp. 509, 512–13.

5 For example *bHag*. 12b; further discussion below.

midrashim, these narratives present a unique and rather systematic theology of a celestial afterlife. The characteristics of this system are: 1) a clear shift of the afterlife from a terrestrial to a heavenly location; 2) the transportation of the dead from here to the hereafter in an instant, not in the distance future with the 'world-to-come' referring to a heavenly realm rather than a temporal event; 3) a clear depiction of the nature and structure of heaven; 4) all the dead forming a living community in heaven; and 5) the activities of the dwellers in heaven, both as individuals and as a group, being made transparent.[6]

The references to heaven are numerous and the imagery is rich. Heaven is where the martyrs who sanctified God's Name receive their rewards. The transition from the terrestrial to the celestial world takes place 'in a brief moment'. In such a moment, a world of darkness is exchanged for a world of light, a world of sorrow for one of joy, a transitory world for an eternal one. The enemy's sword may strike at anytime. But it cannot kill because the indissoluble soul continues to exist eternally in the luminous speculum of the Garden of Eden.[7]

When reading medieval Hebrew texts, one must pay attention to the etymological use of words and how the authors play on these words. In a brief moment, the 'Supreme God' (*El 'Elyon*) turned those victims on earth into 'the pious on high' (*ḥasidei 'elyon*). The phrase *ḥasidei 'elyon* functions on two levels. It describes the members of the Ashkenazi communities as most pious. At the same time, the phrase shows that the entire community ascended to heaven. *El 'Elyon* and *ḥasidei 'elyon* are taken literally to mean the dwellers in heaven. Calling the martyrs 'burnt offerings', *qorban 'ola*, is another indication of the belief that they ascended to heaven. Those who sanctified the 'Name of *El 'Elyon*' are in *'olam ha-ba*; their souls are in *Gan 'Eden*, bound up in the 'bond of life'.[8]

An explicit desire to ascend to God is ascribed to Asher ben Yosef, the *gabbai*. Asher declared: 'Let anyone among you of the people of the Lord – may God be with him – go up [*we-ya'al*] (2 Chr 36:23; Ezra 1:3). Let anyone who wishes to receive the countenance of the Divine Presence [go up]. Behold, a world full of bounty in a brief moment.' Upon hearing this, R. Meir ben Shemuel responded: 'Wait for me! I wish to come with you, into a world that is entirely light.'[9]

---

6 On the concept of the afterlife in these accounts see Shmuel Shepkaru, 'From After Death to Afterlife: Martyrdom and Its Recompense', *Association for Jewish Studies Review*, 24/1 (1999), pp. 1–44; 'To Die for God: Martyrs' Heaven in the Hebrew and Latin Crusade Narratives', *Speculum*, 77 (2002), pp. 311–41.

7 Haverkamp, *Hebräische Berichte*, pp. 325–27, 363, 431, 477.

8 Haverkamp, *Hebräische Berichte*, pp. 289, 317, 389.

9 Haverkamp, *Hebräische Berichte*, p. 477.

R. Eli'ezer bar Nathan concluded his account of the events in the Rhineland with the view that 'it was all at one time, from the month of Sivan till the month of Tammuz, that they [all the Jewish communities] *ascended to God* (*la'alot el ha-Elohim*) in sanctity and purity ... Their souls are bound in the bond of life in the King's sanctuary.'[10]

An emphasis on the existence and survival of the eternal soul did not prevent the narratives from ascribing to the heavenly dwellers material rewards. These material rewards imply that the dwellers of heaven have assumed a physical form. The devastation in the Rhineland, lamented the sources, turned the Jews naked, dressed only in horror. Their great golden crowns, a metaphor for their greatness, had fallen from their heads. Heaven represented a reversal of this troubled reality. In heaven, the dead entered the divine palace and ran to enjoy individual rewards. Each head was adorned by a golden crown, or even by two. Everyone received precious stones, golden necklaces, and golden thrones. Upon their entrance into the palace, they were dressed in the eight vestments from the clouds of glory.[11] In addition to the bestowal on them of individual rewards, they are described as a community in heaven. Such descriptions revolve around the 'meeting-again' motif. The entire community of Mainz, for instance, is said to have ascended to God (*la'alot el ha-Elohim*), all the members together, young and old, the learned and the lay folk, men and women, children, converts and slaves. The community of Speyer, lamented R. Eli'ezer bar Nathan, became beautiful on high (*ba-'elyonim*), as it had been on earth.[12]

In addition to the martyrs of 1096 and the relatives who will join them in the future, the community of heaven consists of past heroes. Abraham, Daniel, Hananiah, Azariah, and Mishael represent the biblical heroes in heaven. Talmudic and midrashic heroes are represented by R. Akiva and his companion, namely, the ten martyrs of the midrashic tradition, and more specifically R. Teradyon. The martyrs of 1096 could now join the martyrs of old in the heavenly palaces.[13]

Yet, the greatest reward in heaven was to be with God and have a vision of Him. A speech attributed to a certain Moshe in the town of Xanten contains the celestial motifs I have mentioned. Moshe urged the assembly to 'rise up and ascend to the house of the Lord' (Gen 35:3), a reference to both martyrdom

10 Haverkamp, *Hebräische Berichte,* pp. 467–69 (emphasis mine).

11 Haverkamp, *Hebräische*, p. 469. This description evokes several *midrashim* (see Haverkamp's notes there). The description opens with the ascension of all the Jewish martyrs to God.

12 Haverkamp, *Hebräische*, in Mainz, p. 313; in Speyer, p. 265.

13 Haverkamp, *Hebräische*, p. 325 and pp. 387–89, for example.

and reward. In return for their martyrdoms, Moshe promised his group, they would reside in the heavenly *Gan 'Eden*. There they would 'see him [God] eye to eye (*we-nirehu 'ayin be-'ayin*), in his actual glory and greatness ... Each one will point at God with his finger and say: Behold this is our God Whom we hoped for. Let us rejoice and be glad in His salvation.' [Isa 25:9; *bTa'an.* 31a].[14] The account then confirms that the martyrs' wish has been granted. They come before God. And what do they do in the innermost heavenly chamber? They gaze at God. Pertaining to these martyrs, continues the account, the prophet prophesied: 'No eye has seen God except you who act for him who wait for him' (Isa 64:3).[15]

This medieval account draws on a discussion in *bBer.* 34b about the nature of the messianic era, and what will take place in the Garden of Eden.[16] At the same time, it reveals an essential departure from the Talmud. The text in *bBer.* 34b, as several other talmudic discussions, employs Isa 64:3 to stress that the world to come is known only to God. Second, the medieval passage ascribes *heavenly rewards specifically to martyrs*. Finally, 'We shall see Him eye to eye' is another alteration by the twelfth-century Jewish author.[17] The biblical verse intended to show that no human being, but only God, has seen God's terrifying wonders that humans dare not hope for. In the medieval syntax this verse is read as, 'No eye has seen God, except you ...', i.e., the martyrs.

What this reading suggests is that heaven is a hierarchical structure. Personal merit determines one's position in this hierarchy. Martyrs who stood the test like Abraham

> shall be of that *section* (*kat*), preferred by Him more than any other. They are destined to *stand and sit in the shadow of the Holy One, standing on His right*. Regarding them, the verse states: In Your presence is bounteous (*sova'*) joy, delights are ever *in Your right [hand]* (Ps 16:11). Read not 'bounteous' (*sova'*) but 'seven' (*sheva'*). These are the *seven sections of the saintly ones*, each [section] ranking above the other ...[18]

High in the hierarchy of heaven are the martyrs. But as the last two quotations suggest, not all martyrs receive equal recompense. Only the martyrs that stood

---

14 Haverkamp, *Hebräische*, p. 437. On the events on Xanten see Eva Haverkamp, 'Martyrs in Rivalry: the 1096 Jewish martyrs and the Thebean Legion', *Jewish History*, 23.4 (2009), pp. 323–27.

15 Haverkamp, *Hebräische*, pp. 439–41.

16 *bTa'an.* 31a does not refer to the dead; it is a description of the end of days.

17 In contrast, *bBer.* 10a: 'As the Holy One, blessed be He, sees but cannot be seen'. Also *Midrash Tehillim* to Ps 103:1; p. 217a: 'The Holy One, blessed be He, sees the works of His hands but they cannot see Him'. This is, of course, one of the talmudic opinions.

18 Haverkamp, *Hebräische*, p. 459. See *Leviticus Rabba*, 30.2. See also *Numbers Rabba* 15.11 for 'seven' and *sova'* in the context of the messianic era.

the test, like Abraham, enter God's preferred section. In our texts, Abraham's test, the *'aqeda*, is the one that applies to those who have sacrificed loved ones. In this section dwell those who chose active martyrdom for themselves and those who agreed to be sacrificed. Unlike in the other active sections, existence in the preferred section is marked by inactivity. In contrast to the situation in other sections, these dwellers do not appear to be aware of each other. The interaction here appears to be mainly between the individuals and God.

Missing in these medieval accounts is the older rabbinic views of physical resurrection. The phrase *teḥiyyat ha-metim* and its variants are missing. Nor are there attempts to conflate the two rabbinic visions of the terrestrial resurrection and the celestial afterlife. Moreover, the medieval accounts make use of rabbinic texts, which do mention resurrection, but omit the rabbinic references to *teḥiyyat ha-metim.*

Take, for example, the aforementioned martyrs of Xanten. Before undergoing martyrdom, they are reported to have recited the Grace after Meals. The Grace after Meals mentions the *'olam ha-ba* of the messianic era and alludes to resurrection, based on a talmudic exposition of the patriarchs' blessing 'with everything in everything'. In *bB. Bat.* 16b–17a, the phrase indicates that even the patriarchs were granted only an inkling of the world to come, and that the denial of bodily resurrection is a cardinal transgression. As everyone else, the patriarchs had to wait for their resurrection in the world to come. The speech of the medieval rabbi ignores such references and speaks only of the heavenly realms.

Let us now deal with other celestial images in our texts, such as the seven heavens, the seven sects, God's treasure, and the treasures of life. Several talmudic and midrashic discussions could have inspired our medieval texts. In several places (as on Lev 30:2 and Num 15:11) *Midrash Rabba* refers to God's creating the groups (כתות) of the those who sing before Him in heaven. Equally important in these discussions is the promise that God will resurrect the dead.

According to R. Yehuda, 'There are two firmaments, for it is said: Behold, unto the Lord thy God belongeth heaven, and the heaven of heavens' (*bḤag.* 12b–13a). Resh Laqish added that there are seven heavens. God did not create these heavens for humans. In the heaven called *ma'on* ('a dwelling place'), dwell the sections (כתות) of the ministering angels who praise God night and day. Additionally, the discussion distinguishes between celestial and terrestrial treasures. The first are reserved entirely for God, the second 'are to be found on earth'. Those who study Torah in this world will receive in the next world *ḥesed* ('loving-kindness'), a term associated with resurrection or life in the *gevurot* prayer. God's resurrection of the dead is His greatest act of *ḥesed.* The tractate affirms the biblical view that Heaven is God's exclusive dwelling place. The treasury of life in heaven *('aravot)* is where 'the souls of the righteous and the spirits and the souls that are yet to be born' are located. The treasury of life is designated as 'the fountain of life'. More significant is the promise that God 'will hereafter revive the dead', like the dew revives the earth, because the souls of the righteous originate in Him (*bḤag.* 12b). The medieval texts have left out such references to resurrection.

Tractate *bŠab.* 152b also states in the name of R. Eli'ezer, 'The souls of the righteous are hidden under the Throne of Glory ... they shall be bound up in the bond of life' (1 Sam 25:29). The discussion, however, concludes with R. Mari's view that [even] the righteous are fated to be dust and return to the earth from which they originated. But eventually God will 'open your graves' and one hour before the resurrection of the dead the body will reappear intact to be resurrected. That passage in *bŠab.* gave the medieval authors another possible reason to link the notion of 'the bond of life' with bodily resurrection. They chose not to do so.

Two questions now occur: 1. How can this sudden and unique booming of heavenly imagery be explained? 2. Why did the medieval accounts disregard resurrection, even though the rabbinic texts they appear to have incorporated do mention resurrection?

A comparison between the Hebrew accounts of the First Crusade and the Latin Crusade narratives reveal a great deal of resemblance.[19] As in the Hebrew accounts, the Christian accounts promised the Crusaders personal rewards should they die in their holy war against the Muslims. It was believed that, upon death, Crusaders would ascend to heaven, also called 'the celestial paradise', or the luminous speculum, immediately to obtain everlasting life. Regardless of how or why they died, all were considered martyrs and holy living sacrifices for God. In his call for the First Crusade, Pope Urban the Second labeled potential casualties the proper sacrifice (*recta quidem oblatio*).[20] And, therefore, those who 'gave up their souls to God with joy and gladness' deserved celestial recompense.[21]

The Latin accounts note the same kind of material rewards as found in the Hebrew accounts. The bodies of the Christian martyrs were preserved in

---

19 See again, Shepkaru, 'To Die for God'.

20 In his letter to the Monks of the Congregation of Vallombrosa. Robert Somerville, *The Councils of Urban II, i: Decreta Claromontensia* (Amsterdam: Hakkert, 1972), p. 74.

21 *Gesta Francorum et aliorum Hierosolymytanorum*, ed. and trans. by Rosalind Hill (London: Nelson, 1962), p. 17.

heaven. In body, they are reported to have descended to help their comrades fight the Muslims. The 'meeting-again' motif is at play. Crusaders were believed to re-unite in heaven with their fallen comrades and with their heroes of the past. Biblical heroes, such as the patriarchs, especially Abraham, as well as Daniel, are among the shared icons. As in the Hebrew accounts, fallen Crusaders could find their bliss in the 'companion of the saintly'. The supreme heavenly reward took place in the presence of God. As with the Jewish martyrs, the Christian martyrs received their seats at the right hand of God. They could see him face to face and enjoy the *Viso Dei*.[22]

Such celestial rewards were received according to merit. This meant that the Jewish and Christian heavens shared a similar hierarchy. Those who died together on earth sat together in heaven; those who sacrificed the most, sitting with God. The highest level in heaven, thus, is marked by contemplation and inactivity.

To be sure, the correspondence between the Jewish and the Christian images was not accidental. Already the gospel of Luke (Luke 16:22) made it clear that the God of Abraham, Isaac, and Jacob, was the God of the living patriarchs. They are alive with God. When the poor man Lazarus died, he was carried by the angels into the bosom of Abraham. Medieval Christian accounts applied similar stories to Crusaders and placed the martyrs in the bosom of Abraham (*in sinu Abrahe*).[23] The Hebrew accounts also placed Jewish martyrs in the bosom of Abraham (*be-ḥeqo shel Avraham avinu*).[24] This is in contrast to some talmudic sayings, and especially to the saying of the Palestinian *amora*, R. Pinḥas ben Ḥama. According the R. Pinḥas, 'If the patriarchs had wished that their resting place should be in the above realm, they could have had it there: but it was here below, when they died and the rock closed on their tombs, that they deserved to be called saints' (*Midrash Tehillim* 16.2). While R. Pinḥas wished to refute a contemporaneous Christian view of the patriarchs in heaven, the medieval Jewish author recognized the value of this view for his own purposes.

Another parallel is the presentation of martyrdom as weddings or celebrations. Martyrdom was not a tragedy. After the battle of Antioch in June 1098, Emperor Alexius wrote to the Abbot of Monte Cassino that the dead continued living in their celestial 'Eternal Tabernacle' and, therefore, 'we ought not at all to consider them as dead, but as living and transported to eternal and

---

22 Shepkaru, 'To Die for God', pp. 315, 320, 322.

23 Peter Tudebode, *Historia de Hierosolymitano Itinere*, publié par John Hugh Hill et Laurita Hill (Paris: Geuthner, 1977), pp. 79–81. Shepkaru, 'To Die for God', p. 321.

24 Haverkamp, *Hebräische*, pp. 285, 431.

incorruptible life' *(sed ut uiuos et in uitam aeternam atque incorruptibilem transmigratos)*.[25] A contemporary Hebrew liturgical poem by a certain R. Avraham admonished: 'We ought not question [the destiny of] the dead (*redumim*, literally, 'the sleeping'), for they have been set [placed?] and bonded in everlasting life.'[26] Avrhaham's designation of the dead as *redumim* appears to coincide with Peter Tudebode's use of the term. In his account of the First Crusade, Peter reported that Adhemar, Bishop of Le Puy,

> by God's will fell mortally ill and by God's nod, resting in peace, fell asleep in the Lord (*obdormivit in Domino*), namely, in the bosom of Abraham, Isaac, and Jacob, on the Feast of Saint Peter in Chains (*in Abrahe videlicet sinu et Isaac et Iacob, in sancti Petri a Vinculis Sollempnitate*). His most happy soul rejoiced with the angels.[27]

These illustrations, among others, reveal the influence that the crusading milieu had on the writing style and theological thinking in Ashkenaz. The notion of celestial recompense helped both Jews and Christians rationalize their many losses. They had to reassure their co-religionists that friends and loved ones did not die in vain. Better yet, Jews and Christians reassured their co-religionists that their heroes did not die at all. Heavenly recompense would vindicate both God and the dead.

Polemical exchanges between Jews and Christians made this question of theodicy even more acute. The issues of salvation and damnation stood at the core of such theological conflict. Christian doctrine offered postmortem salvation only to Christians. A Crusader slogan maintained that those who died in Christ's service never died.[28] Damnation was the fate of those who died unbaptized. The bodies of Christians might have been destroyed, but not their souls. Non-believers, however, died in body and soul. When the Crusaders, therefore, gave Jews the ultimatum of death or conversion, they did not offer them just life, but also eternal life. From the Christians' point of view, Jewish martyrdom, not to mention self-inflicted martyrdom and the taking of others' lives, resulted in damnation rather than salvation.

---

25 'Epistula II Alexii I Komneni ad Oderisim I de Marsis abbatem Casinensem', in Heinrich Hagenmeyer, *Epistulae et Chartae ad Historiam Primi Belli Sacri Spectantes. Die Kreuzzugsbriefe aus den Jahren 1088–1100* (Innsbruck: Wagner, 1901, repr. Hildesheim: G. Olms, 1973), p. 153.
26 Abraham Meir Habermann and Yitzhak Baer, *Sefer Gezerot Ashkenaz We-Ṣarefat: divre zikhronot mi-benei ha-dorot shebi-tequfat masa'e ha-ṣelav u-mivḥar piyyuṭehem* (Jerusalem: Sifre Tarshish and Mossad Harav Kook, 1945), p. 62.
27 Tudebode, *Historia de Hierosolymitano Itinere*, p. 116.
28 '*Equidem non moriuntur illi, qui in Christi servicio vitam finiunt.*' Raymond of Aguilers, *Historia Francorum Qui Ceperunt Iherusalem* in *Le Liber De Raymond D'Aguilers*, pubilié par John Hugh Hill et Laurita Hill (Paris: Geuthner, 1969), p. 109.

Bishop Egilbert urged the Jews of Trier to convert, but: 'if you persist in this faithlessness, you will lose your body as well as your soul.'[29] Bernard of Clairvaux, who laboured to protect the Jews during the Second Crusade, restated this point. Those who died for the Lord are joined to the Lord. In contrast, 'he who dies without sacrificing his life to God, remains in death (*manet in morte*)'. Bernard believed that Israel would be saved when the time was ripe, because they would then acknowledge Christ. Those who die unbaptized before that time will remain in death.[30] Ashkenazi Jews were familiar with such Christian arguments and obviously could not accept them. Paradoxically, then, Jews adopted and adapted the very same Christian imagery of heaven to dispute the Christian anti-Jewish message that intended to keep them out of heaven.

The urgency to vindicate God and the dead, as well as the need to refute Christian arguments, made resurrection an unattractive proposition. The suffering and the potential doubts, triggered by the massacres, required an immediate solution for the Jewish victims, not a reward that might take place in an uncertain future and be determined by a tentative judgement.

Additionally, the Hebrew narratives often mention the attackers' systematic practice of mutilating Jewish bodies, and leaving them unburied. The Latin documents confirm this claim.[31] Such mutilation and lack of burial might have complicated the mechanics of resurrection in the minds of the Jews. Early Christian martyrologies struggled with similar questions.[32] Some suggested Abraham's bosom as an interim place for the martyrs. Others preferred heaven as the best alternative solution to resurrection.[33]

Moreover, many of the Jewish replies to the offers of conversion emphasize, in unflattering terms, Jesus's mortality and the destruction of his body.

---

29 *Gesta Treverorum, MGH S.* 8:190–91 and *Patrologiae Cursus Completus Latina*, ed. by Jacques-Paul Migne and Georg Heinrich (Paris: Garnier, 1881), p. 154: 1207a–b.

30 Bernard of Clairvaux, 'De Laude Novae Militiae Templi Liber', Sancti Bernardi Opera (Rome: Ed. Cisterciensis, 1963), 3:215 and Letter 363, 8:316.

31 Haverkamp, *Hebräische*, pp. 275–77, 283–85, 361, 369, 389, 433. Regarding the Jewish martyrs in Xanten, Eva Haverkamp has suggested that the same burial motif is followed in Sigebert's *Passio* about the Christian martyrs there. 'Martyrs in Rivalry: the 1096 Jewish martyrs and the Thebean Legion', *Jewish History* 23.4 (2009), 323–7. A poem by R. Abraham depicts similar episodes of men and women being dragged naked in Mainz, Habermann, *Sefer Gezerot*, p. 62. This is also confirmed by the *Annalista Saxo, MGH S.* 37:491. '... eratque miseria spectare multos et magnos occisorum acervos efferri in plaustris de civitate Mogontia.'

32 See for example, the story of the Christian martyrs of Lyon by Eusebius, History of the Church, 5:1.

33 Jerome Baschet, 'Medieval Abraham: Between Fleshly Patriarch and Divine Father', *Modern Language Notes*, 108 (1993), pp. 738–58.

David, the *gabbai*, for instance, rejected his attackers' proposal to believe in the 'crucified one' and proclaimed his belief in a God who lives forever and resides in the highest heavens.[34] Such replies conveyed not only a refusal to convert, but also a refutation of the attackers' belief in Jesus's sacrifice and resurrection. Apparently, the Crusaders demanded of the potential converts that they proclaim their belief in the living Jesus. At al-Barah, for example, the Crusaders offered captured Muslims their lives, if they would agree to be baptized and acknowledge the living Christ as the saviour.[35] Another reason for the absence of resurrection in the Hebrew accounts may be found in its theological function in Christianity, during the Crusade in particular. Pope Urban II compared the First Crusade to Jesus's passion and resurrection.[36] The Holy Land in the hands of Muslims was in a state of death. The recapture of Jerusalem equalled Jesus's resurrection. One Crusader joined the campaign to 'seek that sepulchre from which our redemption, having overcome death, wished to arise'.[37] A sermon on Christ's ascension and resurrection motivated the Crusaders during their march to the Mount of Olives.[38] When Jesus, in a vision, asked the priest Stephen 'What do these Christians believe?', the latter replied: 'They believe that Christ was born of the Virgin Mary and endured agony on the Cross, died, was buried, rose from the grave on the third day (*et resurrexisse tercia die*) and ascended to heaven'.[39] Even when Jesus himself reportedly promised the Crusaders a seat with him on God's right, the Latin text still maintained that Jesus's resurrection occurred first (*post resurrectionem*).[40]

A Latin account describes the capture of Jerusalem in the following terms: 'A new day, new gladness, new and everlasting happiness ... This day ... changed our grief and struggles into gladness and rejoicing ... This is the day which the Lord has made; we shall rejoice and be glad in it (Isa 25:9; Ps 118:24) ... because on this day God shone upon us and blessed us (Ex. 32:29). At this time we also chanted the Office of the Resurrection (*officium de resur-*

34 Haverkamp, *Hebräische*, p. 371.
35 Robert the Monk, 'Historia Iherosolimitana', *RHC Oc.* 3:840.
36 Guibert of Nogent, *RHC Oc.*, 4:137–39. In a letter, Urban complained about the Muslims' control of those Christian sites that were glorified by Jesus's passion and resurrection. Urban urged the Crusaders to re-establish Christianity in the Holy City. Hagenmeyer, *Epistulae*, p. 136.
37 Abbaye de Saint-Vincent du Mans, Robert Charles, and Samuel Georges Jean Maurice Menjot d'Elbenne. *Cartulaire de l'abbaye de Saint-Vincent du Mans (ordre de Saint Benoît)* (Mamers: Imprimerie Fleury, 1886), 1:69.
38 '*in locum unde Dominus post resurectionem ascendit in celum* ...'. Raymond D'Aguilers, *Historia Francorum*, p. 145.
39 Raymond D'Aguilers, *Historia Francorum*, p. 73.
40 Raymond D'Aguilers, *Historia Francorum*, p. 114.

rectione), since on this day he, who by his might, arose from the dead (*mortuis resurrexit*), restored us through his kindness.'[41] The restoration of Jerusalem was believed to have been made possible because of Jesus's resurrection. Through the Crusades, God's kingdom in Jerusalem was resurrected.

The Hebrew accounts also used the very same verses from Ps 118: 'This is the day ...' and from Ex. 32:29: 'the Lord this day ... bestow a blessing upon us this day' *(we-latet 'alenu ha-yom berakha)*.[42] Unlike the function of these verses in the Latin account, their use in the Hebrew account demonstrated the martyrs' jubilation with their sacrificial act and their transportation to the new heavenly Jerusalem. The centrality of resurrection in proving Jesus's divinity, the Christian theological fusion of martyrdom and resurrection, and the association of resurrection with the revival of Christianity in the Holy Land, I suspect, gave the Hebrew accounts additional reasons to omit the topic of resurrection.

The choice of the Jewish author to use the same verses to shift the location and nature of victory was probably not accidental. In the war of words, it was crucial for each side not only to ratify its own beliefs, but also to refute those of others. On several occasions, the Jewish martyrs are said to have ridiculed the ideas of Jesus's immaculate conception, his death, the destruction of his body, his resurrection and his ascension.[43] They proclaimed that Jesus had descended to hell and scorned the absurdity of the belief in a doomed dead man. The Jewish texts made these assertions without actually mentioning the word resurrection, in a Christian or a Jewish context. For the same reason, the Hebrew texts refused to acknowledge the Crusaders' victory in Jerusalem, or the 'resurrection' of Christianity in the Holy City, as the Christians saw it. The Jewish denial was a response to the Christian theological argument that compared the Crusaders' victory to Christ's resurrection in order to prove that God was on their side. The need to reward the Ashkenazi victims instantly on the one hand, and to deprive the Crusaders' victory of any theological meaning on the other, prompted the Hebrew chronicles to favour the ethereal, but instant, heaven over the corporeal, but distant, resurrection as the place of bliss for their martyrs.

---

41 Raymond D'Aguilers, *Historia Francorum*, p. 151.

42 Haverkamp, *Hebräische*, 437.

43 Haverkamp, *Hebräische*, pp. 253, 333, 353. See also Anna Sapir Abulafia, 'Invectives against Christianity in the Hebrew Chronicles of the First Crusade', in *Crusade and Settlement: Papers Read at the First Conference of the Society for the Study of Crusades and the Latin East and Presented to R. C. Smail*, ed. by R. C. Smail and P. W. Edbury (Cardiff: University College Cardiff Press, 1985), pp. 66–72.

Section 2: **Texts in Society: Liturgy and Ritual**

Andreas Lehnardt

Christian Influences on the *Yahrzeit Qaddish*

1 Introduction

It is well known that the *qaddish* prayer serves in the Ashkenazi rite primarily as a conclusion of the entire service, and as a closing element of its main sections. Additionally, it marks the ending of a Torah reading and is also recited after the study of religious texts. As reflected in early rabbinic literature, it may have developed from a prayer of so-called *bet midrash* origin.[1] Today, however, it is mainly known as a prayer recited by mourners or one mourner during or at the end of the service, or after a burial. Since this usage is not attested in early rabbinic sources, it is certainly a later medieval development.[2] Obviously, the text of the *qaddish*, which is known in at least four main versions – *ḥaṣi qaddish*, *qaddish shalem*, *qaddish de-rabbanan* and *qaddish le-(it)ḥaddeta* – has undergone considerable changes, has been used from time to time in changing contexts, and could have fulfilled different purposes.

This article aims to shed light on the existence of the *yahrzeit qaddish* – the latest development in these uses of the *qaddish* – as a custom for commemorating the anniversary of a parent's death, which seems to have emerged only in thirteenth-century Ashkenaz. To my knowledge the liturgical custom of saying *qaddish* on a *yahrzeit*, which should not be confused with the older and related custom of saying *qaddish yatom* (the orphan's *qaddish)*, or the

1 On the early development of the *qaddish* as reflected in rabbinic literature, see: David de Sola Pool, *The Old Jewish Aramaic Prayer: The Kaddish* (Leipzig 1909, repr. New York: Sivan Press, 1964); Jacob Hübscher, *Das Kaddisch-Gebet, dessen Sinn, Bedeutung und Tendenz erklärt und commentiert* (Berlin: Cernauti, 1912); Joseph Heinemann, *Prayer in the Talmud. Forms and Patterns*, Studia Judaica 9 (Berlin: de Gruyter, New York, 1977), pp. 251–75; Andreas Lehnardt, *Qaddish. Untersuchungen zur Entstehung und Rezeption eines rabbinischen Gebetes*, Texts and Studies in Ancient Judaism 87 (Tübingen: Mohr-Siebeck, 2002).

2 Cf. Israel M. Ta-Shma, 'Some Notes on the Origins of Kaddish Yatom' in idem, *Early Franco-German Ritual and Custom* (Hebrew; Jerusalem: Magnes Press, 1994), pp. 299–310; Shmuel Glick, *Or Le-Avel. Le-hitpatḥutam shel iqqare minhagei avelut be-mesorot Yisrael me-le-aḥar ha-qevura ad tom ha-shiv'a* (Efrat: Keren Ori, 1991), pp. 147–58; see also Lehnardt, *Qaddish*, pp. 278–95. On the recitation of the *qaddish* after burial, see also idem, 'Tzidduq Ha-Din und Kaddish. Beobachtungen zur Entwicklung der jüdischen Begräbnisliturgie im Mittelalter', *Trumah. Zeitschrift der Hochschule für Jüdische Studien Heidelberg*, 12 (2002), pp. 1–33.

qaddish said after burial,[3] has never been the subject of rigorous investigation. What can be found in articles and books on Jewish liturgy concerning the *yahrzeit qaddish* is marginal.[4] This is rather surprising, since the custom is widely practised in all the Jewish liturgical rites, and the Middle-High German '*iar-zit*' or the Yiddish '*Yohrzayt*'[5] is undoubtedly one of the most famous German words in the Jewish world. Furthermore, the lack of interest is surprising because in the early nineteenth century Christian and Jewish scholars such as Gustav Dalman (1855–1941),[6] Israel Abrahams (1858–1924),[7] Moritz Güdemann (1835–1918),[8] and Jacob Obermeyer (1845–1935)[9] were already hinting in articles and notes that some *yahrzeit* customs, like kindling a light, were inspired by, or adopted from Christian, or more precisely Catholic, mourning rites.

Remarkably, in publications that emerged from a more traditionally observant perspective, as in a Hebrew article by Avraham Hoffer,[10] a certain interest

---

3 See on this also Andreas Lehnardt, 'Die Qaddish *yitkele harba*-Versionen und ihr Verhältnis zu biblischen Texten' in *Orient als Grenzbereich? Rabbinisches und außerrabbinisches Judentum*, ed. by Annelies Kuyt and Gerold Necker (Wiesbaden: Harrassowitz, 2007), pp. 51–64.

4 See, e.g., Eliezer (L.) Landshut, *Vollständiges Gebet- und Andachtsbuch zum Gebrauch bei Kranken, Sterbenden und Leichenbestattungen sowie beim Besuchen der Gräber von Verwandten und Lieben* (Hebrew; Berlin, Adolf 1867), p. LXVI; Adolf Kurrein, *Das Neschamoth-(Seelen)-Licht. Eine Abhandlung* (Frankfurt a.M.: J. Kauffmann, 1898), pp. 27 ff.; Kaufmann Kohler, 'Kaddisch-Gebet, Jahrzeit und Seelen-Gedächtnißfeier', *Jewish Reformer*, V,1 No. 11 (1886), pp. 11–12; Y. L. Avida (Zlotnik), '*Perakim Be-'Inyane Ha-Azkara (Jahrzeit)*', *Sinai*, 25 (1949), pp. 59–68; 330–48; Maurice Lamm, *The Jewish Way in Death and Mourning* (New York: Jonathan David Publishers, 1969), pp. 201–06; J. S. Sperka, *Hayye Nesah. Eternal Life. A Digest of all Jewish Laws of Mourning. Complete Funeral, Burial and Unveiling Services, Kaddish, Yizkor, and El Mohle in Hebrew, Translation and Transliteration* (New York: Bloch, 1961), pp. 91–94; Isaac Klein, *A Guide to Jewish Religious Practice*, Moreshet 6 (New York: Ktav, 1979), pp. 294ff; Judith Hauptman, 'Death and Mourning: A Time for Weeping, a Time for Healing', in *Celebration and Renewal*, ed. by R. M. Geffen (Philadelphia: Jewish Publication Society, 1993), pp. 226–51, esp. p. 247.

5 Cf. M. Lexer, *Mittelhochdeutsches Handwörterbuch* (Leipzig 1872, repr. Stuttgart: Hirzel, 1974), p. 1476 s.v.; see also Uriel Weinreich, *Modern English–Yiddish Yiddish–English Dictionary* (New York: Schocken, 1977), p. 589 s.v.

6 Gustav Dalman, 'Jüdische Seelenmesse und Totenanrufung', *Saat auf Hoffnung*, 27 (1890), pp. 69–190.

7 Israel Abrahams, *Jewish Life in the Middle Ages* (Philadelphia 1896, repr. Philadelphia, Jerusalem: Jewish Publication Society, 1993), p. 140 n. 2.

8 Moritz Güdemann, *Geschichte des Erziehungswesens und der Cultur der Juden in Deutschland während des XIV. und XV. Jahrhunderts*, Vol. 3 (Vienna, 1888, repr. Amsterdam: Philo Press, 1966), p. 132.

9 Jacob Obermeyer, *Modernes Judentum im Morgen- und Abendland*, Vienna (Leipzig: C. Fromme, 1907), pp. 126–28.

10 Avraham Hoffer, 'Yesodo u-meqoro shel yom mitat ha-av we-ha-ben mi-de shana be-shana', *Ha-Zofe le-Hokhmat Yisrael*, 10 (1926), pp. 116–21.

prevails in explaining all Jewish anniversary customs on the basis of earlier Jewish sources. For example, Hoffer stresses fasting on the anniversary of a death as a custom that was described in earlier rabbinic writings,[11] and therefore understands all other related practices as having developed from this older rite. In studies written by more liberal authors, however, at least the term *yahrzeit* and some of the related *minhagim* are explained as the result of influences from the Christian environment in Ashkenaz in which they evolved.[12]

With an awareness that any inquiry in this field may be used polemically or apologetically, the current study aims to present suggestions regarding the possible historical development of the *yahrzeit qaddish*. The author intentionally limits his focus here to the prayer *minhag* of reciting *qaddish*, without tackling the questions of whether and how similar *yahrzeit* customs, like the kindling of lights, may be explained.[13]

2 *Where and when did this custom emerge?*

The information available for answering this question is scanty indeed. Encyclopaedia entries and academic articles yield different responses, and even the topic of who first used the term '*yahrzeit*' has not yet been thoroughly researched.[14] From the outset, one must distinguish between two related questions: who first mentioned the custom of reciting an additional *qaddish* at the end of the service on the anniversary of the death of a loved one; and who first used the name '*yahrzeit*' to describe this practice.

---

11 Cf. *bNed.* 12a; 14a; *bŠebu.* 20a; Hoffer also refers to the older custom of fasting on the anniversary of the death of Gedalya (*Ṣom Gedalya*), cf. Jer. 40; 2 Kings 25.

12 For a review article that is remarkable in this regard, see P. Rieger on I. Elbogen, *Der jüdische Gottesdienst in seiner geschichtlichen Entwicklung* (Frankfurt a. M.: Kauffmann, 1913), *Allgemeine Zeitung des Judentums*, 78 (1914), p. 468.

13 On this, see Abrahams, Jewish Life, p. 140 n. 2; Steven Oppenheimer, 'The Yahrzeit Light', *Journal of Halacha and Contemporary Society*, 37 (1999), pp. 101–16; S. L. Silver, *An Investigation into the Origins of Jahrzeit Practices*, Rabbinic Thesis, Hebrew Union College 1984 (n.v.).

14 Cf. Jehuda D. Eisenstein, Art. 'Jahrzeit', *Jewish Encyclopaedia* 7 (1904), pp. 63–65; idem, *Ozar Dinim u-Minhagim. A Digest of Jewish Laws and Customs in Alphabetic Order* (Hebrew; Tel Aviv: Shilo, 1938), pp. 154 ff.; D. Flattau, Art. 'Jahrzeit', *Encyclopedia Judaica* (Deutsch) 8 (1931), pp. 779–81; L. I. Rabinowitz, Art. 'Yahrzeit', *Encyclopaedia Judaica* 16 (1971), pp. 702–3; see also: 'Yortsayt', *The Oxford Dictionary of Jewish Religion*, ed. R. J. Z. Werblowsky et al. (Oxford: University Press, 1997), p. 753; Abraham E. Millgram, *Jewish Worship* (Philadelphia: Jewish Publication Society, 1971), pp. 448 ff.; Catherine Hezser, Art. 'Jahrzeit', *Religion in Geschichte und Gegenwart* 4 (2001), pp. 351 f.

It has often been noted that Ya'aqov ben Moshe Moellin (c. 1360–1427), better known by his acronym 'Maharil', the leading rabbinic authority of central Europe in the fourteenth century, seems to have been the first to mention the custom of saying *qaddish* on the anniversary of the death of a father or a mother.[15] One should, however, recall that his *Sefer Maharil* was compiled only later by one of his students, Rabbi Zalman of St. Goar, and printed even later, in Italy in 1556. Furthermore, the term *yahrzeit* does not appear in his book. The only portion that refers to the commemoration of the anniversary of a death leaves open the question of whether the *qaddish* said on a *yahrzeit* should be differentiated at all from the 'usual' *qaddish yatom*.

The passage in *Sefer Maharil* that is of interest for this study alludes only to the problem of who would be the appropriate person to say *qaddish* during a Sabbath service when there are visitors from another community who are present and may also wish to say *qaddish*. *Sefer Maharil* does not discuss whether this additional *qaddish* by a mourner after an eleven- or twelve-month period could be interpreted as a sign of disrespect. Neither does it mention the effect of this *qaddish* on the souls of the dead. Its sole focus is on the dilemma concerning the synagogal presence of more than one mourner obligated to honour the *yahrzeit* of a parent.[16]

Additionally, there is evidence from the responsa of the 'Maharil'[17] that some people would recite this form of *qaddish* – which is today called the *yahrzeit qaddish* – twice in a leap year, if the anniversary of the parent's death fell during Adar I.[18] But in a short comment in a responsum by the 'Maharil', which has been attributed to Rabbi Yehuda he-Ḥasid and resembles a similar remark in *Sefer Ḥasidim*,[19] the term *yahrzeit* is not mentioned. It therefore seems that R. Ya'aqov Moellin knew the custom of an additional recitation of

15 Cf. *The Book of Maharil. Customs by Rabbi Ya'aqov b. Moshe Moellin. Published According to the First Edition with Additions and Variants from Various Manuscripts with References, Notes, and Indices*, ed. by Shlomo Y. Spitzer (Jerusalem: Makhon Yerushalayim, 1991), p. 608, where it is mentioned that one is obligated to say *qaddish* on an anniversary only once; the term 'yahrzeit', however, is not used. See also pp. 446 ff.

16 On the custom of saying *qaddish* for only eleven instead of twelve months, the estimated time of being judged in *Gehenna* (cf. *m'Ed.* 2.10), which was inspired by the *Zohar*, cf. Obermeyer, *Judentum*, p. 123; Ismar Elbogen, *Jewish Liturgy. A Comprehensive History* (New York, Jerusalem: The Jewish Publication Society, 1993), p. 408 n. 9; Lehnardt, *Qaddish*, p. 279 n. 6.

17 See *Responsa of Rabbi Ya'aqov Moellin-Maharil. Revised and Corrected with Additions According to Previous Editions and Various Manuscripts with Introduction, References, Notes, and Commentaries*, ed. by Y. Satz (Jerusalem: Makhon Yerushalayim, 1979), p. 29 (§ 39).

18 On this problem, see eg, Hübscher, *Kaddisch-Gebet*, p. 42.

19 Cf. *Sefer Ḥasidim she-Ḥibber Rabbenu Yehuda he-Ḥasid*, ed. by Reuven Margaliot (Jerusalem: Mossad Harav Kook, 1957), p. 440 (§ 712).

qaddish yatom by a mourner on anniversary of a death, but he did not call it '*yahrzeit*', nor did he ascribe to it any new religious intent, as in subsequent kabbalistic writings.

Caution is, however, essential lest the conclusions drawn from this observation be too far-reaching. The term *yahrzeit* can already be found in the writings of a teacher of the 'Maharil', namely in the responsa of the Austrian, Rabbi Shalom of Wiener Neustadt[20] who died in 1415/16. According to Shlomo Spitzer in his edition of the responsa of Shalom of Neustadt, it is here that one finds the first mention of *yahrzeit*, and not, as is often claimed, in a responsum by Moshe Mintz (fifteenth century), nor in a statement erroneously ascribed to Meir of Rothenburg.[21] Yet in the responsum of Shalom of Neustadt, *yahrzeit* refers only to fasting on the anniversary of a dead relative, but not to the *yahrzeit qaddish*. And the same holds true for the occurrences of the word *yahrzeit* in the *minhag* book written later by Yiṣḥaq of Tyrnau (who died no earlier than 1408).[22] This famous Austrian rabbi also mentions *yahrzeit* in relation to fasting, but without connecting this with the recitation of *qaddish* on that specific day.[23] It may therefore only be surmised that he, like his teacher Shalom, knew the custom only from oral tradition, probably assuming that the *yahrzeit qaddish* should be recited only as an additional *qaddish yatom*.

The next scholar to use the term *yahrzeit* in connection with mourning customs seems to have been the great Eastern European talmudist and kabbalist, Mordekhai ben Avraham Jaffe (c. 1535–1612) in his *Levush Tekhelet* on the *Arba'a Ṭurim* (Berdiczew, 1821, § 133). It should, however, be noted that already in his teacher's main work, *Darkhei Moshe* (printed in Fürth in 1766), a commentary on Ya'aqov ben Asher's *Ṭurim* written by Moshe Isserles (c. 1525–72, acronym: 'Rema'), it is explained that 'in the case of a *yahrzeit*, *qaddish* may

---

20 Cf. Decisions and Customs of Shalom of Neustadt, ed. by Sh. Spitzer (Jerusalem: Makhon Yerushalayim, 1977) (Hebrew), § 457.

21 See on this Abraham Berliner, '*Die mittelhochdeutsche Sprache bei den Juden*', *Jahrbuch für jüdische Geschichte und Literatur*, 1 (1898), pp. 162–82, esp. p. 164: 'Seit den Zeiten des R. Meir aus Rothenburg wird das Wort ‚Jahrzeit' in jüdischen Quellen bekannt, das dann sich so sehr eingebürgert, daß man es nur als eine specielle jüdische Bezeichnung erkennen mag.' Cf. on this, however, Avida, *Sinai*, 25 (1949), p. 56. On Mintz (sometimes spelled: Münz), cf. also Jakob Zimmels, *Studies in Jewish History and Booklore* (New York: JTS New York, 1944), pp. 119–27.

22 Cf. *Sefer Ha-Minhagim (Rulings and Customs) of Rabbi Eisik Tirna Published according to the First Edition with Additions and Variants of Various Manuscripts with Introduction, References, Notes, and Commentaries*, ed. by S. J. Spitzer (Hebrew; Jerusalem: Makhon Yerushalayim, 1979). See also Eisenstein, Art. 'Yahrzeit', p. 64, who suggests that Yiṣḥaq Tyrnau was the first who used the term '*yahrzeit*'.

23 Cf. his *Sefer Ha-Minhagim*, ed. by Spitzer, p. 119 n. 1 on § 183.

be recited even when the anniversary falls on a Sabbath'.[24] This is an opinion that the Rema, like earlier authorities, connects with the legend about a dead man's son who was ordered by Rabbi Akiva to say *qaddish*, the well known founding legend for reciting the orphan's *qaddish*.[25]

Evidently, all these early sources for the recitation of *qaddish* by a relative on the anniversary of a death reflect the close linkage between *qaddish yatom* and the older custom of fasting on a *yahrzeit*. Furthermore, all these references are found in Ashkenazi writings, namely, in texts that originated in southern Germany or in Austria and were written at the beginning of the fourteenth century.

An important witness to this change in attitude towards *qaddish* in Ashkenaz is Binyamin Ze'ev ben Matitya of Arta, the early 16th century Greek halakhic scholar, who writes in his *Shu"t Ḥinukh bet Yehuda*.[26]

> It is correct with regard to fasting (on *yahrzeit*) that it is an important thing ... but saying *qaddish* (on *yahrzeit*) is only a local custom in those lands (i.e. Ashkenaz), and it is not (a custom) in other places, (which means) in the land of Yishma'el.

A similar reference to the Ashkenazi origin of the *yahrzeit qaddish* is found in a famous passage in Menashe ben Yisrael's (1604–57) *Nishmat Ḥayyim*.[27] This celebrated Sefardi writer and resident of Amsterdam makes abundantly clear that *yahrzeit qaddish* was not only a disputed Ashkenazi custom but also a *minhag* that found many opponents. Being Sefardi and a kabbalist, he seems to have been reluctant to adopt this custom. Nonetheless, he is probably the first writer who tries to have this practice adopted among non-Ashkenazi congregations. Underlying his position, he cites Yedidya Gottlieb ben Avraham's *Lewiat Ha-Derekh*, printed in Cracow in 1644, providing a completely new explanation of this liturgical usage of the *qaddish* that was originally ascribed to Yiṣḥaq ben Shelomo Luria Ashkenazi (c. 1510–74), the famous kabbalist from Safed. Gottlieb ben Avraham writes:

---

24 Cf. D. Telsner, *The Kaddish. Its History and Significance* (Jerusalem: Tal Orot Institute, 1995), p. 229.

25 Cf. the version of this *ma'ase* in: *Sefer Or Zarua', ḥibbero ga'on tif'eret ḥakhmei Yisrael R. Yiṣḥaq ben Moshe mi-Wina*, ed. by Abraham Lehrn, Vol. 2 (Zhitomir 1862, repr. Benei Braq: Hekhal Ha-Sefer, 1958), pp. 11c–d; the dating and origin of this story are disputed, cf. Myron B. Lerner, '*Ma'ase Ha-Tanna We-Ha-Met. Gilgulaw ha-sifrutiim we-ha-hilkhatiim*', *Asufot*, 2 (1988/89), pp. 29–70; Rela Kushelewsky, '*Ha-Tanna We-Ha-Met ha-Noded: ha-omnam aggada lo yehudit?*', *Criticism and Interpretation*, 30 (1994), pp. 41–63.

26 Amsterdam 1708, § 83.

27 Menashe ben Yisrael, *Sefer Nishmat Ḥayyim* (Leipzig 1862, repr. Tel Aviv, 1968), p. 55a (II 27) = Idem, *Sefer Nishmat Ḥayyim Ha-Menuqqad* (Jerusalem: Yedid Ha-Sefarim, 1995), p. 150.

> The sages of Eretz Yisrael complain about the minhag that exists in our lands (ie Ashkenaz), that we say *qaddish* on the anniversary of the death of a father and a mother, what we call in German '*yahrzeit*', from year to year (ie every year). And [this custom] appears to mock [the dead], because the Sages ordained saying *qaddish* for a period of only eleven months and not more, so that one's father should not look like a wicked person, [given that] the judgement in *Gehenna* lasts twelve months. And if this would be a (correct use of the *qaddish*) when one's father or mother has died, how can one hold (his father) to be a wicked man for several years, saying *qaddish* (all that time) for him, to release him from the punishment in *Gehenna*. Would this not shame his father? And according to our ways it is correct, for the intention (of saying *qaddish* on the anniversary is) to elevate the (souls of the) righteous from one level to the next.

The 'new' idea referred to in this statement is that a *qaddish* said on a *yahrzeit* not only atones for the sins of the deceased relatives in *Gehenna* but also elevates the souls to higher spheres in *Gan 'Eden*. This understanding of the *yahrzeit-qaddish*, nowhere mentioned in the legend about Rabbi Akiva and the dead man's son, must be understood against the background of Lurianic Kabbala and its mythic messianism of *tiqqun*. According to *Sefer Ha-Kawwanot*, written by a disciple of Luria, prayers like the *qaddish* not only save one's soul from *Gehenna* but they are also effective in raising souls from the lower levels of *Gan 'Eden* to the upper ones.[28]

The Lurianic explanation referred to by Gottlieb ben Avraham and Menashe ben Yisrael reflects, then, how in later times (ie a significant period after Ya'aqov Moellin's writings) kabbalistic narratives offered to balance the conflicting traditions of limiting the recitation of *qaddish yatom* to the first eleven months after the death of a relative and of saying an additional *qaddish* on the anniversary of the death each year. This kabbalistic interpretation seems to have been one of the main reasons for the ultimate acceptance of the *yahrzeit qaddish* among Oriental, Italian and Sefardi Jews.[29] This stance was also later strengthened because the *yahrzeit qaddish* was introduced in a gloss by Moshe Isserles to *Shulḥan 'Arukh, Yore De'a* (376,4).[30] Opinions that remained

---

28 Cf. Yiṣḥaq ben Shelomo [Ashkenazi] Luria, *Sefer Ha-Kawwanot le-ha-Rav ha-Elohi qadosh yomar lo Yiṣḥaq Luria* (Korzec: Silberman, 1784), pp. 22b–23a. On the mystical interpretation of the *qaddish* by Luria, cf. also *Siddur me-ha-AR"Y ha-Nikra be-Shem Kol Ya'aqov* (Slavuta: Pavloitsch, 1804), pp. 51a–54b. On the importance of these interpretations of the *qaddish*, cf. D. Assaf, *Sefer Ha-Qaddish* (Haifa: Maimonides Research Institute, 1966), pp. 202 ff.

29 For the Italian rite, cf. A. Berliner, *Gesammelte Schriften, Vol. 1: Italien* (Frankfurt a. M.: Kauffmann, 1913, repr. Hildesheim, Zürich, New York: Olms, 1988), pp. 179 ff.; for the Sefardi communities, cf. Pool, *Kaddish*, p. 106 and H. J. Zimmels, *Ashkenazim and Sephardim. Their Relations, Differences, and Problems as Reflected in the Rabbinical Responsa* (London 1958, repr. Farnborough: Gregg, 1969), pp. 186 ff.

30 See *Shulḥan 'Arukh, Yore De'a*, 376,4 [*Hilkhot Avelut*] (299b). On the reception of the word 'Yahrzeit' in oriental congregations, cf. also J. Press, 'Schebua Ha-Ben', *Monatsschrift für Geschichte und Wissenschaft des Judentums*, 76 (1932), pp. 572–77, esp. p. 576. See also Yiṣḥaq

critical of the introduction of this custom may also be found in sources written long after this rather official statement of support in the *Shulḥan 'Arukh*.[31]

3 Christian 'influences'?

What does Christianity have to do with these motivations for saying *qaddish* on a *yahrzeit*? Is it not somewhat odd to ask if the additional use of *qaddish* on the anniversary of a dead relative was influenced by Christianity? The question arises especially in the light of the previous analysis, which indicates that this custom is obviously connected with the development of *qaddish yatom*, a similar use of the *qaddish* usually assumed to have emerged in the Rhineland during the persecutions by the Crusaders in the eleventh century, with their lasting effects on liturgy and prayer?

It is significant that at the very time when various *yahrzeit* customs were being adopted by Ashkenazi Jews in the thirteenth and fourteenth centuries, comparable developments were also occurring in Catholic Christianity. Those changes seem to have been motivated on the one hand by the spread of diseases, such as the plague, and on the other hand by social conditions. Additionally, the commemoration of the deaths of relatives was a major field of concern in Christian churches from antiquity onwards.[32] From the time of the early Church fathers, such as Polycarp, Tertullian and Cyprian,[33] until the thirteenth and fourteenth centuries, the death of a relative or a saint would always have been commemorated and celebrated by special masses and

---

ben Shmuel Lampronti, *Paḥad Yiṣḥaq. Real-Wörterbuch zum Talmud und den Dezisoren* (Posekim), Vol. 10 (Hebrew; Lyck 1874), pp. 158a–b.

31 On this, cf., e.g. Y. Galis, *Minhagei Ereṣ Yisrael* (Jerusalem: Mosad Harav Kook, 1968), p. 63 (§ 25) on conflicts over the right to say *qaddish* in the *qehillot* of Amsterdam and London, where the *yahrzeit qaddish* was said only by a *sheliaḥ ṣibbur* (see Rabbi Shem Tov Gaguin, *Keter Shem Tov* [Kidan 1934]); see also p. 312, on drawing lots to determine who has the right to say *qaddish*. On similar problems, see also W. S. Jacobson, *Über das Qaddish-Gebet* (Frankfurt a. M.: Verlag des Israelit; Hermon, 1932, repr. Basel: Goldschmidt, 1974), p. 52. For further material on discussions regarding who has the right to say *yahrzeit qaddish*, cf. Louis Jacobs, *Theology in the Responsa* (London, Boston: Routledge, Kegan, 1975), p. 273, on a responsum by Joseph Ḥayyim from Baghdad (1835–1909) which addresses the question of whether the *yahrzeit qaddish* is effective even twenty years after the death of a parent.

32 Cf. Reiner Kaczynski, Art. 'Gedenken der Toten', *Lexikon für Theologie und Kirche3* 4 (1995), p. 339; H.-J. Ignatzi, Art. 'Jahrgedächtnis', *Lexikon für Theologie und Kirche* 5 (1996), pp. 711 ff.

33 Cf. Peter Karpinski, *Annua dies dormitionis. Untersuchungen zum christlichen Jahrgedächtnis der Toten auf dem Hintergrund antiken Brauchtums*, Europäische Hochschulschriften XXIII 300 (Frankfurt a. M., Bern, New York: Lang, 1987).

prayers. The commemoration rites of fasting, praying or celebrating a mass on the seventh or the thirtieth day following death, and on the anniversary, were rooted deeply in the belief that the deeds of the living could have a direct effect on the fate of the dead in their place – be it in hell, in a state of *limbus*, or in heaven.

In Christianity, however, these mourning customs were a pagan heritage, especially originating in Roman rites. Some Christian theologians succeeded in retroactively basing these practices on biblical examples and laws: for instance, with regard to the commemoration on the seventh, they relied on the law demarcating seven days of impurity after contact with a corpse; and in the case of the thirtieth day, they pointed to the bereavement period of thirty days for both Aaron and Moses – meaning the period of time the community spent mourning each of their deaths. Given the early stages of development of mourning customs, Christianity was clearly influenced by two spheres of belief: a Gentile and a Jewish one.[34] After a long period of relative stability, with only slight changes in mourning rituals, we find in Christian sources, especially from the thirteenth century onwards, a new and strengthened interest in special prayers and masses for the dead.[35] This renewed interest in masses for the dead parallels the invention of further customs of mourning like memorial donations, which gained a prominent place in the social, political and theological culture of the Catholic Church during the thirteenth and fourteenth centuries.[36] As has been well researched in recent decades, these

---

34 Cf. on this Emil Freistedt, *Altchristliche Totengedächtnistage und ihre Beziehung zum Jenseitsglauben und Totenkultus der Antike*, Liturgiegeschichtliche Quellen und Forschungen 24 (Münster i. W.: Aschendorf, ^{2}1971), pp. 53 ff.

35 On this disputed question, cf. P.-M. Gy, 'Der Tod des Christen' in *Handbuch der Liturgiewissenschaft*, vol. 2, *Die übrigen Sakramente und die Sakramentalien. Die Heiligung der Zeit*, ed. by A.-G. Martimort et al. (Freiburg, Basel, Vienna: Herder, 1965), pp. 164 ff.; on the other hand, see Franz-Joseph Dölger, Ichtys. *Der Heilige Fisch in den antiken Religionen und im Christentum. Textband II* (Münster i. W.: Aschendorf, 1922), p. 565: 'Es gewinnt also den Anschein, als ob die Lehre von der Erbsünde mitbestimmend gewesen wäre, um den Geburtstag der antiken Totenliturgie zu verdrängen und ihn durch das Jahresgedächtnis des Todes zu ersetzen. Im Hintergrund steht aber das jüdische Jahrgedächtnis, das die stärkste Unterlage bot.' See also, however, the rejoinder to this statement, by Karpinski, *Annnua dies dormitionis*, p. 191 n. 1, who denies Old Testament examples of any of the anniversary rites in Christianity.

36 Cf. Karl J. Merk, *Die messliturgische Totenehrung in der römischen Kirche. Zugleich ein Beitrag zum Mittelalterlichen Opferwesen, I. Teil* (Stuttgart: Schloz, 1926), pp. 87–108; Ludwig Ruland, *Die Geschichte der kirchlichen Leichenfeier* (Regensburg: Manz, 1901), pp. 146 ff. For different rites and their intentions, cf. also Arnold Angenendt, 'Theologie und Liturgie der mittelalterlichen Toten-Memoria', in *Memoria. Der geschichtliche Zeugniswert des liturgischen Gedenkens im Mittelalter*, ed. by K. Schmid and J. Wollasch (Munich: Fink, 1984), pp. 79–199, esp. pp. 179 ff.

innovations changed the character and status of the Catholic Church in medieval society, especially in southern Germany and Austria[37].

Berthold of Regensburg, a famous ascetic, itinerant preacher and member of the *Ordo Fratres Minores* who died in 1272,[38] provides an exemplar for this change. He seems to have paved the way, especially in southern Germany, the Danubian region, Bohemia, and Austria, for a new theology of '*do, ut des*' (I give, that you might give), that strongly emphasized the effects of prayers for the dead, specifically those recited in an anniversary mass, such as the *Paternoster* ('Our Father'), the *Ave Maria* ('Hail Mary') and the *Credo* (The Apostles' Creed). His German sermons, which are an important source for any reconstruction of the *Volksfrömmigkeit* – the piety of the common people – at that time, reflect a remarkable concern about death, and a growing interest in the whereabouts of souls in hell.

In one of his German sermons, that was edited posthumously by his adherents, we find that Berthold recommended praying three additional Paternosters silently, after the celebration of the mass.[39]

> Three *Paternosters* in silence after the *Paternoster* [of the mass]: And he should say the first one to praise and honour almighty God and to praise and honour the Holy Mother, my Holy St. Mary, and all the heavenly armies; and the second *Paternoster* you should recite to honour almighty God, a blessing for all Christian people on earth; and a third *Paternoster* you should recite to comfort all souls and as a help for them in purgatory.

---

37 Cf. O. G. Oexle, 'Die Gegenwart der Toten', in – *Death in the Middle Ages*, ed. by H. Braet/ W. Verbke, *Mediaevalia Lovaniensia I Studia IX* (Leuven: Leuven University Press, 1983), pp. 19–77; Norbert Ohler, *Sterben und Tod im Mittelalter* (Munich, Zürich: Artemis, 1990), p. 37 and p. 129. G. Hölzle, 'damit och unser gedechtnus [...] nit mit dem glocken ton zergang'. 'Totengedenken in Bruderschaften Bayerisch Schwabens und Altbaierns anhand literarischer und liturgischer Quellen', in *Totengedenken und Trauerkultur. Geschichte und Zukunft des Umgangs mit Verstorbenen*, ed. by M. Herzog (Stuttgart, Berlin, Cologne: Kohlhammer, 2001), pp. 87–110; Karl Müller, 'Die Esslinger Pfarrkirche im Mittelalter', *Württembergische Vierteljahrshefte für Landesgeschichte, Neue Folge*, 16 (1907), pp. 237–326, esp. pp. 313–23; H. Lentze, 'Begräbnis und Jahrtag im mittelalterlichen Wien', *Zeitschrift der Savigny-Stiftung für Rechtsgeschichte 67 Kanonistische Abteilung*, 36 (1950), pp. 328–64.

38 On him, cf. F. G. Banta, Art. 'Berthold von Regensburg', in *Die deutsche Literatur des Mittelalters. Verfasserlexikon*, ed. by Kurt Ruh, vol. 1, Berlin, New York 1978, pp. 817–23.

39 Cf. Berthold von Regensburg. *Ausgewählte Predigten. Mit einer Einleitung* by H. Hering (Leipzig: Richter, 1893), p. 128 [on the mass]; *Berthold von Regensburg. Vollständige Ausgabe seiner deutschen Predigten mit Anmerkungen und Wörterbuch* by F. Pfeiffer, Vol. 1 (Vienna 1862, repr. Berlin: de Gruyter, 1862, pp. 501 f. On the literary difficulties of these sermons and their historical value, cf. also Werner Röcke, *Berthold von Regensburg. Vier Predigten* (Stuttgart: Reclam, 1983), pp. 235–64.

The third *Paternoster* mentioned in this sermon is not known to older prayer orders, such as the commonly accepted *Missale Romanum*[40]. The slightly different *Regensburger Missale*[41], notes that it should be said to comfort the souls of the believers and to save the souls of the departed in purgatory.

Similar additions to the standard prayer recitations may be found in many other Christian documents from that time.[42] For example, in a Franciscan *Missale* from Southern Germany we find prescriptions for the seven Gregorian masses that stress the importance of fifteen sets of '*Pater noster cum totidem Ave Maria et Credo*' for the dead.[43] Of interest in this regard is also that at the end of the fourteenth century, the sheer quantity of masses said for the dead dramatically increased. This is confirmed not only by the large number of donations usually connected with the reading of masses for the dead but also by the many last wills whose primary concern focuses on making reliable arrangements for reading such anniversary masses.[44] This case in point is also affirmed in several documents from Wiener Neustadt, a place that is, as noted above, closely connected with the development of the reception of the term *yahrzeit*. Remarkably, in this small town, that might serve for many reasons as a typical model of a Catholic environment, the '*Jahrtag*'-masses were held in high esteem by the public.[45]

---

40 Vgl. *Missale Romanum cum lectionibus III. Tempus per Annum Hebdomadae VI–XXI*, (Vatican: Libr. Ed. Vaticana, 1977), pp. 1854 ff.; *Die Feier der Heiligen Messe [Messbuch] für die Bistümer des deutschen Sprachgebietes. Authentische Ausgabe für den liturgischen Gebrauch*, Teil II: *Das Messbuch deutsch für alle Tage des Jahres außer der Karwoche* (Linz: Herder, 1975), pp. 1129–34; *Enchiridion Liturgicum Compectens Theologiae Sacramentalis et dogmata et leges iuxta novum codicem rubricarum*, concinnavit P. Rado, Tomus Primus (Rom, Freiburg, Barcione: Herder, 1961), pp. 372 ff. For the older rites see M. Fearotin, *Le Liber Ordinum. En Usage dans l'Église wisigothique et mozarabe d'Espagne du cinquième au onzième siècle*, Bilbiotheca 'Ephemerides Liturgicae' Subsidia 83, Istrumenta Liturgica Quarreriensia 6 (Rom: Ed. Liturgiche, 1996), pp. 447 ff. [6.–8. cent.]; Judith Frei, *Das Ambrosianische Sakramentar D 3-3 aus dem Mailändischen Metropolitankapitel. Eine textkritische und redaktionsgeschichtliche Untersuchung*, Corpus Ambrosiano-Liturgicum 3 (Münster: Aschendorf, 1974), pp. 419 ff. [10. cent.]; Odilo Heiming, *Corpus Ambrosiano Liturgicum I. Das Sacramentarium Triplex. Die Handschrift C 43 der Zentralbibliothek Zürich* (Münster: Aschendorf, 1969), pp. 349–51.

41 Cf. Anton Beck, *Kirchliche Studien und Quellen* (Amberg: Bös, 1903), esp. pp. 246–54.

42 Cf., for example, Rieger in his review article on Elbogen, *Gottesdienst*, where he hints at a Nekrologium Monasterii S. Crucis Ratisbonensis. There we find written in Middle High German on fol. 229: 'Hie sint angeschriben die tôten, den wir gebunden sin, daz wir iarcit mit vigilien und mit messen alle iar begên.'

43 Cf. Adolf Franz, *Die Messe im Deutschen Mittelalter. Beiträge zur Geschichte der Liturgie und des Religiösen Volkslebens* (Freiburg i. B.: Herder, 1902), p. 257.

44 See Merk, *Messliturgische Totenehrung*, pp. 102–4.

45 Cf. Helga Skvarics, *Volksfrömmigkeit und Alltagskultur. Zum Stiftungsgeschehen Wiener Neustädter Bürger im Spätmittelalter und in der frühen Neuzeit (14.–16. Jh.)*, Beiträge zur neu-

The assumption that Jews who lived in a town like Wiener Neustadt would not have noticed any of the aforementioned changes and developments in their Christian environment in late thirteenth century seems not only to be naive, but arises out of an extremely uncritical picture of how Jews lived in a Christian environment. In a town like Wiener Neustadt, that housed a considerable Jewish population from the late thirteenth century until the expulsion in the mid-fourteenth century, Jews lived not in a ghetto, but in close proximity to their Christian neighbours. According to numerous documents from this location, Jews shared strong economic ties with their fellow residents and, despite all limitations, it is attested that the Jews also adopted local behaviours and customs.[46]

Is it therefore too far-fetched to assume that the inclusion of the *qaddish* at the anniversary of a death, as attested in *Sefer Maharil* (not yet kabbalistically re-interpreted), might have been influenced by its Christian environment?

Admittedly, it is impossible to prove whether Jews from Wiener Neustadt, or from similar places in Southern Germany and Austria, were directly influenced by their neighbours' mourning customs. Furthermore, it must, of course, be taken into consideration that at the end of the thirteenth century, the boundaries between the Christian and the Jewish hemisphere were not easily permeable. But even if we take into account the strong barriers between the Jewish and the Christian worlds at that time, one cannot totally deny the possibility of influences that sometimes left behind only slight traces, like, in our case, the remarkable adoption of the German word *yahrzeit* itself.

4 Conclusion

This study is best summed up with both cautions and evidence. With regard to the trace developments in *Volksfrömmigkeit*, research in this area necessarily remains shaky. For methodological reasons, it must be emphasized that inquiring into direct influences on local *minhagim* should always be considered a

eren Geschichte Österreichs 15 (Frankfurt a. M., Berlin, Bern, Brussels, New York, Oxford, Vienna: Lang, 2000).

46 On the close relationship between Jews and Christians in Wiener Neustadt during thirteenth century, cf. Martha Keil, 'Juden in Grenzgemeinden: Wiener Neustadt und Ödenburg im Spätmittelalter', in idem and E. Lappin (eds.), *Studien zur Geschichte der Juden in Österreich*, Handbuch zur Geschichte der Juden in Österreich, Reihe B, Vol. 3 (Bodenheim: Philo-Verlag, 1997), pp. 9–33, esp. pp. 15 ff. See also *Germania Judaica*, Vol. 3: 1350–1519, 2. Ortschaftsartikel Mährisch-Budwitz – Zwolle, ed. by A. Maimon/M. Breuer/Y. Guggenheim (Tübingen: Mohr, 1995), p. 1621.

very problematic task.[47] The use of the word 'influence' itself may be misunderstood in so far as it seems to involve directionality. Of course, one cannot speak of a Christian intention to change Jewish mourning practices. Rather, the use of that term here points to the fact that any environment leaves its imprint on culture, and, in this case, a majority of Christians may have had such an impact on a smaller group of Jews.[48]

In the case of the *yahrzeit qaddish*, the current sources are still so meagre that any definite answer of who adopted it, why they made that choice, or whether they were influenced by certain local customs remains guesswork. The development of a custom, such as the *yahrzeit qaddish*, cannot, however, be explained by intrinsic developments within the Jewish culture alone, particularly since these *yahrzeit* customs developed in Christian lands but not in the Islamic world.

As this paper aims to demonstrate, the custom of reciting *qaddish* on the anniversary developed from an older custom, the *minhag* of saying *qaddish yatom*.[49] This disputed and often criticized custom of *yahrzeit qaddish*[50] cannot, however, be fully understood on the basis of known explanations of this *qaddish*. Obviously the use of the *qaddish* as an annual prayer for mourners was widely accepted only after it was re-interpreted on the basis of kabbalistic thinking. But these concepts certainly do not reflect the original intention of saying *qaddish* on an anniversary; there is an evident gap in the chain of interpretation for saying the *qaddish* on the *yahrzeit*, that can best be explained by a lack of knowledge about the real motivations for this liturgical development. Thus, if we deal with this apparently 'very' Jewish custom, we can and must take into account that its development may also have been stimulated by a spiritual atmosphere and culture then dominated by the Catholic Christianity and by *Volksfrömmigkeit*, with its own cryptic ways of transmitting cus-

47 On a similar problem, which refers to the reconstruction of Christian 'influence' on an apparent Jewish motif, cf. Peter Schäfer, 'Daughter, Sister, Bride, and Mother: Images of the Femininity of God in the Early Kabbala', *Journal of the American Academy of Religion*, 68 (2000), pp. 221–42. See on this question also Peter Schäfer, Die Geburt des Judentums aus dem Geist des Christentums (Tübingen: Mohr-Siebeck, 2010), p. 178.

48 As already mentioned above, the use of candlelights for the commemoration of the dead also seems to have been a custom developed in a cultural environment where the use of candles was common. See on this very custom an overview cited by Katrin Seidel, *Die Kerze. Motivgeschichte und Ikonologie* (Hildesheim, Zürich, New York: Olms, 1996), pp. 67–73. For an uncritical study of the Jewish use of lights, see the article by Oppenheimer, mentioned above, n. 12.

49 Cf. already Moshe Isserles on *Shulḥan 'Arukh, Yore De'a*, 376.4 [*Hilkhot Avelut*] (299b).

50 See on this, e.g., Jakob J. Petuchowski, *Prayerbook Reform in Europe. The Liturgy of European Liberal and Reform Judaism* (New York: World Union for Progressive Judaism, 1968), pp. 324 ff.

toms and religious practices. People during the time focused on in this study were very concerned about the afterlife and the well-being of the dead. This intense preoccupation, so typical of Christian belief during that period, seems to have left its mark by introducing an additional *qaddish* among its neighbours, the Jews.

Ruth Langer

Investigation into the Early European Forms of the *Ṣidduq ha-Din*

1 History

The concept of justifying God's judgement at the time of death by the recitation of appropriate biblical verses appears in tannaitic literature, apparently as a *novum*. *Sifre*, in its commentary on Deut 32:4, records the following teaching regarding the Hadrianic persecutions in the early second century:

> כשתפסו את רבי חנינה בן תרדיון נגזרה עליו גזירה לישרף עם ספרו. אמרו לו: נגזרה עליך גזירה לישרף עם ספרך. קרא המקרא הזה: הצור תמים פעלו. אמרו לאשתו: נגזרה על בעלך גזרה לישרף ועליך ליהרג. קראה המקרא הזה: אל אמונה ואין עול. אמרו לבתו נגזרה גזירה על אביך לישרף ועל אמך ליהרג ועליך לעשות מלאכה. קראה המקרא הזה: גדול העצה ורב העליליה אשר עיניך פקוחות. אמר רבי: כמה גדולים צדיקים אלו, שבשעת צרתם הזמינו שלשה פסוקים של צידוק הדין, מה שאין כן בכל הכתובים. כיוונו שלשתם את לבם וצידקו עליהם את הדין ...

> When they arrested Rabbi Ḥanina ben Teradion, ... they told him that it had been decreed that he should be burned with his book [Torah scroll]. He recited this verse: 'The Rock – His deeds are perfect!' [Deut 32:4a] They informed his wife that it had been decreed that her husband should be burned and that she should be killed. She recited the verse: 'A faithful God, never false, true and upright is He.' [Deut 32:4b]. They told his daughter that it had been decreed that her father should be burned and that her mother should be killed and that she should be enslaved. She recited this verse: 'Wondrous in purpose and mighty in deed, whose eyes observe all the ways of men, to repay every man according to his ways and with the proper fruit of his deeds.' [Jer 32:19] Rabbi reflected: How great were these righteous people that in their hour of trouble, they were able to summon these three verses of '*ṣidduq ha-din*' (justifying the judgement), unlike any others in the Scriptures. The three of them justified the judgement with full intentionality ...
> (*Sifre Devarim* 307; *b'Avod. Zar.* 17b)

The term *ṣidduq ha-din* carries several overlapping valences in ongoing Jewish practice. Here, it obviously speaks to martyrs' own verbal acceptance before their deaths of their personal fate. The model for Jewish martyrdom, however, came to be another victim of these persecutions, Rabbi Akiva, who recited *shema*' (Deut 6:4) rather than the verses discussed here. In rabbinic tradition, *ṣidduq ha-din* also refers to the ritual recitation upon receiving bad news of the blessing ברוך דיין האמת ('Blessed [is/are You, Eternal our God, Ruler of the universe,] the true Judge'). The Mishna (*Ber.* 9.2) dictates the recitation of this blessing and the Babylonian Talmud explicitly connects it with receiving news of one's father's death (*bBer.* 59b), but without this specific title.[1] This blessing later becomes associated with the ritual of tearing one's clothing as a gesture of mourning, and a preference for this application apparently underlies the restriction on expressing *ṣidduq ha-din* before a person has actually died.[2] Finally, *ṣidduq ha-din* becomes the name of a liturgical text (or a cluster of such texts) that have at their core precisely the verses mentioned in this *baraita*. This prayer is our focus here. Although the evidence is scanty, there are signs that the prayer underwent not insignificant transformations as it took on the forms found in medieval liturgical manuscripts.

By the time of the Rishonim, this prayer is presumed as one of the few fixed elements of European funeral liturgies, recited in conjunction with burial itself and preceding the burial *qaddish*. Evidence does, however, suggest that this may have been a fairly new custom, even at the time of Rashi. When we look at geonic sources, we see that the prayer's appearance in the *Seder Rav Amram Gaon* is a later addition, appearing in two different versions in two manuscripts.[3] Sa'adya similarly does not mention the *ṣidduq ha-din* in his prayer-book and is dismissive of the recitation even of *qaddish* at a burial.[4] Robert Brody notes that the Babylonian Geonim knew of the prayer only from the questions that they received about it;[5] their answers, therefore, do not really relate to the text of the prayer itself and sometimes show uncertainty about its precise liturgical context. This applies to Rav Naṭronai's more detailed responsum about the mode of its performance on a minor holiday that looks only to mishnaic precedents and permits the prayer on those days only if it is recited in unison, rather than as a call and response (whether of the same words or of a refrain is not clear).[6] Similarly, an anonymous geonic responsum suggests that

1 David Kraemer, *The Meanings of Death in Rabbinic Judaism* (London, New York: Routledge, 2000), p. 46, p. 135, suggests that the concept existed in the tannaitic period but cannot be precisely documented. *t.Ber.* 6.3 describes the bad news as a judgement of retribution.

2 *Evel Rabbati* 3.1.

3 *Seder Rav Amram Gaon*, ed. by Daniel Goldschmidt (Jerusalem: Mossad Harav Kook, 1971), # 156, p. 186.

4 *Siddur Rav Sa'adya Gaon*, ed. by I. Davidson, S. Assaf, and B. I. Joel (Jerusalem: Mekize Nirdamim, Reuven Maas, 1985), p. 359.

5 *Teshuvot Rav Naṭronai bar Hilai Gaon* (Jerusalem; Cleveland: Ofeq Institute, 5754), p. 237 n. 5 (to Responsum 118), p. 425 n. 2 (to Responsum 284). For a fuller discussion of this issue, though one less definite in its conclusions, see Andreas Lehnardt, 'Tzidduq ha-Din und Kaddisch. Beobachtungen zur Entwicklung der jüdischen Begräbnisliturgie im Mittelalter', *Trumah: Zeitschrift der Hochschule für Jüdische Studien Heidelberg [Studien zum jüdischen Mittelalter]*, 12 (2002), pp. 6–14.

6 Responsum 118. This was widely cited. See, for example, the Meiri to *b.Mo'ed Qat.* 27b.

this is a prayer recited *after* returning from the cemetery and that each *ḥazzan* recites it however he wishes. The text suggests that this is somehow connected to the *birkat avelim* or perhaps to the additions to the *birkat ha-mazon* recited in the house of mourning, or perhaps to the Mishna's prescription of a liturgy that requires standing and sitting.[7] Support for Brody's assertion is Rav Haya Gaon's claim not to know the custom of reciting this prayer at all, and his presumption that any earlier geonic discussions of it were referring to the custom of their questioners, somewhere outside of Babylonia.[8]

Genizah sources support this picture. While there are numerous fragments with the header '*ṣidduq ha-din*', most of these are *piyyuṭim* on the general theme of our prayer that could function as eulogy texts as well, with little or no connection to our more fixed liturgical text.[9] Andreas Lehnardt perhaps overreads the evidence when he points to these *piyyuṭim*, some composed in Babylonia, as proof that the *ṣidduq ha-din* was recited there (as a fixed liturgical element) by the end of the geonic period.[10] I think it is also questionable, without specific evidence, to presume as he does that the prayer had its origins in the Land of Israel just because it seems not to have originated in Babylonia.[11] As we shall see, the style of the prayer and the variations in its actual text and performance suggest a late and not particularly authoritative origin. See Peter Lehnardt's article in this volume for the history of this prayer in Italy, a point of possible origin for it in this form, although, especially because of

---

7 *Newly Discovered Geonic Responsa and the Writings of Early Provencal Sages*, ed. by Simcha Emanuel (Jerusalem; Cleveland: Ofeq Institute, 5755), p. 78, #68.

8 *Oṣar Ha-Genim*, ed. by Lewin, *Mashq*. pp. 40–41, #115, and p. 55, #156, citing from Naḥmanides, *Torat Ha-Adam* and *Hilkhot Rabbi Yiṣḥaq Ghiyyat, Hilkhot Evel* (Jerusalem: Chatam Sofer Institute, 1998), p. 218.

9 A query posed to Maimonides suggests that this conflation of *ṣidduq ha-din* and dirges (*qinot*) was customary before the burial in the courtyard of the synagogue in Alexandria. (*Shu"t Ha-Rambam* #161) According to searches in 2010 of the catalogues of the Friedberg Genizah Project and the Institute for Microfilmed Hebrew Manuscripts (and a check of all the fragments listed), one fragment, MS Philadelphia University of Pennsylvania HB Genizah NS12, begins with the opening line of our prayer, ... הצור תמים בכל פועל, but the rest of the text appears to differ significantly and offers a refrain אמרי אנוש בשם טוב ילך. Another version of this text may appear in the badly preserved fragment, MS Paris – Collection Jacques Mosseri II, 268.2. Another fragment, MS Paris Collection Jacques Mosseri IV, 157/1 contains a text beginning אמנם חסד ורחמים כולו that has the literary structure that seems to underlie our text (see below). It does not, however, contain any parallel language. A text that consists primarily of a collection of verses contains significant parallels in language, but essentially because its verses appear also in our text. See MS Cambridge University Library Or. 1080.9.2 and MS Manchester, John Rylands University Library MS A 53.

10 Lehnardt, 'Tzidduq ha-Din und Kaddisch', p. 28.

11 Lehnardt, 'Tzidduq ha-Din und Kaddisch', pp. 16 ff.

the poetic additions it attracted there, that version subsequently became much more elaborate there than anything known elsewhere in Europe.

Discussions among the Rishonim frequently address whether this prayer may be recited on semi-festive occasions, like at burials during the intermediate days of festivals and on minor holidays when public mourning is forbidden as inconsistent with the joyfulness of the day. One of the most widely cited traditions surrounding this prayer recalls that when at an actual funeral during the intermediate days of a festival, someone protested that the prayer should not be said, Rashi himself recited the *ṣidduq ha-din* as well as the *qaddish* following it, giving the explanation that the *ṣidduq ha-din* is neither an act of eulogizing nor otherwise something destructive of the festive nature of the day; it is fundamentally no more than praise of God and acceptance of the heavenly judgement.[12] Recitation of *qaddish*, even in its special funeral form, was at best a secondary issue in these halakhic discussions; the rabbis understood it to function as a response to the recitation of verses in this prayer and not to be an independent act of mourning.[13] In other words, in Rashi's late eleventh-century France, people knew a *ṣidduq ha-din* preceding burial whose essential element was its biblical verses, but they were unsure whether to consider its recitation an act of mourning. Other texts, unfortunately not associated with any datable figure, indicate that the Jews of Mainz did not follow Rashi's precedent, or perhaps, that Rashi was acting counter to their precedent.[14] While we could simply attribute this to the typical, local nature of Ashkenazi *minhag*, the very fact that Rashi had to determine the French *minhag* suggests that recitation of this liturgy was itself a fairly new custom.[15]

---

12 One wonders whether Rashi's move was pastorally motivated, to avoid distress in the midst of a funeral itself. It was not, however, treated as such in subsequent halakhic discussions.

13 *Shu"t Rashi* 189:2; *Sefer Ha-Orah* II, p. 146; *Mordekhai, Mo'ed Qaṭ.* 838, and numerous parallels.

14 Rosh, *Mo'ed Qaṭ.* 3.87 documents the various different customs about how this prayer was or was not recited on minor holidays. He notes a difference between Mainz and Worms that appears also in *Sefer Ma'ase Ha-Geonim*, ed. by Avraham Epstein, Schriften des Vereins Mekize Nirdamim 3. Folge, Nr. 3 (Berlin: Mekize Nirdamim, 1909) p. 49, #58.

15 There was, similarly, some attempt to allow the recitation of the prayer only for important people on these minor holy days. See *Sefer Ha-Roqeaḥ, Hilkhot Avelut*, #316. R. Yiṣḥaq Ghiyyat indicates that the custom in Spain was not to recite it at all, for drawing the line between different sorts of people (simple people and Moshe Rabbenu) is not legitimate in this situation (*Hilkhot R. Yiṣḥaq Ghiyyat, Hilkhot Evel*, p. 241). His real concern here is, however, that on these minor holidays, when *taḥanun* is not recited, one also does not recite, at the Sabbath afternoon service, the verses of *ṣidduq ha-din* recited in memory of the Sabbath afternoon death of Moses. This becomes his precedent for establishing the Spanish custom. Naḥmanides rejects this and rules according to Rashi (*Torat Ha-Adam, Sha'ar Ha-Sof, 'Inyan Hoṣa'a*, ed. I. Melzer, Zikhron

How was this text performed? Medieval manuscripts are typically very sparing in their instructions for the performance of the texts they record. All versions of the prayer open with the verse, Deut 32:4, that which Rabbi Ḥanania and his wife divided between them. All but the latest French manuscripts indicate that this verse is to function as a congregational response between the other lines. That this instruction is lacking elsewhere may mean only that the scribal tradition omitted it, not that the community performed the prayer differently. One unique Sefardi manuscript (S2) divides the prayer over different stages of the burial process. Two sections of it are recited in the home of the deceased as a liturgical accompaniment surrounding the mourners' tearing of their clothes before leaving for the cemetery, that is, in a context that all acknowledge requires a *ṣidduq ha-din*. The remainder is recited at the cemetery before the burial itself. *Qaddish* follows the burial. Because the liturgy in this manuscript also contains a different content and organization of the lines, we cannot presume that the other two Sefardi exemplars represent the same practice.

There is evidence for significant variation as to where, and hence when, our text is recited. The Tosafist, R. Shimshon of Sens, locates the *ṣidduq ha-din* in the Mishna's *sede bokhim*, a field where the funeral procession customarily halts before the burial at some distance from the grave for people to say farewell to the deceased and to recite this prayer. As the Mishna did not know of the *ṣidduq ha-din*, we have to assume that this reflects R. Shimshon's own French reality of the twelfth-thirteenth century.[16] This is confirmed in the responsum of a R. Meshullam, presumably of the Rhineland Kalonymide family, and several generations earlier, who presumes that reciting the *ṣidduq ha-din* requires setting the bier down in the street (that is, in an open place), something forbidden on minor holidays. On these days, therefore, one may recite the prayer only for a very prominent person.[17] Apparently in response to this ruling, the Worms community recited the prayer on minor festivals while walking to the cemetery, that is, without setting down the bier, allowing them to recite *qaddish* at the cemetery itself.[18]

In contrast, the Rosh and R. Yeruḥam report that Ashkenazi and French Jews recite *ṣidduq ha-din* and *qaddish* after forming lines following the burial,

Ḥinukh Torani, 1994. Thus, the Sefardi custom was no more firmly established even two centuries later.

16 See his commentary to Tractate *Ohalot*, ch. 18. The Ritva, *Mo'ed Qat*. 5b, cites this with approval.

17 He adds that if one does not recite the *ṣidduq ha-din*, one also may not recite *qaddish*, because it may be recited only after words of Torah like the recitation of verses in this prayer. *Sefer Ma'ase Geonim*, ed. by Epstein, p. 49; *Sefer Ha-Roqeaḥ*, *Hilkhot Avelut* #316.

18 *Sefer Ha-Roqeaḥ*, *Hilkhot Avelut* #316, *Ravi"ah*, part III, *Hilkhot Evel* 841.

a point at which others (Sefardi Jews?) only recite *qaddish* (presumably having recited the *ṣidduq ha-din* before the burial, but they are not explicit on this point).[19] This is not confirmed, though, by the ruling of their near contemporary, an exemplar of the French rites, R. Ya 'aqov ben Yehuda Ḥazzan of London, who instructs 'that before they bury the deceased, they stand around him and the *Ḥazzan* recites ...'. He proceeds to indicate the text, complete with congregational responses of Deut 32:4. The burial follows immediately, suggesting that the locus of this ritual is the graveside.[20] The Ramban's discussion in his *Torat Ha-Adam* is not particularly helpful on this point, as he is trying to integrate all his received sources into what is probably a new instruction for his community rather than reflecting on actual custom.[21] In his *Orḥot Ḥayyim*, Aharon Ha-Kohen of Lunel, born in Narbonne but exiled to Spain after 1306, describes our prayer as one that the community recites to the mourner in his home immediately after the death, as well as one that is recited during the procession to the grave within the cemetery. Apparently this was the custom of Narbonne.[22] It is plausible that some version of this custom is that reflected in S2. This mélange explains why the Ṭur begins his discussion of this question saying, 'All these things are dependent on *minhag* (custom), and therefore each and every place should follow its own custom.'[23]

1 The text

The liturgical composition beginning with Deut 32:4 and entitled '*ṣidduq ha-din*' appears in relatively stable and mature forms by the time we can docu-

---

19 Rosh, *Mo'ed Qat.* 3:86; Rabbenu Yeruḥam, *Sefer Toldot Adam we-Ḥavah*, Netiv 28, part 2, p. 221d.

20 *'Eṣ Ḥayyim*, ed. by Israel Brodie (Jerusalem: Mossad Harav Kook, 1962), *Hilkhot Evel*, ch. 6, p. 394.

21 *Sha'ar Ha-Evel*, *'Inyan Ha-Hatḥala* #46. He suggests the following order for all the customs (without geographical or chronological distinction) that he has listed: after the burial, they go to a place near the cemetery called 'the place where the family stands' where the community arranges itself in lines of ten opposite the mourners, petitions for mercy for the deceased, and recites *qaddish*; then they move to the place where they do the 'standing and sitting' and recite brief words of *ṣidduq ha-din* during its seven iterations; then they go to a place nearby designated for eulogies and dirges; then to the city square (or the synagogue if a village lacks a square, or to the mourner's home) where they recite the *birkat avelim* over a cup; and finally to the home of the mourner to comfort him.

22 *Hilkhot Evel* 5. 11. See also the *Kol Bo* #114 which presents the recitation while walking to the grave as a regional custom; others recite *qinot* or *hashkavot*.

23 *Yore De'a* § 376.

ment the medieval European rites. Peter Lehnardt's article in this volume presents the Italian materials, and I will not enter into them here. Given the focus of this volume, the centre of this discussion will be the rites of medieval Greater Ashkenaz, which I identify as Western Ashkenaz, that is, the Rhineland, Northern France,[24] and Eastern Ashkenaz, that is, the 'Canaanite' rites, initially of Bohemia and eventually of Poland. These cannot be understood properly, though, without comparison with other rites. Our primary point of comparison will be Spain, although I found only three manuscripts from there, all from the fifteenth century, that contained the prayer. No manuscripts including this prayer of identifiable provenance appear to have been preserved from the medieval Romaniote or non-European rites.[25]

There is no consistency in any rite as to whether this prayer appears in the *siddur* or *maḥzor*, or where it appears, if it does, although it frequently appears along with other lifecycle rituals and/or the prayers in response to a bad dream (הטבת חלום) and *birkat kohanim*. Two possible reasons suggest themselves: the total omission of the prayer perhaps reflects a hesitancy to include death-related rituals in *siddurim*; the inconsistency in its location likely comes because death rituals were introduced into the European *siddur* after its basic organization had become standardized.[26]

Clearly, the texts represented in these various rites are related. The western, Rhineland Ashkenazi text, like the rite itself, is extremely stable. The earlier manuscripts already present the prayer as it appears in later prayerbooks.[27] The only significant variation in the order of its lines is recorded in a comment in a manuscript from Worms that notes the variants in nearby Cologne. We, however, lack any manuscript directly reflecting this custom. In

24 I do not include French manuscripts dated after the fourteenth century because of the final expulsion of that community by the end of that century.

25 A text essentially identical to our Sefardi base text appears in the 1527 Venice printing of the Aleppo *siddur* (facsimile edition: *Siddur Tefillot Kefi Minhag Q"Q Aram Ṣova* [Jerusalem: Yad Ha-Rav Nissim, 2007]), pp. 771b–72a. However, this prayer does not appear in either of the surviving manuscripts of this rite. MS Cincinnati Hebrew Union College 407, NLI f 18689 (1410) does include death-related rituals on a folio that may be a later addition at the end, but these begin with a prayer titled *birkat ha-shurah* directed to the mourners (and followed by the burial *qaddish*) but not a *ṣidduq ha-din*. It is possible that the inclusion of this prayer in the 1537 Venice printing results from Sefardi influence.

26 This organization generally follows that of the *Seder Rav Amram Gaon*. *Ṣidduq ha-din* does appear in manuscripts of this text, but in varying forms that are recognizably those of later European rites. See the edition of Daniel Goldschmidt (Jerusalem: Mossad Harav Kook, 1971), II:#156, pp. 186–7.

27 See for instance, Seligman Baer's *Seder 'Avodat Yisrael* (Roedelheim, 1868 and many reprints), p. 586.

Worms itself, line five precedes line four, but these two lines have the same opening word, making this a less significant variant than many. Moving first westwards, we see that all the exemplars of the Northern French rites have a totally different text for line four, a line beginning with the address to God as *ha-ṣur* ('the Rock') in continuation of the theme of the opening lines. Like the Sefardi rites, this rite in most exemplars uniquely clusters toward the end those lines that explicitly echo the Mishna's blessing of *ṣidduq ha-din* (but with a different order and an additional line: 7, 9, 6) and concludes only with a single verse. Jer 32:19 (line 11) usually appears earlier in the composition, and the two Ashkenazi verses (lines 12 and 13[28]), not mentioned in the *baraita*, do not appear at all. That this organizational logic appears in Spain, but nowhere else in Ashkenaz, is consistent with the development of local customs in Europe and their tendencies, like linguistic dialects, to blend at the boundaries.[29]

This also suggests that the precedent for this prayer that shaped all the European rites was received as a model, more than as a fixed composition. While many individual lines appear in essentially identical form from one European rite to another, their order, and which of them are included, varies. Indeed, when we look to the eastern Ashkenazi rite, we see a wide variation, particularly in the second half of the prayer, from a list of verses identical to that of the Rhineland, to lists with significant re-orderings and omissions (though no additions). The Sefardi rites do contain a number of lines identical to the Ashkenazi text, but also include lines that do not at all appear in Ashkenaz, and variants of parallel lines. They also omit altogether the verse recited by Rabbi Ḥanina's daughter! Nevertheless, even the lines that do not appear in Ashkenaz fit the literary pattern of this prayer. This variation in the order of the lines means that the meanings communicated by the composition as a whole are not fully consistent from one rite or even sub-rite to another.

What is more consistent are the literary characteristics of the prayer. Following their opening verse, all continue with a poetic rephrasing of it, appearing in France and Ashkenaz as: הצור תמים בכל פועל. מי יאמר לו מה תפעל.

28 This is particularly surprising because line 13, Job 1:21b, is itself a justification of the Divine judgement, although it may also be noted that this verse's language does not inform the rest of the prayer in any way in any of the versions.

29 Although we frequently lack sufficient information to establish the provenance of a manuscript, this conclusion is also supported implicitly by the data gathered and presented in my articles, 'Sinai, Zion, and God in the Synagogue: Celebrating Torah in Ashkenaz', in *Liturgy in the Life of the Synagogue: Studies in the History of Jewish Prayer*, ed. by Ruth Langer and Steven Fine, Duke Judaic Studies 2 (Winona Lake, Indiana: Eisenbrauns, 2005), pp. 121–59; in the appendices of my *Cursing the Christians?: A History of the Birkat HaMinim* (Oxford; Oxford University Press, 2012); and in a forthcoming article on mapping medieval rites.

השליט במטה ובמעל. ממית ומחיה מוריד שאול ויעל: ('The Rock is just in all action; who can say to Him, "What will you do?"; He rules below and above; He causes death and [renews] life, lowers to Sheol and raises up.') This line models the literary characteristics of much of this composition. The lines, with the exception of two in Ashkenaz (3, 5) and one in Sefarad (8), consist of four rhymed stichs, with the rhyme frequently being more a word play emphasizing the theme than anything more complex. Some lines – all those unique to either Ashkenaz or Sefarad, including line 4 where France and Ashkenaz differ – have proper rhymes rather than repetition or plays on the same word (Ashkenaz 4, 7; France 4; Sefarad 6, 9 11), and two lines lack any rhyme (Sefarad 5, 10). That these lines are those not shared by various rites only underlines the degree to which they do not represent the prayer's native pattern and may suggest that they are later additions. The list of lines not shared does not, however, include others where the characteristic rhyming pattern is present. Beyond issues of rhyme, there is no metre of any sort. Our exemplar line, like many but not all others, ends with a biblical citation, and many also incorporate earlier in the lines biblical language directly or barely altered, but interspersed liberally with non-biblical phrases. In general, this composition does not approach or even try to imitate the literary standards of a top-flight *payyeṭan*.

The different traditions, in their own ways, apparently elaborated on a core group of lines, each of which they treated independently. Several lines appear in both places in virtually identical language: אדם אם בן שנה יהיה ('Whether a person lives a year ...') appears as line 6 in Ashkenaz and 12 in Sefarad and is the line on which the Italian poet, Amittai elaborated;[30] דיין אמת ('True Judge ...') appears as line 9 in Ashkenaz and 13 in Sefarad; נפש כל חי בידך ('The soul of all the living is in Your hand ...') appears as line 10 in Ashkenaz and 7 in Sefarad. Line 8 in Ashkenaz (ידענו ה' כי צדק משפטיך, 'We know, Eternal, that Your judgements are just ...') appears in Italy and in one Sefardi manuscript (S2). Line 3 in Sefarad, beginning הצור פעל is a clear cognate to Ashkenazi line 2, beginning הצור תמים בכל פועל. These lines also all fit the basic poetic model described above. Thus, just over half of the Ashkenazi poetic text is identical to just under half of the Sefardi one.[31] Yet, the degree of difference in what is identifiably the same prayer also indicates the freedom that accompanied the basic model.

30 See Peter Lehnardt's essay in this volume.
31 5/9 vs. 5/12 of the lines that are not fully biblical verses.

2 Meanings

When we turn to the content of this prayer, we need to ask how it functions as *ṣidduq ha-din*. While some of its themes obviously fit this context, others do not. The opening verse describes God as a God of judgement, and variations on this language of *mishpaṭ* echo throughout Ashkenazi lines 8 and 9 and Sefardi line 6. A more common theme expresses that God is absolutely in charge of the world, including the action of decreeing life and death. This appears in Ashkenaz, lines 2, 3, 5, 7, and 10, in Sefardi line 4 and 9 (plus Ashkenazi cognates 3 and 7), as well as in several of the biblical verses. The opening verse also describes God as *ṣaddiq*, righteous, that is, decreeing judgement justly, and this specific language echoes in the introductory words of Ashkenazi lines 4 and 5 as well as in lines 8, 9, and 10. In the Sefardi text, this language begins lines 4, 5, and 6 (as well as in Ashkenazi cognates 7, 7a, and 13). The connection between declaring God a *ṣaddiq* and God's deeds as *ṣedeq* on the one hand and the human action of *ṣidduq* on the other lies in the human recognition of God's qualities of justice. The explicit language of *din* (judgement) echoes less frequently here, appearing primarily in variations on the language of the rabbinic blessing *barukh dayyan ha-emet* ('blessed is the true Judge') in Ashkenazi lines 6, 7, and 9 and Sefardi cognate lines 12 and 13. That this ends the prayer, in Sefarad and France, emphasizes the importance of the allusion in this particular setting. That the Ashkenazi texts scatter the language throughout (except in E3) is more surprising.

What becomes more interesting are the moves beyond a simple acceptance of divine judgement in the prayer. A death has occurred, and it must be accepted. But is this the end of the story? These texts in the forms here examined were all functioning in a wider medieval Christian context with its deep concerns about the fate of a person after death. We know that later funeral prayers, most notably the *El male raḥamim*, also pray most explicitly for a good afterlife for the deceased. Does any of that occur here?

Resurrection of the dead is of course an ancient theme in rabbinic theology and liturgy, and it is here alluded to in the ends of Ashkenazi lines 2 and 6 (= Sefardi 3 and 12) and the beginning of Ashkenazi line 5.

Of more immediate implication, though, is the emphasis throughout this prayer on God's mercy and willingness to forgive. This theme operates on four levels. First, it operates simply as part of the *ṣidduq ha-din*, declaring human assurance that God has already acted with justice regarding the deceased; in this sense, it is still simply a praise of God's qualities, that which various sages found acceptable even on minor holidays. Second, this same language may also operate as a prayer for the deceased, asking God to be merciful and forgiving in the ultimate divine judgement about this person's fate. There is an ambiguity in the grammar of this prayer that allows many of its phrases to be read as petitions rather than as statements of praise. Third, the prayer embeds within it overt petitions that God turn this mercy also to the still-living community, a theme that has nothing directly to do with the deceased. Finally, the Sefardi text turns to members of the living community, reminding them how to access this justice and mercy for themselves.

The first two levels are self-evident, implicit in almost every element of the prayer, especially the shared ones, and need no discussion. The third and fourth, however, provide an important key to the history of the text. The petition on behalf of the living community is particularly evident in Ashkenaz in:

- the second half of line 3: חסד חנם לנו תעשה, ובזכות הנעקד כשה הקשיבה ועשה ('act out of gracious lovingkindness for us, and through the merit of the one who was bound like a ram' [i.e., Isaac], listen and act');
- line 4: חמול נא וחוס נא על אבות ובנים, כי לך אדון הסליחות והרחמים ('please have pity and mercy on parents and children, for Yours is the mastery of forgiveness and mercy');
- the French version of this line: הבט נא ממרומים ותושיע מעוטי עמים כי לך ה' הצדקה והרחמים ('peer down from the heavenly heights and save the least of the peoples, for with You, Eternal, are righteousness and mercy');
- the second half of line 5: חלילה לך זכרוננו למחות, ויהיו נא עיניך עלינו פקוחות, כי לך אדון הרחמים והסליחות ('God forbid that You erase our memory; may Your eyes be looking over us, for Yours is the mastery of mercy and forgiveness');
- line 10's petition: רחם על פלטת צאן ידך ותאמר למלאך הרף ידך ('have mercy on the remnant of the flock of Your hand, and say to the angel [of destruction], let your hand be weak!').

Only the last of these examples has a direct parallel in Sefarad line 7, but that rite contributes its own list in:

- the second half of line 6: עלינו יהמו רחמיו. כי כלנו מעשה ידיו ('His mercy will yearn for us, for we are all the work of His hands')
- line 8: צור תמים חמול ממרומים. ועשה ברחמים. כאבות על בנים מרחמים. עצור רוגזך מעוללי תמימי' ומחתומי דמים. הבט נא במְעַטי עמים. כי אתה מלא רחמים. ולאבלים תן ניחומים ('Perfect Rock, have mercy from on high and act in mercy, like parents have mercy on children. Withdraw Your wrath from the innocent nurslings and those sealed with blood [martyrs]; look please to the least of the peoples, for You are full of mercy; and give comfort to the mourners').

Finally, we find only in Sefarad a set of themes that takes this one step further, giving direction to the living community on how to live their lives to encourage divine mercy for themselves after their deaths. Line 9 encourages the living to perform acts of *ḥesed*, lovingkindness, and line 10, similarly, to pursue *ṣedaqa* (justice, particularly economic justice) because *ṣedaqa taṣil mi-mawet* (acts of economic justice, ie, charity, save one from death).

The preponderance of lines expressing the petition for the living community, without parallels between the rites, strongly suggests that these are additions to the original and hypothetical *Vorlage*. We can argue that they may well reflect the theological needs of the Jewish communities of the High Middle Ages living in Europe. Their introduction reflects an interest in gaining some control over the individual's fate after death, an area of theological competition with Christians.

This reconstruction also helps explain the halakhic move to restrict the recitation of this prayer on minor festivals.[32] Where the original prayer was solely a praise of God's justice in the face of the current experience of death, appropriate for recitation even on minor festivals, with these additions it becomes instead a voice of worried concern over the fate, both of the immediately deceased and of the living. The prayer thus ceases to be one of praise, and becomes, as the *Shibbolei Ha-Leqeṭ* declares in his Italian context, 'full of words that sorrow a person's heart' with the purpose of 'breaking a person's heart and reminding him of his own day of death, in order to humble his inclination.'[33] Such a proactive, petitionary prayer is no longer a simple praise of God that may be recited on days when public acts of mourning are prohibited.

3 Appendix

3.1 Critical presentation of Medieval European texts from Ashkenaz and Sefarad

These critical tables use two base texts, the earliest western Ashkenazi text and the Sefardi text that gives the clearest basis of comparison with the other two of similar dates. I do not note differences in spelling, abbreviations, or errors in the transcription of verses, where the intended word is obviously the

32 As discussed by Lehnardt, 'Tzidduq ha-Din und Kaddisch', p. 29.

33 *'Inyan Ḥanukka*, #192, 'Rules of Eulogy, *Ṣidduq Ha-Din* and Sustaining the Mourners on Hanukkah; *Hilkhot Semaḥot* #13', 'Rules of the *Ṣidduq Ha-Din* that is Recited over the Deceased and the Days on which is is Appropriate to Recite It.'

same. Because of the variation in which lines individual manuscripts include, I indicate the order of the lines and which lines are included separately after the list of manuscripts for each rite. Each manuscript is indicated by its cataloging in its home library as well as by its film number in the Institute for Microfilmed Hebrew Manuscripts at The National Library of Israel (NLI). While there are numerous variants for the text of each line, these are almost entirely those characteristic of orally transmitted or scribal texts and do not change the meaning of the lines or their form except in error. The variations in the order of the lines is much more significant. For ease of comparison, I have divided the critical notes themselves between the three main Ashkenazi subrites and have designated the texts accordingly.

3.1.1 *Ashkenazi rites (Western, Northern France, and Eastern)*

1 הצור תמים פעלו כי כל דרכיו משפט אל אמונה ואין עול צדיק וישר הוא:[34]

2 הצור תמים בכל פועל. מי יאמר לו מה תפעל. השליט במטה ובמעל. ממית ומחיה מוריד שאול ויעל:

3 הצור תמים בכל מעשה. מי יאמר לו מה תעשה. האומר ועושה. חסד חנם לנו תעשה. ובזכות הנעקד כשה הקשיבה ועשה:

4 צדיק בכל דרכיו הצור תמים ארך אפים ומלא רחמים. חמול נא וחוס נא על אבות ועל בנים. כי לך אדון הסליחות והרחמים:

4) מנהג צרפת: הצור תמים מלא רחמים הבט נא ממרומים ותושיע מעוטי עמים כי לך ה' הצדקה והרחמים)

5 צדיק אתה ה' להמית ולהחיות. אשר בידך פקדון כל רוחות. חלילה לך זכרוננו למחות. ויהיו נא עיניך ברחמים עלינו פקוחות. כי לך אדון הרחמים והסליחות:

6 אדם אם בן שנה יחיה. או אלף שנים יחיה. מה יתרון לו כלא היה יהיה. ברוך דיין האמת ממית ומחיה:

7 ברוך הוא כי אמת דינו. ומשוטט הכל בעינו. ומשלם לאדם חשבונו. והכל לשמו הודיה יתֵנו:

8 ידענו ה' כי צדק משפטך. תצדק בדברך. ותזכה בשָׁופטך. ואין להרהר אחר מדת שָׁפטך. צדיק אתה ה' וישר משפטיך:

9 דיין אמת. שופט צדק ואמת. ברוך דיין האמת. כי כל משפטיו צדק ואמת:

10 נפש כל חי בידך. צדק מָלְאָה ימינך וידך. רחם על פליטת צאן ידך. ותאמר למלאך הֶרֶף ידך:

11 גדול העיצה ורב העליליה. אשר עיניך פקֻוחות על כל דרכי בני האדם

---

34 Deut 32:4.

לתת לאיש כדרכיו וכפרי מעלליו:[35]
12 להגיד כי ישר ה' צורי ולא עולתה בו.[36]
13 ה' נתן וה' לקח יהי שם ה' מבֹרך.[37]
14 והוא רחום יכפר עון ולא ישחית והרבָּה להשיב אפו ולא יעיר כל חמתו:[38]
וקוברין את המת לאחר קבורת המת אומ': [קדיש]

3.1.1.1 Western Ashkenaz

Except in the Worms and Cologne rites (W6), all the manuscripts include all the lines, in the order listed in the base text.

4 **ומלא]** W5 מלא. **ועל בנים]** W4, W5, W6, W7, W8 ובנים. **אדון הסליחות]** W3, W5 הסליחות

5 **ה']** W5, W6 חסר. **כל]** W6 לכל. **רוחות]** W8. הרוחות. **זכרוננו]** W8 זכרינו. **למחות]** W7 מלמחות. **ויהיו ... פקוחות]** W6 חסר. **עיניך ברחמים עלינו]** W3 ברחמים עיניך. W4, W5, W7 ברחמים עיניך עלינו. **אדון הרחמים]** W6, W8 הרחמים.

6 **אדם ... יחיה]** W4, W6 אדם ... יהיה. **או]** W7 או אם. **מה]** W7 ומה. **לו]** W5 לו סופו.

7 **הכל בעינו]** W5 בכל עינו. **חשבוננו]** W3, W6 לפי חשבוננו. W5 כפי חשבוננו.

8 **ידענו ה']** W6 ידענו. **ותזכה]** W4 תזכה. **ואין]** W4, W5, W7 אין.

9 **שופט צדק]** W6 ושפט צדק צדק. **משפטיו צדק ואמת]** W6 משפטיו חסד ואמת. W8 משפטיו אמת.

W1. MS Vatican – Biblioteca Apostolica ebr. 329, NLI f 11636 (13c., Western Ashkenazi rite, calendar begins with *maḥzor* 264, year 995 = 1235 CE), ff. 172b–75b = base text with the exception of the French version of line 4.

W2. MS Paris – Bibliothèque Nationale héb. 644, NLI f 11540 (calendar begins with 1264), beginning missing, f. 166a begins in middle of line 7; no significant variants beyond spelling.

W3. MS London – British Library Add. 27556, NLI f 6091 (13–14c.), f. 85a–b, with a few errors in the original manuscript corrected in the margins perhaps by the original scribe and not included in the variants here.

W4. MS Vatican – Biblioteca Apostolica ebr. 326, NLI f 373 (14c., Western Ashkenazi), ff. 40b–41a.

---

35 Jer 32:19.
36 Ps 92:16.
37 Job 1:21b.
38 Ps 78:38.

W5. MS Parma – Biblioteca Palatina Cod. Parm. 1904 (605), NLI f 13061 (14c, Western Ashkenazi), ff. 144b–45a.

W6. MS Paris – Musée Cluny 12290, NLI f 14772 (early 14c, Western Ashkenazi, Worms), ff. 65b–66b. Line 5 precedes 4. The introduction to the text lists the order of the lines in Worms (ג' הצור. ב' צדיק. אבידן גל אדם ברוך ידענו דיין נפש גדול להגיד) followed by a note about the variants in Cologne. In Cologne the order is 1, 2, 3, 6, 7, 11, 9, 8, 10, 5, 4 (ג' הצור אדם ברוך גדול דיין ידענו נפש צדיק אתה צדיק בכל), which is not represented in any manuscripts I located.

W7. MS Jerusalem – The National Library of Israel MS Heb. 4°681–2, microfilm B 398 (14c.), ff. 43a–44b.

W8. MS Oxford – Bodleian Library MS Can. Or. 86 (Neubauer 1103), NLI f 17709 (14c. Western Ashkenazi), folios unnumbered, text follows fast day liturgy and then *haṭavat ḥalom*.

3.1.1.2 France

All the lines of this sub-rite appear in the Western Ashkenazi sub-rite and vice versa, with one exception. Instead of the Ashkenazi line 4 (צדיק בכל דרכיו) this rite's fourth line continues to echo the opening verse and reads: הצור תמים מלא רחמים הבט נא ממרומים ותושיע מעוטי עמים (כי לך ה' הצדקה והרחמים). One manuscript also lacks line 8 entirely, and none include lines 12–13, both biblical verses. The order of the lines in the second half of the prayer is also different, with two of the earlier witnesses showing more variety, especially in the placement of line 11 (a verse of *ṣidduq ha-din*), which in this rite tends to be clustered with line 10 instead of presented as a biblical verse concluding the prayer. Lines 9 and 6, with which this sub-rite concludes in five of six exemplars, are those that contain the most specific language of *ṣidduq ha-din*. F1, F2, F3, and F4 call for the recitation of this prayer in an open space outside the cemetery, with the assembled gathered around the deceased, while F5 explicitly places the prayer when the casket has reached the grave but before the burial.

2 **פועל]** F3 מפעל. F4 פעל. F5 מעשה. **השליט]** F1, F4, F5 שליט. F2 צדיק אתה. F3 צדיק. **ממית ומחיה]** F4 ח'. F5 אל ממית ומחיה.

3 **האומר]** F1 ובזכות הנעקד כשה אומר (כנראה ט"ס). F3, F4, F5 אומר. **חנם לנו]** F2 עמנו. F3, F5 חנם עמנו. F4 חנם עלינו. **תעשה]** F1, F3, F4, F5 עשה. **הקשיבה]** F3, F5 ה' הקשיבה.

4 **מעוטי]** F3 מעטי. **כי לך ה' הצדקה והרחמים]** F1, F2, F3, F4 ח'.

5 **ה']** F1, F2, F3, F4, F5 ח'. **כל רוחות]** F2, F4 הרוחות. F3 רוחות. **לך]** F3 ח'. **זכרונינו]** F2, F4 ז(י)כרינו. **למחות]** F1, F2, F3 להמחות. F5 מלהמחות. **עיניך ברחמים עלינו]** F1, F4 ברחמים עיניך עלינו. F2 ברחמים עינינו אליך. F3 ברחמים עלינו עיניך. F5 ברחמים עלינו. **אדון]** F1, F2, F3, F4 ח'. F5 ה'.

6 **אדם ... אלף שנים יחיה]** F3 אדם אם אלף שנים יחיה, אחריתו לקבר יהיה. **אם]** F2 ח'. **שנה יחיה]** F1 שנה יהיה. **או]** F1 או אם. **לו]** F3 לו סופו. **כלא היה יהיה]** F1 כי לא יהיה. F2 חיה כלא יהיה. F4 כלא יהיה. F5 כלא חיה יחיה.

7 **ברוך הוא]** F2 ברוך. **אמת]** F1 צדיק אמת. **הכל בעינו]** F2, F3, F4, F5 בכל עינו. **ומשלם]** F1 ומשלם הכל. **לאדם]** F2 לאיש. **והכל לשמו]** F1 והכל יתנו. F2, F3, F4 והכל ישנו. F5 וכל אשר ישנו. **הודייה יתנו]** F1, F2, F4, F5 והודייה יתנו. F3 והודייה לשמו.

8 **ידענו ה']** F3 ידענו. **ותזכה]** F1, F2, F3, F5 תזכה. **ואין]** F2, F3 אין. **מדת שפטך]** F1 מידותיך כי. F2 מות שפטיך. **ה' וישר]** F1 ויושר. F2 ה' ביושר. F3 וישר. F5 אל וישר.

9 **שופט צדק]** F3 שופט. **משפטיו צדק ואמת]** F2 משפטיך אמת. F4 משפטיו אמת.

10 **ימינך וידך]** F2, F3, F4, F5 ימינ(י)ך. **ורחם על]** F1 ורחם. F4 רחם על.

F1. MS Oxford – Corpus Christi 133, NLI f 39535 (12c.), ff. 328b–30a. This text calls for the assembled to repeat line 1 (Dt. 32:4) as a refrain after each line.

F2. MS Sassoon 535, NLI f 9278 (12c.), ff. 145a–146a, *Maḥzor Vitry*. This text calls for the assembled to repeat line 1 (Deut 32:4) as a refrain after each line.

F3. MS Leipzig – Universitätsbibliothek B.H. 14. 40, NLI f 20965 (13c.) as published by Israel Brodie, *Ets Hayyim of Rabbi Jacob Hazan of London* (Jerusalem: Mosad Harav Kook, 1962), p. 394. This text calls for the assembled to repeat line 1 (Deut 32:4) as a refrain after each line.

F4. MS Paris – Bibliothèque Nationale 632, NLI f 31298 (13c.), ff. 71b–72b. This text calls for the recitation of this prayer in the square outside of the cemetery itself by a community that gathers around the deceased. The assembled repeat line 1 (Deut 32:4) as a refrain after each line.

F5. MS Oxford – Bodleian MS Opp. 759, NLI 17724 (13–14c.), ff. 60b–61a. The text calls for a communal response after the first line, but it is not clear what they respond.

F6. MS Moscow – Russian State Library, MS Günzburg 728, NLI f 48037 (14–15c.), ff. 130b–131a. This text is an addition to the original prayer-book and is not well preserved. Too many words are illegible to identify precise textual variants.

Orders of the lines

F1: 1, 2, 3, 4 (French text), 5, 6, 8, 7, 9, 10, 11, 14
F2: 1, 2, 3, 4 (French text), 5, 8, 10, 11, 7, 9, 6, 14
F3: 1, 2, 3, 4 (French text), 5, 8, 10, 7, 9, 6, 11, 14
F4: 1, 2, 3, 4 (French text), 5, 10, 11, 7, 9, 6, 14 (no line 8)
F5: 1, 2, 3, 4 (French text), 5, 8, 10, 11, 7, 9, 6, 14
F6: 1, 2, 3, 4 (French text), 5, 8, 10, 11, 7, 9, 6

3.1.1.3 Eastern Ashkenaz

This sub-rite adds no content to that found in the Western Ashkenazi texts. There is, however, significant variation from one manuscript to another in the order of the lines and sometimes also in what is included. Only one (E6) is fully identical to the western model.

2 **מי]** E4 ומי. **השליט]** E2 שליט.

3 **האומר ועושה]** E2 הגוזר ועושה. E6 ה'. **חסד חנם לנו]** E2 חנם לנו חסד. **ובזכות]** E1, E2, E4, E5 בזכות.

4 **וחוס נא]** E1, E6 וחוס. **ועל בנים]** E1 ושלימים. E2, E4, E5, E6 ובנים.

5 **ה']** E1, E2, E3, E4, E6 ה'. **אשר בידך ... רוחות חלילה ... למחות]** E2 חלילה ... למחות כי בידך ... רוחות. **למחות]** E1 ומחות. E4 מלמחות. **עיניך ברחמים עלינו]** E1 ברחמים עלינו עיניך. E3, E6 ברחמים עיניך עלינו. **אדון]** E3 ה'.

6 **שנה יחיה]** E1, E2, E4,E5, E6 שנה יהיה. **או אם]** E4 או. **היה יהיה]** E1 היה ויהיה. E3 חיה יחיה. **ברוך ... ומחיה]** E1 ה'.

7 **ברוך הוא]** E1 ברוך. **ומשוטט]** E1 ומשיט. **הכל בעינו]** E4 בכל עינו. **חשבונו]** E1 חשבונו ודינו. E6 לפי חשבונו.

8 **צדק משפטיך]** E4 צדק דיניך. **תצדק בדוברך ותזכה בשופטך]** E1 ותצדק בשופטך ותזכה בדוברך. **תצדק]** E6 ותצדק.

9 **משפטיו]** E3 ברכיו משפטיו.

10 **ימינך וידך]** E3 ימינך. **רחם]** E1 ורחם. E6 חמול. **ותאמר]** E4 תאמר.

E1. MS Vatican – Biblioteca Apostolica ebr. 323, NLI 372 (13–14c., calendar begins with 1295), ff. 110b–112a

E2. MS Jerusalem – Schocken Institute for Jewish Research 13160, NLI 74219 (1306), no folio numbers, but follows the Purim blessings.

E3. MS St. Petersburg – Russian National Library Evr. I 143, NLI f 51934 (Reel 15), (14–15c., middle Ashkenazi), 2b–3b. This manuscript consists of five folios from the additions made to the end of a siddur.

E4. MS St. Petersburg – Russian National Library Evr. IV 1, NLI f 69479 (1480), ff. 55a–56a, following the wedding blessings

E5. MS Hannover – Kestner-Museum MS 3953, NLI f 69252 (15c.), partial text on recto of folio apparently added at the very end of the prayer-book, verso is blank.

E6. Ms Oxford – Bodleian Library MS Opp. 646 (Neubauer 1123), NLI f 17729 (15c.), ff. 77b–78b.

Order of the lines

E1: 1, 2, 3, 6, 7, 8, 9, 10, 5, 4, 11, 12, 13, 14
E2: 1, 3, 2, 6, 10, 7, 8, 4, 5, 11, 12, 13, 14 (no line 9!)
E3: 1, 2, 3, 5, 10, 11, 7, 9, 6, 12, 13, 14 (no lines 4 or 8)
E4: 1, 2, 3, 5, 4, 6, 7, 8, 9, 10, 11, 12, 13, 14
E5: 1, 2, 3, 4, 7, 6
E6: 1, 2, 3, 4, 5, 6, 7, 8, 9, 10, 11, 12, 13, 14

3.1.2 Sefarad

צדוק הדין
1 הצור תמים פעלו כי כל דרכיו משפט אל אמונה ואין עול צדיק וישר הוא
2 הצור תמים פעלו כי כל דרכיו משפט אל אמונה ואין עול צדיק וישר הוא
לבדו זך ויחיד במפעליו. חנון ורחום צדיק בדינו
3 הצור פעל מי יאמר לו מה תפעל. הכל למענו פעל. כי הוא מוריד שאול
ויעל
4 צדיק יוצר כל מעשה וחסיד בכל אשר יעשה. שליט בכל חפצו עושה.
מי יאמר לו מה תעשה
5 צדיק וישר אין בדרכיו עול. כי הוא הנקרא צדיק תמים. זך פעלו.
צדק אֹרחֹתיו אין להסתר מפני פועל כל.
6 צדק ומשפט כל דרכיו. ואמת ארחותיו. משׂא פנים אין לפניו. עלינו
יהמו רחמיו. כי כֻלנו מעשה ידיו
7 נפש כל חי בידך. צדק מלאה ימינך. רחם פלטת צאן ידך. ותאמר למלאך
הרף ידך
8 הצור תמים חמול ממרומים. ועשה ברחמים. כאבות על בנים מרחמים.
עצור רוגזך מעוללי תמימי' ומחתומי דמים. הבט נא במְעַטי עמים.
כי אתה מלא רחמים. ולאבלים תן ניחומים
9 זו היא דרך כל העולם הֵאָספו ועשו חסד כֻלם כי אין דבר מאל נעלם
נשמתו לחיי עולם
10 זו היא לקטֹן ולגדֹל. כי אין לפניו משוא פנים. אשרי אדם רודף צדקה.
וצדקה תציל ממות

11 זו היא לעשירים ודלים. לקטנים ולגדולים. אמנם הם ספים וכלים. כי הכֹל הֶבל הבלים.

12 אדם אם בן שנה יהיה. או אלף שנים יחיה. מה יתרון לו סופו כלא היה יהיה. ברוך דין האמת ממית ומחיה

13 דיין אמת שופט צדק ואמת ברוך דיין האמת. כי כל משפטיו צדק ואמת.

14 והוא רחום יכפר עון ולא ישחית והרבה להשיב אפו ולא יעיר כל חמתו

2 **במפעליו]** S3 במפעלו.

3 **כי הוא]** S2 ח'.

4 **שליט]** S3 צדיק. **מי]** S3 ומי.

5 **הנקרא צדיק]** S3 נקרא הצור.

6 **ואמת]** S2, S3 חסד ואמת. **עלינו]** S2 ועלינו.

7 **ותאמר למלאך]** S2 ואמור למלאך המשחית.

8 **עצור ... תמימי']** S2 ח'. **ומחתומי דמים]** S3 ח'. **במעטי]** S2 למעטי.

9 **הֶאָספו ... כֻּלם כי אין ... נעלם]** S2 כי אין ... נעלם האספו ... כלם. **נשמתו]** S2 נשמתו של זה.

10 **לקטן ולגדל]** S2 דרך קטון וגדול. S3 דרך לקטון וגדול. **לפניו משוא פנים]** S3 משוא פנים לפניו.

11 **זו היא לעשירים ודלים]** S3 זו היא דרך לעשירים ולדלים. **הם]** S3 ח'.

12 **שנה יהיה]** S3 שנה יחיה. **סופו]** S3 וסופו. **היה יהיה]** S2, S3 חיה יחיה.

13 **צדק]** S2 בצד'.

S1. MS Nimes 13, NLI f 04418 (14c. *siddur*), ff. 184b–186a, = base text. The prayer here precedes an extensive and elaborate series of additional burial prayers, including an additional prose *ṣidduq ha-din*.

S2. MS Montreal – Elberg 24, formerly MS Sassoon College 24 (299), NLI f 9293 (14c.), ff. 179–82. This text divides the prayer over various stages of the pre-burial process as follows:
Lines 1, 2, 3, 4, 13, followed by the instructions: וקורעין כל החייבים לקרוע ומעומד ובגלוי
Lines 6, 14, 8, followed by the instructions: עד כאן אומ' בבית המת ובבית הקברות מוסיפין
Lines 7, 7a (ידענו יי כי צדק משפטיך ואמונה עִנּוּ' שבטיך אין להרהר אחר שפטיך צדיק אתה יי וישר משפטיך), 12, 10, 9, followed by the instructions: וקוברין את המת.
(Lines 5 and 11 do not appear; a line not found in the other manuscripts follows line 7)

S3. MS Oxford – Bodleian MS Opp. Add. Oct. 18 (Neubauer 1133), NLI 16594 (14c., Catalonia), ff. 251a (2–3), 251b (3), 251a (4). The prayer appears here in a larger context of burial liturgies, preceding the *hashkava*.
Order of the lines: 1, 2, 3, 4, 5, 6, 8, 7, 9, 10, 11, 12, 13

Peter Sh. Lehnardt

Ha-Ṣur Tamim be-khol Po'al: On some Italian roots of the Poetic *Ṣidduq Ha-Din* in the Early Ashkenazi rite

Dedicated to Shlomo Simonsohn and
Cesare Colafemmina, two pioneers in
uncovering new sources
for our understanding of Jewish culture
in Italy

1

Ashkenazi literary tradition is connected by its navel to the beginnings of the Hebrew culture of medieval Europe in southern Italy. This unique area of encounter between Byzantine, Romano-Germanic and, later on, even Arabic culture, was not only the cradle of Middle-Latin as officialese but also saw the emergence of Hebrew as the language of Jewish literacy in the western hemisphere of the Mediterranean.[1] The Latin part of this southern Italian renaissance was based on the collection and reproduction of manuscripts from Antiquity and Late Antiquity while its Hebrew part depended on the acquisition and copying of written material from the two creative literary centres in the Orient, the Land of Israel and Babylonia. This nexus between the older and newer Hebrew worlds was revealed for the first time in one of the earliest historico-critical studies by the nestor of the *Wissenschaft des Judentums*, Shelomo Yehuda Leib Rapoport (1790–1867). It was Rapoport who traced back Ashkenazi knowledge about Ele'azar Bi-Rebbi Qillir, the major contributor to

1 For the cultural importance of the transition from the use of Hebrew as icon in Antiquity and Late Antiquity into Hebrew literacy, see Shlomo Simonsohn, 'The Hebrew revival among early medieval European Jews' in *Salo Wittmayer Baron Jubilee volume* ed. by Saul Lieberman (Jerusalem: American Academy for Jewish Research, 1974), II, pp. 831–858 and for much of the new epigraphic evidence attesting this process in Southern Italy see the bibliography (up to the year 2000) of Cesare Colafemmina: http://www.humnet.unipi.it/medievistica/aisg/AISG_Colafemmina/Colafemmina.html (01. 08. 10) and up to the year 2005: 'Bibliografia di Cesare Colafemmina', in *Hebraica Hereditas: studi in onore di Cesare Colafemmina*, ed. by Giancarlo Lacerenza, Series Minor, 70, (Napoli: Istituto universitario orientale, Dipartimento di studi asiatici, 2005), pp. [xi]–xxv.

the earliest stratum of the liturgical poetry in the Ashkenazi rite, to its earliest European origins.[2]

Even after more than 150 years of research, this general picture of the transmission and tradition of synagogue literature having taken place in the east and travelled via southern Italy to central Europe requires only little refinement.

This article has two purposes. Firstly, it deals with the flow of Jewish liturgical traditions into Italy, and deeper into Christian Europe, and traces how the *ṣidduq ha-din* ceremony in the early Italian rite may have influenced later Ashkenazi developments. Secondly, it presents a critical edition of the complex textual element of the burial ceremony in the rite of Rome, thereby offering an analysis not only of textual, but also of ceremonial, evolution. This will draw attention to the scientific need to examine the ongoing relationship between words and rituals and their mutual impact. It will also set an example that can then followed in the close study of texts and ceremonies in other rites.

As already indicated, the early stratum of Ashkenazi liturgical poetry came from its classic predecessor in the Land of Israel during the late Byzantine period, and was augmented with an important layer of creative response in ninth- and tenth-century Italy. Thus, Ashkenazi Judaism learned from the Italian tradition not only how to embellish public prayers with the liturgical poetry of old but also how *piyyuṭ* could provide an arena in which to perform a living tradition of replacement and local creativity. Although the main route of tradition was from Apulia through Lucca – traditionally associated with the famous Qalonymos family – to Ashkenaz, we should also consider, especially for the second half of the tenth century, the existence of an additional path by which Babylonian poetical traditions made their way from the East not via Italy but via Byzantium, or most probably via France. This may be exemplified by the prooemia for the groom, a genre that evolved in Babylonia[3] and was embraced by the early Ashkenazi poets but is completely absent from the Italian tradition.[4]

---

2 S. Y. L. Rapoport, *'Zeman u-Meqom R. Ele'azar Ha-Kallir we-'Inyyanei Piyyuṭaw u-Fiyyutei Zulato, u-Qeṣat 'Inyyanei Ha-Tefillot'*, *Bikkure Ha-Ittim*, 10 (1830), pp. 95–123, 11 (1831), pp. 92–102 [repr. as, *'Toldot R. Ele'azar Ha-Kallir'*, in Rapoport, *Toldot Gedolei Yisrael*, Warsaw 1913, pp. 125–95].

3 See Tova Beeri, *'Reshit Ha-Yeṣira Ha-Payṭanit Be-Bavel: Piyyuṭei R. Ḥayyim Al-Baradani'*, *HUCA*, 68 (1997), [1]–[33] (Hebrew part), esp. p. [30].

4 Menahem Schmelzer, 'Wedding *Piyyuṭim* by the Early Sages of Ashkenaz', in *Studies in Hebrew Poetry and Jewish Heritage In Memory of Aharon Mirsky*, ed. by Ephraim Hazan and Joseph Yahalom (Hebrew; Ramat Gan: Bar-Ilan University, 2006), 173–85 [reprinted in Schmelzer, *Studies in Jewish Bibliography and Medieval Hebrew Poetry: Collected Essays* (New York, Jerusalem: The Jewish Theological Seminary of America, 2006), 190–208 (Hebrew part).

Even bearing in mind his French origin, the poetical œuvre of the head of the *yeshiva* of Magenza, Rabbenu Gershom Meor Ha-Gola (*c.* 960–*c.* 1028/1040), may nevertheless be wholly explained against the background of the Italian tradition, especially that of Shelomo Ha-Bavli, the transmitter of Apulian tradition to the northern parts of Italy.[5] For its part, however, the corpus of *piyyuṭim* written at least a generation earlier by Shim'on Bar Yiṣḥaq (Magenza, late tenth century) already attests to a perfect and creative blend of the sources mentioned above, namely, the Land of Israel, Italy and Babylonia.[6] This occurred two or three generations before Ashkenazi culture began its creative phase of writing in other genres, and developed its literary identity, at the beginning of the eleventh century.[7] Liturgical poetry was in Ashkenaz, like in Italy, one of the earliest components of Hebrew literary response. Such a response involved the absorption of corpora of texts from the Mishna, Talmudim and *midrashim*, as well as from liturgical poetry and constituted an astonishing approach, given liturgical poetry's complexity of expression and its intertextuality with these books. It went far beyond the first steps of acquiring a library of canonical texts through copying, commenting or rearranging them.

The process of outlining the genres of liturgical poetry in each rite has two different aspects to it. The first concerns which genres are existent in a rite and for which specific liturgical locus, for example, the questions as to whether there is a proem for the reading of a *hafṭara* on the Passover festival, and whether there are *zemirot* for the Sabbath? The other aspect concerns which genres are 'imported' from other rites, which are not, and which are reflected in local creative response and which are local developments, eg the *bikkurim* supplements for the *ma'ariv* compositions.

Another important criterion concerns the hierarchies of the different liturgical loci. One such hierarchy may be detected in the cycle of the year, eg Yom Kippur vs. an ordinary weekday; another in the different services of a day, eg *shaḥarit* vs. *minḥa*; and a third in the place during the service eg the congrega-

---

5 See Ezra Fleischer (ed.), *The Poems of Shelomo Ha-Bavli: Critical Edition with Introduction and Commentary* (Hebrew; Jerusalem: The Israel Academy of Sciences and Humanities, 1973), and *The Yozer: Its Emergence and Development* (Hebrew; Jerusalem: Magnes Press, 1984), esp. pp. 615–23, 647–53, 686–701; *Preces Poenitentiales quae Selichoth vocantur*, ed. Avraham Fraenkel (Hebrew; Jerusalem: Mekize Nirdamim, 1993), pp. 598–608, 814–24.

6 See Elisabeth Hollender, *Synagogale Hymnen: Qedushta'ot des Simon b. Isaak im Amsterdam Mahsor*, Judentum und Umwelt, 55 (Frankfurt a. M.: Lang, 1994), pp. 19–24.

7 Cf. Israel Moses Ta-Shma, *Ritual, Custom and Reality in Franco-Germany, 1000–1350* (Hebrew; Jerusalem: Magnes Press, 1996), pp. 13–16, and 'Rabbinic literature in the Middle Ages, 1000–1492', in *The Oxford Handbook of Jewish Studies*, ed. Martin Goodman (Oxford: Oxford University Press, 2002), pp. 221–24.

tional *qedusha* vs. private preparations leading up to the service. But there is one more distinction that challenges Ezra Fleischer's clear-cut definition of *piyyuṭ* as the poetry used for the embellishment of public prayer in the synagogue as distinct from the secular poetry with religious themes that was never intended to be included in the agenda of such synagogal rites.[8] There are in fact other sequences of texts in liturgical settings that are not connected to the statutory synagogal prayers promoted by Rabbinic Judaism. They include the Grace after Meals, and other ceremonies such as those of a circumcision and a wedding, that are nevertheless public and may be performed by the same persons as those who lead the the synagogal liturgy. The Jewish communities of the Middle Ages also applied the idea of a clear hierarchy to such services and ceremonies, as is reflected again and again in the poetic embellishments. It is not only the sheer length that clearly distinguishes between a *qedushta* for the morning service of the Day of Atonement and a *zemer* for a meal after a wedding; it is also the composition's complexity of structure, the number and complexity of the literary events in terms of prosody, figurae and tropoi per line, and the levels of density, sophistication and horizon concerning the intertextuality employed that confirmed for those whose literacy extended to medieval Hebrew poetry where to locate the centre and the margins of the synagogal literature.[9] Moreover this synchronic hierarchy was made even more manifest in the diachronic tradition and creative response represented in the acts of choice made for maintaining established custom or creating new poems.

Against the background of such considerations, we have to evaluate the fact that the Ashkenazi rite demonstrates no creativity in liturgical poetry used for the rubric of the burial ceremony but restricted its tradition to one famous poem '*Ha-Ṣur Tamim Be-Khol Po'al*' which it inherited, apparently in earliest times, from outside. The following discussion is intended to explore the historical, literary and cultural background of this *piyyuṭ* in the early Apulian tradition and to promote a better understanding of the possible functions of the *ṣidduq ha-din* as public ceremony, such as is reflected in the texts that occur

8 Ezra Fleischer, *Hebrew Liturgical Poetry in the Middle Ages* (Hebrew; Jerusalem: Magnes Press, 20072), pp. 7–8.

9 This awareness, as manifest in thousands of text throughout generations of tradition and creation, is the reason why a distinction between liturgical poetry used for the embellishment of the public prayer texts in the synagogue service, and the para-liturgical poetry employed for the embellishment of religious ceremonies beyond the institutional frame of the synagogue, is valid for Hebrew liturgical poetry. The problem of the enforcement of centralistic authority in world liturgy is not an intrinsic problem of Jewish liturgy but arises under the ecclesiastical influences of Catholicism and Orthodoxy.

as standard elements in the literary sources of the Italian rite. Beginning with a review of the literary sources available to us for our reconstruction, the article will then include a critical edition of the textual elements of the burial ceremony based on liturgical manuscripts from Italy from the thirteenth to the sixteenth centuries CE. The edition will serve as the basis for a literary analysis of the poetical texts, against the background of the historical development of Hebrew liturgical poetry, and especially as a test case for a new way of reading Hebrew liturgical poetry in the context of ceremony.[10]

2

The burial ceremony may be seen as an act of religion, using the word 'religion' in its basic etymological sense, as developed from the Latin *religio* meaning 'obligation', 'reverence', 'bond': describing something that has to be done, according to what has traditionally been done, and thereby meeting one's obligation to the deceased. The pious need to act according to the will of the deceased, within the basic concept of *gemilut ḥasadim*,[11] imposes on this ceremony the kind of fundamentally conservative attitude that might explain the slow and limited developments at this liturgical locus within all the liturgical rites. Consideration should also, however, be given to another tendency that might encourage literary creativity within the traditional framework of the ceremony in order to stress the unique personality of the deceased, or the special circumstances of their death.[12]

---

10 For the methodological considerations see Peter Sh. Lehnardt, 'Studies in the Emergence of the Tradition of Hebrew Liturgical Poetry in Italy' (Hebrew; doctoral dissertation, Ben-Gurion University of the Negev, Beer-Sheva, 2006), pp. 19–30.

11 For an overview of concepts associated with *gemilut ḥasadim*, see Jack D. Spiro, 'An Exploration of *Gemilut Ḥasadim*', *Judaism*, 33 (1984), pp. 448–57, esp. p. 450. For the beginnings of the *ṣidduq ha-din* as attested in rabbinical literature, see Ruth Langer's contribution to this volume.

12 In the matter of the dialectics of unique dirges *ad personam* and generic laments for different kinds of people, compare the classical study of Emanuel Feldman, 'The Rabbinic Lament', *JQR*, 63 (1972–73), pp. 51–75 with the Aramaic corpus of texts published by Michael Sokoloff and Joseph Yahalom (eds.), *Jewish Palestinian Aramaic Poetry from Late Antiquity: Critical Edition with Introduction and Commentary* (Jerusalem: The Israel Academy of Sciences and Humanities, 1999), pp. 282–329. (For an introduction see Joseph Yahalom, '"Syriac for Dirges, Hebrew for Speech": Ancient Jewish Poetry in Aramaic and Hebrew', in *The Literature of the Sages: Second Part: Midrash and Targum, Liturgy, Poetry, Mysticism, Contracts, Inscriptions, Ancient Science and the Languages of Rabbinic Literature*, ed. Shmuel Safrai, Assen; Philadelphia: Van Gorcum, 2006, pp. 375–91, esp. pp. 375–80.) See also Harry Sysling, 'Laments at the Departure of a Sage: funeral songs for great scholars as recorded in rabbinic

What may serve as a starting point for our 'literary excavation' of the antiquities of the Italian rite is the rubric of the *ṣidduq ha-din* in the *editio princeps* of the *Maḥzor Roma*, Soncino–Casal-Maggiore, 1486.[13] Most of the later editions seem to be reprints, in full or in part, or adaptations of this form to match the multi-rite reality of the Italian Ghetto with its mutual influences.[14] What is interesting, however, is that a review of some 600 manuscripts has clarified that this edition represents, by way of this rubric, the final stage of canonization of the rite of Rome as known in the second half of the thirteenth century and as attested in the earliest existing manuscripts.[15] To date I know of no form of text to be habitually recited after a death, and during the burial ceremony, other than the one attested in one of the earliest dated liturgical manuscript of the Jews in Italy, Ms Paris, Bibliothèque Nationale héb. 599, from the year 1265.[16] This includes what appear to be the latest prints from the end of the seventeenth century.[17] This redaction was obviously based on

---

literature', in *Studies in Hebrew Literature and Jewish Culture: Presented to Albert van der Heide on the Occasion of His Sixty-Fifth Birthday*, ed. by Martin F. J. Baasten and Reinier Munk (Dordrecht: Springer, 2007), pp. 81–102.

13 See the description of J. Joseph Cohen, '*Bibliyografya shel Maḥzorim we-Siddure Tefilla le-fi Minhag Benei Roma*', in *Samuel David Luzatto, Introduzione al Formulario delle Orazioni di rito italiano pubblicata in ebraico, a Livorno nel 1856*, ed. by Daniel Goldschmidt (Tel Aviv: Dvir, 1966), p. 111 (# 1) and, for bibliography and reference of copies, see Gesamtkatalog der Wiegendrucke M19921 (http://gesamtkatalogderwiegendrucke.de/docs/M19921.htm, last change 2010-08-10). See the facsimile: *Mahzor Ke-Minhag Roma Soncino – Casalmaggione, 1485–1486*, Jerusalem: Magnes, 2012.

14 This is at least the first and foremost impression although the general prevalence of a uniform rite of Rome through northern Italy in the age of printing might be misleading. See, however, the print from Bologna 1540–1541 with the commentary *Qimḥa De-Avishuna* attributed to Yoḥanan b. Yosef Trèves (see: J. Joseph Cohen, *Bibliyografiya*, pp. 113–114 [#7]) which seems to reflect an independent manuscript source.

15 See Peter Sh. Lehnardt, 'Redactions of the Prayer Book according to the Italian Rite: First Reconsiderations on the Basis of the Different Outlines of the Liturgical Poetry', *Italia*, 20 (2010), pp. 31–66.

16 For a palaeographic description, see Malachi Beit-Arié and Colette Sirat, *Manuscrits Médiévaux en Caractères Hébraïques portant des indications de date jusqu'à 1540, II. Bibliothèques de France et d'Israël, Manuscrits de petit format jusqu'à 1470* (Jerusalem; Paris: Centre National de la Recherche Scientifique; Académie Nationale des Sciences et des Lettres d'Israel, 1979), # II, 10.

17 The *Siddur Mi-Berakha Ke-Minhag Italiyani* (Ferrara: [Girolamo] Filoni, 1693), deserves a brief mention. Another octavo print without page numbering is partly preserved in a copy in the Library of the Jewish Theological Seminary in New York (SHF 1907:26 / RB 5802) and bound with another siddorello with a colophon mentioning Mantova שנת כי א'ת'כ'ם' אני = תס"א (with an apparently more complete copy to be found in the Valmadonna Trust Library, London). I have found no bibliographic reference to this print, but the minor prints of prayer-books in Italy are still worthy of study, even after the bibliographic work of Jacob J. Cohen.

earlier material emanating from the circles of the Min Ha-'Anawim/Piattelli family at the *yeshiva* in Rome which arranged prayer forms and halakhic traditions for the book now known as *Maḥzor Benei Roma*, the *maḥzor* of the rite of Rome. The revision of prayer texts and liturgical poetry in mid-thirteenth-century Rome and the arrangement of the halakhic traditions are both to be seen as a reaction to halakhic material, or even a form of *siddur/maḥzor*, from the school of Rashi (eg *Siddur Rashi*[18] or *Maḥzor Vitry*[19]) introduced into Italy through the authority of Yesh'aya di Trani ben Mali (the Elder) (*c.* 1180–*c.* 1250)[20] that evolved an intensive literary activity out of formulating the regulations for the ceremony of the *ṣidduq ha-din*:

- *Seder Ḥibbur Berakhot* (Rome, late 12th/early 13th cent.), MS Torino, Biblioteca Nazionale Universitaria A. III. 2, [first part of a] *maḥzor*, Italian rite (thirteenth century – lost, partly copied by and for Solomon Schechter in MS New York – JTS Library Ms. 8401) – [presumably in the missing second part];
- Yeḥiel b. Yequtiel (Rome, mid thirteenth century), *Halakhot* (written soon after 1240 and no later than 1260), [not part of the subjects in the unique, remnant source MS Munich, Bayrische Staatsbibliothek hebr. 232, Collectanea (Italy, thirteenth-fourteenth centuries), ff. 97a–142b];[21]

All that may confidently be stated about the copy is that it seems to be one of the local reprints of the *Siddur Mi-Berakha* of (Venice: Pietro e Lorenzo Bragadin, 1618). The latest partial reprint of this form should also be considered in the context of its research; see Leser M. Landshuth, *Vollständiges Gebet- und Andachtsbuch zum Gebrauche bei Kranken, Sterbenden und Leichenbestattungen, sowie beim Besuchen der Gräber von Verwandten und Lieben* (Berlin: Adolf Cohn, 1867), pp. LVIII–LIX.

18 See *Siddur Raschi: Ritualwerk Salomo ben Isaak zugeschrieben*, ed. by Salomon Buber, Schriften des Vereins Mekize Nirdamim, 3,11 (Berlin: Mekize Nirdamim, 1911) and Andreas Lehnardt, '"Siddur Rashi" und die Halacha-Kompendien aus der Schule Raschis', in *Raschi und sein Erbe; internationale Tagung der Hochschule für Jüdische Studien mit der Stadt Worms*, ed. by Daniel Krochmalnik, Hanna Liss, Ronen Reichman (Heidelberg: Universitäts-Verlag Winter, 2007), pp. 65–99.

19 See, for a late augmented version of this work, *Machsor Vitry: nach der Handschrift im British Museum (Cod. Add. No. 27200 u. 27201) zum ersten Male hrsg. und mit Anm. vers.*, ed. Simon H. Hurwitz (Hebrew; Berlin: Mekize Nirdamim, 1888–1897; repr. Nürnberg: Bulka, 1923).

20 For the major shift in talmudic scholarship after the establishment of the *yeshiva* in Rome in the eleventh century promoted by Yesh'aya di Trani, see Israel Moses Ta-Shma, 'Rabbinic literature in the Middle Ages, 1000–1492', in Martin Goodman (ed.), *The Oxford Handbook of Jewish Studies* (Oxford: Oxford University Press, 2002), p. 229.

21 Edited by Israel M. Ta-Shma, '*Sefer Halakhot Iṭalqi Qadmon le-Rav Yeḥiel b"r Yequtiel*', *Kobez al Yad*, n.s. 15 (25) (2000), pp. 143–206 [repr. in Ta-Shma, *Studies in Medieval Rabbinic Literature, 3. Italy & Byzantium* (Hebrew; Jerusalem: Bialik Institute, 2005), pp. 76–148].

- Ṣedaqia b. Avraham Anaw (Rome, *c.* 1210–1275), *Shibbolei Ha-Leqeṭ Ha-Qaṣar* (*c.* 1250) [not part of the printed edition of this version of the book, Venice 1546];
- Yeḥiel b. Yequtiel, *Tanya Rabbati*, [a redaction of the former to be copied on the margins of forms of prayer]: *'Inyan Ṣidduq Ha-Din*;[22]
- Ṣedaqia b. Avraham Anaw, *Shibbolei Ha-Leqeṭ Ha-Shalem*, [the final edition of this work by its author from *c.* 1260]: *Din Ṣidduq Ha-Din She-Omrim 'Al Ha-Met We-Yamim Ha-Reuyim Le-Omro*;[23]
- Anonymus, *Hilkhot Avel* (before 1265) in the *maḥzor* MSS;[24]
- Moshe b. Yequtiel (Rome, fourteenth century), *Sefer Ha-Tadir*, chap. 34, *Dinei Ha-Avelut*.[25]

The most important characteristic of all these texts is that they are written to report traditional halakhic rulings and to facilitate future ones concerning the *ṣidduq ha-din* and do not reproduce the actual texts to be recited. Despite the impression that the text of the *ṣidduq ha-din* is to be found in the *maḥzor* manuscripts and prints of the Roman rite in a section of rulings for *rites de passage*, it has to be stressed that even here the Italian literary tradition is clearly manifest. The basis for the halakhic decision and the format of the textual element of the ceremony are to be found in two distinct literary genres. Additionally, the texts are in different genres but are not intended for different readers, since we find on the one hand no historical evidence of any professional distinction in the world of prayer in medieval Italy between a rabbi and a precentor and, on the other hand, we see an effort to arrange both kinds of texts side by side in *maḥzor* manuscripts with the *Tanya Rabbati*.[26] But even

22 See *Tanya Rabbati*, ed. Shim'on Horovitz (Warsaw: I. Goldmann, 1879), ff. 70c–71a. And see now *Tanya Rabbati, le-Rabbi Yeḥiel B"R Yequtiel Ha-Rofe mi-Mishpaḥat Ha-'Anawim*, ed. Yisrael Braun, (Jerusalem: Mossad Harav Kook, 2011), pp. 267–69.

23 *Shibbolei Ha-Leqeṭ Ha-Shalem*, ed. S. Buber (Vilna: Witwe und Brüder Romm 1887), ff. 172b–173a.

24 Among the more comprehensive manuscripts and prints, see editio princeps Soncino – Casal-Maggiore: Benei Soncino, 1486, II, f. 149a–150b or ed. Bologna: Menahem ben Avraham Mi-Modena; Yeḥiel Ben Shelomo; Dan Ariye Ben Shelomo Ḥayyim MiMonticelli, 1541, f. 387a.

25 Moshe J. Blau, *Shiṭat Ha-Qadmonim* (New York: author's edition, 1992), pp. 237–38. The chronological arrangement and the attribution to the authors of the sources listed here is based on Israel M. Ta-Shma, '*Sefer Shibbolei Ha-Leqeṭ u-Khfilaw*', *Italia*, 11 (1994), pp. 39–51 [reprinted in Ta-Shma, *Studies in Medieval Rabbinic Literature, 3. Italy & Byzantium*, (Hebrew; Jerusalem: Bialik Institute, 2005), 63–75].

26 For a basic survey of the sources of the *Tanya* see Israel Z. Feintuch, '*Tanya Rabbati*', *Sinai*, 90 (1977), pp. 14–25 [reprinted in his *Mesorot we-Nusḥaot Ba-Talmud: Meḥqarim*, ed. by Daniel Sperber (Hebrew; Ramat-Gan: Bar-Ilan University, 1985), pp. 65–76, 77–88].

if both categories of information are to be found on the same page, a clear and graphical distinction is maintained between the layout of the text to be performed in the ceremony, with its minimal interspersed instructions, and the comments being offered with regard to the halakhic aspects; and, even if the halakhic texts are transmitted in a separate bibliographic unit, they do not reproduce the liturgical text to which they refer. Therefore, we too have to pay particular attention, if we want to learn something about the textual part of the *ṣidduq ha-din* in the rite of Rome, to the copies of the *maḥzor*.

For the purposes of our investigation of the different (and habitual) textual elements of the *ṣidduq ha-din* and their interrelations, the texts are given here in a critical edition according to the earliest, and almost complete, manuscript of the Roman rite that is available to us and that has already been mentioned above.[27]

27 This is an appropriate place for a caveat for the reader: the version of MS Paris is, on the one hand, the earliest that is available but, on the other hand, it does not represent the popular version that should serve as the basis of any critical edition of the Roman rite. The purpose of using this version here is not because it is the 'original' text; its importance lies rather in the fact that it may represent an early (thirteenth century!) redaction that shows by its almost unique interconnection (*Verschränkung*) of the various elements their relative independence, as well as the intention of arranging them in such a way as to blur the borders, especially between the first two textual elements. The text has been transcribed from the manuscripts but obviously with the addition of modern, critical apparatus and method of presentation. For an edition of the first text '*Ha-Ṣur Tamim be-khol Po'al*', not only according to sources from the Italian rite but from all medieval European rites, see the contribution of Ruth Langer to this volume.

וזהו צידוק הדין

[א] הַצּוּר תָּמִים פָּעֳלוֹ, כִּי כָל דְּרָכָיו מִשְׁפָּט;
אֵל אֱמוּנָה וְאֵין עָוֶל, צַדִּיק וְיָשָׁר הוּא (דב' לב 4).

הַצּוּר תָּמִים בְּכָל פּוֹעַל
וּמִי יֹאמַר לוֹ: 'מַה תִּפְעָל'? –

מקורות: [מנהג איטליה:] • כ"י פריז, הספרייה הלאומית héb. 599, מחזור, מנהג איטליה (משנת 1265), דף 143ב–144ב [= נוסח הפנים, **פ1**]; • כ"י וטיקן, הספרייה האפוסטולית Cod. Neofiti 9, מחזור, מנהג איטליה (מאה י"ג/ט"ו), דף 425א-426ב [=**נ**]; • כ"י לונדון, הספריה הבריטית Or. 14055 (לשעבר Sassoon 408), תפילות לעת מצוא, מנהג איטליה (מאה י"ד), עמ' 125–141 [=**ל**]; • כ"י מודנה, ספריית אסטנזה α.F.10.13 (ברנהיימר 30), מחזור, מנהג איטליה (מאה י"ג/י"ד), דף 221ב–222ב [=**מ**]; • כ"י לונדון, ג'וס קולג', אוסף מונטיפיורי Halberstam 69 (הירשפלד 217), מחזור, מנהג איטליה (שנת 1300 לערך), דף 299אב [=**ט1**]; • כ"י ירושלים Heb. 8º 4281 (לשעבר ברסלאו בהמ"ד לרבנים לוינגר-ויינרב 194), מחזור, מנהג איטליה (משנת 1381), דף 252ב–253א [= **י1**]; • כ"י פריז, הספריה הלאומית MS héb. 598 מחזור, מנהג איטליה (מאה י"ד), דף 310ב–314א [= **פ2**]; • כ"י מוסקבה, ספריית המדינה Guenzburg 255, מחזור, מנהג איטליה (מאה י"ד/ט"ו), דף 263ב–264ב [= **מ10**]; • כ"י רומא, קזנטנזה Cod. Casanat. 2873 (סצ'רדוטה 70), מחזור, מנהג איטליה (מאה י"ד/ט"ו), דף 246ב–247א [= **ר1**]; • כ"י ניו-יורק, ספריית בהמ"ד לרבנים Ms. 4750 (ENA 4153), מחזור, מנהג איטליה (מאה ט"ו), דף 209ב–211א [= **נ10**]; • כ"י וינה, הספריה הלאומית Cod. Hebr. 172 (שוורץ 98), מחזור, מנהג איטליה (המאה הט"ו), דף 180א–181ב [= **ו1**]; [דפוסים:] • מחזור כמנהג בני רומא, שונצין-קזאלמיורי רמ"ו, דף ב[149]ב–[150]א [=**ש"ק**]; • מחזור רומא, עם פירוש קמחא דאבישונא, בולונייא ש'-ש"א, דף [387]א [=**ב"ו**];

שינויי הנוסח צוינו רק להבדלים בעלי השלכות לפרוזודיה או למשמעות הדברים.
נוסח: [א] כותרת: סדר צידוק הדין **נ** צידוק הדין שאומרים על המת **ל מ** צידוק הדין **י1 פ2 מ10 ט1 ו1 ב"ו** צדוק הדין **נ10 ש"ק**.

פירוש: [א] 3 **הצור תמים בכל פועל:** אלהים ישר בכל מעשה, שילוב בין לשון שתי הצלעיות הראשונות של דב' לב 4. 4 **מה תפעל:** לצירוף השוו: 'גבהי שמים מה תפעל עמקה משאול מה תדע' (איוב יא 8) 'הבט שמים וראה ושור שחקים גבהו ממך. אם חטאת מה תפעל בו ורבו פשעיך מה תעשה לו' (איוב לה 5–6) והשוו

הַשַּׁלִּיט בְּתַחַת וּבְמַעַל,
מֵמִית וּמְחַיֶּה, מוֹרִיד שְׁאוֹל וַיָּעַל.

[הַצּוּר תָּמִים פָּעֳלוֹ, כִּי כָל דְּרָכָיו מִשְׁפָּט;
אֵל אֱמוּנָה וְאֵין עָוֶל, צַדִּיק וְיָשָׁר הוּא (דב' לב 4).]

הַצּוּר תָּמִים בְּכָל מַעֲשֶׂה
וּמִי יֹאמַר לוֹ: 'מַה תַּעֲשֶׂה'? –
הַגּוֹזֵר וְעוֹשֶׂה / חִינָּם לָנוּ חֶסֶד תַּעֲשֶׂה
וּבִזְכוּת הַנֶּעֱקַד כְּשֶׂה – / הַקְשִׁיבָה וַעֲשֵׂה!

[הַצּוּר תָּמִים פָּעֳלוֹ, כִּי כָל דְּרָכָיו מִשְׁפָּט;

5 **ובמעל**] ומעל מ. 7–8 השימוש של פסוק הפתיחה כרפרין נשתמר רק בכ"י צרפתי אחד, ראו בפירוש. 11 **הגוזר ועושה... תעשה**] חסר ר1.

שורה 10. 5 **בתחת ובמעל**: כמו בארץ ובשמים, השוו: 'יִדַעְתָּה כִּי מוֹשְׁלָךְ בְּמַעַל [וְשִׁלְ]טוֹנָךְ בְּתָ[חַת] וְהִישְׁמַדְתָּה [פְּרְ]יָים מִמַּעַל וְשָׁרְשָׁם מִתַּחַת' (יניי, הטור השלישי במשלש בקדושתא 'ארץ מנוחה לנו תרתה' לשבת הסדר 'ראה החלתי' [דב' ב 31], השוו: צבי מאיר רבינוביץ, מחזור פיוטי רבי יניי לתורה ולמועדים, ב, ירושלים תשמ"ז, עמ' 132 שורה 31). 6 **ממית ומחיה... ויעל**: על פי 'ה' ממית ומחיה מוריד שאול ויעל' (שמ"א ב 6). 7–8 פסוק הפתיחה אינו נרמז במקורות של מנהג איטליה מן המאה הי"ג ואילך כרפרין בין מחרוזות השיר אלא בכ"י אוקספורד קורפוס קריסטי 133, מחזור מנהג צרפת (אנגליה, מחצית הראשונה של המאה הי"ב), דפים 328ב–330א (וכאן לאורך כל השיר גם לאחר הפסוקים) והצבתי אותם כאן לשם המחשה לדגם אפשרי של ביצוע משולב בין פסוקים למחרוזות השיר. 9–10 **הצור תמים... תעשה**: וריאציה על שורות 3–4 וראו לפירוש שם. 10 **ומי יאמר... תעשה**: על פי 'באשר דבר מלך שלטון ומי יאמר לו מה תעשה' (קה' ח 4). 11 **הגוזר ועושה**: השוו 'ברוך שאמר והיה העולם, ... ברוך אומר ועושה, ברוך גוזר ומקים' (ברכת השיר לפני פסוקי דזמרא). **חינם לנו חסד תעשה**: הצירוף 'ע.ש.ה. חסד' הוא מקראי והשוו לצירוף 'חסד' ו'חינם': 'עושה חסד חנם בכל דור ודור' (מתוך התחנון לשני וחמישי). 12 **ובזכות הנעקד כשה**: כינוי ליצחק על פי המסופר בבר' פרק כב. **הקשיבה ועשה**: צירוף מתוך: 'ה' שמעה ה' סלחה ה' הקשיבה ועשה אל תאחר למענך אלהי כי שמך נקרא על עירך ועל עמך' (דנ' ט 19) פסוק מרכזי בתחנון ובסדר הסליחות.

אֵל אֱמוּנָה וְאֵין עָוֶל, צַדִּיק וְיָשָׁר הוּא (דב' לב 4).]

הַצּוּר תָּמִים פָּעֳלוֹ אֱמֶת,
כִּי כָל דְּרָכָיו חֶסֶד וֶאֱמֶת;
הוּא אֱמֶת וּמִשְׁפָּטָיו אֱמֶת
אֶרֶךְ אַפַּיִם וְרַב חֶסֶד וֶאֱמֶת.

וְהוּא רַחוּם, יְכַפֵּר עָוֹן וְלֹא יַשְׁחִית
וְהִרְבָּה לְהָשִׁיב אַפּוֹ, וְלֹא יָעִיר כָּל חֲמָתוֹ (תה' עח 38).

בָּרוּךְ כִּי אֱמֶת דִּינוֹ
וּמְשׁוֹטֵט הַכֹּל בְּעֵינוֹ
וּמְשַׁלֵּם לְאָדָם חֶשְׁבּוֹנוֹ –
וְהַכֹּל לִשְׁמוֹ הוֹדָיָה יִתְּנוּ.

רְאוּ עַתָּה כִּי אֲנִי אֲנִי הוּא, וְאֵין אֱלֹהִים עִמָּדִי

23 חשבונו] כחשבונו נ10.

15 **פעלו אמת:** וריאציה על שורת הפתיחה, הצירוף השגור יותר במקרא הוא 'ע.ש.ה. אמת'. 16 **כל דרכיו חסד ואמת:** השוו: 'כל ארחות ה' חסד ואמת' (תה' כה 10) ולצירוף חסד ואמת השוו שורה 18. 17 **הוא אמת:** השוו: וה' אלהים אמת' (יר' י 10). 18 **ארך אפים... ואמת:** על פי 'ויעבר ה' על פניו ויקרא ה' ה' אל רחום וחנון ארך אפים ורב חסד ואמת' (שמ' לד 6) אזכור י"ג המידות מתוך סדר התחנון וסדר הסליחות. 19–20 הפסוק הפותח את סדר התחנונים. 22 **ומשוטט הכל בעינו:** והכול גלוי לפניו, הניסוח על פי 'שבעה אלה עיני ה', המה משוטטים בכל הארץ' (זכ' ד 10), 'כי ה' עיניו משטטות בכל הארץ להתחזק עם לבבם שלם אליו' (דה"ב טז 9). 23 **חשבונו:** גמולו לפי החישוב של מה שמגיע לו. 24 **לשמו הודיה יתנו:** הודאה והודיה הן צורות מתחלפות בספרות הבתר מקראית, ובמקום: 'יאמרו לו תודה (=שבח)' ונראה שיש כאן לגרוס כמו: '(וכולם) יכירו בו (כדיין)'. 25–26 **ראו עתה... מציל:** למשמעות הבאת הפסוק בהמשך למחרוזת הקודמת בעניין הכרה באל כבורא וכדיין, השוו: "אנכי יי אלהיך (שמ' כ 2) - למה נא<מר>? [...]שלא ליתן פתחון פה לאומות העולם לומר: שתי רשויות הן. אלא 'אנכי יי אלהיך' - [...] אני לשעבר, אני לעתיד לבא, אני בעולם הזה, אני לעולם הבא, שנ<אמר>:

אֲנִי אָמִ[י]ת וַאֲחַיֶּה, מָחַצְתִּי וַאֲנִי אֶרְפָּא, וְאֵין מִיָּדִי מַצִּיל (דב' לב 39).

אָדָם אִם בֶּן שָׁנָה יִהְיֶה
אוֹ אִם אֶלֶף שָׁנִים יִחְיֶה
מַה יִּתְרוֹן לוֹ הֱיוֹת כְּלֹא יִהְיֶה? –
בָּרוּךְ דַּיַּין הָאֱמֶת, מֵמִית וּמְחַיֶּיה.

נֶפֶשׁ כָּל חַי בְּיָדֶךָ
צֶדֶק מָלְאָה יְמִינֶךָ,
רַחֵם עַל פְּלֵיטַת צֹאן יָדֶךָ
וְתֹאמַר לַמַּלְאָךְ: 'הֶרֶף יָדֶךָ'.

זְכוֹר לְאַבְרָהָם וְהַבֵּט מִמְּרוֹמֶיךָ

26 אמית] אמת (טעות סופר) **פ1**. 28 אם] נוסף מעל השורה **ט1** חסר **פ2 ר1 נ10 ו1**. 29 כלא] נוסף היה **מ**. 34 ידך] בידך **פ2**. 35 ממרומיך] ממרומך **נ מ ט1 י1 פ2 נ10**. 37 תמימך] תמימיך **פ 2**.

'ראו עתה כי אני אני הוא' וגו' (דב' לב 39)' (מכילתא, מסכתא דבחדש (יתרו), ה [מהד' הורוביץ-רבין, עמ' 220]). 27–29 **אדם אם... יהיה**: השוו: 'ואלו חיה אלף שנים פעמַים וטובה לא ראה הלא אל מקום אחד הכל הולך' (קה' ו 6). 29 **מה יתרון לו**: השוו: 'מה יתרון לאדם בכל עמלו שיעמל תחת השמש' (קה' א 3), 'כאשר יצא מבטן אמו ערום ישוב ללכת כשבא ומאומה לא ישא בעמלו שילך בידו. וגם זה רעה חולה כל עמת שבא כן ילך ומה יתרון לו שיעמל לרוח' (קה' ה 14–15). **ברוך דיין האמת**: מלשון ברכת ההודאה, השוו: 'ועל שמועות הרעות הוא אומר: ב' דיין האמת' (משנה, ברכות ט, ב). **ממית ומחיה**: ראו לעיל לשורה 6. 31 **נפש כל... בידך**: כינוי לאל, על פי 'אשר בידו נפש כל חי' (איוב יב 10). 32 **צדק מלאה ימינך**: על פי 'תהלתך על קצוי ארץ, צדק מלאה ימינֶך' (תה' מח 11). 33 **פליטת צאן ידך**: שארית עמך ישראל, הכינוי מבוסס על צירוף מקראי כגון 'שאר ישראל ופליטת בית יעקב' (יש' י 20) ולשון הפסוק 'ואנחנו עם מרעיתו וצאן ידו' (תה' צה 7). 34 **ותאמר למלאך... ידך**: ותאמר למלאך המוות, על פי 'וינחם ה' אל הרעה ויאמר למלאך המשחית בעם רב: עתה הרף ידך' (שמ"ב כד 16). 35 **זכור לאברהם**: רמיזה לבקשת המחילה מתוך אזכור ברית האבות מאת משה לפני האל: 'זכֹר לאברהם ליצחק ולישראל עבדיך אשר נשבעת להם בך ותדבר אלהם ארבה את זרעכם ככוכבי השמים וכל הארץ הזאת אשר אמרתי אתן לזרעכם ונחלו לעלם' (שמ' לב 13). **והבט ממרומיך**: השוו: 'שוב נא הבט משמים וראה ופקד גפן זאת'

וּלְיִצְחָק הַנֶּעֱקָד עַל שְׁמֶךָ |
[144א] וּלְמַעַן יַעֲקֹב הַנִּקְרָא תְּמִימֶךָ –
לְמַעַנְךָ וּלְמַעֲנָם חוּסָה וַחֲמוֹל עַל עַמֶּךָ.

אָמְנָם עַל שְׁלֹשָׁה דְבָרִים
יְסוֹדֵי עוֹלָם מְיֻוסָּדִים
עַל הַתּוֹרָה וְעַל הָעֲבוֹדָה וְעַל גְּמִילוּת חֲסָדִים –
בָּרוּךְ מְשַׁלֵּם שָׂכָר טוֹב לְגוֹמְלֵי חֲסָדִים.

מַה יִּתְרוֹן לְאָדָם בְּכָל עֲמָלוֹ
כִּי עַל כָּל אֵלֶּה מָוֶת גּוֹרָלוֹ;
וּבְיוֹם הַמָּוֶת אֵין עוֹזֵר לוֹ
כִּי אִם הַצּוּר תָּמִים פָּעֳלוֹ.

צַדִּיק בְּכָל דְּרָכָיו הַצּוּר תָּמִים

שורות 43–46 אחרי שורה 50 **נ ט1 י1 פ2 מ10 ר1 נ10 ו1 ש"ק ב"ו**. 46 אם] חסר **פ2**.

(תה' פ 15) 'הוא מרומים ישכן' (יש' לג 16). 36 **על שמך**: משמעות הביטוי בלשון חז"ל כמו 'על קידוש שמך' בלשון ימי-הביניים. 37 **הנקרא תמימך**: השוו: 'שדה ויעקב איש תם ישב אהלים' (בר' כה 27). 38 **למענך ולמענם**: מלשונות סדר התחנונים והסליחות, השוו דנ' ט 19 (לעיל לשורה 12) ולשונות כמו: 'אבינו מלכנו עשה למענך אם לא למעננו'. **חוסה וחמול על עמך**: השוו מתוך תיאור מקראי של מעמד של תענית: 'חוסה ה' על עמך ואל תתן נחלתך לחרפה למשל בם גוים למה יאמרו בעמים איה אלהיהם. ויקנא ה' לארצו ויחמל על עמו' (יואל ב 17–18). 39–41 **אמנם על... חסדים**: על פי 'שמעון הצדיק [...] היה אומר: על שלשה דברים העולם עומד, על התורה ועל העבודה ועל גמילות חסדים' (משנה, אבות א, ב). 42 **ברוך משלם... חסדים**: במקביל ללשון ברכת השיר: 'ברוך משלם שכר טוב ליראיו' והשוו בניסוח של ברכה בהקשר של מנהגי אבלות: 'ורואין את האבל ויושבין לארץ כדי שישבו ויצאו כל ישראל ידי חובתן בגמילות חסדים, ועליהם הוא אומר: ברוך אתה ה', נותן שכר טוב לגומלי חסדים' (פרקי דרבי אליעזר, פרק 'גמילות חסדים לאבלים מנין' (יז) [ורשה תרי"ב, דף מא ע"ב]). 43 **מה יתרון... עמלו**: ראו לעיל לשורה 29. 44 **כי על... גורלו**: השוו גם 'גורלך תפיל בתוכנו כיס אחד יהיה לכלנו' (מש' א 14). 45 **וביום המות... לו**: השוו: 'ובא עד קצו ואין עוזר לו' (דנ' יא 45). 46 **כי אם... פעלו**: על פי דב' לב 4 (לעיל שורה 1). 47 **צדיק בכל דרכיו**: על פי

אֶרֶךְ אַפַּיִם וּמָלֵא רַחֲמִים,
חֲמוֹל-נָא חוּס נָא עַל אָבוֹת וּבָנִים
כִּי לְךָ, [אָדוֹן], הַסְּלִיחוֹת וְהָרַחֲמִים.

צַדִּיק וְיוֹצֵר כָּל מַעֲשֶׂה
חָסִיד בְּכֹל אֲשֶׁר יַעֲשֶׂה,
שַׁלִּיט חֶפְצוֹ עוֹשֶׂה
וּמִי יֹאמַר לוֹ: 'מַה תַּעֲשֶׂה ?'

צַדִּיק וְיָשָׁר וְאֵין בִּדְרָכָיו עָוֶל
כִּי הוּא נִקְרָא הַצּוּר תָּמִים;
זַךְ פָּעֳלוֹ וְצֶדֶק אוֹרְחוֹתָיו
וְאֵין לְהִסָּתֵר מִפְּנֵי פּוֹעֵל כֹּל.

צֶדֶק וּמִשְׁפָּט כָּל דְּרָכָיו
חֶסֶד וֶאֱמֶת אוֹרְחוֹתָיו
מַשּׂוֹא פָּנִים אֵין לְפָנָיו

49 חוס נא] חוסה נ ר1 חוס מ10 נ10 ו1. 50 לך] נוסף אדון נ מ ט1 י1 פ2 מ10 ר1 נ10 ש"ק ב"ו נוסף מתן ל. שורות 51–54 אחרי שורה 58 נ ט1 י1 פ2 מ10 ר1 נ10 ו1 ש"ק ב"ו. 53 שליט חפצו עושה] חסר ל. 54 ומי] מי ב"ו. 55 וישר] ישר פ2. 56 נקרא] הנקרא פ2 מ10 ר1 נ10 ו1. 59 צדק] צדיק(!) פ2 כל] בכל ש"ק. 60 אורחותיו] כל אורחותיו ב"ו. 61 פנים] פניו פ2.

'צדיק ה' בכל דרכיו וחסיד בכל מעשיו' (תה' קמה 17). **הצור תמים:** כינוי לאל, על פי דב' לב 4. 48 **ארך אפים:** ממידות האל, השוו לעיל לשורה 18. **ומלא רחמים:** השוו את לשון סדר נפילת האפים: 'רחום וחנון חטאתי לפניך, ה' מלא רחמים, רחם עלי וקבל תחנוני' עם פתיחת תפילת יזכור: 'אל מלא רחמים'. 49 **חמול נא חוס נא:** מלשונות הפנייה בסדרי הסליחות. 50 **לך אדון.. והרחמים:** השוו: 'לה' אלהינו הרחמים והסלחות' (דנ' ט 9). 51–52 **צדיק ויוצר... יעשה:** כינוי לאל, על פי תה' קמה 17 (לעיל לשורה 47). 53–54 **שליט חפצו... תעשה:** על פי 'באשר דבר מלך שלטון ומי יאמר לו מה תעשה' (קה' ח 4). 55–57 **צדיק וישר... אורחותיו:** פרפרזה על דב' לב 4 (לעיל שורות 1–2). 58 **ואין להיסתר:** השוו 'כי עיניו על דרכי איש וכל צעדיו יראה. אין חשך ואין צלמות להסתר שם פעלי און' (איוב לד 21–22). 59–60 **צדק ומשפט... אורחותיו:** פרפרזה לדב' לב 4. 61 **משוא פנים**

וְעָלֵינוּ יֶהֱמוּ רַחֲמָיו / כִּי כּוּלָּנוּ מַעֲשֵׂה יָדָיו.

דַּיַּין אֱמֶת,
שׁוֹפֵט צֶדֶק וֶאֱמֶת,
בָּרוּךְ דַּיַּין הָאֱמֶת,
כִּי כָל מִשְׁפָּטָיו חֶסֶד וֶאֱמֶת.

[רְאוּ חֲכָמִים וְהָבִינוּ עַל לֵב
כִּי אֵין שִׁלְטוֹן בְּיוֹם הַמָּוֶת
כְּמוֹ דִבֵּר אִישׁ תָּם וְיָשָׁר:
יְיָ נָתַן וַייָ לָקָח יְהִי שֵׁם יְיָ מְבוֹרָךְ].

[יָדַעְנוּ יְיָ כִּי צָדְקוּ מִשְׁפָּטֶיךָ

62 מעשה] מעשי **נ**. שורות 67–70 שולבו ב-[ב] לפני שורה 13 ויד שנייה הפנתה בגיליון בעזרת הציון 'ראו – רד' שמקום הדברים כאן **פ1 ל מ** (ללא הפנייה). 67 על לב] חסר **פ1**. 69 דבר] דם(!) **פ1** דיבר **ט1 י1 פ2 ר1 נ10** וישר] חסר **ש"ק**. שורות 71–74 שולבו ב-[ב] לפני שורה 9 **פ1** לפני שורה 13 בהמשך לשורות 67–70 **מ** והחזרתי אותם לכאן לפי רוב עדי הנוסח. 71 צדקו] צדק **נ ט1 פ2 מ10 ר1 ו1 ש"ק**.

אין לפניו: על פי 'אין עם ה' אלהינו עולה ומשא פנים ומקח שחד' (דה"ב יט 7) והשוו: "ויאמר יי אל משה הן קרבו ימיך למות' (דב' לא 14) – ר' שמעון בן יוחי אום<ר>: ברוך דיין אמת, אדון כל המעשים שאין עוולה ומשוא פנים לפניו' (ספרי דברים, נצבים, סי' שד [מהד' פינקלשטיין, עמ' 323]). 62 **ועלינו יהמו רחמיו**: השוו נוסח של ברכת הצדיקים: 'ועלינו יהמו רחמיך ה' אלהינו'. **כי כולנו מעשה ידיו**: על פי 'אשר לא נשא פני שרים ולא נִכַּר שוע לפני דל כי מעשה ידיו כֻּלם' (איוב לד 19) וזה בהמשך ישיר לשורה הקודמת. 63–66 **דיין אמת... ואמת**: ואריאציה על נושא ברכת ההודאה, ראו לעיל לשורה 61. 67 **ראו חכמים**: השוו: 'איזהו חכם? – הרואה את הנולד!' (תלמוד בבלי, תמיד לב ע"א). **והבינו על לב**: כמו ושימו על לב והשוו 'שמועה רעה לא יירא נכון לבו בטח בה'' (תה' קיב 7). 68 **כי אין... המות**: על פי 'אין אדם שליט ברוח לכלוא את הרוח ואין שלטון ביום המות' (קה' ח 8). 69 **איש תם וישר**: לפי הציטוט בשורה הבאה כינוי פריפרסטי לאיוב. 70 **ה' נתן... מבורך**: איוב א 21 בספרות חז"ל מופת לאמירת הודאה. 71 **ידענו ה'... משפטיך**: על פי 'ידעתי ה' כי צדק משפטיך' (תה' קיט 75). 72 **תצדק בדוברך... בשופטך**: על פי 'לך לבדך חטאתי והרע בעיניך עשיתי למען תצדק בדברך תזכה בשפטך' (תה' נא 6).

תִּצְדַּק בְּדָוּבְרֶךָ, תִּזְכֶּה בְּשָׁופְטֶךָ
וְאֵין לְהַרְהֵר אַחַר מִידַּת שְׁפָטֶיךָ
צַדִּיק אַתָּה יְיָ וְיָשָׁר מִשְׁפָּטֶיךָ].

[ב] אָדָם אִם-יִחְיֶה אֶלֶף שָׁנִים
וְשִׁלְטוֹן מָשְׁלוֹ בְּכָל-צַד וּפִינִים

מִבְּלִי עָשְׁרוֹ יֵרֵד בָּאַשְׁמַנִּים
וּבַדִּין יָועֳמַד לִפְנֵי אֵל אֲשֶׁר לֹא יִשָּׂא פָּנִים.

תַּקִּיף שְׁמוֹ מְיֻוחָד
וּלְפָנָיו קָטוֹן וְגָדוֹל שָׁוִים יַחַד

יְצִיר, זֹאת יָשִׁיב אֶל-לִבּוֹ וְיִפְחַד
כִּי יִתְוַוכַּח לִפְנֵי שׁוֹפֵט אֲשֶׁר לֹא יִקַּח שׁוֹחַד.

[ב] 1 אם] כי ר1. 2 ושלטון] שלטון נ ל מ ט1 י1 פ2 מ10 ר1 נ10 ו1 ש"ק ב"ו צד] חסר י1 ופינים] ופנים ט1 ב"ו. 3 מבלי] ומבלי ל חבלי ש"ק באשמנים] במשמנים ש"ק. 4 ובדין] ופנים ר1 יועמד] יעמד ט1 יעמוד י1 יעמֹד ש"ק. 5 מיוחד] ומיוחד נ ל מ ט1 פ2 מ10 ר1 נ10 ו1 ב"ו. 6 ולפניו] לפניו ל ב"ו קטון] קטן ל ט1 י1 ש"ק ב"ו. 7 ישיב] ישים פ2. 8 שופט] אל מ פ2 ר1 נ10 יקח שוחד] ישא פנים ולא יקח שוחד נ ל מ ט1 פ2 מ10 ר1 נ10 ו1 ב"ו.

73 **ואין להרהר**: השוו את שתי הדרשות למילים 'הצור' ו-'תמים פעלו' בעניין שאין להרהר במידת הבורא ובמידת הדיין בספרי דברים, האזינו, פסקה שז (מהד' פינקל-שטיין, עמ' 344–345) ולצירוף הלשון 'להרהר אחר מידות' שמ"ר ו, א (מהד' שנאן, עמ' 184–185). 74 **צדיק אתה... משפטיך**: תה' קיט 137.
[ב] 1 **אם יחיה אלף שנים**: על פי קה' ו 6 ראו לעיל [א] שורות 27–29. **יחיה**: כמו תחיה. צורת הנסתר מקנה כאן לתוכחה ממד אוניברסלי יותר מאשר צורת הנוכח, השוו שורה 7. 2 **ופינים**: ופינות, מתוך התאמה לחריזה. **ירד באשמנים**: ירד לקבר, על פי 'נגששה כעורים קיר וכאין עינים נגששה כשלנו בצהרים כנשף באשמנים כמתים' (יש' נט 10), ובתרגום יונתן: '... כמא דאחידין קבריא באפי מתיא'. 4 **אשר לא ישא פנים**: על פי 'כי ה' אלהיכם הוא אלהי האלהים ואדני האדנים האל הגדל הגבר והנורא אשר לא ישא פנים ולא יקח שחד' (דב' י 17), השוו לעיל [א] שורה 61. 8 **יתווכח**: יישפט, על פי 'ושפט בצדק דלים והוכיח במישור לענוי ארץ' (יש' יא 4). **לא יקח שוחד**: על פי דב' י 17 כמו לסיום המחרוזת הקודמת.

* יָדַעְנוּ יְיָ כִּי צָדְקוּ מִשְׁפָּטֶיךָ
תִּצְדַּק בְּדָובְרֶךָ תִּזְכֶּה בְשָׁופְטֶךָ
וְאֵין לְהַרְהֵר אַחַר מִידַּת שְׁפָטֶיךָ
צַדִּיק אַתָּה יְיָ וְיָשָׁר מִשְׁפָּטֶיךָ .

חַי וְקַיָּים, בְּחַרְתָּנוּ
וּבְחַרְנוּךָ חֵלֶק מְנָתֵינוּ;
עַל-דְּבַר כְּבוֹד שְׁמֶךָ הַצִּילֵנוּ
וְכַפֵּר עַל-חַטֹּאתֵינוּ.

** וּלְמַעַן דַּם עֲבָדֶיךָ הַשָּׁפוּךְ בִּשְׁנַת תַּתְּנ"וּ
אֲשֶׁר נַפְשָׁם וּמְאוֹדָם עַל יִיחוּד שֵׁם קָדְשֶׁךָ נָתְנוּ.
זְכוּת עָקוּד בֶּן שְׁלֹשִׁים וָשֶׁבַע הַמְּיֻוחָד

* שורות אלה הועברו לכאן מ-[א] ראו לעיל [א] שורות 71–74 **פ1** ולפני כן השורות המסומנות ב-*** (= [א] שורות 67–70) **ל מ**. 11 הצילנו] והצילנו **ל מ10 ר1 נ10 ב"ו**. ** שארית של מחרוזת וחצי מסליחה בענייני גזרות תתנ"ו 1** ולמען] למען **ל פ2 ר1 נ10 ב"ו** תתנ"ו] שמונה מאות וחמשים וששה **ש"ק**. 2** שם קדשך] קדשך **מ** שמך **ש"ק ב"ו** נתנו] נַתַנוּ (צ"ל נָתְנוּ השווה יח' כז 19) **נ**. 3** זכות] זכור **ל י1** בן] בין **ב"ו**.

* למחרוזת זו ראו במדור חילופי הנוסח והשוו [א] שורות 71–74. 9 **חי וקיים:** פנייה לאל, כינוי פריפרסטי המשמש בתפילות הקבע (ברכת מעריב, נשמת וכדומה). 10 **חלק מנתינו:** כמו מנת חלקינו בסמיכות הפוכה. 11–12 **על דבר... חטאותינו:** על פי 'עזרנו אלהי ישענו על דבר כבוד שמך והצילנו וכפר על חטאתינו למען שמך' (תה' עט 9); במהלך המסירה התאימו את לשון הפיוט ('הצילנו') ללשון הפסוק ('והצילנו') ושיבשו בכך את התחביר עד שב' קלאר ראה צורך להשלים בראש הטור 'עזרנו' גם על פי לשון הפסוק. ** תוספת של מחרוזת וחצי שנכתב בעקבות הגזרות בשנת תתנ"ו (1096) באשכנז. 1** **למען דם עבדיך השפוך:** על מנת להפריך את הטענה הגלומה בדברי הפסוק ביסוד הניסוח: 'למה יאמרו הגוים איה אלהיהם יודע בגוים לעינינו נקמת דם עבדיך השפוך' (תה' עט 10). 2** **נפשם ומאודם:** השוו: 'ואהבת את ה' אלהיך בכל לבבך ובכל נפשך ובכל מאדך' (דב' ו 5). **על ייחוד... נתנו:** מתו על קידוש השם. 3** **עקוד:** יצחק, כינוי פריפרסטי על פי המסופר בבר' כב. **בן שלושים ושבע:** על פי מסורת מדרשית לסיפור העקדה, ראו מדרש תנחומא, וירא, כג (מהד' ורשה, עמ' 78) ולמקבילות בראשית רבא, נה, ה (מהד' תיאודור-אלבק, עמ' 588) ושם בפירוש.

וּבְצִיוּוּיֶךָ נִמְסַר לְטֶבַח וּלְבַסּוֹף אַיִל תְּמוּרוֹ נֶאֱחַד
הִבְטַחְתָּה הֱיוֹת שָׁמוּר לְדוֹרֵי דוֹרוֹת לְעוֹבְדֶיךָ בְּאַהַב וּבְפַחַד
כֹּל שֶׁכֵּן כַּמָּה אַלּוּפֵינוּ אֲשֶׁר בִּשְׁנַת כל"ו כֻּלּוֹ יַחַד.

***רְאוּ חֲכָמִים וְהָבִינוּ [עַל לֵב]
כִּי אֵין שִׁלְטוֹן בְּיוֹם הַמָּוֶת
כְּמוֹ דַּם אִישׁ תָּם וְיָשָׁר:
יְיָ נָתַן וַייָ לָקָח יְהִי שֵׁם יְיָ מְבוֹרָךְ (איוב א 21).

זוֹ הִיא דֶּרֶךְ כָּל-הָעוֹלָם
הֵאָסְפוּ וַעֲשׂוּ חֶסֶד כּוּלָּם
כִּי אֵין דָּבָר [מִ]מֶּנּוּ נֶעְלָם |
נִשְׁמָתוֹ לְחַיֵּי עוֹלָם. [144ב]

4** ובציויך] בצווייך **נ** איל] אל **ש"ק** תמורו] תמורתו **ל**. 5** לדורי דורות] **חסר נ10** לעובדיך] לעבדך **נ** לעובדך **פ2**. 6** כל] וכל **פ2** כל"ו] כְּל"וּ **נ** קלו (כלומר שנת 1176!) **ב"ו**. *** שורות אלה הועברו לכאן מ-[א] שורות 67–70 ונרמז שם בגיליון שמקומם ברצף שם **פ1**. 15 ממנו] מנו **פ1 ט1 ש"ק**. 16 נשמתו] ונשמתו **נ מ10 ר1 נ10 ו1 ב"ו** (ומכאן ואילך נרשמו בגיליון סיום המלים הנדרשות התאמה למין נקבה: כגון –תה וכו') **נ ל ט1** (רק התחלה) **ר1 ו1**.

6** **בשנת כל"ו**: כמו נ"ו, כלומר תתנ"ו, השוו: 'ובימיו נגזרה גזרה כלו שנת תתנ"ו לפרט' (שו"ת מהרש"ל סימן כט [מהד' לובלין של"ד, דף [55] ע"ב]), לנדסהוט, סדר בקור חולים, עמ' LIX *** לארבע שורות אלה ראו במדור חילופי הנוסח והשוו [א] שורות 67–70. 13 **זו היא... העולם**: רמיזה לחוקיות המוות וגם לטכס ההלוויה. 14 **האספו ועשו חסד**: פנייה לקהל לגמול חסדים למת, כמו 'ולמה זכו להעמיד אליהו הצדיק? - בשביל שעשו חסד עם עצמותיו של שאול' (דברים רבה, פרשת עקב (מהד' ליברמן, עמ' 73). 15 **כי אין... נעלם**: על דרך הלשון 'לא היה דבר נעלם מן המלך' (מל"א י 3) מתוך הסבת הדברים על אלהים ורמיזה לזכות שבקיום המצווה או שמא לאור המעבר המפתיע לקביעה על אודות נפשו של הנפטר מדובר כאן באמונה שאף על פי שמטמינים את המת בקבר ומסתירים אותו, זהותו ידועה לפני האל, והשוו לקשר בין קבורה, ידיעת זהות הנקבר וחיי עולם: מסכת חיבוט הקבר א, ו. 16 **נשמתו לחיי עולם**: ככל הנראה רמז לסיום טכס האשכבה, השוו את התיעוד הספרותי: 'וכשבקש יהושע רבו [את משה] ולא מצאו היה בוכה ואומר: 'הושיעה ה' כי גמר חסיד כי פסו אמונים מבני אדם' (תה' יב 2),

קוֹל נִשְׁמַע מְבַשֵּׂר שָׁלוֹם
רְצוֹן יְרֵיאָיו עוֹשֶׂה שָׁלוֹם
שִׁמְעוּ דְבַר שָׁלוֹם
תָּנוּחַ נַפְשׁוֹ בְּמִשְׁכָּבוֹ בְּשָׁלוֹם.
יִשְׁכַּב בְּשָׁלוֹם / וְיִישַׁן בְּשָׁלוֹם
עַד-יָבוֹא מְנַחֵם מַשְׁמִיעַ שָׁלוֹם.

18 עושה] יעשה **נ ר1 ש"ק ב"ו**. 20 במשכבו] ומשכבו **מ פ2 ש"ק**. 21–22 ישכב בשלום... שלום] השורות הועברו לאחר [ג] שורה 6 **ל מ**. 22 מנחם] מבשר **נ10**.

ומלאכי השרת אומרים: 'צדקת ה' עשה' (דב' לג 21), וישראל היו אומרים: 'ומשפטיו עם ישראל' (שם); אלו ואלו היו אומרים: 'יבא שלום ינוחו על משכבותם הולך נכוחו' (יש' נז 2), 'זכר צדיק לברכה' (משלי י 7) ונשמתו לחיי עולם הבא. אמן כן יהי רצון, ברוך ה' לעולם אמן ואמן' (דברים רבה יא, ט (הוצ' וילנא, דף קכ ע"ד) והשוו ילקוט שמעוני, וילך (רמז תתקם) [מהד' הימן-שילוני, עמ' 605]). 17–20 שילוב של סיום של פיוט אלפביתי קדום (קרש"ת), השוו כבר התרשמותו של א"ל לנדסהוטה, סדר בקור חולים, עמ' LVIII. 'ארבע שורות אלה מופיעות (בשינוי קל – 'ינוח' במקום 'תנוח' מתוך הסבת הפועל על המנוח בעקבות הביטוי 'hic requiescit n. n.') על מצבתו של ר' ברוך בן רבי יונה מברינדיזי מן המאה התשיעית, ראו: Cesare Colafemmina, 'Archeologia ed epigrafia ebraica nell'Italia meridionale', Italia Judaica, 1 (1983), p. 205. ממצא זה מחזק את הרושם שלטקסט היה קיום עצמאי לפני שהוא שולב בפיוטו של אמתי. לאפשרות של חיבור פתיחה חדשה של קינה למת שתוביל אל סיום מסורתי השוו את דרך ההבאה של קינתו של אמתי ב"ר שפטיה 'אי אכסניה אי גלות' במגילת אחימעץ (מהד' בונפיל, עמ' 311). 17 **קול נשמע... שלום:** על פי 'מה נאוו על ההרים רגלי מבשר משמיע שלום מבשר טוב משמיע ישועה אמר לציון מלך אלהיך' (יש' נב 7). 18 **רצון יריאיו... שלום:** על פי 'רצון יראיו יעשה ואת שועתם ישמע ויושיעם' (תה' קמה 19). 19 **דבר שלום:** הצירוף על פי 'והכרתי רכב מאפרים וסוס מירושלם ונכרתה קשת מלחמה ודבר שלום לגוים ומשלו מים עד ים ומנהר עד אפסי ארץ (זכ' ט 10). 20 **תנוח נפשו:** לצירוף השוו את המובא אצל Jean-Baptiste Frey, Corpus Inscriptionum Iudaicarum: I. Europe [Suddidi allo Studio delle Antichita Cristiane, 1], Roma: Pontificio Istituto di Archeologia Cristiana 1936, p. 422. 22 **מנחם:** המשיח, הכינוי על פי איכה א 16 השוו: 'ויש אומרים מנחם בן חזקיה שמו, שנאמר: 'כי רחק ממני מנחם משיב נפשי' (איכה א 16)' (תלמוד בבלי, סנהדרין דף צח ע"ב).

[ג] אֲבוֹת עוֹלָם, יְשֵׁינֵי חֶבְרוֹן,
שַׁעֲרֵי גַן עֵדֶן פִּתְחוּ לוֹ וְאִמְרוּ לוֹ: 'שָׁלוֹם בּוֹאוֹ'.

[ג] שורות 1–6 סדר השורות 5–6 1–4 **ל מ** 1–2 5–6 3–4 **פ2 ר1**. שורות 3–6 סדר השורות 5–6, 3–4 **פ1** וסידרתי אותם כברוב עדי הנוסח. 2 בואו] בציוני ההתאמה למין נקבה רשום בגיליון בואך **נ**.

[ג] 1 **אבות עולם**: לפי ההמשך כינוי לאברהם, יצחק ויעקב הקבורים במערת המכפלה בחברון. לפי ההקבלה ל-'גבעות עולם' (שורה 3), השימוש 'שבח אבות עולם' בבן-סירא (העברי) מד 1 (מהד' סגל, עמ' שב) והכינוי 'אבות העולם' להלל ושמאי במשנה עדויות א, ה, תלמוד ירושלמי, חגיגה ב, ב (דף עז ע"ד) ועוד, משמעות הצירוף: גדולי תבל. אבל השוו: ''ארץ חמדה' (במ' טו 2) - שנתחמדו לה אבות העולם אברהם יצחק ויעקב' (מדרש תנחומא-ילמדנו [מהד' גינצבורג, קטעי מדרש והגדה מן הגניזה שבמצרים (גנזי שכטר, א), ניו-יורק תרפ"ח, עמ' 101]). **ישיני חברון**: הקבורים בחברון, השוו 'ורבים מישני אדמת עפר יקיצו' (דנ' יב 2), והצירוף ככינוי לאבות בפיוטים כגון: 'חוננו למען ישיני חברון' (אלעזר ברבי קליר, 'איילותי אקראך בגרון', משלש של הקדושתא 'אזרחי ידעך מכל אומות' ליום כפור [אלכסנדר שייבר, 'פיוט קלירי המובא ע"י קרקסאני', בתוך: דוד שמואל לוינגר ואלכסנדר שייבר (עורכים), גנזי קויפמן, א, בודפשט 1949, עמ' 11–12]) והשוו בהקשר איטלקי: 'מניני ישיני חברון' (אחימעץ בן פלטיאל, ספר יוחסין, 2 (מהד' בונפיל, עמ' 239). 2 **שערי גן עדן**: לנרטיב הסיטואציה ביסוד הדברים השוו: 'נשמה כד נפקת מהאי עלמא, אי זכאת עאלת בגנתא דעדן דארעא דנטע קודשא בריך הוא לרוחיהון דצדיקייא כגוונא דההוא גנתא דעדן דלעילא ותמן כל צדיקיא דעלמא. וכד נשמתא נפקת מהאי עלמא, עאלת במערתא דכפלתא דתמן איהו פתחא דג<ן> ע<דן>, פגעת באדם הראשון ובאינון אבהן דתמן. אי זכאת איהי חדאן בה ופתחין לה פתחין ועאלת' (זוהר - סתרי תורה, לך לך [מהד' מרגליות, א, דף פא ע"א] (= נשמה כאשר היא יוצאת מן העולם הזה, אם היא זכאית היא נכנסת לגן עדן של הארץ שנטע הקדוש ברוך הוא לרוחותיהם של הצדיקים כמו אותו גן של מעלה ושם כל צדיקי העולם. וכאשר הנשמה יוצאת מן העולם הזה, היא נכנסת למערת המכפלה ששם נמצא הפתח לגן עדן, פוגשת את האדם הראשון ובאותם אבות הנמצאים שם. אם היא זכאית, שמחים בה ופותחים לה את הפתחים והיא נכנסת); 'ותאנא: שבע פתחים יש לנפשות הצדיקים להכנס עד מקום מעלתם ועל כל פתח ופתח שומרים. הפתח ראשון נכנסת הנשמה במערת המכפלה שהיא סמוכה לג<ן> ע<דן> ואד<ם> הר<אשון> שומר עליו. זכתה, הוא מכריז ואומר: פנו מקום, שלום בואך!' (זוהר חדש – מדרש הנעלם, נח [מהד' מרגליות, דף כ ע"ב–כא ע"א]). וזה רק ניסוח מאוחר ורצוף על סמך מסורות קדומים, השוו: 'אמר ריש לקיש: כל העונה אמן בכל כחו, פותחין לו שערי גן עדן, שנאמר: 'פתחו שערים ויבא גוי צדיק שומר אמונים' (יש' כו 2) – אל תיקרי 'שומר אמונים' אלא 'שאומרים אמן' (תלמוד בבלי, שבת קיט ע"ב).

[גִּבְעוֹת עוֹלָם   מִמַּכְפֵּלָה
שַׁעֲרֵי גַן עֵדֶן פִּתְחוּ לוֹ   וְאִמְרוּ לוֹ: 'שָׁלוֹם בּוֹאוֹ'.
מַלְאֲכֵי שָׁלוֹם   צְאוּ לִקְרָאתוֹ
שַׁעֲרֵי גַן עֵדֶן פִּתְחוּ לוֹ   וְאִמְרוּ לוֹ: 'שָׁלוֹם בּוֹאוֹ'].
שׁוֹמְרֵי גִּינְזֵי גַּן עֵדֶן,
שׁוֹמְרֵי גִּינְזֵי גַּן עֵדֶן,
פִּתְחוּ לוֹ שַׁעֲרֵי גַן עֵדֶן.
וְיָבוֹא ר' פל'וני' בְּגַן עֵדֶן
וְיִישְׁתַּעֲשֵׁיעַ מִפְּרִי גַּן עֵדֶן
מַחְמַדִּים בִּימִינוֹ   וּמַמְתַּקִּים מִשְּׁמוֹאלוֹ –
זֹאת תַּעֲנֶה וְתֹאמַר לוֹ:   'שָׁלוֹם בּוֹאוֹ'.

3–4 גבעות עולם... בואו] חסר **ו1**. 5–6 מלאכי שלום... בואו] חסר **י1 נ10 ש"ק ב"ו**. 7 שומרי] לפני השורה ישכב בשלום ויישן בשלום עד יבוא מנחם **ל** יישן בשלום וישכב בשלום עד יבוא מנחם משמיע שלום **מ** (השווה שורות [ב] 21–22). 8 שומרי גינזי... עדן] חסר **ר1**. 10 ר'] זה מר **ל** זה **ט1** רבי **ש"ק** חסר **ב"ו** פלוני] נוסף זה **מ פ2 ו1**. 11 עדן] חסר **ל**. 12 בימינו] מימינו **נ ט1 מ10 נ10 ו1 ש"ק ב"ו** וממתקים] ממתקים **ש"ק** משמאלו] בשמאלו **ש"ק**. 13 זאת] זו **ש"ק**.

3 **גבעות עולם:** כינוי לאבות ולאמהות, שרה, רבקה ולאה, השוו: "וממגד גבעות עולם' (דב' לג 15) – מלמד שאבות ואימהות קרויין גבעות, שנאמר: 'עד שיפוח היום ונסו הצללים אלך לי אל הר המור אל גבעת הלבונה' (שה"ש ד 6)' (ספרי דברים, וזאת הברכה, פסקה שנג [מהד' פינקלשטיין, עמ' 414]). 5 **מלאכי שלום:** צירוף מקראי (יש' לג 7) בניגוד למלאכי חבלה. 7 **שומרי גנזי גן עדן:** פנייה אל הדמויות הממונים על מתן רשות כניסה לזכאים להיכנס בדומה לשומרי הסף בספרות ההיכלות. **גנזי גן עדן:** השוו: "בכל ביתי' (במ' יב 7) – מלמד שהפקידו הקב"ה למשה על כל ישראל, ועל כל גנזי התורה, ועל כל גנזי חכמה, ועל כל גנזי תבונה, ועל כל גנזי מזימה, ועל כל גנזי מדע, ועל גנזי גן עדן, ועל כל גנזי חיים, והראהו כל חמודות שבעולם הזה וכל חמודות שבעו<לם> הב<א>' (אלפא ביתא דרבי עקיבא [א], צ [מהד' ילינק, עמ' 43–44]). 11 **וישתעשע:** השוו 'בחֻקֹּתיך אשתעשע' (תה' קיט 16), 'ואשתעשע במצותיך' (תה' קיט 47). **מפרי גן עדן:** לפי ההקשר כאן: מפרי עץ הדעת, כלומר בתלמוד תורה. 12 **ממחמדים... וממתקים:** כינויים לדברי תורה, השוו: 'משפטי ה' אמת צדקו יחדו. הנחמדים מזהב ומפז רב ומתוקים מדבש ונפת צופים' (תה' יט 10–11) והשוו: 'חכו ממתקים וכֻלו מחמדים זה דודי וזה רעי בנות ירושלם' (שה"ש ה 16). **זאת תענה:** לפי ההקשר אולי התורה כדמות מואנשת.

[ד] יִתְגַּדַּל וְיִתְקַדַּשׁ שְׁמֵיהּ רַבָּא בְּעָלְמָא דְהוּא עָתִיד לְחַדָּאתָא וּלְאַחֲיָיָה מֵתַיָּא
[וּלְשַׁכְלָלָא הֵיכְלָא] וּלְמִבְנֵי קַרְתָּא דִירוּשְׁלֵים וּלְמֵיעְקַר פּוּלְחָנָא נֻוכְרָאָה מֵאַרְעָנָא
וְלַאֲתָבָא קֻודְשָׁא בְּרִיךְ הוּא מְשִׁיחֵיהּ בְּמַלְכוּתֵיהּ וִיקָרֵיהּ לְאַתְרֵיהּ
בְּחַיֵּיכוֹן וּבְיוֹמֵיכוֹן [וּבְחַיֵּי] דְכָל בֵּית יִשְׂרָ‹אֵל› [בַּעֲגָלָא וּבִזְמַן קָרִיב וְאִמְרוּ אָמֵן]
[יְהֵא שְׁמֵיהּ רַבָּא מְבָרַךְ לְעָלַם וּלְעָלְמֵי עָלְמַיָּא]
יִתְבָּרַךְ וְיִשְׁתַּבַּח [וְיִתְפָּאַר וְיִתְרוֹמַם וְיִתְנַשֵּׂא וְיִתְהַדָּר וְיִתְעַלֶּה וְיִתְהַלָּל
שְׁמֵיהּ דְּקֻדְשָׁא בְּרִיךְ הוּא]
לְעֵילָּא לְעֵילָּא [מִן כָּל בִּרְכָתָא שִׁירָתָא תֻּושְׁבְּחָתָא וְנֶיחֱמָתָא דַּאֲמִירָן בְּעָלְמָא
וְאִמְרוּ אָמֵן].
יְהֵא שְׁלָמָא [רַבָּא מִן שְׁמַיָּא וְחַיִּים טוֹבִים עָלֵינוּ וְעַל כָּל יִשְׂרָאֵל וְאִמְרוּ אָמֵן].
עוֹשֶׂה שָׁלוֹם [בִּמְרוֹמָיו הוּא בְּרַחֲמָיו יַעֲשֶׂה שָׁלוֹם עָלֵינוּ וְעַל כָּל יִשְׂרָאֵל אָמֵן].

[ד] הרישום ב-פ1 ש"ק מקוצר והשלמתי על פי נ ומרבית עדי הנוסח. 1 לחדאתא] לאיתחדתא נ נ10 לחדתא ל מ ט10 י1 מ10 לאתחדתא פ 2 ר1 ב"ו לאיתחדתא ו1 לאדדתא ש"ק ולאחייה] ולאחייא ב"ו. 1–2 מתיא] מותייא ר1 נוסף ולשכללי היכלי נ ולשכללא היכלא ל מ ט10 י1 פ2 מ10 נ10 ו1 ש"ק ב"ו. 2 דירושלים] דירושלם ל י1 ר1 ו1 ש"ק ב"ו מארענא] מארעא ר1. 3 במלכותיה] למלכותיה ר1. 4 ובימיכון] או ביומיכון ש"ק. ובחיי] חסר פ1 והשלמתי על פי נ. 6 ויתהדר ויתעלה] ויתעלה ויתהדר מ ר1. 10 עלינו ועל כל ישראל] על כל ישראל ל מ ר1. 10 אמן] נוסף ועתה יי אבינו אתה אנחנו החומר ואתה יוצרנו ומעשה ידך כלנו (יש' סד 7). מודה אני לפניך [- -] יי אלהי שאני עפר ואפר רמה ותולעה עץ יבש צל עובר. ואתה יי לעולם תשב כסאך לדר ודור (איכה ה 19*) [- - -] (מטושטש – מן האמירות בשעת החזרה מבית הקברות) מ.

[ד] במקום פירוש תרגום של החלק הראשון: יתגדל ויתקדש שמו הגדול, בעולם שהוא עתיק לחדש ולהחיות את המתים / ולהקים את ההיכל, ולבנות את העיר ירושלים, ולעקור את העבודה הזרה מארצנו / ולהביא הקדוש ברוך הוא את משיחו במלכותו ובכבודו למקומו / בחייכם... .לנוסחים אחרים השוו: Andreas Lehnardt, Qaddish: Untersuchungen zur Entstehung und Rezeption eines rabbinischen Gebetes, Texts and Studies in Ancient Judaism, 87, (Tübingen: Mohr Siebeck, 2002), pp. 33–39, 309, 313–15.

Even at first glimpse it becomes clear that we have before us even with these habitual texts – not to mention occasional dirges or funeral orations which are not mentioned in the form at all – a composite *agenda mortuorum*:

[A] *Ha-Ṣur Tamim Be-Khol Po ʿal* – a Bible verse opens a long row of quatrains, sometimes in rhyme, and with many variations of a few basic sayings;

[B] Amittai, *Adam Im Yiḥye Elef Shanim* – a poem with a clear-cut opening, signed on every second line with the letters of the name of his author AMi-TaY'. What seems to be the plain continuation, with the strophic acrostic blessing *ḤaZaQ* ('be strong'), shows already indicates a digression in content and form in the direction of the persecutions by the Crusaders in the Rhine valley in the summer of 1096 and towards a quatrain with an acrostic using the last four letters of the Hebrew alphabet at the head of each line;

[C] *Avot Olam Yeshenei Ḥevron* – another poem with a complex structure but united in its elaboration of one situation by way of a dialogic lyric;

[D] Qaddish *Le-Itḥaddeta* – a variation of the most important Aramaic prose prayer in the synagogal liturgy.[28]

And so the question arises whether this is a mere accumulation of texts or whether we assume a kind of composition, but, in the case of the latter, we must also ask how the assumption of a composition can tolerate such a blatant doublet as:

[A] Man whether one year (old)
Or living a thousand years
What real value has he, when he ceases to exit?
Blessed be the true judge!

[B] (A) Man, if you could live a thousand years
exercising your reign forward and back,
(*Mi*) bereft of your fortune you will go down to darkness
and stand in trial before God who shows no kindness.

Duplicate passages are not uncommon in Hebrew liturgy. The high esteem accorded to tradition even in the case of parallel, or 'rival', formulations is demonstrated by the tendency to coalesce such variations, or as Rav Papa, the mid-fourth-century Babylonian Amora put it: *hilekakh nimrenhu le-trawehu*. But there was also a system of constantly replacing such passages by reformulating them either in artificial prose or in poetic form and the doubling was the result of retaining the former text together with its later substitute. This amounted to a rejection of the basic concept of Hebrew liturgical poetry, which

28 For versions, sources and development of this form of the *qaddish*, see Andreas Lehnardt, *Qaddish: Untersuchungen zur Entstehung und Rezeption eines rabbinischen Gebetes*, Texts and Studies in Ancient Judaism, 87 (Tübingen: Mohr Siebeck, 2002), pp. 39–42, 235–43.

came into being, and continued to be a creative force in synagogal literature, for the following four basic reasons:

a. replacing prose sentences in benediction(s) of the long form within a composition of benedictions like the *qeriyat shema'* and its surrounding blessings, the *'amida* etc;[29]
b. replacing prose 'bridges' to fixed biblical verses in statutory prayers;
c. adding proems before statutory text units;
d. replacing *piyyuṭ*.

Bearing in mind that these four considerations define the framework for the creation of some ten thousand pieces of liturgical poetry in medieval Hebrew literature, we may assume that there was also a text at the end of the ninth century in southern Italy that was routinely used in the burial ceremony and that could be replaced with a poetical alternative.

3

Adam Im Yiḥye Elef Shanim – the *piyyuṭ* of Amittai as attesting to *Ha-Ṣur Tamim Be-Khol Po 'al*

A poem for the burial ceremony was apparently composed by a poet named Amittai who is seems to be known to us from other poems but mainly through the *Chronicle of Aḥima'aṣ*, even if it remains uncertain whether he was Amittai the Elder (Oria, mid ninth century) or his grandson, Amittai birebbi Shefaṭya (Oria around 900 CE) mentioned there.[30] As already shown, this poem resembles parts of *Ha-Ṣur Tamim Be-Khol Po'al*, especially the central part, lines 27–42:

- a rebuke (*tokheḥa*) that leads to the acknowledgment that God is the eternal judge ([A] lines 27–30 / [B] lines 1–8);

29 For the criteria used in the analysis of the different forms of benedictions in order to distinguish between the statutory and the private in rabbinic prayer, see Joseph Heinemann, *Prayer in the Talmud: Forms and Patterns*, Studia Judaica, 9, (Berlin, New York, DeGruyter, 1977), pp. 158–92.

30 The source of the discussion concerning this identification is in Robert Bonfil, *History and Folklore in a Medieval Jewish Chronicle: The Family Chronicle of Aḥima'az ben Paltiel*, Studies in Jewish History and Culture, 22 (Leiden, Boston, Brill, 2009), p. 384. I prefer to regard the grandson as the author, mainly because of the author's prosodic sophistication in signing his name at the head and in the middle of the strophes and thus dividing the quatrains into hemistichs. For the patterns of strophic acrostics by the ninth-century Apulian *payyeṭanim* Silano or Shefaṭya BiRebbi Amittai, see Peter Sh. Lehnardt, 'Studies' (n. 10 above), pp. 36–38

- a section with the rhetoric of a penitential poem (*seliḥa*) that articulates a plea for forgiveness in the forthcoming trial of the deceased, while recalling the merits of the fathers ([A] lines 31–38 / [B] lines 9–12 and the part marked by**;
- an invitation to earn merit by taking part in the burial and by escorting the dead body to its resting place ([A] lines 39–42 / [B] lines 13–16).

In spite of these common topoi, the two compositions later develop in different directions. While *Ha-Ṣur Tamim* turns into a reprise designed to bring the escorting congregation and the mourning relatives to an acceptance of the death as a deed of divine righteousness ([A] lines 43–74), the continuation of Amittai's poem focuses on the place of the deceased in his grave but not without broadening the horizon into a quest for redemption and peace for the whole congregation.

Such a variation of focus might reflect the different settings of the two compositions, one a confrontation with death while escorting the dead to the cemetery, the other an attendance at the interment and a recital of the first words of consolation. If the two texts had even slightly different settings within the ceremony the recurrence of topics in the cumulative line-up would be less disturbing. A similar argument might be used in connection with the iterative character of *Ha-Ṣur Tamim*, especially if the congregation was not standing listening but, rather, making progress toward the cemetery, at a more expeditious rate than the rhetoric of the poem.

Turning once more to the rhetoric of the poem written by Amittai, we can (as already noted) discern between, on the one hand, the two quatrains divided into two hemistichs by the four-letter acrostic yielding the name of its author, and, on the other, the three quatrains yielding in their opening letters the word *ḥazaq*. The copyist-redactor of MS Paris inserted at the point of transition a quatrain that serves in the popular tradition as a final concord of *Ha-Ṣur Tamim* and thus becomes at this point a response constituting a congregational consent to the rebuke about the *condition humain* issued by Amittai.

After the first subsequent quatrain (to the letter *ḥ*, lines 9–12) – a plea formulated in the first person plural for the forgiveness of sins as befitting the final section of any penitential poem – we find in all Italian testimonies the relic of a half quatrain and then a complete quatrain of a *seliḥa*-like poem that recalls, among the 'merits of the fathers', not only the binding of Isaac but also the martyrdom of the congregations in Ashkenaz in the summer of 1096:

[B**] For the sake of the blood shed in the year 856 (= 1096 CE)
Who gave their life and their goods to make Your Holy Name one.
The merit of the only son, bound at the age of thirty seven
And according Your command handed over for slaughter
and in the end a ram was singled out instead of him

5 You promised (that he would be) kept (in mind) for generations to come
for the sake of those who worship You with love and fear
Just like our teachers who were in the year KaLU (= [48]56 = 1096 CE)
extinguished all together

These lines are characteristic of the penitential poems written in and around the Rhine valley after the persecutions of 1096 during the twelfth century, even if the precise poem has not yet been identified in any of the Ashkenazi sources.[31] What we may assume is that these lines, together with a number of liturgical compositions, either originated in the first centre of Ashkenazi Judaism that was established in Italy as early as the eleventh and twelfth centuries[32] or were brought by one of the Italian scholars studying in thirteenth-century Ashkenaz, such as Yesh'aya di Trani or, more likely by members of the Anaw family of Rome, given the crucial influence they had on the final redaction of the Roman rite.

The copyist-redactor of MS Paris transcribed, after this martyrological passage, one of the last 'quatrains'[33] of *Ha-Ṣur Tamim*. He seems to have been guided by an association of ideas. After mentioning *allufenu* ('our teachers', 'our masters'), he turns in direct speech to the *ḥakhamim* ('the skilled', 'the learned') of the (broader) congregation:

*** See, wise man, and prepare in the heart[34]
Because there is no test at the day of death
Like the blood[35] of a honest and righteous man:
'The LORD has given, and the LORD has taken away,
blessed be the name of the LORD' (Job 1:21).

---

31 Cf. Leopold Zunz, *Literaturgeschichte der synagogalen Poesie* (Berlin: Louis Gerschel Verlagsbuchhandlung, 1865), p. 167–68, Abraham David, 'Historical Records of the Persecutions during the First Crusade in Hebrew Printed Works and Hebrew Manuscripts', in Yom Tov Assis [et. al.] (eds.), *Facing the Cross: The Persecutions of 1096 in History and Historiography* (Hebrew; Jerusalem: Magnes, 2000), pp. 199–200.

32 See the fragment of an Italian *maḥzor* with Ashkenazi elements in the eleventh-century MS Cambridge, CUL T-S H12.23, but the most important document for this phenomenon of Ashkenazi 'feedback' to Italy is the *Seder Ḥibbur Berakhot*, mentioned above on p. 7.

33 This four-liner is structured not with a rhyme but according to a four-unit rhythm (*Ha-Miqṣav Ha-Merubba'*), a basic feature in the Hebrew poetry of Late Antiquity, in which the biblical clausula is here stressed by adding, as in many *silluq* endings, an extra third unit.

34 The strange expression *we-hakhinu 'al lev* seems to derive from a combination of the more idiomatic phrase שימו על לב ('take to heart') with the wording of a verse like: משמועה רעה לא יירא נכון לבו בטח בה' (Ps 112:7) according to an interpretation influenced by the use of the phrase שמועה רעה in *mBer*. 9. 2.

35 Taking into account that all other manuscripts read *dibber* ('he said'), the phrasing *dam* is an interesting interweaving of ideas by the redactor, or a slip of the pen caused by dragging the subject of the former strophe into this line.

The original continuation of the *ḥ* strophe (lines 9–12) with its penitential rhetoric was far more focused on the situation of the burial ceremony. The *z* strophe (lines 13–16) parallels the two courses, that of man towards death and that of the congregation escorting the dead to their final rest. It appeals to the public to earn merits in a last act of solidarity since such an act, like the fate of the one to be buried and to be hidden from the eyes of the living, is known before God.

This combination of the concrete and the universal is continued in the final *q* strophe (lines 17–22) taking the *Vorlage* in *Ha-Ṣur Tamim* into new directions. The word 'peace' serves as a bridge between the wish expressed over the last resting-place of the dead in the grave and the hoped-for announcement of the redemption. And all this would fit well with the image of Amittai of Oria as a skilled author of liturgical poetry if we had not before us a ninth-century epitaph for Rabbi Barukh from nearby Brindisi:

Epitaph of Rebbi Barukh ben Rebbi Yona	Final section of the poem of Amittai
[מ]שכב רבי ברוך בן רבי יונ[ה]	[ב]
פה הרגיע במרגוע נפש ר[בי]	
ברוך בן רבי יונה נוח נפש	[...]
מבן שישים ושמונה שנים	קוֹל נִשְׁמַע מְבַשֵּׂר שָׁלוֹם
יהי שלום על מנוחתו	רְצוֹן יְרֵיאָיו עוֹשֶׂה שָׁלוֹם
קול נשמע מבשר שלום רצון	שִׁמְעוּ דְּבַר שָׁלוֹם
יראיו עושה שלום שמעו	תָּנוּחַ נַפְשׁוֹ בְּמִשְׁכָּבוֹ בְּשָׁלוֹם.
דבר שלום ינוח נפשו משכבו	יִשְׁכַּב בְּשָׁלוֹם / וְיִישַׁן בְּשָׁלוֹם
בשלום	עַד יָבוֹא מְנַחֵם מַשְׁמִיעַ שָׁלוֹם.

It seems to me that Amittai took the well-known ending, as attested by the epitaph, of an older and anonymous alphabetical poem – which had a different prosodic allocation of the acrostic, in the form of one letter per line[36] but basically the same four unit rhythm scheme – and used it, in a typically medieval process of thought and craftsmanship, as a literary spolia for the rhetorically elaborated cap-stone of his poem. If this, or any subsequent, precentor was the sole speaker who was addressing his rebuke to the public (lines 1–8), his use of a familiar element of tradition by way of conclusion turned his voice

36 Compare the archaic styled dirges in Aramaic as in *Jewish Palestinian Aramaic Poetry from Late Antiquity* ed. by Michael Sokoloff and Joseph Yahalom (Aramaic and Hebrew; Jerusalem: The Israel Academy of Sciences and Humanities, 1999), pp. 282–323, and see, for an example in Hebrew based on this pattern, *Iggeret Ḥatuma Ha-Yom Niftaḥat*, as in Israel Davidson, *Genizah Studies in Memory of Doctor Solomon Schechter, III: Liturgical and Secular Poetry*, Texts and Studies of the Jewish Theological Seminary of America, 9 (New York: The Jewish Theological Seminary of America, 1928), pp. 263–64.

into one of public consent, similar to the use of the first person plural at the end of the *Ha-Ṣur Tamim* (lines 71–74) in the popular version of the Roman rite.[37]

Of central significance for our understanding of the literary aspect of the burial ceremony in southern Italy is the fact that in the days of Amittai there was a living tradition of poetic embellishment within a given frame and there is even an eleventh-century source concerning this period that appears to support such a suggestion:

> Once, he (= Amittai b. Shefaṭya) went out to his vineyard and to his estate (= outside Oria), and on that day a stranger (*akhsenai*) died, a wise and God-fearing man, and the elders of the community sent word to him, to join them in attending the dead who had nobody else to attend him, to proceed to bury him, to mourn, eulogize and honour him, as is commanded by the Law. He sent word to them: 'You go out of the city and I will await your arrival and will come with you to the cemetery and recite well-ordered lamentations.'
>
> All the community came out to bury him, R. Amittai prepared a eulogy to mourn him, and all the community cried and mourned for him. R. Amittai eulogized him with a dirge that he composed for him, and this is the beginning of the dirge that he began to recite:
>
> אִי אַכְסַנְיָא, אִי גָלוּת
> מִי לֹא יַכִּירֵךְ יַעֲשֶׂה מִמֵּךְ הוֹלֵלוּת
> וּמִי יַכִּירֵךְ יְקוֹנֵן בִּילָלוֹת
>
> O (temporary) lodging, O exile
> He who does not know you may speak superficially of you,
> But he who knows you will mourn with moaning.[38]

The discrepancy between the religious duty to escort the bier of a Torah scholar (*ḥakham*) and the fact that the man is nameless and defined only as stranger is a challenge for the Jewish community of Oria and for Amittai. How could the latter bring the congregation from a mere act of human solidarity to an honest mourning of the fate of a stranger. Amittai accepted the challenge, as he had promised, and makes a connection by means of the word *akhsaniya* – a lodging facility for the wayfarer – the situation of the stranger, the *akhsenai* – both words based on the Greek word ξένος – with the existential situation of the Jews in Italy. They for their part were living as strangers in exile from Ereṣ Israel under Byzantine rule and Amittai is therefore able, in the absence of family ties, to encourage the congregation to weep by appealing

---

37 Compare the far less skilled use of the Italian tradition in a Genizah fragment of the *Seder Rav Amram*, MS Oxford, Bodleian Library Heb. c. 20, f. 16; see *Seder Rav Amram Gaon*, ed. by Daniel Goldschmidt (Hebrew; Jerusalem: Mossad Harav Kook, 1972), p. 187.
38 Robert Bonfil, *History and Folklore* (see n. 30 above), pp. 308–11 (§ 41).

to an existential common denominator. While we may assume in the case of the poem *Adam Im Yiḥye Elef Shanim* that the private and public ties to the deceased are a given fact and that Amittai therefore opens with a universal *tokheḥa* based on the *condition humain*, such a universal appeal could not work in this case where the stranger has no family or other social ties. The use of a foreign word, even if well established in Hebrew and Aramaic from talmudic times onwards, in a Hebrew ceremony that demonstrates by the use of Hebrew poetry the new Jewish cultural group identity as a Hebrew literate people among a Greek speaking majority, may serve as a trigger for the release of feelings of estrangement[39] and may arouse a longing for the peace referred to in the final stanza (lines 17–22) as well as an agreement to 'mourn with moaning'.

This scene might also shed some light on the agenda of the ceremony and permit a possible reconstruction: (a) the community (*'eda*) brought the deceased to the cemetery outside the town; (b) here Amittai joins the funeral and takes the lead with a new composed dirge; and (c) from here on the ceremony continues with the interment. If we parallel this agenda with the order in the Roman rite, we may be justified in seeing in the long formula of [A] *Ha-Ṣur Tamim* a kind of litany that routinely accompanied the escorting of the bier to the cemetery. There, as the subject changed from a justification of the deeds of God towards the fate of man, a precentor like Amittai could insert [B] a dirge that was specific to the deceased, from a stock of dirges for a man, woman, child, *kohen* or *levi* etc[40] or was written ad hoc,[41] and then the ceremony would continue with texts like [C] *Avot 'Olam* and [D] a final *qaddish*.

The analysis of *Adam Im Yiḥye Elef Shanim* by Amittai leads to our first important conclusions for the understanding of the history of *Ha-Ṣur Tamim Be-Khol Po'al*. There was a version used as a matter of routine at burial ceremonies in Southern Italy in the ninth century. This version was obviously understood as having two parts, with an opening focusing on God as performing

---

39 The background to this is recorded in the *Chronicle of Aḥima'aṣ* which reports that the Jews have lived for generations in Oria and have, as reported about Amittai, houses in the town and land or agricultural estates in the countryside.

40 Compare the collection of dirges mentioned above in n. 36, and see also, for rich collections of Hebrew *misped* poems, examples in the Yemenite rite: *Sefer Ha-Tikhlal: Siddur Tefilla Qadmon ke-Minhag Yehudei Teyman* (*Tikhlal Qadmonim*) (Jerusalem: Joosef S. Habareh, 1964), ff. 81a–84b.

41 This may mean that on the one hand only the strophes signed AMiTaY ([B] lines 1–8) are undoubtedly his, the *ḤaZaQ* strophes ([B] lines 9–22) constituting an already traditional poetic bridge to the following texts, as seems in any case very likely for the final stanza. On the other hand, Amittai is the first known *payyeṭan* in Italy to use the letters of the term *ḥazaq*, which is already known from acrostics of the classical period in Byzantine Ereṣ Yisrael, as the opening letters of three subsequent strophes.

just deeds in creation and judgement and a second section reflecting the *condition humain* and leading into the ceremonial frame and the texts that accompanied the act of committing the deceased to his final rest. Thus, we may take the year 900 as a *terminus ante quem* for the institutionalized use – and existence – of a version of *Ha-Ṣur Tamim Be-Khol Po'al*. The tempting question that therefore arises is whether there are any hints that might help to determine the original date of a first version of this poem.

4

For most, if not all, Hebrew poetry we have virtually no autographs before the eleventh century and this latter date is possible mainly because of the extraordinary existence of the fragments from the Cairo Genizah.[42] If we acknowledge that Amittai wrote his *Adam Im Yiḥye Elef Shanim* in creative response to some of the strophes of the anonymous *Ha-Ṣur Tamim*, we may hardly expect to find an 'original' copy by the author himself, or from soon after its date of creation, that could give us a clue as to its place and date of origin. But there are features of prosody and style that might enable us to determine its approximate place on the line of development of liturgical poetry up to the ninth century.[43]

The obvious fact that the poem is written in quatrains defines the earliest possible date as in the second half, if not the end of, the sixth century, when the arrangement in strophic forms, especially in quatrains, became predominant and subsequently the most popular form in the history of Hebrew poetry. But even a dating at this early period of the so-called classical (= strophic) *piyyuṭ* in Ereṣ Yisrael is hard to accept, given the fact that the strophic poems are mostly arranged in an alphaetic acrostic or signed with the name of the author, and that only very distinct parts of compositions (such as *Piyyuṭ* IV or a *silluq*) could be denied this literary device.

Another criterion in the prosodic development of Hebrew liturgical poetry is the matter of the rhyme. While this norm dates from the sixth century and

---

42 See, for example, Shulamit Elizur, *Poet at a Turning Point: Rabbi Yehoshua Bar Khalfa and His Poetry* (Hebrew; Jerusalem: Yad Ben-Zvi, 1994), pp. 19–25, 82–89, pl. 7, 8, 9–11 (drafts in cursive), 1–2, 3–6, 13–14, 15–16 (clean copies in a square script).

43 Any attempt of this kind with regard to a later period would be more difficult due to the fact that the ninth century saw the beginning of the regional diversity of creative centres of Hebrew liturgical poetry, and the recognition that a *piyyuṭ* found only in southern Italy gives no hint about its place of origin.

is based on the identity of sound made by the consonant before the last vowel at the end of each prosodic unit, the poets of the classical period in Ereṣ Yisrael, and later in the classicistic renewal of their norms in Italy and Ashenaz in the tenth to the twelfth centuries, knew how to adjoin to this combination of sounds in the rhymed syllable one or more sounds based on an additional root consonant, even where this sequence was interrupted by another vowel, or even consonant, and thus to create rich assonances that augmented the basic rhyme.[44] For a moment it seems that we also find in *Ha-Ṣur Tamim* augmented rhymes, but almost immediately it becomes clear that any stanzas do not comply even with the minimal principle of rhyme. Rhyming primarily means an act of abstraction under one formal aspect of words, namely, their sequence of sounds. This abstraction enables the poet to create – and the listener to experience – new combinations of words having in common the final sound(s). Here we find iterations if not of the same root then of exactly the same word. Together with the numerous repetitions of the same opening words, this prosodic device calls to mind the lining up of sounds in the so-called pre-classical (= non strophic) Hebrew liturgical poetry. A *payeṭan* like Yose ben Yose could choose a relevant *Leitwort* to end all the lines of a non-strophic composition with an alphabetic acrostic,[45] but a closer look reveals that the rhymes of *Ha-Ṣur Tamim* are not reminiscent of the early strata of Hebrew liturgical poetry but of the post-classical strata from the ninth century onwards. Besides two plain 'quatrains' (lines 55–58, 67–71), which resemble in their rhythmic division both the surrounding quatrains and the opening biblical verse, the basic rhyme norm is consonant-vowel (cf. lines 43–46) or consonant-vowel-consonant (cf. lines 3–6).[46] Any shift of stress is irrelevant to the rhyme (cf.

44 A description of the historical development of Hebrew prosody and much of its terminology was first suggested by Benjamin Hrushovski, 'Prosody, Hebrew', *Encyclopaedia Judaica* (1970), 13, cols. 1195–1240. See now *Encyclopaedia Judaica* 2nd ed. (2007), 16, cols. 595–623, abridged in T. Carmi (ed.), *The Penguin Book of Hebrew Verse* (London, New York: Penguin, 1981), pp. 57–72. For a new enlarged edition of this analytic survey, see Benjamin Harshav, *The History of Hebrew Versification: From Bible to Modernism* (Hebrew; Ramat-Gan: Bar-Ilan University, 2008).

45 For his *Teqi'atot* for Rosh Ha-Shana (New Year), see *Maḥzor La-Yamim Ha-Noraim, Le-Fi Minhagei Benei Ashkenaz Le-Khol Anfehem, I. Rosh Ha-Shana*, ed. by Daniel Goldschmidt (Jerusalem, New York: Koren, Leo Baeck Institute, 1970), pp. 238–42, 251–56, 265–70; *Yosse Ben Yosse: Poems*, ed. Aharon Mirsky, (Hebrew; Jerusalem: Mossad Bialik, 1991), pp. 93–117.

46 All Hebrew poets, especially but not exclusively in the area of liturgical poetry, adhered to this norm of Hebrew rhyme until even the twentieth century when the rhyme norm of the majority culture was from the last vowel onward as in Arabic poetry, or in the poetry of Romance or Germanic languages. This may be one of the seemingly marginal testimonies to the centrality of liturgical poetry for training the ears of Hebrew poets, whatever the differences in their emerging pronunciations, over a period of some 1400 years.

3–6).[47] But the rhyme may also be based solely on suffixes;[48] only on the common sound of a grammatical ending;[49] or on similar vowels like o/u/.[50] Another technique of 'rhyming' in *Ha-Ṣur Tamim* involves using variations of the same root, which may be found fairly often as a local solution according the morphology of Semitic languages, but seldom occurs in classical poetry as a solution for complete strophes (cf. lines 9–12), or simply the same word. All these are found in the corpora of liturgical poetry from the end of the ninth to the eleventh century, the period of the so-called post-classical late oriental *piyyuṭ*.[51] From this era we also have the first Hebrew poems that were written not for the embellishment of the statutory prayers but as songs to be sung during gatherings to perform a *miṣwa* especially within the life cycle, such as circumcision,[52] marriage, and the final escort towards burial, as well as for the Sabbath and festival meals.[53]

In a world of intensive creativity on the part of Hebrew liturgical poetry mainly up to the twelfth-thirteenth century), we find consistent incursions by liturgical poetry and, even when poetic versions of most of the services became more and more canonized in the different rites, the genres of occasional poetry for the life cycle and for paraliturgical gatherings was still left in the hand of the precentors. This general and well-attested picture of a transition of the focus of creativity from the liturgical ceremonies to their margins and to paraliturgical contexts, seems to require at least a minor correction with regard to the burial ceremony and the Jewish culture of Christian Europe, especially in Ashkenaz. Although we have texts and testimonies for the composition of per-

---

47 This is the norm for all Hebrew rhyme until the encounter with distinctly tonic poetry in Romance languages, as in Christian Spain or Italy.

48 The syllable of the rhyme may be based on four different consonants -KhAW, -TAW, -NAW and -DAW in one quatrain (cf. lines 59–62)!

49 Again, the syllable of the rhyme may be based on different consonants: -RIM, -DIM (lines 39–40) or -NIM, -MIM (lines 49–50).

50 See lines 23–24: -NO (3×) -NU.

51 Cf. for an examination of a cycle of *yoṣerot* compositions from about the year 900 in Ereṣ Yisrael or Syria, see Shulamit Elizur, *The Piyyutim of Rabbi El`azar Birabbi Ḳillar* (Hebrew; Jerusalem: Magnes, 1988), pp. 64–66 and for a thorough description of the use of rhyme toward the end of the classical period, see Elizur, *The Liturgical Poems of Rabbi Pinḥas Ha-Kohen: Critical edition, Introduction and Commentaries* (Hebrew; Jerusalem: Word Union of Jewish Studies; The David Moses and Amalia Rosen Foundation, 2004), pp. 166–76.

52 See, for example, one of the earliest datable *Shirei Zemer* for this occasion: *Panaw Yaer Ṣur Le-ḥonnehu*, in Elizur, *The Liturgical Poems of Rabbi Pinḥas Ha-Kohen* (above n. 51), p. 740 and compare pp. 20–21.

53 See, example, for Italy of the ninth and tenth centuries. Zvi Malachi, '*Qoveṣ Shirei-Zemer shel Payṭanei Italya Ha-Qadmonim*', in *Yad Le-Heman: The A. M. Habermann Memorial Volume*, ed. Zvi Malachi (Lod: Habermann Institute, 1984), pp. 73–102.

sonal creations or the rewriting of traditional ones for the mourning ceremonies of the Jews in the Arabic-speaking Mediterranean culture,[54] and, as we have seen above, a specifically documented case in Apulia around the year 900, Ashkenazi Judaism finally opted for an approach that did not tally with these others. It saw *Ha-Ṣur Tamim* not as liturgical poetry that could be replaced at least in part but as a statutory text to be recited (by the individual) in the hour of death and at the funeral.[55] This might go back to a process attested in a halakhic responsum attributed to Rashi:

> I found in the name of Rabbenu Shelomo z"l: It is customary to say the *ṣidduq ha-din* at the moment the soul departs but one should wait for the sake of [according] honour and say it in the courtyard of the cemetery or at the opening of the burial cave, may you rest in peace [*sic*]. Once they conducted a burial on the intermediate days of a festival and they did not want to say either a *ṣidduq ha-din* or a *qaddish*, because the *qaddish* is recited because of the (biblical) verses of the *ṣidduq ha-din*. And a Rabbi stood up and said over him the *ṣidduq ha-din* and a *qaddish*, because they are neither eulogy nor dirge and this is not a case of a desecration of the festival but a confession and an acceptance of the judgement from heaven [...] And I do not know a reason for this severity (of implementing the religious rules), but the people of Israel are sages, and are the children of sages, and if they are not prophets, they are the children of prophets, and a custom that hey learned from their fathers is religious law that may not expanded or contracted. [...] so far the words of Rabbenu Shelomo z"l.[56]

The *ṣidduq ha-din* mentioned here is certainly to be identified as *Ha-Ṣur Tamim Be-Khol Po ʿal*, the only such known text in the Ashkenazi tradition, and it reveals another aspect of its nature that goes beyond the dialectics of personal performance versus more general, public participation. It is not only the halakhic concept that you have to recite something that might be referred to as study of Torah in order to fulfil the conditions for reciting a *qaddish* that makes *Ha-Ṣur Tamim* part of a dialogue. A closer look makes it clear that this dialogue is not only against the background of *halakha* or *piyyuṭ*, or like Amittai's dialogue with the congregation's particular agenda; it has, as a matter of fact, a

54 See, for example, Menaḥem Ben Saruq, *Afqid Ḥamasi Be-Yad El*, his letter for help from Ḥasdai Ibn Shaprut (ed. Schirmann, p. 23, lines 281–88).

55 Cf. for example: 'Tzidduk Hadin. A declaration of submission to the justice of the Divine judgement, by which the Burial Service is called. This faith is derived from such verses embodied in the text, *Hatzur tamim po'alo* (Deut. 32:4) [...] Following this prayer [...]', Macy Nulman, *The Encyclopedia of Jewish Prayer: Ashkenazic and Sephardic Rites*, (Northvale, NJ; London: Jason Aronson, 1993), pp. 326–27 (citation, p. 326) – nothing remains of the original setting within liturgical poetry.

56 *Shibbolei Ha-Leqeṭ Ha-Shalem*, ed. S. Buber (Vilna: Witwe und Brüder Romm, 1887), fol. 172b; cf. the annotated reprint in *Responsa, Rashi, Solomon ben Isaac* ed. by Israel Elfenbein (New York: Schlesinger, 1943), p. 301.

very literary character. Precisely what we described as predictable rhymesat a very low level of innovation are paralleled by the frequent use of biblical idioms and expressions. Both these styles, together with the possible use of a biblical verse as a refrain, create an intensive dialogue between the text as it plays out and the anticipation felt by the community members according to their literary knowledge and even if they have only a basic Hebrew. Maybe all this disqualifies *Ha-Ṣur Tamim* as a specimen of classical Hebrew liturgical poetry but it might explain its success as congregational poetry and as a canonical text-form only a few generations after its first formulation.[57] Even if *Ha-Ṣur Tamim* may hardly serve as an example of the sublime in Hebrew poetry, it certainly functions successfully as the correct text for a situation that is based on the participation not only of the intellectual elite but of all kinds of members in a local congregation.

5

The period under discussion constituted a new era in which Jewish communities not only followed the classical option of renewal according to older traditions but also developed new patterns of presentation – especially with musial aspects – involving various forms of participation on the part of the congregation. We shall now attempt to demonstrate how we can, on the threshold of such a period, read *ṣidduq ha-din* in the Italian rite as the reception of an obviously non classical text which amounted to a ceremony with the proposed purpose of public participation.

For this task we have to introduce into our research a basic shift of perspective on the burial ceremony. It has now to be viewed not only as the framework for the inhumation of the dead in Jewish tradition but also as a '*rite de passage*' of the mourners according the model of the ethnographer and folklorist Arnold van Gennep.[58]

He basically identifies three phases of the ceremony: (a) the *préliminaire* separation from a statically perceived 'world of old'; (b) a central *liminaire* phase of transition; and (c) the *postliminaire* re-incorporation in a new status quo. In the course of the past hundred years, his identification has proved to

57 See, in this volume, Ruth Langer's study of the different textual traditions in the European rites.

58 Arnold van Gennep, *Les rites de passage: étude systématique des rites de la porte et du seuil* (1909) (Paris: Gallimard, 1981) and see, for an application of this approach: Margaret Alexiou, *The Ritual Lament in Greek Tradition* (London: Cambridge University Press, 1974).

be a helpful tool for understanding ceremonies as a routine framework employed by the congregation in order to cope with the uncertainties of the liminal stage.

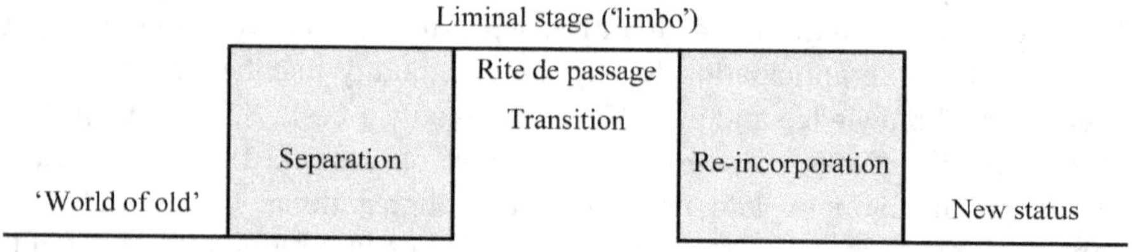

And implemented at a funeral:

death → burial ceremony → grave

or:
confrontation with the death → burial ceremony → living without the deceased

The liturgical texts within the ceremony function, in a manner of speaking, as a bridge over the troubled waters of the liminal stage of the mourning[59] not only by their form ('because something has to be said') but also by their content and – as reflected in the basic choice of language in the Hebrew renaissance in southern Italy – by the *religio* of the national and ancient literary tradition.

Looking again at the *ṣidduq ha-din* in the Roman rite of Rome as a composite *agenda mortuorum*, we can discern that the different parts are focused on, or append different subjects:

[A] *Ha-Ṣur Tamim Be-Khol Po 'al* is focused on the righteousness of the powerful deeds of God, the creator and judge, as foundations of the world order;

[B] Amittai, *Adam Im Yiḥye Elef Shanim* adds the perspective of the vacuity of mankind in the world order and the need for a plea for mercy and for a reference to the merits of former generations;

59 Some of the texts in the ceremony also refer also to the deceased's change of status, as if he is to be seen as the subject of a transition, but we here follow the basic approach of van Gennep to a society of human beings. Thus, the report of what happens to the deceased, his body or his soul, is primarily considered as a process in the world of the mourners. The puzzling Janus-faced *rites de passage* at a funeral and the related literary reflections within the community concerning the fate of the dead and the living in the liminal phase after a death should be mentioned here only as a broader theme to be dealt with elsewhere; but see, for an example of literary and imaginary communication between these mirrored worlds: Varda Padva, 'The Voice of the Dead in the Elegy', *Jerusalem Studies in Hebrew Literature*, 10–11 (Hebrew; 1987–1988), pp. 629–59.

[D] *Qaddish Le-Itḥaddeta* strikes a more positive note, beyond the limits of the specific burial, and speaks about the timeless holiness of God and the hope for holiness within the time and space of Israel, and for peace.

So what might be the special contribution of *Avot 'Olam Yeshenei Ḥevron* as the third section, between the last lines of the poem opened by Amittai and closing with the phrase 'may he rest in peace on his bier', and the final universal sounds of the *qaddish*?

We have already encountered epitaph evidence from Southern Italy as an early testimony to texts otherwise attested, at the earliest, only in late thirteenth-century manuscripts:

Epitaph of Lea, daughter of Yefe Mazal

פה שכ[ב]ת לאה בת יפה מזל
שתהא נפשא בצרור החיים
שהיא נפטרת משחרב בית
המקדש עד מותה שבע מאות
וששים וארבעה שנה וימי חייה
היו שבע עשר שנה והק'ב'ה' יזכה
אותה להקים נפשה עים הצדקת[ה]
ותבוא שלום ותנוח על מנוחתה.
שומרי גינזי גן עדן פיתחו לה שער[י]
גן עדן ותבוא לאה לגן עדן פיתחו
לה שערי גן עדן מחמדים בימינה
וממתקים בישמואלה זאת תענה
ותאמר לה זה דודי וזה ריעי[60]

Part of the *ṣidduq ha-din* ceremony

[C] אֲבוֹת עוֹלָם, יְשֵׁנֵי חֶבְרוֹן,
שַׁעֲרֵי גַן עֵדֶן פִּתְחוּ לוֹ וְאִמְרוּ לוֹ: 'שָׁלוֹם בּוֹאוֹ'.
גִּבְעוֹת עוֹלָם מִמַּכְפֵּלָה
שַׁעֲרֵי גַן עֵדֶן פִּתְחוּ לוֹ וְאִמְרוּ לוֹ: 'שָׁלוֹם בּוֹאוֹ'.
מַלְאֲכֵי שָׁלוֹם צְאוּ לִקְרָאתוֹ
שַׁעֲרֵי גַן עֵדֶן פִּתְחוּ לוֹ וְאִמְרוּ לוֹ: 'שָׁלוֹם בּוֹאוֹ'.
שׁוֹמְרֵי גִּינְזֵי גַן עֵדֶן,
שׁוֹמְרֵי גִּינְזֵי גַן עֵדֶן,
פִּתְחוּ לוֹ שַׁעֲרֵי גַן עֵדֶן.
וְיָבוֹא ר' פל'וני' בְּגַן עֵדֶן
וְיִשְׁתַּעֲשֵׁיעַ מִפְּרִי גַן עֵדֶן
מַחְמַדִּים בִּימִינוֹ וּמַמְתַּקִּים מִשְּׂמוֹאלוֹ –
זֹאת תַּעֲנֶה וְתֹאמַר לוֹ: 'שָׁלוֹם בּוֹאוֹ'.

This epitaph from Brindisi, as that of Rabbi Barukh of Oria, mentioned above, is bipartite: a first part with the personal data and a second one with a literary text. We learn from the first part (lines 1–8) that the epitaph is dedicated to the memory of Leah, the daughter of Eutychos – here in the hebraized form *Yefe Mazal*, who died at the age of 17 in the year 764 after the destruction

60 First published by Graziadio Isaia Ascoli, 'Iscrizioni inedite o malnote, greche, latine, ebraiche, di antichi sepolcri giudaici del Napolitano', in: *Atti del IV Congresso Internazionale degli Orientalisti, tenuto in Firenze nel settembre 1878*, I, (Firenze: Arnaldo Forni, 1880), pp. 298–299 (# 24), pl. VIII, cf. Shlomo Simonsohn, 'The Hebrew revival among early medieval European Jews', in: Saul Lieberman (ed.), *Salo Wittmayer Baron Jubilee Volume*, (Jerusalem: American Academy for Jewish Research, 1974), II, pp. 853, n. 60; Cesare Colafemmina, 'Hebrew Inscriptions of the Early Medieval Period in Southern Italy', in: Bernard D. Cooperman – Barbara Garvin (eds.), *The Jews of Italy: Memory and Identity* (Studies and Texts in Jewish History and Culture, 7), (Bethesda: University Press of Maryland, 2000), pp. 78, 81.

of the temple (= 832 CE) – while in the second part we see again a partial adaptation of a text from the *ṣidduq ha-din* ceremony.

[C] Fathers of the world,[61] sleepers in Hebron,
open the gates of paradise for him and say to him: 'He shall come in peace!'
Eternal hills,[62] from Makhpela,
open the gates of paradise for him and say to him: 'He shall come in peace!'
Angels of peace, go to meet him,
open the gates of paradise for him and say to him: 'He shall come in peace!'
Guardians of the hoards of paradise,
Guardians of the hoards of paradise,
open the gates of paradise for him
and Rabbi n. n. shall enter paradise
and take enjoyment in the fruit of paradise
with delights on his right and sweetmeats on his left –
'He shall come in peace' is the reply that you will offer him.

This audio drama of appeals to different characters, to humans, to angels and to cosmic principles such as the Torah, for them all to issue a direct invitation to the deceased to leave limbo and to enter paradise, is based on a situation that must have been known to the congregation in ninth-century southern Italy, even if the full narrative is known to us only from much later sources.[63] While the body of the deceased is put to rest in the grave, his soul seeks to reach the paradise. The entrance to paradise is in the Makhpela cave in Hebron near the graves of (Adam and Eve, in some traditions,) Abraham and Sarah, Isaac and Rebecca and Jacob and Leah, the forefathers and mothers of (mankind and of) Israel. The entrance to paradise is like the entrance to the palace of a king and the guards have to summon the one who wants to enter, if he is worthy in their eyes. At first the poem refers to the human relatives of the deceased, still at the threshold between the known world and paradise. A second plea, made as in a hallway, is addressed to the angels of peace, those opposed to the angels of wrath,[64] and the third is already to the guardians at the entrance to paradise. What is more, paradise is not an empty place but has treasures and fruit to offer to anyone worthy of entering it. The metaphor is not spelt out but the epithet *maḥmadim* may provide a hint that the study

61 This may also yield the sense 'principles of the world', but is here defined by the context as Abraham, Isaac and Jacob, who are buried in Hebron.
62 Payyetanic, metonymic antonomasy based on Gen 49: 26 and referring to the forefathers or the four mothers of the tribes of Israel. Cf. *bRoš. Haš.* 11a.
63 For the sources, see the Hebrew commentary to the edition.
64 For similar traditions, see Aharon Berekhia of Modena, *Ma'avar Yabboq* (Modena: Yehuda Shemuel Mi-Perugia, 1626), fols. 38a, 42a.

of the words of the Torah, the ultimate fruit of the tree of knowledge, are meant. This lofty, lyrical style with its hints at an allegedly identifiable situation leaves us puzzled with regard to the last character addressed: is he, who has to issue the final invitation to the soul of the deceased, the messiah, or perhaps God Himself? It becomes quite clear that, as with every lyrical text, the meaning changes with our knowledge of the situation. Therefore, every additional testimony that clarifies the situation in the early Middle Ages is important. The epitaph for Leah, for instance, reveals not only the fact that the text was part of the burial ceremony in southern Italy at the beginning of the ninth century, but also that it also no mere citation but an adaptation made to fit the special situation of a father burying his young daughter.

> Guardians of the hoards of paradise,
> open the gates of paradise for her
> and Leah shall enter paradise
> open the gates of paradise for her
> and sweetsmeats in her left and delights in her right –
> this is the reply that you will offer her: 'Such is my beloved, and such is my darling'.

First, we can see how the draft format was completed, with 'Rabbi n.n.' being replaced by the name of the young woman. Secondly, the metaphorical fruit, that we interpreted as fruit of the tree of knowledge, is not mentioned here and thus the 'sweetmeats' and the 'delights' in her hands may be not so much the words of the Torah referred to as 'the judgements of the LORD are true, righteous altogether, more delightful (*neḥmadim*) than gold, than much fine gold; sweeter (*metuqim*) than honey, than drippings of the comb' (Ps 19:10–11) but, rather, the intercessional deeds of righteousness that she had performed. But the combination of the words *mamtaqim*/*maḥmadim* in the poem was for the one who formulated the epitaph an allusion to the climactical description of the groom in one of the songs of the bride in the Song of Songs: "His mouth is sweetmeats (*mamtaqim*), and all of him is delights (*maḥmadim*). Such is my beloved, and such is my darling, O maidens of Jerusalem!" (Song 6:3). The entrance to paradise becomes the realization of the prolonged marriage metaphor that lies at the basis of an allegorical reading of Song of Songs. Here, the father, who was denied the opportunity of escorting his daughter to the bride's canopy (*le-hakhnis la-ḥuppa*) because she died at the age of seventeen, rephrases the text of the burial ceremony, the very text said that is recited after interment to accompany her journey that is hidden from human eyes. Thus the ceremony of passing each of the different kinds of intercessors and guardians on the way to paradise ends differently with an intertextual allusion that replaces Torah study before God with a *hieros gamos*. The act of passing through the world of death into the world near the tree of life, in paradise, has become a transition from a father's house to a groom's house. Paradise makes good what is deficient in life; Eros takes over from Thanatos.

The fact that the formula could be adapted in such a way demonstrates that the Jews in southern Italy did not use such texts as quasi-magical spells but paid heed to them according to their literary style. This kind of attention to the text is also reflected in the *variae lectiones* of the manuscripts more than 400 years later. One aspect is the censoring out of the guardian angels, which might be explained as a polemic against angelic intercession.[65] Another aspect is the adaptation of the form according the gender of the deceased. Thus we find on the margins of the text in some manuscripts a predominance of notes concerning the changes of the suffixes and verbal forms that are necessary in order to use the text for a woman. This is summarized in a brief note of instruction at the end of the text in one of the manuscripts:

> ואין מנהג לומ<ר> שומרי גינזי גן עדן על הקטין. ואם רוצה אביו לכבודו אומרין אותו. ואם היא נקיבה אומ<רין>: 'ונשמתה לחיי עולם', 'תנוח נפשה' ו'משכבה', 'תשכב בשלום ותישן בשלום'; 'צאו לקראתה', 'פתחו לה', 'ואמרו לה שלום בואך', 'ותבוא מרת פלנית בגן עדן', 'ותשתעשע', 'מחמדים מימינה וממתקים משמאלה', 'ואת תענה ותאמרי לה שלום בואך'.[66]
>
> And it is not an accepted custom to recite 'Guardians of the hoards of paradise' over a minor.[67] But if his father wants it in his honour, you say it.[68]
>
> And if she is female, you say: 'And her soul for eternal life' ([B], line 16), 'May her soul' and 'her rest' ([B], line 20), 'May she rest in peace and sleep in peace' [B], line 22), 'go to meet her' ([C], line 5), 'open for her', 'and you say to her: Come in peace' ([C], lines 2, 4), 'And may Mrs. n.n. come into paradise' ([C], line 10), 'and she shall take enjoyment in' ([C], line 11), 'And delights on her right, and sweetmeats on her left' ([C], line 12), 'And You(!) shall reply to her: Come in peace' ([C], line 13).

Another way of adapting the text to the gender of the deceased is found only in late sources like the influential *Siddur Mi-Berakha Ke-Minhag Q"Q Italiyani*, Venice 1618 (and its reprints). There *Avot 'Olam* is assigned '*le-zakhar*' ('for a

65 The idea that such 'intercessors' were censored out of the liturgy needs special attention, particularly when it occurred against the background of the Italian tradition, and this will have to be done in another context. Meanwhile, compare similar poems for this occasion like *Raḥem Na Alaw El Elohim Ḥayyim* or *Ṣur Mi-Me'ono Ṣaddiq Hu We-Ṣaddiq Dino*; see eg Joseph Shalom Galliano, *Imrei No'am* (Amsterdam: Menashe Ben Yosef Ben Yisrael, 1628–1630), fols. 131b–33b.

66 MS Paris, Bibliothèque nationale héb. 598, *Maḥzor*, Italian rite (14th cent.), fol. 314a.

67 This may relate to its different status in the context of religious duties and study of the Torah.

68 It is noteworthy that this is exactly the position adopted by Eutychos with regard to his daughter in Brindisi, and it may be that the detail of custom recorded in this passage was brought to his special attention.

male') and *Giv'ot 'Olam* 'Le-Neqeva' ('for a female').[69] This is an interesting gender-biased interpretation of the term *Giv'ot 'Olam* against the background of the tradition concerning the graves in the Makhpela cave. If the fathers, Abraham, Isaac and Jacob are mentioned in the term *Avot 'Olam*, then the phrase *Giv'ot 'Olam* must refer to the mothers, Sarah, Rebecca and Leah who are also buried there. And the next step is to see the fathers as intercessors for the male deceased and the mothers for the females so that they can all find their final resting place in paradise.

Thus we may now summarize our interpretation of the texts of the *ṣidduq ha-din* ceremony at a funeral according the Italian rite as a balanced *rite de passage*, in which

[A] *Ha-Ṣur Tamim Be-Khol Po 'al* creates a community with a common background and world view;

[B] Amitay, *Adam Im Yiḥye Elef Shanim* evokes the attitudes and deeds of solidarity, and accompanies the inhumation of the dead;

[C] *Avot 'Olam Yeshenei Ḥevron* dramatizes a narrative dealing with the reincorporation of the dead,[70]

[E] *Qaddish Le-Itḥaddeta* turns the focus from the graveyard to future hopes and to the vision of '*shalom*' in both contexts.

Even if we use the modern concept of *rite de passage* to explain how the ceremony stayed the course, it seems plausible that it was not only a conservatively pious attitude to the matter of burial that kept this *agenda mortuorum*, with only minor changes, as part of the Italian Jewish tradition for some 800 years. Even when literary style changed and became more refined over the ages, the texts of the ceremony were not replaced until the age of baroque with its kabbalistic elements and a new focus on personal ceremonies leading to new forms of staging 'proper' deaths and burials.[71]

6

So what has this ceremony according the Italian rite, with its roots in ninth century Byzantine Apulia and its canonization in thirteenth century Rome, to

---

69 Cf. also the fragment of the print at the Jewish Theological Seminary Library in New York, already mentioned in n. 17 above.

70 A narrative, because other notions were also apparently attached to the term *Ṣeror Ha-Ḥayyim*, which is already found on some of the earliest epitaphs in southern Italy and develops later into the famous תנצב"ה formula.

71 See Avriel Bar-Levav, 'The Concept of Death in *Sefer Ha-Hayyim (The Book of Life)* by Rabbi Shimon Frankfurt' (Hebrew; doctoral dissertation, Hebrew University of Jerusalem, Jeru-

do with the Ashkenazi rite, where *mutatis mutandis* only the first element *Ha-Ṣur Tamim Be-Khol Po ʿal* and the final *Qaddish Le-Itḥaddeta* gained a foot-hold? If replacements of text in the funeral ceremony by *piyyuṭ* compositions were unacceptable, or not customary, in Ashkenaz, and appealing to intercessors was perhaps problematic according some theological concepts of Jewish prayer, we need testimonies from elsewhere that might show a link between both traditions.

Such a testimony has survived in the margins of an illuminated Haggada manuscript from thirteenth-century southern Germany, Ms Jerusalem, Israel Museum 180/57, the so-called 'Birdhead Haggadah'. On fol. 33a we find as an illustration to the verses 'Open the gates of justice for me that I may enter and praise the LORD. This is the gateway to the LORD – the righteous shall enter through it' (Ps 118:19–20), the depiction of three bird-headed persons turning into the gate of a two-storey building. At the gate stands the figure of an angel and in each of the two inner spaces of the roofed and castellated structure stands another angel. Above them, we see depictions of the sun and the moon and the inscription זה הגן עדין ('This is the paradise'). It is quite clear that anyone who attempting to explain the situation dramatized in the lyrical poem from southern Italy or the illustration in the Ashkenazi manuscript was faced with a basically similar story of passing by gates, angels, spaces and voices on the way to paradise.[72]

Thus a study of the Italian roots of *Ha-Ṣur Tamim Be-Khol Poʿal* may on the one hand promote our understanding of the text as part of a composite *agenda mortuorum* and of its function as part of a public ceremony while on the other hand emphasizing the choices made in the Ashkenazi tradition according to halakhic concepts and depending on how it was followed by individuals.

---

salem, 1997) and Bar-Levav, 'Ritualisation of Jewish Life and Death in the Early Modern Period', *Yearbook of the Leo Baeck Institute*, 47 (2002), pp. 69–82.

72 This narrative stands within an interesting dialogue between motifs connected to the ascent before the chariot in the Hekhalot literature and Byzantine monumental art; see eg the depiction in a ninth-century Byzantine mosaic of the archangel Gabriel, St. Peter and St. Paul at the Gates of Paradise on the triumphal arch in Santa Prassede, Rome. This may demonstrates just how much we need, for our understanding of the Jewish Middle Ages, studies like that of Peter Dronke, *Fabula: Explorations into the Uses of Myth in Medieval Platonism*, Mittellateinische Studien und Texte, 9 (Leiden: Brill, 1974) that combine analyses of thought, art and literature.

Joseph Isaac Lifshitz

Av ha-raḥamim: On the 'Father of Mercy' Prayer

אַב הָרַחֲמִים שׁוֹכֵן מְרוֹמִים,
בְּרַחֲמָיו הָעֲצוּמִים הוּא יִפְקֹד בְּרַחֲמִים
הַחֲסִידִים וְהַיְשָׁרִים וְהַתְּמִימִים,
קְהִלּוֹת הַקֹּדֶשׁ שֶׁמָּסְרוּ נַפְשָׁם עַל קְדֻשַּׁת הַשֵּׁם,
הַנֶּאֱהָבִים וְהַנְּעִימִים בְּחַיֵּיהֶם וּבְמוֹתָם לֹא נִפְרָדוּ,
מִנְּשָׁרִים קַלּוּ, מֵאֲרָיוֹת גָּבֵרוּ,
לַעֲשׂוֹת רְצוֹן קוֹנָם וְחֵפֶץ צוּרָם.
יִזְכְּרֵם אֱלֹהֵינוּ לְטוֹבָה עִם שְׁאָר צַדִּיקֵי עוֹלָם,
וְיִנְקֹם בְּיָמֵינוּ לְעֵינֵינוּ נִקְמַת דַּם עֲבָדָיו הַשָּׁפוּךְ,
כַּכָּתוּב בְּתוֹרַת מֹשֶׁה אִישׁ הָאֱלֹהִים:
"הַרְנִינוּ גוֹיִם עַמּוֹ, כִּי דַם עֲבָדָיו יִקּוֹם.
וְנָקָם יָשִׁיב לְצָרָיו, וְכִפֶּר אַדְמָתוֹ עַמּוֹ".
וְעַל יְדֵי עֲבָדֶיךָ הַנְּבִיאִים כָּתוּב לֵאמֹר.
"וְנִקֵּיתִי דָּמָם לֹא-נִקֵּיתִי, וה' שֹׁכֵן בְּצִיּוֹן".
וּבְכִתְבֵי הַקֹּדֶשׁ נֶאֱמַר:
"לָמָּה יֹאמְרוּ הַגּוֹיִם אַיֵּה אֱלֹהֵיהֶם,
יִוָּדַע בַּגּוֹיִם לְעֵינֵינוּ נִקְמַת דַּם-עֲבָדֶיךָ הַשָּׁפוּךְ".
וְאוֹמֵר: "כִּי-דֹרֵשׁ דָּמִים אוֹתָם זָכָר, לֹא-שָׁכַח צַעֲקַת עֲנָוִים".
וְאוֹמֵר: "יָדִין בַּגּוֹיִם מָלֵא גְוִיּוֹת,
מָחַץ רֹאשׁ עַל-אֶרֶץ רַבָּה: מִנַּחַל בַּדֶּרֶךְ יִשְׁתֶּה, עַל-כֵּן יָרִים רֹאשׁ".

The Father of mercy who dwells on high
in His great mercy
will remember with compassion
the pious, upright and blameless
the holy communities, who laid down their lives
for the sanctification of His name.
They were loved and pleasant in their lives
and in death they were not parted.
They were swifter than eagles and stronger than lions
to carry out the will of their Maker,
and the desire of their steadfast God.
May our Lord remember them for good
together with the other righteous of the world
and may He redress the spilled blood of His servants
in our sight, in our time,
as it is written in the Torah of Moses the man of God:
'O nations, make His people rejoice
for He will redress the blood of His servants
He will retaliate against His enemies
and appease His land and His people'.
And through Your servants, the prophets it is written:
'Though I forgive, their bloodshed I shall not forgive

When God dwells in Zion'
And in the Holy Writings it says:
'Why should the nations say, "Where is their God?"'
Let it be known among the nations in our sight
that You avenge the spilled blood of Your servants.
And it says: 'For He who exacts retribution for spilled blood
remembers them
He does not forget the cry of the humble'.
And it says:
'He will execute judgement among the corpse-filled nations
crushing the rulers of the mighty land;
from the brook by the wayside he will drink
then he will hold his head high'.

1 Introduction

The prayer, *Av ha-raḥamim* ('Father of Mercy'). recited to this day in Ashkenazi communities during the Sabbath morning prayers,[1] is mentioned in the Worms community records as a prayer that was composed in memory of those killed in the riots that took place during the First Crusade (1096). In this paper I intend to show how *Av ha-raḥamim,* though initially composed as a memorial prayer, was later invested with a variety of deeper theological meanings. It were these theological meanings that gave it the importance that it has carried into our own days.

Av ha-raḥamim appears in later halakhic writings as a memorial for those who were killed during the First Crusade. Thus we find in the writings of the 'Maharil' (R. Ya'aqov Moellin, 1360–1427): 'In all the Rhineland they say the prayer *Av ha-raḥamim* only on the Saturday before Pentecost, for this is the time that the holy ones of the decree of תתנ"ו (the year 5856/1096) are commemorated'.[2] That is, *Av ha-raḥamim* is recited only when those murdered during the First Crusade are being commemorated. What is the meaning of the prayer *Av ha-raḥamim,* as recited throughout those generations, until our own times? What was meant by its composers, and how did it come to be

1 In most communities, *Av ha-raḥamim* is recited every Sabbath except for those which fall before the new month (according to the Hebrew calendar), on the first day of the month, and during the month of Adar. In the Jewish-German custom, *Av ha-raḥamim* is recited only before Pentecost and before the Ninth of Av.

2 R. Ya'aqov son of Moshe Moellin, *Sefer Maharil* (*Minhagim*), ed. by Shlomo J. Spitzer (Jerusalem: Makhon Yerushalayim, 1989), p. 159 (*Hilkhot Shavu'ot*).

preserved? Was it meant, as some say, as a memorial prayer, or, as others suggest, as a polemical prayer, – or is it maybe something altogether different?

In order better to understand the meaning of *Av ha-raḥamim*, we must consider the significance of the First Crusade for the Jewish communities. During the First Crusade, as is well known, some of the crusaders attacked Jewish communities on their way to the Holy Land. During these attacks, the attackers demanded that the Jews convert to Christianity; those who refused to do so were killed. Some Jews indeed converted, some were executed and some took their own lives rather than convert. This period became instilled in Jewish consciousness as a particularly traumatic episode – nothing less than the destruction of the Jewish community in the Rhineland.

According to Robert Chazan,[3] the events were not as widespread as tradition would have it; that is to say, that in comparison with much of Jewish history, which was so full of disasters, the 1096 events do not count among the worst. They were regarded as especially disastrous only in the subjective perception of medieval Jewry. Chazan's view has been challenged by Avraham Grossman who contends that Jewish sources relate, not only by poetry but by chronicles that state evident that are grave indeed.[4] Regardless of this disaster's objective degree of severity, it constituted a trauma that inspired the extensive acts of memorialization by medieval Rhineland Jewry. That is why they wrote the names of those who were killed in *Memorbücher*, and why they wrote prayers of commemoration like *Av ha-raḥamim*. But there, is more to it than that. Beyond the emotional experience involved, there was also a theological crisis that drove the Jews to emphasize these events. The existence of the small Jewish community in Christian Europe was possible due to the Christian 'Doctrine of Witness'. According to this doctrine, the humiliation of the Jews proved the truth of Christianity, and that is why their existence as a lowly people was necessary, as it provided reassurance for Christians. At the same time, the humiliated Jews felt that the truth of their religion was becoming

---

3 Robert Chazan, *European Jewry and the First Crusade* (Berkeley, Los Angeles, London: University of California Press, 1987), pp. 62–63. See also Simon Schwarzfuchs, *A History of the Jews in Medieval France* (Hebrew; Tel Aviv: Hakibbutz Hameuchad, 2001), pp. 109–13; Simon Shwarzfuchs, 'The Place of the Crusades in Jewish History', in *Culture and Society in Medieval Jewry, Studies Dedicated to the Memory of Haim Hillel Ben-Sasson*, ed. by Menachem Ben-Sasson, Robert Bonfil, Joseph R. Hacker (Hebrew; Jerusalem: Shazar Center, 1989), pp. 251–67.
4 Avraham Grossman, *'Shorshaw shel Qiddush Ha-Shem be-Ashkenaz Ha-Qeduma'* in *Sanctity of Life and Martyrdom, Studies in Memory of Amir Yekutiel*, ed. by Isaiah M. Gafni and Aviezer Ravitzky (Hebrew; Jerusalem: Shazar Center, 1992), pp. 102–3.

undermined. The experience of a disaster like that of 1096 made it difficult for the medieval mind to justify the truth of Judaism. The Jews were constantly being faced with their image in the eyes of the Christians. In the famous artistic depiction, Judea leans on a broken staff with her eyes covered, while Ecclesia stands straight, holding a staunch staff, her eyes wide open. If the reality of daily events serves as a theological proof, how could the Jews maintain their religion? The way they battled against such so-called proofs was by assuming a postponment of good fortune to the future. So, while misery is the property of the present, good fortune is the property of the future. In this messianic theodicy, not only will the Jewish condition improve in the future, but whoever oppresses the Jews in the present will be punished in the time to come. Thus, revenge was very much a central motif in medieval Jewish Ashkenazi theology. This brief overview of Jewish perspectives regarding the 1096 riots provides us with a solid background of the *Av ha-raḥamim* prayer. As already noted, and as I shall demonstrate in more detail, both aspects of the Jewish condition in the Rhineland after 1096 – the emotional trauma and the theological humiliation – found their expression in this prayer. *Av ha-raḥamim* has a strong element of commemoration and, at the same time, an element of revenge that serves a theodicy, and as a polemical claim against the Christian attack on Judaism based on the Jews' physical misfortune. Often, these two elements are presented as mutually contradictory, but, in fact, they did not necessarily coexist in time, but, rather, were emphasized in different eras. That having been said, it must be noted that these two elements in *Av ha-raḥamim* are not the only ones that were to be identified among those reciting this prayer over the years. As I shall demonstrate, the martyrs were viewed as holy people, and their merits were counted as assets before the Almighty. Prayers in their memory were essentially prayers for the sake of the people who remained.

2 Commemoration

For a long time Torah scholars interpreted *Av ha-raḥamim* as a commemoration of the 1096 riots. Reading halakhic sources from the end of the thirteenth century in Ashkenaz, one cannot avoid seeing the connection between *Av ha-raḥamim* and the martyrs of 1096. One should note, however, that the first appearance of the prayer is in this century, and not earlier. This gap of at least a century and a half between the time the events took place and the appearance of the prayer should engage our attention, as it makes it difficult to claim that the prayer served as a sort of documentation of the dead.[5] But it is not only the time gap that arouses our suspicions. A careful reading of the sources reveals that this prayer was not written exclusively as a memorial. If we start with the *Sefer Minhagim* ('Book of Customs'), based on the customs of R. Meir of Rothenburg ('Maharam' ~1220–1293), one can identify a distinction between *Av ha-raḥamim* and the memorial prayer recited before it:

> There is a tradition that on the last days of the pilgrim festivals, while the cantor is sitting on the *migdal* (central podium), holding the Torah, before reciting *Ashrei* (Psalm 145), the leading member of the community takes an object and a book in his hand and goes from one [person] to another, and blesses everyone, one by one, separately, for the merit of promising to give a donation for the sake of God and the festival. *And in places where it is customary to do so, they [also] commemorate the dead and say Av ha-raḥamim* [my italics].
> מנהג שבכל יומי[ם] אחרוני[ם] של רגלים בעוד החזן יושב על המגדל והס"ת [= והספר תורה] בידו קודם אשרי הגדול שבעיר לוקח חפץ [ו]ספר בידו והולך מזה לזה ומבורך כל העם אחד ואחד בפני עצמו בעבור שיתן נדר לכבוד המקום ולכבוד הרגל **ובמקום שנהגו מזכירין נשמות ואומ[רים] אב הרחמים**.[6]

A similar citation is found in the *Sefer Minhagim* of R. Yiṣḥaq Tyrnau (end of the fourteenth century to the beginning of the fifteenth century). Here, too, *Av ha-raḥamim* appears as a prayer separate from the one that commemorates the dead:

> On the Sabbath before the first day of the month, they offer a blessing for the new month and say 'May the One who performed miracles for our patriarchs etc ...' And then they do not commemorate the dead nor do they say *Av ha-raḥamim*. The same rule applies to a wedding and all the more so to the first day of the month and to *Ḥanukka*.
> בשבת שלפני ראש חדש מברכין החדש מי שעשה נסים וכו', ואז אין מזכירין נשמות, ואין אומרים אב הרחמים וכן בחתונה, וקל וחומר ראש חדש וחנוכה ...[7]

---

5 On mentions of the dead in prayer-books see Avriel Bar Levav, 'The Concept of Death in the 'Book of Life' (*Sefer Ha-Hayyim*) by Rabbi Shimon Frankfurt' (doctoral dissertation, submitted to the Hebrew University of Jerusalem, 1997), pp. 160–225, Regarding a prayer for commemorating the dead, see Bar-Levav, pp. 177–79; Susan L. Einbinder, *Beautiful Death: Jewish Poetry and Martyrdom in Medieval France (Jews, Christians, and Muslims from the Ancient to the Modern World)*, (Princeton: Princeton University Press, 2002), pp. 17–44.

6 *Sefer Minhagim Devei Maharam, Minhagim ben Pesaḥ Le-Shavuot*. And further: 'And after Nisan is over, one says *zulatot* every Sabbath ... and on the Sabbath before Pentecost the **souls of the murdered of the [1096] decrees are commemorated and *Av ha-raḥamim* is said**.'
'ולאחר שעבר ניסן אומרי' בכל שבתות זולתות כגון אזכרה דודי אלהי אל דמי לך עד שבועות ובשבת שלפני שבועות **מזכיר (הרוגי גזירות) נשמות של הרוגי (גז') גזירות ואומ' אב הרחמים**'.

7 R. Yiṣḥaq Tyrnau, *Sefer Ha-Minhagim*, by S. Y. Spitzer, *Minhag shel Shabbat* (Jerusalem: Makhon Yerushalayim, 1979), p. 26.

The separation appears even more clearly in the *Qoveṣ Minhagim* ('Collection of Customs') of R. Zalman Jent, who lived in the same time and place as Yiṣḥaq of Tyrnau and towards the end of his life moved to Italy:

> The Sabbath before Pentecost, [the custom is to] wake up early and say *pesuqe de-zimra* (the Psalms recited at the beginning of the prayers) quickly in order to commemorate the murdered and the burned of the communities of Speyer, Worms and Mainz. And *Av ha-raḥamim* is said, as well as, in the *yoṣer* (additional poetry inserted in that particular section) in *Ahava Rabba* – 'It is You that we were eager for all day' and the *zulat* (additional poetry inserted in that particular section) – 'My God! We heard it in our own ears'.
> שבת שלפני שבועות משכימין וממהרין פסוקי דזמרה כדי להזכיר הרוגי ושרופי קהילות שו"ם, ואומרים אב הרחמים ואומרים ביוצר באהבה רבה אותך כל היום קוינו וזולת אלהי באזנינו שמענו.[8]

In all the passages I have cited above, the recitation of *Av ha-raḥamim* is mentioned together with that of the commemoration of the martyrs, although they are clearly perceived as separate prayers. From the next citation I can demonstrate that the recitations were separate from each other:

> In the Sabbath that falls after the [fast-day] of Seventeenth of Tammuz, ... after the Torah reading, the decrees against the murdered are commemorated and the community is blessed. And Ashrei (Psalm 145) is recited, and afterwards *Av ha-raḥamim* is said, and special Sabbath clothes are not worn.
> בשבת אחר י"ז בתמוז ולאחר קריאת התורה מזכירין גזירות ההרוגי[ם] ומברכין הקהל, ואומרי[ם] אשרי ואח"כ [= ואחר כך] אומרי[ם] אב הרחמים ואין לובשין בגדי שבת.[9]

These sources indicate that *Av ha-raḥamim* is not only about commemoration. The next source appears to contradict my claim and to make a halakhic connection between *Av ha-raḥamim* and the commemoration of the dead: R. Zalman Jent teaches us that *Av ha-raḥamim* is recited only on those days when the dead are commemorated. Hence we learn that *Av ha-raḥamim* is also considered a sort of commemoration:

> On *Shabbat Teshuva* (the Sabbath before Yom Kippur), the *yoṣer* (an added piyyuṭ to the prayer) 'Light of the World' [is said] [...] and the dead are not commemorated and *Av ha-raḥamim* is not said. This is the rule: on every Sabbath that has a *yoṣer*, the commemoration of the dead is not recited and *Av Ha-raḥamim* is not recited. That is also the case on a Sabbath when the benediction of the new month is recited.
> בשבת תשובה היוצר אור עולם קראו והאופן כי אם שם אדיר ולא אמת ויציב די"ט [= דיום טוב – של יום טוב] והזולת אל לבבנו והפטרה שובה ולא יאמר אותה נער. ואין מזכירין נשמות ואין אומרי[ם] אב הרחמים, וזה הכלל בכל שבת שיש בו יוצר אין מזכירין נשמות, וכן בשבת שמברכין בו ראש חדש אין מזכירין.[10]

---

8 R. Zalman Jent, *Qoveṣ Minhagim*, included in the edition of Tyrnau's *Minhagim* ed. by S. Y. Spitzer (Jerusalem: Mekhon Yerushalayim, 1979), p. 179.
9 Ibid.
10 Ibid.

The same rule can be found in the writings of R. Ya'aqov Moellin, based on R. Jent, where the link between *Av Ha-raḥamim* and the mention of the dead is very clear – *Av ha-raḥamim* is recited only when the martyrs of 1096 are mentioned:

> In all Rhineland *Av ha-raḥamim* is not said, except on the Sabbath before Pentecost, when the martyrs of the 4856 [1096] decree are mentioned, and on the *Shabbat Ḥazon* [the Sabbath preceding the Ninth of Av] these martyrs are also commemorated and *Av ha-raḥamim* is said.
> בכל מדינתריינוס א"א [= אין אומרים] אב הרחמים אלא בשבת דלפני שבועות דמזכירין את הקדושים גזירת תתנ"ו. ובשבת חזון ישעיהו מזכירין ג"כ אותן הקדושים ואומר אב הרחמים.[11]

In the next source, R. Ya'aqov Moellin connects the commemoration of the dead with *Av ha-raḥamim*, without any separation:

> In Mainz, on *Shabbat Ḥazon* they recite 'It is you that we love ...' and the *zulat* 'Lions they expelled' (names of *piyyuṭim*) and they commemorate these holy martyrs of 5856 [1096], *Av ha-raḥamim*.
> במגנצא בשבת חזון ישעיהו אומר אותך כל היום לאהבה, וזולת אריות הדיחו, ומזכירין קדושים תתנ"ו, אב הרחמים.[12]

These sources reveal a link between *Av ha-raḥamim* and the commemoration of the dead, though almost all of them present *Av ha-raḥamim* as a separate prayer. *Av ha-raḥamim* is not necessarily presented in these sources as a prayer commemorating the martyrs; that commemoration was done separately. But nonetheless, it is clear that there is an association between the two. Thus, both tradition and allusions in the above-mentioned texts connect *Av ha-raḥamim* to the 1096 events.

At the same time, it seems that *Av ha-raḥamim* was not perceived solely as a prayer of commemoration. The names of the communities are not even mentioned, although they are mentioned elsewhere. Even their acts of martyrdom are described anonymously as 'the holy communities, who laid down their lives'. We thus have to proceed to the other meaning inherent in *Av ha-raḥamim* – the polemic one.

3 The polemical-theological purpose

In his book, *Two Nations in Your Womb*, Yisrael Yuval points out two motifs in *Av ha-raḥamim*. The liturgist prays for redressing 'the spilt blood of His ser-

11 *Sefer Maharil (Minhagim)*, p. 159 (*Hilkhot Shavu'ot*).
12 *Sefer Maharil (Minhagim)*, p. 243 (*Hilkhot Shiv'a 'Asar be-Tammuz we-Tisha be-'Av.*

vants in our sight, in our time. This prayer is a request for redemption that includes revenge (as distinct from redemption that includes conversion of the Gentiles).[13] The second motif appears in the liturgist's prayer to God to remember, as opposed to human beings remembering: 'The Father of Mercy who dwells on high, in His great mercy, will remember with compassion the pious, upright and blameless ...'.[14] Regarding the first motif, Yuval puts a special emphasis on the words, that 'He redress the spilled blood of His servants in our sight, in our time'. The quest for a redressing to take place in our time is closely tied to a certain kind of redemption. Yuval's main attention is focused on the idea of revenge and its very close connection with redemption.

Borrowing Avraham Grossman's distinction between two perspectives of redemption that were common in the Middle Ages – a redemption of revenge and a redemption of conversion[15] – Yuval understands the revenge in *Av ha-raḥamim* as being of the former type.

According to Grossman, both redemptions provide a solution for the difficult state of the Jews in the Middle Ages. But according to Yuval, the two kinds of redemptions are typical of the differences between West and East, between Jews in the Christian world and Jews in the Islamic world.

For the Jews under Christian dominion, the difficulty was not only physical but also theological. As mentioned above, the 'Doctrine of Witness' played an important role in the Christian's perception of the Jews. Christianity used the miserable situation of the Jews to prove Judaism's fallacy. The Jewish reply to this claim was that although the present seems bad, the future will change the picture. In the future, not only will the Jews benefit from a better life, but God will take revenge on the Christians for oppressing the Jews. This messianic solution is a redemption of revenge, unique to Ashkenaz. Hence, according to Yuval, we find an emphasis on revenge in Ashkenazi liturgy.

In the East, on the other hand, we find a different messianic expectation. R. Hai Gaon, for instance, claims that at the end-time, all the Gentiles will convert to Judaism. That kind of redemption involving conversion knows no violence or revenge of the sort we find in the Ashkenazi world.

The second motif is expressed in the words: 'The Father of Mercy who dwells on high, in His great mercy will remember with compassion the pious, upright and blameless ...'[16]. As Yuval explains: 'The purpose of the ritual is

---

13 Yisrael Y. Yuval, *Shnei Goyim be-Vitnekh* (Tel Aviv: Alma, Am Oved, 2000), p. 152.
14 Ibid.
15 Avraham Grossman, 'Redemption of Conversion in the Writings of the Early Sages of Ashkenaz' (Hebrew), *Zion*, 59 (1994), pp. 325–42.
16 Ibid.

not to augment human memory but, rather, Divine memory. The liturgical meaning ... does not relate to human beings remembering, but to God who remembers.'[17]

In saying that, Yuval is in effect criticizing the opinion that holds that *Av ha-raḥamim* was meant to commemorate the dead. When the communities were praying for the memory of the deceased, they were not engaging in an active act of remembering as in Marcel Proust's works, but, rather, in a religious act, requesting that God should remember.

I find Yuval's claims convincing, not only because rituals of self-commemoration in this context sound anachronistic, but also because of the very special wording of the prayer: 'In His great mercy will remember ...'.

4 Tremendous mercy

Simha Goldin has already shown the early roots of the expression 'Father of Mercy'.[18] But the idea of remembering with *tremendous* mercy has no precedence. In *Av ha-raḥamim* the liturgist is not satisfied with mercy as a means of remembering the deceased; he needs 'tremendous mercy'. The question that arises, then is, why? Why does God need all His mercy in order to remember them with compassion?

It seems that the people of that generation were sure that the acts of the martyrs did not deserve just any kind of mercy; but that only tremendous mercy could assure Divine remembrance.

There is no doubt that the liturgist of *Av ha-raḥamim* was well acquanted with the talmudic source that tells us, with regard to the martyrs of the city of Lod, that 'no creature can stand in their place'.[19] The common explanation of this source is that these martyrs gave their lives for the sake of the Jews of Lod, and thus achieved great spiritual heights.[20] If martyrdom is so respected,

17 Ibid.

18 Simha Goldin, *The Ways of Jewish Martyrdom* (Hebrew; Ganei-Aviv; Lod: Dvir publishing House, 2002), pp. 131–36.

19 *bPesaḥ*. 50a; *bB. Bat*. 10b. Parallel *midrashim* appear in *Midrash Qohelet Rabba* 9.10 (24b), and *Midrash Zuṭa – Qohelet* 9 (ed. Buber, 74a).

20 Rashi, *bTa'an*. 18b: 'And that is what is said in every place (*bB. Bat*. 10b): As for the martyrs of Lod, no creature can stand close to them in *Gan 'Eden*, and there are those who say that they were killed because of a princess who was found murdered. It was said that the Jews had murdered her, and there was a decree against the enemies of Israel [euphemism for the Jews themselves], and these [two] stood up and rescued Israel, saying "We murdered her," and the king killed only those.'

why is tremendous mercy necessary? It is not unlikely that the liturgist could not think of the praise deserved by the Ashkenazi martyrs without feeling that their act also warranted some criticism. Although he praised them for being 'pious, upright and blameless' he also indicated that they required tremendous mercy. What sort of criticism, then, is being levelled at them?

The answer is that the martyrs not only committed suicide, but also killed others, in a collective attempt to prevent forced conversions. It is this element that raises questions, halakhic as well as moral.[21]

Despite all this, love and appreciation of the martyrs should also be recorded. The following sentences express a respect and a love that reflects something much powerful than the prayer's polemical elements:

> They were loved and pleasant in their lives, and in death they were not parted. They were swifter than eagles and stronger than lions to carry out the will of their Maker, and the desire of their steadfast God.

Commemoration, polemics, controversy – all are present. But one issue still remains – that of the prayer's continued presence in the prayer-book. Is there some content in it that goes beyond these time-connected elements? In the next section I will explore additional aspects of the prayer, which may serve to answer this question.

---

21 R. Meir son of R. Barukh of Rothenburg, *Teshuvot, Pesaqim u-Minhagim* (*Responsa, Rulings and Customs*), ed. by Isaac Z. Cahana, Jerusalem, vol. 2 (Jerusalem: Mosad Harav Kook, 1960), p. 54, section 59. Moshe Aryeh Bloch included the following responsum at the end of the collection as one transmitted to him by Rabbi Dr Gross, who had received it from Dov Goldberg without any indication of the location of the original manuscript. See *Sha'arei Teshuvot Maharam ben Rabbi Barukh z"l*, pp. 346–47. The explanations in brackets are in the original:

> I do not know how to assess this matter properly, for certainly one who kills himself for the sake of the unity of God is permitted to harm himself thus ... But it has become common to permit killing family members for the purpose of sanctifying God's name, for we have heard and read about many great people who slaughtered their sons and daughters ... And whoever says that he must atone for this is slandering the earlier generations. His intention was worthy; arising out of his great love for our Creator, that is why he struck down his loved one ...
>
> לא ידענא שפיר מה אידון ביה [= איני יודע כיצד לדון בדבר כראוי], כי ודאי ההורג עצמו על ייחוד ה' רשאי לחבול בעצמו ... מיהו דבר זה פשט היתירו [= ברם התפשט ההיתר – להרוג בני משפחה כדי לקדש את השם], כי שמענו ומצאנו שהרבה גדולים שהיו שוחטין את בניהם ואת בנותיהם ... ואחרי שכוונת(ו) [יצרו] היה לטובה; מרוב אהבת יוצרינו יתברך שמו פגע ונגע (במעמד) [במחמד] עינו. גם הם חילו פניו על ככה ... ואין להחמיר עליו כלל.

On this responsum see Goldin, *Jewish Martyrdom*, pp. 228–42, Haim Soloveitchik, 'Religious Law and Change: The Medieval Ashkenazic Example', *AJS Review*, 12 (1987), pp. 205–21.

5 The merit of the forefathers

Defining the communities 'who laid down their lives for the sanctification of His name' as holy gives the impression that they were truly great people in Jewish history: patriarchs, people whose merits go beyond simple human virtues. It seems to me that *Av ha-raḥamim* was intended for the living much more than for the dead. The martyrs' merits are therefore mentioned as a way of according them a status that will benefit the living.

Requesting that the deceased serve as our advocates in heaven was common in medieval Ashkenaz. Thus, R. Mordekhai Yaffe at the end of the sixteenth century teaches us to remember the acts of the dead:

> One remembers the acts of the dead and says: 'If this dead man were alive, he would have been giving charity.' When this is said, his merits are remembered. If the deceased was poor but generous and would have given this charity on his own, if he had had money, then giving this charity can bring him some merit, because the living can ask for a more lenient judgement of the dead. That is why charity is given on their behalf, so that they, too, if they were righteous [in their lives], will speak up for their offspring and relatives. But if one gives for a confirmed sinner, it will not help him.
> זוכר מעשה המתים ואומר, אם היה אותו המת בחיים היה ג"כ נותן צדקה ואגב זוכר לו זכותו, ואם היה עני אותו המת אך היה לבו טוב והיה נותן לרצונו אם היה לו, אז תועיל לו קצת, כי החי יכול לבקש להקל דין המת, כדוד על אבשלום [סוטה י ע"ב] וכר' מאיר על אחר [עי' חגיגה טו ע"ב], הלכך נותנים לכבודם כדי שגם הם אם היו הם צדיקים יהיו מליצים על צאצאיהם וקרוביהם, אבל אם נותן בעבור רשע אין מועיל לו.[22]

Remembering the acts of the dead was meant to grant them atonement and improve their state in the afterworld. At the same time, it might help their living relatives in this world.

This source from the end of the Middle Ages was based on perspectives from the earlier High Middle Ages. R. Eleazer of Worms (~1165–~1230) related to the custom to pray for the merits of the deceased as common knowledge:

> And regarding the giving of charity on behalf of the dead, on Yom Kippur and not on Yom Tov, there is a source for it in the Torah ... And how does it help the deceased that the living give charity on his behalf? Well, the Lord examines the hearts of the living and the dead. If this deceased person gave charity when he was alive, or if he was a poor but generous man who would have given charity, then the merit of charity will help him somewhat.
> ומה שפוסקין צדקה עבור המתים ביום הכפורים ולא ביום טוב יש להם אסמכתא שכתוב בסוף פרש' ואתה תצוה הכפורים אחת בשנה יכפר וסמיך ליה ונתנו איש כופר נפשו לײ' בזמן שיתן לכפר' הנפש. ומה מועיל למת שהחי נותן צדקה בעבורו אלא השם בוחן לבות

22 R. Mordekhai Yaffe, *Levush*, *Oraḥ Ḥayyim*, 621.

החיים והמתים אם אותו המת בחיים היה נותן צדקה ואם היה עני אותו המת אך לבו בטוב והיה נותן אם היה לו אז תועיל לו קצת.[23]

Both R. Mordekhai Yaffe and R. Ele'azar are relating to the custom, common in their times, of giving charity on High Holy Days. According to them, charity is beneficial to the deceased only if they would have acted similarly when they were alive. And only the righteous can be advocates for their relatives. They are, then, not recommending the custom, but, rather, trying to justify it. This shows the extent to which viewing the dead were viewed as possible advocates in heaven was common in the Rhineland, even from the beginning of the thirteenth century.

The usefulness of seeking such advocates is not necessarily a given; but it seems that the general approach was that there was nothing wrong with the custom. R. Ṣidqiya, the son of Avraham Ha-Rofe (1210–1275) recommends, in his *Shibbolei Ha-Leqeṭ* in the name of Rashi, that one should make efforts to receive all possible help from such sources. Actually, Rashi was referring to angels, but angels, too, can serve as go-betweens:

> R. Yoḥanan said: A person should always seek full encouragement from earthly powers, as well as having no enemies on high. And Rabbenu Shelomo explained this to mean that the heavenly angels should assist him by asking for mercy, and that he should have no antagonists above. And also in the *Midrash Shir Ha-Shirim*, on the verse 'I adjure you', it says, *The community of Israel* says to the angels that stand at the gates of prayer and the gates of tears: 'Bring my prayer and my tears before the Holy One, Blessed be He, and be my true advocates before Him, so that he will forgive me for my intentional and unintentional transgressions. And it says, 'If there is one advocating angel for him out of a thousand etc.'
>
> אמר ר' יוחנן לעולם יבקש אדם שיהו הכל מאמצין את כחו מלמטה ואל יהי לו צרים מלמעלה ופי' רבינו שלמה זצ"ל שיסייעוהו מלאכי השרת לבקש רחמים ושלא יהיה לו משטינים מלמעלה וגם במדרש שיר השירים על פסוק השבעתי אתכם אומרת כנסת ישראל למלאכים העומדים על שערי תפלה ועל שערי דמעה הוליכו תפלתי ודמעתי לפני הקב"ה ותהיו מליצי יושר לפניו שימחול לי על הזדונות ועל השגגות ונאמר אם יש עליו מלאך מליץ אחד מני אלף וגו'.[24]

The request that the dead serve as advocates is, then, what was at the base of commemorating the dead. It seems to me that this meaning has also affected the understanding of *Av ha-raḥamim*. Including the martyrs with other righteous people in the words 'May our Lord remember them for good together

---

23 R. Ele'azar of Worms, *Sefer Ha-Roqeaḥ Ha-Shalem*, ed. by Barukh Shneurson (repr. Jerusalem: Otzar Posqim, 1967), p. 110 (*Hilkhot Yom Ha-Kippurim*). On giving charity on behalf of the dead on Yom Kippur, see Bar Levav, *The Concept of Death*, pp. 226–30.

24 R. Ṣidqiyahu the son of R. Avraham Ha-Rofe, *Sefer Shibbolei Ha-Leqeṭ Ha-Shalem*, ed. Buber (Wilna, 1887; repr. Jerusalem: Pe'er Ha-Tora, 1959), p. 133b (*Rosh Ha-Shana*, section 282).

with the other righteous of the world' carries with it the notion of the merit of the forefathers. The request is not only for these particular martyrs, but also for the benefit of those living today. This explanation of mine may help explain another phenomenon that developed with regard to *Av ha-raḥamim*. As mentioned above, this prayer was said on those days of the year on which the 1096 events occurred, namely before Pentecost, as described in R. Zalman Jent's collected customs, already cited above.

This also helps us to understand the custom to say *Av ha-raḥamim* immediately before the Ninth of Av, as mentioned in the book of customs of the Maharam of Rothenburg: 'And there are places where *Av ha-raḥamim* is said only on the Sabbath before the Ninth of Av'.[25]

And so also in the 'Maharil', in continuation of the passage quoted above:

> ... And on *Shabbat Ḥazon Yesha'yahu* (the Sabbath preceding the Ninth of Av), those martyrs are also mentioned, and *Av ha-raḥamim* is said. And so Maharaz Jent instituted ...
> ... ובשבת חזון ישעיהו מזכירין ג"כ אותן הקדושים ואומר אב הרחמים. וכן הנהיג מהר"ז ייענט ...[26]

But it is difficult to understand the role of *Av ha-raḥamim* in the prayers of the three festivals, as cited above from the Maharam's customs, namely, that 'there is a tradition that on the last days of the holidays, while the cantor is sitting on the *migdal* (central podium), holding the Torah ... and in places where it is customary to do so, they [also] commemorate the dead and say *Av ha-raḥamim*.'[27] In my opinion, the fact that saying *Av ha-raḥamim* also became common on the festivals supports my thesis – that the point of this prayer, as viewed by these people, was to mention the merits of the forefathers, and therefore it is to be said not only on days when tragic events occurred, but on the festivals too. On days that are considered days of judgement there is a special need for the merits of our forefathers, and therefore a special role was also assigned to the Rhineland forefathers.

---

25 R. Meir son of R. Barukh, *The Book of Customs from the Sphere of the Maharam*, section on Seventeenth of Tammuz.

26 R. Ya'aqov b. Moshe Moellin, *Sefer Maharil, The Book of Customs*, section of the laws of Shavu'ot, ed. Shlomo Y. Spitzer (Jerusalem: Makhon Yerushalayim, 1989), p. 199.

27 R. Meir of Rothenburg, Ibid, section of Customs Between Pesaḥ and Shavu'ot, p. 28, and later in p. 29: "and after the month of Nisan they say ... and mention the souls of the murdered of persecutions, and say *Av ha-raḥamim*".

6 Summary

The recital of *Av ha-raḥamim* is a custom that persists to this day. Its historical survival teaches us about its deep and varied levels and about its powerful meaning. Unlike during the Middle Ages, not everyone is aware of its connection to the events of 1096, and it is generally viewed as a general commemoration of the many communities that were destroyed during the long exile. Our Sages have taught us that recent troubles make us forget earlier ones.[28] It seems that the 1096 events went through a similar process, one that affected *Av ha-raḥamim*. The terror of the Crusades began to wane. The prayer then became meta-historical and absorbed memories of other massacres, of other communities. In the meantime, the original memory, together with its connection to the 1096 events, weakened. Its general wording forced the Ashkenaz communities that wished to remember that particular memory to do so by way of saying a separate prayer of commemoration for the dead. As mentioned above, this process may be seen in the separation that occurred during thirteenth and fourteenth centuries between the 1096 riots and the introduction of *Av ha-raḥamim*.

But beyond those two meanings, *Av ha-raḥamim* acquired an additional meaning. The 1096 martyrs became figures whose merits protected the living. *Av ha-raḥamim* gradually lost the personal connection to the martyrs of the Crusades. They became holy figures – not mere mortals who need mercy – and their memory became a source of strength for the Jews, not only when facing their Christian neighbours, but mainly when facing the Creator Himself. The merit of those martyrs is seen as what provides one with the necessary power to stand before God and the heavenly court.

28 *bBer*. 13a.

Abraham Gross

Liturgy as Personal Memorial for the Victims in 1096

One would be hard-pressed to find a topic in recent medieval Jewish historiography that equals, in terms of abundance, scores of books and articles, ranges of treatment, numbers of scholars involved, and innovative methodologies, that of the Crusaders' persecutions of the Jews of the Rhineland during 1096. It seems that, beyond martyrdom, the denominator common to almost every aspect of historiographical coverage, is that of memory. This is so because one of the only views that has achieved consensus among scholars is that the tragic events of 1096 left their mark on the collective religious psyche of Ashkenazi Jewry. One would therefore certainly have expected a fully-fledged study analysing the memory of 1096 in the immediately following generations within the Jewish communities of Germany. Yet, despite the considerable attention that has been given to collective memory in Jewish historiography in the past three decades, such a comprehensive study on 1096 remains a *desideratum.*[1]

Recent studies have discussed the memory of 1096 mostly in connection with assessments of the extent of damage suffered during the persecutions (such as loss of lives and physical destruction), and its impact on the communities. The discussion of memory is limited to the chronological and geographical dimensions, namely, to the questions whether the persecutions were remembered in the long range (in terms of centuries), and how far away from the Rhenish 'ground zero' this memory operated? Generally, it may be said that the present trend is to minimize the losses, the repercussions of the persecutions, and the memory of the entire ordeal.[2]

The present study is not concerned with the memory of 1096 but with its memorialization. My interest is in what I conceive to have been the massive,

---

1 Among those who have treated aspects of 1096 memorialization in the twelfth century are: Simha Goldin, *The Ways of Jewish Martyrdom* (English translation; Turnhout: Brepols, 2008); Nati Barak, 'The Book of Memory of the Jewish Communities in Ashkenaz in the Middle Ages (Memorbuch): Its Origin, Aims, and Role in the Ceremony of Memorialization' (master's dissertation, Tel Aviv University, 2003); David Wachtel, 'The Ritual and Liturgical Commemoration of Two Medieval Persecutions' (master's dissertation, Columbia University, 1995). A short exchange between Ezra Fleischer and Yisrael Yuval concerning the *Memorbuch* can be found in *Zion*, 59 (1994), p. 294, n. 89, p. 384, n. 81.

2 The long-range memory of 1096 is briefly discussed in the introduction to a forthcoming edition of 1096 liturgical poetry by Avraham Fraenkel and myself. The present article stems from that study.

versatile, and unprecedented effort at the memorialization that was undertaken by the generations that immediately followed 1096 in Germany. The survivors of 1096 saw themselves as the ‘remnant.’ Expressions such as *she'erit* or *she'erit ha-pleṭa* are common in post-1096 liturgy and other literary sources. Those generations constructed a system of memorialization for the events and for the victims. It was unique and unprecedented in its comprehensiveness and included a number of innovative elements.

A central question that I will try to answer, at least in part, is: Was the memorializing effort simply a product of the religious mind of Ashkenazi society or was there another motive, based on a human impulse equally well-known to modern society? In other words, were liturgy, customs, and *halakha* designed as means to ends that cannot justifiably be described as ‘religious’, and, if so, to what degree?

I am here concerned only with liturgy, and in this context we should ask whether the sole intention of the liturgical poets [henceforth: *payyeṭanim*] was to request divine forgiveness, mercy, revenge, and redemption. If the answer is in the affirmative, then the historiographical significance is that we are limiting our understanding of their words to a basic level that defines them in exclusively religious terms. That is how liturgy is often read. After all, religious poetry is written in accordance with traditional forms, its language is by and large that of biblical and post-biblical sacred literature, and it is meant to be recited in the synagogue. There is, however, the other possibility that the intention of the entire liturgical system, or at least parts of it, was to soothe the emotional needs of a people that had lost its community, its revered rabbis, its close friends and dear relatives. To what extent can we identify in the liturgical heritage of the 1096 remnant this need for a preservation of memory that is distinct from explicitly religious language and content?

This explains why I preferred to use in the title of this article the neutral term ‘victims’, rather than ‘martyrs’, which has an exclusively religious connotation. The ‘victims’ (or ‘dead’, for that matter) need not be classified as ‘martyrs’, certainly not by historians, and the memorializiation of such persons may be, but need not be, restricted to the religious sphere.

The source material of this present study is the liturgy written about the events of 1096. That liturgy, dedicated wholly to 1096, numbers about thirty poems that were composed during the twelfth century. Some explicitly mention the date (תתנ"ו, תנו"ת רנ"ו, כל"ו), while others simply describe the destruction and martyrdom. There are some additional poems that mention 1096 together with later persecutions of the twelfth century, such as those of the Second Crusade (1147) and the blood libel at Blois (1171).

Liturgical poetry relating to the First Crusade may be divided into three main genres: *qinot*, *seliḥot*, and *zulatot*. The *qinot* were to be recited on the fast of the Ninth of Av, in addition to the traditional *qinot* on the destruction of the two Jerusalem temples. The *seliḥot* were written for days of communal commemoration of the 1096 catastrophe, as well as for the *yamim nora'im*, and especially for Yom Kippur. *Zulatot* were to be recited in the morning prayer [*shaḥarit*] of the sabbaths during the month of Iyyar, and until the festival of Shavu'ot (Pentecost), corresponding to the period of the attacks on the major Jewish communities.[3]

A communal *ḥazzan* [*sheli'aḥ ṣibbur*] was expected to write liturgy. Yet, not all the liturgical poems [henceforth: *piyyuṭ/piyyuṭim*] were written by 'professional' *payyeṭanim*. For example, David bar Meshullam who wrote *Elohim al domi le-dami*, one of the most famous and imposing 1096 *piyyuṭim*, was a communal leader. This is the only *piyyuṭ* we have by him. We may assume that he created it to satisfy his own emotional need, or that he believed that it was important for the community. We may also safely assume that anyone who wrote a 1096 *piyyuṭ*, the communal *payyeṭan* included, had an agenda that guided his writing. If so, then we must treat liturgy just as historians have been treating the 1096 Hebrew chronicles, and ask two questions. How did the 1096 *payyeṭanim* perceive their communal-religious duty in the post-1096 Ashkenazi milieu? What were the results they were attempting to achieve in writing '1096 liturgy'?

A partial list of of their possible aims would have to include: to call upon God for forgiveness through the merit of the martyrs; to avenge their death; to hasten the Redemption; to evoke in the communal audience the memory of the catastrophe; to mourn the desecration of the Torah scrolls, the killing of scholars, women, and nurslings; to remind the audience what the Christians did and thus broaden the gap between the two faiths; to contribute to internal social cohesion; to impart an implicit message of religious loyalty unto death as exemplified by the martyrs; to strengthen faith in the ongoing covenant between God and Israel; to justify divine judgement; to raise feelings of pride in belonging to the chosen people; to 'prove' the veracity of Judaism out of the readiness of the martyrs to die for their faith; to preserve the memory of the persecutions; to lend meaning to current suffering by linking it with the ancient chain of martyrological tradition from the times of Rabbi Akiva, Rabbi Ḥanina ben Teradion and their colleagues; and to equate the status and reward of the martyrs in the present with those of their ancient predecessors.

At times, depending on the *piyyuṭ*'s specific genre and its conventional aims, the *payyeṭan* may say why he is writing. But not everything is by any

3 On the strictures associated with mourning customs during the month of Iyyar, specific to Ashkenazi Jewry, and their relation to 1096, see: Daniel Sperber, *Jewish Customs: Origins and History* (Hebrew; Jerusalem: Mosad Harav Kook, 1989), pp. 110–11.

means explicit. It seems that all too often, central aims remain implicit. As one examines the *payyeṭan*'s intentions, one thing becomes apparent. He does not detail the religious and social agenda that he is trying to impart to the audience. By 'implicit' intentions, I refer not only to intentionally hidden messages, but also to those that play a role in the creative process of the composition without the conscious consideration of them by the *payyeṭan*.

Now that we have a tentative list of aims, we must ask, of course, how important the element of memorialization is within this framework. A detailed answer to the question is beyond the limited scope of the present article. In general, however, I would suggest the following:

a. the answer might vary from *piyyuṭ* to *piyyuṭ*, from *payyeṭan* to *payyeṭan*, and from generation to generation.
b. analysis of the entire poetical corpus appears to me to suggest that the element is more central than most historians have acknowledged to date.

Let us take, for example, Qalonymos bar Yehuda. Qalonymos, a member of the community of Mainz, wrote at least five (!) 1096 liturgical poems. He may certainly be given the honorary title of the foremost 1096 *payyeṭan*. The time of composition is estimated to be between ten and twenty years after the events.

Now, why would one write five *piyyuṭim* (two *qinot* for the Ninth of Av, and three *seliḥot*)?[4] Why does he relate the self-slaughter in one *qina* while completely ignoring it in the other? Why does he transcribe in one *qina* the names of the major communities and the dates on which they were attacked? It would seem that Qalonymos intended to produce a series of *piyyuṭim* designed to complement each other and to create one whole poetic narrative. This narrative's aim was, primarily, to serve as a poetical memorial to the destroyed communities. One might say that, in this respect, he was attempting a poetical parallel to the Hebrew prose accounts of 1096.

A comprehensive assessment of 1096 liturgy as a collective memorial requires an independent study. I would like to present here only one side of the issue, namely, the phenomenon of personal memorialization in that liturgy. In this instance, I will refer mainly (but not exclusively) to Qalonymos bar Yehuda's *piyyuṭim*.

One of the most discussed martyrological episodes related in the 1096 Hebrew chronicles is that of Rachel of Mainz, who slaughtered her children in order to prevent their baptism. The story is extant in two versions. It seems

4 It is unlikely that he wrote any *seliḥa* for the memorial day observed by the Mainz community because he seems to advocate in one *qina* (*mi yiten roshi mayyim*) a collective mourning for all the communities on the Ninth of Av.

that Qalonymos bar Yehuda refers to it in his *Amarti she'u*. In this *qina* he describes scenes of self-slaughter in Mainz and uses expressions and lines that appear in the long version of the Rachel narrative in Shelomo bar Shimshon's chronicle [henceforth: Chronicle A]. Isaiah Sonne concluded from his detailed literary analysis that in this instance Chronicle A is based on the version of the chronicle of the Mainz Anonymous [henceforth: Chronicle C] and the author embellished it with lines from Qalonymos's *piyyuṭ*. Yitzhak Baer, on the other hand, insisted that Qalonymos based his *piyyuṭ* on Chronicle A's version. In fact, both positions are untenable. Elsewhere, I have suggested a tentative solution for this literary problem.[5] Be that as it may, one thing is beyond controversy: Qalonymos was aware of, and refers in his *qina* to the Rachel story. Let us look at the relevant lines:

נְוַת בַּיִת הַיָּפָה בְּתוּלַת בַּת יְהוּדָה
צַוָּארָהּ פָּשְׁטָה וּמַאֲכֶלֶת הִשְׁתִּיזָה וְתִדְּדָה
עַיִן רָאֲתָה וַתְּעִידָהּ
סִיגְּפָה הָאֵם וּפָרְחָה רוּחָהּ
וְנַפְשָׁהּ הִשְׁלִימָה לָטֶבַח אֲרוּחָה כְּאֵרְחָה
אֵם הַבָּנִים שְׂמֵחָה
עָלְצוּ הַבָּנוֹת כְּנוּסוֹת וַאֲרוּשׂוֹת
לְאִבְחַת חֶרֶב דָּצוֹת וְשָׂשׂוֹת
דָּמָם עַל צְחִיחַ סֶלַע לְבִלְתִּי הִכָּסוֹת
פּוֹנֶה הָאָב בִּבְכִי וִילָלָה
עַצְמוֹ עַל חַרְבּוֹ לִדְקוֹר וּלְהַפִּילָה
וְהוּא מִתְגּוֹלֵל בַּדָּם בְּתוֹךְ הַמְּסִלָּה
צִדְקָה דִינָהּ פּוֹרִיָּה כְּהִקְרִיבָהּ עֲנָפֶיהָ
וּתְמוּר מִזְרָק דָּם קִבְּלָה בִּכְנָפֶיהָ
תִּתְיַפֵּחַ תְּפָרֵשׂ כַּפֶּיהָ

The beautiful one who dwells within,
the maiden daughter of Judah,
stretched her neck and honed and sharpened her knife;
An eye saw and testified.
Tormented was the mother and her spirit flew away
she submitted her soul to the slaughter
as if she was preparing a meal.
The mother of children rejoices.
The daughters exulted, those wed and those betrothed,
they rushed joyfully and gladly to the scourging sword,
their blood [shed] on a smooth rock, never to be covered over.
The father turns away with weeping and wailing,
throwing himself on the sword to be stabbed.

---

5 Abraham Gross, 'Historical and Halakhic Aspects of the Mass Martyrdom in Mainz: An Integrative Approach', in *Facing the Cross; The Persecutions of 1096 in History and Historiography*, ed. by Y. Assis et al. (Hebrew; Jerusalem: Magnes Press, 2000), pp. 187–91.

He wallows in his own blood on the street.
The fruitful [mother] proclaimed the righteousness of her judgement as she offered her scions.
And instead of the consecrated basin she caught [the blood] in the hem of her garment, sobbing and spreading out her arms.[6]

Now the *payyeṭan* did not reveal any specifics. He did not provide personal names. He did not even mention the name of the community in this particular *piyyuṭ*. In following such a policy, he uprooted, so to speak, the story from its original personal domain and endowed it with a collective dimension. Moreover, since the anonymity of the martyrs and of the community was maintained, all readers, even those who did not have a direct personal or communal connection to the events, including Jewish mourners in generations to come, would be able to identify with the non-personal, collective martyrdom described by Qalonymos. But the basic dimension of the *piyyuṭ* is communal. His Mainz audience knew intimately the historical background of this *piyyuṭ*. Clearly, there were others in Mainz who had experienced, had seen, or had heard of, similar events and could identify parts of the *piyyuṭ* with specific episodes or persons within the collective catastrophe.

If my analysis of the *payyeṭan*'s intentions is so far accepted, another question occurs. True, he wished to compose a poetic account of the 'epic' dimensions of the martyrdom. But did he intend to reveal, or at least hint, to his contemporary audience about Rachel's personal martyrdom? The composition of this influential *piyyuṭ* and the beginning of its communal use in the Mainz synagogue service apparently date to no later than the two decades after 1096. Therefore, we may assume that some of the Mainz elders who survived the persecutions were still alive. This being the case, it is highly improbable that they had neither heard nor read of the incident.

It is fashionable to set the Rachel story, in the long version of Chronicle A, in the context of Jewish-Christian polemics and interpret it as a literary attempt to construct a typological image of a superior Jewish woman-martyr. This line of historiography notwithstanding, one fact should be stated clearly: Rachel was not an imaginary figure. She was a woman of flesh and blood. She and her children are mentioned in the *Memorbuch* among the martyrs of 1096 in Mainz. Moreover, both accounts state that she was the 'daughter of Rabbi Yiṣḥaq bar Asher'. Mentioning two generations of her genealogy is not a com-

6 The translation of this *piyyuṭ* is based mainly on earlier translations by Abraham Rosenfeld, *Kinot for the Ninth of Av* (London: Labworth, 1965), and Avrohom C. Feuer and Avie Gold, *The Complete Tishah B'av Service* (ArtScroll Mesorah Series), (New York: Mesorah Publications, 1991).

mon characteristic. It is plausible that the reason for it is that Rabbi Yiṣḥaq bar Asher was none other than one of the foremost scholars of that generation.[7] If this is the case, then we may say that it is highly probable that Qalonymos indeed chose to relate the collective communal martyrdom through virtual citations of entire lines from the Rachel prose narrative as a memorial to the exceptional daughter of a revered rabbinic leader.

It seems to me that we may similarly interpret yet another section of the same *piyyuṭ*. Following the Rachel lines, Qalonymos raises, in a very novel poetic manner, a theological discussion of the problem of burial of the corpses:

רַעְיוֹנַי נִבְהֲלוּ וַאֲחָזַתְנִי פַּלָּצוּת וָשֶׁבֶר
בְּאַחַת נִמְצָא הַכָּתוּב בּוֹ תִּקְוָה וָסֶבֶר
כִּי זֶה לְבַדּוֹ יָבֹא לְיָרָבְעָם אֶל קֶבֶר
שָׁלֵם נִמְצָא בְּכָל פָּעֳלוֹ
נַפְשׁוֹ הִשְׁלִים לָטֶבַח מִפַּחַד חֵילוֹ
וְגַם קְבוּרָה לֹא הָיְתָה לוֹ
תַּתִּי לִבִּי מְצוֹא תֹּכֶן עִנְיָנָיו
יָדַעְתִּי אֲנִי צֶרֶק וְיֹשֶׁר דִּינָיו
יִהְיֶה טוֹב לְיִרְאֵי הָאֱל-הִים אֲשֶׁר יִירְאוּ מִלְּפָנָיו
קְדוֹשָׁיו לֹא יַאֲמִין הִשְׁלִים עֲוֹנוֹתָיו לְשַׂעֲרָה
סִימָן טוֹב בְּאָדָם בְּלֹא נִסְפַּד וְנִקְבַּר כַּשּׁוּרָה
בְּיוֹם עֶבְרָה לֹא יִירָא

My thoughts are confounded shuddering and distraughtness take hold of me,
because of one single [good deed] found in him Scriptures gives hope and expectation,
for he alone of Jeroboam's [stock] shall come to the grave.
[Yet] one found perfect in his every deed,
submitted himself to the slaughter in awe of God,
for him there was not even a proper burial!
I have set my mind to find the reason for His dealings,
For this I do know: His judgements are righteous and just,
and it will be good for the God-fearing that they may be awed in His Presence.
He puts no trust in His holy ones, rather He punishes their sins even to a hair.
Indeed it is a good sign for a man if he is not eulogized or buried properly.
[Such a man] should not fear on the day of reckoning.

We have here the poetic discussion of what seems like a divine injustice in that the Jewish corpses were thrown into the streets (temporarily) in a further act of humiliation. An extreme sensitivity to the need for proper, immediate burial is also highly conspicuous throughout the 1096 Hebrew Chronicles. While we might expect a general discussion in broad terms, Qalonymos surprisingly uses the third person singular form:

7 This identification has recently been suggested by Mataniah Y. Ben-Gedalyah, 'The Sages of Speyer During and After the Persecutions of 1096: Their Biographies, Communal Leadership, and Spiritual Works' (doctoral dissertation, Bar-Ilan University, Ramat Gan, 2007), p. 64.

שָׁלֵם נִמְצָא בְּכָל פָּעֳלוֹ
נַפְשׁוֹ הִשְׁלִים לָטֶבַח מִפַּחַד חֵילוֹ
[...] וְגַם קְבוּרָה לֹא הָיְתָה לּוֹ
קְדוֹשָׁיו לֹא יַאֲמִין הִשְׁלִים עֲוֹנוֹתָיו לְשַׂעֲרָה
סִימָן טוֹב בְּאָדָם בְּלֹא נִסְפַּד וְנִקְבַּר כַּשּׁוּרָה
בְּיוֹם עֶבְרָה לֹא יִירָא

I think it may well be that the *payyeṭan* is here hinting at the death of the revered communal leader, Rabbi Qalonymos the Parnas, probably his relative. The circumstances surrounding his death were recorded in several oral traditions. According to all of these traditions, he died in, or close to, Rüdesheim, not in Mainz. In Chronicle A, where the accounts of his death are recounted, it is not clear that his corpse was ever brought to Mainz for burial, in contradistinction to other martyrs who eventually received proper burial.[8] In this way, then, Qalonymos found a way to mention, mourn, and memorialize a revered communal leader.

From all of this, it follows that it is possible to ascribe to some of 1096 poets the writing of lines that were understood by all readers as general descriptions but also contained hints of an individual and personal nature.

Indeed, the mode of interpretation here offered, which presupposes an allusion to a specific woman, when the lines themselves seem to betray no such intention, is not unique. *Al domi le-dami*, one of the first of the 1096 *piyyuṭim*, was written by Rabbi David bar Meshullam. The context is the cruel massacre of Jewish women by the Crusaders:

יִרְאֶה יֵרָאֶה פְּעֻלַּת בָּנוֹת בּוֹטְחוֹת
בְּחֹם הַיּוֹם עֲרֻמּוֹת לַשֶּׁמֶשׁ נִשְׁטָחוֹת
יָפָה בַּנָּשִׁים מְבֻקָּעֵי כָּרֵס וּמְפֻלָּחוֹת
מִבֵּין רַגְלֶיהָ שִׁלְיָהּ וָלָד מַפְרִיחוֹת

Let this sight come before You: young women who put their trust in You
were stripped naked in broad daylight;
the fairest of women – their wombs slashed open
letting out the unborn from between their legs.[9]

To whom did that 'fairest of women' refer? *Prima facie*, the *payyeṭan* describes all young women, some of whom were pregnant and who were brutally murdered. The fact that the poem moves from the plural to the singular form, and then alternates between these two forms, with no apparent reason, is puzzling.

---

8 Concerning other members of his group, it is related that they intended to return to Mainz in order at least to be buried in a Jewish cemetery, but were killed on the way.

9 This translation is based on T. Carmi, *The Penguin Book of Hebrew Verse* (New York: Penguin Books, 1981), p. 375.

The commentary on these lines in one manuscript, citing oral tradition, states: 'And I have heard that this maiden was the daughter-in-law of Rabbi Meir bar Yiṣḥaq Shaṣ'[10] Rabbi Meir bar Yiṣḥaq was a much revered *payyeṭan* and scholar in the second half of the eleventh century, and therefore it stands to reason that David bar Meshullam would think of memorializing the Rabbi's daughter-in-law.[11] Obviously, this tradition, with a precise identification of the woman, does not stem from the syntactic problem. There is, however, a hint that ties that beautiful, pregnant woman with Rabbi Meir bar Yiṣḥaq Shaṣ. The poetic expression *yir'e yera'e*, which opens the verse above, is special and had been coined by Rabbi Meir himself in his *'aqeda* poetry. Thus, the *payyeṭan*, while formulating his description in a generalized way, planted a clue that many of his audience would have understood, thereby making a connection to individuals.[12]

Rabbi Eli'ezer bar Nathan was one of the important scholars in post-1096 Mainz (died *about* 1153). He composed two *piyyuṭim* about the 1096 persecution and alludes to them in two others. He also compiled one of the 1096 Chronicles. This literary work differs from the other Chronicles in that the author inserted short *qinot* about the major communities. After a short description of the limited killing in Speyer, a short *qina* is inserted. Beyond some general praise of the community the *qina* is, in effect, a summary of the prose description that precedes it. It includes the following factual lines:

[...] עֵדָה הַמְיֻוחָדָה
אֲשֶׁר יִחֲדָה צוּרָהּ
כַּהֲרוּגֵי מַלְכוּת עֲשָׂרָה [...]
זוּג קוֹדֶשׁ
בְּזִיו חוֹדֶשׁ
בִּכְבוֹדָהּ נִתְחַבְּרָה
בִּצְרוֹר הַחַיִּים לְהִתְאַצְּרָה

the special community
which unified its Rock
just like the Ten Martyrs [...]
Holy [Sanctified] wife
In the month of Ziv (Iyyar)

10 ושמעתי שהיתה כלתו של רבינ' מאיר שליח ציבור אותה הנערה – Ms. Bodley 1209, fol. 84b. It is referred to in Abraham Grossman, 'The Roots of Kiddush Ha-Shem in Ancient Ashkenaz', in *Sanctity of Life and Martyrdom*, ed. by I. Gafni and A. Ravitzky (Hebrew; Jerusalem: Shazar Center, 1992), p. 103 n. 9.

11 Avraham Grossman, *The Early Sages of Ashkenaz. Their Lives, Leadership and Works (900–1096)*, (Hebrew; Jerusalem: Magnes Press, 1988), pp. 292–96.

12 I owe this insight to Avraham Fraenkel.

Attached herself to her honour
To be bound in the Bond of Life

In both, the prose narrative and the *piyyuṭ*, the number of people who were killed, is ten. While the *piyyuṭ* likens the martyrs to the famous 'Ten Martyrs' of antiquity, the chronicle specifies that it is also the actual number of martyrs in Speyer. Those men are followed by one woman who committed suicide. She is not included in the initial ten, all of whom are men, and therefore this does not contradict Chronicles A and C which talk about eleven having been killed.

Now *zug* is a short form of *bat-zug*, 'wife', 'spouse'. So, who is the woman? Whose wife was she? According to one source, her name was Sarah, wife of Rabbi Shabbetai bar Qalonymos, the Gabbai, one of the ten martyred men.[13] If this is correct – and we have no good reason to doubt it – then the *payyeṭan* hinted at the identity of the woman by calling her *zug*. This is a good clue in the case of this particular suicide – not to be confused with the common 1096 self-slaughter – since the source mentioned above says that she killed herself in an extreme act of grief when she heard of her husband's death. The word *zug* is very precisely and appropriately chosen.[14]

One of the *piyyuṭim* that was interpreted as referring in some of its lines to historical details and figures is *berit keruta*. This *seliḥa* was composed by Binyamin bar Ḥiyya. This *payyeṭan* is otherwise unknown but was clearly a talmudic scholar. Two of his lines read thus:

יְדִידַי שְׁלְפֵי שְׁמַד בְּמַחֲבָא בַּחֲרָדָה מִבֹּא
דֶּרֶךְ יִקָּרֵא לָמוֹ לַעֲבוֹר בּוֹ

How are we to understand, let alone translate, these two difficult lines? The only general conclusion one can reach is that they are somehow related to persecution and concealment. An early thirteenth-century commentary, preserving an otherwise unknown tradition, interprets it as referring to the author himself:

זה עשה ר' בנימין על עצמו ועל שאר בני אדם שניצלו מן השמד על ידי בריחה כמו שהוא ניצול עם אנשי נישנא בכרך ועם אנשי שפירא בבריחה. שילפי, זה בריחה במחבה, שנתחבאו בכרך ובשאר המקומות שיכלו להנצל

13 For the citation of this relatively unused source, a discussion of its authenticity, and an interpretation of the poetic lines, see Ben-Gedalyah [above, n. 7], pp. 166–78.

14 This would also indicate that 'her honour' refers to her husband (although a reference to God cannot be ruled out).

> This was written by Rabbi Binyamin about himself and about others who had been saved from the persecution by escaping, just as he had been saved along with the people of Neuss in the city and with the people of Speyer through such an escape. *Shilpei* means escaping into hiding, since they hid in the city and in any other place where they could thus be saved.

The information as it here appears cannot be entirely accurate.[15] Inaccuracy occurs all too often in the process of transmitting facts over more than a century. It should not, however, lead us to discount the general historical information imbedded in these lines according to that tradition. People were aware of the *payyeṭan*'s intentions, either through knowledge of his personal ordeal during the persecutions, or through information that he himself passed on to his own community or circle. In any event, the nature of this description is personal and 'informative'. It may seem strange to find it in a *seliḥa*, the addressee of which is God. Why the need to tell Him this detail? This *piyyuṭ* has other historical references, all of which make sense only in the context of a poetic narrative for which the undercurrent element of memorialization is central.

It seems to me that the interpretations given by the commentators of the twelfth and thirteenth centuries reflect, by and large, credible traditions that date back to the composition of the *piyyuṭim*. Moreover, the *payyeṭanim* themselves could have been the initial oral decipherers of the clues to individuals. Chronologically, we are on the threshold of the *Ḥasidei Ashkenaz* movement with its rigorous interpretation of every word and nuance in the prayer-book, including *piyyuṭim*. Like many elements that characterize this movement, how-

15 Chronicle C tell us that the Speyer community had been led away and hidden by its Bishop, in his 'fortified towns' until the Crusaders gave up and continued their journey on from there. This should not be connected in any way with the hideaway at Neuss, which was one of the towns of the Bishop of Cologne. Indeed, it was one the seven places where that Bishop hid his Jews. Chronicles A and B tell us about those who were not saved and died as martyrs and – as is all too often true about 1096 – we lack serious information about the events in Neuss. Our *payyeṭan* may have belonged to the group that had been sent from Cologne by the Bishop to hide in Neuss. The *Memorbuch* does record a martyr from Cologne by the name of Mar Moshe bar Ḥiyya (Siegmund Salfeld, *Das Martyrologium des Nürenberger Memorbuches*, Berlin: Leonhard Simion, 1898, p. 9). On the other hand, there may be an indication of a local Jewish presence in Neuss prior to 1096 in Chronicles A and B, where there is the story of a martyr whose son was hanged with his sons on the door of 'his house' (Eva Haverkamp, *Hebräische Berichte über die Judenverfolgungen während des Ersten Kreuzzugs*, Hannover: Hahnsche Buchhandlung, 2005, p. 409). Otherwise there is no indication of a pre-1096 Jewish community in Neuss (See: Alfred Haverkamp, *Geschichte der Juden im Mittelalter von der Nordsee bis zu den Südalpen*, Teil 2 Ortskatalog, Hannover: Hahnsche Buchhandlung, 2002, p. 253). I thank Professor Andreas Lehnardt for this reference.

ever, the centrality of the *piyyuṭ* and close attention to its nuances date back to the eleventh century.

Admittedly, some of those oral interpretations were not intended by the *payyeṭan*. The following seems to be a case in point. Efrayim bar Yiṣḥaq of Regensburg (mid-twelfth century) includes in a *seliḥa* (*ani ani ha-medabber*) a description of the persecutions of 1096, although the reference to them is not explicit. One lines reads as follows:

רְמוּסִים נִגְלָלוּ / בְּדָמִים נִבְלָלוּ / וּבְלוּלִים יַעֲלוּ / מְסִילָּה בַּעֲרָבָה

This describes trampled bodies as if they were dung, their blood mixing together, and the joint ascent of their souls to Heaven. In a thirteenth-century commentary we do, however, find:

> **רמוסים נגללו**, בדם אשר ברגלי סוסים היו נופלים ומבללים עצמם בדם, שיסברו שנהרגו, והיו שוכנים כך. **ובלולים יעלו**, כשהשונאים הלכו להם וסבורים שנהרגו כולם, היו הבלולים בדם עומדים והולכים בערבה וביער להחבות.[16]
>
> [...] They fell and rolled in the blood [...] so that they would think that they were dead, and they lay this way. [...] and when the enemy left, thinking that they were all dead, those who had rolled in the blood got up and went to hide in the fields and forests.

There is no intrinsic problem with the line of poetic text that should force us to look there for this far-fetched interpretation. It is simply *eisegesis*. The commentator found a line into which he could read the historical information that Ashkenazi tradition had transmitted to his generation. Here, then, we have evidence of the serious nature of public interest in the *piyyuṭim* and its expectation of finding within it a hidden store of information about 1096 that was neither religiously significant nor of any relevance to the *piyyuṭ* as liturgy.[17]

I have posed a question concerning the weight of memory and memorialization intended by the *payyeṭanim* in composing 1096 liturgical poetry. While acknowledging the difficulty of answering this question in all its complexity, let alone in a short paper, I have attempted to establish a basic working assumption that has far-reaching implications for our understanding of the Ashkenazi medieval individual and society.

The sheer volume of the liturgical corpus should already be appreciated as an initial indication that their basic emotions and response to the mass-killing and the loss of family and friends, alongside the destruction of a pros-

---

16 Efraim E. Urbach, *Arugat Ha-Bosem*, vol. 3 (Jerusalem: Mekize Nirdamim, 1963), p. 368, n. 70.
17 Compare Urbach, *Arugat Ha-Bosem*, vol. 4, pp. 182–84.

perous and proud community, are rooted in the human condition. In this sense, I contend, the needs of medieval man are not much different from our own.[18]

We can find in the liturgical poetry more than a few references to historical details surrounding the events of 1096. Those include the recording of dates, names of communities, allusions to the Pope and his declaration of the Crusade at Clairmont, the developing stages of the Crusade, and Count Emicho. Some of the facts mentioned may be understood in religious terms as addressing either God or the community, such as I have listed above. Some data may, however, also be explained – and perhaps even primarily explained – as arising out of a need to memorialize the events separately from any practical, religious context.

Singling out, as I have done above, references to well-known martyred individuals, identifiable to the community of survivors, supplies us with unequivocal proof of my claim for an areligious memorialization, and leads to the unavoidable conclusion that they had a need to memorialize as much as possible, no matter what the literary genre. It was not only for the sake of perpetuating the memory of martyrdom, of fighting an existing trend towards apostasy, of setting up a model response for their own and for future generations, or of defining Jewish-Christian relations. Taking a religious literary medium and using it to memorialize individuals can emerge only from an emotional need that is identical to our own, that is, a desire to preserve the memory of people dear to us. Appreciating how this was achieved in a covert fashion teaches us not only the art and subtlety of the *payyeṭanim* but also the difficulty of including such personal material, which was immaterial, indeed alien, to the religious aims of *piyyuṭ*. In this respect, then, 1096 liturgical poetry tries to do in a constrained fashion – given the narrowness of the religious-literary medium – what the 1096 chroniclers could do freely.[19]

What still await analysis and characterization are the diverse expressions of response to the events of 1096. It seems to me that every type of response,

18 For a most valuable illustration of emotions of grief expressed by a father during the Black Death, see Ron Barkai, 'On Children's Death in the Black Death', in *Women, The Aged, and Children: Festschrift in Honor of Shulamit Shahar*, ed. by Y. Hen and Miri Eliav-Feldon (Hebrew; Jerusalem: Shazar Center, 2001), pp. 67–84.

19 An exception to the rule is the (relatively late) *adabra be-ṣar ruḥi* which describes the martyrdom at Mainz and mentions two public figures who are also named in the Chronicles. From the second half of the twelfth century, we encounter the explicit naming of martyrs. This applies to cases of persecutions on a smaller scale than 1096, such as the blood libel and the host libel. One should also take into account that the very writing of *piyyuṭim* (especially of *qinot*) on local persecutions is in itself a daring novelty, and the mentioning of names should be seen as a further stage in the development of this genre.

be it literary or behavioural, has its parallel in contemporary modes of memorialization, especially of the victims of terror and those who have fallen in the military. The differences are cultural. Thus, secular society, devoid of religious beliefs in, or concern with, the afterlife, the eternity of the soul, reward and punishment and related matters, cannot memorialize the dead within the system of beliefs and the language of generations past. Hence, contemporary modes of memorialization have come into being. Modern culture has adapted itself but has not invented anything new, save for technological innovations that enable new formats of memorialization. These modern means hardly change the essence of things. Twelfth-century Ashkenazi society needed, and therefore developed, a variety of vehicles of memorialization. These included, among others, general customs to strengthen the folk memory, the rituals of memorial days, and the compilation of a *Memorbuch,* that is, a list of the names of the victims to be read in the synagogue on certain occasions.

Although the *Memorbuch* is not the focus of the present article, a short comment on its nature will illustrate the point I am trying to make concerning 1096 liturgy. According to Yisrael Yuval, the *Memorbuch* testifies to 'the deep penetration of the revenge concept into the religious ritual of Ashkenazi Jews in the Middle Ages'. This assessment was rejected by Ezra Fleischer who preferred to see in it a testimony to their simple wish to remember their dead martyrs on certain dates. Yuval's reply was: 'Emotionally, this is certainly true. Nevertheless, the ritual significance of *hazkarat neshamot* [and not *zekhirat neshamot*] in the *Memorbuch* does not relate to the memory of man but to that of God [*yizkor Elohim*] [...].'[20] Yuval was saying that, if Fleischer was right, then the ritual of memory of the dead should have been called *zekhirat* (= 'remembering', or, 'mentioning') and not *hazkarat* [= 'reminding'] *neshamot*. Reminding can be directed only to God, and, according to Yuval, this is for the purpose of avenging the death of the victims.

If we adhere closely to the written word, Yuval is certainly right. After all, it is a double-edged prayer to God, requesting Him to remember the victims and to avenge their death. Since, however, there is a wide recognition of the presence of an emotional dimension beyond the religious one, we need to pose a number of questions. How important is the emotional element in the *Yizkor* prayer? Is it central, or secondary to the ritual? Why, according to Fleischer, is this dimension absent from the words of the prayer? The answer to the last question is, in my opinion, fairly simple – because it is a prayer, and not a modern civic memorial service whose explicit focus is the expression of collective grief and pain.

---

20 See above n. 1.

Yet, the medieval ritual is no different from the *hazkarat neshamot,* still practised today, 900 years after 1096. A strong expression of human and personal emotions is present, even if the language and contents are religious. In other words, we encounter here a ritualization of emotions. The expression of emotions passes through a religious vortex, so to speak, and the result is a ritualistic expression. What we therefore meet here is a traditional outer shell of language that hides within itself human impulses and emotions. These are destined to receive their direct, personal, and unmediated expressions, as we know them, only in the modern-secular era.

This seems to hold true for the *piyyuṭim*, the main topic of the present article. The language they knew best was religious.[21] And so, liturgy had to be the choice, and in accordance with the forms dictated by synagogal tradition. However, the impulse beneath this religious surface was one of grief, loss, and longing. I suggest that we should view the *Memorbuch* in the same vein. I believe that this is the correct approach to the entire issue of the medieval Jewish memorialization of victims that is concealed in all genres of post-persecution literature.[22]

21 Cf. Lucette Valenci, 'From Sacred History to Historical Memory and Back: The Jewish Past', *History and Anthropology* 2 (1986), pp. 283–91. I thank Amnon Raz-Krakotzkin for bringing this article to my attention.

22 Elsewhere, I have suggested that memorialization is a crucial motivating factor in the composition of the Hebrew Chronicles of 1096 (Abraham Gross, 'Reflections on Halakhic and Non-Halakhic Aspects of Kiddush Ha-Shem in 1096', in *Be'erot Yitzhak: Studies in Memory of Isadore Twersky*, ed. by Jay M. Harris (Cambridge MA: Harvard University Press, 2005), pp. 24–25).

Yechiel Y. Schur

'When the Grave was Searched, the Bones of the Deceased were not Found': Corporeal Revenants in Medieval Ashkenaz

Dear dead! – Not as before will Elijah come
To stretch out upon you with burning lips and eyes.
You are cold. No voice cries out. There is not one to listen.
And you will never rise.

Raḥel, 'Elijah'[1]

1 Introduction

Reassuring and comforting indeed is the biblical scene about Elijah resuscitating the deceased child. But as the poet Raḥel touchingly reminds us, this biblical scene is but a heartening fantasy; in real life the dead remain dead and will never come back. Or will they?

The belief that the dead will come alive in the unknown future has been traditionally regarded as a foundational religious belief in Judaism, and various tenets of this belief are shared by Christianity and Islam.[2] According to the Mishna, a person who denies this belief has no share in the world to come.[3] In their efforts to validate the belief in the resurrection of the dead, and in large part in response to sectarian groups who denied this belief, the sages of the Talmud marshalled various verses as prooftexts for this religious tenet.

Medieval Jewish thinkers, most notably Sa'adya and Maimonides, elaborated the theme of the resurrection of the dead far more extensively than earlier writers. Sa'adya devotes an entire chapter in his *Book of Doctrines and Beliefs* to discussing the concept of bodily resurrection[4] and Maimonides discusses it

---

1 *Flowers of Perhaps*, Eng. trans. by Robert Friend and Shimon Sandbank (New Milford, CT: Toby Press, 2008), p. 51. I thank Ephraim Kanarfogel, Yonatan Moss, Amnon Raz-Krakotzkin, Sabine Schmidtke, and Galili Shahar for reading an earlier draft of this article.

2 For Christianity, see Caroline W. Bynum, *Resurrection of the Body in Western Christianity, 200–1336* (New York: Columbia University Press, 1995). For Islam, see Jane I. Smith and Yvonne Y. Haddad, *The Islamic Understanding of Death and Resurrection* (Oxford; New York: Oxford University Press, 2002), esp. pp. 31–61. I thank Sabine Schmidtke for this latter reference.

3 *mSanh.* 10.1, ed. by Ch. Albeck (Tel Aviv: Devir, 1953), p. 202.

4 Sa'adya Gaon, *The Book of Beliefs and Opinions*, Treatise VII, Eng. trans. by Samuel Rosenblatt (New Haven: Yale University Press, 1948), pp. 264–89. On Sa'adya, see Arthur Hyman,

in his *Mishne Torah*, the *Commentary on the Mishna*, and in a treatise devoted exclusively to this topic, commonly known as the *Treatise on Resurrection*.[5]

One commonality in the texts about the resurrection of the dead written by these two Jewish philosophers is that they have treated the topic as part of a broader discussion of the days to come and the messiah. Sa'adya's chapter on the resurrection precedes a chapter on redemption whereas Maimonides' discussion in the *Commentary on the Mishna* appears in his introduction to the tenth chapter of *Tractate Sanhedrin*, where he extensively expands the talmudic discussion about the world to come.

The various and somewhat contradictory statements of Maimonides, in particular, about the resurrection of the dead have led scholars to debate his real stance regarding the belief in a bodily resurrection. On the one hand, Maimonides famously claims in his *Commentary on the Mishna* that 'the delights of the soul are everlasting and uninterrupted, and there is no resemblance in any possible way between spiritual and bodily enjoyments.'[6] Similarly, since according to the *Mishne Tora*, there are in the other-world no 'bodies and forms, but souls of the righteous only without body, like the angels on high',[7] the concept of bodily resurrection is rendered futile and meaningless. On the other hand, Maimonides affirms in his *Treatise on Resurrection* and elsewhere the traditional rabbinic belief in bodily resurrection, thereby echoing his

Eschatological Themes in Medieval Jewish Philosophy (Milwaukee, Wis.: Marquette University Press, 2002), pp. 45–51; Steven Harvey, 'Logistical and Other Otherworldly Problems in Saadya', in *Esoteric and Exoteric Aspects in Judeo-Arabic Culture*, ed. by Benjamin Hary and Haggai Ben-Shammai (Leiden; Boston: Brill, 2006), pp. 55–84; Henry Malter, *Saadia Gaon: His Life and Works* (Philadelphia: Jewish Publication Society, 1942), pp. 230–37. Note that the definition of the resurrection of the dead as an occurrence that '[...] will take place in this world of ours as a natural phenomenon' in Malter's discussion of the seventh chapter of Sa'adya's *Book of Opinions and Beliefs* (p. 231 in Malter's book) differs from the way the phenomenon of revenants is understood in this paper. Malter means that the resurrection will take place in this world rather than in the world to come but still maintains an eschatological dimension with regard to the question as to when the resurrection of the dead will occur.

5 On Maimonides, see Hyman, *Eschatological Themes*, pp. 75–79; Albert Friedberg, 'Maimonides' Reinterpretation of the Thirteenth Article of Faith: Another Look at the Essay on Resurrection', *Jewish Studies Quarterly*, 10:3 (2003), pp. 244–55; Alexandra Wright, 'Immortality and Resurrection: Maimonides and the Maimonidean Controversy', *Aspects of Liberal Judaism*, ed. by David J. Goldberg and Edward Kessler (London; Portland, OR: Vallentine Mitchell, 2004), pp. 159–69. I thank my Penn colleague Marc Herman for sharing with me his unpublished article 'Evaluating Maimonides' Treatise on Resurrection.'

6 Maimonides, *Commentary on the Mishna*, vol. 4, Heb. trans. by Yosef Kafaḥ (Jerusalem: Mosad Harav Kook, 1965), pp. 204–205. See Joshua Abelson, 'Maimonides on the Jewish Creed', *Jewish Quarterly Review*, 19:1 (1906), p. 38.

7 Maimonides, *Mishne Torah*, Laws of Repentance, 8.2.

commitment to the traditional view, which may be the result of his religious role in the Jewish community as a major halakhic figure and communal leader.

Without attempting to reconcile the seeming contradictions in Maimonides' treatment of the resurrection of the dead, it becomes evident that, by considering bodily resurrection in the context of the days to come and the messianic period, Maimonides was able to remain, perhaps intentionally, vague and inconclusive. Only in the unknown future will the exact nature of the days to come become clear and, therefore, one is advised not to spend much time worrying about such issues as the nature of the messianic period and the world to come.[8]

Modern scholars have also conventionally treated the topic of bodily resurrection in the context of eschatological and messianic beliefs. To mention but one example, E. E. Urbach situates the bulk of the discussion about the resurrection of the dead in the book's last chapter under the title 'On Redemption'. Resurrection is grouped with topics such as redemption, apocalyptical literature, and messianism in ancient Judaism.[9] This tendency is easily identified in many other scholarly discussions of resurrection in biblical,[10] talmudic,[11] and medieval texts.[12]

The association of bodily resurrection with eschatology and the days to come is so common that it is nearly impossible to deal with the topic in any other way. But, historically speaking, people in pre-modern society commonly accepted the phenomenon of the dead coming back to life not merely as part of a traditional belief in the resurrection of the dead, but as part of everyday experience. With regard to Western Europe during the Middle Ages, several studies have shown the commonality of beliefs in revenants (the dead coming undead) and, more generally, the acceptance of beliefs in frequent encounters between the living and the dead.[13]

---

8 Maimonides, *Mishne Torah*, Laws of Kings and Wars, 12.2.

9 Ephraim E. Urbach, *The Sages, Their Concepts and Beliefs*, Eng. trans. by Israel Abrahams (Cambridge, MA.: Harvard University Press, 1987), pp. 649–92; pp. 990–1009.

10 Lloyd R. Bailey, *Biblical Perspectives on Death* (Philadelphia: Fortress Press, 1979), pp. 73–4.

11 Jacob Neusner, 'Death and Afterlife in the Later Rabbinic Sources: The Two Talmuds and Associated Midrash-Compilations', in *Judaism in Late Antiquity*, vol. IV (Leiden, New York: E. J. Brill, 2000), pp. 267–91.

12 Julius Guttmann, *Philosophies of Judaism: The History of Jewish Philosophy from Biblical Times to Franz Rosenzweig*, Eng. trans. by David W. Silverman (New York: Schocken, 1973), pp. 82–83.

13 See Ronald C. Finucane, *Appearances of the Dead: A Cultural History of Ghosts* (London: Junction Books, 1982), esp. pp. 29–89; Aaron Gurevich, *Historical Anthropology of the Middle Ages*, ed. Jana Howlett (Chicago: University of Chicago Press, 1992), esp. pp. 65–89; Nancy Caciola, 'Wraiths, Revenants and Ritual in Medieval Culture', *Past and Present*, 152 (1996), pp. 3–45; Jean-Claude Schmitt, *Ghosts in the Middle Ages: The Living and the Dead in Medieval*

In this paper I argue that medieval Jews, like their non-Jewish counterparts, believed in the phenomenon of revenants. Like Christians, Jews believed that a dead person could come alive in the relatively near future after that person's demise (as opposed to returning in the unknown eschatological time frame). Moreover, like Christians, some Jews believed that a revenant comprised *actual* corporeal elements of the deceased, rather than a spiritual entity, such a ghost, which may appear as a human being but is lacking any actual corporeal elements.

I also submit that a belief in the phenomenon of revenants was held by the rabbinic elite and not merely by ordinary, 'superstitious' folk. This contention is in line with other studies on medieval Ashkenaz that have called into question any bifurcated division between the elite and the populace.[14] Such a scholarly effort at challenging the two-tiered distinction between the perceptions of the elite and those of the populace is also apparent in more general works on pre-modern society.[15] As Peter Brown has shown in a different context, the two-tiered model can rarely be sustained and is rather a scholarly construct with limited correspondence to the historical reality of late antiquity or medieval Europe.[16]

My focus on revenants in medieval Ashkenaz stems from two reasons. First, the exegetical approach known as *peshaṭ* and championed by a number of Ashkenazi scholars lends itself to interpreting biblical passages about the undead in a more literal and factual way than, for example, the alternative

Society, Eng. trans. Teresa L. Fagan (Chicago: University of Chicago Press, 1998). For a discussion of the phenomenon of revenants in a later period, see Paul Barber, *Vampires, Burial and Death: Folklore and Reality* (New Haven: Yale University Press, 1988).

14 See Avriel Bar-Levav, 'Death and the (Blurred) Boundaries of Magic: Strategies of Coexistence,' in *Kabbalah: Journal for the Study of Jewish Mystical Texts*, 7 (2002), pp. 51–64; idem, 'We are Where We are Not: The Cemetery in Jewish Culture,' in *Jewish Studies*, 41 (2002), pp. 15–46; Moshe Idel, *Golem: Jewish Magical and Mystical Traditions on the Artificial Anthropoid* (Albany, N.Y.: State University of New York Press, 1990), esp. pp. 57–80; Ephraim Kanarfogel, *Peering Through the Lattices: Mystical, Magical, and Pietistic Dimensions in the Tosafist Period* (Detroit: Wayne State University Press, 2000); Dov Schwartz, *Astral Magic in Medieval Jewish Thought* (Hebrew; Ramat Gan: Bar Ilan University Press, 1999); David Shyovitz, "'He Has Created a Remembrance of His Wonders': Nature and Embodiment in the Thought of the Hasidei Ashkenaz" (Philadelphia: doctoral dissertation, University of Pennsylvania, 2011).

15 Robert Darnton, *The Great Cat Massacre and Other Episodes in French Cultural History* (New York: Basic Books, 1984); Carlo Ginzburg, *The Cheese and the Worms: The Cosmos of a Sixteenth-century Miller*, Eng. trans. by John and Anne Tedeschi (Baltimore: Johns Hopkins University Press, 1980).

16 Peter Brown, *The Cult of the Saints: Its Rise and Function in Latin Christianity* (Chicago: University of Chicago Press, 1981).

exegetical approaches of various commentators from medieval Spain.[17] Furthermore, even specific references to the resurrection of the dead in rabbinic texts are treated by Ashkenazi scholars (most notably by Moshe Taku) in a manner that is more factual and empirical than that found in parallel discussions of the topic by Sefardi thinkers.[18]

2 Corporeal revenants

In a short anonymous treatise from Ashkenaz on the use of Divine names for conjurations (*hashba'ot*), we find the following intriguing passage:

> Said R. Yiṣḥaq: It occurred that Eliyahu, the son of R. Todros from the town of *Qeranot*[19], was killed at the age of twenty inside the city. The son was buried promptly while the father was away but when the father returned he refused to eat or drink anything until the great sages, R. Ya'aqov [b. Meir] of Ramerupt and R. Eliyahu [b. Yehuda] of Paris permitted him to call upon (*le-ha'alot le-fanaw*) his son by using the Divine Name in the presence of the entire community [...] After receiving the consent of the rabbis, the father immersed himself in a ritual bath, wore white clothes and, together with the community, fasted on a Thursday[20] and went to the synagogue. Having inserted the Name between the Torah scrolls [inside the Holy Ark], the father conjured up the deceased son after which the son appeared between the Torah scrolls. Having *removed his son* (*we-laqaḥ beno le-horido*) from the Holy Ark with the entire community witnessing, the father spoke to the son as the father had wished and then *returned him* (*heḥziro*) back to the Holy Ark [...][21]

Relating the moving story of a father who could not attend his son's funeral and wished to bid farewell to the deceased son, the text raises several issues

17 See Sarah Kamin, *Rashi: Peshuṭo shel Miqra u-Midrasho shel Miqra* (Jerusalem: The Magnes Press, 1986); Sara Japhet, *Dor Dor u-Parshanaw: Asufat Meḥqarim Be-Parshanut Ha-Miqra*, *Asufot* 1 (Jerusalem: Mosad Bialik, 2008), pp. 133–309. For a recent comparison of the different exegetical approaches in Spain and Ashkenaz, see Eric Lawee, 'The Reception of Rashi's Commentary on the Torah in Spain: The Case of Adam's Mating with the Animals', *Jewish Quarterly Review*, 97:1 (2007), pp. 33–66.

18 Compare the discussion of the resurrection of the dead in Moshe Taku's *Ketav Tamim* with Maimonides' *Treatise on Resurrection*. *Ketav Tamim*, ed. by Joseph Dan (Jerusalem: The Dinur Center, 1984); *Treatise on Resurrection*, in *Crisis and Leadership: Epistles of Maimonides*, ed. and trans. by Abraham Halkin and David Hartman (Philadelphia: Jewish Publication Society, 1985), pp. 211–33; 233–45.

19 This is the Hebrew spelling of the place but, regrettably, I am unable at this point to identify the town.

20 *mTa'an*. 1.4.

21 Kanarfogel, *Peering Through the Lattices*, p. 171.

noted in previous scholarly discussions. Most apparently, it attests to the involvement of Ashkenazi authorities in magical activities. In addition to the activity described here, other forms of magic were attributed to R. Todros.[22] R. Eliyahu of Paris was known for his piety and the use of mystical traditions concerning the end of days. But even such a normative authority as R. Ya'aqov b. Me'ir of Ramerupt (commonly referred to as 'Rabbenu Tam') ruled in favour of this mysterious practice. Moreover, what seems like an esoteric practice – the use of a Divine name for calling upon a dead person – was not done privately in a hidden place but in public, in front of the entire community, thus undermining the possible classification of the ritual as an esoteric kabbalistic activity performed in secrecy.

One additional, and rather unnoticed aspect of the text is the corporeality of the revived son. While it is not possible to know from this text the 'matter' from which the undead son was made (that is, spiritual elements only,[23] or real flesh and blood), the verbs employed to convey how the father interacted with his son by physically removing him from the holy ark and returning him there arguably allude to some form of corporeal existence.

If the corporeal essence of the undead son may seem at least speculative, if not unimaginable, additional texts from medieval Ashkenaz confirm this interpretation and show that at least some Ashkenazi Jews believed in the phenomenon of corporeal revenants. But before considering the medieval textual evidence, it is necessary to consider briefly and generally biblical and post-biblical references to post-mortem existence.

In the Hebrew Bible at least two different views concerning post-mortem existence may be identified. According to one approach, life is the joining of body and spirit and death is the separation of the two. With the departure of the soul, the body 'returns to the ground' and the soul 'returns to God who bestowed it.'[24] The rewards and punishments mentioned in the Bible are commonly promised in this world, with few instances of otherworldly incentives for obeying God or of otherworldly punishments for disobeying Him. But the Bible also alludes to various forms of post-mortem existence such as resurrec-

22 See reference in *ibid*, p. 171, no. 96.

23 This is suggested by Kanarfogel who refers to the miraculous incident as a resurrection of '(the image of) the son' but how can an image be resurrected? Although the word 'resurrection' would have been in line with my interpretation of the text as a revival of an embodied figure, and not merely the revival of an image, I refrained from using the word in my translation since the corresponding Hebrew words *teḥiyya* (see Ezek 37:3) or *le-haqiṣ* (see Dan 12:2) do not appear in the Hebrew text.

24 Eccl 12:7.

tion of the dead ('many of those that sleep in the dust of the earth will awake'[25]), the underworld (*she'ol*)[26], and the prohibition on any communication with the dead.[27] In addition, there are several scriptural stories of dead people returning to life, most notably the episode about Samuel and the medium in Endor (I Samuel 28) to which I shall return later. These instances demonstrate deep familiarity with, and awareness of, the world of the dead, although, in comparison with references to post-mortem existence in post-biblical texts, the Bible has relatively little to say about the otherworld.[28]

References in rabbinic texts to various forms of post-mortem existence are legion.[29] Among the many expressions of such beliefs are the various passages about bodily resurrection of the dead in the days to come[30]; the soul visiting the body of the deceased during the first twelve months after death[31]; and several stories about dead people appearing to the living as ghosts.[32] The rabbis clearly not only formulated and constructed their theoretical views of post-mortem existence but prescribed some concrete halakhic requirements directly related to their perceptions of death. For instance, they prohibited the conducting of certain rituals in the vicinity of the dead, since this is regarded as teasing the dead who are unable to partake in religious rituals. The Talmud formally grounds this prohibition in the dictum 'worms are as painful to the dead as a needle in the flesh of the living',[33] thus asserting that the deceased are capable of sensing physical pain.

Nevertheless, in spite of the engagement of ancient Jewish sages with issues pertaining to life after death, the evidence about their belief in the existence of corporeal revenants is rather limited. This assertion may be explained through the rabbinic discussion of the appearance of Samuel to the necromancer in Endor – arguably the most pronounced encounter with the undead in the Bible – where very little is said about the nature of the revealed prophet. The rabbis mention that due to Saul's elevated status the dead prophet appeared

25 Dan 12:2.

26 As in Gen 42:38.

27 As in Deut 18:11.

28 Joshua J. Adler, 'The Bible and Life After Death', *Jewish Bible Quarterly*, 22:2 (1994), pp. 85–90; John Day, 'The Development of Belief in Life After Death in Ancient Israel', in *After the Exile*, ed. by John Barton and David J. Reimer (Macon, Ga.: Mercer University Press, 1996), pp. 231–57.

29 For general discussion, see Julius Guttman, *Philosophies of Judaism*, Eng. trans. by David W. Silverman (New York: Schocken, 1973), pp. 82–83.

30 *bSanh.* 90b–92b.

31 *bŠabb.* 152b–153a.

32 For arguably the most famous story, see *bBer.* 18a–18b.

33 *bBer.* 18b.

to the necromancer upright rather than upside-down, which explains how the woman recognized Saul's attempt to deceive her by not identifying himself at the outset. The sages also comment on the cloak the undead prophet was wearing, asserting that it was the same cloak his mother made for him as a child, and the same cloak in which he was buried. But in both instances the rabbis raise exegetical questions – how the medium recognized Saul or why Samuel was wearing a cloak – that are solved with fairly characteristic methods of interpretation.

Keeping this background in mind, let us consider how Jews in medieval Ashkenaz viewed and explained the phenomenon of dead people coming back to life, and what mechanisms they employed to cope with the dangers posed by corporeal revenants. Writing on certain biblical and post-biblical texts about encounters between the living and the dead, Ashkenazi commentators explained such encounters and explored the nature of revenants by asking what precisely they are: spiritual entities lacking any physical attributes, or corporeal entities that are made of the real body parts of the deceased.

A text about the nature of revenants appears in a commentary on the Pentateuch written by the fourteenth-century Ashkenazi writer Menaḥem b. Me'ir Ṣiyyon.[34] Commenting on the arrival of the three angels to visit Abraham (Gen. 18:1–22), Ṣiyyon explains the nature of prophetic revelations in general but also discusses in this context apparitions in biblical and post-biblical texts. The following passage is cited by Ṣiyyon but is attributed to Yehuda b. Shemuel of Regensburg (Yehuda He-Ḥasid, 1140–1217):

> Regarding such instances as the vision of the necromancer in Endor, and concerning similar occurrences, Yehuda He-Ḥasid has maintained that if one were to search inside the grave no corporeal remains would have been found until after the revenant sheds its clothing (*malbushaw*). This is the meaning of the verse 'he feels only the pain of his flesh [and his spirit mourns in him].'[35] A spirit called 'animal spirit' (*nefesh behemit*) remains in the grave, mourning over its palace that returned to the ground. About this the sages say that 'worms are as painful to the dead as a needle in the flesh of the living' and speak allegorically about the lame and the blind.[36] This is the interpretation of the words 'I see a divine being coming up from the earth',[37] meaning that the spirit remains with the body in the grave but that the soul, which is 'bound up in the bundle of life'[38], will not separate itself by the forces of impurity from the divine splendour.[39]

34 See the discussion about him in Israel J. Yuval, *Ḥakhamim Be-Doram: Ha-Manhigut Ha-Ruḥanit shel Yehudei Germania Be-Shilhei Yemei Ha-Benayim* (Jerusalem: Magnes Press, 1988), pp. 282–311.

35 Job 14:22.

36 *bSanh.* 91a–91b.

37 I Sam 28:13.

38 I Sam 25:29.

39 Menaḥem Ṣiyyon, *Sefer Ṣiyyuni* (Jerusalem, 1963), p. 10c.

The key element in this passage is the animal spirit and its outer garment. The assertion that, were someone to search the grave of Samuel during his appearance to the medium at Endor, the prophet's corporeal remains would not have been found in the grave, suggests that the prophet's outer garments were ostensibly composed of the prophet's corporeal remains. This reading of the text is reaffirmed by the previous passage where, in explaining the talmudic story about Yehuda Ha-Nasi (*c.* 200 CE) appearing to his family every week, Ṣiyyon asserts that the Nasi's bones would doubtlessly have been found in the grave were one to have searched for them.[40] This suggests a difference of opinion regarding the nature of encounters with the dead. According to Yehuda He-Ḥasid, the dead may appear as revenants – physical entities embodying the animal spirit and the corporeal remains of the dead – whereas, according to Ṣiyyon, the dead may leave the grave only in the form of apparitions – spiritual entities composed of the spirit of the deceased clothed in outer garments that appear real but are, in reality, a mere illusion.

Before probing deeper into the belief in corporeal revenants, let us explore briefly Ṣiyyon's view and his likely source of influence.[41] While Ṣiyyon himself never quite explains the mechanism by which a ghost can look real without being made of any tangible material, one should keep in mind the discussion of Ele'azar of Worms concerning the scent of the deceased.[42] According to Ele'azar, after a person is buried and that person's soul departs the body, two entities remain in the grave: the person's spirit (*ruaḥ*) and a quasi-physical entity referred to as scent (*reaḥ*). Due to the quasi-physical characteristics of scent – being tangible and intangible at the same time – it surrounds the formless spirit, thereby giving it the appearance of a physical body.[43] Ele'azar's concept of the corpse retaining the authentic and unique scent of the deceased originally appears in his discussion of the physical punishment of the wicked in hell. Rabbinic texts describe hell as a place where the souls of the wicked are burned but, if the soul is a metaphysical entity, how can it possibly be consumed by fire as a form of corporeal punishment? Ele'azar explains that what is being burned in hell is not merely the formless soul, that in itself cannot be subjected to any physical punishment, but rather the soul joined

40 *Ibid.*

41 For Ele'azar of Worms's impact on the work of Ṣiyyon, see Joseph Dan, *Torat Ha-Sod shel Ḥasidut Ashkenaz* (Jerusalem: Mosad Bialik, 1968), p. 259.

42 *Ḥokhmat Ha-Nefesh* (Ṣefat: 1913; repr. Jerusalem: 1968), pp. 5d–6a, 6d.

43 See Joshua Trachtenberg, *Jewish Magic and Superstition: a Study in Folk Religion* (Cleveland: Meridian Books, World Pub. Co., 1961), pp. 61–68. See also Moshe Idel, 'Gazing at the Head in Ashkenazi Hasidism', in *The Journal of Jewish Thought and Philosophy*, 6 (1997), pp. 289, 294–98.

with the scent of the body that makes it possible to exact physical punishment from the wicked in the afterlife.[44] Thus, by adopting Ele'azar's concept of scent, Ṣiyyon is attempting to explain the nature of apparitions.

Ashkenazi references to the biblical episode at Endor, and its relevance for their understanding of the phenomenon of revenants, parallel contemporary and earlier treatments of the topic by Christian writers. The approaches of Christian writers are succinctly summed up in the words of the twelfth-century theologian Peter Comestor (d. 1169):

> On the subject of this evocation some say that the evil spirit appeared looking like Samuel, or that it was his fantastic image (that is, raised up by the devil) that appeared there, which was called 'Samuel'. Others say that with God's permission it was indeed the soul of Samuel, covered by a body that appeared; but for others it was a body that was resuscitated and received the life of a spirit, while Samuel's soul remained in its resting place.[45]

The multiple Christian interpretations of this biblical episode are also reflected in a series of iconographic representations. While in some illuminations Samuel appears as if he is still alive, walking and wearing ordinary clothing,[46] in other artistic depictions he rises out of his grave wrapped in shrouds.[47] In one image of the latter kind, Samuel's face is uncovered, the eyes and mouth are open, but the rest of the body is completely covered in shrouds, and he is standing upright in his grave. Similarly, in one fourteenth-century manuscript, Samuel is standing upright in his grave and the shrouds cover almost the entire body, but not his face. There is no clear evidence that Jewish writers were familiar with Christian texts or with Christian artistic representations of the topic but the possibility that Jews and Christians held in common beliefs about revenants remains plausible.

This may also be illustrated in a text from *Sefer Ḥasidim* that raises the question of how, when seeing a revenant, one can tell whether the revenant is the actual embodiment of the deceased or a pretender, that is, a demon appearing falsely and deceitfully in the image of the dead person. As the tale is told in one exemplum, a dead master appears to his servant and requests that the servant return the master's contested property, in order to alleviate any chastisement of the servant in the afterlife. When asked by the servant for verifica-

44 *Ḥokhmat Ha-Nefesh*, p. 7a. For a discussion of the mind-body duality in earlier rabbinic literature, see Nissan Rubin, *The End of Life: Rites of Burial and Mourning in the Talmud and Midrash* (Hebrew; Tel Aviv: Hakkibutz hameuchad, 1997), pp. 59–76.

45 Schmitt, *Ghosts in the Middle Ages*, p. 15.

46 *Ibid.*, illustrations # 1, 3, 5, and 6.

47 *Ibid.*, illustrations # 2 and 4.

tion, the dead master promises to appear on a certain tree on the morrow and indeed he appears there as promised. In their effort to verify the true identity of this revenant, the people of the town search the master's grave and, as predicted, the corporeal remains of the master cannot be found.[48]

What is most striking about this exemplum is the relatively neutral or indifferent tone employed by the writer to describe the undead Christian master. Rather than challenging the belief in revenants as a superstitious and credulous idea believed by Christians but not by Jews, the transmitter of the exemplum merely says 'true or not', meaning that there is no real way of verifying the truth, even by searching the grave to see if the body is still there. The writer of this exemplum remains modestly sceptical about revenants but does not altogether reject the phenomenon.

Jews (and non-Jews) who believed in revenants had to overcome the puzzling question of how bodies subjected to natural decay and degeneration can suddenly appear intact. The governing solution for this problem is the miraculous involvement of an omnipotent God in the process, which renders moot any questions about feasibility. More worldly solutions were, however, also offered, especially with regard to the issue of natural decay. One approach was to challenge in different ways the empirical assumption that the human body is always subject to corporeal decay after death. The persimmon, for example, was considered a deadly fruit that preserves the body of the person who would surely die after eating it.[49] In addition, the religious status of the deceased, whether the person was considered righteous or wicked, was believed to have an impact on the state of the corporeal remains. The following quotation from a book describing the norms and customs of R. Shalom b. Yiṣḥaq of Wiener Neustadt (d. 1413) demonstrates how religious status and the state of the corporeal remains were regarded as highly related issues in the minds of Jews and Christians alike:

> Once an unmarried woman (*betula*) apostatized (*nishtamda*) in the Principality of Austria and died in her wickedness. They (the Christians) buried her in the churchyard (lit. 'in the courtyard of their idolatry'). After many years passed, they came to pile bones into a mound (of dry bones) as their custom and law dictates, but the flesh [of the woman] had not yet decomposed. They approached the extremely pious R. Shalom of Neustadt and inquired about the matter but he put them off. To his disciples, however, he explained that she was still being punished (in hell); and that only once her sin had been atoned, would the woman's flesh fully decompose [...] Yet, there is no reason to wonder about the pious people whose bodies remain intact in the grave even after they die. Quite

48 *Sefer Ḥasidim*, ed. by Judah Wistinetzki and Jacob Freimann (Berlin: H. Itzkowski, 1891), p. 37, § 35.
49 *Sefer Ḥasidim*, p. 101, § 320–21.

> the contrary, this is the goodness and righteousness of the pious; they die instantly with the 'kiss of death' and their bodies remain intact until a short while prior to the resurrection of the dead. So I heard from my master and teacher Ya'aqov Moellin ('Maharil', ca. 1360–1427), may he rest in peace.[50]

The crux of this text is the belief of Jews and Christians alike in the connection between the state of the corporeal remains and the spiritual status of the deceased. It demonstrates that even an 'objective' empirical phenomenon such as the decomposition of the body after death was infused in the minds of medieval people with religious assumptions and, in this case, with polemical undertones as well. Such beliefs in the immunity of some dead to the process of natural decay clearly complicate any empirical assumptions that one might have about the fate of the corporeal remains after death. The case of the apostate woman is obviously an extreme one but it does show that the dichotomy between 'life' and 'death' was regarded as rather vague – at least concerning the spiritual status of the living and the fate of the body after death.[51]

Beliefs in revenant were often associated with concerns about their hazardous nature. That Jews in medieval Ashkenaz were anxious about revenants may be seen in various rituals, some of which seem quite bizarre to the modern reader. *Sefer Ḥasidim* prescribes a method for preventing a witch from causing harm by stabbing her with a stake in her (open) mouth or by filling her mouth with rocks.[52] Noteworthy is the underlying assumption that the same organ that causes the damage must be dealt with, in order to prevent such dangers from recurring. Therefore, the mouth of a woman whose children died in succession was filled with stones to prevent her from biting or eating any living beings, or a deceased witch's corpse was anchored to the ground to stop her ever leaving her grave and causing further damage.

While the treatment of the witch's body may seem extreme and unrepresentative, it was fairly common in Ashkenaz to confront the danger stemming from the dead through the recitation of special conjurations. What in *Sefer Ḥasidim* appears simply as an antidote for unexpected or undesirable encounters with the undead becomes in a later text – *Hilkhot u-Minhagei Rabbenu*

---

50 *Hilkhot u-Minhagei Rabbenu Shalom mi-Noishtat*, ed. by Shlomo Y. Spitzer (Jerusalem: Makhon Yerushalayim, 1996/7), p. 206, §2.

51 See Avriel Bar-Levav, 'The Concept of Death in Sefer Ha-Ḥayyim (The Book of Life) by Rabbi Shimon Frankfurt' (Hebrew; Jerusalem: doctoral dissertation, Hebrew University, 1997), pp. 125–35.

52 Joseph Dan, 'Demonological Stories in the Writings of R. Yehuda He-Ḥasid', *Tarbiz*, 30:3 (1961), pp. 278–79, §2; p. 280, §5. On witches in *Sefer Ḥasidim*, see Susanne Borchers, 'Hexen im "Sefer Hasidim"' in *Henoch*, 16.2–3 (1994), pp. 271–93.

Shalom mi-Noishtat – part of the funerary ceremony to be recited in the presence of a quorum (*minyan*). The conjuration includes the following text:

> 'In the name of the heavenly court, in the name of the earthly court, and in the name of so-and-so, I conjure you in the name of the God of heaven and earth and all His holy names that you will not kill any person [lit. bring with you], neither man nor woman, neither minor nor adult, neither a relative nor a stranger. Cause them no harm either *with your body* or with your spirit or soul. *Your body must remain in the grave until the resurrection of the dead.* Your soul should remain in its proper place and likewise your spirit should remain in its proper place. You should take an oath with sanctions from now until the end of days.' Following the ceremony the participants replied 'Amen'. I saw that they conjured the father-in-law of Shalom [of Neustadt] at the house where the bodies of the dead are ritually cleansed before the ritual cleansing in the present of ten people. On another occasion I saw that they conjured the great-granddaughter of Shalom's wife in his courtyard where they left the body on the ground before carrying her to the cemetery.[53]

This ritual conjuration recited before the body of the deceased and in the presence of ten men, who upon hearing it responded 'amen', reveals concrete fears about the re-appearance of the dead. Strikingly, the people at whose funerals the conjuration is reported to have been recited are none other than the father-in-law of Shalom of Neustadt's child, and the great grandchild of a female neighbour of Shalom of Neustadt. This suggests that concerns about the hazardous potential of revenants was not restricted to distinct elements in Jewish society (such as criminals or, not to mention the two in the same breath, women) but included men and women, young and adult, distinguished and less distinguished people alike.

References to dead bodies departing physically from their graves appear as a matter of fact in at least two halakhic texts. The texts formally discuss prohibitions concerning sorcery and magic. Any communication with a dead corpse (*doresh el ha-metim*) – either when the body remains in the grave, or in the case of necromancy, which involves communicating with a body that has left the grave – is considered an idolatry and is, therefore, strictly prohibited. If, however, one requests a dying person to appear after death, or attempts to communicate with the spirit of the dead (*doresh le-ruḥo*) this is not prohibited, since communicating with the spirit of the dead is not the same as communicating with the body of the deceased.[54]

---

53 *Hilkhot u-Minhagei Rabbenu Shalom mi-Noishtat* (Jerusalem: Makhon Yerushalayim, 1996), pp. 159–60 (§544).

54 Eli'ezer b. Shemuel of Metz, *Sefer Yere'im*, ed. by Abraham A. Schiff (Vilna: Katzenellenbogen, 1892–1904), pp. 187a–187b, §334–335.

3 In conclusion

In conclusion, I would like to discuss briefly another practice that may not seem at first glance related, but a closer look will reveal the connection. This practice, too, appears in the compilation of rulings and customs of Hilkhot u-Minhagei Shalom mi-Noishtat. The custom concerns the ritual discarding of the foreskin after circumcision:

> 'Who can ascend to the heaven for us?'[55] I heard from R. Shalom that [the first letters of the words in this quotation] form the acronym MILA (circumcision). When Ashkenazim circumcise a child they cast the child's foreskin in a hole dug under the ark since they believe that the foreskin ascends to heaven. This is the true meaning of R. Shalom's comment about the acronym of the verse. [Note also that] the last letters of the words in this verse, YHWH, form the name of God.

In an article entitled 'Marking the Flesh', Elisheva Baumgarten describes two traditions concerning the disposal of the foreskin after circumcision. The first involved circumcising the child over sand or water after which the foreskin was buried, and the second permitted barren women to swallow the foreskin after they attend a circumcision ritual as a way of inducing fertility.[56] In addition to the two practices mentioned by Baumgarten one should add a third one reported in the text above concerning R. Shalom. Rather than being buried in the ground or swallowed, the foreskin was kept in a *locus sanctus* under the ark. It should be mentioned that according to this text, the custom was practised by Ashkenazim of other localities and not only by the community of Wiener-Neustadt. This rather obscure custom raises many questions. What is the purpose of casting foreskins into a hole under the ark? How can foreskins or, for that matter, any other objects ascend to heaven? Is the designation of a location underneath the ark for disposal related to the Christian tradition of burying the most elevated saints and ecclesiastical figures under the altar?

This custom clearly merits a separate and longer discussion but I would like to call attention to the confluence of a bodily object – the foreskin – with the heavenly world. As with the earthly soul of the deceased that resides with the corporeal remains in the grave, or the phenomenon of revenants, here too the boundaries between a corporeal object – the foreskin – and the heavenly world are crossed and become blurred. In a reversal of terms, just as the spirit of the dead remains in the earthly world after death, so too the bodily object,

---

55 Deut 30:12.

56 Elisheva Baumgarten, 'Marking the Flesh: Circumcision, Blood, and Inscribing Identity on the Body in Medieval Jewish Culture', *Micrologus*, 13 (2005), pp. 313–30.

the foreskin, ‘resides’ in the spiritual, heavenly world. In both instances, the heavenly and the worldly intersect, not in the unknown eschatological future but in the immediate future, in the here and now.

Nati Barak

The Early Ashkenazi Practice of Burial with Religious Paraphernalia

In his research dealing with initiation rites in medieval Jewish society, Ivan Marcus mentioned that these rites had a starting point and an ending point. These points might serve, according to Marcus, as indicators of the changes undergone by the culture of which they were part.[1]

Burial practices, according to which the dead were laid to rest with paraphernalia of a spiritual-religious meaning, probably appeared in Ashkenaz in the first quarter of the eleventh century, when Rabbenu Gershom Me'or Ha-Gola died. Rabbenu Gershom was probably the first to practise the custom of burial with a *ṭalit*, and thus pioneered a custom that came to be observed by both leaders and laymen.[2] One may also claim that the practice of burial with religious paraphernalia in the Jewish world is of authentic Ashkenazi origin. As with many other practices to be addressed below, which were mainly or exclusively chracteristic of Ashkenaz, this practice, too, is an entirely Ashkenazi one.

This eleventh-century practice of burial with such paraphernalia continued into the late Middle Ages, and was observed by the generations that followed the Black Death, in the fourteenth and fifteenth centuries and subsequently. What are the lines of continuity, and what are the points of discontinuity and change, between the way this practice was implemented by the generations that preceded the Black Death, and how it was pursued in the period that followed it? The answer to this question is a crucial one, since it may help to provide the historian of these and, by extension, similar practices, with a clear picture of the changes in the design of Ashkenazi death rituals in the generations that followed the Black Death.

Robert Scribner has discussed, in his research, the folkloristic traditions of the late Middle Ages, or, as he defines it, the development of 'unofficial religion' in that period. One of the important fourteenth-century changes that he emphasizes, concerns the manner in which women in Christian society became more religiously devout and more dominant. They achieved this by

---

1 I. G. Marcus, *Rituals of Childhood: Jewish Acculturation in Medieval Europe* (Hebrew; Jerusalem: Shazar Centre, 1998), p. 32.

2 Maharam, *Responsa, Rulings and Customs*, ed. I. Z. Cahana, (Hebrew; Jerusalem, 1957–62), vol. 2, p. 36. N. Barak, 'Time of Rage. Changing Attitudes Toward Death in Ashkenaz Communities: from the first Crusade to the Black Death' (Hebrew doctoral dissertation, Tel Aviv University, 2010), pp. 40–98.

utilizing, on the one hand, more channels of spiritual development, and by expanding, on the other, their capacity to influence mundane affairs. This view, and Philippe Ariès's treatment of the rise in the use of the dead person's room as a public place for communicating messages, may facilitate our understanding of one of the most intriguing literary documents of the age of the Black Death, the document named *Evel Rabbati*.[3]

This document, written by R. Ya'aqov ben Shelomo Ha-Ṣarfati, describes the last hours of his beloved daughter, who died in a late wave of the plague at the end of 1382. His essay combines elements of a testament – the daughter having expressed final wishes on her deathbed – with those of lamenation, since the father lamented his daughter in the presence of a multitude of people who were present: 'It would have been unbelievable had it not been heard by the crowd of men, women and children standing in the gallery. Those who came to console me heard a speech that was inspired by the Almighty.' And all this, out of an explicit wish to convey to the listeners an appropriate set of values and form of behaviour in the event of such a loss.

Before I further examine the custom that is at the heart of our discussion, I would like to correct something that seems to me crucial for our understanding of the original text. Ron Barkai, who analysed and closely read this document, remarked, among other things:

> The book *Evel Rabbati* has great importance, since it presents us with first-hand evidence of practices, that were common in the communities of fourteenth-century Provence, and that relate to the event of any person's death in general, and to the case of Esther, the daughter of Ya'aqov, in particular.[4]

Evel Rabbati was indeed written in the city of Avignon in southern France, but it is difficult to define the practices described in it as exclusively those of Provençal communities. First of all, Ya'aqov ben Shelomo is not a Provençal Jew, but belongs to those who were expelled from northern France, where he had gained some of that education that his deceased daughter also absorbed. Secondly, the daughter's names also testify to the French origin of this man.

---

3 R. W. Scribner, 'Elements of Popular Belief', in *Handbook of European History: 1400–1600 Late Middle Ages, Renaissance and Reformation*, ed. by T. A. Brady, Heiko A. Oberman, J. D. Tracy (Leiden: Brill, 1994–95), pp. 244–49; P. Ariès, *Western Attitudes toward Death: From the Middle Ages to the Present* (London: Boyars, 1974; repr. Baltimore: The John Hopkins Press, 1990), p. 12; R. Barkai, 'A Medieval Hebew Text on the Death of Children', in *Women, Children and the Elderly: Essays in Honour of Shulamit Shahar*, ed. by M. Eliav-Feldon, Y. Hen (Hebrew; Jerusalem: Shazar Center, 2001), pp. 76–84 (includes an edition of Paris, Bibliothèque Nationale de France, Ms. Heb. 733, 61r–67r).

4 Barkai, 'A Medieval Hebrew Text' (see n. 2 above), p. 71.

The names given in a such family are not only names that commemorate a deceased relative, but also those that point to the social identity of the people who applied them to their descendants. One of the names in this testament is Yentish, a clearly Ashkenazi name, and the dying daughter's other name is Trina, which is also an Ashkenazi name. These are Ashkenazi names that occur frequently in memorial books of Ashkenazi communities in this period.[5]

The conflict between the essay's writer and those who indulge in polemics is not uniquely Provençal in this period. It is a conflict that is represented among many of the leaders of the period, the most prominant among them being Yom Ṭov Lipman from Muelhausen, undoubtly an Ashkenazi scholar. Another example of this conflict may be found in Shim'on ben Shemuel, the Ashkenazi author of the kabbalistic essay, *Hadrat Qodesh,* who struggled against the philosophers and 'scholars of nature'. Furthermore, in his essay (*Evel Rabbati*) the father describes the large crowd of people who came to be with his daughter in her last hours, a crowd ['standing in the gallery']. The custom to stand while a person is dying is an Ashkenazi one that is echoed in the customs book of R. Shalom of Neustadt, one of the most prominent leaders of Ashkenaz in the period following the Black Death. Some of the practices mentioned in the testament cannot be regarded as Provençal, since they were not familiar in that region.

According to her testament, Esther wished to take to her grave her scarf and her wedding ring. This reflects the burial practice that was followed in Ashkenaz during the period that preceded the Black Death, a practice rejected by the Sefardi tradition that influenced the Provençal Jews. Furthermore, in the period that followed the plague, many Ashkenazi women asked to be buried with items very similar to those requested by Esther, the daughter of R. Ya'aqov (as we shall later see).

Before dealing with her requested manner of burial, we should take note of the fact that Esther wished to be buried with her scarf. The scarf and the girdle (belt) are items known from the Ashkenazi *Sivlonot* practice, according to which, a day before the wedding, the groom sends his first gift to the bride through the rabbi or one of the community leaders. This present was known as *Sivlonot*, and usually comprised several items, such as a scarf and a girdle. I am not suggesting that the *Sivlonot* was practised in southern France, but the choice that Esther made, to be buried with her scarf, has a particularly Ashkenazi flavor. The girdle had another function in Ashkenaz, that is detailed

---

5 S. Salfeld, *Das Martyrologium des Nürnberger Memorbuches* (Berlin: Leonhard Simion, 1898), pp. 73–77; S. Cooper, 'Names as Cultural Documents', in *These are the Names*, ed. by A. Demsky and J. Tabory (Hebrew; Ramat Gan: Bar Ilan University, 2000), pp. 13–22.

below. Thus, one cannot regard these practices in general, and certainly not her request to be buried with her ring and scarf, as particularly Provençal wishes, and distinct from Ashkenazi ones.

The essay *Evel Rabbati* goes further and reports additional wishes expressed by Esther:

> Indeed you will cry for Sarah, my lady, my sister, the fairest among women, my dove, my undefiled one. Beside her, make a place to bury my body, because she taught me knowledge. And you, my father, please take from me my rings, that are on my fingers. They should be removed so they do not fall or get lost, and so that you do not suspect any innocents, while everybody cries aloud like the Philistines. But on my small finger, leave the ring with which my husband married me and designated me as a married woman among women. This you will do, and furthermore, put the pure turban on my head, to serve as an example, and as a good omen for the life of my man, my husband.

Esther presented several requests, some to her family members and the people who were close to her, and some of them direct orders referring to her burial. For our historical purposes, the important thing is that she expressed not only a wish about where to be buried and next to whom, but also, and more significantly, what she chose to take with her to her grave. The headgear, 'the pure turban' and the wedding ring, both obviously symbols of her married status, and her adherence to the *miṣwot*, are to accompany her to her grave. Esther is an example of an educated, medieval Jewish woman. Her father also wrote that his daughter 'knew how to read the Bible, שניים מקרא ואחד תרגום, and eloquently to pronounce the verse with its accents and vocalization without stammering'. The fact that Esther was an exemplary scholar supports the assumption that she used in her testaments phrases that originated from the talmudic and midrashic sources, and this has profound meaning, given that her father appears to have quoted her actual words. Thus, when she instructed him, 'on my small finger, leave the ring', Esther knew that the phrase 'on my small finger' was familiar to a medieval Jew as an allusion to the strict practice of menstruation rules by the Jewish woman. Thus, according to a talmudic and midrashic legend, when a God-fearing man died and his wife expressed her resentment at his death, the prophet Elijah appeared to her, to address her distress. She emphasized to him that during her menstrual periods, her husband had not touched her 'even with his *small finger*'. When the profundity of the phrases is understood, it becomes clear that Esther takes with her objects that testify to her careful fulfilment of her religious obligations as a woman.

There are further examples from Ashkenazi areas of women who wished to take with them on their last journey some meaningful items . The collection *Leqeṭ Yosher*, written by a disciple of R. Yisrael Isserlein, Yosef ben Moshe of Münster, contains the following paragraph, reporting a similar female practice:

> An important woman died, and some of her household members said that they heard her voice in her room, and said that this was because she had ordered in her will that her hair, which she kept concealed all her life, as something that was part of her own body, should be buried with her. The 'Gaon', may he rest in peace, ordered that the hair that she had kept should be buried within her tomb, at a depth of a hand-fist below the ground, and this event took place thirty days after her burial.[6]

Some details of this event require further clarification. Firstly, the reference to her having concealed her hair 'all her life' probably means that she had done so since her marriage. In addition, there can be little doubt that this woman, like the one mentioned in *Evel Rabbati*, belongs to a social elite ('an important woman'), of religiously educated, strong-minded and influential Jewish women (further discussed below). Presumably, her family members had not initially carried out her request, and thus her ghost returned home. This incidentally reveals a belief, common at that period and shared by Jews and Christians, regarding ghosts and demons. The origin of the custom of a 'watch night', dedicated to the study of Torah on the night before a baby's circumcision, may be traced to the popular belief that on this night the demons might harm the baby. The belief in demons and angels was at that period so strongly rooted among the Jewish public in Ashkenaz, that many Jews, when they wished to execrate someone, did not refrain from cursing the victims by employing the names of angels of destruction who are not at all known in the Jewish tradition. Güdemann has drawn attention to the central place occupied by demons and the fear of ghosts in the Jewish-Ashkenazi culture of that period. Elisheva Baumgarten, too, has referred several times to the influence of popular beliefs in demons, witchcraft, and hobgoblins, and their impact on the formation of birth rituals in the thirteenth and fourteenth centuries.[7] Such a popular belief is echoed in the paragraph just cited, since after her death 'they heard her voice in her room', and this was clearly understood to be an angel or a demon

6 *Sefer Leqeṭ Yosher le-Rabbi Yose bar Moshe; kolel minhagim pisqei halakhot we-teshuvot shel ba'al Terumat Ha-Deshen, ḥeleq Yore De'a*, ed. J. Freimann (Berlin: Mekize Nirdamim, 1904), p. 82:

> פ"א מת' אשה חשובה ואח"כ אמרו מקצת בני ביתה ששומעים קולה בחדר שלה ואמרי' שהוא מחמת זה שצותה לקבור עמה שער שלה שגנזה כל ימיה מה שבאה מגופה וא' הגאון ז"ל קברו שער שלה שגנזה בתוך קבר שלה למטה מן הקרקע טפח וזה המעשה היה לאחר ל' יום לקבורתה.

7 M. Güdemann, *The Tora and Life* (Hebrew; Warsaw: Ahiasaf, 1896) p. 84; M. Güdemann, *Geschichte des Erziehungswesens und der Cultur der abendlandischen Juden, wahrend des Mittelalters und der neueren Zeit* (Wien: A. Hölder, 1880), pp. 199–227; E. Baumgarten, *Mothers and Children: Jewish Family Life in Medieval Europe* (Hebrew; Jerusalem: Shazar Center, 2005), pp. 143–55; E. Baumgarten, *Mothers and Children: Jewish Family Life in Medieval Europe* (Princeton: Princeton University Press, 2007), pp. 126–38.

who was delivering her message, and her opinion that the separation from her would not be complete until her request had been fulfilled. As far as a relationship between the living and the dead is concerned, the story describes the woman's return to her home after her death. The 'Gaon' (R. Yisrael Isserlein) ordered the opening of her tomb, thirty days after the burial, and the burial of her hair, as she had requested.[8] The pattern that we earlier identified is here repeated and we again encounter a woman who wishes to be buried with an object that symbolizes the fulfillment of her religious obligations to her husband and her God. Again, a rabbinic order is issued to complete the burial and the separation process, that would be deficient without the addition of this object.

Note should be taken of the complexity of the event under discussion. The household members of this deceased woman were trying to make a clear separation of the living from the dead. They felt uneasy about the dead still being among them, as evinced by the sound of her voice in the room. The rabbinic solution was intended to prevent her return to the living environment, but at the same time contributed to a blurring, albeit temporarily, of the border between the living and the dead, precisely the border that the family of the woman wished to delineate. This blurring of borders is exemplified by the opening of her grave, and by the surviving family endowing the dead woman with a gift after her burial. These measures clearly meet the requirements of Arnold van Gennep's definition of an action that blurs the borders between the living and the dead, and disturbs the peace of the dead.[9]

Another example of a woman who wished to take with her to her grave a meaningful object, is given by the 'Mahari'. R. Yisrael Bruna describes an event that occured in Regensburg, where he served as a rabbi. The event occurred on *Ḥol Ha-Mo'ed* (intermediate days) of Sukkot (Tabernacles), 'when Rabbi Yiṣḥaq Dinar died', and the report is mainly concerned with the Jewish religious laws concerning burial during *that semi-festive period.* In passing, R. Israel Bruna provides us with the following details:

> And the Jews dug the grave, though Gentiles could have done it. And when they were intent on burying her in the grave, they clothed her with a girdle. Afterwards, they found her own girdle that she had herself made so that she could to be clothed with it after her death. Some wished to cut off the girdle and clothe her with her own girdle, and some objected, arguing that the custom was to put her girdle in the grave too, and so they did.[10]

---

8 *Leqeṭ Yosher, Yore De'a,* p. 100.

9 A. van Gennep, *The Rites of Passage* (London: Routledge, 1977), p. 165.

10 Yisrael Bruna, *She'elot u-Teshuvot*, ed. M. Hershler (Jerusalem: Tif'eret Ha-Tora, 1960), no. 191:

והיהודים חפרו הקבר אע"ג שהיה אפשרי על ידי גויים. וכשרצו לשומה בקבר חגרוה בח"א

Here again we encounter a woman who had previously prepared a girdle for her burial and wished to be buried with it. The items that people took with them to their graves had meaning. In Ashkenaz, the girdle of the woman was a gift, or a part of the *Sivlonot* gift, that the groom gave the bride before the wedding, and that has already been described earlier in this study. When the gift was given to the bride, the person who gave it to her said, 'Listen, o bride; the groom has sent you this (gift) to be yours after the wedding and not now.' The girdle was, then, the first gift that the bride had received from her future husband, even before the wedding ring, and this gift represented the first act that symbolized the connection between the two.[11]

The customs book of Yuspa, the beadle of the Worms community (1604–1678), carefully documented many communal practices, in order to ensure, among other reasons, their proper maintenance. The *Sivlonot* custom is there dealt with at length, as the first step in making the process of marriage a public one through the first gift given to the bride by the groom. The woman in our story chose to take with her on her last journey this first expression of her marriage and her loyalty to her husband.[12]

It should also be noted that the girdle had another function. In the Middle Ages, Jewish women believed that they could prevent harm coming to them during pregnancy and birth – processes that often involved popular beliefs – by carrying with them talismans and stones that allegedly had special magic powers. Some of the women wore their husbands' belts, and wrote on them spells and magical words that were meant to prevent abortions. This practice was also common among Christian women. In addition to indicating that spontaneous abortions were very common at that period, such a practice also supports our thesis that the woman's girdle could then have religious and cultural significance.[13]

ואח"כ מצאו חגור שלה שעש' לה לעצמה לחגר בו אחר מיתה, יש שרצו לחתוך חגור זה ולחוגרה בחגור שלה, ויש שמיחו ואמרו שנוהגים לשום חגור שלה גם כן אצלה בקבר וכן עשו.

11 Moshe ben Yiṣḥaq Mintz, *She'elot u-Teshuvot Rabbenu Moshe Mintz*, ed. by J. S. Domb, 2 vols. (Jerusalem: Mekhon Yerushalayim, 1991); M. Güdemann, *The Tora and Life* (see n. 6 above), pp. 96–97.

12 Yosef ben Shelomo Colon ('Maharik'), *Teshuvot Maharik* (Jerusalem: Mekhon Yerushalayim, 1984, p. 215.

13 C. Rawcliffe, *Medicine and Society in Later Medieval England* (Gloucestershire: A. Sutton, 1995); M. Klein, *A Time to be Born: Customs and Folklore of Jewish Birth in Israel* (Philadelphia PA: Jewish Publication Society, 1998), pp. 90–3; E. Baumgarten, *Mothers and Children* (see n. 6 above), pp. 137–38; B. Bolton, '*Mulieres Sanctae*', in *Sanctity and Secularity: The Church and the World*, ed. by D. Baker (Oxford: Blackwell, 1973), pp. 77–95.

In discussing the status of the women in Jewish society of the thirteenth century, Elisheva Baumgarten suggests that the woman's place in public rituals and in the practice of personal *miṣwot* was limited, as may be proved by a comparison of the Jewish and Christian customs relating to godparents. A similar situation applied in Christian society in the late twelfth century. It may be that the examples that we have examined, in which women made demands as to the way they should be buried, reveal a certain change regarding the practice of private *miṣwot* or customs by women. This important issue is, however, beyond the scope of the current study that is centred on the perception of death. Perhaps the fact that most of the communities in the generations following the Black Death had small numbers enabled women to make such burial requests. And it may be that this freedom was granted them only towards their deaths or afterwards.

We have dealt with three cases of women who influenced the nature of their burial by expressing an explicit request regarding the items that should be interred with them. Assuming that many requests were orally transmitted before burial, and/or that many others did not survive the passage of time, we should give such examples a wider meaning within the Ashkenazi Jewish community of the fourteenth and fifteenth centuries. In the halakhic literature from this period, we encounter numerous cases of women with a high scholarly status and treated as such by society. These examples may serve as partial evidence relating to the overall scholarly status of Jewish women in the period under discussion. Thus, for example, we find that Rabbi Isserlein's daughter-in-law studied Torah with a scholar, and that his wife (Schöndlein) wrote an answer to a question concerning religious rules relating to women. There are also testimonies relating to women who wore a *ṭalit*, and to a woman who funded a Jewish school. When she died and was being laid to rest, *yeshiva* students studied Torah at the same platform on which her body had been purified for burial as a token of respect for her. In written testimonies of the period there are references to women who independently donated money to the poor of Jerusalem, with no mention of any man making the donation with them. There is also an example of a later continuation of this trend, when a woman, at the turn of the fifteenth century, taught Torah to 'learned students', with a curtain separating her from them.

This period is also witness to an attempt by Ḥayyim Ṣarfati to compose a book on 'female purity' in German, an initiative that was set aside due to the severe objections of the 'Mahari'. Nevertheless, the attempt itself testifies clearly to the fact that women were interested in knowing the religious rules concerning menstruation but found it hard to understand them in the Hebrew language.[14] Further evidence of the difficulty that Ashkenazi women had with Hebrew may be found in the letters of appointment carried by the messengers whose mission was to bring the soil of the Holy Land (for burial purposes too) to the Diaspora. These letters of appointment included official appeals for donations made by the Jewish community in the Holy Land to the communities abroad. All these documents, whether they were sent to Europe, Eastern Europe, North Africa, or Yemen, were written in Hebrew. But in 1650, the Ashkenazi women from Jerusalem sent an epistle to the Ashkenazi women of Germany, appealing for support. This epistle is the only letter of its kind that is not written in Hebrew that has survived to this day![15] This letter attests to the existence of an Ashkenazi community in Jerusalem, and to the fact that other women, in far away communities, were capable of collecting donations (in forms of sisterhood). But more than that – it represents further evidence of the continuing difficulty (since the time of Ḥayyim Ṣarfati, in the mid-fifteenth century) that some Ashkenazi women had in understanding the Hebrew language.

In sum, close examination of the religious behaviour of women in early Ashkenazi society is historically informative, testifying as it does to the dynamic nature of their religious practices and to the way in which they were influenced by external as well as internal factors.

14 S. J. Spitzer, 'Rabbinical Leadership in South Germany and Austria at the Beginning of the 15th Century' (Hebrew), *Bar Ilan* 1960, pp. 267–79; I. J. Yuval, *Scholars in their Time: The Religious Leadership of German Jewry in the Late Middle Ages* (Hebrew; Jerusalem: Magnes Press, 1988), pp. 311–18; A. Grossman, *Jewish Women in Medieval Europe* (Hebrew, Jerusalem: Shazar Center, 2001).

15 A. Yaari, *Sheluḥei Ereṣ Yisrael* (Hebrew; Jerusalem: Mossad Harav Kook, 1951), pp. 8–91.

Section 3: **Re-Placing the Dead**

Avraham (Rami) Reiner

The Dead as Living History: On the publication of *Die Grabsteine vom jüdischen Friedhof in Würzburg 1147–1346*[1]

A tombstone fragment bearing the word *amen* appears on the cover of the book *Open Closed Open*, that was published toward the end of the life of the Israeli poet Yehuda Amichai.[2] This tombstone comes from the cemetery of Würzburg, Amichai's birthplace, where close to 1,500 tombstones from the twelfth to the fourteenth centuries, either whole or fragmentary, were found and examined. Their discovery began in 1987, as a consequence of the destruction of an old structure that had formerly served as a monastery, in the Pleich district in the centre of Würzburg. A passerby named Rudolph Erben saw that some of the stones removed from the débris bore Hebrew inscriptions. Erben collected a number of the stones and gave them to David Schuster, who headed the city's Jewish community from the 1950s until his death in 2001. When the nature of the stones and their source became clear, Schuster, together with Professor Karlheinz Müller of the Catholic Theology Department of the University of Würzburg, achieved the intervention of public and academic figures to ensure that the stones would be carefully dismantled from the building and moved to a location where they could in the future be studied. Some of the close to 1,500 stones bearing Hebrew inscriptions taken from the building contain whole tombstone inscriptions, and others are partial tombstones that underwent later cutting for the construction of the building in which they were found, many centuries later. These are not the first Hebrew inscriptions to come to light in Würzburg. In 1965, Zvi Avneri published an article entitled 'Medieval Hebrew Inscriptions',[3] in which he reported on fifteen tombstones and tombstone fragments that had been discovered before the Second World War, some of which were lost in the Allied bombing of the city close to the end of the War. Together with additional tombstones, that were already known before the war but of which Avneri was unaware, the Hebrew

1 On cemeteries as a source for cultural and historical research, see Elizabeth Valdez del Alamo and Carol Stamatis Pendergast (eds.), *Memory and the Medieval Tomb* (Aldershot: Ashgate, 2000); Avriel Bar-Levav, 'We Are Where We Are Not: The Cemetery in Jewish Culture', *Jewish Studies*, 41 (2002), pp. 15*–46*.

2 Yehuda Amichai, *Open Closed Open* (Hebrew; Tel Aviv: Schocken, 1998).

3 Zvi Avneri, 'Medieval Hebrew Inscriptions', *Proceedings of the American Academy for Jewish Research*, 33 (1965), pp. 1–34 (Hebrew).

inscriptions that originated in the Würzburg cemetery currently number more than 1,500. (This number refers to the quantity of stones that were found. Since some of the stones complement each other and are actually part of a single inscription, the number of extant whole and partial inscriptions comes to some 1,450.) Hebrew inscriptions are most likely incorporated in the walls of another structure in the city, but for the present we cannot determine the extent of this material. The 'new' stones that were discovered in 1987 were transferred to the storerooms of the University of Würzburg, and their initial documentation was carried out by Professor Müller and his students. Funded by the German-Israel Foundation for Scientific Research and Development (GIF), preparations for the scientific publication of this discovery began in 1996. Professor Müller was joined in this effort by Professor Simon Schwarzfuchs of Bar-Ilan University and myself, with the participation of Dr Edna Engel of the Jewish National and University Library in Jerusalem for the palaeographic-epigraphic aspects of the research. Since then, each tombstone has been read and interpreted, and the fragments have been pieced together, to provide scholars and the public at large with texts as complete and as comprehensible as possible. This corpus was published, together with a comprehensive introduction, in the winter of 2011–2012.[4] In this article I will briefly describe the scope of the discovery, together with a number of representative examples. In *Sefer Zekhira* (Memorial Book), R. Efrayim of Bonn credits Bishop Siegfried with aiding in the establishment of the cemetery, immediately following the massacres of the Second Crusade. He writes:

> The following day, the bishop ordered that all the slaughtered martyrs should be collected in carts, including all substantial remains, thighs and shoulders as well as fingers and toes, and that they were to be purified with sacred oil, and all that could be found of their bodies and limbs, and he gave instructions to bury them in his garden. Afterwards, R. Ḥizqiyahu the son of *Rabbenu* Elyaqim and his wife *Marat* [= Mrs] Yehudit purchased that 'Garden of Eden' from the bishop, and they designated it as a permanent cemetery. 'The generous man is blessed, because he gives' [Prov 22:9].[5]

The participants in the Second Crusade attacked the Würzburg community on 24 February, 1147, and close to forty of the city's Jews were killed that day. We

4 Karlheinz Müller, Simon Schwarzfuchs, and Avraham (Rami) Reiner, *Die Grabsteine vom jüdischen Friedhof in Würzburg aus der Zeit vor dem Schwarzen Tod* (Neustadt an der Aisch: Verlagsdruckerei Schmidt, 2011).

5 Efrayim ben Ya'aqov of Bonn, *Sefer Zekhirah* ('Memorial Book'), in Avraham Meir Habermann, *The Persecutions of Germany and France: Memoirs by those from the Generations of the Crusades and a Selection of their Poems* (Hebrew; Jerusalem: Sifre Ofir, 1971), pp. 119–20.

know most of their names from the *Memorbuch* that was published in 1898.[6] In contrast to what we would expect on the basis of R. Efrayim's description, none of the extant tombstones can be definitely attributed to any of the victims of the Second Crusade. Furthermore, we do not possess even a single tombstone from the Hebrew year 4907 (roughly corresponding to 1147), in which the cemetery was established, the two earliest tombstones dating from the Hebrew year 4908 (corresponding to 28 August, 1147 – 15 September, 1148). Only some four hundred tombstones (that is, less than a third) bear a date; the other Würzburg stones (some 1,100) are merely tombstone fragments of different sizes, that lack the part of the tombstone recording the year of death.[7] These fragments might include tombstones from the year of the cemetery's founding, and possibly even those of victims of the Second Crusade, for whom the cemetery was established. It is evident, however, that we do not possess the tombstones of most of those murdered in 1147. It seems that the large number of those murdered in a single day made it impossible for the surviving members of the community to arrange separate burials for all the victims, and a tombstone was not therefore erected for each of them. Another possible explanation for the lack of tombstones for the Second Crusade victims is to be found in the manner in which the tombstones came to us. In order to clarify this possibility, we should describe the last days of the cemetery of medieval Würzburg.

On 21 April, 1349, during the time of the Black Death, the Würzburg community came to an end, when its members burned themselves to death in their homes rather than face the fury of the rioting mob outside. Close to that year, the wall encompassing the new quarters of the city was erected, and its builders took tombstones from the Jewish community's abandoned cemetery as building material. Two centuries later, in 1576, 430 years after the establishment of the cemetery by Bishop Siegfried, his successor at the time, Bishop Julius Echter, appropriated the area of the cemetery in order to build the hospital that bears his name to the present day: the Julius Echter Spital. The stones that remained in the cemetery after the construction of the wall in 1349 were incorporated in the nearby building in 1576, where they were finally found about twenty-five years ago. The discovery of the stones matched their disappearance in its two stages. The wall that had been erected in 1349 was demolished in 1854, and a number of tombstones came to light, and found their way

---

6 S. Salfeld, *Das Martyrologium des Nürnberger Memorbuches* (Berlin: Leonhard Simion, 1898), p. 12.

7 The undated inscriptions were dated on palaeographic grounds by Dr Edna Engel of the National Library of Israel, and they appear in our edition in accordance with this dating.

to the city museum, and to the home of a Würzburg resident. These were the fifteen tombstones listed by Avneri in his article. The second phase was the great discovery of 1987, in the building in the Pleich quarter. While most of the tombstones published by Avneri date to the early fourteenth century, only seven of the 1455 tombstones that came to light in 1987 are from that century, with the decisive majority from the twelfth and thirteenth centuries. The significance of this fact is that stones were taken from different areas of the cemetery at different periods, as they were needed at the time. The fifteen tombstones published by Avneri came to the city wall from the new section of the cemetery, that had been in use in the beginning of the fourteenth century, while the other extant inscriptions came from other parts of the cemetery, which explains the paucity of extant tombstones from that period. In the light of this, any scholar who uses the Würzburg tombstones must realize that the collection, despite its impressive size, paints an incomplete – and even somewhat misleading – picture of the community from its inception to its destruction during the time of the Black Death. We may reasonably assume that if the wall built in 1349 had been dismantled more carefully in 1854, as the other structure was disassembled in 1987, we would possess a more comprehensive knowledge of the community in the first years of the fourteenth century. Likewise, if additional structures in the Pleich quarter were dismantled, including the foundation of a structure that was only partly taken down in 1987, we would undoubtedly have in our possession additional inscriptions that would shed light on the history of the community, mainly in the twelfth and thirteenth centuries.

The argument that the extant collection of tombstones reflects only a proportion of the tombstones in the Würzburg cemetery dating from 1147 to 1349 is supported from another point of view. More than seventy names of individuals who were active in Würzburg during that period are known to us from the rabbinic literature of the time, but we have only about fifteen tombstones of these people. This strengthens the argument that the extant collection of Würzburg tombstones, despite its impressive size, does not represent the entire picture. Possibly, some of the individuals whose names are known from the literature left Würzburg at some point. It is also likely that even if they spent their entire lives in the city, they might have died while travelling or on a visit to another city, and were buried where they died, just as a person from 'the islands of the sea' (= England) died in Würzburg and had a tombstone erected over his grave, and just as tombstones were erected over the graves of a woman from Strasbourg and other visitors who died in Würzburg.[8] Regardless,

8 The names of the localities mentioned on the Würzburg tombstones, in most instances specifying the place of origin of the deceased, are: Bamberg, France, Frankfurt, Göttingen, Grüns-

the large quantitative disparity indicates that the extant tombstone collection does not fully document all the members of the community who died in their city.

As regards the quantity of the tombstones, we should also point out another lacuna: the extant collection of tombstones does not include a single tombstone erected over an infant's grave. Only four tombstones describe the deceased as a boy or girl, in contrast to the sixteen that portray the deceased as a *na'ar* or *na'ara* (male or female youth, respectively) and more tombstones that depict the deceased as a *baḥur* or *baḥura* (young man or woman, respectively). All this clearly indicates that tombstones were hardly ever raised over the graves of young children, thus revealing the status of children while alive, and even more, after their death. It should be mentioned in this context that, with a single exception, the age of the deceased is not specified on the tombstones; and the birth date is never mentioned. This lack of information prevents us from determining from what age a person was entitled to have a tombstone erected over their grave.

Despite these deficiencies and methodological difficulties, the development of the Würzburg community can be charted by charting the number of tombstones from the time when the cemetery was active along a time axis: between 1147 and 1200: 13 tombstones; 1201–1250: 109 tombstones; 1250–1298: 268 tombstones.[9] Three tombstones date from the end of the Hebrew year 1298, toward the end of which more than 900 members of the community and their guests were murdered in a single day (23 July, 1298) in the Rindfleisch massacres. The names of more than 600 of the victims are known from the *Memorbuch* mentioned above, but we apparently cannot match any of these three tombstones to the names in the list of the dead. The large number of victims most likely prevented the individual interment of the dead and the erection of tombstones over their graves. We do not have a single tombstone from the time of the massacre in July 1298 until December 1306, while from then until December 1346, the time of the last tombstone in the collection, we possess only nineteen tombstones. The numerical disparity between the years preceding 1298 and those following it indicates that, even if the Würzburg community was finally destroyed only during the time of the Black Death riots in 1349, already by 1298 all that remained in the city were remnants of the community that had once flourished, both demographically and creatively, during the

feld, Halle, Hammelburg, Hassfurt, Möckmühl, Mühlhausen in Thüringen, Nürnberg, Regensburg, Röttingen, Speyer, Tauberbischofsheim, Ulm, Wertheim.

9 These numbers relate only to the tombstones on which dates appear, and not to those dated by palaeographic means.

course of the thirteenth century – and from that period we possess a few tombstones of individuals that are known to us from various literary sources.[10]

Thus, R. Yiṣḥaq ben Moshe of Vienna was one of the leading authorities of Ashkenaz in the first half of the thirteenth century, and owed his renown to his monumental work *Or Zaru'a*. In his youth R. Yiṣḥaq frequently travelled between different talmudic academies in Europe, and testimonies to his stay in Würzburg, as a teacher and as a student, appear in the contemporary literature. In Würzburg he almost certainly studied under R. Yonathan ben Yiṣḥaq,[11] whose widow's tombstone was found in its entirety in Würzburg, bearing the following inscription:

1 'On the full moon
2 of our feast day'
3 died *Marat* [Mrs] Hanna
4 our mother, the widow of Yonathan
5 *Rabbenu* [our master], the daughter of R. [an honorific title, not meaning 'Rabbi'] Yeḥiel our grandfather the *kohen* [i.e. of the priestly class] the year
6 *ma.l.k.o.* by the minor count, may her [s]oul
7 be bound up in the bond of everlasting life

The wording *ba-kese* for our feast day (ll. 1–2)[12] refers to Ps 81:4: 'Blow the horn *ba-kese* for our feast day.' The BabylonianTalmud (*Roš. Haš.* 8a–b) expounds this verse as relating to the New Year, the only Jewish holiday that begins a month, and on which, therefore, the moon is 'covered' (*mekhuse*). This woman's death on Rosh Ha-Shana led the writers of the epitaph to use the world *malko* (literally, 'his king'; l. 8) to denote the year, in order to allude to God's kingship in the world, a very pronounced motif in the Rosh Ha-Shana liturgy. The woman apparently died on Rosh Ha-Shana, in the year *mem-lamed-khaf-waw* (with the numerical value of 96), ie, 5096, that fell on 19–20 September, 1335. A palaeographic analysis, however, along with the location of the tombstone in the Pleich quarter, in which most of the tombstones are from the twelfth and thirteenth centuries, preclude any possibility of dating this tombstone to the fourteenth century. This Hanna most likely died a century earlier, on Rosh Ha-Shana of 4996 (1235). The tombstone writers omitted

---

10 For the history of the Würzburg community in this period, see Z. Avneri, *Germania Judaica* II/2 (Tübingen: Mohr, 1968), pp. 928–36; K. Müller, *Die Würzburger Judengemeinde im Mittelalter* (Würzburg: Freunde Mittelfränkischer Kunst und Geschichte, 2004).

11 On R. Yiṣḥaq's studies in Würzburg with R. Yonathan, see U. Fuchs, 'Studies in the Book *Or Zarua* by R. Isaac ben Moses of Vienna', (Hebrew; master's dissertation, Hebrew University of Jerusalem, 1993), p. 16.

12 In MT, this word is spelt with a final letter *he*. The spelling here, with a final *alef*, is known from *midrashim* emanating from the Land of Israel.

the letters denoting the centuries in their desire to denote the year by means of the world *malko*, which was connected to the day (Rosh Ha-Shana) of her death. Thus, Hanna died on Rosh Ha-Shana 4996, which fell on 15–16 September, 1235.

Who was this Hanna? The tombstones in the Würzburg collection usually relate women only to their fathers, while no mention is made of the husband. Only two tombstones are exceptions to this rule, and in both of them the husband's standing was the reason for the change from the accepted practice. 'Yonathan *Rabbenu*' was such a husband, to the extent that Hanna's children based their mother's prestige on her marriage to a man who was not their father, for if they were the children of 'Yonathan *Rabbenu*', they would undoubtedly have mentioned this, and not merely written the title, without indicating their connection with him. 'Yonathan *Rabbenu*' was the leading sage in Würzburg in the early thirteenth century. He did not leave a distinguished literary legacy, but he was the teacher of many other sages, the most famous of whom was R. Yiṣḥaq, the author of *Or Zaru'a*. The sage's importance motivated the tombstone writers to adorn their mother's memory with the name of one of her husbands, and not that of another of her husbands, who was their father, but lacked the renown of R. Yonathan.

Hanna's prestige came from her husband, while other women's tombstones depict them and their actions, and not only their families. The following is such a tombstone:

1 She left her father
2 [.] in the Rock of Israel
3 [..] dwells in the bosom
4 of our father [Abraha]m, her father, on the day
5 [A]dar, year 10
6 [M]ay her soul rest
7 [.] *Amen A[men] Se[lah]*

This woman was a convert: like Ruth the Moabite, she left her father and mother (following Ruth 2:11) and came to the Rock of Israel (ie, the God of Israel, following Isa 30:29). The presence of a woman convert in this period in Ashkenaz is in itself of special interest; but the wording chosen by the tombstone writers, who place this convert 'in the bosom' of the patriarch Abraham, is also worthy of our attention. The midrashic work *Pesikta de-Rav Kahana*[13] connects this wording with those circumcised: at the time of the circumcision, the one undergoing this act is in the bosom of Abraham, who was the first to

13 *Pesikta de Rav Kahana*, ed. by B. Mandelbaum (New York: The Jewish Theological Seminary of America, 1987), 1:44.

undergo circumcision and to circumcise. A different and more charged use appears in the *Midrash Lamentations Rabba*, in a narrative that portrays the actions of Miriam daughter of Tanḥum, whose seven sons died for refusing to bow down before an idol. When Miriam gazed upon her six-year-old seventh son as he was deliberating with the Roman soldiers, she is cited as telling him: '*Let not your courage falter* [Deut 20:3]. You are going to your brothers, and you will be in the bosom of Abraham'.[14] In the consciousness of Miriam (or perhaps that of the author of *Lamentations Rabba*), the bosom of Abraham is the place where martyrs are expected to arrive. A similar consciousness is indicated in another source from Ashkenaz. The chronicle portraying the massacre in Worms in 1096 quotes a man named Meshullam ben Yiṣḥaq who tells his wife, before he slaughters his son: 'I shall not delay for even a moment; the One who gave him to us will take him to his portion, and place him in the bosom of our father Abraham.'[15] Once again, as in *Lamentations Rabba*, Abraham's bosom is the place that is assured to those who die a martyr's death.

A completely different consciousness emerges from this epitaph. The bosom of Abraham is not promised here to martyrs, but to converts. The connection between converts and Abraham is deeply rooted in rabbinic teachings, since Abraham, as the first convert, is always identified as their father.[16] The innovation introduced by this epitaph is the use of the wording 'in the bosom', in the bosom of Abraham, as the intended destination of converts in the world to come; such a usage is unprecedented in rabbinic literature and in the literature of early Ashkenaz.

A number of years ago Jérôme Baschet indicated the distribution of the expression 'the bosom of our father Abraham' in Christian literature and art during the eleventh to thirteenth centuries.[17] He maintained that in the Christian world during that period this verbal and artistic expression symbolized the spiritual bond between Abraham, the ancient father, and those who accepted Christianity, while consciously foregoing their biological paternity, that of the flesh. As in the Jewish tradition, Christian tradition's identification of Abraham as the father of those converting to Christianity throughout the ages is quite distinct, and has ancient roots. Additionally, the phrase 'the bosom of Abraham' already appears in Luke 16:22–4, when the poor man Lazarus, tormented

14 *Midrasch Echa Rabbati*, ed. S. Buber (Vilna: Romm, 1899), p. 84.

15 E. Haverkamp, (ed.), *Hebräische Berichte über die Judenverfolgungen während des Ersten Kreuzzugs* (Hannover: Hahnsche Buchhandlung, 2005), p. 285.

16 See, eg, *yBik.* 64a (1d).

17 J. Baschet, *Le sein du père: Abraham et la paternité dans l'Occident médiéval* (Paris: Gallimard, 2000). See also S. Schwarzfuchs, 'Le sein d'Abraham', *Revue des études Juives* 163 (2004), pp. 283–88.

and rejected, is said to be in the bosom of Abraham after his death. Towards the beginning of the millennium, however, the expression 'the bosom of Abraham' assumed a new meaning in the Christian conceptual world, and became the place assured to those who accepted Christianity. This consciousness intensified during the course of the twelfth and thirteenth centuries.

The writers of the convert's epitaph did not need to borrow the identity of Abraham as the father of converts, or the expression 'the bosom of Abraham', from the surrounding Christian world, since they could have been quite familiar with them from the internal Jewish tradition. On the other hand, the conception of the bosom of Abraham as the place of the converts in the afterlife almost certainly originated in the Christian environment, in which the notion that this bosom is the proper place for those entering Christianity made its appearance close to this time. This convert's sons accordingly infused the early Hebrew expression with a meaning that came from the Christian cultural field, which they had known before their conversion. The family members therefore acted as 'cultural agents' who, either consciously or unwittingly, transferred language and meaning from their original Christian family to the Jewish community that they had entered and in which they died – the Würzburg community.

The role of converts as cultural agents who bring values from their first world into their new one can also be understood from a responsum by R. Yoel Ha-Levi, who was active in Ashkenaz in the last third of the twelfth and the early thirteenth centuries. The responsum appears in the collection of responsa of his son, R. Eli'ezer ben Yoel Ha-Levi of Bonn:

> A spirit came from the Lord and rested in the heart of this person, R. Abraham son of our father Abraham. Now when the spirit rested upon him, he drew near to the Lord's work, to seek the Lord, to study the book [i.e., Torah] and the holy tongue. He dwelt with us for a long time, and he was a blameless and upright man, who stayed inside [see Gen 25:27]. One day I, the undersigned [R. Yoel Ha-Levi, the father of R. Eli'ezer] found him sitting and copying the Pentateuch from an impure book of priests [i.e., a Latin Bible that had been copied by monks or priests]. I said to him: 'What is this in your hand?' He replied: 'I know the language of priests [= Latin], but I do not know the holy tongue [= Hebrew]. Now, this [the Latin Bible] is like an explanation for me, and, what is more, the sages of Speyer lent me priests' books to copy, and they did not try to prevent this. If this seems bad to you, I will cease and not continue.' I responded to him: 'You should know that I find this act to be evil.' He asked me to write on his behalf to my masters in Speyer, who might perhaps permit this to him. I knew that his intent was for Heaven's sake. I acted childishly, and I was impudent to my teachers, perhaps I erred.[18]

This convert lived in the second half of the twelfth century, and, as usual for converts in the medieval period, moved between different Jewish communities.

---

18 *Sefer Ravyah*, ed. D. Dvelaitsky (Bnei Brak: D. Dvelaitsky, 2005), p. 166.

The passage indicates that he lived in Cologne, Speyer, and Würzburg. During his stay in Speyer he obtained from the local Jewish scholars books of the Bible in Latin, from which he copied the Pentateuch for himself, so that he could learn something from it. Latin books of the Bible came to Jews as pledges for loans, and their being in the possession of Ashkenazi Jews does not indicate the latter's interest in them. Even if the Jewish sages in Ashkenaz had been interested in the biblical interpretations written in these books, they would have had difficulty in studying them, since they were not sufficiently proficient in Latin. Abraham the convert functioned as an intermediary through whom the members of his new community, the Jews, could become acquainted with the biblical interpretations of Christian scholars. Thus, Abraham the convert may have filled the same role that the converted woman had filled in Würzburg. They and the members of their families served as conduits for the transmission of cultural content; it is unclear whether the Jewish sages of the time were pleased by this transmission.

R. Yoel, whose responsum is cited above, was active for most of his life in Cologne, but his daughter's tombstone is among the collection from Würzburg:

1 In sorrow
2 with stylus incised, in the rock hewn
3 at the head of the dignified woman, *Marat* Hanna
4 [daughter of] our master, R. Yoel, the grandson of a Kehat [i.e., a Levite]
5 and Momona, the daughter of our master *Aban*
6 May her soul have repose
7 [b]irth pangs struck her, she died in the month [...]
8 and is gone, it shall be congenial for her soul
9 She shall be deemed among the righteous women

The tombstone of Hanna, daughter of R. Yoel Ha-Levi, who died in the year [5]914 (21 September, 1153 – 8 September 1154), the numerical value of which is expressed in the Hebrew for 'it shall be congenial for my soul', is singular in its size, the attempts at rhyme made in the epitaph, and in that it is the only tombstone that mentions the name of the deceased's mother. Momona, the wife of R. Yoel Ha-Levi, was the daughter of R. Eli'ezer, son of Nathan, 'our master *Aban*' (known as *Raban*), the leading Jewish sage in the Rhine communities of the eleventh century. The desire of the epitaph writers to trace the deceased's lineage to her renowned grandfather led them to go beyond the accepted practice in the Würzburg tombstones, both by mentioning the name of the deceased's mother, and by adding the grandfather's name, while normal practice called for mentioning only the father of the deceased. The epitaph, however, is not limited to lineage and her distinguished family. Hanna died when 'birth pangs struck her', thus joining other women on whose tombstones this fact was inscribed. The cause of death was generally not mentioned on the Würzburg tombstones, except for women who died during childbirth, or men and women who were murdered by non-Jews, as in the following tombstone:

1 Cherished in their life and in [their] death
2 Never parted, may He wreak their [vengeance]
3 Moshe son of R. Eli'ezer and R. Ya['aqov]
4 son of R. Ele'azar against whom
5 the sons of Esau arose and whom they killed
6 in the month of Elul 403, by the minor count

Two men who were killed by 'the sons of Esau' in the late summer of 1243 are buried under this tombstone. The mention of the cause of their death, and the prayer for vengeance that appears in l. 3, are not unique. A similar content appears on a tombstone from 1297:

1 This tombstone
2 was erected for
3 R. Moshe who was killed
4 son of R. Avraham die[d]
5 13 Adar II
6 57 by the minor count. May there be vengeance
7 by the Lord speed[ily] in [our] days
8 *A[men] A[men] A[men] S[elah]*

These and similar tombstones suffice to reveal that violence, murders, and wishes for vengeance were an integral part of the life of Würzburg's Jews, even in the intervals between the Second Crusade, the Rindfleisch massacres, and the Black Death. And this is not all. These tombstones demonstrate that the Jews of Ashkenaz had no qualms about pleading for divine revenge in a text that was in plain view, in a highly accessible cemetery. Weren't the Jews of Würzburg afraid to carve their request for vengeance in stone, and erect such an inscription in the cemetery? The answer is obviously that they were not deterred from taking such a step, and this in itself is highly instructive.[19]

A second point: this tombstone concludes without the blessing of the 'slain ones'[20] to accompany them on their way to the world of the dead; also absent

19 On the centrality in Ashkenaz of the motif of revenge, see I. J. Yuval, *Two Nations in Your Womb: Perceptions of Jews and Christians in Late Antiquity and the Middle Ages*, Eng. trans. B. Harshav and J. Chipman (Berkeley: University of California Press, 2006), pp. 91–134.

20 'Slain' (*ha-neherag*) teaches that the deceased died in violent circumstances at the hands of non-Jews. See A. Reiner, '"A Tombstone Inscribed": Titles Used to Describe the Deceased in Tombstones from Würzburg between 1147–1148 and 1346', *Tarbiz*, 78 (2008), pp. 144–45.

are 'may his abode be honoured', as well as 'may his honoured abode be in the Garden of Eden', and 'may his soul be bound up in the bond of everlasting life'.[21] These and similar blessings were inscribed on **all** the tombstones found in Würzburg, with the exception of some of those 'slain' by non-Jews, apparently against a background of interreligious hostility. This raises a question. Was a person's murder against the background of such tension sufficient, in the minds of Ashkenaz Jewry, to ensure the victim's place in the Garden of Eden or in the bond of everlasting life, to the extent that the blessings could be waived? An examination of the contemporaneous rabbinic literature teaches that these omissions were not by chance. We read in a responsum by R. Yiṣḥaq ben Ḥayyim, the grandson of the author of *Or Zaru'a*, who lived in Ashkenaz in the thirteenth century:

> The relative of my friend R. Naḥman the son of R. Shemarya came to me and showed me a letter from R. Moshe the son of R. Meir, of blessed memory, reporting that our master and teacher, R. Shemarya son of R. Ḥayyim,[22] of blessed memory, ordered that the *qedoshim* were not to be mourned.[23]

The *qedoshim* (literally, 'holy ones', i.e., martyrs) were those killed by Christians. According to R. Shemarya, mourning practices were not to be observed upon learning of their murder. R. Shemarya's ruling was subject to scathing criticism by R. Yiṣḥaq, who wrote: 'I say that atonement and contrition are required for what issued from his mouth.' The wording of R. Yiṣḥaq's reaction indicates the confusion and opposition generated by R. Shemarya's ruling. What is of importance for us, however, is the existence in Ashkenaz at that time of a halakhic determination that those who died a martyr's death were not to be mourned. Echoes of this ruling, and of its distribution, are also to be found in a responsum by R. Ya'aqov Moellin ('Maharil'),[24] thus demonstrating the way of thinking that regarded martyrdom as such a fit and exonerating death that there was no need to mourn the martyr, nor even to recite the

---

21 On blessings for the dead on tombstones in Ashkenaz and on the changes they underwent in the medieval period, see A. Reiner, 'From Paradise to the Bonds of Life: Blessings for the Dead on Tombs in Medieval Ashkenaz', *Zion*, 76 (2011), pp. 5–28.

22 On R. Shemarya, see Naftali Ha-Cohen, *Oṣar Ha-Gedolim Alufei Ya'aqov* (Haifa: Ha-Cohen, 1967–70), vol. 9, p. 54.

23 *She'eilot u-Teshuvot Ma-ha-raḥ Or Zarua'*, ed. M. Avitan (Jerusalem: Avitan, 2002), para. 14, p. 18. My thanks to Dr Maoz Kahana for drawing my attention to this responsum.

24 *Responsa of Rabbi Ya'aqov Moellin-Maharil*, ed. Y. Satz (Hebrew; Jerusalem: Mekhon Yerushalayim, 1979), pp. 189–90. This responsum indicates, not only that some sages ruled against mourning, but also that there was such a popular practice: 'I heard from my masters that it happened in the riots in Prague that some desired not to mourn for the martyrs, and, in the end, the leading authorities at the time agreed to mourn.'

qaddish prayer for his benefit.[25] The absence of a blessing for the dead on the tombstones of martyrs almost certainly originated in the same mindset. Since they died sanctifying the name of God, there was no longer any need for a blessing to send them on their way, neither on the journey to Paradise nor for their attachment to the bond of everlasting life. The manner of their death ensured them of their place in the world of everlasting life after death.[26]

---

25 *Responsa of Rabbi Ya'aqov Moellin*, pp. 189–90: 'I wish to know, my master, what I heard in the name of R. [...] of Tronbork, may the Lord avenge him, who ruled and established that *qaddish* is not to be recited for one's father who died a martyr's death.'

26 It nonetheless should be emphasized that three additional tombstones that state that the deceased was 'slain' do not contain a wish for vengeance, but do contain a blessing of the dead in the usual forms. Possibly, therefore, the request for revenge contained a degree of daring that was not exhibited by all, and the epitaph writers therefore chose not to write it on the tombstone. This said, however, the appearance of the blessing of the dead on these tombstones should be seen against the background of the halakhic dispute, with its practical implications, briefly mentioned in this article.

Nathanja Hüttenmeister and Andreas Lehnardt

Newly Found Medieval Gravestones from Magenza

The Jewish cemetery in the city of Mainz/Mayence, known to the Jews as Magenza, one of the famous three SHUM-cities[1] in the Rhineland, is one of the oldest, or maybe even the oldest, Jewish cemetery in medieval Ashkenaz. It is situated in the vicinity of the medieval city, on a hillside along an old Roman road leading to town from the north-west, near, or maybe even above, the remains of a Roman necropolis. Due to the sandy soil, the cemetery has been called 'Judensand' since the thirteenth century. Burials can be traced back to *c.* 1000 CE, but the Jewish cemetery could be even older. In the course of the persecution of the Jews in the First Crusade, the Jewish community of Magenza was almost completely destroyed, resulting in the depredation of its cemetery. When the Jews returned to Mainz, they replaced some of their famous forefathers' lost gravestones with (undated) memorial stones.

In 1438 the Jews were expelled from Mainz, the cemetery was destroyed again, the gravestones being spoilt and used for building purposes. In 1449 the premises were partly returned to the Jewish community that had returned to Mainz, and they served the community until 1880 when a new cemetery was inaugurated.

Over 200 medieval Jewish gravestones have been found in Mainz in the past two hundred years, dating from the years 1049 to 1421, among them a stone from the year 1049, constituting the oldest Jewish gravestone ever found in Germany.

Most of the recovered gravestones had been built into edifices from the fifteenth century, or were found underground in the gardens adjacent to the Jewish cemetery, obviously in an area that was part of the medieval Jewish cemetery before the expulsion of the Jews in 1438.

Some of these stones are currently on exhibition in the Landesmuseum Mainz, but most of them were in 1926 returned to their places of origin and assembled in a field adjacent to the Jewish cemetery, as a memorial cemetery ('Denkmalfriedhof') to commemorate the glorious past of the Jewish community of medieval Magenza.[2] This section of the memorial site was formerly part

---

1 SHUM, after the first Hebrew letters of Shpira (Speyer), Wormayza (Worms) and Magenza (Mainz). – The present paper is a preliminary report. A longer and more detailed report has been accepted for publication by the Generaldirektion Kulturelles Erbe in Mainz.

2 Sali Levi, *Beiträge zur Geschichte der ältesten jüdischen Grabsteine in Mainz* (Mainz: Walter, 1926).

of the medieval Jewish cemetery, as has been proved by excavations done under the supervision of Rabbi Sali Levi.[3]

In 1952, when an agricultural school was built in an area adjacent to the Jewish cemetery and the memorial graveyard – an area that had obviously also once been part of the medieval Jewish cemetery – additional gravestones were found and documented by Professor Eugen Rapp. In 2008, this agricultural school was demolished to give way to luxurious city mansions. In the pit that was dug for the mansion basements, more medieval gravestones turned up, together with other fragments.[4]

1 The newly found gravestones

Twenty-nine gravestones and fragments of gravestones were discovered, intact and partly intact, as well as some small parts, made of reddish, yellowish or grey sandstone. Other stones that were excavated appear not to have any connection with the Jewish cemetery but originate in the nearby Roman necropolis.

Twelve tombstones are intact; while a further twelve stones bear a date from the era between the end of the eleventh century and the middle of the thirteenth century (see the list below).

Most of the gravestones are of fairly elaborate design, while some are only roughly worked. They close, as far as can be seen today, with straight closures, three have a semi-circular arch and one a kind of asymmetric triangular pediment. On most of the gravestones the text area was sunken and on two gravestones auxiliary text lines can still be seen.

In order to achieve a systematic analysis of the newly found gravestones, the tombstone inscriptions were entered into 'Epidat', the epigraphical database of the Salomon Ludwig Steinheim-Institute for German Jewish History,[5] together with over 200 medieval Magenza tombstone inscriptions previously discovered.

---

3 Levi, *Beiträge*, p. 6.

4 A complete list is provided below. Details of these newly found gravestones and their inscriptions will be published in 2014 by Nathanja Hüttenmeister and Andreas Lehnardt from the Johannes Gutenberg-University of Mainz.

5 Although the digital edition of the medieval gravestones of Mainz (www.steinheim-institut.de/cgi-bin/epidat) is not yet publicly accessible, the reference numbers provided there will be used below for future reference when publication is completed.

Some of these have already been published[6]: in 1834, the first discovery was announced.[7] In 1860/62, Marcus Lehmann, Rabbi of Mainz, published more medieval Magenza tombstone inscriptions *inter alia* in the monthly journal *Jeschurun* and in his weekly journal *Der Israelit*, the 'central organ for orthodox Judaism'[8]. He was followed by Sigmund Salfeld, who published a list of all the then known stones and a few inscriptions in his well-known volume *Das Martyrologium des Nürnberger Memorbuchs* in 1898[9]. When Sali Levi, then Rabbi of the Mainz community, founded the memorial grave site in 1926, he published additional inscriptions[10] as well as a list of all 188 gravestones,[11] that had been assembled at the memorial site.

After World War II, the concern and effort of the Protestant theologian, Eugen Ludwig Rapp (1904–1977), resulted in the medieval gravestones not being forgotten. He collected every newly found item and ensured that everything was photographed and documented.[12]

Last but not least, the publication of 104 tombstone inscriptions in the memorial volume for Zvi Avneri, that appeared in 1970, also deserves to be mentioned.[13]

More than 240 medieval gravestones and gravestone fragments have been found to date in Mainz, including the twenty-nine newly discovered items. Two of the new stones date from the eleventh century and so rank among the

---

6 A more or less complete overview of all the publications until the year 2005 is offered in: Falk Wiesemann, *Sepulcra Judaica. Jewish Cemeteries, Death, Burial and Mourning from the Period of Hellenism to the Present. A Bibliography* (Essen: Klartext, 2005), pp. 293–95.

7 Georg Christian Braun, 'Über einen auf dem jüdischen Begräbnisplatz zu Mainz gefundenen Stein', *Annalen des Vereins für Nassauische Alterthumskunde und Geschichtsforschung* 2 (1834), vol. 2, 163–66.

8 Marcus Lehmann, 'Die in der Nähe des Ludwigsbahnhofes in Mainz aufgefundenen jüdischen Grabsteine', *Zeitschrift des Vereins zur Erforschung der Rheinischen Geschichte und Altertümer* 2 (1859/1864), 226–32; and in *Jeschurun* (old series) 1859–1860, vol. 4 (January 1860), 204–10; and see also 'Mitteilung aus Mainz von Marcus Lehmann', *Der Israelit* (1862), vol. 19 (7 May 1862), 150–51.

9 Siegmund Salfeld, *Das Martyrologium des Nürnberger Memorbuchs* (Berlin: Simion, 1898).

10 Levi, *Beiträge*.

11 'Verzeichnis der alten jüdischen Grabsteine auf dem „Judensand"', compiled by Rabbi Dr S. Levi (Mainz, 1926).

12 His cardboard box with photographs and transcriptions is kept at the 'Seminar für Judaistik' of the Johannes Gutenberg University of Mainz. See also Eugen Ludwig Rapp and Otto Böcher, 'Die ältesten hebräischen Inschriften Mitteleuropas in Mainz, Worms und Speyer', *Jahrbuch der Vereinigung der "Freunde der Universität Mainz"* (1959), 1–48.

13 Zvi Avneri, 'Medieval Jewish Epitaphs from Magenza', *Studies in the History of the Jewish People and the Land of Israel in Memory of Zvi Avneri*, eds. A. Gilboa, B. Mevorach, U. Rappaport and A. Shochat (Hebrew; Haifa: Haifa University, 1970), pp. 141–61.

oldest gravestones ever found in Magenza and even in Ashkenaz. Altogether, six dated gravestones from the eleventh century have now been found in Mainz: The oldest seems to be from the year 1049, another is dated to the Jewish year (4)824 (1063–64), three stones bear dates from the 1080s (1080, 1084 and 1089), and one is from the year 1094/95. Recently, two new gravestones were found from the year 1085/86. Of the first, only the lower part remains, where the year of death and a closing blessing indicate that the stone was erected for a woman.[14]

This inscription provides no exact date, but only the year of death. Four of seven legible Magenza gravestones from the second half of the eleventh century carry an exact date, three only the year of death. In the first half of the twelfth century, it was common in Magenza for only the year of death to be engraved on the gravestones, while years later the month in which the deceased passed away was added. Only from the middle of the thirteenth century onwards did the exact date, with day, month and year of death, appear more frequently on the gravestones.

The second gravestone[15] from the year 846 (1085/86) was erected for R. Amram *ha-baḥur*, son of Yona, who came from the Holy City, most likely the R. Amram Yerushalmi mentioned in the responsa literature: It was R. Amram Yerushalmi who delivered a responsum from R. Nathan b. Makhir to R. Shemuel Ha-Kohen, a contemporary of Rashi in Magenza.[16] If this identification is correct, this is the only one of the newly found Magenza gravestones whose 'owner' can be identified from other sources.

R. Amram is said to have been murdered ביום הזעם, 'on the day of wrath', the eighteenth day of the month of Elul in the year 846, that is, Monday, August 31, 1086. No hint has been found in any other source that might explain the term 'day of wrath' and it may have been used to refer to a single day of pogrom against the Magenza Jews, of which no other record has survived.

Another of the newly found Magenza gravestones was erected for a martyr: Mar Avraham bar Shemuel Kohen[17] was murdered 'in the year 7 of the counting'. This might be the year 1246/47, the seventh year of the new, that is, the sixth millennium of the Jewish era, but the term 'of the sixth millennium',

---

14 Digital Edition – Jewish Cemetery of Mainz, Medieval Gravestones (1049–1421 / 248 items), no. 0014.

15 Digital Edition – Jewish Cemetery of Mainz, Medieval Gravestones (1049–1421 / 248 items), no. 0011.

16 *Pardes* 23, *Or Zaru'a* II, 389. See also Avraham Grossman, *The Early Sages of Ashkenaz* (Hebrew: Jerusalem: Magnes, 1988), pp. 187, 201, 206, 365, 393, 427.

17 Digital Edition – Jewish Cemetery of Mainz, Medieval Gravestones (1049–1421 / 248 items), no. 0004.

which was common in Magenza at least from the 1250s onwards, is missing here.[18] Given the style of the gravestone and the place it was found, the date may also be read as 'in the year 7 of the new, that is, the tenth century', meaning the year 907, that is, 1146/47, the year of the Second Crusade, that claimed at least two casualties in the Magenza Jewish community.[19]

What is extraordinary is the gravestone of David bar Yiṣḥaq Ha-Kohen.[20] It was clearly found for the first time in the 1950s when the agricultural school was built. At that time, the upper left corner of the stone was cut off, as is proved by traces of concrete that are still visible today. The stone was left at its place of origin and was buried under the concrete basement of the school. In 2007 it was rediscovered after the demolition of the school, with the part yielding the year of death missing. In the pit that was dug for the erection of the planned new building, two graves were found right next to the stone just mentioned. One of the graves is covered by a layer of flat stones,[21] while on the other one an elaborate construction of stones was created to stabilize the gravestone, whose base was still in place, in this sandy slope. Already at first sight, the gravestone of David bar Yiṣḥaq Ha-Kohen seemed to match the stone base on this second grave, as could be proved thanks to the technical assistance of the State Department for the Preservation of Historical Monuments ('Landesamt für Denkmalpflege Mainz') [Fig. 1]. This gravestone points directly to the east, in the direction of Jerusalem, while the direction of the second grave shows a small variation.

As a token of respect for the dead, the hole was covered up without any excavations being done, and the stones were transferred to the storehouse of the State Department for the Preservation of Historical Monuments.

Among the newly found stones was also the gravestone of Rivqa bat Qalonymos[22], who might, according to her father's name, be a descendant of the famous Qalonymos family which founded the Magenza community [Fig. 2]. Her stone was photographed on its original site but was obviously not trans-

18 There is only one more stone from the 1240s, but it is badly damaged, with missing text after the year.

19 *Germania Judaica I. Von den ältesten Zeiten bis 1238*, eds. I. Elbogen, A. Freimann and H. Tykocinski (Tübingen: Mohr Siebeck, 1963), p. 181.

20 Digital Edition – Jewish Cemetery of Mainz, Medieval Gravestones (1049–1421 / 248 items), no. 0001.

21 It has not been possible to ascertain whether this grave is of Jewish, or of older Roman, or Celtic origin.

22 Digital Edition – Jewish Cemetery of Mainz, Medieval Gravestones (1049–1421 / 248 items), no. 0003. See also Nathanja Hüttenmeister, 'Riwka Tochter des Kalonymos aus Mainz. Ein zweimal verschwundener Grabstein', *Kalonymos* 12 (2009), vol. 3, pp. 13–16.

Fig. 1: David bar Yiṣḥaq Ha-Kohen, Photo © Andreas Lehnardt.

Fig. 2: Rivqa bat Qalonymos, Photo © Andreas Lehnardt.

ferred to the storehouse. The stone disappeared and probably fell back into the hole and was covered by sand, before the hole was filled up again. A more thorough research revealed that the stone, which now shows clear signs of damage, was first discovered in 1952, when the agricultural school was built, and was at that time not yet damaged. Pictures of the stone were taken[23], and the text was copied, but it seems that the gravestone was left at the building site and later covered up again.

The inscription fills only two and a half of at least eight auxiliary lines that were prepared for it. Such auxiliary lines are also to be found on other Magenza gravestones, mainly on stones from the twelfth century. The form and design of Rivqa's gravestone resemble those on the gravestone of the famous liturgical poet, R. Meshullam b. Moshe b. Itiel, who died in 1094/95.[24] Both are square stones with a straight closure, with a sunken area for the inscription and with auxiliary lines, which appear on R. Meshullam's stone only on the first two out of a total of six lines of inscription.

The word נחללת, 'the slain one', that follows the opening phrase, indicates Rivqa's fate; the term is used in biblical and talmudical texts for death in a fight and is still used today for IDF soldiers killed in combat. This leads to the assumption that Rivqa died a martyr's death. Since the inscription gives us no date, no further circumstances can be determined, but there might be a connection with the pogroms accompanying the First Crusade.

This gravestone seems never to have included a date of death, as is the case with another one of the newly found gravestones; that is the rectangular, partly damaged stone for Moshe b. Elyaqim Kohen[25], whose design resembles the oldest Magenza gravestones and is probably to be counted among the above-mentioned memorial stones, erected by the Jewish community as substitutes for lost gravestones when the Jews returned to Mainz in the twelfth century after the expulsions of the First Crusade. They were meant as a commemoration of the outstanding forefathers who were known to all so that there was

---

23 In Professor Rapp's cardboard box are two pictures of this gravestone.

24 Eugen Ludwig Rapp, 'Mainzer hebräische Grabsteine aus dem Mittelalter. Die neuen Funde im Altertumsmuseum', *Mainzer Zeitschrift. Mittelrheinisches Jahrbuch für Archäologie, Kunst und Geschichte* (1957), pp. 42–45 (p. 42 and p. 43, no. 1: photograph, transcription in Latin letters and translation into German). Eugen Ludwig Rapp, 'Die Mainzer hebräischen Epitaphien aus dem Mittelalter', *Jahrbuch der Vereinigung „Freunde der Universität Mainz"*, 7 (1958), 73–90 (pp. 82–87: 'Übersicht über alle datierbaren Mainzer Inschriften von 1064 bis 1420', no. M 005). Rapp/Böcher, pp. 16–17, no. 12 (Transcription in Latin letters, translation into German and commentary), and p. 25, fig. 10. Avraham Zvi Roth, 'The gravestone of Rabana ben R. Moshe ben Rabana Itiel from Magenza', *Zion*, 28 (1962/63), 233–35 (Hebrew).

25 Digital Edition – Jewish Cemetery of Mainz, Medieval Gravestones (1049–1421 / 248 items), no. 0012.

no need to mention a date on them. Among them is the liturgical poet Shim'on b. Yiṣḥaq the Great (died around 1000)[26], the liturgical poet Meshullam b. Qalonymos, grandson of R. Moshe of Lucca in Italy, the ancestor of the Qalonymos family who played a prominent role in early Ashkenazi history (died before 1027)[27], the talmudist and halakhist Rabbenu Gershom, the 'light of the exile' (died 1028/1040)[28], who in his day turned Magenza into a center of Jewish intellectual and religious life, and R. Yaqar, father of Rashi's teacher Ya'aqov b. Yaqar (died before 1050)[29].

Also Rivqa, 'the praised one', was the daughter of a man called Qalonymos, who perhaps was a descendant of this renowned Qalonymos family. And the fact that her inscription is one of few known inscriptions in Magenza that is rhymed, could indicate her noble ancestry, with the rhyme seen as a special honour for this martyr of high lineage. One more of the newly found gravestones bears the name Qalonymos: the stone of Qalonymos *ha-baḥur* b. Yoel who died in the year 905 (1144/45).

Among the newly found stones, eight are designed for men, and nine for women. Out of these, three were erected for *baḥurim*, bachelors, and another three for *baḥurot*, perhaps 'virgins'. On thirty-three out of all the medieval gravestones found in Mainz until now, the deceased are referred to as *baḥurim*

---

26 Siegmund Salfeld, 'Mainzer jüdische Grabsteine, gefunden im Jahre 1922', *Mainzer Zeitschrift. Mittelrheinisches Jahrbuch für Archäologie, Kunst und Geschichte* 17–19 (1922–24), 62–65 (p. 63, no. 2). Levi, 'Verzeichnis', no. 116 (field VIII): 'Rabban, R. Simon, Sohn des R. Isak, ohne Jahr'. Oscar Lehmann, 'Der alte jüdische Friedhof in Mainz', *Aus alter und neuer Zeit* 55 (1926), 436–37 (p. 436). *Germania Judaica I*, p. 189 (no. 5).

27 M. Lehmann, *Jeschurun*, p. 205. 'Der alte israelitische Friedhof in Mainz', *Der Israelit* (1876), vol. 9 (1.3. 1876), pp. 201–2. Eliakim Carmoly, 'Die Juden zu Mainz im Mittelalter. V. Der uralte Friedhof', *Der Israelit* (1865), vol. 39 (27.9. 1865), 563–65. M. Lehmann, *Der Israelit*, p. 150. Salfeld, *Martyrologium*, p. 434, no. 25: 'Rabban Meschullam, Sohn des Rabban R. Kalonymos'. Jonas Bondi, 'Der alte Friedhof', in *Magenza. Ein Sammelheft über das jüdische Mainz ...* (Mainz, 1927), 22–32 (p. 27); also as special edition in *Menorah. Jüdisches Familienblatt für Wissenschaft/Kunst und Literatur* V (1927), vol. 12 (December 1927), 718–28 (p. 723). Levi, 'Verzeichnis', no. 1 (field I): 'Rabban Meschullam, Sohn des Rabban, Rabbi Kalonimos, ohne Jahr'. Bernd Andreas Vest, *Der alte jüdische Friedhof in Mainz* (Mainz: Vest, 1988), p. 14 (transcription), p. 15–16 (photographs) and p. 87 (no. 30).

28 Levi, *Beiträge*, p. 12–13, no. I (transcription, translation, commentary and photograph). Salfeld, *Martyrologium*, p. 434, no. 29: '12. Gerschom, Sohn Meirs (?)'. Levi, 'Verzeichnis', no. 164 (field XI): 'Rabbi Gerschom bar Jehudah (ohne Jahr)'. *Germania Judaica I*, p. 189–191 (no. 7). Vest, p. 16 (photograph), p. 19 (translation), p. 69 and p. 88 (no. 33).

29 Salfeld, *Mainzer Zeitschrift*, p. 65, no. 25). Levi, *Beiträge*, p. 14–15, no. II (transcription, translation, commentary and photograph). Levi, 'Verzeichnis', no. 3 (field I): 'Rabbi Jakar (Fragment)'. *Germania Judaica I*, p. 189 (no. 6). Vest, p. 41 and 42 (photograph, transcription and translation), p. 68 and p. 88 (no. 31).

or *baḥurot*, with a balanced spread between the sexes: sixteen *baḥurim* and seventeen *baḥurot*. In most of the cases, these terms probably indicate that the deceased were not married, but the possibility cannot be ruled out that this term is sometimes used as a honorary title meaning 'special'. This could for example be the case with '*Ṣippora*, the special, the modest, daughter of R. Moshe', who died in the year 878 (1117/18).[30]

Two signs are carved in the head of her stone that resemble the Latin letters V and L. These could be a symbol of the stone cutter who prepared the gravestone but more probably go back to older, Roman times. Another gravestone[31], that of Orgie, 'the special (or virgin) and modest daughter of Shneor', who died in 1137/38, shows clear signs of previous use. The gravestone's base shows one half of a neatly carved text area that contrasts with the upper part of the stone that has only roughly been treated. So it seems that parts of these stones were originally used as Roman gravestones and were taken from the nearby Roman necropolis and made into gravestones for the Jewish cemetery.

The described gravestones were found on the grounds of the medieval Jewish cemetery, and survived, covered by sand. Some of the gravestones show signs of damage, but this damage occurred when the agricultural school was built in 1952 or when it was demolished in 2007. But one of the newly found gravestones has damage that seems to be much older: The inscription in memory of Binyamin Ha-Kohen or of his son[32] from the year 1105 is only partly legible, the stone around the letters having been chipped off. Has this been caused by weathering or was the inscription intentionally obliterated? There is another medieval gravestone from Magenza that exhibits similar damage: the gravestone of Bat Sheva'[33] from the year 1141, first described by Eugen Rapp in 1957.[34]

It seems reasonable to assume that these gravestones were set aside after the expulsion of the Jews from Magenza and were worked on in preparation

---

30 Digital Edition – Jewish Cemetery of Mainz, Medieval Gravestones (1049–1421 / 248 items), no. 0002.

31 Digital Edition – Jewish Cemetery of Mainz, Medieval Gravestones (1049–1421 / 248 items), no. 0017.

32 Digital Edition – Jewish Cemetery of Mainz, Medieval Gravestones (1049–1421 / 248 items), no. 0006.

33 Digital Edition – Jewish Cemetery of Mainz, Medieval Gravestones (1049–1421 / 248 items), no. 2210.

34 Rapp, *Mainzer Zeitschrift*, p. 42 and p. 43, no. 2 (photograph, transcription in Latin letters, translation). Rapp, *Jahrbuch*, p. 82–87: 'Übersicht über alle datierbaren Mainzer Inschriften von 1064 bis 1420', no. M 007. Rapp/Böcher, p. 27 (transcription in Latin letters, translation, commentary). Vest, p. 65 and p. 86 (no. 11).

for building purposes. But for unknown reasons, the stones were left on the cemetery grounds, covered by sand and forgotten.

Most of the medieval Ashkenazi gravestones known to us today were preserved because they were victims of acts of depredation perpetrated on the cemeteries of their origin and were reused in sacral and secular buildings alike, as trophies after the expulsion of the Jews, as visible symbols of the victory of the church over the synagogue, and as cheap and available building material.

But the gravestones on this site, though invisible, survived on the grounds of the medieval Jewish cemetery until they were rediscovered in our own days.

2 The newly found gravestones from Magenza

A woman (died 1085/86) [0014, fragmental]

Amram ben Yona from the Holy City (died 31. 08. 1086) [0011, intact]

Son of Binyamin Ha-Kohen (died 11. 10. 1105) [0006, damaged]

A man (died 1105/06) [0015, fragmental]

A man? (died 1105/06?) [0024, fragmental]

Ṣippora bat Moshe (died 1117/18) [0002, intact]

Menaḥem ben Yosef (died 1121/22) [0005, intact, but weathered]

Meir ben Ele'azar Ha-Kohen (died 1132/33) [0021, slightly damaged]

Orgie bat Shneor (died 1137/38) [0017, intact]

Qalonymos ben Yoel (died 1144/45) [0018, intact]

Avraham ben Shemuel Kohen (died 1146/47) [0004, slightly damaged]

Sara bat Shim'on Ha-Kohen (died July 1152) [0019, intact, but weathered]

Orgie bat Ele'azar (died 1181/82) [0007, fragmental]

Rivqa bat Qalonymos (undated, probably one of the oldest gravestones) [0003, damaged]

David Ha-Ko(hen) ben Yiṣḥaq Ha-Ko(hen) (died between 1041–1139) [0001, damaged]

Gita bat Yosef (undated) [0008, fragmental]

Moshe ben Eliaqim Kohen (undated) [0012, damaged]

A man (undated) [0022, fragmental]

A woman (undated) [0009, fragmental]

A woman (undated) [0010, fragmental]

Ten undated fragments, some of them very small (they may not all represent parts of Jewish gravestones) [0013, 0020, 0023, 0025, 0027–0030, 0032, 0033]

Thirteen fragments of rectangular flagstones, made of reddish sandstone, with engraved ornamental designs, probably of Roman origin [0026, 0031, 0034]

David Malkiel

The Structures of Hebrew Epitaph Poetry in Padua

Simple prose inscriptions, noting the name of the deceased and the date of death, are the most common variety found in Jewish graveyards of the pre-modern era. These monuments are valuable tools for the study of demographic patterns and social structures, as well as for genealogical research. Far more precious to the student of literature and thought, however, are the poetic inscriptions. Italy is home to the largest surviving corpus of such documents, dating from the early modern era.

The largest volume of Italian Hebrew verse, in print and manuscript, was produced to honour social or communal religious events, such as weddings or the dedication of synagogues. This kind of poetry deploys Spanish and Italian forms and makes liberal use of biblical language and motifs to articulate religious ideals, both theological and ethical. This genre, known as occasional poetry, is the broader category within which the epitaph poem is subsumed.

For three centuries, from 1529 to 1830, epitaph poems constitute more than half of Padua's tombstone inscriptions, and sometimes as much as three quarters. After that, the epitaph poem drastically declines. In the final thirty years of our period (1830–1862) the epitaph poem drastically declines, with poems numbering just over ten per cent of the total corpus.

1 Form

1.1 Prose, rhyme and metre

The material from the 1530s to the 1560s represents a discrete period in the literary development of Padua's Hebrew inscriptions. The series of tombstones in our corpus dates from 1529. For the first thirty years or so the corpus of inscriptions divides fairly evenly between simple prose inscriptions and rhymed prose or unmetered poetry. There are about forty inscriptions from this initial period, after which time the rhymed and metered poem becomes the most common form.

Presumably, this material represents continuity with the literary form employed in the monuments of the previous Jewish cemetery, at least in its later years. Rhymed prose is common in medieval Hebrew literature, especially in lamentations and penitential texts composed in Germany, the native land of most of Padua's Jews. The predominance of prose and rhymed prose texts comes, therefore, as no surprise.

The rhymed prose and poetry display a broad range of linguistic and poetic elements. Inscriptions are studded with biblical expressions and with snippets of biblical verses, mostly expressing sorrow and often drawn from Lamentations or Job. 'For these things do I weep' (Lam 1:16) and 'the crown has fallen from our head ... because of this our hearts are sick' (Lam 5:16–17) are examples of such usages.

Another common feature is the acrostic, which, like rhymed prose, is common in the lamentation and penitential writings of medieval Germany and hence not unexpected in Padua. The letters of the acrostic denote the first name of the deceased, and occasionally the patronym too. Texts with an acrostic also sometimes deploy a rhyme scheme; the short couplet is a common rhyme scheme, with each pair of lines rhyming in its own sound.

Hebrew metered epitaph poetry appears in Padua in the 1530s and dominates the corpus of Paduan inscriptions for the next three hundred years. Hebrew metre is based on the division of vowels into short vowels – the *shewa* and *ḥaṭaf* – and long ones, namely all the rest. The basic principle is that the stichs must present a single pattern of long and short vowels.[1] The Hebrew poets of early modern Italy usually ignored the distinction between long and short vowels. Instead, they measured the number of syllables in a line and required that lines uniformly conclude in either *milra'* or *mil'el*, namely accented on either the ultimate or penultimate syllable.

The Italian taste generally preferred stichs of eleven syllables, known as *endecasillabo,* and preferably those ending in *mil'el*, known as *endecasillabo piano*. Sometimes poets did pay attention to the distribution of long and short vowels. Thus, the favoured *endecasillabo piano* scheme appears in a number of variations, of which the layout with short vowels at syllables three and seven was especially popular and thus is appropriately known in Hebrew poetics as 'standard 11-*mil'el*.'[2]

The inaugural text of Padua's metered epitaph poetry is that of Naftali ben Yosef Kohen (1.58, d. 1538). This epitaph is carefully constructed in six stichs

1 See Benjamin Hrushovski, 'Prosody, Hebrew', *Encyclopaedia Judaica* (Jerusalem: Keter, 1971), vol. 13, col. 1212; Dvora Bregman, *The Golden Way: The Hebrew Sonnet during the Renaissance and the Baroque*, Eng. trans. by Ann Brener (Tempe, Arizona: Arizona Center for Medieval and Renaissance Studies, 2006), pp. 31–41.

2 The scholarly literature on the subject of Hebrew metered poetry is prodigious. Indispensable is: Dan Pagis, *Change and Tradition in the Secular Poetry: Spain and Italy* (Hebrew; Jerusalem: Keter, 1976), pp. 289–355. See also the writings of Dvora Bregman, particularly 'The Metrical System of Immanuel of Rome', *Tarbiz*, 58 (1989), pp. 413–52; and *The Golden Way* (see n. 1 above).

of sixteen syllables, each line divided into four units of four syllables, always ending in *milra'*. A single rhyme threads its way through the poem (*-rah*), and there is also an internal rhyme scheme: in three of the six lines the fourth and eighth syllables rhyme. This poem is built exclusively with long vowels, and hence termed 'simple' in the language of Hebrew poetics. The structure of four-times-four syllables per line, in *milra'* and monorhyme, is the legacy of medieval Spanish Jewry. Thus the very first clear instance of metered Hebrew epitaph poetry from Padua exhibits Iberian influence, which is surprising, in view of the population's German origins.

The second metered poem in the Paduan corpus is that of Neḥemya Saraval (1.76, d. 1544). This inscription presents a metrical scheme of twelve syllables with a *milra'* ending ('12a'). Like its predecessor, the Saraval text lacks an acrostic, and this is a prominent characteristic of Padua's metered epitaph poetry. Between 1532 and 1573 eighteen epitaph poems are adorned with an acrostic, but later in the sixteenth century there are only two more, one in 1594 and another undated. The acrostic's disappearance coincides with the adoption of metre. From a purely literary point of view, the appearance of metre may explain it, for metre guarantees a larger measure of form and discipline than acrostic, compensating for its disappearance and perhaps for some practitioners rendering it dispensable. The switch from acrostic to metre is significant evidence of the Italianization process of Padua's German Jewish population, a cultural trend that began with their immigration from Ashkenaz over a century earlier and was clearly still underway.

This kind of literature was not new in the sixteenth century; a rich and varied corpus of metered verse had accumulated since its introduction and development by Immanuel of Rome in the latter thirteenth century. The novelty lay rather in the choice of genre, in the decision to craft epitaph inscriptions using these particular poetic tools. In this regard, it appears that the German Jews of Padua were *au courant*, for although little information is available about the Hebrew tombstone inscriptions of Italy in the thirteenth to fifteenth centuries, the metered epitaph poem becomes a staple of Italian Jewish epigraphy in the early modern era, from the sixteenth century onwards. This tendency cuts across ethnic and geographical lines; the primary sources evince no clear distinction between the ethnic affiliations of communities or individuals in the matter of the inclusion of a poem in one's epitaph.[3]

The trail having been blazed, nineteen years were to pass before metre came to dominate the Padua graveyard. Between 1544 and 1563 twenty-one

3 See: David Malkiel, 'Epitaph Poems from Northern Italy in the Sixteenth and Seventeenth Century', *Pe'amim*, 98–99 (2004), pp. 121–54.

gravestones were added, not one of them in metre but ten in rhyme and several with acrostic, indicating a preference for the familiar over the novel. These inscriptions, some of which have been described above, are highly creative, presenting a wide range of rhyme schemes, from monorhyme to couplets, to a sequence as complex as ABABBACCC.

It is with the epitaph of Eli'ezer Hefetz (1.68, d. 1563) that metered epitaph poetry becomes a consistent feature of Padua's Hebrew inscriptions. His is a modest effort, just a quattrain, but exhibiting a metrical scheme in *endecasillabo tronco*, or the short eleven-syllable scheme (10a). Moreover, unlike the compositions surveyed earlier, Hefetz's poem has an enclosed rhyme scheme (ABBA), which is very common in the eight-stich poem, the *ottava*, which was an extremely popular form in Italian Hebrew verse, as well as in the Paduan graveyards. In effect, then, Hefetz's poem is a half-*ottava*.

A year later we find the metered poem of Meir Katzenellenbogen (1.2), the famous 'Maharam mi-Padova'. His poem is in the simple Spanish style, with lines of four-times-four syllables in long vowels. Given his stature, the composition of his epitaph poem in a classic Spanish form is powerful testimony to the cultural shift we are examining. His son Shemuel's epitaph (1.1, d. 1597), has twenty two lines, which is unprecedented and hardly paralleled in the Padua graveyards. The metre is classic *endecasillabo piano* (11b), and a rhyme scheme stitches together the even lines, while in each of the odd-numbered lines the two hemistichs share a rhyme of their own.

The epitaph poetry of the seventeenth century exhibits new forms of increasing complexity. In 1604 the poetic inscription of Hanna Rava (1.230) is structured in a 12a syllabic metre, but it also adheres to one of the quantitative metrical schemes adopted by the Hebrew poets of medieval Andalusia from the conventions of Arabic poetics. These dictate that lines be composed of hemistichs (*delet* and *soger*), with matching sequences of long and short syllables. But poets were to deploy only particular metrical patterns, which are listed by name in Spanish works of Hebrew poetics. In the scheme known as *ha-arokh b*, a short vowel ('◡') precedes five long vowels, with a caesura after the third syllable, such as (proceeding from right to left):[4]

לְאוֹת צוּר זֶה הוּשַּׂם לְגוּטְלֶן נִפְטְרָה
'- - - / - - ◡ // - - - / - - ◡ // - - - / - - ◡ // - - - / - - ◡

A quick count reveals that the sequence comprises twelve syllables, and thus dovetails with the syllabic format of the Rava inscription. The author of this

4 See Jefim Schirmann, *Hebrew Poetry in Spain and Provence* (Hebrew; Jerusalem and Tel Aviv: Magnes, 1971), vol. 4, p. 722.

text was thus able to meld the Spanish and Italian forms, and organize the inscription in both 12a and *ha-arokh b*. Ten more such texts survive for the period until 1700.[5]

In like fashion, the 1629 poem memorializing Aharon Heilperon (1.188) has an *endecasillabo piano* pattern identical to the Spanish metre known as *ha-shalem c:*

אֶשְׁמַע בְּקוֹל דָּמִים אֲשֶׁר יִצְעֲקוּ
- '- - / - ◡ - - / - ◡ - - // - - - / - ◡ - - / - ◡ - -

There are a number of variations on the 11b sequence, depending on the positions of long and short vowels, and Heilperon's matches *ha-shalem c* because it is constructed in the pattern known as 'standard 11-*mil'el*' (mentioned above), which requires short vowels at syllables three and seven.

Other Spanish quantitative metre sequences found in the Padua corpus include: *ha-merube, ha-marnin, ha-mitpasheṭ c, ha-mahir b* and *ha-doher b*:

נְדוּנְיָתָהּ בִּזְכֻיּוֹת מְרֻבּוֹת
ha-merubeh: '- - ◡ - - - ◡ - - - ◡

וְהוּא הָיָה וְהוּא הוֹוֶה וְהוּא יִחְיֶה בְּתִפְאָרָה
ha-marnin: '- - - ◡ / - - - ◡ // - - - ◡ / - - - ◡

הוּא מָל בְּשַׂר עָרְלָה כָּל פָּעֳלוֹ נִשְׁלַם
ha-mitpasheṭ c: '- - / - ◡ - - // - - / - ◡ - -

חַיֵּי תְּמוּתָה תֹּאמְרוּ אַחַי
ha-mahir b: '- - / - ◡ - - / - ◡ - -

נִחַם עֲגוּמִים בְּשִׂכְלוֹ רָם
ha-doher b: '- - ◡ - ◡ - - ◡ - -

The texts are from 1618 (1.161), 1694 (1.281), 1622 (1.111), 1711 (2.34) and 1717 (1.30), respectively.

A number of blended poems exhibiting syllabic and quantitative metre, do not match any of the accepted Andalusian patterns. Two of the exceptional patterns appear twice: in one set the two poems are chronologically adjacent to one another, while in the other the two are numbered sequentially:

כְּמוֹ אֶבֶן סַפִּיר וְאַחְלָמָה
1667 (1.303): '- - - ◡ / - - - - - ◡

---

5 1604 (1.230); 1605 (1.223); 1606 (1.112); 1609 (1.222); 1610 (1.116; 1.243); 1614 (1.183); 1622 (1.126); ? (1.124); 1.25: 1668. The inscriptions have now appeared in a volume entitled *Shirei Shayish* (*Poems in Marble*) (Jerusalem: Ben Zvi Institute, 2013).

לְבֵית קְרִישְׁקַשׁ הָיָה לְרֹאשׁ פִּנָּה
1668 (1.314): '- - - ◡ / - - - - - ◡

תַּחַת אֶבֶן הַזֹּאת מְקוֹם הַקֶּבֶר
1616 (1.255): - '- - - ◡ - - - - - -

לֹא אֶבְכֶּה ... כִּסְּתָה פָּנֶיהָ
1657 (1.254): - '- - - ◡ - - - - - -

Although the latter pair are adjacent to one another, the individuals they commemorate were unrelated: 1.255 is for Shemuel Kohen da Pisa and 1.254 is for Dina Segal, wife of Daniel Ferro. Furthermore, the poems are similar only in metrical structure: Dina's poem is a sonnet (the only sonnet in the early part of our period), while Shemuel's consists of two stanzas of four stichs each, and a 'girdle' rhyme scheme of AAABCCCB.

The remaining five patterns bear no relationship to one another:

אָהַב נַפְשׁוֹ מֵת בְּנִקְיוֹן כַּפַּיִם
1667 (1.274): - '- - - - ◡ - - - - -

יִרְאַת אֵל בְּקִרְבּוֹ תּוֹרָתוֹ בְּלִבּוֹ
1603 (1.137): '- - ◡ - - - / - - ◡ - - -

אַשְׁרֵי אָדָם הַמְחַכֶּה עֵת וּזְמַן אֵין בּוֹ מְבַכֶּה
1629 (1.164): '- - ◡ - - - - - / - - ◡ - - - - -

פֹּה לָנִים בְּסֵתֶר בְּצֵל אֵל שַׁדַּי
n.d. (1.123): '- - - - ◡ - - ◡ - - -

עָזְבָה בֵּיתָהּ וְהָלְכָה לָהּ
n.d. (1.294): '- - - ◡ - - - -

Although these quantitative patterns are not among those listed in the poetic manuals of Muslim Spain, their consistent use within these particular poems leaves no doubt that their authors strove to blend syllabic and quantitative metre.

The canons of Hebrew poetics do not define or restrict the number of lines in a poem, and yet some models of length were more popular than others, especially the *sestina* and *ottava*, poems of six and eight lines respectively. Apart from displaying a specific number of lines, the *sestina* and *ottava* also adhere to a rhyme scheme in which the rhyme alternates three or four times and then concludes with a couplet in a different rhyme altogether: ABABCC for sestina and ABABABCC for *ottava*. In a *sestina* the first four lines can also appear in an enclosed rhyme scheme (ABBA), followed by a couplet (CC).

The epitaph poem of Hanna Aziz, from 1625/26, is the earliest *ottava* in the Padua corpus. The *ottava* then disappears for several decades, but it returns in

1667 (1.312) and occurs ten more times by the end of the century.[6] The *sestina* makes its first appearance in 1649 (1.133) and its second a year later. Like the *ottava*, it then vanishes for about two decades, appearing again in 1668 and then sixteen more times, at evenly distributed intervals, by 1700.[7]

One additional form to appear in the seventeenth century is the dramatic epitaph, employing dialogue, which appears in the inscription memorializing Simḥa Trèves (1.221, d. 1681). The text resembles the epitaph poems and rhymed prose inscriptions in its liberal use of biblical language. It is, however, the first dramatic epitaph in Padua, although a few others appear in later centuries.[8]

A further level of complexity is introduced in 1614, in the epitaph of Doña Reina, whose surname is not supplied (1.91), but who was clearly of Sefardi ethnicity. It is a quattrain, in monorhyme, but the text is organized as two couplets, each with its own metrical scheme: the first pair of lines are structured in 10a and the second in 8a, with no particular pattern for the placement of long and short vowels.

The undated poem in memory of Fraidella Kohen (1.198) also exhibits multiple metrical schemes. This text is formed of eight stichs, with two rhyme schemes: there is a monorhyme at the end of even lines, and in addition, the first three out of four hemistichs of each pair of lines display a secondary rhyme scheme. The metrical structure is no less complex than the rhyme scheme:

[1]–2: 10a; **3–4:** 14a; **5–6:** 10a; **7–8:** 12a

The reference to the first line is bracketed because the text is fragmentary and its structure is thus conjectural, based on the overall pattern. Obviously the metrical structure, like the rhyme scheme, organizes the text into couplets, but the particular metres assigned to the various pairs do not seem to be in any sort of logical progression. Of the three cases of poems with multiple metrical structures, the last one is by far the most complex, and therefore arguably also the most beautiful.

The material thus far presented exhausts the forms found in Padua's Hebrew epitaph poetry in the early part of our period, more or less in their

6 1670 (1.301); 1673 (1.257); 1674 (1.256); 1676 (1.83); 1690 (1.19); 1695 (1.313); 1697, (1.279); 1699 (1.21a–b). There is also the undated poem in 1.123.

7 The chronological spread is as follows: 1650 (1.234); 1668 (1.25), 1676 (1.268,143); 1684 (1.253); 1685 (1.84a–b); 1687 (1.225); 1687 (1.238); 1688 (1.235); 1694 (1.259, 260); 1695 (1.263, 290); 1696 (1.233); 1700 (1.288, 13).

8 See: 3.290, d. 1746; 4.26, d. 1824; 3.222, d. 1814; 3.238, d. 1815.

chronological order of appearance. All appear in the seventeenth century, by approximately 1625. The century or so from about 1560 to 1650 is thus the most creative period within the time-frame of the Paduan corpus. The period that follows is one of stability, that lasts for over a century, until approximately 1830. Epitaph poetry then declines in both quantity and quality, until it all but disappears after about 1830.

The decline in the quality of Padua's Hebrew epitaphs is evident, for example, in the epitaph's conclusion. By far the most common ending is the Hebrew formula: 'May his/her soul be bundled in the bundle of life.' There is a drop in the number of appearances of afterlife expressions in 1680–1729, followed by recovery in 1730–1779, and a quantum leap in occurrences in 1780–1804. But at that point there is a shift from the fully articulated formula of the 'soul bundle' prayer to its acronym (TNṢBḤ), which becomes almost universal. The move from full expression to acronym generally signifies that the power and significance of the usage for the average reader has been greatly diminished, rendering its appearance automatic and conventional. The widespread adoption of the 'soul bundle' acronym in the late eighteenth century thus indicates a general drop in creativity in epitaph composition.

The decline in the quality of Padua's Hebrew epitaphs is also apparent in the repetitive use of rhymes, a marked tendency from approximately the middle of the eighteenth century. For example, the rhymes *gever-qever* and *refesh-nefesh* appear over and over, becoming lifeless and tiresome.

The same period also witnesses an increased use of stock phrases. For an expression to become a formula it must reach a high degree of acceptance, which implies that at one time it packed a powerful conceptual and literary punch. A prime example is the phrase 'to be illuminated with the light of eternity' (*le'or be'or 'olam*), a biblicism based on Job 33:30. This phrase came into vogue in the early eighteenth century. As the hereafter is the subject of the phrase, it typically appears in either the ultimate or penultimate line. More specifically, the phrase is found at the start of the last or next-to-last line, and therein lies its appeal, for it supplies the first six syllables of the standard *endecasillabo piano* sequence: two long vowels, one short and three long. As this was the most popular metrical scheme, and as the sentiment was suited the concluding section of the epitaph poem, the expression was felicitous indeed.

The increased use of stock expressions, phrases and rhymes signifies an important cultural shift. For two centuries, Padua's epitaph poetry had been a fountain of creativity and inspiration, offering comfort and guidance to readers in an impressive array of literary forms and formulations. By the latter eighteenth century the composition of such epitaph had stagnated into a mindless act of mass production.

2 Content

The following section surveys the principal themes presented in the main body of the Paduan corpus. *Memento mori,* the notion that inscriptions should terrify viewers by confronting them with the reality of their own inevitable destruction, receives stark expression in the epitaph of Stella Scaramella (1.193, d. 1676), in which Stella herself addresses the visitor:

> Passerby!
> I was like you yesterday;
> tomorrow you will be like me.

The adjuration of the wayfarer to stop and contemplate the grave is a new Hebrew version of a genre as old as ancient Greece and Rome. In the ancient world, graves often lined the roads, and thus 'Stop, passerby, and read' was a common epigraphic formula, urging the wayfarer to pause and read the inscription, thereby momentarily rescuing the deceased from oblivion.

After getting the wayfarer's attention, Stella's inscription reminds the visitor that death comes to everyone. This implies that everyday joys and anxieties are fleeting, as the poem for Simḥa Leoncin (2.27, d. 1709) makes plain:

> Such is the fate of all who are born, for all is vanity.
> Joy and rejoicing must end in sorrow and mourning.

The sentiment is essentially moralistic, rather than religious.

The prime expression of the *memento mori* motif in medieval Europe is the *transi*, the depiction of the decomposing corpse.[9] In the Hebrew epigraphy of Padua we encounter this genre in the gloomy epitaph of Avraham Ben Porat (2.30, d. 1705):

> Death shall cast and extend her net,
> burst through and smash with great destruction.
> The garments of the naked shall she strip away,
> slashing and burning everything until no memory remains;
> sharply, a full finger length, into my bones.
> I raise my voice before the Ark, saying:
> Friend, mighty father, garland on my head:
> 'Return, Oh Lord, deliver my soul.'

The text describes the body's destruction in violent and powerful terms. Death strips us of our garments, meaning our skin, reaching into our bones until nothing remains of our mortal self.

---

9 See Kathleen Cohen, *Metamorphosis of a Death Symbol: The Transi Tomb in the Late Middle Ages and the Renaissance* (Berkeley: University of California Press, 1973).

The *memento mori* tradition is replaced in our Hebrew texts by the search for sources of consolation, and a variety of motifs are deployed in pursuit of this objective. Many texts stress the beauty of the body deposited beneath the stone, denying the process of physical decomposition; this is the opposite of the *transi* motif. The epitaph of Brünlein Levi (1.206, d. 1602) declares: 'a pure, clean body lodges here.' The prose text of Barukh Kohen (1.52, d. 1535) insists that corpse as well as spirit will dwell in the bosom of Abraham.

Among the most popular themes is that death is universal and hence unavoidable. The following poems, in memory of Abram Torres (1.92.d. 1624) and Yosef Coneian (1.121, d. 1649) respectively, offer more succinct statements of this theme:

> This is the law of all flesh, this is the Torah:
> rich and poor shall return to the earth,
> for so it was decreed from the time of Creation.
> From the day [Adam], father of the world, sinned,
> death was decreed for all who enter the world.

The epitaph poem of Perla Terni (3.182, d. 1801) demonstrates the continued relevance of this motif at the turn of the nineteenth century:

> Death is a wheel that has slid from the scales of justice.
> For, seeking cumin, it sorely pursues every body.
> The soul, however, enjoys adornment and joy;
> for its labour it shall receive eternity.

This text takes up the theme of the dualism of body and soul, consoling the bereaved with the knowledge that the soul not only survives the body but goes to eternal bliss.

Another road taken in the search for consolation is the view of death as liberation. We find this idea in the poem of Reichele mi-Shalom (1.249, d. 1639):

> He [Death] opened a door to the house of my body.
> As a candle from prison, he took me out.

The body as a prison is a well-known dualistic motif, as is the likening of the soul to a candle (Prov 20:27), or more generally to spirit and hence to light.

Another tack is the motif of death as offering a state of repose and tranquility, that effectively neutralizes the image of corporeal destruction. This attitude is eloquently articulated in the epitaph poem of Smeralda Aziz (3.306, d. 1741):

> Why do people fear
> to come dwell here,
> if they have never seen

tranquility in life?
Such a fear is folly,
for here one finds repose.
Here sound understanding abounds,
here every light shines.

The obverse of the association of death with rest and tranquility is the image of this world as the site of toil and travail. The themes of life's travails and the grave's repose suggest the idea that the terms life and death should actually be reversed. This is the message of the quattrain in memory of Shemuel Ḥai meha-Ḥazzanim (2.34, d. 1711):

A life of death, you, my brothers, shall call
the days on earth, days of dread.
Life, death: Exchange names!
Call me now Shemuel Ḥai!

This text exemplifies the tendency of the classical epigram to end with a point, or satirical twist. In this case the poem's punch is rooted in the name Ḥai, which like Vita, its Italian equivalent, means life. The poem is saying that, paradoxically, only now, in death, is the name Ḥai truly apt.

Other texts reject as futile the pursuit of worldly success, echoing the Stoics or Ecclesiastes. The poem for Shemuel Franco (1.224, d. 1650) observes that, realistically, economic success is not proportional to toil:

See how people move through days as they do through seas.
Some labour at length and some in just a little while
attain their heart's desire: emerald, onyx and amethyst.

The opening couplet of Ya'aqov Jaffe's epitaph poem (1.34, d. 1648) condemns pride, rather than materialism, as pointless:

See the tower, mountain and city!
Oh mortal mortal, do not be proud!

A petition to the wayfarer to beg forgiveness of God is stated briefly in the prose epitaph of Shim'on Parent (1.102, d. 1551): 'May his virtues count in our favour.' This theme is more elaborate in the poem for Asher Ha-Kohen (3.357, d. 1751):

Gather at my grave, my brothers and friends
and see what happened to me in my life.
Pray for me before the One who dwells in my abode;
perhaps on your account he will accept me.

Apart from the assumption that the dead are able to intercede on behalf of the living, to what other notions did Padua's Jews subscribe with regard to the nature of life after death and the 'End of Days'?

The ethereal or spiritual realm is often described in terms of light, an image rooted in both the biblical and classical traditions, and in the Middle Ages in texts influenced by neoplatonic thought. Light imagery is used in a number of Paduan epitaph poems to describe the post-mortem experience. A neoplatonic image of the light of the afterlife is put forward in the epitaph of Tzirleh (1.109a, d. 1641), whose surname is not given and whose son seems to have predeceased her:

> Tzirleh, the mother here
> roosting on her son,
> in her Garden of Eden
> returns to light.

The last line conveys the neoplatonic view that the human spirit returns to its original state, in light, as it longed to do during its mortal imprisonment in the body.

More information about the source of the supernal light is found in the epitaph of the Venetian rabbi and communal leader, Leib Saraval (1.17, d. 1617): 'his spirit was extinguished and his soul ascended to God to dwell in light, the glow of the divine presence his rest.' Here the divine presence, the *Shekhina,* is the source of the light to which the righteous go after death.

The Saraval poem concludes with an allusion to the state of rest that follows life. We have already examined the theme that people find repose when life's struggles are past, but the Saraval text refers to a rest that is an objective, spiritual state, rather than merely the cessation of toil. This idea is familiar from the phrase 'his rest is in Eden' (*nuḥo 'eden*), a ubiquitous euphemism in rabbinic literature for the death of an esteemed individual. It receives poetic expression in a number of Paduan epitaphs, as in the inscription of Rachel Ṣarfati (1.167, d. 1566): 'May her spirit rest in relief and [be] at rest before the King.' More elaborate and poetic is the formulation in the epitaph of Gioia Ferarese (1.308, d. 1671), which echoes that of Leib Saraval: '[She] departed the corporeal prison for the supernal rest beneath the wings of the *Shekhina*.' In a unique text, the statement that Ya'aqov Alperon (1.216, d. 1588) 'ascended to serve God' refers to the afterlife in terms of activity rather than repose.

Learned discussions of the epigram generally agree on the importance of a pointed conclusion, one that is both pithy and powerful. The Padua epitaph poems generally articulate this value in the final line or two, as the poet turns from a lugubrious discussion of the death of the body to an upbeat declaration about the everlasting delight of the soul in paradise.

The Paduan corpus offers almost no references to the messiah and messianic advent, in contrast to resurrection. In the same vein, the epitaph poem for Asher Marini (2.48, d. 1716) offers the only explicit reference to the return of the Jewish people to its ancestral homeland. The silence regarding national redemption resounds loudly because the Jews of early modern Italy are known to have expressed intense interest in messianism, both political and mystical. Resurrection is only a little more popular, appearing in just 10%–15% of the inscriptions until the mid-seventeenth century, not at all in the latter seventeenth century, and hardly ever thereafter.

3 Final Generation

The inscriptions of the final generation, 1830–1862, depart markedly from Padua's tradition. Epitaph poetry, as against prose inscriptions, declines sharply in the final generation, from above fifty per cent in 1805–1829 to barely ten per cent. Even S. D. Luzzatto ('Shadal'), for all his passion for the Hebrew poetry of the Middle Ages, elected to inscribe a prose text on the tombstone of his son Filosseno. Biblicisms disappear too, as do stock rhymes and phrases. What we are witnessing is a complete overhaul, a response to the sense that the venerable tradition of epitaph poetry had become a dead letter and no longer addressed the tastes and values of the age.

The epitaphs of the final generation differ radically in both form and content from what came before. The new form is a prose text, but one much longer than the traditional epitaph, running well over ten lines and sometimes double that length. The new epitaph is also considerably more personalized than the traditional one. Authors not only strive for personalized rhetoric, avoiding traditional formulae, but also focus on the character and achievements of the individual, apparently signalling a new sense of the singular nature of each person.

The central characteristic of the new variety of inscription is the attribution to the departed of three particular qualities. The three-attributes string is nowhere accompanied by a rationale, but it bears a striking resemblance to the famous slogan of the French Revolution: *Liberté, Egalité, Fraternité*. Hence the new epitaph may have been intended to do more than immortalize the deceased; it may have also communicated the sense that a new, modern, era had dawned.

The inscriptions of the final generation also break with tradition in supplying far more information. It becomes quite normal for the names of the sponsor or sponsors of stone and inscription to appear below the inscription. A number of texts now provide the time of death.

The prominence of the Italian language is yet another departure from tradition. Hitherto a marginal phenomenon, the use of Italian becomes ordinary in the final generation, primarily in prose texts, and to a lesser degree in verse. Clearly the level of acculturation had risen significantly in comparison with the early modern era. On the other hand, for this to become obvious only in the second third of the nineteenth century is powerful testimony to the respect Italian Jews had for tradition, at least in the graveyard, if not in other venues and genres.

4 Conclusion

Our period ends in 1862, with the closing of the cemetery in Via Canal and the inauguration of the new cemetery in Via Sori. The geographical shift was accompanied by a transformation of the epitaph no less revolutionary than the innovations of the final generation. The perimeter of the new cemetery is lined with elaborate tombstones and inscriptions, most even more bombastic and grandiose than those of the final generation. These are, however, few and exceptional, as almost all of the tombstones and inscriptions are their polar opposite. In the years immediately following our period the gravestone and epitaph are almost completely standardized: they are quite small and supply only the most basic particulars. Needless to say, epitaph poetry disappears, but so do the detailed personalized epitaphs that had only just appeared in the previous generation. The new epitaphs from Via Sori are thus devoid of literary and cultural value; their latent demographic data is their sole merit.

The preceding analysis of the Padua corpus has yielded an image of a body of literature that went through four stages of development. Simple prose inscriptions, with nothing more than the basic particulars, appear during the first half of the sixteenth century, along with a sizeable corpus of inscriptions in rhymed prose and unmetered poetry. The second stage, lasting roughly a century from the middle of the sixteenth century, witnesses the arrival and blossoming of metered epitaph poetry in the style of early modern Italian Jewry. Thus our corpus affords a unique opportunity to witness a major cultural transformation, as Padua's largely Ashkenazi constituency acculturated to its Italian environment. With the passing of the decades, the inscriptions become ever more sophisticated, increasing the range of the literary devices employed, to maximal aesthetic effect.

The tradition continues for another century, roughly from 1650 to 1750, before there are signs of stagnation and ennervation. In the latter eighteenth century, the third stage, epitaph poems are more numerous than ever, but for the most part they are no longer creative and original. Rhymes and tropes become formulaic and lifeless, and there is a marked use of stock expressions and phrases. The early modern tradition seems to have lost its vibrancy and appeal, and presumably it had become disconnected from the social and cultural values of the age. If Italian Jewry underwent a period of decadence, the corpus of epitaphs from Padua suggest that it was centred in the second half of the eighteenth century.

Revival came in the final stage of our period, when a new type of epitaph appears, with a fresh range of features. These are revolutionary not only from a strictly literary point of view, but also in terms of the values they project. They are written in rolling prose, rather than rhymed and metered verse, and their salient characteristic is their effort to characterize the deceased as an individual, in stark contrast to the impersonal, didactic tone of the early modern epitaph poem. These texts mark the entrance of Paduan Jewry squarely into the modern era and bring our era to a close.

The inscriptions of Paduan Jewry do not generally reflect the broader cultural currents set down in studies of the death culture of early modern Europe. There are some exceptions to this rule. Instead of focusing on the degradation of the body and the request for intercessory prayer, the humanist epitaph depicts death in neoplatonic terms, as liberation from the flesh and reunion with God. For the righteous, death is actually the beginning of true living.[10] These ideas appear in some of the texts cited above, such as the inscription of Rabbi Leib Saraval.

The final generation seems more in step with the broad cultural developments of European society. The communal view of the deceased, as representing shared social and ethical values, gives way to a more personalized image, as inscriptions emphasize the particular virtues and achievements of the deceased. Religious values recede, and the unfavourable comparison of the turmoil and travail of this world with the repose and delight of the afterlife is abandoned.[11]

---

10 Kathleen Cohen, *Metamorphosis*, pp. 127–28.

11 Philippe Ariès, *The Hour of Our Death*, Eng. trans. by Helen Weaver (New York: Knopf, 1981), pp. 449, 467, 605–9; Armando Petrucci, *Writing the Dead: Death and Writing Strategies in the Western Tradition*, Eng. trans. Michael Sullivan (Stanford: Stanford University Press, 1998), pp. 114–6. See also: Michel Vovelle, *La mort et l'Occident de 1300 à nos jours* (Paris: Gallimard, 1983), pp. 425–31; Joshua Scodel, *The English Poetic Epitaph: Commemoration and Conflict from Jonson to Wordsworth* (Ithaca: Cornell University Press, 1991), pp. 312–14.

The shift in the final generation suggests that Jews of Padua were not so much disconnected from the cultural trends of the surrounding milieu as out of step. Perhaps profound cultural change penetrated the Jewish community somewhat later than it appeared in the general community.[12] I am, however, hesitant to draw far-reaching conclusions from our corpus of inscriptions about the nature of Italian Jewish culture, and more inclined to ascribe significance to the genre. The epitaph developed along its own lines, integrating some formal and substantive elements from other types of writing and ignoring others. The context of grave and epitaph gave tradition an inordinate degree of power, blunting the forces of social and cultural change and rendering the tastes of Padua's Jews especially conservative.

12 A similar dynamic would explain the appearance of characteristics of Renaissance culture among the Jews of Italy in the early seventeenth century.

Mauro Perani

The *Corpus Epitaphiorum Hebraicorum Italiae* (CEHI): A Project to Publish a Complete Corpus of the Epitaphs Preserved in Italian Jewish Cemeteries of the Sixteenth–Nineteenth Centuries

Les cimetières sont remplis
de personnes indispensables

1 Introduction

Italy's Jewish cultural heritage is one of the most important in the western world. For geographical and historical reasons, the Jewry of the Italian peninsula is the most ancient in Europe and the Mediterranean basin. The presence of Jewish communities in Rome, Sardinia and the southern region of Apulia and Sicily goes back two thousand years, dating from the first years of the Christian era, and even earlier in the case of Rome. Although Italian Jewry, compared with other European countries, never achieved high numbers, it always played a major role because of its cultural importance, and due to a successful co-existence on Italian soil of the three major cultural and geographical European traditions: the Italian, the Sefardi and the Ashkenazi. As has commonly occurred in the field of non-Jewish culture, Italy has also produced about half of all resources in the field of Jewish cultural heritage, and the relevant treasures are today kept in Jewish and non-Jewish museums and libraries all over the world, as well as in the Italian Peninsula. Italian Jewish inscriptions play an important role in this rich legacy, with regard to both the first 1,540 years of the current era, predominantly in southern Italy, and the cemeteries of the Italian Jews between the sixteenth and nineteenth centuries. From the sixteenth century onwards, and well into the seventeenth century, the art of writing epitaphs in Hebrew became a true literary genre, practised in rhyme and rhythm, by rabbis and learned scholars. The writing of these texts was commissioned by people requesting epitaphs for their dead relatives, as well as for literary and fictional purposes. We have to take into account that the epitaphs – sometimes more and sometimes less artistically elaborated – constituted, starting in the sixteenth century, the first registration of people, in both the Christian and the Jewish worlds. They were therefore equally

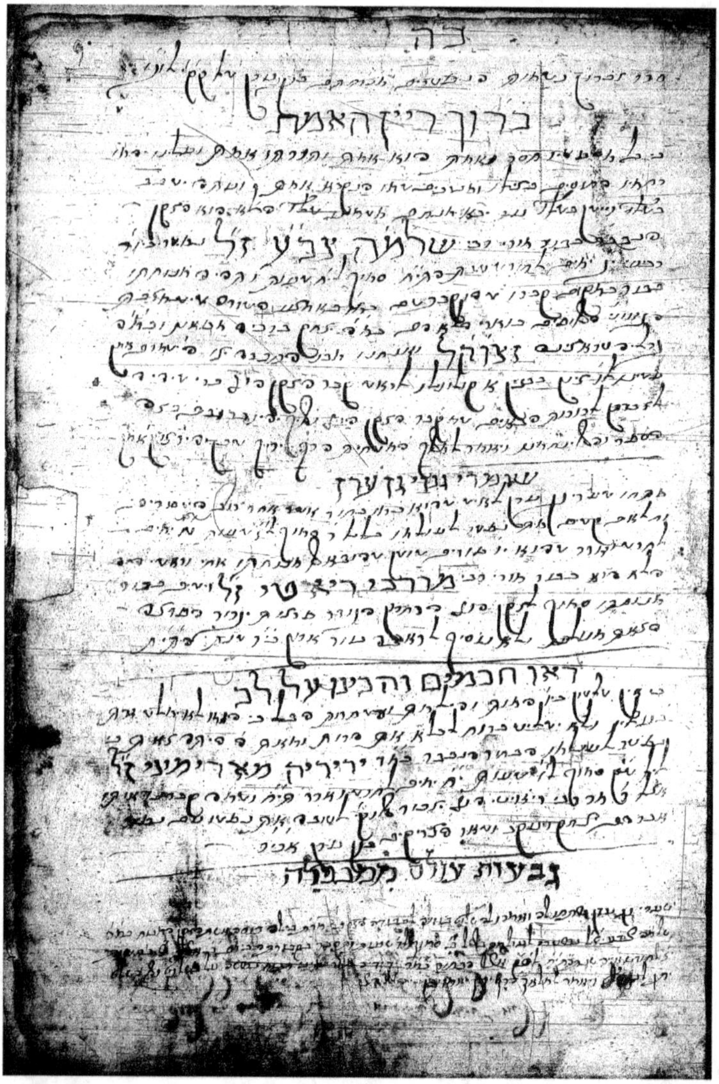

Fig. 1: The first page (fol. 9r) of the *Pinqas Ha-Nifṭarim* of the Jewish Community in Lugo, recording its deaths and ranging from 1658 to 1825; Ms. n. 3960, of the Jewish Theological Seminary in New York. The first record belongs to Shelomo Ṣeva‘, who passed away on 4 Ḥeshvan, in 1658. The lines 12–13 read as follows: ... עשינו לו ציון בבנין א׳ קולונילו לראש קבר הזקן הנ״ל כדי שיהיה לזכרון לדורות הבאים שמקבר הזקן הנ״ל אליך יהיו זכרונם בזה הספר והאל ינחמנו ויאמר למאלך המשחית הרך ידיך שכן יהי רצון אמן that is: “... *we have made for him a* colonnello [pillar] *as sign to indicate the tomb of this old man, as an everlasting memory for all those who in future generations, from the tomb of this old man forward, are to be recorded in this book, and God will console us and will tell the exterminating Angel: ‘Loosen your hand’, and so be it, amen*”.

Fig. 2: Tombstones at the Jewish cemetery of Cardeto in Ancona, in the shape of cylindrical pillars, made from erosion resistant Istria stone and therefore in a good state of preservation. This cylindrical style probably originated in northern Africa and was adopted by Sefardi Jews. After the expulsion, this tombstone style, brought to this region by Jews from Sefarad and from Turkey, became almost unique among the Marches communities.

important as compilations of births, marriages and deaths, written and archived by priests and rabbis. In the Christian world this practice was formally imposed on all parish priests in the middle of the fifteenth century by the Council of Trent, and implemented during the second half of that century. At the same time, the Jewish communities of Italy started to write minutes of the council assemblies and to compile registers of dead Jews. A very interesting example is found in the *Pinqas Ha-Nifṭarim* (פנקס הנפטרים), Ms. 3960, of the Jewish Theological Seminary in New York, comprising eighty-three folios of the Jewish *ḥevra qaddisha* (burial society) of the town of Lugo. This charitable body was charged by the Jewish community to bury its dead and the manuscript contains the death records of almost two centuries, from 1658 until 1825 (Fig. 1). I shall later present an example of the importance of cross-checking information from different sources so as to enrich our knowledge not only of the active Jewish communities of Italy, but also of their death, burial and mourning liturgy in the early modern period. Because the tombstones are mostly made from less solid stone than the *pietra d'Istria,* that is particularly used in the Jewish cemeteries of the Marches region (Fig. 2), this cultural heritage has in the course of the past fifty years been more severely damaged by air pollution and acid rain than in the previous five centuries. Immediate action is required to save this precious heritage and to avoid the legacy being irremediably lost for future centuries and generations. Several Jewish *maṣevot* are already almost impossible to decipher, and consequently lost forever. It should not be forgotten that the texts of the epitaphs have the potential to make an important contribution to our knowledge of Hebrew epigraphy in Italy and the western Jewish civilization as a whole.

2 The Italian Jewish inscriptions of the first millennium and until 1540 CE

The work carried out by my late friend, Professor Cesare Colafemmina, is of great importance for Italian inscriptions of this period. Professor Colafemmina has published for the first time numerous southern Italian inscriptions, some discovered by himself, as is the case in the matter of the inscriptions found in the catacombs of Venosa. Unfortunately, these articles were published in various Italian reviews and journals which remain difficult of accession. The corpus includes catacomb inscriptions painted or engraved on the plaster of arcosolia, as in Jewish catacombs of Sant'Antioco (Fig. 3), in Sulcis region of southern Sardinia, dating back to the late Roman period (fourth-fifth century CE). The Hebrew epigraphy of Sicily, the Venosa sepulchral inscriptions on stone in the Basilicata Region, and similar inscriptions in Apulia, Calabria, and other southern Italian regions, provide data until 1540, which is the starting-point for the documentation then coming from the Jewish cemeteries of central and northern Italy. The inscriptions from the third to the seventh centuries were mainly published by Jean Baptiste Frey in his *Corpus inscriptionum iudaicarum. Recueil des inscriptions juives qui vont du IIIe siècle avant Jésus-Christ au VIIe siècle de notre ère*, in Rome, Pontificio Istituto di Archeologia Cristiana, 1936. More recently, David Noy published two volumes: *Jewish Inscriptions of Western Europe: Volume 1, Italy (excluding the City of Rome), Spain and Gaul*, Cambridge University Press, 1995, and *Jewish Inscriptions of Western Europe: Volume 2, The City of Rome*, Cambridge University Press, 1995. For Italy, Noy based himself mainly on Colafemmina's studies. The main studies by Colafemmina are listed hereunder, with only one of them, no. 23, appearing in English. For this reason, following an invitation received some

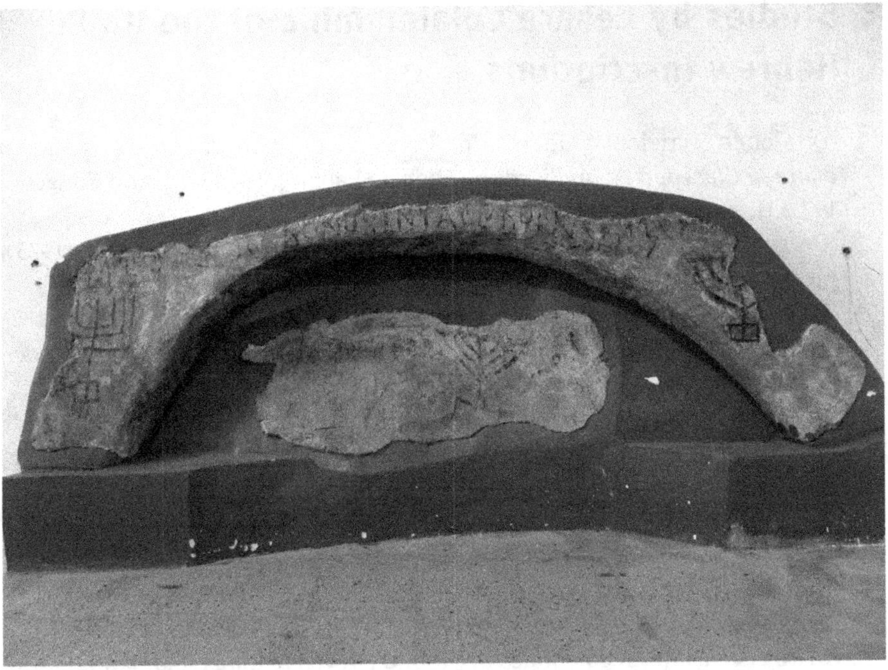

Fig. 3: Inscriptions in Hebrew and Latin, discovered in 1894, in the Jewish catacomb of *Bonus*, Roman period, (4th–5th centuries), at Sant'Antioco, in southern Sardinia. During the restoration of the two arcosolia of *Bonus* and *Beronice*, about 40 years ago, the restorer wrongly placed the inner painted *menorah* and inscription of Beronice's arcosolium under the arch of the arcosolium of Bonus (this image) and vice versa. In the upper arc, on the right, we read *shalom*, and in the inscription of the central part, to the left of the *menorah*, is clearly readable: *shalom 'al* [...] whereas the other words, probably incorrectly reconstructed, are difficult to decipher; they perhaps mean: [*mishkavo amen*], according a well known formula.

time ago from Colette Sirat, the general editor of this Jewish series, I very much hope that we can soon see the republication of all Italian epigraphs of the first 1.500 years of the common era in one English volume in the prestigious series *Monumenta Palaeographica Medii Aevi: Series Hebraica* (SHEBA) printed by Brepols in Turnhout (Belgium) whose policy is to publish original-size facsimiles of the documentary heritage of Europe.

3 Studies by Cesare Colafemmina of the Italian Hebrew inscriptions

1. 'Di alcune iscrizioni giudaiche di Taranto', in *Studi di storia pugliese in onore di Giuseppe Chiarelli*, ed. by Michele Paone (Galatina: Mario Congedo, 1972), I, pp. 233–42.
2. 'Un'iscrizione ebraica inedita di Trani', in *Augustinianum*, 13 (1973), pp. 339–43.
3. 'Iscrizioni ebraiche a Brindisi', in *Brundisii res*, 5 (1973), pp. 91–106.
4. 'Documenti epigrafici inediti o mal noti della "Regio Secunda"', in *Cenacolo*, 3 (1973), pp. 147–151, figg. 1–5.
5. '*Nova e vetera* nella catacomba ebraica di Venosa', in *Studi storici*, ed. by Cesare Colafemmina (Molfetta: Ecumenica Editrice-, 1974), pp. 87–94, tab. I–IV.
6. 'L'iscrizione brindisina di Baruch ben Yonah e Amittai da Oria', in *Brundisii res*, 7 (1975), pp. 295–300.
7. 'Nuove iscrizioni ebraiche a Venosa', in *Studi in memoria di p. Adiuto Putignani* (Cassano M.: Ecumenica Editrice, 1975), pp. 41–46, tab. XII–XV.
8. 'Di una iscrizione greco-ebraica di Otranto', in *Vetera Christianorum*, 12 (1975), pp. 131–37.
9. 'Iscrizioni paleocristiane di Venosa', in *Vetera Christianorum*, 13 (1976), pp. 149–65.
10. 'Gli ebrei a Taranto nella documentazione epigrafica (secc. IV–X)', in *La Chiesa di Taranto*, I: *Dalle origini all'avvento dei Normanni*, ed. by C. D. Fonseca (Galatina: Congedo Editore, 1977), pp. 109–27.
11. 'Un'iscrizione venosina inedita dell'822', in *La Rassegna Mensile d'Israel*, 43 (1977), pp. 261–63.
12. 'Di un'iscrizione biblica (Ps. 125,1) e di altri graffiti', in *Il santuario di S. Michele sul Gargano dal VI al IX secolo. Contributo alla storia della Langobardia meridionale. Proceedings of the congress held in Monte Sant'Angelo (9–10 dicembre 1978)*, ed. by Carlo Carletti and Giorgio Otranto (Bari: Edipuglia, 1980), pp. 337–45, figs. 1–6.
13. 'Una nuova iscrizione ebraica a Venosa', in *Vetera Christianorum*, 21 (1984), pp. 197–202.
14. 'Iscrizione ebraica inedita di Lavello', in *Vetera Christianorum*, 23 (1986), pp. 171–76.
15. 'Tre nuove iscrizioni ebraiche a Venosa', in *Vetera Christianorum*, 24 (1987), pp. 201–209.
16. 'Note su di una iscrizione ebraico-latina di Oria', in *Vetera Christianorum*, 25 (1988), pp. 641–51.

17. 'Le iscrizioni ebraiche nel cimitero di Tarsia', in Ferramont: un lager nel Sud', in *Proceedings of the International congress held in Cosenza (15–16 maggio 1987)*, ed. by Francesco Volpe (Cosenza: Edizioni Orizzonti Meridionali, 1990), pp. 101–17.
18. 'Una nuova epigrafe ebraica altomedievale a Lavello', in *Vetera Christianorum*, 29 (1992), pp. 411–21.
19. 'Epigraphica Hebraica Venusina', in *Vetera Christianorum*, 30 (1993), pp. 411–21.
20. 'Due nuove iscrizioni sinagogali pugliesi', in *Vetera Christianorum*, 21 (1994), pp. 383–95.
21. 'Iscrizioni ebraiche su una lucerna e su un amuleto rinvenuti nel Salernitano', in *Apollo. Bollettino dei Musei Provinciali del Salernitano*, 10 (1994), pp. 56–58.
22. 'Ipogei ebraici in Sicilia', in *Italia judaica. Gli ebrei in Sicilia sino all'espulsione del 1492, Proceedings of the V congress held in Palermo (15–19 giugno 1992)*, Publications of the Archivi di Stato, Saggi, 32 (Rome: Ministero per i Beni Culturali e Ambientali, 1995), pp. 304–29.
23. 'Hebrew Inscriptions of the Early Medieval Period in Southern Italy', in *The Jews of Italy. Memory and Identity*, ed. by Barbara Garvin and Bernard Cooperman, Studies and Textes in Jewish History and Culture, 7 (Bethesda: University Press of Maryland, 2000), pp. 65–81.
24. 'Un frammento di iscrizione ebraica sinagogale', in *Palazzo Adorno. Storia e restauri*, ed. by Regina Poso (Matera; Spolent: R&R Editrice), 2000, pp. 24–29.
25. 'Di alcune iscrizioni ebraiche a Trani', in *La Rassegna Mensile d'Israel*, 67 (2001), pp. 305–312.
26. 'Nota sull'iscrizione ebraica rinvenuta nella chiesa di S. Giovanni Battista a Siracusa', in A. Scandaliato and N. Mulè (eds.), *La sinagoga e il bagno rituale degli ebrei di Siracusa*, con una nota epigrafica di Cesare Colafemmina, Associazione Italiana per lo Studio del Giudaismo, Testi e Studi dell'AISG n. 13 (Florence: Giuntina, 2002), pp. 129–33.
27. 'Le catacombe ebraiche nell'Italia meridionale e nell'area sicula: Venosa, Siracusa, Noto Lipari, Malta', in M. Perani (ed.), *I beni culturali ebraici in Italia. Situazione attuale, problemi e progetti per il futuro*, Proceedings of the Congress of Ravenna (22–24 maggio 2001) (Ravenna: Longo editore, 2003), pp. 119–46.
28. 'Le testimonianze epigrafiche e archeologiche come fonte storica', in *Materia giudaica* IX/1–2 (2004), pp. 37–52.
29. 'Tre iscrizioni ebraiche altomedievali a Matera', in M. Perani (ed.), *Una manna buona per Mantova. Man Tov le-Man Tovah*. Studi in onore di Vittore Colorni per il suo 92° Compleanno (Florence: Olschki, 2004), pp. 101–14.

30. 'Sull'iscrizione di Berakah ben Sa'adyah Ha-Zaqen Faqqas di Siracusa', in *Materia giudaica* X/2 (2005), pp. 313–17.
31. 'Una rilettura delle epigrafi ebraiche della Sardegna', in C. Tasca (ed.), *Gli ebrei in Sardegna nel contesto mediterraneo. La riflessione storiografica da Giovanni Spano ad oggi*, Atti del XXII Convegno Internazionale dell'AISG, published in *Materia giudaica*, XIV/1–2 (2009), pp. 81–99.

4 *The new series* Corpus Epitaphiorum Hebraicorum Italiae (CEHI) *of the sixteenth–nineteenth centuries*

For the reasons already noted, and particularly because of the precarious state of preservation of the epitaphs of the past four centuries on the *maṣevot* of Italian Jewish cemeteries that may be lost forever, I decided to set up a project whose aim is the publication of all the funerary texts of Jewish tombstones in Italy. The research material is mainly located in the central and northern regions of Italy. In southern Italy in the modern era there are no Jewish cemeteries because of the expulsion of the Jews from these lands during the *Gerush Sefarad* of 1492, that stretched as far as Sardinia and Sicily, and included the sixteenth-century reign of Naples and other kingdoms. On the other hand, as already pointed out, southern Italy holds almost all the Hebrew epigraphic documentation of the first 1,500 years of the current era.

This precious heritage of texts written on stone must not be lost but should be archived and published, also on the Internet, so that it can be preserved for and available to future generations. This is exactly the aim of the newly established Series of CEHI, published by La Giuntina Press in Florence, where the whole corpus of Jewish epitaphs extant in all the Jewish cemeteries of Italy will be gathered and published. As pointed out earlier, the series will not include the corpus of the Jewish inscriptions of the first millennium before 1540, found predominantly in the regions of southern Italy, and almost entirely already published. The volumes of the CEHI Series Project are each devoted to a particular cemetery or to several small cemeteries in the same area. They include editions of the Hebrew texts of the epitaphs, the identification of biblical sources and rabbinic quotations, with explanatory notes and an Italian translation.

Each cemetery will have an introduction to its local Jewish community and its history, in order to contextualize the funerary inscriptions against their historical background. In addition, a rich apparatus of colour and black/white images will illustrate the editions of the texts. An online edition on a website will be created and developed in parallel, to complement the printed hard copy, presenting the content of each volume and allowing for an online electronic search of the names of Jews, both in Hebrew and in Italian. Under my supervision, the project, beginning with a survey of the *status quaestionis* and of research in cooperation with the *Fondazione per i Beni Culturali Ebraici* and the *Unione delle Comunità Ebraiche Italiane* (UCEI, Union of Italian Jewish Communities), and covering the period from the sixteenth to the nineteenth centuries, aims at producing a census of all the Jewish cemeteries in Italy. Each cemetery has been catalogued on electronic cards that show the state of preservation, list the existing studies, refer to the related Jewish communities, and include maps of geographic locations, a complete bibliography, digital photographs of the epigraphs, with comments on their state of conservation and legibility. During the past ten years, I have assigned a number of MA and BA dissertations to research on the following cemeteries of the Emilia Romagna and Marches regions: Lugo, Ancona, Senigallia, Pesaro, Correggio, Finale Emilia, Cento. Each of these studies contains an introduction on the Jewish communities, a description of each site with historical notes, and details of the social institutions and structures that have characterized the communities over the centuries. They also deal with the reasons for their foundation and their subsequent history, as well as tracing the development of their cemeteries over the centuries, and often also the reasons for their disappearance. These dissertations include transcriptions of the sepulchral inscriptions found, their Italian versions, and photographic reproductions. The whole process is then completed with indices of names and places in Italian and Hebrew. As far the research methodology is concerned, the first step required an inspection of the Jewish cemeteries under examination, in order to ascertain the condition of the epitaphs, which were often in a bad state of preservation, many of them destroyed by overgrown vegetation and the neglect that characterizes numerous Jewish cemeteries. During the inspection, the tombstones were partially cleaned by the removal of plaque, moss, lichen and grimy patina. Through these efforts, fragments of accidentally damaged and overgrown gravestones have been recovered as far as possible, Jewish epitaphs have been made legible, and have thus reclaimed their importance as documents, testifying to the history of the Jewish communities that have, over time, populated that place.

5 *Planning of the series* CEHI

The *Corpus Epitaphiorum Hebraicorum Italiae* was inaugurated in September 2008 with the publication of the first volume entitled: *Il 'giardino' degli ebrei. Cimiteri ebraici del Mantovano*, edited by La Giuntina Press, in Florence. The volume brings together about two years of research on the cemeteries of Mantua and the Mantovano and includes the Jewish cemeteries of Mantua, Bozzolo, Gazzuolo, Ostiano, Pomponesco, Revere, Rivarolo Mantovano, Sabbioneta, Sermide and Viadana[1]. Two new volumes, devoted to the cemeteries of Lugo and Finale Emilia, have been published at the beginning of 2011.

The volumes already published are:

1. *Il 'giardino' degli ebrei. Cimiteri ebraici del Mantovano*, ed. by C. Bonora Previdi and A. Mortari, CEHI n. 1 (Florence: La Giuntina, 2008).
2. M. Perani, A. Pirazzini and G. Corazzol, *Il cimitero ebraico di Lugo*, CEHI n. 2, (Florence: La Giuntina, 2011).
3. M. P. Balboni, M. Perani, A. Creatura, *Sigilli di eternità. Il cimitero ebraico di Finale Emilia*, n. 3 (Florence: La Giuntina, 2011).

The following volumes are scheduled to be published in the coming years:

4. *Padova*
5. *Senigallia*
6. *Ancona*
7. *Pesaro*
8. *Urbino*
9. *Triveneto*
10. *Venice*

The volumes next listed are already planned for following years:

11. *Correggio*
12. *Roma*
13. *Cento*
14. *Bologna*

And at a later date attention will be given to the Jewish cemeteries of: Modena, Ferrara, Pisa, Asti, Perugia, Vercelli, and whatever else is extant in the Italian regions of Piedmont, Umbria, Tuscany, Lombardy.

---

1 I have published additional material but I am unable to include it in this article; see *Addenda ai cimiteri ebraici di Mantova e di Rivarolo Mantovano e l'epitaffio incompiuto del Museo Ebraico di Bologna*, in *Materia giudaica*, 13/1–2 (2008), pp. 281–99.

6 The information contained in the text of the epitaphs and their importance for the new science of genealogy

The valuable documentation obtained from the epitaphs constitutes a sort of archive written on stone, yielding important information about family relations and other, sometimes rather explicit details, often almost impossible to find in official historical sources, such as the causes of death. The epitaphs tell stories of fathers, mothers, brothers and sisters, sons and daughters. They provide interesting insights into such causes of death: as child-bearing, a bad cold, etc. Most interestingly, the epitaph represents a more popular documentation that is not related exclusively to riches, power and communal importance. The epitaphs retrace Jewish genealogy and are of importance for the relatively new academic discipline of genealogical research. This 'registration', 'engraved on stone' was the first to be extended to all the people, regardless of their social background. In previous centuries, with archival documentation starting basically in the thirteenth and fourteenth centuries, the sources related primarily to rich and important people: scholars, leading rabbis, and bankers. The poor, both of the Jewish and Christian communities, had less relevance and were often neither registered nor formally archived. Historical documents are in fact rarely representative of the history of the common people, but more commonly records of the rich and powerful, of princes, popes, the leading classes, bankers and merchants. Officially registering the dates of circumcision or baptism, and extending this process even to those of low social rank, and reporting marriages, deaths and other events in their daily lives, represented an important turning point in the drive towards a certain democratization in the production of historical documents. Although it remains true that the most beautiful and artistically and literarily valuable *maṣevot* and epitaphs are those composed for important people, they do nevertheless also reveal some general information on the lower ranks of society. It is from these epitaphs that I gleaned pieces of information that enabled me to reconstruct the puzzling genealogy of some families, such as the Fano or Forlì households, as documented in the Jewish cemetery of Lugo. I achieved this by combining the data from the epitaphs with the above-mentioned register of deaths diligently compiled for about two hundreds years by scribes of the *ḥevra qaddisha* charged with the task of burying the dead.

7 Incorrect and misleading conservation work that has damaged the inscriptions

During my research on the Italian Jewish cemeteries, I have, more than once, discovered Hebrew texts that have been rewritten in black paint by someone with little or no command of Hebrew, in an attempt to save the epitaphs that has unintentionally had the opposite effect. This practice not only ruins the tombstone, but more frequently also damages the text, since those rewriting it have not understood the meaning of the epitaph, which is often in poetry or in the exalted language of past centuries, from Baroque until the Ottocento. Among these attempts at preservation, I have found many exchanges of similar-looking Hebrew letters such as, for example, *zayin* for *waw*, *kaf* for *bet*, *he* for *ḥet* or vice versa, and others. Zealous and well-meaning volunteers, taking care of the cemetery and its maintenance, while acting in good faith, have caused serious damage. Those erroneous corrections, or the confusion of Hebrew letters and words, have meant that tremendous effort and time have been required to read and decipher the (original) text, often much more than would have been necessary to decipher and translate the epitaphs in their original (albeit poor) state of preservation. In other cases, I noted that the *maṣevot* had been cleaned by using a muriatic acid solution and wire brush, which seriously abrased and damaged the stone, erasing forever the traces of engravings, that had suffered the continuous erosions of time and weather. Here, I wish also to add that in Italy there are many Jewish cemeteries in places from which Jewish communities have long since disappeared, and it has often been Christians who have preserved these artefacts and their cultural heritage. It may appear strange to the large Jewish communities of the United States or Israel that in Italy and other European countries Jewish studies are pursued mainly by non-Jewish scholars. It is also a sad fact that Italy, a country richer than most in cultural heritage, whether Jewish or non-Jewish, invests less than many other countries in its conservation. In addition, there are absurd laws that prevent the protection and preservation of Jewish cemeteries. In Mantua, for example, a city where the Jewish population in the sixteenth century reached ten per cent, the municipality, to this very day, cannot supply (or support) a custodian for the Jewish cemetery, since the cemetery is not situated on public land but on land owned by the Jewish community. This is, in a way, an act of discrimination against the Jewish citizens of Mantua who for centuries paid their taxes like everyone else.

8 A diwan of poetry in rhyme and rhythm

Starting from the sixteenth century, and in particular during the Baroque period, the writing of poems and epitaphs in rhyme and rhythm became an accepted literary mode. As Michela Andreatta has shown in her article on the Jewish epitaph as literary genre,[2] it was the rabbis and leading scholars who, in these centuries, wrote collections of sepulchral inscriptions either for themselves, or as commissioned by others. Epitaphs, both true and fictitious, were worthy of publication as poetry. This precious heritage certainly must be saved from decline and falling into oblivion. A device used by the Jewish poets who composed these *piyyuṭim* is the separation of two parts of a word for poetical reasons. There follow a few examples of such poems.

A fine poetical composition is found in epitaph no. 9 from the cemetery of Lugo, written for Refael Ḥizqiya of Forlì, who passed away in 1592 (Fig. 4). The text is structured according a metrical scheme in octave: AB, AB, AC, AC, where A ends in *-ìm*, B in *-èreṣ* and C in *-arùṣ*. As a matter of fact, the beauty and rhetoric of these poems can be appreciated only in their original Hebrew.

Hebrew text:

אָדָם יְלוּד אִשָּׁה קְצַר יָמִים[3]
הַבֵּט אֱנוֹשׁ קָם עַל וְנִכְבָּד אֶרֶץ
אִישׁ *תָּם וְיָשָׁר*[4] אַף נְדִיב עַמִּים
טוֹב שָׁב לְדַל *תִּקְוָה*[5] וְגוֹדֵר פֶּרֶץ[6]
הוּבַל בְּקֶבֶר זֶה בְּ[שֵׁ]ם תָּמִים
עִם כָּל *כְּבוֹד עָשְׁרוֹ*[7] כְּעַפְרוֹת חֶרֶץ
אֵין טוֹב לְאִישׁ כִּי *אִם* לְבָב רָמִים
לְשָׂא לְמַד תַּכְלִית אֲשֶׁר לוֹ תֶּרֶץ

הנעלה כמה״ר רפאל חזקיה זצ״ל
מיפורלי עלה אל האלהים יום
י״א ניסן השנ״ב תנצב״ה

2 M. Andreatta, *L'epitaffio come genere letterario*, in *Il 'giardino' degli ebrei: Cimiteri ebraici del Mantovano*, ed. by A. Mortari and C. Bonora Previdi, series *Corpus Epitaphiorum Hebraicorum Italiae* (CEHI), created and directed by Mauro Perani, n. 1 (Florence: Giuntina, 2008), pp. 9–23.
3 Job 14:1.
4 Job 1:8.
5 Job 5:16.
6 Isa 58:12.
7 Esth 5:11.

Fig. 4: Tombstone in the Jewish cemetery of Lugo with epitaph of Refael Ḥizqiya from Forlì, who passed away in 1592.

English version:
Poetic part:

1. *Short is the life of man born of woman* (Job 14:1).
2. Regard a fine man who is high among the nobles of the land.
3. *A man right and just* (Job 1:8), a true *prince of the nations* (cf. Ps. 47:10);
4. Good, *restoring hope to the poor* (Job 5:16), and *repairer of the breach* (Isa 58:12)
5. laid in this tomb with an honest name.
6. Despite *the splendour of his richness* (Esth 5:11), the gold is as his dust.
7. There is nothing good for men (see Eccl 8:15) than to be exalted of heart[8],
8. to bring knowledge of the fate you are running to.

Prose part:

9. The excellent, honoured Refael Ḥizqiya, may the memory of the righteous be a blessing,
10. from Forlì, rose to God on 11 Nisan 5352 (March 23, 1592). May his soul be bound up in the bundle of life.

Comment:

As we can see, the classic structure of the text of the epitaph is composed of two parts: the first is in poetry which, in the epitaphs of the late sixteenth century, the golden era of Baroque, until the eighteenth century, is in rhyme and rhythm, and constructs a eulogy of the deceased. The poetic part is an ottava rima where the lines 1, 3, 5 and 7 are decasyllabic composed of 5 iamb verses; lines 2 and 6 are hendecasyllables composed by 3 iambs, 1 anapaest and 1 iamb verses; line 4 is an dodecasyllabic verse, the central one adopting a different rhythm and is composed of 1 anapaest, 2 iambs, 1 anapaest and a trochee. So we have a wonderfully elaborate structure, with the composer making the most of the rhyme and rhythm, as well as of parallelism. There is a connection between lines 1 = 3 = 5 = 7 which all end in *-im*, and 2 = 4 = 6 = 8 all ending in *-eṣ*.

9 The structure and various registers of the speaker in the epitaphs

In the epitaphs, the deceased's virtues are often celebrated with words quoted from the Bible, but at the same time the poet invites the visitor to consider the vanity of the human condition, emphasizing the shortness of human life because of the *fuga temporis*, as is made evident by the inevitability of death,

8 Text inspired by Exod 35:21: וַיָּבֹאוּ כָּל אִישׁ אֲשֶׁר נְשָׂאוֹ לִבּוֹ וְכֹל אֲשֶׁר נָדְבָה רוּחוֹ.

Fig. 5: The entrance to the former Pizzeria “La Stalla” in Cerese, not far from Mantua, with two cylindrical Jewish funerary pillars, reused as ornamental elements. On the right side, the one of Avraham Yedidya Basilea, brother of the Mantua kabbalist, Avi‘ad Sar Shalom Basilea, who passed away in 1748, in July. On the left side, that of Avraham Ḥayyim Norsa, who died in 1783, both leading Rabbis in Mantua during the 18th century. Despite my efforts to obtain permission to bring the funerary pillars to the Jewish community in Mantua, with the intention to putting them in a museum, together with other Mantua *maṣevot* of the 16th–18th centuries, the two pillars remain, up to now, at the place where the picture was taken.

and invites visitors and passers-by to reflect on that, to spare a thought for the deceased, and to follow his moral example. The second part is in prose and gives general information about the deceased’s name, his characteristics, often his main family relations, the date of death and sometimes also its causes. The order of these two parts is interchangeable and each part can be placed either at the beginning of the epitaph, or at its end. Who is speaking in the text of the epitaph? There are several possibilities: sometimes it is either the tombstone that speaks for itself, inviting the passer-by to reflect on the fugacity of life and to turn his mind to the dead and pray for him; but the speaker, in the literary representation, is occasionally the dead himself, asking the visitor to enjoy his life, to thank God for being still alive and to consider the vanity of events that make men rush through life, following in particular the religious reflections of Qohelet and Job, which are, not by chance, and together with Proverbs, the most quoted books in the epitaphs; a hidden voice sometimes speaks to the visitor, describing the situation of the dead in macabre terms such as 'consumed by worms' and as in a state of decomposition, in order to make an impression on the visitor and to encourage him to be attached in his present life to eternal and important values, and to everlasting things. *Havel havalim ha-kol-havel* of Eccl 1:2 is used as a refrain, to remind the living of the vanity of all existing things.

I discovered a most interesting epitaph in Cerese, near Mantua, where a cylindrical pillar, probably at the beginning of the Ottocento, was reused as an ornamental element at the entrance of the Pizzeria 'La Stalla' (Fig. 5). The dead, Avraham Ḥayyim Norsa, was a prominent rabbi in Mantua during the eighteenth century and had passed away on the eighth day of the month of Shevat in 5543, equivalent to 11th January 1783 (Fig. 6). Here its text is presented, with an interpretation that improves on the one I published in my book on the Jewish cemeteries of Mantua[9]:

Hebrew text:

רְאֵה חַיִּים[10]

1. עַד מָה אַנְשֵׁי לֵבָב חָבֹל תְּחְבָּלוּ
לִרְאוֹת עָמָל[11] יְגוֹן חַיִּים תִּשְׂבָּעוּ
2. עַד אָנָה אֶל אֵימוֹת מָוֶת תִּשְׁתָּעוּ
בִּינוּ כִּי טוֹב לָכֶם מַה תִּתְחַלְחָלוּ

מצבת
קבורת הזקן הנעלה ונשא פנים עמו ירא
אלקים כמה"ר חיים ב"ר אברהם נורצי
שנקרא אל השמים מעל אור ליום ד' ח'
שבט ש' תקמ"ג לפ"ק תנצב"ה אכי"ר

9 See *Il 'giardino' degli ebrei: Cimiteri ebraici del Mantovano*, quoted in n. 2 above, p. 148, epitaph no. 16; after a more precise examination of the epigraph, which is still located in Cerese near Mantua, in front of the former pizzeria 'La Stalla', I achieved the improved reading *yegon* instead of the previous *we-gan*.

10 Eccl 9:9.

11 Compare. Eccl 1:3: מה יתרון לאדם בכל עמלו שיעמל תחת השמש.

Fig. 6: The cylindrical pillar, engraved with the epitaph of Avraham Ḥayyim Norsa, a prominent rabbi in Mantua during the 18th century, who passed away on 8 Shevat in 5543 (11 January 1783). See fig. 5 above.

Opening biblical motto:

Enjoy life (Eccl 9:9).

English version

Poetic part:

How long, o men of understanding, will you devote yourselves to the struggle / taking your fill of painful desires and anguished life / how long will you fear the terrors of death / why be afraid of what is good for you

Prose part:

Sepulchral stone / of the distinguished elder, revered by his people and fearing / God, R. Ḥayyim, the son of Avraham Norsa, / summoned to heaven above during the night of Wednesday 8 / Shevat in the year 5543 (= 1783) of the minor computation. May his soul be bound up in the bundle of life. Amen and so be it.

Comment:

This epitaph is addressed to the passer-by, or the visitor, who sees the memorial stone at the cemetery. The sense of this epitaph, characterized by a sympathetic vein of Qoheletic cynicism, can be succinctly summarized as an invitation not to be afraid of death but to contrast this life with the eternal life. The poetic part is a quatrain that follows the rhythmical scheme A B B A (known as enclosed rhyme) with an ending in *-lu* and B in *-ʿu*. As for the metrical structure, the stanza is composed as follows: line 1 is dodecasyllables (3 iambs, 1 trochee, 2 iambs); line 2 is of fourteen syllables (all 7 iambs); line 3 is hendecasyllabic (3 iambs, 1 trochee, 1 anapaest); and finally line 4 is hendecasyllabic as well (3 iambs, 1 anapaest, 1 iamb). As far the rhyme is concerned, the ending vowel is always identical through the quatrain. Each line of the poem has eleven syllables, stressed *milraʿ*, all with long vowels. The word 'life', in Hebrew *ḥayyim*, is also the name of the deceased, and the composer of the epitaph is making a play on the double meaning of the term. In the literary fiction, the poet invites the passersby to 'consider *ḥayyim*', citing Eccl 9:9, which opens as the motto of the first poetic part.

10 The integration of data found in the epitaphs with other sources recording a death

I wish to offer here an interesting example of the fruitful integration of historical information contained in the epitaph of a leading rabbi of the Jewish community in Lugo with the important information given in the text dealing with his death in the above-mentioned manuscript of New York containing the

Fig. 7: Jewish cemetery in Lugo with, on the left, the tombstone of Rabbi Shelomo David Del Vecchio (*me-ha-Zeqenim*), son of Moshe, who lived between the second half of the 18th and the beginning of the 19th century and passed away on 10 Adar 5583 (February 1823). He was one of a dozen Italian Rabbis who attended the second session of the Grand Sanhedrin convened by Napoleon Bonaparte in 1807 in Paris.

Pinqas Ha-Nifṭarim of the Jews of Lugo. I am speaking of Rabbi Shelomo David Del Vecchio (*me-ha-zeqenim*), son of Moshe, who lived between the second half of the eighteenth and the first quarter of the nineteenth century and passed-away on 10 Adar 5583, i.e. 21 February, 1823. He was one of the leading rabbi of Lugo, the last member of his family, which was one of the most ancient among the Jewish families of Lugo. This small city developed great importance for the local presence of Jews after an ecclesiastical ordinance, ordering a concentration of all the Jewish population of the new *Legazione pontificia* after the *Devoluzione* of Ferrara, from the Estense Duchy, to Papal territory. In fact, Lugo passed from the Duchy of the house of Este to the Church's State, where many of the rights, previously enjoyed by the Jews, were cut back. Pope Urbanus VIII in 1638 ordered the Jews to concentrate and relocate in only the three cities of Lugo, Cento and Ferrara. For this reason, Lugo's small Jewish community increased substantially and became one of the most important centres of Jewish presence and culture in north Italy, starting from the seventeenth century and lasting for about two hundred years. According to a population census carried out in Lugo in 1638, the Jews represented 10 per cent of the whole population. Rabbi Shelomo David, the last of the great rabbis of this community, was a theologian, philosopher and poet. At eighteen, he became the spiritual leader of the community of Lugo and he was the head of the local rabbinical academy. When Napoleon Bonaparte summoned

Fig. 8: The last part of the epitaph of Rabbi Shelomo David Del Vecchio, indicating the year of his death, using the last verse of the book of Esther: שנת דרש טוב לעמו ודבר שׁלום לכל זר̇ע̇ו̇ in which the words indicating the date are written in a finer and larger script, and the letters to be calculated are highlighted by a stroke.

the second session of the Grand Sanhedrin in 1807, in Paris, he was one of the participants. In 1815, he was sent to Rome to negotiate less severe conditions for the Jews after the restoration of pontifical rule. He owned a library of great value. Let us now see how much valuable information can be found in the record of his death contained in manuscript no. 3960 of Jewish Theological Seminary in New York, in addition to what we read in his epitaph. This is the text engraved on his tombstone, kept in the Jewish cemetery of Lugo (Figs. 7 and 8):

Hebrew text:

השר ונגיד בין החכמים
עטרת זקנים[12] ורב בגאונים
זקן וישיש איש האלהים
כמהר"ר שלומה דוד מהזקנים
זצוק"ל
שעלה למרום בי' באדר
שנת
דרש *טוב לעמו ודבר שלום לכל*
זרעו[13]

We see that the above text is fairly concise and succinct, when compared with the information gathered from of the New York manuscript's record of his death, which contains a fine *piyyuṭ* in rhyme and rhythm, longer than that of the epitaph, and a lengthy report of the funeral ceremony. (Fig. 9):

12 Prov 17:6.
13 Esth 10:3.

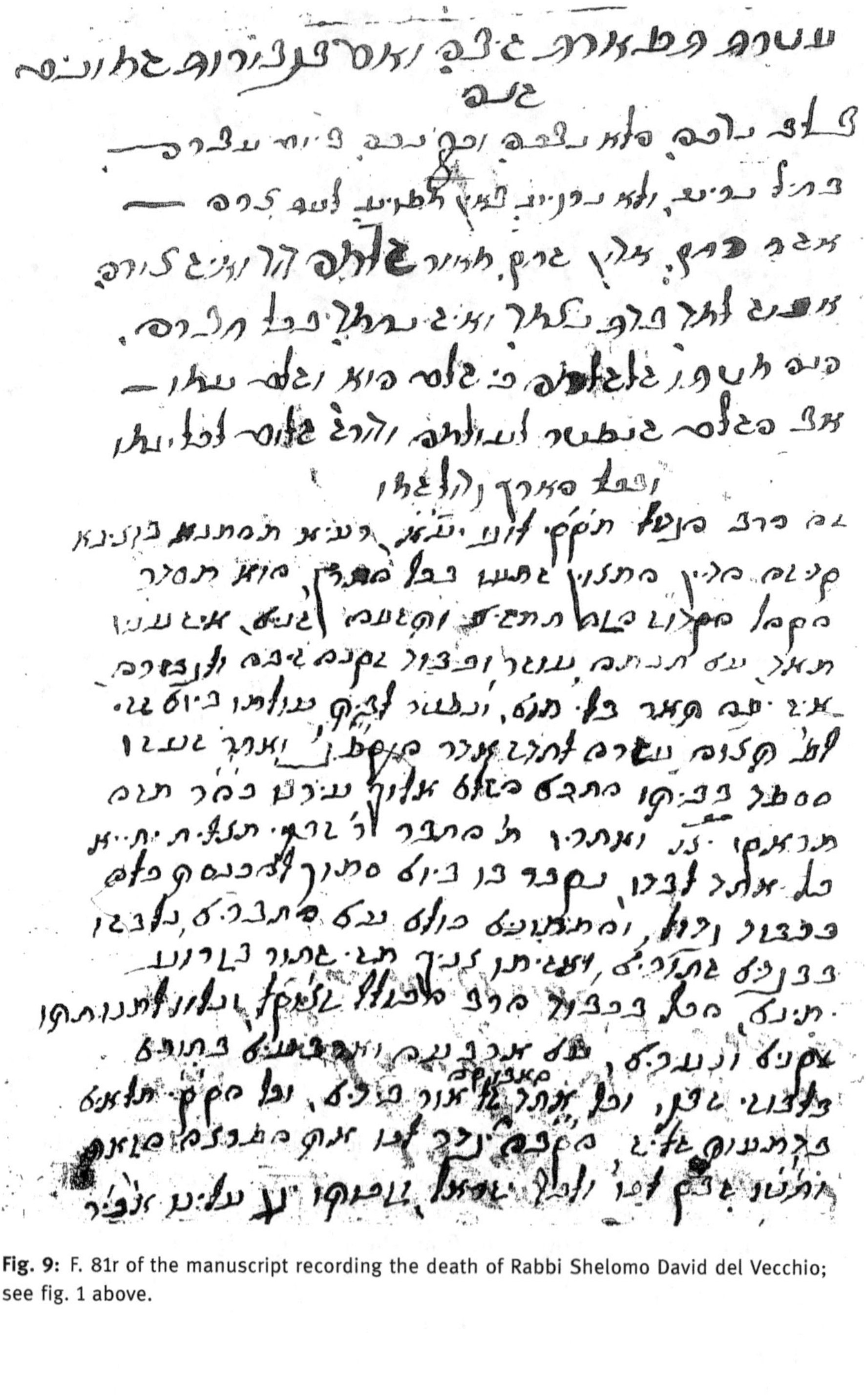

Fig. 9: F. 81r of the manuscript recording the death of Rabbi Shelomo David del Vecchio; see fig. 1 above.

Opening biblical motto:

עטרת תפארת שיבה[14] *ואם בגבורות שמונים*
שנה[15]

Hebrew text:
Poetic part:

1. בְּלֵב נִדְכֶּה הֲלֹא נִבְכֶּה וְכַף נַכֶּה בְּיוֹם עֶבְרָה
בְּחַיִל נָרִיעַ [נָרַע?] וְלֹא נַרְגִּיעַ [נַרגַּע?] בְּאֵין *מַפְגִּיעַ*[16] לְעֵת צָרָה
2. אֲשֶׁר רִחק אֲדוֹן שָׁחָק מָאוֹר שְׁלֹמֹה דּוֹד וְאִישׁ צוּרָה
אֱנוֹשׁ לָמַד בְּדָת נִצְמַד וְאִישׁ נֶחְמָד בְּכָל חֶבְרָה
הִנֵּה מִטָּתוֹ שֶׁלִּשְׁלֹמֹה[17] כִּי שָׁלֵם הוּא וְשָׁלֵם עִמּוֹ
אָב הַשָּׁלֵם שֶׁנִּפְטַר לְעוֹלָמוֹ[18] וְדוֹרֵשׁ שָׁלוֹם לְכָל עַמּוֹ
וּבְכָל הָאָרֶץ גָּדוֹל שְׁמוֹ.

Prose part:

זה הרב הגדול מק״ק לוגו יע״א רעיא מהמנא בוצינא
קדשה הדיין המצוין שמעו בכל הארץ הוא מסדר
הקהל הקדוש הזה חמשים ותשעה שנים איש עניו
מאד עם הנחה עושר וכבוד זקנה שיבה ולגבורה
איש יפה תאר בלי מום ונפטר לבית עולמו ביום ששי
לפ׳ תצוה עשרה לחדש אדר התקפ״ג ואחר שעשו
הספד בביתו החכם השלם אלוף עירנו כה״ר משה
מראקו יצ״ו ואחריו מ׳ החבר ר׳ שבתי מצליח יחייא
כל אחד לבדו נקבר בו ביום סמוך להכנסת כלה
בכבוד גדול והממונים כולם עם החברים נלבשו
בבגדים שחורים וישימו צניף משי שחור בזרוע
ימינם הכל בכבוד הרב הכולל זצוק״ל ונלוו למנוחתו
זקנים ונערים עם ארבעה וארבעים בחורים
בלבושי שבת וכל אחד ‹האבוקה› של אור בידים וכל הק״ק מלאים
בדמעות שליש הקב״ה יגדר לנו את הפרצה הזאת
וחיים טובים וארוכים[19] שבק לנו ולכל ישראל וזכותו ייגן עלינו אכי״ר.

The poem is in the Spanish style of sixteen syllables, structured as 4 × 4, with some deviation in lines 5–6 and considerable variation in the last line.

---

14 Prov 16:31.
15 Ps 90:10.
16 Compare Isa 59:16.
17 Cant 3:7.
18 The manuscript has לעולמה instead of לעולמו which seems to be wrong, possibly influenced by the word שלשלמה *she-li-Shelomo* in which the final *-o* cited from Cant 3:7 in the name Shelomo ends in *-h*.
19 The manuscript has the abbreviation: וחט״ו.

English version:
Opening biblical motto :

> *The hoary head is a crown of glory* (Prov 16:31), *He who has the strength arrives at eighty* (Ps 90:10)

Poetic part:

> With a broken heart we cry and smite our palms on the day of anger, / and powerfully we cry, we do not rest, because there is no one who can intercede in time of trouble, / in which [time of trouble] the Lord has turned away, he has extinguished the light of Shelomo David, who was a worthy and learned man, attached to religion, a man most pleasant among the whole brotherhood. / This is the bier of Shelomo, for he was perfect, and peace was with him – he was the perfect father and he departed for the eternal life, *he sought peace for all its people* (see Esth 10: 3), / and his name was great over all the earth.

Prose part:

> He was the great rabbi of the holy community of Lugo – may the Most High protect, Amen – the faithful shepherd, holy light, incomparable judge, known throughout the world. He led this holy community for fifty-nine years. He was a very humble man as well as blessed with satisfaction, wealth, honour, old age, gray hair and seniority. He was a handsome man, impeccable, and he departed on the sixth day (Friday) of the *parasha Teṣawweh*, on 10 Adar 5583. After eulogies had been separately delivered at his home by the wise leader of our city, the respected Rabbi Moshe Morocco – may God, his Rock, protect and maintain him – and, after him, by our teacher and colleague Rabbi Shabbetai Maṣliaḥ Yaḥya, he was then buried on that same day with great honour just before the arrival of the bride (the Sabbath).
> All the officer bearers and all the members (of the burial society) were clothed in black and wore a black silk arm-band on their right arms. They did this in honour of the most learned rabbi – may the memory of the righteous and the holy be a blessing. The old men and, with them, the boys, and forty-four young men dressed in Sabbath clothes, with each of them holding a candle, then accompanied him to his grave. All members of the holy community shed abundant tears [Ps 80:6]. May the Holy One, blessed be He, repair this breach for us. And he left with us and with all Israel (the memory of) a good and long life. May his merit protect us. Amen; may God's will be done.

Comment:

The poetic part in the manuscript places on the same line what I have edited as 1a and 1b; ends the first four lines with *-rah* (... ביום עברה, ... לעת צרה, ... ואיש צורה, ... בכל חברה), and the last three lines with *-mo* (... ושלם עמו, ... לכל עמו, ... גדול שמו), with the same word *'ammo* 'his people' occurring twice, and *shemo* 'his name' in the last line. It is interesting to note that the poem written in the manuscript report of his death is longer, richer in detail, and rather different from that engraved on the tombstone of Rav Del

Vecchio, which is much shorter and basic. Both versions, however, regard as a crucial a citation, with some variations, of the last verse of the book of Esther: *doresh shalom le-khol 'ammo*, 'he sought peace for all his people', for the original *doresh ṭov le-'ammo we-dover shalom le-khol zar'o*. The emphasis is of course here being placed on *his people*: the rabbi had been a good shepherd for the community of Lugo that he served for almost sixty years. His cultural standing and the public role he played on the occasion of the second session of the Grand Sanhedrin, in which he had been invited to participate together with a dozen other leading rabbis as a representative of the Jewish communities of the northern Italy under the Napoleonic empire, is pointed out and celebrated in both the epitaph and in the record of his of death, so that his role can be compared there with that of Mordechai in the Bible.

From the manuscript record of his death we glean new information (some of it perhaps somewhat hyperbolic) not included in the epitaph, namely, that he served as rabbi the Jewish community of Lugo for fifty-nine years, that he was a very humble man, a faithful and impeccable shepherd, a holy light, an incomparable judge known throughout the world, blessed with many distinguished attributes. There is in this source even a somewhat unexpected note in which the scribe-poet tell us that he was a handsome man. Two rabbis of the community gave funeral orations, and he was buried with great honour at the auspicious time of Friday afternoon. This description of the whole funerary procession is most impressive and charming.

11 Palaeography and style of the Jewish epitaphs on burial stones

Like any manuscript or other text, funerary inscriptions must also be studied as palaeographic documents taking due account of the style and shape of their letters. We have to treat the Hebrew sepulchral inscriptions of Italy with the same reasoning that we use for Italian Hebrew manuscripts. While the Hebrew manuscripts, epitaphs and inscriptions found in the Ashkenazi area are written exclusively in Ashkenazi style, and those found in Sefardi countries are only in Sefardi style, the contrary situation applies in Italy, where there is evidence not only of the Italian style but also of the other two, both Ashkenazi (Fig. 10) and Sefardi (Fig. 11). In other words, we observe in the texts of funerary inscriptions the same phenomenon encountered in Hebrew manuscripts of Italy: they are written in all three main types of script used in the Western world, ie Italian (Fig. 12), Sefardi (Fig. 13) and Ashkenazi (Fig. 14). This multicultural nature of Italy is due to its central geographical position in the Mediterranean basin, and also has cultural and historical reasons. Italy, in fact,

Fig. 10: An example of Ashkenazi-style engraved letters in the *maṣeva* of Azriel Kohen Ṣedeq, who died at the age of 83 on *Lag ba-ʻomer* 5407 (1647 CE), at the Jewish cemetery of Padua.

Fig. 11: Examples of Sefardi letters in the *maṣeva* of Mrs Felice, the daughter of Yisrael Yehuda from *Sermene* (ancient name of Sermide in the Mantovano) and spouse of R. Eli'ezer. No clearly indicated date. It is unclear whether the points highlighting the *lamed* in the proper names *Felice* and *Sermene*, and perhaps the letter *ṣade* in the eulogy *y''ṣ*, indicate the figure representing the year of death 5330 (= 1460 CE or without the value of *lamed* in *Felice*, 5300 = 1430 CE). More probable is that the total numerical value of the name Sermene yields the date 5430/5400 (= 1670/1630 CE).

Fig. 12: Examples of Italian letters in the *maṣeva* of R. Yehuda (Leone) ben Eli'ezer Briel (1643–1722), disciple of Moshe Zacuto and kabbalist, as his master.

Fig. 13: Another example of a Sefardi script with Italian influence in the tombstone of Gentile the wife of Shelo[mo], who died on 3 Adar II in the year 5385 (1625 CE), preserved in the Jewish cemetery of Padua.

Fig. 14: Beautiful example of Ashkenazi letters in gem style (*stile gemmato*), used to engrave the epitaph of the "master and father of the town" (*rosh we-av medina*) Asher Levi, who died on 1 Iyyar in the year 5292 (1532 CE), at the Jewish cemetery at Padua. The stone has been cut into two, probably for re-use. In this text we can detect two rhetoric and scribal devices. The name of the deceased and the eulogy *z"l* can be read as an acrostic of the first letters of the initial eight lines. Moreover, in the sixth line at the end of the right half of the stone, the sculptor has, for metrical reasons, written *-im* of the word *reḥoqim* separately in the line spacing above; see the next figure below.

saw the immigration of many Jews from Spain, France and Germany, who had come for various reasons. They had been expelled from their homelands, they were using Italy as a transit point on their way to the Middle East, or they were attracted by Italy's culture in the Renaissance period and in modern time. This is documented by the abundance of Jewish epitaphs engraved in Ashkenazi style in the Italian Jewish cemeteries of the northern regions. Actually, following expulsions from their countries, many Ashkenazi Jews immigrated into northern and central Italy. Likewise, the presence of many funerary inscriptions sculpted in Sefardi characters, testifies to the expulsion of Jews from the Iberian peninsula. Their arrival enriched the Italian communities, and brought with it their Sefardi writing style, as used on their the epitaphs. The parallel situation between manuscripts and epitaphs, as just described, is attested in the major and large Jewish communities of northern and central

Fig. 15: Detail of the word of the word *reḥoqim* with *-im* detached and written in the spacing above, in the epitaph of Asher Levi, who died in 1532, as found in the Jewish cemetery of Padua; see previous figure.

Italy, such as Mantua, Venice, Ferrara, Rome and various others. A curious device is the separation of two parts of a word for metrical reasons, as we can see in some tombstones, and another characteristic, as also found in manuscripts, is the writing of a word in small letters, upwards from the line, for reasons of physical justification (Fig. 15).

12 Evolution, language and style of the Italian Jewish epitaphs

Obviously, the style of Hebrew epitaphs in Italy was influenced by the culture of the ongoing centuries. The oldest tombstones, especially those of the sixteenth century, display the art and beauty of the Renaissance, are written in a beautiful calligraphy, embellished by the engraving of letters in a way similar to gem (*stile gemmato*) and with fine serifs, similar to the crowns used on the text of a *Sefer Torah* (Figs. 16, 17 and 18). Of course, such impressive monuments

Fig. 16: A wonderful example of letters sculpted in Ashkenazi *stile gemmato* at the beginning of the 16th century in the tombstone of the Bolognese banker, Avraham Yagel from Fano, who died on 24 Tammuz 5268 (1508 CE). The tombstone is kept in the Medieval Museum of Bologna.

were primarily reserved for the rich and for leading personalities, because their construction was a highly expensive exercise. There are also many examples of beautiful texts engraved in Sefardi letters, with the round shapes of their characters. As for as the language of the epitaphs is concerned, Hebrew was the only one used until the nineteenth century, when a short summary of the Hebrew starts to be written in Italian. Slowly, the Italian part prevails over that of the Hebrew, until the sacred language completely disappears. This cultural phenomenon reflects the progressive loss of the Hebrew language by many Jews. This process culminates in the second half of the nineteenth and the first half of the twentieth century with the almost total abandonment of Hebrew in

Fig. 17: A detail of some letters with wonderful serifs and small circles in sculpted Ashkenazi *stile gemmato* at the beginning of the 16th century in the tombstone of the Bolognese banker Avraham Yagel from Fano, who died in 1508. We see the gem-shaped upper and lower part of the letters, especially *ṣade* and *alef* and the curled lower part of the *qof*; the tombstone is kept in the Medieval Museum of Bologna.

Fig. 18: A verse from Psalms 120:2 sculpted in Ashkenazi gem-shaped style on the wall of Palazzo Bocchi in Bologna, together with Latin and Greek verses, built by the humanist Achille Bocchi (1488–1562). The building, designed by Jacopo Barozzi da Vignola, was inaugurated in 1546 and became the seat of the Hermathena Academy that he founded years before, and the name of which is a fusion of Hermes and Athena.

Fig. 19: The top of a cylindrical tombstone in Istria stone from the Jewish cemetery of Cardeto in Ancona, with a figure of a sixteen-petal-flower or of a sun with sixteen rays. This image is very frequently used in the tombstones of the Marches, but it is unclear whether it is purely ornamental or whether it has some other, unknown meaning.

favour of Italian. Only a few words of Hebrew remains, such as *shalom*, or the abbreviation of the eulogy *tehi nafsho/-a ṣerura bi-ṣeror ha-ḥayyim*.

This unfortunate phenomenon is connected with the loss of Jewish culture by the Italian communities after the proclamation of Italy as a unified state in 1861, and reflects the climate of secularization and of modernism that characterized that century. After the emancipation, and after leaving the ghettos, the Jews wanted finally to be citizens with full civil rights like everyone else and they were attracted by modern life and science, often abandoning their culture and religion, to become assimilated into the external world. A particular problem that I wish to point out is the transition of *maṣevot* from the classical marble slab to that of the cylindrical pillar that occurred at the end of the sixteenth century in some Italian regions, especially in the Marches. In my research on the Jewish cemeteries of the Marches, and especially on the largest one of Ancona, I was surprised to see that the shape of the tombstones in the last decade of the sixteenth century passes quickly to the cylindrical (Fig. 19), a new form which, at the end of sixteenth and in the seventeenth century accounted for 95 % of the total. The Marches tombstones, as already indicated, are very well preserved because they were made using the hard Istria stone (*pietra d'Istria*), transferred by ship from the Istria peninsula to the centres on the Marches coast of the Adriatic Sea. This is a very hard stone, resistant to temperature changes and extremely durable. But how do we explain this sudden change in the community of the Marches? At the moment I can only speculate. The cylindrical shape is typically used by the Sefardi Jews, who probably borrowed it from North Africa. We know that many Sefardi Jews who were expelled in 1492 went to Italy and to the Levant region of Turkey. The style was probably imported by the Sefardim who came to Ancona and other towns of the Marches, and its adoption was then strengthened by the trade relations between the great commercial port of Ancona and the cities of the East, such as those of Turkey. While the phenomenon is prominent in the Marches, other Jewish communities display only rare examples of the cylindrical pillar among Jewish tombstones.

We shall now discuss the persecutions, the expulsion of the Jews and the new hygienic and sanitary laws at the end of the eighteenth century as reasons for the loss of *maṣevot* and their reutilization as building material

12.1 Persecution and the expulsion of Jews and the loss of memory

The history of the Italian Jewish cemeteries, as of the Jews themselves, has been strongly affected by the persecution and expulsions experienced by the Jews. To give an example, if the Jews had a rich and beautiful cemetery, and were expelled from the city in which they lived, they were forced to abandon it. In such circumstances, normally the *maṣevot* were lost to the Jewish community, either being reused by Christians for other purposes, or even re-written on the reverse for the Christian dead.

An example of the abandonment of a cemetery is that of the important Jewish community in Bologna under the rule of the Papal State, which, after centuries of pacific coexistence with the Christians, was expelled in 1569. Many Jews took refuge in the nearby city of Ferrara, still under the benevolent rule of the house of Este. We know that their cemetery was bought by the nuns of St. Peter Martyr, and that most of the tombstones were lost or sold for secondary use. Only a few tombstone of the rich Jewish bankers of Bologna survived, and they are now kept at the Medieval Museum in Bologna. One of them, that of Yoav Ṣeruya from Rieti, who died in 1547, was re-used twenty-four years later to mark the burial place of the Christian Rinaldo Duglioli (Fig. 20). His son, Albizio Duglioli, bought from the Sisters of St. Peter's a marble headstone

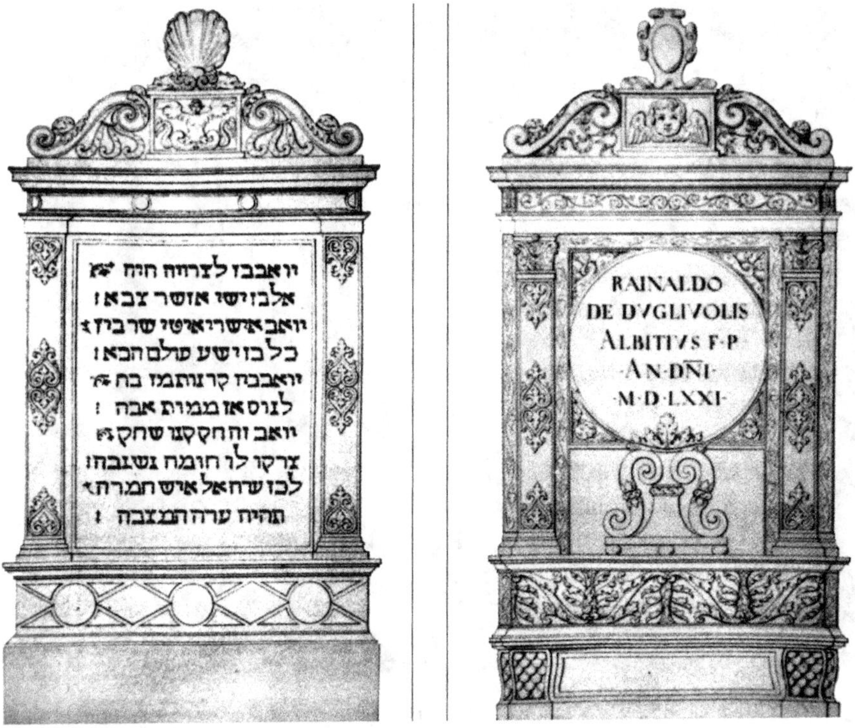

Fig. 20: A picture, depicting both the original front side tombstone of Yoav Şeruya from Rieti, who died in 1547, and of the reverse, which was re-used 24 years later, in 1671, to mark the burial place of the Christian Rinaldo Duglioli; from the book *Eletta dei monumenti più illustri e classici*, published in Bologna in 1840, vol. 2.

with a large thickness. It was cut in the thickness direction, leaving about two-thirds for a new peace of marble to be engraved, and separating the original side written in Hebrew, which had broken during the cutting process. Recently this tombstone was examined with an Enhanced Compton Spectrometer, scanning it with an electronic microscope.[20] Also, the remarkable tombstone of Avraham da Fano, a rich banker who died in Bologna on 24 Tammuz 1508 (see Fig. 16), was re-used 152 years later in 1660 for engraving on the reverse side of the marble the Latin epitaph of the tomb of Carlo De Tassis (Fig. 21). and his wife Anna Linder. Today, this beautiful funerary stone is mounted on a pivot so that the visitor can rotate and view the two sides, the Hebrew and the Latin (Fig. 22).

---

20 G. Maino (ed.), *Antichi marmi e nuove tecnologie. La lapide di Yoav da Rieti nel Museo Civico di Bologna* (Torino, London, Venice, New York, Turin: Umberto Allemandi, 2007).

Fig. 21: The tombstone of Avraham da Fano, a rich banker who died in Bologna on 24 Tammuz 1508 (see fig. 16). In 1660, some 60 years after the expulsion of the Jews from Bologna in 1569 and 152 years after the death of Avraham, the stone was re-used for a Christian tomb on which is engraved on the reverse side of the marble the Latin epitaph of Carlo De Tassis and his wife Anna Linder.

The re-use of the stone and marble of tombstones was a normal practice all over the world. Some of the ancient *maṣevot* from the twelfth-fourteenth centuries now kept in the Nachmanides Museum of Gerona were found in a building not far from the old Jewish cemetery. A dedicatory stone with the inscription of the donor was re-used as building stone in the synagogue structure of Syracuse when it was transformed into the Church of San Giovannello (Fig. 23). Some sepulchral inscriptions from Matera (southern Italy) dating back to the ninth century, were re-used as building elements, as evidenced by seven holes[21]. In Venosa, many tombstones of the same period were bricked into the walls of the church of the Holy Trinity. The examples could continue. The

21 C. Colafemmina, *Tre iscrizioni ebraiche altomedievali a Matera*, in M. Perani (ed.), *Una manna buona per Mantova. Man Tov le-Man Tovah*. Studi in onore di Vittore Colorni per il suo 92° Compleanno (Florence: Olschki, 2004), pp. 101–14.

Fig. 22: Today the beautiful tombstone, formerly of Avraham da Fano (front side, see fig. 16) and later of the De Tassis family (reverse side), is mounted on a pivot so that the visitor can turn the two sides, and see both the Hebrew and the Latin.

Fig. 23: A dedicatory stone of the 15th century, with an inscription about the donor who gave a piece of ground for the enlargement of the synagogue at Syracuse. After the expulsion of the Jews from Sicily in 1492, when the synagogue was transformed into the Church of San Giovannello, the inscription was re-used as a building stone in the apse of the church.

Nazis also re-used the tombstones of the ancient Jewish cemetery of the 'Remu' in Krakow to pave the streets after cutting into two parts those that that were too large for this. After the Second World War many of them were recovered and partially restored.

Since ancient times Egyptian papyri have been re-used to make pasteboard for the mummies or to function as packaging for goods. Parchment and skin, first used as to record writing and then recycled as bindings, ties, belts or straps; in addition, sheets of paper with handwriting, when no longer interesting as texts, were glued together to make fillings for the binding of books, just to give some examples. There is no doubt that in the history of civilization, the re-use of materials for secondary, cultural purposes represented a major element in their conservation.

12.2 The new hygienic and sanitary laws of Europe at the end of eighteenth century and the dispersion of Jewish tombstones

In 1804, with the Edict of Saint-Cloud, Napoleon Bonaparte imposed on the lands of his empire, including the Italian regions under his rule, the displacement of cemeteries to sites outside the populated centres. This legislation, requiring the construction of cemeteries outside the town, derived from both a hygienic consideration and from a Jacobin egalitarianism, and it ordered not only that the tombs should be located outside the town but also that they should have similar stones. The extension of the edict to Italy also aroused controversy and discussion, in the course of which the poet Ugo Foscolo intervened with the composition of his work *I sepolcri*, 'The tombs'.

But as far as Mantua was concerned, already some time before, in the eighties of the eighteenth century the Emperor Franz Joseph of Austria imposed on his domains of the Lombardo-Veneto these new hygienic rules. So in the town surrounded by three lakes formed by the River Mincio, both the Christian and Jewish communities were forced to move their cemeteries outside the town. The Jews of Mantua, after several attempts to find a suitable area for the new cemetery made between 1786 and 1789, finally succeeded in finding a suitable field and in January 1790 they began to bury their dead in the new area outside the San Giorgio port, where the cemetery is located up to the present. However, according to Jewish religious law, the dead are not usually removed from their place of burial, and consequently for a while even the old cemetery continued to be guarded. But over the years it was abandoned, and those tombstones that were beautiful from the artistic point of

Fig. 24: The funerary cylindrical pillar, engraved in beautiful Sefardi letters, of the famous Mantua kabbalist, Moshe Zacuto, chief rabbi of Mantua from 1673 until his death on 1 October 1697. Mutilated on two-thirds of the upper part, it had been used as building material before being purchased by Vittore Colorni and Shlomo Simonsohn and brought into the Jewish cemetery. It was later lost but recently rediscovered by the author in the Diocesan Museum of Mantua, where it had remained unidentified.

view or more valuable for the literary texts and poems of their inscriptions – generally those of the most important personalities of the community, such as rich bankers, learned and famous people and educated rabbis – were transported to the new cemetery of St. Giorgio.

That area was, however, a strategic point for military defence, and a few years later, during the Austrian wars with the French, the Jews had to move back to the place in which they had formerly buried their dead. Later, under Napoleonic rule in 1802, they returned permanently to the new cemetery. In this period the Jewish community of Mantua buried sixty of its dead each year. In 1816, the walls in the new cemetery collapsed and for a short time the Jews were again forced to bury their dead in the old area of the district of Gradaro, near the church of San Nicole. These constant shifts obviously led to the loss of many tombstones. After the Jewish cemeteries had been definitively abandoned, the abundant marble tombstones became a free quarry for non-Jews who required a marble slab for one purpose or another. In a house in Mantua (see below), in which a tombstone from the eighteenth century is now the base of a barbecue, there are also fragments of other tombstones with epitaphs in Hebrew that have been re-used as paving in its courtyard (Fig. 24). All these factors, together with the problematic historical context, explain the loss of most of the Italian Jewish tombstones of the ancient cemeteries from the period ranging from the sixteenth to the end of the eighteenth centuries, before the application of the new sanitary regulations of the Austrian and French rulers in northern Italy. We shall now examine two re-used *maṣevot* from Mantua.

12.3 The cylindrical funerary pillar of Moshe Zacuto (d. 1697)

An amazing story about the re-use of a tombstone concerns the cylindrical pillar of the famous Mantua kabbalist Moshe Zacuto (Fig. 25), who was the chief rabbi in Mantua from 1673 until his death on 1 October, 1697. This funerary pillar is unfortunately mutilated in more than two-thirds of the upper part. Born in Amsterdam in 1639, Zacuto studied in the rabbinical academies of Eastern Europe and left Venice in 1645 for appointment as rabbi of Mantua. He wrote extensively in the fields of Hebrew learning, law, poetry and esoteric kabbala, and in Mantua he introduced a group of disciples, notably Yehuda Briel and Aviad Sar Shalom Basilea, to kabbala. Thanks to Dvora Bregman, all his poetry is now published, and she has also written about the epitaphs that

Fig. 25: Tombstone of Ya'aqov ben Matitya Ashkenazi from Brescia, in the magnificent *stile gemmato*, probably from the beginning of the 16th century, held in the Museum of the Jewish Community of Ferrara. In its epitaph we read: והאבן הזאת הוקם על ראש / הצדיק כמ״ר יעקב זצ״ל ב״ר / מתתיה מברישי אשכנזי ז״ל / [נאסף] אל עמיו יום ו׳ י״ט ניסן / [שנת ...] English version: *This stone was erected at the head of the righteous, R. Ya'aqov, the memory of the righteous be a blessing, son of Matitya from Brescia Ashkenazi, of blessed memory, gathered to his people on Friday 19 Nisan* [*of the year* ...]. The final lacuna is because secondary use had been made of the stone.

he himself composed.[22] During S. Simonsohn's studies in Mantua in 1952/53 he and Vittore Colorni found in Mantua, in a shop selling building material not far from the cemetery, the cylindrical pillar of Zacuto, already mutilated but not as it is at the present. They bought it, in order to transfer it to the Jewish cemetery in Mantua. But when I recently researched the tombstones of that ancient cemetery of Mantua, it was missing. The stone had previously disappeared in the second half of the nineteenth century, when Abba Appelbaum, author of a book on the kabbalist (*Moshe Zakut*, published in Lvov in 1926), had asked the chief rabbi of Mantua, Marco Mortara, for the tombstone of Zacuto, and Mortara had said that it was lost. During my researches in 2007, I was informed that the Diocesan Museum of Mantua possessed two funerary Hebrew cylindrical pillars in Hebrew. I went to check these and fortunately rediscovered Zacuto's mutilated tombstone. Another cylindrical pillar, found in Mantua, had been re-used to act as a support of the missal in a Catholic

22 D. Bregman, *I Raise my Heart: Poems by Moses Zacuto* (Hebrew; Jerusalem: Ben Zvi, 2009), pp. 8, 367–434, and her Hebrew article 'Dimness and Clarity in *Tofteh Aruch* by Rabbi Moses Zacuto', *Pe'amim*, 96 (2003), pp. 35–52.

Fig. 26: The wrongly written and consequently unfinished tombstone of Ya'aqov Ḥayyim dalla Volta, who died in 1735. It was re-used in 1950 as the base of a barbecue in a house located in what had once been the area of the old Jewish cemetery of Mantua.

chapel in a village near Mantua (Fig. 26). The text surviving at the bottom of the pillar contains only the last four lines out of a total of thirteen and is presented below. The first lines are in prose, and contain the information about the death of the leading kabbalist. There follows an ottava rima ending in AB AB AB CC, with A -*'u*, B -*ver* and C -*hah*.

מצבת קבורת הרב הגדול שברבנים
המקובל החסיד והקדוש מרנא ורבנא
משה זכות זצוק"ל אשר נסע
למנוחה ועזב אותנו לאנחות
יום ב' סכות התנ"ח

1. הָעוֹבְרִים עִמְדוּ וְאַל תִּפְרְעוּ
2. שִׂימוּ לְבַבְכֶם אֶל קְבוּרַת גֶּבֶר
3. גָּבַר בְּעוֹז עַל כָּל אֲשֶׁר נוֹדָעוּ
4. בַּסּוֹד וּבַנִּגְלֶה וּמַשְׁבִּיר [23] שֶׁבֶר [24]

23 Prov 11:26.
24 Gen 42:1–2.

5. כָּל שׁוֹמְעָיו יִשְׁתַּעְשְׁעוּ יִשְׂבָּעוּ
6. עַל כֵּן שְׂפָתָיו דּוֹבְבוֹת בַּקֶּבֶר
7. עוֹמֵד כְּמוֹ *מֹשֶׁה* בְּעֵת הַדַּחַק
8. לָנוּ *זְכוּתוֹ* יַעֲמוֹד בַּשַּׁחַק

12.4 The wrong and consequently unfinished tombstone of Ya'aqov Ḥayyim Dalla Volta (d. 1735)

On July 26, 2008, I went to Mantua to visit the location of the ancient Jewish cemetery, in the Gradaro quarter of the city, where the Jewish community buried its dead from its foundation until the end of eighteenth century. I had been informed of the existence of a *maṣeva* which had been re-used in 1950 by the owner of an house as the base of a barbecue (Fig. 27). The precious fireplace obtained by re-using a seventeenth-century tombstone was located at *vicolo* Maestro no. 10, in Mantua. Having arrived there, I started to clean the upper part of the stone, on to which had been engraved the Hebrew text of a epitaph

Fig. 27: Detail from the text on the epitaph of the tombstone of the Mantua Jewish pharmacist Ya'aqov Ḥayyim Dalla Volta (from Volta Mantovana in Mantua Province), unfinished because the engraver erroneously sculpted *qevuvat* instead of *qevurat*.

Fig. 28: The cylindrical pillar, found recently in Mantua, which had once been the tombstone of Yehoshua ben Mahalalel Norsa, banker in Mantua where he died on 16 December 1713. It had been re-used as a support for the Gospel volume in a Catholic chapel in a village near Mantua.

(Fig. 28). When the marble was cleaned, I could read the text, starting on line 1 with a standard formula commonly used in epitaphs:

מצבת קבובת (sic!) היקר איש תם וישר
כמה"ר יעקב חיים מלאוולטה ז"ל
נפטר לעולמו ביום שני בסיון
התצ"ה ליצירה תנצב"ה

Ya'aqov Dalla Volta died on 2 Siwan of the Jewish year 5495 which, according the Gregorian Calendar, was 23 May of the Christian year 1735. Finally, the last four lines, in rhyme and rhythm, also became legible. This part, celebrating the virtues and the goodness of the dead, was written in poetry, according to an alternate rhyme scheme: A-B, A-B, in which A ends in *-im* and B ends in *-ov*. The Hebrew text of the tombstone reads:

1. אִם יַעֲקֹב שִׁמְךָ וְעוֹד חַיִּים
2. לֹא עַל פְּנֵי תֵבֵל תְּקַו טוּב רָב
3. כִּי רַק בְּאוֹר עֶלְיוֹן בְּעֵץ חַיִּים
שָׁם תֶּהֱסֶה תָּמִיד {בְּשָׁלוֹם רָב}[25]

The poem has ten syllables, alternating rhymes, and metrical structure that twice has two long vowels followed by a short and long, and then two long vowels (*mahir*).

English version:
Prose part*:*

> Tombstone of the dear *right and perfect man* (Job 1:1) / the honoured R. Ya'aqov Ḥayyim Dalla Volta, may his memory be blessed, / who died on 2 Siwan / 5495 of the creation, may his soul be bound in the bundle of life. /

Poetic part*:*

> If Ya'aqov is your name and, in addition, Ḥayyim, / not on the face of the earth can you expect great good, but only in the light of God and in the tree of the life / there you will find refuge forever in an everlasting peace.

Comment:

I was surprised to see that the engraved text of the epitaph started from about the middle of the *maṣeva*, leaving the upper part unwritten and unfinished. This appeared to me fairly strange. Perhaps the engraver had intended

25 The last two word are not completely legible, being partially walled in, and consequently they are conjecturally reconstructed, according to rhyme and rhythm requirements.

to add in the upper part a decoration, an ornamentation or even a family stemma. If so, why he did not finish his work? After these considerations, I realized that the word for sepulchre in Hebrew *qevurat*, was wrongly engraved as קבובת instead of the correct קבורת. I found it difficult to believe that such an error had been made but finally accepted that the engraver had written a *bet* instead of the required *resh*. At that point I imagined the scene. Normally in Italy the engraving of *maṣevot* was not done by Jews, but by Christian artisans who obviously did not know Hebrew, but only knew the shape of the Hebrew letters, after having sculpted them for years. The engraver who prepared the tombstones for the deceased of the populous Jewish community of Mantua, which at that time numbered about two thousand people, had his shop next to the cemetery. He engraved the inscriptions by copying a model prepared by a rabbi or by a learned member of the community capable of composing poems in rhymes. After he had finished his work, he called the relatives to choose what they wished to place in the upper part of the *maṣeva* as an element of ornamentation or a family stemma. When, in this case, the relatives of the deceased arrived, they read the inscription and noticed the mistake *qevuvat* in the text. Of course it was unfeasible to repair the error. It would have been easy to transform a *resh* into a *bet* adding a horizontal line at its base, but it was simply impossible to do the opposite and correct a *bet* into a *resh*. Consequently, the only solution was to engrave a new tombstone with the correct text. So the upper half of the incorrectly engraved tombstone remained unfinished and, as a consequence, it was never placed in the cemetery to mark the tomb of the rich Mantua pharmacist, Ya'aqov Dalla Volta. A new tombstone with the correct text was engraved and placed in the cemetery, but it was lost together with the majority of the sepulchral inscriptions. Our wrong *maṣeva* was stored in the engraver's shop, in the hope that it could at some stage be used for a new different inscription on the reverse side and placed in a wall. But this never happened, and it was abandoned on that site from 1735 until 1950, when Mr Rodolfo Grizzi bought the house and its garden where the engraver's shop had been, and re-used it as a basis for his barbecue.

To conclude, significant work remains to be done in order to save this precious Jewish heritage (Figs. 29 and 30), and it is of enormous importance to transmit to future generations the memory contained in these stones.[26]

---

26 The author of this article is deeply grateful to Professor Dvora Bregman and Professor Yaakov Bentolila for their important assistance with the transcription, presentation and pointing of the poetic texts cited above.

Fig. 29: The tombstone of Menaḥem ben Avraham da Ventura, Jewish banker in Bologna where he died on 3 Tammuz 1555; sculpted in the magnificent style of the Renaissance and of the humanistic *Zeitgeist* of the mid-16th century, the tombstone is kept in the Medieval Museum of Bologna.

Fig. 30: The tombstone of Shabbetai Elḥanan da Rieti, a leading Jew of Bologna, who died on Monday 23 Elul 1546, in the monumental style of that period with angels and fantastic figures. The large blocks in the lower part perhaps evoke those of the western wall in the Herodian basement of the Temple in Jerusalem, depicted in funerary monuments according to a style that is also found on some Italian *maṣevot* in subsequent centuries. The tombstone is kept in the Medieval Museum of Bologna.

Minna Rozen

Romans in Istanbul Part 1: Historical and Literary Introduction

This article considers several possible avenues of research arising from the systematic study of large cemeteries, and combines the resultant findings with knowledge derived from other sources. The material used in this study was assembled and processed from four cemeteries in Istanbul where Jews were buried during the Ottoman era: Hasköy, Ortaköy, Kuzguncuk, and the Italian cemetery in Şişli.[1] But the sheer abundance of that material obliged us to choose a single case study that would best serve as an examplar. The case that we selected is a specific group from the Jewish community of Istanbul, with the surname of 'Romano', and one of its branches in particular, whose members were buried in the Hasköy cemetery and were known by the name 'Roman'. 'Roman' or 'Romano' is a generic name referring to one who comes from the city of Rome. This identification of the source of the name is supported, for example, by the commentary of Immanuel the Roman (*'Immanuel Ha-Romi*, 1270–*c.* 1328) on the Book of Proverbs, which makes reference to his brother Yehuda ben Moshe Romano.[2] In several sources, the name appears as 'Roman', a shortened form characteristic of Italian surnames. Thus, the name of the well-known family of printers, Soncino, appears in Istanbul with a different spelling than the accepted form in Italy, reflecting the way it was pronounced in Istanbul, Ṣonṣino; but in the various Hebrew sources, it also appears as Ṣonṣin. In the Veneto region of Italy, such shortened forms appear frequently among the Christians, e.g., Bragadin for Bragadino, Margaran for Margarano, and the like.[3] Inscriptions in the Jewish cemetery of Venice testify to ties with the 'Roman' family.[4] The name 'Romano' or 'Roman' also appears

1 Documentation Project of Turkish and Balkan Jewry, Computerized Database of Jewish Cemeteries in Turkey (Tel Aviv: Goldstein-Goren Diaspora Research Center, Tel Aviv University) (hereafter: TAU DP).

2 Printed in Naples in 1487, and published in facsimile by the Jewish National and University Library, and Magnes Press in 1981, with an introduction by David Goldstein; see that Introduction, pp. 9, 14, 15, 21.

3 Minna Rozen, 'Metropolis and Necropolis: The Cultivation of Social Status among the Jews of Istanbul in the Seventeenth and Eighteenth Centuries', in Rozen, *A Journey Through Civilizations: Chapters in the History of Istanbul Jewry*, 1453–1923, (Brepols, forthcoming).

4 Aldo Luzzato, *La communità ebraica di Venezia e il suo antico cimitero* (Milano: Edizioni Polifilo, 2000), pp. 568–71.

among non-Jews from Rome who lived in other parts of Italy,[5] and is sometimes used simply to indicate ties to the ruling powers of the Roman Empire.[6] Since 'Roman' or 'Romano' is a generic surname, we cannot conclude that all who went by this name in Istanbul were from one family, and we should treat with caution any family-tree drawn up on the basis of material assembled from the city's cemeteries.

This being the case, what exactly can the material at our disposal tell us? To answer this question, it is necessary to supplement the information derived from the cemetery with external sources. The more plentiful the latter, the richer the portrait of the past that emerges from the cemetery. It is important to note that the picture can never be complete, for the types of sources at our disposal are not of equal quantity or quality; likewise, parts of certain sources were destroyed over time, so that the remaining material is liable to provide us with a somewhat distorted impression. It is thus imperative that we combine the knowledge derived from the cemetery with that obtained outside its walls; and though that too can yield only partial answers, these latter can certainly be instructive and bring us closer to a picture of the past.

In approaching our topic, the following questions should be considered:

- How far did the families bearing the surname Romano spread?
- From when did families with the surname Romano reside in Istanbul?
- Was there a common denominator for the locations where the Romanos resided in Istanbul?
- Can we identify the family burial plots of the Romanos?
- What can the epitaphs teach us about the values and life circumstances of the dead and those who mourned them?
- What knowledge can be gleaned from the material aspects of the tombstones?
- What can we learn by merging the information derived from the tombstones with that drawn from other sources?

Let us now examine each of these questions in turn.

5 Thus, for example, a non-Jew named 'Piero Roman' appears in a discussion between two Jews regarding the payment of taxes in Casale Monferrato in the fifteenth century. See R. Yosef Colon, *Responsa*, D. Pines edition (Jerusalem: A. Joseph, 1970), sec. 37.

6 See, for example, the fictitious correspondence etween King Virsuris and Alphonso the 'righteous' regarding his investigations in the libraries of Rome: 'Booklet of Marcus Consul Romano who sits in judgement on the Jews in Jerusalem' (Salomone Aben Verga, *Liber Schevet Jehuda*, ed. by M. Wiener [Hannover: Carol Rümpler, 1855], sec. 64, p. 97).

1 How far did the families bearing the surname Romano spread?

The dispersal of the Romano family took place quite early, and extended beyond what later became the boundaries of the Ottoman Empire; most certainly, it followed at some point the general arrival of the Jews in Rome. In addition to the aforementioned Immanuel the Roman and his brother Yehuda Romano, from the thirteenth century, we find the following statement at the end of the *Tosefot Ha-Rosh* (*bḤul.* 141b): 'I, Mordekhai son of R. Menaḥem (may God protect and redeem him), known as Romano, have written these addenda for myself in the state of Tulitula, and completed them on the fourth day [of the week], the tenth day of the month of Shevaṭ in the year 5106'. In other words, Mordekhai ben Menaḥem of Rome completed these addenda on 12 January 1346, in the city of Toledo, Spain. It should be recalled that if the descendants of the author of these addenda found their way to Istanbul after the Expulsion of 1492, they carried the name Romano, though it is most likely that from a cultural standpoint they were by then distinctly Spanish.

If we consider the Mediterranean Basin as a whole in the late Middle Ages and the dawn of the modern era, it becomes clear that what is true of the city of Istanbul is true of the larger region as well. We have available to us two types of sources: in addition to the epitaphs, there are onomastic materials derived from the community records, Hebrew legal and other documents, poetry, homiletic literature, and commentary, as well as archival material of non-Jewish provenance. Obviously, both types of documents, separately and together, do not offer a consummate picture of the dispersion of the Jews of Rome in the Mediterranean Basin in general and the Ottoman Empire in particular, for the same reasons enumerated above concerning Istanbul.

The computerized catalogue of tombstones of Turkish Jewry, which comprises 60,000 tombstones from 1582 to 1991, includes 248 stones with the name Romano or Roman. A total of 227 of these tombstones are found in Istanbul, thirteen in Izmir,[7] three in Edirne, three in Bodrum, one in Çorlu, and one in Tekirdağ. Of 7,157 marriages registered in Istanbul between the years 1903 and

7 It is important to note that the 'old' cemetery of Izmir is in fact new and burials apparently began there only in 1880. The ancient cemetery in Bahrı Baba, which existed from the seventeenth century, was destroyed in the city's development, and it is possible that there were additional Romano family tombstones there. Shmuel Roman of Izmir is also mentioned in 1617 in Izmir. *Responsa of the Maharit* [R. Yosef ben Moshe Mi-Trani], part II (Tel Aviv, 1959; facsimile, Lemberg, 1861), Even Ha-'Ezer, sec. 43; *New Responsa of the Maharitaṣ* [R. Yom Ṭov Ṣahalon] (Jerusalem: Jerusalem Institute, 1981), sec. 25.

1922, 59 individuals bore the name Romano. There are numerous Romanos in the Jewish communities of Bulgaria, in particular Sofia and Plovdiv.[8] In the birth registry of the Belgrade community, which includes a total of 7,623 births from 1819 to 1941, by contrast, only two Romanos are listed. The marriage registry of this same community, which numbers 2,859 records covering the period from 1864 to 1941, contains ten Romanos. The death listings of that community, which begin in 1888 and end in April 1941, and comprise 1,574 deaths, show only two Romanos. Similarly, we find small numbers of them in Serbia, Bosnia, and northwestern Greece (Macedonia and Epirus).[9] We find one Romano in Cyprus at the end of the 16th century.[10] And in 1683, a *dayyan* (Jewish religious-court judge) by the name of Yisrael Romano is mentioned in Egypt.[11] From the late eighteenth century, we find references to members of the Romano or Romani family in Benghazi, Libya.[12] A number of the family members are buried in the Mount of Olives cemetery in Jerusalem.[13] The earliest mentions of the name that we have in our possession from the Ottoman era are from Istanbul, Epirus, Thrace, and Macedonia; in Thrace, the name appears mostly in Edirne, while in Macedonia, most of the instances are found in Salonika. If we may here generalize, it can be assumed that the majority of people bearing this surname but living in other places emigrated from the above locations. In any event, most of the examples available to us should be treated as secondary and tertiary emigrants (or beyond).

8 Among the Jews of Bulgaria too, the common assumption was that those bearing the name Romano originated from Rome (H. Keshales, *History of the Jews of Bulgaria* [Hebrew], pt. 1 [Tel Aviv: Davar, 1971], p. 241). A few examples of such members of the Romano family are given in Appendix 1 below.

9 Romanos in these centres are exemplified in Appendix 2 below.

10 R. Eliyahu ibn Ḥayyim, *Responsa* (Jerusalem, 1960), sec. 31.

11 R. Mordekhai Halevi, *Responsa Darkhei No'am* (Jerusalem, 1970; facsimile, Venice 1697), *Ḥoshen Mishpaṭ*, sec. 56–57; see also R. Avraham ben Mordekhai Halevi, *Responsa Ginat Veradim* (Jerusalem, 1970; facsimile Istanbul, 1716), EH 3:8; R. Ya'aqov Faraji, *Responsa* (Jerusalem, 1999), sec. 23, 61.

12 See http://www.roumanifamily.co.il

13 R. Asher Leib Brisk, *Ḥelqat Meḥoqeq*, pt. I (Jerusalem, 1901), p. 7. In the section for Jews from Rouse, Bulgaria, in the Mount of Olives cemetery in Jerusalem, Sara de Romano bat Ya'aqov Medini is buried (d. 1897). The burial of Yehoshu'a (1814) is mentioned in the book's index (ibid., p. 1) (line 15, sec. 17). Also mentioned (ibid., p. 3) without a year of burial but in proximity to tombstones from 1827, and among graves of Jews from Istanbul and Bursa, are the graves of Yosef Romano, Señora de Elia Romano, and Elia Romano himself (line 17, sec. 13, 14, 15). In a group of graves of the Medina family, the graves of Rivqa de Romano and Reina de Romano are mentioned (ibid., p. 4, line 18, sec. 23 and 26). Alongside them are tombstones from the 1820s.

2 From when did families with the surname Romano reside in Istanbul?

An overview of the material before us indicates that in the sixteenth and seventeenth centuries, the majority of the Jews by the name of Roman or Romano who migrated in the direction of the Ottoman Empire settled in Istanbul, from where they spread far and wide. In relating to the findings of the Istanbul cemeteries, we must bear in mind that the ancient Jewish cemetery in Balat was built over by new construction in the 1950s, and that of Kasım Paşa seems already to have fallen into ruin in the late sixteenth century. Consequently, we are unable to date the earliest presence of the Roman-Romano families in Istanbul based on cemetery findings. In the late 15th century, even before the Spanish Expulsion, there were already Jews in the city who had come from various parts of Italy, but it is not possible to determine precisely from where.[14] The earliest Roman family tombstone that we discovered is that of Kalomira, wife of David Romano, who died on 20 Tammuz 5343 (10 July 1583). Her burial was apparently one of the first at the Hasköy cemetery, which was inaugurated by sultanic decree in November 1582. Like the other tombstones from this and subsequent decades, it is a simple stone bearing a brief inscription that reveals little about the deceased [Photograph No. 1].[15]

3 Was there a common denominator for the locations where the Romanos resided in Istanbul?

Of the 227 tombstones of people bearing the surname Romano in Istanbul, 131 are found in the Hasköy cemetery; 82, in the cemetery in Kuzguncuk (on the Asian side of the Bosphorus Strait); 13, in Ortaköy (on the European side of the Bosphorus); and 6, in the cemetery of the 'Italian' foreign community, in the Şişli quarter.

---

14 See, for example, the mention of Q. Q. [Qahal Qadosh] Talian (corruption of 'Italian') in Istanbul by R. Eliyahu Capsali as quoted in the *Responsa of R. Yosef Colon* (Venice, 1519), sec. 83, p. 84b. See also M. Benayahu, *Rabbi Eliyahu Capsali of Crete, Chief Rabbi and Historian* (Hebrew; Tel Aviv: Diaspora Research Institute, 1983), pp. 28–29. The quote makes reference to anti-Jewish rioting that took place prior to 1480, the year that R. Yosef Colon died.

15 See on this topic: Minna Rozen, *Hasköy Cemetery: Typology of Stones* (Tel Aviv: Tel Aviv University and The Center for Judaic Studies, University of Pennsylvania, 1994), pt. I, p. 14.

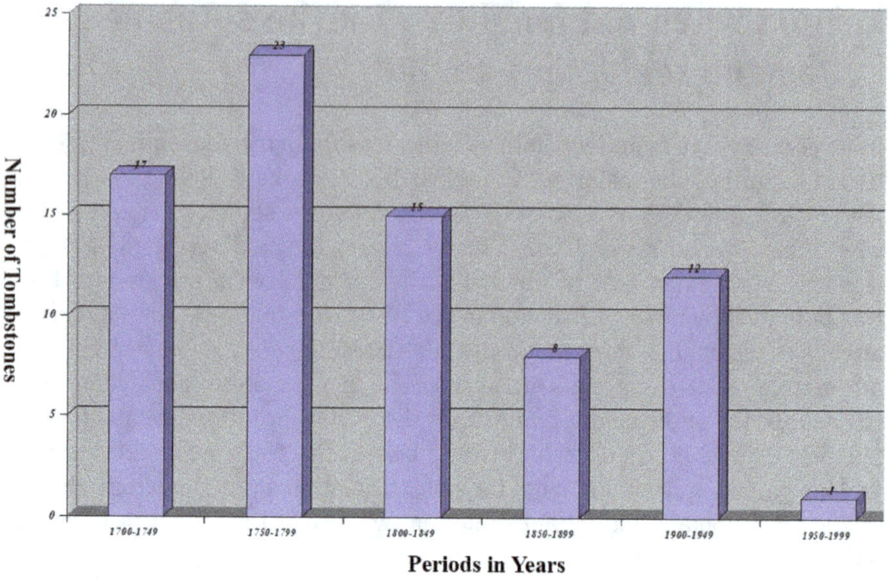

Fig. 1: Breakdown of the tombstones of Romano family in the Kuzguncuk Cemetery, by period.

The burial of individuals with the surname Romano in the Kuzguncuk cemetery apparently began at the start of the eighteenth century;[16] the earliest Romano burial there for which we have a precise date is that of Alta Donna (Italian for 'exalted lady')[17], wife of Nissim Romano, who died of the plague on 22 Ḥeshvan 5465 (20 November 1704) [Photograph No. 2]. The earliest tombstone that we discovered in the Ortaköy cemetery bearing an exact date is that of Rivqa, widow of Shelomo Romano, who died on 19 Elul 5477 (26 August 1717). The conclusion that emerges from this material is that the familial-geographical ties of the emigrants were closely connected with their area of residence in Istanbul, even generations after the migration. During the sixteenth and seventeenth centuries, the place of residence of the emigrants from the province of Rome and their descendants was clearly the Hasköy neighbourhood, and they began to relocate to other neighbourhoods only in the mid-seventeenth century at the earliest, with their new destination being primarily the Kuzguncuk neighbourhood. Ostensibly, this migration can shed light on

16 See Photograph No. 1, above.

17 The Italian origin of this name is substantiated by Shlomo Simonsohn's study *Between Scylla and Charybdis: The Jews of Sicily* (Hebrew; Jerusalem: Magnes Press, 2011), pp. 347, 400–401, 476, 478, 483, 485–86, 489.

Fig. 2: Aynalı Kavak Kasrı [The Palace of Mirrors].

the socio-economic status of these families. Until 1660, Hasköy was characterized by residents of high social and economic standing. Members of ancient families in the city, who were repelled by the overcrowding in the Jewish neighbourhood near the palace walls, built themselves spacious homes in Hasköy,[18] which was the private property of the Sultan and, as such, enjoyed favourable treatment during the early centuries of Ottoman rule. Mehmet the Conqueror ordered the planting of 12,000 cypress trees, and orchards of peaches and pears, on its hills sloping down to the Golden Horn, and Sultan Ahmet I (16032–1618) built his Palace of Mirrors, Aynalı Kavak Kasrı, near the orchards.

In the sixteenth century, the neighbourhood was described as having 3,000 splendid homes, some on the waterfront and a number of them sur-

18 See for example the actions of the family of Lady Khrisula the Karaite during the sixteenth and seventeenth centuries. Minna Rozen, 'The Trust of Lady Khrisula of Istanbul: Urban Reality and Dynastic Continuity', in Rozen, *Journey Through Civilizations*, forthcoming.

Fig. 3: Seafront homes in Kuzguncuk, in the nineteenth century.

rounded by expansive fruit gardens, with some even boasting greenhouses where oranges and lemons were grown. The Hamon family, physicians to the Sultan, built a two-story stone house there. Following the fires that struck the ancient Jewish Quarter near Topkapı palace in 1569 and 1589, many elected to rent out their destroyed properties and build a new home in Hasköy. [19] But from 1660 onward, again after a huge fire that consumed the old Jewish quarter, Hasköy was inundated with thousands of Jews, and its character was drastically altered. Originally a village on the outskirts of the city, it became the largest Jewish quarter in Greater Istanbul, with all that that implied. For the next two hundred years, Hasköy became a place of the lower classes, and ultimately, the quintessential slum neighbourhood of Jewish Istanbul.[20]

This was, more or less, the point at which the Jews began to relocate to Kuzguncuk, on the Asian side of the Bosphorus. This now became the stylish neighbourhood where wealthy Jews resided, at first only in the summer months, and later, year-round, in magnificent villas on the seashore (*yalılar*, in Turkish). This movement of populations testifies to the social standing of the Romano families in the city.

19 Minna Rozen and Benjamin Arbel, 'Great Fire in the Metropolis: The Case of the Istanbul Conflagration of 1569 and its Description by Marcantonio Barbara' in *Mamluks and Ottoman: Studies in Honour of Michael Winter*, ed. by David Wasserstein and Ami Ayalon (New York: Routledge, 2005), pp. 134–63.

20 On the Hasköy neighbourhood, see: M. Rozen, *A History of the Jewish Community in Istanbul: The Formative Years, 1453–1566* (Leiden, Boston: Brill, 2002), pp. 216–17.

4 Can we identify the family burial plots of the Romanos?

A thorough examination of all tombstones bearing the name Roman or Romano in Istanbul's Jewish cemeteries offers some idea of the ties within this group, and between the Romanos and Jews from other places of origin, in the neighbourhoods where they resided. In Hasköy, the primary neighbourhood inhabited by the Romanos, we were able to identify several major blocs of family members. One of the first methods of identification is through burial plots. In the first centuries of the Hasköy cemetery's existence, distinguished families would purchase burial plots that would be sufficient for several generations; this was a sign of status, no less than a splendid mansion.[21]

It should be recalled that due to damage to the cemetery over the generations, tombstones were moved, washed away, relocated, or uprooted, so that the picture that meets our eyes is not an exact one; nonetheless, it can be indicative of trends. In our field work, we divided the cemetery into sections of 25 square metres; thus, the presence of a group of stones bearing the same family name within a given section can attest to chronological proximity in death, but apparently also to family ties. In many instances, this is substantiated by the inscription on the tombstone. Out of 131 Roman or Romano tombstones in Hasköy, we can see on the map before us [Map 1] concentrations of tombstones, consisting in most cases of the nuclear family only.

Of particular interest is the concentration of tombstones bearing the shortened version of the surname (Roman) in section 6-5 and in the adjacent section 5-5, which is reminiscent of the pattern of the family residences in life. This would appear to be a group whose members all have blood or marriage ties [Map 2].

The first woman with the surname Roman to be buried in Hasköy (or at least, the earliest one whose grave we found) was Mazal Ṭov, wife of Mevorakh Roman, who died in 1641. Near her is the tombstone of her elderly husband, who died on 10 Av 5403 (26 July 1643) [Photograph No. 3]. Adjacent to them is their niece, a young betrothed woman, Mazal Ṭov bat Teshuva Roman, who was only 15 years old when she died on 22 Ḥeshvan 5404 (2 November 1643) [Photograph No. 4]. Her bereaved parents passed away not long after her. We were unable to find the father's tombstone, but we did locate that of her mother near her: Simḥa, widow of Teshuva Roman, who died on 4 Iyar 5404

---

21 See for example: Rozen, *Hasköy Cemetery*, pt. I, pp. 48–51; pt. II, pp. 245–52; R. Yeḥiel Basan, *Responsa* (Istanbul, 1737), sec. 21, p. 31a.

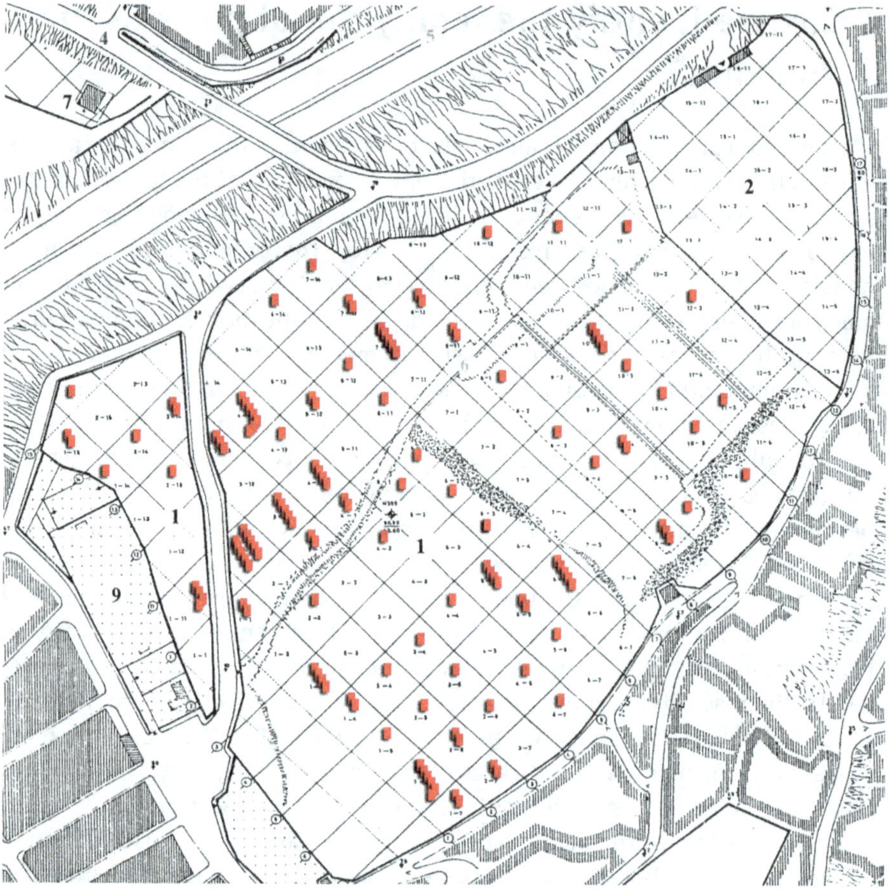

Map 1: Distribution of the Romanos in Hasköy Cemetery, 1582–1989.

(10 May 1644) [Photograph No. 5]. Four years later, on 18 Tevet 5408 (13 January 1648), Sulṭana bat Teshuva ben Moshe Roman, third cousin of Mazal Ṭov and wife of Shelomo Hamon, died [Photograph No. 8]. Near her is buried Mazal Ṭov's second cousin, Mevorakh ben Moshe Roman, d. 6 Ḥeshvan 5409 (23 October 1648) [Photograph No. 10]. Also close to her grave are those of Teshuva ben Mevorakh Roman, who died childless on 18 Adar II 5426 (25 March 1666) [Photograph No. 11], and Reina bat Yiṣḥaq Roman, who died on 18 Tishrei 5436 (7 October 1675) [Photograph No. 12].

The tombstones of two members of the Roman family are found in other sections. One is in a pile of gravestones heaped together when a section of the cemetery was flattened to make way for old-new graves transferred from the

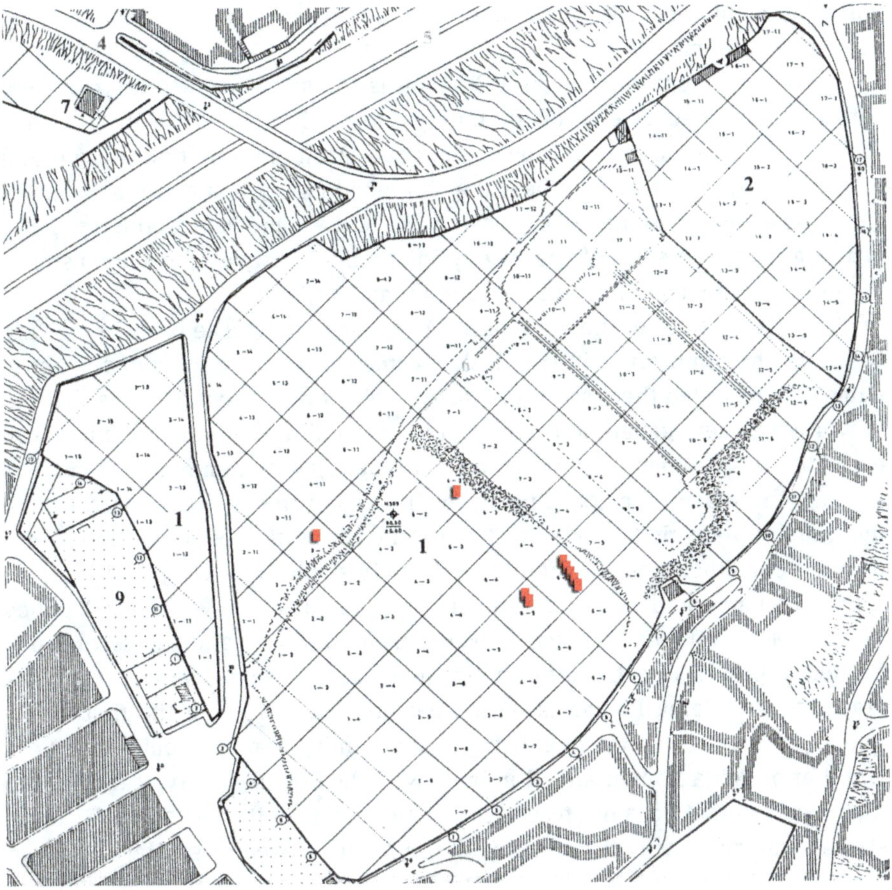

Map 2: Distribution of the Roman family in Hasköy Cemetery, 1582–1703.

area where the ring road around Istanbul was laid (section 6-2);[22] the other is in a distant section (3-1). The latter is the stone of Kalomira, wife of Aharon Roman, who died giving birth to twins, together with the infants, on 22 Ḥeshvan 5444 (12 November 1683) [Photograph No. 13]; the former, the grave of Kalomira bat Aharon Roman, who died on 23 Tishrei 5464 (3 October 1703) [Photograph No. 15]. This indicates that the unfortunate Aharon Roman remarried after the death of his first wife, Kalomira. He had a daughter named Kadın, who did not live long, dying on Sunday, 26 Adar I 5451 (25 March 1691) [Photograph No. 14]. Subsequently, another daughter was born to him, whom he

22 *Hasköy Cemetery*, pt. I, pp. 8–11; plate 1 on p. 1, plate 2 on p. 3, plate 3 on p. 5.

named after his first wife, Kalomira. He did not live to see her marry, dying during her lifetime.

Kalomira, daughter of Aharon Roman, is the last person in the cemetery with the shortened version of the family name. After her death in 1703, this form of the name no longer appears. It is our assumption that all those found in the Hasköy cemetery who bear the shortened family name are members of the same extended family. The repeated use of the same names, the proximity of the graves, the style of the inscriptions, and the style of the tombstones themselves draw a connection between them.

Two family trees of the Romans are presented below. The parts in grey are based on the tombstones in the Hasköy cemetery, and the individuals whose names are recorded there share marital and blood ties. The names highlighted in white represent generations who were not found in the cemetery but whose existence was reconstructed based on traditional Jewish naming patterns. The sections that have no colour appear in the second tree and are based on the literature of the period; in such instances, the connection between the individuals is sometimes not sufficiently well-established. For example, Reina bat Yiṣḥaq Roman could be the grandchild of either Ḥizqiyya Roman or Ya'aqov Roman. Moreover, the connection between the first tree and the second tree cannot be proven directly but only by circumstantial evidence: (1) location of gravestones – Reina Roman is buried near the Romans from the first family tree; (2) style of epitaphs – the epitaphs of the individuals in Family Tree No. 1 and that of Reina Roman are all imbued with the Sefardi poetry of the Golden Age, in a way that does not resemble other epitaphs in the cemetery; (3) social status – members of both branches of the family moved in similar social circles.

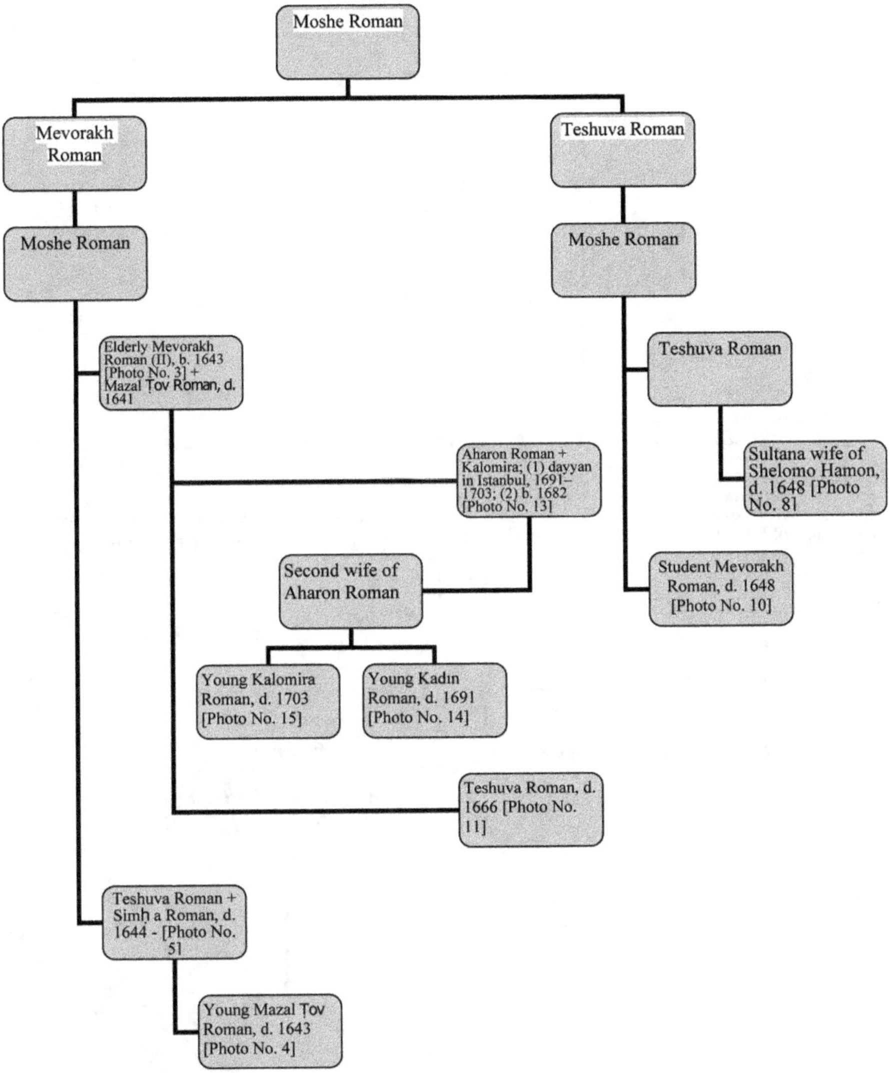

Family Tree 1: A. The Roman family in Hasköy Cemetery (generations highlighted in white are reconstructed).

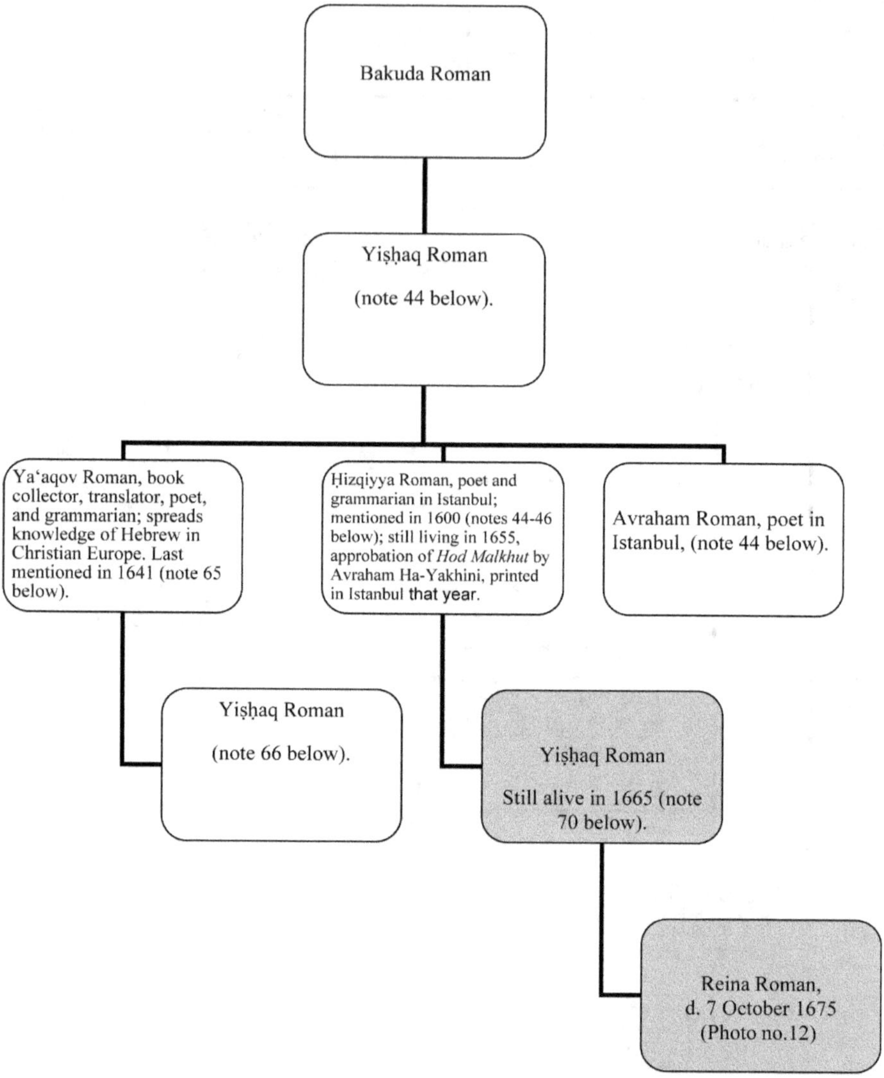

Family Tree 1: B. The Roman family in Istanbul.

5 What can the epitaphs teach us about the values and life circumstances of the dead and those who mourned them?

An examination of the tombstones of both branches of the Roman family, as outlined above, points to the great effort and expense invested in the epitaphs. Lengthy and intricate inscriptions such as these are a sure indication of wealthy and distinguished figures. The high quality and distinctive nature of the epitaphs may also allude to a connection between the two Roman branches depicted in the two family trees; and if we take into account the information derived from external sources on the presence of poets in the family, there are grounds for speculating that the inscriptions were 'homemade'. The richness of the poetry engraved in the family tombstones is particularly noticeable when compared with the stone of Mikri, wife of Yiṣḥaq Hamon [Photograph No. 19]; Mikri was the beloved spouse of a wealthy and powerful man, but not to the extent of purchasing poetry on her behalf such as that found on the Roman family stones. In order to merit such epitaphs, one needed to belong to the Roman family.

On virtually all of these tombstones, we find original poems not seen in the cemetery beforehand, ripe with rich and eloquent images based on the skilful interweaving of biblical passages and fragments of verses, allusions to *midrashim*, and biblical commentary. In several instances, we see conventions similar, or identical, to those of the Sefardi Golden Age poetry.

The inscription on the tombstone of the elderly Mevorakh Roman [Photograph No. 3] directs the following message to passersby: 'As witness to all who will ask: Whose burial cave is this? Think of the end of each and every man, to be chiseled in stone and wrapped in a cloth shroud'; in other words, this is the human state, since we all must hearken to God. The letters inscribed in the stone have no purpose other than to instruct man to worship God. Nonetheless, passers-by will know that every man should feel the pain of his father's death, and especially a father like Mevorakh Roman, who, it is clear, was a good father, and benevolent to all his extended family. Thus the inscription combines acquiescence to the Divine decree, and the duty to uphold God's commandments, with the pain and sorrow felt by all members of his family over the death of a beloved patriarch. All these meanings are understood only when we break down the inscription into the biblical passages of which it is composed, and fully explore their interpretation.

No less elegant is the inscription on the tombstone of Mevorakh Roman's niece, Mazal Ṭov bat Teshuva Roman [Photograph No. 4]. Unlike the inscription on her uncle's stone, there is here no acceptance of fate but a profound sense that the life of her parents has been stripped of all meaning with the death of their beautiful daughter, their first and only offspring, betrothed but not yet married when her life was cut short. The inscription begins with the words: 'This will be called a headstone', which apparently allude to the tombstone itself. But when we pursue the source of the term *even ha-rosha* [literally, 'head stone'] and the *midrashim* concerning its meaning, the expression takes on a deeper meaning. The headstone was the final stone placed at the apex of an arch or dome, as constructed before the introduction of iron. If the headstone was removed, the structure collapsed.

At the same time, according to the *Midrash Tanḥuma*, the headstone is the stone on which the biblical Jacob placed his head when he lay down to sleep en route to Haran.[23] That night, he dreamed his famous dream in which a ladder was set on the ground and its top reached the sky, with angels ascending and descending upon it. There, his inheritance, the Land of Israel, was promised to him. The stone under his head was thus the foundation of Jacob's house and his legacy. Hence, the headstone in the epitaph of the young Mazal Ṭov is the opposite of what it was intended to be. Their only daughter was supposed to be the cornerstone of her parents' existence; and now, by dying before she had fulfilled her destiny of perpetuating their lineage, she had taken from them any reason to live. Their lives had become a useless burden for them.

When the mother of Mazal Ṭov died approximately one year after her daughter's death, she was already referred to as 'the widow of the wise and exalted Teshuva Roman' [Photograph No. 5], meaning that the young woman's father had died a short time after her, and before the death of her mother. Indeed, the grief-stricken father and mother did not live long after the death of their only daughter.

For the mother's epitaph, the poet employed a series of contrasts: The woman was a daughter of kings – an allusion to her lofty origins – but her privileged status did not prevent time from digging 'a pit and a trench in place of burnt and meal offerings, and instead of clothing embroidered with gold mountings, there is a groan, and instead of beaten-work, there is a scream'. The 'burnt and meal offerings' could be referring to what should have been her lot as a daughter of kings, but also to the wedding festivities of her daughter, which did not take place. The poet uses verses that portray a king's daughter secluded in her home, dressed in a garment inlaid with gold; but she is of course concealed in the earth, and instead of clothing embroidered with gold

23 According to Zech 4:7; *Midrash Tanḥuma* (ed. Buber, Vilna: Romm, 1885), *Parashat Toledot*, sec. 20, s.v. *ketiv shir* (Gen 28).

there is a moan of grief. He goes on to allude to the fate of the beloved daughters of Jerusalem at the time of the city's destruction – instead of the upswept hair of a proud young woman comes a shriek of pain.

The use of plays on biblical phrases also continues in the next parallelism, in which the author uses the expression *sar menuḥa* [quartermaster] (Jer 51:59), that is, the king's companion for pleasure and amusement (according to the Radaq's interpretation), turning it into *sha'ar menuḥa* [a gate of rest], which collapses at the sight of the woman's tragedy. The reference is doubtless to the death of her only daughter, which caused her own demise and led to the end of the days of rejoicing, the days of her life. When the poet speaks of the woman whom God rebuked, he is referring not only to her death but also to the punishment she suffered by the death of her only daughter. Of her pain, he writes that her eyes shed 'wells and wells [of tears]', alluding to Abravanel's interpretation of the phrase *be'erot be'erot* (wells whose water cannot be contained, meaning tears without end).[24] In the case of Mazal Ṭov's death, her parents' grief was exceedingly great, since they had no other child.

In general, it would seem that the death of a young son before he had married was an even greater tragedy than that of a daughter, since he would otherwise have carried on the family name. Thus Moshe Roman mourned his son of noble countenance [Photograph No. 10], who died in the prime of life: instead of a wedding canopy, his father was compelled to prepare for him a house of stone. All that remained for him to do was to request that the soul of his son might find peace and thereby atone for the father's sins.

But on the tombstones of the Roman family, the mourning for the death of young daughters not yet married is no less intense than that for sons. It was not only the young Mazal Ṭov Roman who was the object of bitter grief on the part of her parents; the mother of Reina bat Yiṣḥaq Roman also expressed her overwhelming sorrow at her daughter's death. Her words can be understood in two ways, and she was apparently unconcerned about how the inscription on her daughter's tombstone could be interpreted [Photograph No. 12]. Echoing the words of R. Yehuda Alḥarizi, the author (apparently a family member) lamented the treachery of time, which 'drew his bow and killed a queen' – a theme that recurs frequently in Sefardi poetry. The mother decries time, which 'set a trap for my tongue and my lips'. This may be an allusion to words spoken by the mother during the daughter's lifetime, words that she now regrets; or she may be referring to words that denied the will of

24 According to Abravanel's commentary (Warsaw: Levensohn, 1862) on Deut 31, s.v. *we-hine ha-dibbur*: 'For my people have done a twofold wrong: They have forsaken me, the fount of living waters, and hewn them out cisterns, broken cisterns, which cannot even hold water'.

God and His decree, which treacherous time has caused her to utter. From the day that time, the traitor, struck her queen – her daughter – the mother's heart is broken by day and burnt by night. Particularly heart-rending are her words of love to her dead daughter, and the mother's promise to her – the selfsame promise given by a groom on the day of his wedding to recall the destruction of Jerusalem: 'If I forget thee, may my right hand forget its cunning', since 'love is as strong as death'. Likewise, the description of her tortured longings and the nightmares that haunt her sleep, as 'my soul goes to her each night, and returns each morning'.

Life without offspring, and death without offspring, were considered in Jewish society of the early modern period to be a bitter fate. A person who died childless did not fulfill his destiny on earth, and his death was more terrible than any other in that it lacked all meaning.[25]

When the epitaph of Teshuva ben Mevorakh Roman, who died without issue, was composed, the poet had him speak as if he himself were mourning his own death: 'my rivers of tears well up', he states, referring to the floods of his tears, for 'I will die without sons, there is no counsel'. It is written in the Zohar that he who dies without sons is considered dead [for eternity] (*Zohar* III, 34b). The kabbalistic notion is that the sons of a man are what grant him eternal life. If there are no sons, there is no immortality. And for this, there is no remedy, and his soul is gathered unto its Maker in pain.

The next images in the epitaph allude to nature: The heart of the deceased pounded like an endless last rain in the Garden of Eden on the souls of the sons. Sons that were unborn? Sons who were born and died? The dead person does not tell us, but those who mourned him doubtless knew. What is left to the deceased but to study Torah? Thus the author writes that the one who has died will turn his nights into days for the sake of the One who turns nights into days. But in the end, there is no fragrance like the scent of a man's offspring. There is no pain like the pain of a man who died without issue [Photograph No. 10].

For hundreds of years, until the start of the nineteenth century, the death of wives was a common occurrence. Disease was only one reason; failed pregnancies, and childbirth itself, were an additional and not infrequent cause.

---

25 Rozen, *Jewish Community in Istanbul*, pp. 99–111; Minna Rozen, 'The Life Cycle and the Meaning of Old Age in the Ottoman Period', in *Daniel Carpi Jubilee Volume*, ed. by D. Porat, A. Shapira, and M. Rozen (Tel Aviv: Tel Aviv University, 1996), pp. 109–75; J. R. Hacker, 'Pride and Depression: Polarity of the Spiritual and Social Experience of the Iberian Exiles in the Ottoman Empire', in *Culture and Society in Medieval Jewry: Studies Dedicated to the Memory of Haim Hillel Ben Sasson*, ed. by M. Ben-Sasson, R. Bonfil and J. R. Hacker (Hebrew; Jerusalem: Shazar Center, 1989), pp. 541–86.

Married women often died not long after their wedding, in many cases before they had managed to bring a child into the world.[26] Only 33 percent of the women's tombstones in Hasköy from the start of the sixteenth century to the end of the eighteenth century cite a cause of death. Of these, 7 percent died in childbirth, and another 3 percent immediately after giving birth.

Death showed no pity for the young wife of Shelomo Hamon, a member of the well-known family of physicians. And the grieving husband spared no expense on her tombstone or its inscription [Photograph No. 8]. From the epitaph, one cannot deduce whether she had any children; however, it is certain that she was young, that she was not in good health, and that she died shortly after her marriage: 'in place of bridal palaces – ailments'. The images employed by the author of the epitaph are not new, but he used them in an original way and with a rhythm of his own. Thus for example, he employed the image of time as a wheel, which appears in *midrashim*[27] and among such Sefardi poets as Yehuda Alḥarizi,[28] in an intricate and lovely work that combines the notion of the wheel with that of time as traitor, another common motif in Sefardi poetry:[29] 'Spinning around, like the wheel of a wagon, days of agony and months of futility and nights and oracles of delusion and deception[30] deep in their souls, and stumbling blocks and great illnesses. Time betrays [us], its net is spread, and all it desires is to wreak evil.'[31]

Especially poignant are the epitaphs of Kalomira, wife of Aharon Roman, and his daughters by his second wife. Kalomira's excruciating labour pains and harrowing end are graphically described, and the reader can almost hear the unfortunate husband wailing along with his tortured, dying wife, one twin lying dead at her feet and the other still attached between her legs [Photograph No. 13].

---

26 See on this topic: Rozen, *Jewish Community in Istanbul*, pp. 124–27; Ruth Lamdan, *A Separate People: Jewish Women in Palestine, Syria and Egypt in the Sixteenth Century* (Leiden, Boston: Brill, 2000), pp. 83–86.

27 On the theme of the 'wheel of time', see Yehuda David Eisenstein, 'Ma'asiyot', in *A Treasury of Midrashim* (New York, Eisenstein edition, 1915), p. 335.

28 See: Moshe ibn Ezra, *Sefer Ha-'Anaq*, verses 53 and 61 (http://www.benyehuda.org/alxarizi/haanak.html).

29 Time's betrayal of man is a popular motif in Sefardi poetry and literature. See for example the poem *Zeman Boged* ('Treacherous Time') by Shemuel Hanagid (993–1056) (http://www.benyehuda.org/hanagid/index.html), and the poem of the same name by Shelomo ibn Gabirol (c. 1021–1058) (http://www.benyehuda.org/rashbag); Don Vidal Benveniste (fifteenth century), 'Treacherous Time' (http://www.benyehuda.org/benveniste/index.html); Rabbeinu Baḥya ben Asher (1255–c. 1340), introduction to a commentary on the Torah, 'Time as a Treacherous Stream' (Jerusalem: Mosad Harav Kook, 1994).

30 Lam 2:14.

31 Ps 141:4.

One of his daughters, Kadın, from his second wife, died during his lifetime, in 1691 [Photograph No. 14], and it would appear from the phrase 'like the mother of many who is forlorn' at the end of the epitaph that she died after other children born of the same mother.[32] Like his first wife, she was venerated with a poem on her tombstone. The poem composed by her father in her honour is not made up of fragments of biblical passages, like many of the epitaphs; it is written in a lively and totally original Hebrew. The father describes the daughter, small of stature, who broke his heart – she who was his only one and now is beyond his reach. He calls upon passersby to appreciate his love for her and his deep sorrow reflected in the stone he placed on her grave, and not to heed the fact that she was only a young girl, for his pain is great.

His second daughter from the same mother, Kalomira, was already betrothed when she died, and passed away after his death [Photograph No. 15]. She was not privileged to receive a poem at the level of those bestowed on his first wife or his daughter Kadın. The poetic phrasing used in her epitaph suggests that she might have drowned. Without engaging in undue speculation, it is worth noting that most cases of girls drowning in seventeenth- and eighteenth-century Istanbul involved young betrothed women. Of a total of forty-four drownings recorded in the Hasköy cemetery during that period, thirteen were of married men; ten, of unmarried men; three, of married women; and twenty-one, of young women who were engaged to be married – leading us to ponder the possibility that this was a means, however extreme, for young girls to escape unwanted marriages.

6 What knowledge can be gleaned from the material aspect of the tombstones?

The monetary investment in the tombstones of the Roman family is also a topic that calls for discussion. A stone of high calibre was used to mark each of the graves. In most cases, the tombstone was made of choice marble from the Isle of Marmara, transported at great expense, long before regular quarrying was resumed there. In tombstones made up of two parts, one horizontal and the other vertical, the horizontal part – which was naturally much larger – was sometimes brought from a closer source, the quarries of Lala Paşa, near

32 I Sam 2:5.

Edirne. The tombstones that were cut in the shape of a prism, reminiscent of an Ottoman coffin, were all made of Marmara marble.

It is important to recall that at least until the first decade of the eighteenth century, when quarrying was resumed at the Marmara island on a regular basis, such marble was a valuable commodity in Istanbul.[33] In contrast to the epitaph, which reflects a rational understanding of death, the monetary investment in the tombstone – and even the sophistication and elegance of the inscription – may be said to indicate a dichotomy in the attitude of the mourners. The use of expensive marble in tombstones, even those of young boys and girls, shows that, while acknowledging the finality of death, there is the hope that the deceased continues some sort of existence in which he derives pleasure from this investment, coupled with an illusion of immortality. At the same time, this investment should also be seen as a means of bolstering the social status of the surviving family members.[34]

The material aspect of the burial culture of the Roman family also extends to the decorative quality of the tombstones. The majority of these stones did not boast ostentatious ornamentation; even in the late seventeenth century, when overly ornate stones were already beginning to appear, such was not the case with the Roman tombstones. Of the ten gravestones with the shortened family name of Roman, only four – dated 1641[35] and 1643 [Photograph No. 3]; 1644 [Photograph No. 4]; and 1666 [Photograph No. 11] – are made up of a vertical and a horizontal element, with the upper part often serving as a shared tombstone for a couple. But in the case of Mazal Ṭov and Mevorakh Roman, the vertical part is not unified [Photograph No. 3], and with regard to the wife, may not ever have existed. In any event, this notion, which is also found in many modern cemeteries, symbolizes the bed that the couple shared in their lifetime.[36] In the vertical part of Mevorakh's tombstone, the lines of the inscription themselves form the principal decoration; however, in the horizontal part of both tombstones, the epitaph is circumscribed within a *mihrab*-shaped frame. At the sides of the *mihrab* on the wife's stone are also niches, apparently for lighting candles.[37]

---

33 Rozen, *Hasköy Cemetery*, pt. I, pp. 14–17.

34 See Minna Rozen, 'Metropolis and Necropolis: The Cultivation of Social Status among the Jews of Istanbul in the Seventeenth and Eighteenth Centuries', in Rozen, *Journey Through Civilizations*, forthcoming.

35 The tombstone of the wife, Mazal Ṭov Roman, is not illustrated in this article. A plan of the double monument of Mevorakh and Mazal Ṭov Roman can be found in Rozen, *Hasköy Cemetery*, pt. II, p. 79.

36 For the significance of the candle niches, see ibid., pt. I, pp. 55–59.

37 See Rozen, pt. I, p. 92, plate 133, and p. 93, table 14.

The *mihrab* shape indicates that the Muslim world of symbols had been assimilated by Istanbuli Jews of Roman origin. The image of the *mihrab* was not merely a stylistic convention but carried many meanings and associations that apparently occurred to the person commissioning the stone. The *mihrab* is the wall in a mosque that signifies the direction of prayer, facing Mecca. On the stones in question, the head of the *mihrab* points toward Jerusalem. Moreover, the Muslim worshipper prays while kneeling on a prayer rug *(seccade)* [Photograph No. 6], which is decorated precisely in the shape of a *mihrab*.[38] In this way, the stone serves as a form of 'prayer rug' for the relatives of the deceased, with the ornamentation emphasizing the notion that the dead person constitutes a bridge between this world and the next, and can influence the fate of the living. The form of the *mihrab* also recalls a gate of sorts. While in the great mosques, the entrance is in the shape of a *mihrab* [Photograph No. 7], here the association is with the gate of the Holy One, through which only the righteous may pass.[39] In this sense as well, the *mihrab* shape turns the tombstone into an object that symbolically connects not only the deceased and those mourning him or her but, in a more general way, the present world and the hereafter.[40]

Another tombstone, that of Simḥa, wife of Teshuva Roman (d. 1644) [Photograph No. 5], is horizontal, without a vertical element, and is also adorned with the outline of a *mihrab* with two candle niches at its head, mimicking a Muslim prayer rug. The tombstone of Sultana, wife of Shelomo Hamon [Photograph No. 8], who died in 1648, already has an innovation. In addition to the high-quality marble from which it is fashioned, and the poem engraved in it, the *mihrab* surrounding the poem is divided into three pairs of inner frames with rosettes carved between the pairs, as well as in the spaces between the inner frames and the overall outline of the *mihrab*. This is already an adornment whose intent is not to convey meaning but to display wealth, and it brings this type of stone into the realm of the illuminated Ottoman manuscript [Photograph No. 9].

Let us assume, for the purposes of this discussion, that the designs on the tombstones, or at least on the more sophisticated ones, were not created by the stonemasons themselves but by people who specialized in this, devising standard patterns that the engravers followed. Whether it was they or the stone cutters who planned the ornamentation on the stones, how had they come to be familiar with illuminated Ottoman manuscripts? The answer apparently lies

---

38 Ps 118:20.

39 Rozen, *Hasky Cemetery*, pt. I, pp. 55–61.

40 Rozen, p. 82.

in the Ottoman lifestyle. These designs were generally in manuscripts of the Quran, of prayers, or of poetry, the margins illuminated by master artists whose imagination knew no bounds. Such volumes were sold at the book market (*sahaflar*) next to the grand bazaar of Istanbul. Calligraphers would purchase these illuminated works and write the text on the empty space in the center of the page. The Jews of Istanbul were doubtless familiar with the book market, and apparently also visited its stalls, as attested to by a kabbalistic prayer-book from 1734 that was copied into an illuminated book ready for writing [Photograph No. 16]. These patterns were copied from generation to generation for hundreds of years [Photograph Nos 17–18]. It would appear that this was the practice of the Jewish stonemasons as well. An empty ornamental frame was prepared in advance, and upon the client's request, the epitaph was engraved in the stone. The inspiration, both practical and decorative, apparently came from the book market.

Another example of Roman family tombstones is the prism-shaped stone, generally heptagonal, mimicking the form of an Ottoman coffin. This gravestone was usually placed on a stone base, and, from the start of the eighteenth century, on a large, ornamented stone slab. The tombstones of Teshuva ben Mevorakh Roman [Photograph No. 10], Reina bat Yiṣḥaq Roman [Photograph No. 12], Kalomira wife of Aharon Roman [Photograph No. 13], Kadın bat Aharon Roman [Photograph No. 14], and Kalomira bat Aharon Roman [Photograph No. 15] are all of this type. In only one of them [Photograph No. 14] has the bottom slab been preserved. In all cases, the investment in the stones was significant, in terms of detail as well as cost. They were always made of Marmara marble of the finest quality, with stylized frames on each facet of the prism; the decorative ornamentation divided each side into two, so that there were twelve frames in total on each prism. The tombstones of men were generally adorned with rosettes, while those of women were embellished with a belt, symbolizing the engagement belt that the woman received from her betrothed or her groom. On the tombstone of Kadın daughter of Aharon Roman, who was not yet betrothed, we see no such belt.[41] On the sides of the tombstones, there were generally plants representing the Garden of Eden and the hereafter – primarily tulips and lotuses, which were typical symbols of Ottoman art.[42] None of these elements appears by chance or without prior thought, and what characterizes all of these tombstones, in terms of their artistry, is the integration of the Jews who buried their dead at Hasköy into the surrounding cultural space.

---

41 Rozen, pp. 65–81.

42 R. Ya'aqov ben Ḥayyim Alfandari, *Responsa Muṣal me-Esh* (Jerusalem: Mishor, 1997), sec. 2.

7 What can we learn by merging the information derived from the tombstones with that drawn from other types of sources?

Who were the Roman family? We were unable to find information about all of them outside the cemetery, but some indeed left their imprint on the sands of time. One fact stands out from an examination of the Roman family trees (see above) and the sources on which they were based: even if we are speaking of two different families named Roman without blood ties between them, what we have before us is a group of individuals who were extremely well educated, poets, judges, scholars, linguists, and grammarians. In the first Roman family tree, the only individual identifiable in historical sources is the unfortunate Aharon Roman, who was a *dayyan* (religious-court judge) in Istanbul; in late Tammuz 1686, while serving as head of the *bet din* (religious court), he heard testimony concerning the death of a Jew who had drowned in the Bosphorus.[43]

The second Roman family tree raises additional questions. The name Baquda, or alternatively, Paquda, is an Arab one. The first association of the name is with the tenth-century neoplatonic Jewish philosopher, Baḥya ibn Paquda, author of *Ḥovot Ha-Levavot* (Saragossa, 1050–*c.* 1120). It is not clear whether Ya'aqov Roman's plan to publish this work (see below) was connected with the fact that his grandfather, Paquda Roman, was descended from Baḥya ibn Paquda (or wished us to think so), or whether he simply considered it important to publish the book. In any event, the name Paquda indicates that Ya'aqov Roman, along with the other poets who were apparently part of this branch of the family, and perhaps Yiṣḥaq ben Bakuda Roman as well, was not part of the first generation of emigrants from Rome. They might have been scions of a family that immigrated from Rome to the Iberian peninsula generations before the expulsion from Spain, and then moved to Istanbul due to that expulsion. A more conceivable possibility is that they were the offspring of marriages between Roman immigrants who settled in Istanbul and a Sefardi family that may or may not have descended from Baḥya ibn Paquda. The family's Sefardi roots are clear not only from the name Paquda-Baquda (names of Jewish males tended to be preserved for generations, and were not affected by changing fashions, at least until the nineteenth century)[44] but also from

43 See below.

44 The name Baquda was still preserved in the family as of 1707. In that year, Yom Ṭov ben Baquda Roman added an introduction to Eliyahu Ha-Kohen's anti-Sabbatean treatise 'Holy War' (see 'Inyenei Shabbetai Şevi [Hebrew], ed. by A. Freimann, Berlin: Meqize Nirdamim, 1913, p. 2).

the association with Sefardi poetry and the Judeo-Arabic philosophy of Spain as reflected in the epitaphs discussed above, as well as from the Sefardi influence evident in the literary milieu of the individuals on the second family tree.

Almost all the male descendants on that family tree were known as scholars and poets. Avraham Roman, the son of Yiṣḥaq Roman is mentioned as the author of several poems, a letter to the renowned Rabbi Yom Tov Ibn Ya'ish, and an introduction entitled '*Milḥemet Ḥova*' ('Mandatory War') to a polemic work against the Patriarch Kiril, *Sela' Ha-Maḥloqot* ('Bones of Contention'). His brother Ḥizqiyya Roman eulogized him, mentioning his mourning brothers.[45] Ḥizqiyya Roman is cited as the person who completed the copying of *Sefer Otiot Ha-Noaḥ* in 1600,[46] and he was still alive in 1655 when he wrote an approbation for *Hod Malkhut* by Avraham Ha-Yakhini, printed in Istanbul that year. Ḥizqiyya Roman is described in that book as 'the eminent scholar, master of all books and sciences, wonderful and great'.[47]

Ya'aqov Roman was a collector of books, a bibliographer, a linguist, a grammarian, and a well-known poet. The manuscript of an Arabic–Hebrew dictionary that he completed in Istanbul on 27 Tishrei 5390 (11 October 1629) is housed in the National Library of France, in Paris,[48] as is the manuscript of an Arabic–Turkish dictionary that he composed.[49] Ya'aqov Roman also authored a book entitled *Moznei Mishqal* on Hebrew rhyming schemes. The book was written prior to 1634, the year in which it is mentioned several times in the author's correspondence with Johannes Buxtorf the Younger (13 August 1599–16 August 1664).[50] Buxtorf and his father, Johannes Buxtorf (25 December 1564–13 September 1629) were professors of theology at the University of Basel, and among the earliest Christian Hebraists in Europe. Buxtorf the Younger translated Maimonides' *More Nevukhim* (Basel, 1629) and the *Kuzari* (Basel, 1660) into Latin, and corresponded with numerous Jewish scholars in Western Europe and the Ottoman Empire.[51] A friend of Ya'aqov Roman's by the name

---

45 D. S. Sasson, ed., 'Poems and Songs by Ancient Poets', in *Ohel Dawid: Descriptive Catalogue of the Hebrew and Samaritan Manuscripts in the Sasson Library* (Oxford and London: Oxford University Press and Humphrey Milford, 1932), vol. 2, sec. 590, p. 461; and ibid., '*Milḥemet Ḥova*', sec. 793, p. 426.

46 See n. 62, below.

47 P. 2b.

48 *Manuscrits orientaux: Catalogues des manuscrits hébreux et samaritains de la Bibliothèque Impériale* (Paris: Imprimerie Impériale, 1866), no. 1277, p. 230.

49 *Manuscrits*, no. 1278, p. 230.

50 M. Kayserling, 'Richelieu, Buxtorf père et fils, et Jacob Roman', *REJ*, 8 (1884), pp. 89, 94.

51 On the correspondence between Buxtorf and Roman, see M. Kayserling, 'Les correspondants juifs de Jean Buxtorf', *REJ*, 8 (1884), pp. 261–76; 'Moznei Ha-Mishqal', in *Medieval Literature* (Hebrew), ed. by Neḥemya Allony (Jerusalem: Mosad Harav Kook, 1945), p. 88. On Buxtorf (father and son), see Ora Limor, *Jews and Christians in Western Europe: Encounter between*

of Arye Yehuda Leon Sa'aya,[52] who ultimately converted to Christianity, also wrote under the Arab name Nasser a-din Tabib (i.e., physician), and was the court physician of Prince Rakoczy I of Transylvania (1639). Sa'aya was closely acquainted in Istanbul with one Anton Lager, a scholar from Piemonte who was then acting as minister of the Dutch Embassy. Lager subsequently served as a professor of Eastern languages at the University of Geneva, and it was he who put Sa'aya in contact with Buxtorf.[53] Sa'aya later brought together Roman and Buxtorf. From Sa'aya's letter of recommendation to Buxtorf the Younger concerning Ya'aqov Roman, we learn that Sa'aya was of the opinion that 'thanks to his family, riches, dignity, and contacts, this man surpasses all his coreligionists'.[54] It emerges from the correspondence between Ya'aqov Roman and Buxtorf the Younger that Roman asked Buxtorf to send him two copies of the biblical concordance that the senior Buxtorf had composed, and an accurate copy of the Latin translation of *More Nevukhim*.[55] Roman wished to set up a printing press in Istanbul. Among his plans was to publish a trilingual edition of Maimonides' *More Nevukhim*, in Hebrew, Latin, and Arabic in Hebrew transliteration. The reason why the Arabic would appear in Hebrew letters, as he explained, was the Sultanic prohibition against printing Arabic letters. In addition, Roman planned to publish Baḥya ibn Paquda's *Ḥovot Ha-Levavot* and *Sefer Ha-Kuzari* by R. Yehuda Halevi, both in the Latin translation of his friend Sa'aya.[56]

Of particular interest is Roman's plan to publish *Ḥovot Ha-Levavot*, the work written in Arabic in Spain in the eleventh century, translated into Hebrew by Yehuda ibn Tibbon from 1161 to 1180, and published in 1489 in Naples. The book was poorly received due to its numerous neoplatonic concepts, largely in the beginning of the work. It was published in Istanbul in 1550 together with the work *Sefer Tiqqun Middot Ha-Nefesh* by R. Shelomo ibn Gabirol.[57] The idea of also publishing it in Latin is evidence of Roman's desire to reach an

---

Cultures in the Middle Ages and the Renaissance (Hebrew; Tel Aviv: Open University, 1997), pp. 114, 130; A. L. Katchen, *Christian Hebraists and Dutch Rabbis: Seventeenth-Century Apologetics and the Study of Maimonides' Mishne Torah* (Cambridge, MA/London: Cambridge University Press, 1984), pp. 27–28.

52 Avraham Rosanes referred to him as Asseo, but I have not found sources that support this position (A. Rosanes, *Qorot Ha-Yehudim be-Turqyia we-Arṣot Ha-Qedem*, pt. III (Sofia, 1938), p. 259.

53 M. Kayserling, 'Richelieu, Buxtorf père et fils, et Jacob Roman', *REJ*, 8 (1884), pp. 84–86.

54 Kayserling, p. 85.

55 Kayserling, p. 91.

56 Kayserling, p. 93.

57 Baḥya ibn Paquda, *Ḥovot Ha-Levavot* (printed together with Ibn Gabirol's *Sefer Tiqqun Middot Ha-Nefesh* [Istanbul, 1550]); Kayserling, 'Richelieu', p. 88.

audience that read neither Arabic nor Hebrew. Sadly, his plan to establish the printing press and to publish the other two books did not come to fruition, but his multilingual and multicultural aspirations offer evidence of his well-rounded nature – a point also demonstrated by the many manuscripts dealing with Greek philosophy that were in his possession and by several unpublished letters that he left behind as well as the translation from Arabic to Hebrew of several of the works of Yona ibn Janaḥ, the tenth-century grammarian and linguist from Cordoba.[58] Roman collected numerous manuscripts, some of which were purchased by Buxtorf for Jean Tilleman Stella de Téry et Morimont, commercial representative of Cardinal Richelieu, and are now housed in France's National Library. Others found their way to the Bodleian Library.[59] On several of the works, it is written explicitly that they are the property of Ya'aqov Roman.[60] From the legacy of Roman's life's work in the libraries of Europe, it is evident that he was, by any measure, a wealthy man, very distinguished and highly erudite He knew Hebrew, Greek, Spanish, Arabic, Turkish, Latin, and Italian, and was an expert in the literatures of the world. He was fluent in manuscripts of poetry and philosophy in Arabic and Latin, and compared the Arabic *maqama* genre of rhymed prose to the splendid language of Cicero in Latin, and, in its style and imagination, to Boccaccio's *The Decameron*. His connection to Italy was also apparent in his letters to Buxtorf the Younger, and in the fact that he wrote the name of Anton Lager as pronounced in Italian (Antonio Leggero), perhaps because this was the foreign language he was most comfortable with.[61]

An anonymous linguist and anthologist who borrowed a great deal from Roman's *Moznei Mishqal* made reference in his work *Qeṣev u-Moznei Ha-Mishqal* not only to Ya'aqov Roman's book but to other poets of the time: Yiṣḥaq Roman, Avraham Roman, and Ḥizqiyya Roman, whom he placed in the exalted

58 *Manuscrits*, no. 126, p. 224.
59 Kayserling, 'Richelieu', p. 95, nn. 4–5.
60 D. Schwartz, '*Berurim ra'ayoni'im be-farashat ha-pulmusim 'al ha-filosofia ba-me'a ha-shelosh-'esre*', *Qoveṣ 'al Yad*, 14 (1998), p. 344: manuscript of the work *Sefer Yore De'a* by Qalonymos, which was copied during the fifteenth century, possibly before the Ottoman conquest, and was sold in 1481 by Yosef Bekhor Avshalom Bona-Vita to a man by the name of Mordekhai. At the start of the manuscript is the name of its owner, 'Yiṣḥaq Roman ben Baquda z"l, Tammuz 5390', i.e., the summer of 1630. Bodleian ms 267 (Opp. 212). See also the Arabic commentary on Song of Songs by Moshe b. Ḥiyya Kohen, completed on 9 Elul 5195 (1435), colophon in Arabic, apparently written in Granada, property of Ya'aqov b. Yiṣḥaq Roman, 1597 (*Catalogue of the Bodleian Library, Supplement of Addenda and Corrigenda to Vol. I* [A. Neubauer's Catalogue], compiled under the direction of M. Beit-Arié, ed. by R. A. May (Oxford: Clarendon Press, 1994), ms no. 356*, p. 54.
61 Kayserling, 'Richelieu', p. 89.

company of Shelomo ibn Gabirol, Yehuda Halevi, and Moshe ibn Ezra.[62] In *Qeṣev u-Moznei Ha-Mishqal*, there is also a poem by a contemporary of Ya'aqov Roman, R. Yehoshu'a Rafael ben Yisrael Benveniste.[63] Roman's ties with Benveniste are apparent from the latter's remark that he cannot make use of the grammar book entitled *Tevat Noaḥ* because it was lent to R. Ya'aqov Roman, and he himself is ill and cannot go to fetch it from Roman.[64] The work referred to is apparently the *Sefer Otiot Ha-Noaḥ* of R. Yehuda Ḥayuj, the tenth-century Sefardi grammarian and linguist whose book was translated into Arabic by R. Moshe ibn Jiqatilla of Cordoba. This manuscript was copied by Ḥizqiyya ben Yiṣḥaq ibn Paquda Roman in 1600, and was apparently among the manuscripts purchased by Buxtorf the Younger for resale to the agent of Richelieu.[65] I was unable to find Ya'aqov Roman's tombstone in Istanbul, and Buxtorf lost contact with him in 1641.[66] A poem written by Yiṣḥaq ben Ya'aqov Roman is included in the same manuscript of 'Poems and Songs by Ancient Poets' described by David Sasson.[67]

By examining the family tree of the Benveniste family [Tree No. 2, below], we can understand, at least in part, the world of Ya'aqov Roman, and that of

62 Allony, '*Moznei Mishqal*', p. 96.

63 Ibid.

64 Allony., p. 95; Yehoshu'a Rafael ben Yisrael Benveniste, *Responsa Sha'ar Yehoshu'a* (Husiatyn: n. p., 1904), sec. 11, p. 36a.

65 *Manuscrit*, no. 1215, pp. 224–25.

66 An elderly man of eighty from Istanbul by the name of Ya'aqov Romano – a linguist renowned for his brilliance, who knew all six orders of the Mishna by heart – is mentioned in the work of David Conforti (*Qore Ha-Dorot* [Venice, 1746], p. 49a) as living in Jerusalem. The question is whether he is the Ya'aqov Roman of the present work. A person with the same name is referred to in *Ḥorvot Yerushalem* (Venice, 1627; Minna Rozen edition, Tel Aviv: Tel Aviv University, 1981), pp. 35, 103, 106, 140, but again it is unclear whether this is in fact 'our' Ya'aqov Roman, and whether he is the same person mentioned by Conforti. Given the fact that Conforti was born in 1617 or 1618, and came to Jerusalem in 1644, scholars are of the opinion that the Ya'aqov Roman mentioned in Conforti's work and the one cited in *Ḥorvot Yerushalem* are one and the same. While it is possible that the former is 'our' Ya'aqov Roman, one would be hard-pressed to explain how the latter, who is mentioned in *Ḥorvot Yerushalem* in 1625, corresponded with Buxtorf from Istanbul in 1634 and intended to set up a publishing house there. In *Qore Ha-Dorot* (p. 51b), Conforti also refers to 'Ḥayyim Romano, my relative' among the Torah scholars of *Yeshivat Yerushalayim* at the time. Also cited in *Ḥorvot Yerushalem*, in addition to Ya'aqov Roman, are Moshe Romano (Rozen ed., pp. 14, 53, 98, 100), Shelomo Romano (Rozen, pp. 56, 110), and Shemuel Romano (Rozen, pp. 98, 100). Yiṣḥaq Romano is signatory to an agreement not to sow discord and not to besmirch the community leaders, signed in Jerusalem in 1623. See also: Minna Rozen, *The Jewish Community in Jerusalem in the Seventeenth Century* (Hebrew; Tel Aviv: Ministry of Defense Publishing House and Tel Aviv University, 1985), p. 292.

67 See Sasson, *Ohel Dawid*, vol. 2, sec. 590, p. 464.

Yiṣḥaq Roman as well. Yehoshu'a Rafael Benveniste, who was not only a rabbi but also a physician, was the grandson of the physician of Sultan Mehmet III (1595–1603), Dr. Moshe Benveniste. The later was described by his grandson as 'the righteous prince, the flawless sage, the renowned scholar, who devoted his whole life to helping Jews everywhere, facing ministers and judges of the highest rank'.[68] The grandmother of Yehoshu'a Rafael was the daughter of another Jewish luminary from Italy, R. Yehoshu'a Ṣonṣin, a renowned rabbi in Istanbul and a member of the family of printers. Yehoshu'a Rafael Benveniste was also the nephew of another physician of the Sultan, Dr. Nissim Benveniste, who was married to the daughter of the *rav ha-manhig* (generally, if somewhat inaccurately translated as Chief Rabbi) of the Romaniotes, R. Eliyahu ibn Ḥayyim, and the cousin of the *av beit din* (head of the religious court) of Istanbul, R. Moshe Benveniste.[69]

Yiṣḥaq Roman, the father of the young Reina Roman, who died at an early age, was a poet and scholar in Istanbul.[70] In Tammuz 5425 (the summer of 1665), he turned to R. Moshe Benveniste in a dispute over the rights of a female orphan to a house she bought from a leaseholder of the Muslim religious trust (*vakıf*). Moshe Benveniste, grandson of the sultan's physician, was born in 1608. His father, Nissim, died in 1621, when Moshe was a young boy of twelve. It was his mother who endeavoured to see to it that he continued his studies, and he testified of himself that he never engaged in 'vainglorious pursuits' but devoted himself entirely to Torah. He studied at the La Señora *Yeshiva*, established in Istanbul by Doña Gracia Mendes, later teaching there from 1622 to 1660, the year that the *Yeshiva* went up in flames along with the entire Eminönü quarter of Istanbul. He served as a *dayyan* from the age of approximately 24, and as *av beit din* of Istanbul until his death, *c.* 1677.[71]

---

68 See introduction to vol. I of *Penei Moshe*, Moshe Benveniste's responsa, printed in Istanbul in 1669.

69 On the Benveniste family, its pedigree and ties, see M. Benayahu, *Rofe He-Ḥatzer: Rabbi Moshe Benveniste we-ha-shir 'al haglayato la-I Rodos* ['The court physician Rabbi Moshe Benveniste: An elegy on his exile to Rhodes'), *Sefunot* 14 (1970–1973), pp. 125–35. The British merchant John Sanderson bequeathed to his cousin, Samuel Sanderson, several oil paintings of his Istanbuli friends, which he apparently commissioned from an artist in the Grand Bazaar of Istanbul during his stay in the capital of the Ottoman Empire. One of these was of the 'Jewish Physician Dr Benveniste'. John Sanderson, *The Travels of John Sanderson in the Levant 1584–1602*, ed. by W. Foster (London: Hakluyt Society, 1931), p. 35, n. 2. See also Minna Rozen, The Social Role of Book Printing among Istanbul Jews in the Sixteenth through Eighteenth Centuries, in Rozen, *Journey Through Civilizations*, forthcoming.

70 Allony, '*Moznei Mishqal*', p. 96.

71 See R. Moshe Benveniste, *Responsa Penei Moshe*, I (Istanbul, 1669), Introduction.

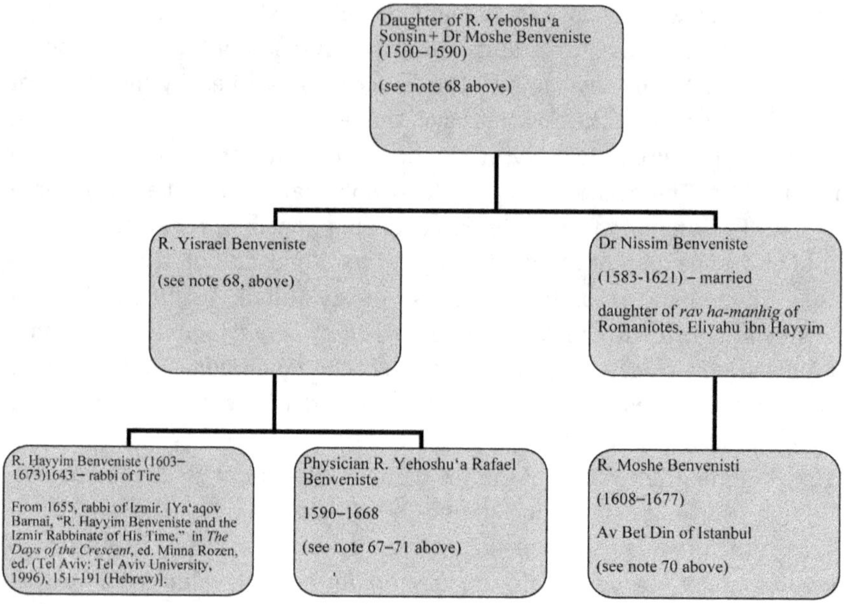

Family Tree 2: Benveniste family of Istanbul.

With the aid of several additional details, we are able to place the Roman family in its rightful position in the Istanbuli Jewish society of the seventeenth century. Aside from the connection to the Benveniste families, another notable connection is through the marriage of Sultana bat Teshuva Roman to Shemuel Hamon. For generations, the Hamons served as physicians to the sultans.[72] The first member of the family to settle in Istanbul was R. Yosef Hamon, who

---

72 On Rabbi Yosef Hamon and the Hamon family, see U. Heyd, 'Moses Hamon, Chief Jewish Physician to Sultan Suleyman the Magnificent', *Oriens*, 16 (1963), pp. 152–70; A. Galante, *Médecins juifs au service de la Turquie* (Istanbul, 1938), 1st ed., in *Histoire des Juifs de Turquie* (Istanbul: Isis, n.d.), vol. 9, pp. 85, 89; A. Dannon, 'Mosheh Hamon and his family', in *Yosef Da'at* (Edirne, 1888), pp. 118–20, 130–34, 146–47, 162–67, 178–83, 194–95; M. Benayahu, 'The House of Abravanel in Salonika' (Hebrew), *Sefunot*, 12 (1971–78), 42–52; Benayahu, 'The sermons of R. Yosef b. Meir Garson as a source for the history of the expulsion from Spain and the Sephardi diaspora', *Michael*, 7 (1981), pp. 124–31; A. Levy, *The Sefardim in the Ottoman Empire* (Princeton, NJ: The Darwin Press, 1992), p. 31; H. Gross, 'La famille juive des Hamons', REJ, 56 (1908), 1–26; 57 (1909), pp. 55–78; A. Rozanes, *History of the Jews in the Ottoman Empire*, vol. I (Hebrew; Tel Aviv: Dvir, 1930), p. 93; vol. 2 (Sofia, 1937–1938), pp. 85–86; vol. 3 (Sofia, 1938), pp. 244–68, 275; M. A. Epstein, *Ottoman Jewish Communities and their Role in the Fifteenth and Sixteenth Centuries* (Freiburg: Klaus Schwartz Verlag, 1980), pp. 86–88, 184–85; L. Bornstein-Makovetsky, 'The Jewish Community in Istanbul in the mid-seventeenth century: Its Sephardi and Romaniot personalities and sages', *Michael*, 9 (1985), pp. 27–54.

immediately upon his arrival in the city (1492/3) entered into the service of Sultan Bayezid II. When Hamon died in Damascus during Selim I's military campaign in the Near East, a sermon was delivered in his memory describing the honour and kindness bestowed upon him by the Sultans he had served, and their great benevolence to the Jews of the Ottoman Empire in general and to those of Istanbul in particular.[73] His son Moshe continued to serve Süleyman the Magnificent, and was rewarded with permission to build a stone house in Hasköy,[74] and a four-storey stone house in the Jewish Quarter near the palace that was leased to the *bailo* of the Republic of Venice.[75] Such permits were generally issued only to viziers and to members of the royal family. The Hamon family constituted a separate fiscal unit (*cemaat*) from all the Jewish communities in Istanbul, and maintained a synagogue of its own in the Hasköy neighbourhood.[76]

There is virtually no direct information on Shelomo Hamon at our disposal, but meticulous detective work based on the scant details in our possession has produced an interesting portrait of the connections between the Hamon, Benveniste and Roman families. Included in the responsa of R. Ḥayyim Benveniste (*Ba'ei Ḥayyai*), brother of Moshe and Yehoshu`a Refael Benveniste, is a decision rendered in 1651 by

> the impeccable wise man, the venerable gentleman, his honour our Teacher, Rabbi Av Hamon, ... the words flowing from the mouth of this flawless wise man, who possesses both a great breadth of knowledge and superior analytical reasoning; the rabbinic

---

73 Benayahu, 'Sermons', pp. 124–31.

74 Hans Dernschwam, *Tagebuch einer Reise nach Konstantinopel und Kleinasien (1554–1555)*, ed. by F. Babinger (Münich & Leipzig: Dünker & Humblot, 1923), p. 113.

75 Regarding the building adjacent to the Sultan's palace, see: Minna Rozen and Benjamin Arbel, 'Great Fire in the Metropolis: The Case of the Istanbul Conflagration of 1569 and its Description by Marcantonio Barbara', in *Mamluk and Ottoman Societies: Studies in Honour of Michael Winter*, ed. by David Wasserstein and Ami Ayalon (New York: Routledge, 2005), pp. 134–63.

76 The Hamon cemaat is mentioned in the tax registers from 1603 (Table 1, ref. in Minna Rozen, *A History of The Jewish Community of Istanbul – The Formative Years (1453–1566)*, (2nd ed. Brill, Leiden, Boston, 2010), p. 51; 1608–09 (Türkiye Cumhuriyeti Başbakanlık Arşivleri, Maliyeden Müdevver [MM] 14932); and 1623 (ibid., MM 286). The tax exemption allegedly received by the Hamons is rather doubtful; see Rozanes, Ottoman Empire, vol. II, pp. 286–88; Bernard Lewis, 'The Privilege Granted by Mehmed II to His Physician', *BSOAS*, 14 (1952), pp. 550–63; Lewis, 'On a Historical Document in the Responsa of Rabbi Shemuel de Medina' (in Hebrew), *Melila*, 5 (1955), pp. 69–76. See also U. Heyd, 'The Jewish Communities of Istanbul in the Seventeenth Century', *Oriens*, VI (1953), p. 303. Heyd's contention that the Hamon family was exempted from taxes is based on the fact that in the 1603 register, no tax scale was assigned to the family; the family was, however, ranked in all of the other registers.

> decisor, ... whose mouth speaks great [words of Torah], as they were given at Mount Sinai; his reasons are good and his justifications are sound and the law is rendered in accordance with his rulings; wherever we may live, we live according to his utterances and we take pleasure in the radiance of his Torah, his Torah teachings are whole, wrapped in a robe of light, the young Av Hamon, the son of our esteemed teacher, Joseph Hamon ...[77]

The fact that the responsum is found in the work of Ḥayyim Benveniste leads us back to the social milieu of the Roman family. Av Hamon, son of Yosef Hamon [the second] and grandson of the physician Moshe Hamon, was a *dayyan* in the community of Aragon who is mentioned in various sources. The Romans moved within the same social circle as the Benveniste and Hamon families, and, as we shall see below, the Vileisid family as well. Yet neither social nor marital ties were able to prevent disputes over property, assets, and influence. At the request of Aharon Hamon, R. Moshe Benveniste sat in judgement in a dispute between him and the wealthy ibn Vileisid brothers, who had earned their riches in the silk trade. One of them sought to be appointed the *sarafbaşı* of Egypt, in response to which Aharon Hamon intruded on their business dealings. Hamon also tried to recruit Yehoshu'a Rafael Benveniste, when he (Hamon) attempted to take control of the Neve Shalom community of Istanbul in 1641.[78]

The connection between the Roman family and the Hamon and Vileisid families also emerges in a different context – the placement of the Roman family's tombstones. A close examination of the concentrations of their gravesites, especially throughout the seventeenth century, and a comparison with those of other families, indicates that members of the ibn Vileisid family were buried specifically in their vicinity. In section 6-5, where most of the burials of the Roman family were conducted in the seventeenth century, we find most of the gravesites of the ibn Vileisid family for this period (nine out of seventeen), with the remainder in close proximity. In addition, four out of six burial sites of the Hamon family are found in these sections. It is possible that there were other ties between the Roman and ibn Vileisid families of which we are not aware, bearing in mind that in the first half of the seventeenth century, members of the Romano family and Avraham Vileisid, all of them from Istanbul, were prominent members and leaders of the Jewish community of Jerusalem.[79] The graves of the Benveniste family are not found at this location, and may have been destroyed during the laying of the ring road around Istanbul.

---

77 R. Ḥayyim Benveniste, *Responsa Ba'ei Ḥayyai* (Salonika, 1791; facsimile, Jerusalem 1970), *Ḥoshen Mishpaṭ* pt. I, sec. 212.

78 Bornstein-Makovetsky, 'Jewish Community in Istanbul', pp. 27–54, esp. pp. 36–38.

79 Avraham ibn Vileisid was a leader of the Jewish community in Jerusalem from at least 1600 to 1618, Rozen, *Jewish Community in Jerusalem*, pp. 120–22, 125, 285; Moshe Hamon, was counted among Jerusalem's notables (1586), Rozen, p. 287; Shemuel Hamon of Jerusalem

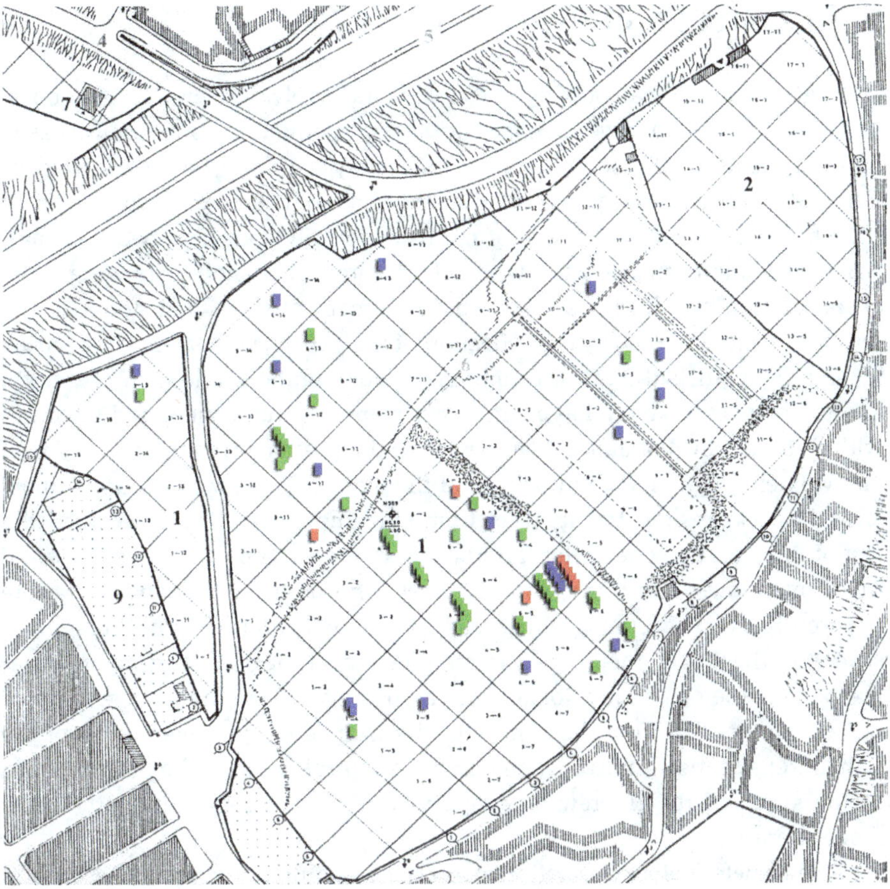

Legend: Red = Roman, Green = Vileisid, Blue = Hamon
Notice the concentration of the three families in lot 6–5, which apparently was the burial plot for distinguished families during the seventeenth century.

Map 3: Distribution of the Roman/Romano, Vileisid, and Hamon families in Hasköy Cemetery, 1583–1700.

---

was entitled to collect taxes from properties in the Diaspora (prior to 1635), ibid., p. 288; Shelomo Romano was among the city's notables (1620), Rozen, p. 291, (1625) *Ḥorvot Yerushalem* (Rozen ed.), p. 98, n. 134, and p. 110; Yiṣḥaq Romano was among the notables of Jerusalem (1623), *Jewish Community in Jerusalem*, p. 292; Ya'aqov Romano was among the city's notables (1631), Rozen., p. 293, (1625) *Ḥorvot Yerushalem* (Rozen ed.), pp. 103, 106; Moshe Romano was one of the city's notables (1623), Rozen., p. 292, (1625) *Ḥorvot Yerushalem* (Rozen ed.), pp. 98–99; Shemuel Romano was also among the city's notables (1623), *Jewish Community in Jerusalem*, p. 292, n. 8.

8 In conclusion

Through the use of painstaking detective work involving manuscripts, books, and tombstones, we have managed to cast a spotlight on one family. Based on their name, the Romans/Romanos ostensibly had their roots in the city of Rome. But, as the inquiry presented in these pages has shown, from the time their forefathers left their place of origin the family spun a network of marriage, social, and business ties with Sefardi families of similar standing – the cream of Istanbuli Jewish society. The placement of their tombstones in the Jewish cemetery at Hasköy is a reflection of their social status. They are buried among distinguished figures, community leaders, rabbis, and men of wealth. The tombstones of the family members demonstrate refinement and restraint, with a similar level of material and emotional investment in the graves of men and women, young girls and boys, and the elderly. Those who mourned them spared no expense in transporting from afar fine stones that have stood the test of time, and devoted effort and imagination to composing the epitaphs of their loved ones. But what is more, those who bore the Roman name were apparently men of letters, with broad intellectual interests. The libraries of several of them contained books and manuscripts brought over from Spain. At least one of them, Ya'aqov Roman, was a polymath whose knowledge of world literature extended from the culture of the Islamic Golden Age to that of the Italian Renaissance. Indirectly, he became a central figure in the promulgation of the study of the Hebrew language in Christian Europe during the early modern era.

The cemetery alone cannot provide all the wealth of information needed to complete this picture. To do that, it is necessary to assemble all of the details piece by piece; researching Jewish cemeteries is only one part of this puzzle.

9 Appendix 1: Data on the Romano family in Bulgaria

'Central Consistory's (Sofia) 1920–1926 Report – Introduction to the Jewish Community of Kiustendil', *Bulgarian State Archives* (hereafter: BSA), Jewish Community, fond 1568, opis 1, file 8944, p. 2, SN 12, p. 1–3 (2–4), no. 520 in the computerized archives of Bulgarian Jewry, Goldstein-Goren Diaspora Research Center, Tel Aviv University (hereafter: CA). Three members of the Romano family are mentioned in the above report, BSA, Jewish Community, fond 1568, opis 1, file 8944–end, p. 2, SN 13, pp. 1–14 (42–55). In 'Review of Jewish Education' (CA, no. 536), there is a reference to an Albert Romano, born in Plovdiv in 1886. He studied law in Geneva and Sofia, served for twenty years as president of the Zionist Organization in Bulgaria beginning in 1921, and died in Tel Aviv in 1965. He was one of the major activists in the Sofia community on the subject of Jewish education. On 23 June 1932, he is cited as one of the individuals elected to the Consistory (BSA, circular letter no. 1258, dd 23/06/1932, Vidin, fond 9k, opis 1, file 80, p. 36, SN 24; CA no. 6769). See also concerning him: Калев Марчел, 'Алберт А. Романо (1886–1965)', в. Ардити Бинямин, *Видни Евреи в България, Галерия на забравените*, Том I, (Хулон, 1970), сс. 111–121 (M. Kalev, 'Albert A. Romano [1886–1956]', in *Notable Jews of Bulgaria* [in Bulgarian], ed. by Benjamin Arditi, vol. I [Holon-Tel Giborim, 1970], pp. 111–121). Albert Çelebi Romano, born in Plovdiv 15 September 1886, completed medical studies in Vienna in 1912, died in Tel Aviv, Ибен Анави, *Извравени от Эабрвата Пловдевски Медици Евреи 1878–1941* (Шалом, 2009), p. 61 (Ivan Eliezer Anabi-Kalev, 'Albert Çelebi Romano', in *Jewish Physicians from Plovdiv Who Were Not Forgotten, 1878–1941, Memoirs and Documents* [in Bulgarian] [Sofia: Shalom Publishers, 2009], p. 61). Sha'ul Bekhor Romano, born in Plovdiv in 1892, completed pharmaceutical studies in 1949 in Sofia (ibid., p. 106). Romano M. Nissim, born in Plovdiv on 15 October 1878, completed his pharmaceutical studies in Prague in 1906 (ibid., p. 105). In an undated registry of foreign subjects residing in Vidin, three Romanos are mentioned, BSA, Vidin, fond 9k, opis 1, file 27, p. 34, SN 20 (CA, no. 2700). In an undated index of all the correspondence between the Consistory in Sofia and the community of Rouse, the name Romano appears once among all 105 names mentioned there (BSA, fond 163k, opis 1, file 39, p. 61, SN 12; CA, no. 8818). In the 1924–1925 registry of all the needy families in Rouse who received firewood from the community, there is a reference to a Rachelle Romano (ibid., file 33, p. 61, SN 6; CA, no. 8628). In a pamphlet about the Zionist movement in Plovdiv dated 2 February 1928, Preciado Romano is mentioned as one of six names (ibid., file 35, p. 61, SN 8; CA, no. 8708). Yakir (Preciado) Avraham Romano was born in Plovdiv in 1866. A lawyer by profession, he was a leader of the Zionist movement, promoted Jewish education, and was a prominent member of the Jewish community of Plovdiv (A. Romano et al., *Bulgaria*, vol. 10, *Encyclopedia of the Jewish Diaspora* [Hebrew] [Jerusalem: Ḥevrat Enṣiqlopediya shel Galuyot, 1967], see index). His signature also appears as vice-president on the charter of Society for the Settlement of Ereṣ Yisrael, 27 December 1893 in Plovdiv (Jerusalem, Archives of Ben Zvi Institute, 1708 L), where he served as chairman of the city's Zionist Federation beginning in 1898. Died in pre-State Palestine in 1933. See also: Ардити Бинямин, 'Пресиадо (якир)

Аврам Романо (1865–1933)' в Ардити Бинямин, *Видни Евреи в България, Галерия на забравените*, Том I, (Хулон, 1970), сс. 122–27 (Benjamin Arditi, 'Preciado [Yakir] Avraham Romano [1865–1933]', in *Notable Jews of Bulgaria*, pp. 122–27). Dr. Marco Romano was also a leader of the Zionist movement in Plovdiv, a lawyer, and a journalist. He immigrated to pre-State Palestine in 1937, and was among the founders of Kefar Ḥittim (*Bulgaria, Encyclopedia of the Jewish Diaspora*, index). A lengthy list of other Romano family members from the nineteenth and twentieth century is also available (ibid.)

10 Appendix 2: Data on the Romano family in other centres

In the city of Arta in the Epirus region, Teshuva and Ya'aqov Romano are mentioned in a legal discourse dating from 1561 (*Responsa of Maharashdam* [R. Shemuel de Medina] [Lvov, 1862], EH sec. 50). There is a reference to a Shabbetai Romano in Manastir (Bitola), Macedonia (in the present-day New Republic of Macedonia) in the mid-sixteenth century (R. Yiṣḥaq Adrabi, *Responsa Divrei Rivot* [Salonika, 1582], sec. 310). Avraham Romano is mentioned in Skopje in 1672 (Eliyahu Kobo, *Shenei Ha-Me'orot Ha-Gedolim* [Hebrew], pt. 1 [*Penei Yehoshu'a*] [Istanbul, 1739], sec. 23). A list of Jewish families on Neofit Bozveli Street in Bitola, prepared by the '*mukhtar*', Vasil Gyorgiev, apparently just before they were sent to their deaths by order of the Bulgarian Commissariat for Jewish Affairs, contained sixteen names, two of which were members of the Romano family (BSA, Bitola, Macedonia, Jewish Community – List of Jewish Families, fond 664, opis 1, file 7, p. 63, SN 7, no. 18; CA, doc. no. 3125). Included in the list of families demanded by the Commissariat from the Jewish community of Shtip is that of Joya and Shemuel Romano (ibid., Shtip, fond 667, opis 1, file 22, SN 9, p. 65, CA. doc. no. 5205). No date was noted, but the list dates from after 7 November 1942. In Sarajevo, a family of rabbis by the name of Romano is mentioned in the nineteenth and early twentieth century (R. Avraham Mercado Romano, *Sefer Avraham Avraham* [Jerusalem, 1927]). In Salonika, a Meir Romano is mentioned in the mid-seventeenth century (R. Ḥayyim Shabbetai, *Responsa Torat Ḥayyim* [Jerusalem, 2004], pt. IV, sec. 34). In a book of Salonika tombstones, which records 1,858 tombstones from 1492 to 1929, five members of the Romano family are found, the earliest from 1557 (Y. S. Emanuel, *Salonika Tombstones* [Hebrew] [Jerusalem, Ben Zvi Institute, 1968], sections 300, 306, 722, 469, 1590). In the records of the Salonika community, located in the archives of the former KGB in Moscow, are 127 references to individuals with the name Romano out of 50,000 documents that have been analyzed and computerized in the TAU DP (see n. 1 above), all of them from the years 1924–1940.

Minna Rozen

Romans in Istanbul
Part 2: Texts and Photographs

These tombstone inscriptions have been copied as precisely as possible, including the few punctuation marks present (colons). All other punctuation marks added to increase the texts' comprehensibility in Hebrew have been added by the author of this article. Abbreviations have been expanded and explained inside square brackets in the Hebrew and translated in full in English. When the beginning of a new row on the tombstone does not match the beginning in the Hebrew text cited below, this has been indicated by a backward slash. The English text follows the Hebrew text as closely as possible in terms of line designations and punctuation, but also makes certain allowances to increase comprehensibility.

Photograph No. 1

Tombstone of Kalomira, wife of David Romano, d. 5 July, 1583, *Documentation Project of Turkish and Balkan Jewry*, Goldstein-Goren Diaspora Research Center, Computerized Database of Jewish Cemeteries in Turkey, Tel Aviv University (hereafter DP), Hasköy Cemetery, lot #4-2, stone #34, film #32 (18 August, 1988). Stone brought from the Köfeke quarries, some 25 km. from Istanbul airport. The use of the quarries was officially restricted to sultanic palaces and mosques. Nevertheless, the frequency of the stone's appearance in the Hasköy Cemetery at this period attests to the Jewish community's considerable investment in the culture of death.

צִיּוּן קְבוּרַת הָאִשָּׁה
מָרַת קָאלוֹמִירָה אֵשֶׁת
דָּוִד רוֹמָאנוֹ נִפְטְרָה
כ' תַּמּוּז השמ"ג ומ"ך [וּמְנוּחָתָהּ כָּבוֹד].

Tombstone [marking] the grave of the lady
Mistress Kalomira, wife of
David Romano, passed away
20 Tammuz 5343. May she rest in dignity.

Photograph No. 2

Tombstone of Alta Dona, wife of Nissim Romano, d. 20 November, 1704, DP Kuzguncuk Cemetery, lot # F-8, stone # 129, film # 186 (26 May, 1989). Marmara marble, hexagonal prismatic stone, decorated with lengthwise protruding inscription lines divided into twelve parts, each one encircled by a separated decorative frame. A symbolic decorative engagement belt divides the frames in the middle of the stone. Although the deceased is a married woman, it is the 'voice' of her father that 'speaks' in the epitaph, a fact attesting to her youth and possibly to her family's social status.

לִבִּי מְאֹד יֵצַר, עַל כִּי בְּמָקוֹם צַר, כָּלָא בְּעַד יָפְיָהּ.
רוּחִי בְּקִרְבִּי סָר, חֶמְדַּת לְבָבִי מַר בָּכָה, בֹּעֵר'[ה]
הַמַּצֵּבָה הַזֹּאת, וְהוֹמִיָּ'[ה] הִיא, וְשָׁמַע אָבִיהָ לָהּ, הֵעִיר
קוֹלָהּ כַּנָּחָשׁ יֵלֵךְ,[1] כִּי הֶחֱרִשׁ לָהּ אָבִיהָ, בְּמַעֲבֵה הָאֲדָמָה
אֶבֶן סְעִפָּיו יֵשׁ בְּיָדוֹ:[2] מָה אֶהֱמֶה לָךְ הַבַּת הַיְקָרָה!
לְזֹאת יִקָּרֵא סֵפֶר הַקִּינוֹת, ה'ה [הֲלֹא הִיא] הַיְקָרָה מָ'[רַת] אַלְטָאדוֹנָה
נ'ב'ת [נַפְשָׁהּ בְּטוֹב תָּלִין], אֵשֶׁת ה'ר [הָרַב] נִסִּים רוֹמָאנוֹ י'ץ [יִשְׁמְרוֹ צוּרוֹ], ב'ש [בָּא שִׁמְשָׁהּ] כ'ב לְח'[דֶשׁ] /

חֶשְׁוָן,
נִקְטְפָה בַּמַּגֵּפָה שְׁנַת ה'תס'ה ומ"ך [וּמְנוּחָתָהּ כָּבוֹד].

My heart is greatly troubled,
that in such a narrow place, her beauty is eternally imprisoned.
My spirit is despondent within me, I weep bitterly for my heart's delight,
this tombstone burns and yearns, and her father heard her, her voice going forth like a serpent,[3] Now her father is silent for her, in the thick of the earth[4] he has offsprings of stone[5]: What can I coo to you, beloved daughter?

---

1 ירמיהו מו:כב.

2 כלומר, במקום צאצאים יש בידו אבן.

3 Jer 46:22.

4 1 Kgs 7:46.

5 That is to say, instead of descendants, he has stone.

For this will be called the book of lamentations, for she is the beloved Mistress Alta Donna, may her soul rest well, the wife of R. Nissim Romano, may his Rock preserve him, her sun set on the twenty-second of the month of Ḥeshvan. Plucked from among us by a plague in 5465. May she rest in dignity.

Photograph No. 3

Tombstone of Mevorakh Roman, d. 26 July, 1643, DP Hasköy Cemetery, lot #5-5, stone #34L, film #34 (11 September, 1987). Marmara marble, vertical part of monument, which had a horizontal element. The only decoration of this part of the monument is the chiseled simple frame and protruding characters. The horizontal part is decorated by a mihrab recess. A plan of the double monument of Mevorakh Roman and his wife Mazal Ṭov, can be seen in Minna Rozen, *Hasköy Cemetery*, Part 2, p. 79.

לְעֵד כָּל שׁוֹאֵל לְמִי הַמְּעָרָה הַזֹּאת?
לְסוֹף אָדָם תַּחֲשׁוֹב, וְתוֹךְ אֶבֶ'[ן] יַחֲצוֹב,
וְתַכְרִיךְ בַּד תַּעֲטוֹף, וְתַעֲמוֹד עַל פִּתְחָהּ,[6]
וְסוֹף דָּבָר תִּשְׁמַע, בְּקֵץ חֶלְדְּךָ[7] תִּסְמֹךְ,
וְזֶה כָּל הָאָדָם.[8] בְּעוֹדוֹ חַי צוֹפֶה,
רָאָה אוֹתוֹת עֲלֵי אוֹתוֹת, בְּאֶבֶ[ן] גִּיר מְנוּפָּצוֹת,[9]
מוֹרִים וְגַם אוֹמְרִים: עֲבוֹד הָאֵל בְּמוֹעָצוֹת.
כָּל אִישׁ יִכְאַב: שֶׁנִּגְנַז אָב: לְכָל מִשְׁפַּחְתּוֹ הוּא
אָב: הָלַךְ לַעֲבוֹד לָאֵל בְּאָב[10]: ה'ה' [הֲלֹא הוּא] הַיָּשִׁישׁ נָבוֹן
כה'ר [כְּבוֹד הָרַב] מְבוֹרָךְ רוֹמָאן תנצ'בה [תְּהִי נִשְׁמָתוֹ צְרוּרָה בִּצְרוֹר הַחַיִּים], נִתְבַּקֵּשׁ
בִּישִׁיבָה[11] בַּעֲשָׂרָה בְּאָב: בְּיוֹם א' שְׁנַת ה'ת'ג' ו'מ'ך' [וּמְנוּחָתוֹ כָּבוֹד].

---

6 על פי ילקוט שמעוני על שופטים, רמז לח "לוז היה עומד על פתחה של מערה".

7 זמנך.

8 על דרך קהלת פרק יב: יג: "סוֹף דָּבָר הַכֹּל נִשְׁמָע אֶת הָאֱלֹהִים יְרָא וְאֶת מִצְוֹתָיו שְׁמוֹר כִּי זֶה כָּל הָאָדָם".

9 על דרך ישעיהו כז:ט: "לָכֵן בְּזֹאת יְכֻפַּר עֲוֹן יַעֲקֹב וְזֶה כָּל פְּרִי הָסִר חַטָּאתוֹ בְּשׂוּמוֹ כָּל אַבְנֵי מִזְבֵּחַ כְּאַבְנֵי גִר מְנֻפָּצוֹת לֹא יָקֻמוּ אֲשֵׁרִים וְחַמָּנִים".

10 כלומר בחודש אב.

11 של מעלה.

As a witness to all [passersby] who will ask: 'Whose burial cave is this?'
Think of the end of each and every man to be chiseled in stone
and be wrapped in a cloth shroud, as you stand at the entrance [of the cave].[12]
And when all is said and done you will learn; at the end of your days, you may rely [on this fact],
for this is the lot of man.[13] In his lifetime he foresees and beholds a multitude of signs punctured in chalk blocks,[14]
instructing and also reciting: 'Worship the Lord in the councils.'
Every person is in pain: That a father has been entombed: He is a
father to his entire family: He went to worship the Lord in [the month] of Av[15]: For he is the old wise one, the honoured rabbi Mevorakh Roman, may his soul be bound up in the bond of eternal life, who was invited to the [heavenly] academy on the tenth of Av, on the first day [of the week], 5403.
And may he rest in dignity.

---

12 Based on *Yalquṭ Shim'oni* on Judges, *Remez* 38 'Luz was stationed at the mouth of the cave.'

13 Echoing Eccl 12:13: 'The sum of the matter, when all is said and done: Revere God and observe his commandments! For this is the lot of man.'

14 Echoing Isa 27:9 this line contains the hepax legomenon *menupaṣot*, translated above as 'punctured' in order to maintain some of the onomatopoeia found in the Hebrew.

15 There is a play words between *av* which is both the name of a Hebrew month and the Hebrew word for father.

Photograph No. 4

Tombstone of Mazal Ṭov, daughter of Teshuva Roman, d. 2 November, 1644, DP Hasköy Cemetery, lot # 6-5, stone # 28L, film # 11 (6 September, 1987). Marmara marble, horizontal slab decorated with lengthwise protruding inscription lines.

לְזֹאת יִקָּרֵא אֶבֶן הָרֹאשָׁה:[16] לִבְכִי וּלְמִסְפֵּד
לְנַעֲרָה בְּכוֹרָה, יְחִידָה וּמְאוֹרָשָׂה: כִּי לְנְהִי וְאוֹי
נֶהְפַּךְ מְשׂשָׂהּ: וּלְאָב וָאֵם כִּי מָרִים הֵם. אֶל ה לֻקְּחָה
מֵאִתָּם בַּת ט'ו שָׁנָה, יָפָה כְּתִרְצָה:[17] אָב לְזֹאת יֶחֱרַד,
וְאֵם תָּחִיל תִּצְעַק, וְחַיֵּיהֶם לָהֶם לְמַשָּׂא: ה'ה' [הֲלֹא הִיא]
בְּתוּלְתָא כַּלָּתָא כְּלִילַת יֹפִי, מַזָּל טוֹב בַּת
הַנָּבוֹן וְנַעֲלֶה ה'ר' [הוּא הָרַב] תְּשׁוּבָה רוֹמָאן יִץ [יִשְׁמְרוֹ צוּרוֹ], נִקְטְפָה
יוֹם ד כ'ב לְמַר חֶשְׁוָן[18] שְׁנַת ה'ת'ד' ו'מ'ך'[וּמְנוּחָתָהּ כָּבוֹד].

---

16 על פי זכריה ד:ז; מדרש תנחומא (בובר) פרשת תולדות, סימן כ דיבור המתחיל "כתיב שיר", האבן אותה שם יעקב. מראשותיו כאשר נטה ללון בדרכו לחרן, שם הובטחה לו בחלום נחלתו ארץ ישראל. האבן היא יסוד נחלתו (בראשית כח). בארכיטקטורה אבן הראשה היא החולייה העליונה בקשת הבנויה באופן מסורתי. כאשר בונים קשת מלבנים על פיגומים, אבן הראשה היא הלבנה המונחת אחרונה ונועלת את הקשת. בלעדיה הקשת לא תישאר יציבה. כעיקרון, לא רק אבן הראשה חיונית ליציבות הקשת אלא כל חלקיה אלא שלאבן הראשה משמעות סמלית. משמעות השימוש במילים אבן הראשה הינה כי אבן המצבה הזאת היא האבן שנלקחה מבניין חייהם של הורי הנערה, שמבלעדיה אין לבניין קיום.

17 שיר השירים ו:ד.

18 מרחשון הוא שמו העתיק של החודש העברי חשון, ומקורו במילה האכדית "וַרְחֻ-שַׁמְנֻ", שפירושה: וַרְחֻ = יֶרַח, חודש; שַׁמְנֻ = שמיני .בעקבות קריאה מוטעית, כנראה, נקרא החודש ברוב תפוצות ישראל מַר־חֶשְׁוָן, מה שהביא להתייחסות ל"מר" כאל קידומת, ובסוף הביא להשמטתה. בכל בתי העלמין שתועדו בתורכיה מופיעים 3801 איזכורים של חשון ,לעומת 119 של מר חשון (עם רווח בין שני חלקי המילה) ו2271 של מרחשון. בתוך 3801 האיזכורים של השם המקוצר 2700 הם משנת 1800 ואילך. כל האיזכורים של הצורה העתיקה הם מן השנים שלפני 1800, והם מהווים כ22 אחוז מכלל איזכורי החודש לפני שנת 1800. המילה מר בשפה העברית פירושה בעל טעם רע, וייתכן שהשימוש בצורה העתיקה במצבות אלה מרמז לביטוי נוסף של צער.

This will be called a headstone:[19] for weeping and eulogizing
a firstborn child, an only child, a young betrothed maiden: for her joy has been transformed into [cries of] lamentation and wailing: and her father and mother are bitter, for the Lord God took her from them [when she was] fifteen years old, as beautiful as Tirṣa.[20] A father fears this and a shocked mother screams, and their life becomes a burden to them: for she is the virgin bride, the epitome of beauty,[21] Mazal Ṭov the daughter of the insightful and exalted R. Teshuva Roman, may his Rock preserve him, plucked [from amongst us] the fourth day [of the week], the twenty-second of the bitter[22] month of Ḥeshvan 5404. May she rest in dignity.

19 Based on Zech 4:7; *Midrash Tanḥuma* (Buber) *Toledot* 20, s.v. *ketiv shir*, the stone that Jacob placed under his head when he lay down to sleep on his way to Ḥaran; there he was promised in a dream that he would receive the Land of Israel as an inheritance. The stone is the foundation of his inheritance (Gen 28). In the field of architecture, a keystone is the wedge-shaped stone piece at the apex of a masonry vault or arch that is the final piece placed during construction, which locks all the stones into position, allowing the arch to bear weight. Figuratively, it refers to the central supporting element of a larger structure, without which the whole structure would collapse. In this context, the headstone is a keystone taken from the parents without which their lives will collapse.
20 Cant 6:4.
21 Lam 2:15.
22 The articulation Marḥeshvan is a distortion of an original Verah shamnu which derives from the Akkadian. In many cases the word was divided and articulated Mar Ḥeshvan, which brought about the omission of the first part altogether. In all the cemeteries documented by me in Turkey I have found 3801 Ḥeshvans, 119 Mar Ḥeshvans, and 227 Marḥeshvans. Out of the 3801 Ḥeshvans, 2700 are post 1800, all the older forms are pre 1800, and comprise 22 % of all the references to this month in all the forms dating before 1800. The use of the ancient form may be an additional expression of grief.

Photograph No. 5

Tombstone of Simḥa, widow of Teshuva Roman, d. 10 May, 1644, DP Hasköy Cemetery, lot # 6-5, stone # 11L, film # 9 (6 September, 1987). Marmara marble, horizontal stone, with mihrab-shaped decorative frame, and lengthwise protruding inscription. The mihrab shape on a horizontal stone creates the image of a Muslim prayer rug, a form assimilated into the Jewish world of images as a gate of heaven. See M. Rozen, *Hasköy Cemetery Typology of Stones* (Tel Aviv University and the University of Pennsylvania, 1996), pp. 55–61.

כְּבוּדָּה בַּת מְלָכִים, בּוֹר וְשׁוּחָה זְמַן כָּרָה מְקוֹם זֶבַח וּמִנְחָה,
וּבִמְקוֹם מִשְׁבְּצוֹת זָהָב אֲנָחָה, וְתַחַת מַעֲשֶׂה מִקְשֶׁה צְוָחָה,[23]
לְנוּדָהּ צָלְלוּ שַׁעֲרֵי מְנוּחָה,[24] בְּיוֹם פָּסוּ יְמֵי מִשְׁתֶּה וְ'שִׂמְחָה,[25]
הִיא הָאִשָּׁה אֲשֶׁר הוֹכִיחַ ה'[26] בְּאַף וּבְחֵמָה בְּאַחַד הַבּוֹרוֹת, וְנוֹתְרָה בַּת צִיּוֹן
מִתַּחַת לָאָרֶץ מַטְמֻנֵי/
מִסְתָּרִים[27] בְּעַד מְעָרוֹת, וְאֶל מַכְאוֹב כְּבוּדָּה בַת מֶלֶךְ, עֵינַי בְּאֵרוֹת בְּאֵרוֹת[28] לְזֹאת

---

23 מליצה אירונית על דרך תהילים מה:יד: "כָּל כְּבוּדָּה בַת מֶלֶךְ פְּנִימָה מִמִּשְׁבְּצוֹת זָהָב לְבוּשָׁהּ" עם ישעיהו ג:כד: "וְהָיָה תַחַת בֹּשֶׂם מַק יִהְיֶה וְתַחַת חֲגוֹרָה נִקְפָּה וְתַחַת מַעֲשֶׂה מִקְשֶׁה קָרְחָה וְתַחַת פְּתִיגִיל מַחֲגֹרֶת שָׂק כִּי תַחַת יֹפִי".

24 מליצה על פי ירמיהו נא :נט "הַדָּבָר אֲשֶׁר צִוָּה יִרְמְיָהוּ הַנָּבִיא אֶת שְׂרָיָה בֶן נֵרִיָּה בֶּן מַחְסֵיָה בְּלֶכְתּוֹ אֶת צִדְקִיָּהוּ מֶלֶךְ יְהוּדָה בָּבֶל בִּשְׁנַת הָרְבִעִית לְמָלְכוֹ וּשְׂרָיָה שַׂר מְנוּחָה". ורד"ק מפרש שר מנוחה:"שהיה ריע המלך והיה עם המלך בעת מנוחתו לשוח ולהתענג עמו וי"ת כמו מנחה שר תוקרבתא".

25 מליצה על שם המנוחה. על פי אסתר ט:כב.

26 על פי בראשית כד:מד.

27 על פי ישעיהו מה:ג.

28 על פי פירוש אברבנאל (ורשה, 1862) לספר דברים לא, ד"ה "והנה הדבור": "כי שתים רעות עשה עמי אותי עזבו מקור מים חיים לחצוב להם בארות בארות נשברים אשר לא יכילו המים". אברבנאל חיבר את הבארות בדברים עם הבֹּארֹת בירמיהו ב:יג.

יְקָרָא אִשָּׁה/ חַכְמַת לֵב.[29] בָּא שִׁמְשָׁהּ בְּעוֹד יוֹמָם לְיוֹם עֶבְרוֹת[30]/
ה'ה'[הֲלֹא הִיא] עֲטֶרֶת תִּפְאֶרֶת חַכְמוֹת
נָשִׁים[31] מָ'[רַת] שִׂמְחָה נב'ת /[נַפְשָׁהּ בְּטוֹב תָּלִין]
אַלְמְנַת הַנָּבוֹן וְנַעֲלֶה ה'ר' תְּשׁוּבָה רוֹמָאן, נִפְטְרָה יוֹם ג' ד' לְחֹדֶשׁ אִיָּר שְׁנַת ה'ת'ד' ו'מ'ך'/
[וּמְנוּחָתָהּ כָּבוֹד].

The dignity of the daughter of kings: Time has dug a pit and a trench in place of burnt and meal offerings, and instead of clothing embroidered with gold mountings,
there is a groan, and instead of beaten-work, there is a scream.[32] Seeing her plight the gates of pleasure[33] have sunk, on the day that the days of feasting and joy[34] have ended.
She is the woman whom God rebuked with wrath and anger in one of the pits, and the daughter of Zion was left beneath the earth in hidden sepulchres,
hidden forever in caves, and at the injury to a king's daughter's dignity my eyes turn into wells upon wells of tears.[35] For she is a lady/ wise of heart.[36] Her sun has set while there is yet day on the day of wrath.[37] For she is the crown of beauty, the wisdom of women,[38] Mistress Simḥa, may her soul sojourn well, the widow of the insightful and exalted R. Teshuva Roman, passed away on the fourth day [of the week] on the fourth day of the month of Iyar, 5404. May she rest in dignity.

---

29 על פי בראשית ב:כג עם שמות לה:כה.

30 איוב כא:ל.

31 על פי משלי יד:א.

32 Ironic poetical allusion based on a conflation of Ps 45:14 – 'The royal princess her dress embroidered with golden mountings' – and Isa 3:24 – 'And then – instead of perfume, there shall be rot; and instead of an apron, a robe; instead of a diadem of beaten-work, a shorn head; instead of a rich robe, a girding of sackcloth; a burn instead of beauty.'

33 Poetic language based on Jer 51:59: 'The instructions that the prophet Jeremiah gave to Seraiah son of Neriah son of Maḥseiah, when the latter went with King Zedekiah of Judah to Babylonia, in the fourth year of [Zedekiah's] reign. Seraiah was quartermaster.' Radaq (= David Qimḥi) comments that the sentence "Seraiah *sar menuḥa*," translated above 'Seraiah was quartermaster', means that Seraiah was the king's friend, who accompanied the king when he went to take his pleasure (*sar menuḥa*). In the epitaph the words *sha'arei menuḥa* ('the gates of rest') tragically echo Radaq's interpretation of *sarei menuḥa*.

34 A poetical allusion to the name of the deceased.

35 Based on Abarbanel's commentary (Warsaw, 1862) on Deut 31, s.v. *we-hine ha-dibbur*: For My people have done a twofold wrong: They have forsaken me, the fount of living waters, and hewed them out cisterns, broken cisterns, which cannot even hold water" (Jer 2:13).

36 Based on a conflation of Gen 2:23 and Ex 35:25.

37 Job 21:30.

38 Based on Prov 14:1.

Photograph No. 6

Ottoman prayer rug made of wool dated to the 18th century. Brooklyn Museum, Gift of the Ernest Erickson Foundation, Inc., 86.227.120.

Photograph No. 7

The Gate of the İnce Minaret Medresesi (1258–1279) in Konya, Turkey.

Photograph No. 8

Tombstone of Sultana, wife of Shelomo Hamon, and daughter of Moshe, son of Teshuva Mevorakh, d. 13 January, 1648, DP Hasköy Cemetery, lot # 6-5, stone # 10L, film # 9 (6 September, 1987). A Marmara marble horizontal stone, decorated with a sunken mihrab shaped frame, divided into six stylized inner frames. The whole structure combines the idea of a prayer rug and an Ottoman decorated manuscript. The characters of the epitaph protrude from the surface of the stone. This is an expensive monument that had much care invested in it, as testified to by the quality of the stone, the quality of the stone masonry, and the intricacy of the epitaph.

תְּסֻבֶּינָה כְּסוֹב אֹפָן עֲגָלוֹת, יְמוֹת עָמָל וְיַרְחֵי שָׁוְא וְלֵילוֹת,
וּמַשְׂאוֹת שָׁוְא וּמַדּוּחִים[39] בְּרוּחָם, וּמַכְשֵׁלוֹת וּמַחֲלוֹת גְּדוֹלוֹת.
זְמַן בּוֹגֵד[40], מְצוּדָתוֹ פְּרוּשָׂה, וְכָל חֶפְצוֹ לְהִתְעוֹלֵל עֲלִילוֹת,[41]
בְּבֹא עֲפָרָהּ בְּמַעֲמַקֵּי מְעָרָה, וּבִמְקוֹם אַרְמְנוֹת כַּלּוֹת מַחֲלוֹת,
לָנוּד אִשָּׁה בְּלֵב אִשָּׁה, פְּלָדוֹת יָקוּד אִשָּׁהּ,[42] וּבִמְקוֹם שִׁיר יְלָלוֹת,
נְהִי נִהְיָה לְשֹׁד רַעְיָה, וּבְכִיָּה בְּפִי בַּעְלָהּ, וּבְכֶנָּה קוֹל כְּחוֹלוֹת,[43]
כִּי קוֹל נְהִי קִנִים וָהֶגֶה וָהִי,[44] וְקוֹל כְּחוֹלָה[45] עַל כָּל רֹאשׁ קָרְחָה,[46] וּפִי קוֹל יְלָלָה עַל תִּפְאֶרֶת/ :

39 איכה ב:יד.

40 בגידת הזמן באדם היא מוטיב מקובל בשירת ספרד וספרותה וראה למשל את שירו של שמואל הנגיד (993–1056) "זמן בוגד"; שלמה ן' גבירול (בערך 1021–1058) "זמן בוגד"; דון וידאל בנבנישתי (המאה החמש עשרה) ,"זמן בוגד"; ורבינו בחיי בן אשר (1255 עד בסביבות 1340), הקדמה לפירושו על התורה "הזמן כנחל בוגד". ראה
http://www.benyehuda.org/hanagid/index.html; http://www.benyehuda.org/rashbag; http://www.benyehuda.org/benveniste/index.html

41 תהלים קמא:ד.

42 על פי נחום ב:ד עם ישעיהו י:טז.

43 על פי ירמיהו ד:לא.

44 על פי ירמיהו ט:יח עם יחזקאל ב:י.

45 על פי ירמיהו ד:לא.

46 עמוס ח:י.

רוּם כְּבֹדָה, בַּת מֶלֶךְ[47] הָעִיר הַהֲלָלָה,[48] ה'ה'[הֲלֹא הִיא] הַמְּעֻטֶּרֶת מָרַת שׁוּלְטַנָּה אֵשֶׁת הַנָּבוֹן וְנַעֲלֶה ה'ר
שְׁלֹמֹה הָמוֹן/ י'ץ [יִשְׁמְרוֹ צוּרוֹ], בַּת הַנָּבוֹן וְנַעֲלֶה ה'ר תְּשׁוּבָה בכ'ר [בֶּן כְּבוֹד רַב] מֹשֶׁה רוֹמָאן נ'ע' [נוּחוֹ
עֵדֶן], נִפְטֶרֶת יוֹם ב' י'ח לְטֵבֵת/ שְׁנַת הת'ח, קֹדֶשׁ מַצַּבְתָּהּ[49] ומ'ך [וּמְנוּחָתָהּ כָּבוֹד].

Spinning around, like the wheel of a wagon, days of agony and months of futility and nights,
and oracles of delusion and deception[50] deep in their souls, and stumbling blocks and great illnesses.
Time betrays [us],[51] its net is spread, and all it desires is to wreak evil,[52]
When her dust arrives in the depths of a burial cave,
and in place of bridal palaces – ailments,
Because of the disaster that befell his wife, in her husband's heart even iron will be wholly consumed in fire[53]
and instead of song [there will be] wailing,
sounds of lament [will arise] at the disastrous end of his wife, and weeping will fill her husband's mouth, and the crying for her [is like] the sound of women in labour,[54] for a cry of lamentations rises up and that of dirges and woes,[55] and the sound of women in labour,[56] and every head will become bald,[57] and the sound of keening over her exalted honour. Daughter of the king[58] of the renowned city,[59] for she is the crowned one, Mistress Sultana, wife of the insightful and exalted R. Shelomo Hamon, may his Rock preserve him, and daughter of the exalted wise man R. Teshuva son of the exalted Rabbi Moshe Roman, may he rest in Eden. Passed away on the second day [of the week], the eighteenth of Tevet/ the year of 5408 *qodesh maṣavata*,[60]
and may she rest in dignity.

---

47 על פי תהלים מה:יד.
48 על פי יחזקאל כו:יז, ומרמז על כבוד אביה:"בת מלך העיר".
49 ישעיהו ו:יג: "קֹדֶשׁ מַצַּבְתָּהּ".
50 Lam 2:14.
51 The notion of time betraying humanity is a popular motif in Sefardi poetry and literature. See, for instance, the following three poems all entitled *Zeman Boged* ['Time Betrays'] written by Shemuel Hanagid (993–1056), (http://www.benyehuda.org/hanagid/index.html); Shelomo ibn Gabirol (c. 1021–1058), (http://www.benyehuda.org/rashbag); and Don Vidal Benveniste (15th century), (http://www.benyehuda.org/benveniste/index.html). See also R. Baḥya b. Asher (1255–c. 1340) in the introduction to his Torah commentary, *Ha-zeman ke-naḥal boged* ['Time betrays like a stream'].
52 Ps 141:4.
53 Based on Nah 2:4 and Isa 10:16. A play on the words *esh*, 'fire', and *ishsha*, 'woman'.
54 Based on Jer 4:31.
55 Based on Ezek 2:10.
56 Based on Jer 4:31.
57 Based on Amos 8:10. In the Bible, baldness is a sign of grief and catastrophe.
58 Based on Ps 45:14.
59 Based on Ezek. 26:17 and alluding to her father's honourable position with the phrase, 'the daughter of the king of the city'.
60 Based on Isa 6:13. The numerical value of 5408 is expressed in letters by *he-taw-ḥet*.

Photograph No. 9

An Ottoman manuscript signed Darwish ‘Ali, Turkey. Dated 945AH/1539AD, Ottoman manuscript on paper, 150 ff. with 15 ll. of fine black nasta‘liq arranged in two columns, within gold border, opening folio with illuminated header, brown morocco binding with gilt tooled medallions – 7 × 4 1/4 in (17.7 × 10.6 cm). Observed at the auction catalogue of Christies sale 5499, lot 16. 8 October, 2010, London, South Kensington. Reproduced courtesy of Christie’s, Inc.

(http://www.christies.com/LotFinder/lot_details.aspx?pos=5&intObjectID=5360223&sid=)

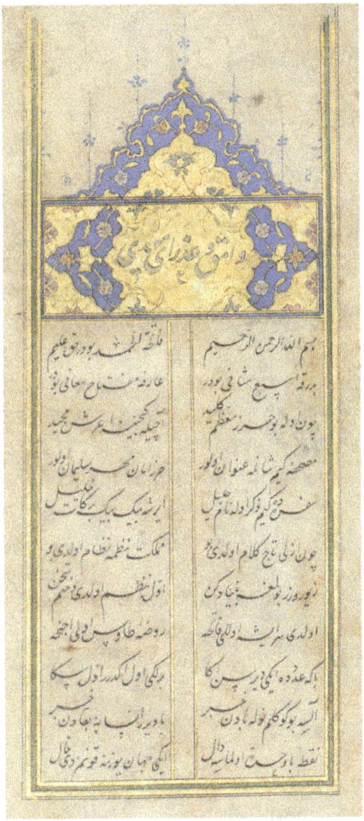

Photograph No. 10

Tombstone of Mevorakh, son of Moshe Roman, d. 23 August, 1648, DP Hasköy Cemetery, lot #5-5, stone #35L, film #34 (11 September, 1987). Marmara marble, heptagonal stone decorated with twelve stylized frames, each pair divided by a different rosette. The characters of the epitaph protrude from the surface of the stone.

לְאֵבֶל נֶהְפַּךְ קוֹל רְנָנִים, וְגַם מִקּוֹל שְׁאוֹנֵי חַיִל שַׁאֲנַנִּים,
בְּעוֹד אֶהְגֶּה הֶגֶא וְקִנִים,[61] וְעֵינַי בִּבְכִי, עֵינַ'[יִם] עֲנָנִים,
אֲהָא נְתָנוֹ בְּאַשְׁמַנִּים,[62] טְמוּנִים פְּנֵי חוֹרְךָ[63] קְצַר יָמִים וְשָׁנִים,
הֲכִינוֹתִי לְךָ חוּפַּת חֲתָנִים, וְיָמִים כּוֹנְנוּ לְךָ בֵּית אֲבָנִים.
לוּ מָצָאתָ פְּדוּתְךָ בְּנִי, תְּהִי לְכָפְרוֹ אַב יְחִידָתִי[64] אֲנִי,
הָהּ יוֹם אֲשֶׁר חָלַף מְשׂוֹשׂ לִבִּי בְּנִי, אוֹמַר לְנַפְשִׁי עַל פְּרֵידָתְךָ אֲנִי.[65]
צִיּוּן קְבוּרַת הַתַּלְמִיד וְנָעִים מְבֹרָךְ נע'[נוּחוֹ עֵדֶן], בֵּן הַמַּר וְנֶאֱנַח הַר'
מֹשֶׁה רוֹמָאן יצ'ו[יִשְׁמְרוֹ צוּרוֹ וְיִגְאֲלוֹ], נִקְטַף יוֹם ו' ו' לְחֹדֶשׁ חֶשְׁוָן שְׁנַת הת'ט.

Sounds of joy have been transformed into mourning, and the tumultuous sounds of terror have frightened serene ones,
While I make woeful sounds and [utter] dirges,[66] and my eyes that have become fountains (due to weeping) become clouded –
Oh! You they have placed among the graves,[67] entombing your noble[68] face that died too young in years.
I prepared a wedding canopy for you, but time prepared for you a house of stone.

---

61 על פי יחזקאל ב:י: "קִנִים וָהֶגֶה וָהִי".

62 קברים ,על פי רד"ק ישעיהו נט:י.

63 יכול להתפרש בשתי דרכים , חורך במובן חיוורונך, או במובן אצילותך.

64 על פי תהילים כב:כא "הַצִּילָה מֵחֶרֶב נַפְשִׁי מִיַּד כֶּלֶב יְחִידָתִי", והמשמעות הינה: לו תמצא נפשך פדות, היא תהיה גם כפרת נפשי.

65 מלשון אֲנִיָּה, קול אבל (ראה איכה ב:ה;ישעיהו יט:ח).

66 Based on Ezek 2:1: 'lamentations and dirges and woes.'

67 'Graves', based on Radaq on Isa 59:10.

68 Because the text lacks the diacritical marks the Hebrew word following the word *penei* can be read *ḥivrekha* or *ḥorkha*. Thus both 'pale' and 'noble' are possible translations. The more likely translation is 'noble'.

If you find eternal rest, my son, may it also be an atonement for your father, my only son[69].
Oh! This is the day on which my heart's joy departed, my son. I say to myself on your departure: Woe is me![70]
The tombstone [marking the grave of] the scholar and congenial person Mevorakh, may he rest in Eden, son of the bitter and groaning R. Moshe Roman, may his Rock and his Redeemer preserve him. Plucked [from among us] on the sixth day [of the week], on the sixth of the month of Ḥeshvan, 5409.

69 Based on Ps 22. Ps 22:21 reads 'Save my life from the sword, my only life from the clutches of a dog'. Here the epitaph means that if the son finds atonement for his soul, he should also function as atonement for his father.
70 In Hebrew a shortened form of *aniyah* – *ani* – is employed to denote lamentation (see Lam 2:5; Isa 19:8).

Photograph No. 11

Tombstone of Teshuva, son of Mevorakh Roman, d. 25 March, 1666, DP Hasköy Cemetery, lot # 6-5, stone # 56L, film # 9 (6 September, 1987), stone brought from Lala Paşa near Edirne, vertical part of monument, which probably also had a horizontal element. The only decoration is the simple protruding frame and the chiseled characters of the epitaph.

בָּעוּ נְבִיעַי,[71] אֵלֵךְ בְּלֹא בָּנִים, אֵין עֵצָה.[72]
נַפְשִׁי נֶאֱסְפָה, גָּוְעָה גַּם דָּאֲבָה.
הִכָּה לִבִּי אַמִּיץ כֹּחַ לְמַלְקוֹשׁ אֵין סוֹף,
בְּגַן עֵדֶן הָלַם עַל בָּנִים גַּם נַפְשָׁם.
נָשִׂים לֵילוֹת כַּיָּמִים עַל מֵשִׂים
לֵילוֹת כַּיָּמִים: וְרוּחַ פְּרִי מְגָדַי
מִכָּל בְּשָׂמִים:[73] גֶּבֶר חָכָם תָּעֹז[74] מִבְּרַק
הָרִים הָרָמִים: מִכְּאֵב כָּזֶה כָּל אִישׁ
קוֹלוֹ יָרִים: בִּבְכִי, כִּי גַּם בֵּן אֵין לִי
בַּשְׂעִפִּים.[75] חַי עַל אֵל אֱלֹד'ים לְגַן עֶדְנוֹ,
הֶחָ'[כָם] הַנַּעֲלֶה ה'ר[הוּא חָרַב] תְּשׁוּבָה רוֹמָאן נ'ע[נוּחוֹ עֵדֶן]/

71 התעבו מקורות דמעותי.
72 "ארבעה חשובים כמתים אלו הן עני סומא ומצורע ומי שאין לו בנים" (בבלי עבודה זרה ה, ע"א). וכן מי שמת בלא בנים קרוי מת (זוהר, ח"ג לד, ב).
73 מליצה ,רוח פרי בטני טובה מכל בושם (על פי שיר השירים ד:י).
74 על פי משלי כד:ה "גֶּבֶר חָכָם בַּעוֹז".
75 במחשבות.

בֵּן ה'ה' [הֶחָכָם הַשָּׁלֵם], ה'ר מְבֹרָךְ רוֹמָאן נ'ע, נִפְטַ'[ר]/
יוֹם ה' ח'י לַאֲדָר ב' שְׁנַת התכ'ו
ומ'ך [וּמְנוּחָתוֹ כָּבוֹד].

My rivers of tears well up, for I will die without sons,[76] there is no counsel.
My soul has been gathered up; it expires and grieves.
The source of great power and unfailing strength has smitten my heart there is no end to the last rains of the season/
in the Garden of Eden it struck on account of [my lack of sons] and their souls.
Days and nights in meditation we shall spend; For him, day and night, let us lament:[77]
And the fragrance of the fruit of my womb is more sweet smelling than any spices:[78]
A wise man will find strength[79] from the lightning of the lofty mountains: Suffering pain such as this, every man in tears will cry out: for I do not even have a son to dream about. Forever alive he will ascend to God, to his Garden of Eden,
The wise one, the exalted R. Teshuva Roman, may he rest in Eden
son of the perfectly wise one R. Mevorakh Roman, may he rest in Eden, passed away on the fifth day [of the week], the eighteenth of Adar II, 5426,
and may he rest in dignity.

76 *b'Avoda Zara* 5a. One who dies without sons is considered dead (*Zohar*, 3:34b).
77 *bMo'ed Qaṭ.* 25b.
78 Poetic language based on Cant 4:10.
79 Based on Prov 24:5: 'A wise man is strength'.

Photograph No. 12

Tombstone of Reina, daughter of Yiṣḥaq Roman, d. 7 October, 1675, DP Hasköy Cemetery, lot #6-5, stone #8L, film #9 (6 September, 1987). Marmara marble, heptagonal stone decorated with twelve stylized frames, divided by a symbolic engagement belt.

לְבַת שַׁמְתִּי בֵּיתָהּ בַּמִּדְבָּר[80] בַּעֲרָבָה, זְמַן שָׁם בִּלְשׁוֹנִי וּבִשְׂפָתַי חַכָּה,[81]
לְזֹאת לִבִּי נִדְכֶּה לְיוֹם, וְלֵיל שְׂרֵפָה, בְּיוֹם דָּרַךְ קַשְׁתּוֹ, וְאֶת מַלְכָּה הִכָּ"ה.[82]
אֲהָהּ בַּת שֶׁכָּרַע הָכְרַעְתְּ עַד נַפְשִׁי דָּאֲבָה! תִּשְׁכַּח יְמִינִי אִם לֹא אֶזְכְּרֵכִי![83]
כִּי עַזָּה כַּמָּוֶת אַהֲבָה,[84] כָּל הַלַּיְלָה נַפְשִׁי הוֹלֶכֶת אֵלַיִךְ, וּבַבֹּקֶר הִיא שָׁבָה.[85]
ה'ה'[הֲלֹא הִיא] הַנַּעֲרָה הַיְקָרָה מָ'[רַת] רֵיינָה בַּת הֶחָכָם הַנַּעֲלֶה ה'ר[הוּא חָרַב] יִצְחָק רוֹמָאן נע[נוּחוֹ עֵדֶן],
נִקְטְפָה יוֹם ג' ב לְחֹל הַמּוֹעֵד שֶׁל סֻכּוֹת התלו ומך[וּמְנוּחָתָהּ כָּבוֹד].

---

80 דהיינו בקבר, על פי מלכים א' ב:לד על רצח יואב בן צרויה:"וַיַּעַל בְּנָיָהוּ בֶּן יְהוֹיָדָע וַיִּפְגַּע בּוֹ וַיְמִתֵהוּ וַיִּקָּבֵר בְּבֵיתוֹ בַּמִּדְבָּר".

81 מושפע כנראה מספר התחכמוני של יהודה אלחריזי, שער שישי בעניין זווג אשה כעורה: "תֵּדַע כִּי אֵין בִּלְשׁוֹנִי רְמִיָּה. וְשׁוּב אָשׁוּב אֵלֶיךָ מָחָר. אַחַר עֲלוֹת הַשַּׁחַר. לְהַשְׁקִיט יְגוֹן לִבְּךָ וְתִילוֹ. וּבֹקֶר וְיוֹדַע ה' אֶת אֲשֶׁר לוֹ. וַתֵּלֶךְ הָאִשָּׁה לְדַרְכָּהּ. וְלִבִּי נִלְכַּד בַּחַכַּת חִכָּהּ".

82 על פי יהושע יא:י.

83 תהלים קלז:ו.

84 שיר השירים ח:ו.

85 על פי אסתר ב:יד.

I made my daughter's house in the wilderness[86] in the waste land,
Time set a trap for my tongue and my lips,[87]
Because of this my heart is oppressed by day and burns at night,
On the day he ['Time'] drew his bow and killed a queen.[88]
Aha! Daughter who is prostrate, my soul will grieve forever.
May I forget my right hand, if I do not remember thee![89]
For love is as fierce as death,[90] the entire night my soul goes [to be with] you and in the morning it returns.[91]
For she is the precious young maiden, Mistress Reina, daughter of the exalted wise one R. Yiṣḥaq Roman, may he rest in Eden. Plucked [from among us] on the third day [of the week] on the second of the Intermediate Days of Tabernacles, 5436.
May she rest in dignity.

---

86 That is to say, in the grave. Based on 1 Kgs 2:34 which records the murder and burial of Yoav ben Şeruya: 'So Benaya ben Yehoyada' struck him down. And he was buried at his home in the wilderness'.

87 The Hebrew word for a trap – *ḥakka* – is very close in sound to the word *ḥika* – 'her palate' – which creats a pun. This line was probably influenced by Judah al-Ḥarizi's *Sefer Taḥkemoni*, sixth gate, regarding the betrothal of an ugly young woman: 'Ah, she smiled, wait till you see her gentleness, this doe that ravens like a lioness; then you will taste of my tongue's truthfulness. I shall be back at dawn to ease your heart and moan: even tomorrow the Lord will shew who are his own. And so she went her way, bearing my heart in her teeth away.' (Judah Alḥarizi, *The Book of Taḥkemoni: Jewish Tales from Medieval Spain*, Eng. trans. D. S. Segal, London: The Littman Library of Jewish Civilization, 2001, p. 75). Obviously, the poetic nature of the translation does not reflect the conflation of images.

88 Based on Josh 11:10.

89 Ps 137:6.

90 Cant 8:6

91 Based on Esth 2:14.

Photograph No. 13

Tombstone of Kalomira, wife of Aharon Roman, d. 12 November, 1683, DP Hasköy Cemetery, lot # 3-1, stone # 58, film # 15* (19 October, 1988). Marmara marble, heptagonal stone, decorated with twelve stylized frames, divided by a symbolic engagement belt, tulips, and rosettes.

צְבִיַּת חֵן וְיָפָה כַלְּבָנָה:[92] וְאִשָּׁה בַּעֲלַת שֵׂכֶל וּבִינָה:
אֲשֶׁר הָיְתָה לְבֵיתִי עֹז וּמִבְצָר: עֲטֶרֶת חֵן בְּרֹאשׁ בַּעְלָהּ[93] נְתוּנָה:
נֶהִי וַ"יְּהִ'י בְּהַ"קְשׁוֹתָהּ בְּלִדְתָּהּ:[94] בְּיוֹם יֵרֵד הֲמוֹנָהּ גַּם גְּאוֹנָהּ:[95]
וְיוֹם לִשְׁכַּב עֲלֵי מִטָּה כְבוּדָּה :בְּגֵשׁ [!][96] עָפָר וְטִיט יָוֵן טְמוּנָה:[97]
עֲלֵי זֹאת אֶצְעֲקָה בֶּכִי וְתַמְרוּר, וְיוֹם יוֹם אֶהְגֶּה מִסְפֵּד וְקִינָה:
יָגַעְתִּי בְקָרְאִי[98] לַיְלָה וְיוֹמָם, שְׁאָגָה כְּלָבִיא[99] לְנֶפֶשׁ חַיָּה:
וַיְהִי בְּלִדְתָּהּ וְהָיוּ תּוֹאֲמִים,[100] נֶהֶפְכוּ/ עָלֶיהָ צִירֶיהָ,[101] תָּחִיל תִּזְעַק בַּחֲבָלֶיהָ,[102] גָּמוּל יָדוֹ הָדָה,[103]
וְכֹחַ אַיִן לְלֵידָה.[104]

---

92. שיר השירים ו:י.
93. משלי יב:ד, "אֵשֶׁת חַיִל עֲטֶרֶת בַּעְלָהּ".
94. מליצה על דרך בראשית לה:יז, אונומטופיאה ב"נהי ויהי".
95. על פי ישעיהו ה:יד:"לָכֵן הִרְחִיבָה שְּׁאוֹל נַפְשָׁהּ וּפָעֲרָה פִיהָ לִבְלִי חֹק וְיָרַד הֲדָרָהּ וַהֲמוֹנָהּ וּשְׁאוֹנָהּ וְעָלֵז בָּהּ". ייתכן שהביטוי 'המונה' מתייחס למי השפיר ,בהשאלה מ"הֲמוֹן מַיִם" (ירמיהו י:יג).
96. צ"ל בגוש.
97. איוב ז:ה עם תהלים מ:ג.
98. תהלים סט:ד.
99. ישעיהו ה:כט.
100. תאומים, על פי בראשית לח:כז-כח.
101. שמואל א, ד:יט.
102. ישעיהו כו:יז:" כְּמוֹ הָרָה תַּקְרִיב לָלֶדֶת תָּחִיל תִּזְעַק בַּחֲבָלֶיהָ".
103. ישעיהו יא:ח.
104. ישעיהו לז:ג.

וָוֵי לְאָזַל אוּרִי לַחֲבָלָא.[105] אֶל/
אֶרֶץ בְּיָדָהּ יָשַׁבְתִּי וָאֶבְכֶּה וָאֶתְאַבְּלָה, יַעַן וּבְיַעַן נִתְפְּרָה הַחֲבִילָה שֶׁחִבְּרָהּ הַיּוֹ"צֵר מְתְחִילָה לִשְׁמָהּ/
וּשְׁאִיָּה:[106] הֲלֹא זאת הָאִשָּׁה עִם בְּנָהּ שׁוֹכֵב מַרְגְּלוֹתֶיהָ, וּבֵן אַחֵר כָּרוּךְ בְּתוֹךְ כְּרָעֶיהָ, הִיא הָאִשָּׁה שְׁלֵמָה בְּתַכְלִית, כְּבוּדָה בַת מֶלֶךְ,[107] וְתִוָּלֵד עֶרְיָה:[108]
ה'ה'[הֲלֹא הִיא] הַיְקָרָה וּצְנוּעָה מָ'[רַת] קָאלוֹמִירָה,/
אֵשֶׁת הֶחָכָם הַנַּעֲלֶה הר' אַהֲרֹן רוֹמָאן נר'ו[נָטְרֵיה רַחֲמָנָא וּפָרְקֵיה], נָפְחָה נַפְשָׁהּ ב'ש[בָּא שִׁמְשָׁהּ] יום ו' כב'
חֶשְׁוָן שְׁנַת נִסְגַּר דַּלְתֵ'י[109] בִּטְנִי/ לפק'[לִפְרָט קָטָן] ומ'ד[וּמְנוּחָתָהּ כָּבוֹד].

A graceful gazelle and beautiful as the moon:[110] A woman of intelligence and understanding:
Who was a stronghold and a fortress for my household:[111] a graceful crown placed on her husband's head:[112]
Woe is me![113] For when her labour was at its hardest:[114] On the day that the tumult [of her waters] came rumbling down and her pride fell low:[115]
The day on which I laid her honour to rest below
Buried in a clod of earth and slimy clay:[116]
On this I will cry out weeping bitterly,[117] and every day I will immerse myself in eulogy and lament:

105 ווי שהלך אורי בחבליה.
106 מליצה כפולה המתחברת לפסוק שלפניה ולפסוק שאחריה, המילה חבלא – במובן חבלי לידה – מתחברת לחבילה, החבילה שחברה היוצר ,האל, שתכליתה הייתה קיום המין, והיא הפכה לשמה ושאיה: האשה שוכבת, ובנה האחד מת למרגלותיה והשני כרוך בין רגליה.
107 תהלים מה:יז.
108 בושת, בניגוד לתחילת התאור של האשה השלמה והכבודה.
109 תמ"ד (1683).
110 Cant 6:10.
111 Amos 5:9.
112 Prov 12:4: 'A capable wife is a crown for her husband'.
113 The word *nehi* – a cry of lament or woe – is found in Jer 31:15.
114 Poetic language based on Gen 35:17. In Hebrew the first two words in the line – *nehi* [Woe is me] *va-yehi* [For when] – demonstrate both alliteration and onomatopoeia.
115 Based on Isa 5:14: 'Assuredly, Sheol has opened its jaws in a measureless gape; And down into it shall go, that splendour and tumult, that din and revelry'. The term *hamon*, translated above as 'tumult' may refer to the amniotic fluid, as alluded to in Jer 10:12–13, 'He made the earth ... *hamon mayim* [rumbling water].' The combination of *hamon* ('tumult') and *gaon* ('pride') echoes a liturgical poem written about Purim by R. Judah Halevi, which is read on the Sabbath before Purim by the Mizraḥi communities, מי כמוך ואין כמוך, מי דומה לך ואין דומה לך ('Who is like you and there is none like you, Who is similar to you and there is none similar to you): 'And when the sea returned to its strength / Pharaoh and his entire multitude (*hamon*) were drowned / for the sea made it difficult for the chariots of his pride (*gaon*) / and he saw that he could not overcome him (Gen 32:26)' (my translation).
116 Job 7:5 and Ps 40:3.
117 Based on Jer 31:15.

I am weary with calling out at night,[118] and during the day I shall roar like a lion for her living soul:[119]
And when she came to give birth, and there were twins,[120] she was seized with labour pains,[121] writhing and screaming in her pangs,[122] a baby sends forth his hand[123] and the strength to give birth was lacking.[124]
Woe is me that my light departed in labour pains.
I sat on the ground next to her and I will weep and I will mourn, since most assuredly the package that the Creator has sown for her from the very beginning has been sown for her destruction:[125]
For this is the woman with her son lying dead at her feet, and her other son wrapped around her knees, she is the perfect woman [maintaining] the honour of the daughter of the king,[126] and nakedness was born:[127]
For she is the precious and modest Mistress Kalomira
The wife of the wise and exalted R. Aharon Roman, may the Merciful One protect him and redeem him, her soul was spent when her sun set, on the sixth day [of the week], the twenty-second of Ḥeshvan, the year of 'the doors[128] of her womb have been closed', excluding the thousands.[129] And may she rest in dignity.

118 Ps 69:4.

119 The phrase *nefesh ḥayya* may also be translated to take into account the rendering of *ḥayya* as midwife.

120 Gen 38:27–28.

121 1 Sam 4:19.

122 Isa 26:17.

123 Isa 11:8. There is a bitter sense of irony in the author's use of this prophetic verse. See *Sifra, Beḥuqotai* 1.2, which fleshes out the ecstatically joyous, messianic message of these words.

124 Isa 37:3.

125 The word לשמה can mean either 'for her' or 'for destruction'. Thus, the phrase לשמה ושאיה, translated above as 'for her destruction', can also mean 'for her and her destruction'. By using the word לשמה the author achieves a double entendre as the package (*ḥavila*) is connected with the labour pains (*ḥavla*) mentioned in the previous line and to the deceased's destruction mentioned in the next line, as the package that God gave to her – designed for procreation – led to her demise.

126 Ps 45:17.

127 In shame, in contrast to the earlier account of the perfect and dignified woman.

128 The Hebrew phrase for 'doors of' (*daltei*) has *the* same numerical value as the Jewish year in which the deceased passed away, 444, if the thousands of years since creation are omitted. That is, she died in 5444 (1683 CE). By linking the number of the year in which she died to a sentence describing her death, special meaning is given to the year in which she died.

129 In the Hebrew, the phrase *li-feraṭ qaṭan* means that this is the enumeration of the Jewish year that omits the thousands of years.

Photograph No. 14

Tombstone of Kadın daughter of Aharon Roman, d. 25 March, 1691. DP Hasköy Cemetery, lot # 5-4, stone # 18L, film # 28 (8 September, 1987). Marmara marble, pentagonal prismatic stone, decorated by four protruding stylized frames and protruding characters.

קִבְרָהּ לְפִי כַּמּוּת: וְהִיא מִתְקַצְּרָה:
שִׂבְרָהּ לְפִי אֱמֶת: וְהִיא מִתְגַּבְּרָה:
רָעָתָהּ כְּמוֹ כַּלֹּ[וֹת]: וְהִיא מִשְׁתַּמְּרָה:
הָיְתָה יְחִידָתִי: וְהִיא מִתְנַכְּרָה:
הָאֶבֶן הַזֹּאת אֲשֶׁר שַׂמְתִּי[130] עָלֵי עֶרְכָּהּ יָעִיד וְלִקְטַנּוּת
אֶל תֵּפֶן, הֲלֹא הִיא כְּרַבַּת בָּנִים אוּמְלָלָה[131] צַהַ [!][132] קָאדוֹן[133]
בַּת הֶחָרָשׁ[הֶחָכָם רַב שָׁלֵם] כמהר [כְּבוֹד מוֹרֵנוּ הָרַב] אַהֲרֹן רוֹמָאן נרו[נָטְרֵיה רַחֲמָנָא
וּפָרְקֵיה], נִפְ'[טַר]
יוֹם א כו לַאֲדָר א שְׁנַת אֶתֵּן לָךְ אֶרֶץ חֶמְדָּה:[134]

She has been buried in accord with her size: And she was tiny:
She earned her true fare: And she won out:
Her bad lot has now quite ended[135]: And she has been preserved forever:
She was my only one: And she has become estranged from me:
The value of the stone which I have placed[136] upon her should testify her worth. Do not pay attention to its size, for she was like the mother of many who is forlorn.[137]

---

130 בראשית כח:כב
131 שמואל א, ב:ה.
132 כך במקור ולא התברר לי.
133 Kadın בתורכית, כלומר נערה צעירה.
134 ירמיהו ג:יט.
135 Proverbs 16:30 (See Rashi and Ibn Ezra), and Esther 7:7.
136 Gen 28:22.
137 1 Sam 2:5. Although she was young, her fate was like the mother of many who is forlorn, because she died before being able to produce any living issue.

Şe[!][138] is Kadon.[139] The daughter of the wise one, the unsullied rabbi, his honour our Master and Teacher Aharon Roman, may the Merciful One protect and redeem him. Passed away on the first day [of the week], the twenty-sixth of Adar I, the year of 'I will give you a desirable land'.[140]

138 The meaning of the Hebrew is unclear and the writer perhaps had in mind the word *zu*, in the sense of 'she is'.

139 In Turkish, this would be *Kadın*, meaning 'young woman'.

140 Jer 3:19.

Photograph No. 15

Tombstone of Kalomira daughter of Aharon Roman, d. 3 October, 1703, DP Hasköy Cemetery, lot #6-2OB, stone #74MA, film #568 (18 January, 1989). Marmara marble, heptagonal stone decorated with twelve stylized frames, divided by a symbolic engagement belt.

אֵיךְ נִגְלוּ כַּנְפֵי גְּאוֹן קִנָּהּ[141] נֶחְפָּה בְּמֵי כֶּסֶף וְאֶבְרוֹתֵיִם:[142]
לֹא עָלָה נַפְשָׁהּ לְמַלֵּט יוֹם: נָפְלָה בְּתוֹךְ רֶשֶׁת שְׁחִיתוֹתֶיהָ:
מַצֶּבֶת קְבוּרַת הַנַּעֲרָה הַמְּאוֹרָסָ'[ה] קָאלוֹמִירָה יְתוֹמַת הֶ"חָ[כָם] הַשָּׁ[לֵם] כְּמ"הָר[כְּבוֹד מוֹרֵנוּ הָרַב]
אַהֲרֹן רוֹמָאן נ"ע[נוּחוֹ עֵדֶן], נִקְטְפָה יוֹם ד' כ'ג' בְּתִשְׁרֵי שְׁנַת ה'ת'ס'ד' ומ"ך[וּמְנוּחָתָהּ כָּבוֹד].

How the proud wings of her nidus were exposed[143] in liquid silver and so [were her] pinions:[144]
Her soul did not manage to escape the day: It was trapped in the net of her corruptions:
The tombstone [marking] the burial [cave] of the young betrothed woman Kalomira, the orphaned daughter of the unsullied wise man, our honoured Teacher and Rabbi Aharon Roman, may he rest in Eden. Plucked [from amongst us] on the fourth day [of the week], the twenty-third of Tishrei, 5464, and may she rest in dignity.

---

141 ירמיהו יג: כב–כו "וְגַם אֲנִי חָשַׂפְתִּי שׁוּלַיִךְ עַל פָּנָיִךְ, וְנִרְאָה קְלוֹנֵךְ" וראה פירושו של הרד"ק הוא משל על כנסת ישראל שהיתה נסתרת תחת כנפי האל ונכבדת בארצה ועתה היא גולה והוסר סתרה מעליה, והנה היא גלויה ונגלה קלונה לעין כל בארצות נכרים. ונראה כרמז על אבריה העירומים שנגלו בעת שנאספה גופתה הטבועה.

142 על פי תהלים סח :יד:"אִם תִּשְׁכְּבוּן בֵּין שְׁפַתָּיִם כַּנְפֵי יוֹנָה נֶחְפָּה בַכֶּסֶף וְאֶבְרוֹתֶיהָ בִּירַקְרַק חָרוּץ:" מרמז על מוות בטביעה.

143 Jer 13:26: 'I in turn will lift your skirts over your face and your shame shall be seen'. See Radaq who notes that this is a metaphor for the house of Israel. The epitaph's author seems to be alluding to the immodest exposure of the deceased's limbs when she was taken out of the water after drowning. The word nidus alludes to her nest, her home, and her private parts.

144 Based on Ps 68:14: 'even for those of you who lie among the cooking pots / [you will be like] the wings of a dove sheathed in silver, its pinions in fine gold.' An allusion to death by drowning.

Photograph No. 16

A colophon of a hand-written kabbalistic prayer-book *Seder Tefillot Yesharot u-Varot* for the winter season (Ḥanuka through Purim; December through March), written by an anonymous scribe in 1734. Quran type illumination done with ink, gouash, and gold leaf. Reproduced courtesy of William Gross, Tel Aviv.

Photograph No. 17

A leaf from an elegantly penned and illuminated copy of the well-known collection of prayers for the prophet Muhammad entitled *Dalā ʻil al-khayrāt* and composed by Muḥammad al-Jazūlī (d. 877 AH/1472 CE). Written on paper in Turkish naskh script, this prayer-book was probably made in the 11th AH/17th century CE.

The Walters Art Museum (Baltimore, Maryland), no. 583. Reproduced courtesy of the Walters Art Museum, Balitmore, Maryland.

Photograph No. 18

Ijazah [License, Authorization, Certificate, Permission], given by Abu Muhammad al-Dhihni 'Uthman Nurī al-Ḥanafī al-Miyāwardī to his student 'Umar Lūtfī ibn al-Ḥajj Muḥammad Ḥilmi known as Munla Isma'ilzadah al Arkhawī. 4 Jumada al-Akhirah 1312 H/3 December, 1894. Reproduced courtesy of the Beinecke Rare Book and Manuscript Library, Yale University.

http://www.library.yale.edu/neareast/exhibitions/exhibit20071.html.

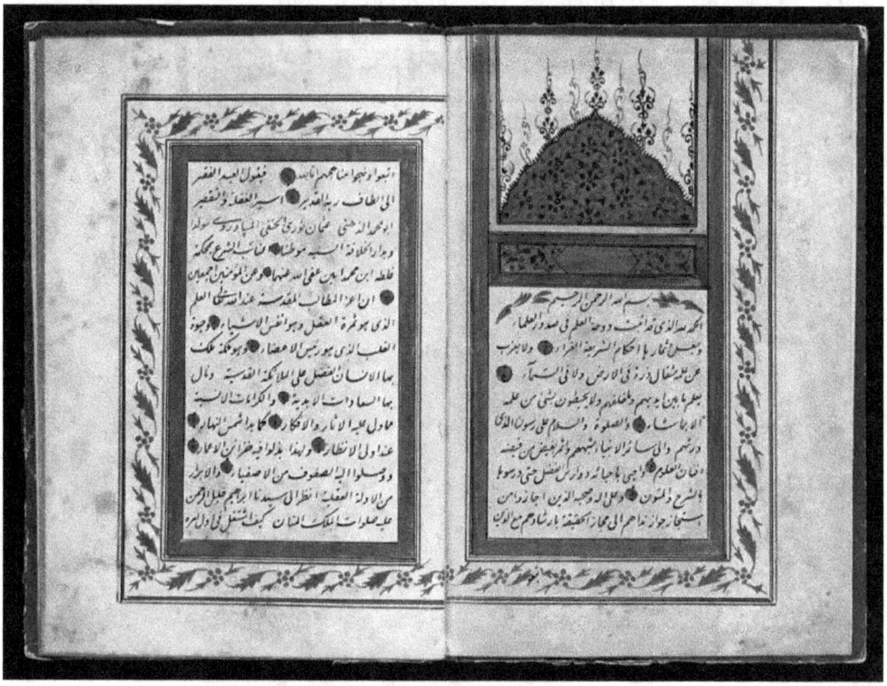

Photograph No. 19

Tombstone of Mikri ('little one') wife of Yehuda Hamon, d. 24 January, 1642, DP Hasköy Cemetery, lot # 6-5, stone # 48L film # 10 (10 September, 1987).

תְּמוֹל אֲנִי מְשַׂחֶקֶת בְּתֵבֵל בְּחֵיק אִישִׁי כְּמוֹ כִּבְשָׂה קְטַנָּה,
וּמַלְאָךְ בָּא טְרָפָנִי בְּזַעְפּוֹ נְתָנַנִי בְּתוֹךְ מִדְבַּר פְּתַנְיָה,
מַצֶּבֶת קְבוּרַת אִשָּׁה חֲשׁוּבָה כְּבוּדָּה בַּת מֶלֶךְ הַמְּהוּלָּלָה, אֵשֶׁת חַיִל עֲטֶרֶת
תִּפְאֶרֶת נָשִׁים, הַגְּבִירָה הַמַּחְצֶבֶת קִבְרָהּ עַל צוּר,[145] הַמַּעֲטִירָה מָרַת מִיקְרִי נ'ב'ת'[נִשְׁמָתָהּ
בְּעֵדֶן תָּנוּחַ],
אֵשֶׁת הֶחָכָם הַנַּעֲלֶה ה'ר' יְאוּדָה הָמוֹן נר'ו[נָטְרֵיה רַחֲמָנָא וּפָרְקֵיה], נִפְטְרָה יוֹם ו' כג לְחֹדֶשׁ
שְׁבָט שְׁנַת
ה'ת'ב'/
ו'מ'ך'[וּמְנוּחָתָהּ כָּבוֹד].

145 "הֲלוֹא אַתְּ הִיא הַמַּחְצֶבֶת רַהַב". על פי ישעיהו נא :ט:

Yesterday I was playing on the earth, in my husband's embrace, like a tiny lamb,[146]
And an angel came and preyed upon me in his wrath, placing me in a wilderness full of snakes.
The tombstone [marking] the burial [cave] of a woman of great consequence,
renowned daughter of the king, a woman of virtue is a crown of glory among women,
You are the woman who quarries her tomb in the rock,[147] the crowned lady, Mistress Mikri, may her soul rest in Eden, wife of the exalted, wise man R. Yehuda Hamon, may the Merciful One protect him and redeem him. Passed away on the sixth day [of the week], the twentythird of the month of Shevat, 5402.
May she rest in dignity.

146 A play on words involving the deceased's name 'Mikri' ('small' in Greek). Also a reference to her tender young age.
147 Based on Isa 51:9: 'Was it not you who hacked Rahab ...'

Indexes

Index of Primary Sources

The Hebrew Bible

as a whole 4, 7 12, 52, 122, 176–177, 190, 204, 207, 208, 255, 265, 340

Genesis
- 2:23 336
- 18:1–22 178
- 22 109
- 24:44 335
- 25:27 112, 207
- 28 304, 334, 351
- 32:26 349
- 35:3 54
- 35:17 349
- 42:1–2 282
- 42:38 177

Exodus
- 20:2 110
- 32:29 61, 62
- 32:13 111
- 34:6 110
- 35:21 255
- 35:25 336

Numbers
- 12:7 120
- 15:2 119

Deuteronomy
- 6:4 79
- 6:5 79, 116
- 10:17 115
- 16:16–17 46
- 18:11 177
- 20:3 206
- 30:12 184
- 31 305, 336
- 31:14 114
- 32:4 79, 83, 84, 91, 94, 112, 113, 132
- 32:39 111
- 33:15 120
- 33:21 118

Joshua
- 11:10 346, 347

1 Samuel
- 2:5 308, 351
- 2:6 109
- 4:19 348, 350
- 25:29 57, 178
- 28 177
- 28:13 178

2 Samuel
- 24:16 111

1 Kings
- 2:34 346, 347
- 10:3 117
- 7:46 329

2 Kings
- 25 67

Isaiah
- 3:24 335, 336
- 5:14 348, 349
- 5:29 348
- 6:13 340
- 10:16 339, 340
- 10:20 111
- 11:4 115
- 11:8 348, 350
- 19:8 343
- 25:9 55, 61
- 26:2 119
- 26:17 348, 350
- 27:9 332
- 30:29 205
- 33:7 120
- 33:16 112
- 37:3 348, 350
- 45:3 335
- 51:9 357, 358
- 52:7 118
- 57:2 118
- 58:12 253, 255
- 59:10 115, 342
- 59:16 263
- 64:3 55
- 64:7 121

Jeremiah
2:13 336
3:19 351, 352
4:31 339, 340
10:10 110
10:12–13 349
13:26 353
31:15 349
32:19 79, 86, 91
40 67
46:22 329
51:59 335, 336
Ezekiel
2:1 339, 342
2:10 340
26:17 340
27:19 116
37:3 176
Joel
2:17–18 112
Amos
5:9 349
8:10 339, 340
Nahum
2:4 339, 340
Zechariah
4:7 304, 334
4:10 110
9:10 118
Psalms
12:2 117
16:11 55
19:10–11 120, 137
22:21 342, 343
25:10 110
40:3 348, 349
45:14 336, 340
45:15 335
45:17 349, 350
47:10 255
48:11 111
51:6 114
68:10 52
68:14 353
69:4 348, 350
78:38 92
79:9 116
79:10 116
80:6 264
80:15 112
81:4 204
90:10 263
92:16 91
95:7 111
112:7 114, 125
115:17 9
118:19–20 140
118:20 310
118:24 61
119:16 120
119:47 120
119:75 114
119:137 115
137:6 346, 347
141:4 307, 339, 340
145 145, 146
145:17 113
145:19 118
150:6 9
Proverbs
as a whole 257, 289
1:14 112
10:7 118
11:26 282
12:4 348, 349
14:1 336
16:30 351
16:31 263, 264
17:6 251
20:27 243
22:9 200
24:5 344, 345
Job
as a whole 226, 256
1:1 285
1:8 253, 255
1:21 86, 91, 125
5:16 253, 255
7:5 348, 349
11:8 108
12:10 111
14:1 253, 255
14:22 178
21:30 336
33:30 232
34:19 113, 114

34:21–22 113
35:5–6 108
Canticles
3:7 263
4:6 120
4:10 344, 345
5:6 52
5:16 120
6:3 137
6:4 334
6:10 348, 349
8:6 346, 347
Lamentations
as a whole 226, 330
1:16 118, 226
2:5 343
2:14 307, 339, 340
2:15 334
5:16–17 226
5:19 121
Ruth
2:11 204
Ecclesiastes
as a whole 235, 256
1:2 257
1:3 111, 257
5:14–15 111
6:6 111, 115
8:4 109, 113
8:8 109, 114
8:15 255
9:9 257, 259
12:7 8, 176
12:13 332
Esther
2:14 346, 347
5:11 253, 255
7:7 351
9:22 335
10:3 261, 264
Daniel
9:9 113
9:14 109
9:19 112
11:45 112
12 xv
12:2 119, 176, 177
Ezra
1:3 53
2 Chronicles
16:9 110
19:7 114
36:23 53

Mishna

as a whole 40, 80, 81, 83, 101, 171, 172, 316
Berakhot
9.2 79, 111, 125
Ta'anit
1.4 175
Sanhedrin
as a whole 172
10:1 51, 171
'Eduyot
1.4 119
Avot
1:2 112
2:10 14
4:16 10

Halakhic Midrashim

as a whole 53, 101, 204, 303, 307
Mekhilta de-R. Ishma'el
Yitro, De-Ba-Ḥodesh, sec. 5 111
Sifra, Levictus
Beḥukotai 1.2 350
Sifre, Deutronomy
Devarim, sec. 307 79
Niṣavim, sec. 304 114
Ha'azinu, sec. 307 79, 115
Ve-zot Ha-Berakha, sec. 353 120

Apocrypha

Ben Sira
44.1 119

Jerusalem Talmud

as a whole 12, 47, 49, 101
Berakhot
5.2 51

Bikkurim
1.4 206
Ḥagiga
2.2 119

Babylonian Talmud

as a whole 47, 49, 101
Berakhot
10a 55
13a 154
17b 43
18a–b 177
18b 177
34b 55
59b 80
Shabbat
88b 52
119b 119
123a 14
152b 57
152b–153a 177
Pesaḥim
50a 149
Rosh Ha-Shana
8a–b 204
Ta'anit
31a 55
Mo'ed Qaṭan
as a whole 49
25b 345
27b 80
Ḥagiga
12b–13a 52, 56–57
Ketubot
111a–b 51
111b 51
Nedarim
12a 67
14a 67
Baba Batra
10b 149
16b–17a 56
17a 11
Sanhedrin
90b–92b 51, 177
91a–b 52, 178
98b 118
Shevu'ot
20a 67
'Avoda Zara
5a 344, 345
17b 79
Ḥullin
141b 291
Tamid
32a 114

Minor Tractates

Semaḥot (Evel Rabbati)
as a whole 49, 80
3.1 80

Aggadic Midrashim

as a whole 53, 101, 204, 303, 304, 307
Alpha Beta de-Rabbi Akiva
[1]90 120
Genesis Rabba
13.6 51
55.5 116
Exodus Rabba
6.1 115
Leviticus Rabba
30.2 55, 56
Numbers Rabba
15.11 55, 56
Deutronomy Rabba
3.1–17, P. 'Eqev 117
11.9 118
Midrash Qohelet Rabba
9.10 149
Midrash Zuṭa
Qohelet, 9 149
Pesikta de-Rav Kahana
as a whole 205
Pesikta Rabbati
1.6 51
Midrash Echa Rabbati
as a whole 206
Midrash Shir Ha-Shirim
as a whole 152
Midrash Tehillim
16.2 58
103.1 55
Pirkei de-R. Eli'ezer
17 112

Tanḥuma
as a whole 119, 304
Toledot, 20 304, 334
Va-Yera, 23 116
Yalquṭ Shim'oni
Exodus, 227 14
Deuteronomy, 940 118
Judges, 38 332

Scriptural Commentaries

Abarbanel
on Deuteronomy
31 336
Baḥya ben Asher
Introduction 307
Ibn Ezra
on Proverbs
16:30 351
Radaq
on Jeremiah
13:26 353
51:59 305, 336
Rashi
on Proverbs
16:30 351

Commentaries on Mishna

Maimonides
as a whole 171–172
Sanhedrin
as a whole 172
R. Shimshon of Sens
Ohalot 18 83

Commentaries on Babylonian Talmud

Beit Ha-Beḥira (Meiri)
on Mo'ed Qaṭan 27b 80
Ḥidushei Ha-Riṭva
on Mo'ed Qaṭan 5b 83
Rashi
on Ta'anit 18b 149
Tosafot Ha-Rosh
on Ḥullin 141b 291
Zohar
as a whole 8, 68
3:34b 306, 344, 345
Zohar – Sitrei Torah
I, 81a 119
Zohar Ḥadash
Midrash Ha-Ne'elam,
20b–21a 119

Codificatory Works

Sefer Ha-Roqeaḥ
as a whole 152
Hilkhot Avelut,
#316 82, 83
Arba'a Ṭurim
as a whole 69
Yore De'a, 376 84
Halakhot (Yeḥiel b. Yequtiel)
as a whole 105
Hilkhot R. Yiṣḥaq (Rits) Ghiyyat
as a whole 81, 82
Kol Bo
#114 84
Levushim
Levush Tekhelet 69
Oraḥ Ḥayyim, 621 151
Maḥzor Vitry
as a whole 94, 105
Mishne Torah
as a whole 172
Laws of Kings and Wars,
12.2 173
Laws of Repentance,
8.2 172
Or Zaru'a
as a whole 204, 205, 210
II, 389 216
Orḥot Ḥayyim
107a 47
Hilkhot Evel 5.11 84
Pardes
23 216
Pisqei ha-Rosh
Mo'ed Qaṭan, 3.87 82
Sefer ha-Ora
II 82
Sefer Ha-Tadir
34, Dinei Ha-Avelut 106
Sefer Ma'ase ha-Ge'onim
#58 82

Sefer (Ha-)Minhagim
as a whole 69, 145
Sefer Minhagim Devei Maharam
as a whole 145, 153
Sefer Mordekhai
Mo'ed Qaṭan, 838 82
Sefer Toldot Adam We-Ḥawah
Netiv 28, II 84
Sefer Yere'im
187a–187b 183
Sefer Yore De'a
as a whole 315
Shibbolei Ha-Leqeṭ Ha-Shalem
as a whole 106, 132, 152
'Inyan Ḥanukka
#192 90
Hilkhot Semaḥot
#13 90
Rosh Ha-Shana
#282 153
Shibbolei Ha-Leqeṭ Ha-Qaṣar
as a whole 106
Shulḥan 'Arukh
Yore De'a, 376, 4 71–72, 77
Teshuvot, Pesaqim u-Minhagim
II, #59 150
Torat Ha-Adam
Sha'ar Ha-Sof, 'Inyan Ha-Hoṣa'a, #25 82
Sha'ar Ha-Evel, 'Inyan Ha-Hatḥala, #46 84
Qoveṣ Minhagim
as a whole 146

Commentaries on Codificatory Works

Darkhei Moshe
as a whole 69
Leqeṭ Yosher
as a whole 190, 191, 192
Yore De'a 84

Books of Ethics, Philosophy and Homilies

Hadrat Qodesh
as a whole 189
Ḥovot Ha-Levavot
as a whole 312, 314
Lewiat Ha-Derekh
as a whole 70
Liqquṭei Maharan
as a whole 10
2.119 10
Maimonides' Treatise on Resurrection
as a whole 172, 175
Milḥemet Ḥova
as a whole 313
Maggid Mesharim
as a whole 8
More Nevukhim
as a whole 313, 314
Nishmat Ḥayyim
as a whole 70
Sefer Avraham Avraham
as a whole 324
Sefer Ḥasidim
35 181
320–321 181
324 9
331 11
335 11
Sefer Ha-Kuzari
as a whole 313, 314
Sefer Hegjon Ha-Nefesch
as a whole 47
Sefer Tiqqun Middot Ha-Nefesh
as a whole 314
Sela' Ha-Maḥloqot
as a whole 313
The Book of Beliefs and Opinions
as a whole 171

Responsa

as a source/literature 71, 72, 81, 216
Hilkhot u-Minhagei Rabbenu Shalom mi-Noishtat
as a whole 69, 184, 189
#2 182
#544 183
Resp. Ba'ei Ḥayyai
I, Ḥoshen Mishpat, #212 320

Resp. Darkhei No'am
#56–57 292
Resp. Divrei Rivot
as a whole 324
Resp. Ginat Veradim
as a whole 292
Resp. Ḥinukh Bet Yehuda
as a whole 70
Resp. Maharashdam
as a whole 324
Resp. Mahari Bruna
as a whole 192
Resp. Mahari Faraji
#23 292
#61 292
Resp. Mahariḥ Basan
#21 297
Resp. Mahariq 193
#37 290
#83 293
Resp. Maharil (including Sefer Maharil)
as a whole 68, 76, 142, 147, 153, 210
Hilkhot Shavu'ot
#39 68
Resp. Maharit
II, Even Ha-'Ezer
#43 291
Resp. Maharitaṣ
#25 291
Resp. Maharshal
#29 117
Resp. Maimonides
#161 81
Resp. Muṣal me-Esh
#2 311
Oṣar Ha-Geonim
Ḥagiga 47
Resp. Penei Moshe
I, Introduction 317
Resp. Penei Yehoshu'a
#23 324
Resp. Ra'anaḥ (Eliyahu ibn Ḥayyim)
#31 292
Resp. Rashi
#189:2 82
Resp. Sefer Ravya
as a whole 207
Resp. Sha'ar Yehoshu'a
#11 316
Resp. Maharam of Rothenburg
as a whole 150
Resp. Maharam Mintz
as a whole 69, 193
Teshuvot Rav Naṭronai
#118 80
#284 80
Resp. Torat Ḥayyim
IV, #34 324

Familial and Communal Chronicles

Chronicles of Eli'ezer bar Nathan 54, 163
Chronicles of Shelomo bar Shimshon 159, 160, 162
Chronicles of the Mainz Anonymous 159, 162
Handbook for William 34
Chronicle of Aḥima'aṣ 118, 119, 123, 128
Nürnberger Memorbuch 189, 201, 215
Pinkas Ha-Nifṭarim of the Jews of Lugo 242, 243, 260
Qore Ha-Dorot 316

Books for the Sick and the Dying

Ma'ane Lashon 8
Ma'avar Yabboq 13, 136
Seder Bikkur Ḥolim 118
Sefer Ha-Ḥayyim 7, 139, 145, 182
Ṣari la-Nefesh u-Marpe la-Eṣem 12

Liturgical Material

Genres

'Aqeda Poetry 163
Piyyuṭ 100, 101, 102, 123, 129, 131, 132, 140, 146, 147, 157–167, 169
Qinot 81, 84, 156–157, 158, 163, 167
Seliḥot 156–157, 158
Silluq 125, 129
Zulatot 145, 156, 157

Poems

Adam Im Yiḥye Elef Shanim 122, 123–129, 132, 134, 135, 139
Afqid Ḥamasi Be-Yad El 132
Amarti She'u 159
Ani Ani Ha-Medabber 166
Avot Olam Yeshene Ḥevron 122
Berit Keruta 164
Elohim Al Domi Le-Domi 157
Ha-Ṣur Tamim Be-Khol Po 'al xv, 99, 102, 107, 123, 128, 129, 140
Ha-Zeman Ke-Naḥal Boged 339,340
Iggeret Ḥatuma Ha-Yom Niftaḥat 126
Mi Kamocha We'Ein Kamocha 349
Mi Yiten Roshi Mayyim 158
Panaw Yaer Ṣur Le-Ḥonnehu 131
Qaddish Le-Itḥaddeta 122, 135, 139, 140
Raḥem Na Alaw El Elohim Ḥayyim 138
Ṣur Mi-Me'ono Ṣaddiq Hu We-Ṣaddiq Dino 138
Treacherous Time (Don Vidal Benveniste) 307, 339, 340
Zeman Boged (Shelomo Ibn Gabirol) 307, 339, 340
Zeman Boged, (Shemuel Hanagid) 307, 339, 340

Prayers and Blessings

'Amida 52, 123
Ahava Rabba 146
Ashrei 145, 146
Av Ha-Raḥamim xvi, 38, 46, 141–154
Barukh Dayyan Ha-Emet 88
Birkat Avelim 81, 84
Birkat ha-Mazon 81
Birkat ha-Shurah 85
Birkat Kohanim 85
El Male Raḥamim 88
Gevurot 52, 57
Hafṭara 101
Hashkava(ot) 84, 97
Hazkarat Neshamot 46, 168, 169
Ma'ariv 101
Minḥa 101
Pesuqei de-Zimra 146
Qaddish 6, 39, 65, 70, 71, 92, 121, 122, 128, 132, 135, 139, 139, 140
Qaddish Yatom xv, xvi, 6, 39, 46, 65–78, 80, 82, 83, 84, 85, 92, 121, 122, 128, 132, 135, 139, 140, 211
Qeriyat Shema' 123
Shaḥarit 101, 157
Ṣidduq Ha-Din xv, 40, 79–97, 99, 140
Taḥanun 82
Yizkor 7, 46, 66, 168

Prayer Books

'Avodat Yisra'el 85
Maḥzor Benei Roma 105
Maḥzor Italian rite –
MS Cambridge, CUL T-S H12.23 125
MS Paris, Bibliothèque nationale héb. 598, fol. 314a. 138
Ms Paris, Bibliothèque Nationale heb. 599 104
MS New York, JTS Library Ms. 8401 105
Seder Ḥibbur Berakhot 105, 125
Seder Rav Amram Gaon 80, 85, 127
Siddur Mi-Berakha Ke-Minhag Q"Q Italyani 138
Siddur Kol Ya'aqov 71
Siddur Rashi 105
Siddur Rav Sa'adya Gaon 80
Siddur Tefillot Kefi Minhag Q"Q Aram Ṣova 85

Liturgical Commentary

Qimḥa De-Avishuna 104

Prayer and Poetry Books

Hod Malkhut 313
Sefer ha-'Anaq
(Moshe Ibn Ezra) 307
Sefer Taḥkemoni 347
Sefer Zekhira 200

Manuscripts

Maḥzor MSS (Anonymous),
Hilkhot Avel 106
MS Paris, Collection Jacques
Mosseri II, 268.2 81
MS Paris, Collection Jacques
Mosseri IV, 157/1 81
MS Cambridge, CUL T-S
H12.23 125
MS Cambridge University Library Or.
1080.9.2 81
MS Manchester, John Rylands
University Library
MS A 53 81
MS Philadelphia University of Pennsylvania
HB Genizah NS12 81
MS Munich, Bayerische Staatsbibliothek
hebr. 232,
Collectanea 105

Others

Eṣ Ḥayim
Hilkhot Evel, ch. 6,
p. 394 84
Ḥokhmat Ha-Nefesh
as a whole 179, 180
Ḥorvot Yerushalem
as a whole 316, 321
Ketav Tamim
as a whole 175
Moznei Mishqal
as a whole 313, 315–316
Qeṣev U-Moznei
Ha-Mishqal 315–316
Sefer Ha-Kawwanot
as a whole 71
Sefer Otiot Ha-Noaḥ
as a whole 313, 316

Christian Primary Sources

New Testament

Luke
16:22 58
16:22–24 206

Prayers

Ave Maria 74–75
Paternoster xv, 74–75
Credo 74–75

Prayer and Custom Books

Liber tramitis 35
Missale Romanum 75
Regensburger Missale 75

Muslim Primary Sources

Quran
as a whole 311, 354
Dalā 'il Al-Khayrāt 355

Index of Names

Abarbanel, Yiṣḥaq ben Yehuda 336
Abelson, Joshua 172
Abrahams, Israel 66–67, 173
Adler, Israel 44
Adler, Joshua J. 177
Alexiou, Margaret 133
Amichai, Yehuda 199
Anaw, family 105, 125
Anaw, Ṣedaqya 106, 125
Andreatta, Michaela 253
Angenendt, Arnold 73
Ariès, Philippe 3, 26–27, 188, 239
Ascoli, Graziadio Isaia 135
Assaf, David 71
Assaf, Simha 80
Assis, Yom Tov 125, 159
Atsma, H. 34
Avida, Y. L. 66, 69
Avitan, Moshe 210
Avneri, Zvi 199, 202, 204, 215
Avraham ben Mordekhai Halevi 292

Baasten, Martin F. J. 104
Baer, Seligman 85
Baer, Yitzhak 59, 159
Bailey, Lloyd R. 173
Banta, F. G. 74
Bar Khalfa, Yehoshua 129
Barak, Nati xvii, 40, 47, 155, 187 ff.
Barber, Paul 174
Barkai, A. 167
Barkai, Ron 188
Bar-Levav, Avriel xiii, 3 ff., 39, 46, 139, 145, 152, 174, 182, 199
Barret, S. 34
Barton, John 177
Basan, R. Yeḥiel 297
Baschet, Jérôme 60, 206
Baumgarten, Elisheva 184, 191, 193–194
Beck, Anton 75
Beeri, Tova 100
Beit-Arié, Malachi 104, 315
Benayahu, Meir 5, 293, 317–319
Ben-Gedalyah, Mataniah Y. 161, 164
Ben-Sasson, Haim Hillel 306
Ben-Sasson, Menachem 306
Ben-Shammai, Haggai 172
Benveniste, Don Vidal 307
Benveniste, Yehoshua ben Yisrael 316
Benveniste, Yehoshua Rafael 317
Berekhia of Modena, Aharon 13, 136
Berliner, Abraham 69, 71
Blau, Moshe J. 106
Bloch, Moshe Aryeh 150
Böcher, Otto 215, 220, 222
Bodel, John 23
Boe, Guy de 32
Bolton, B. 193
Bondi, Jonas 221
Bonfil, Robert 123, 127, 143, 306
Bonora, C. 250, 253
Boynton, Susan 35
Brady, T. A. 188
Braet, H. 74
Braun, Christian Georg 215
Braun, Yisrael 106
Bregman, Dvora ix, xi, 226, 280–281, 286
Brener, Ann 226
Breuer, M. 76
Brink, Laurie 23
Brisk, Asher Leib 292
Brodie, Israel 84, 94
Brody, Robert 80–81
Brown, Peter 21, 24, 27, 31, 174
Bruel, A. 34
Bruna, Yisrael 192
Buber, Salomo 105, 106, 132, 149, 153, 206, 304
Bynum, Caroline Walker 27, 31, 39, 171

Caciola, Nancy 173
Cahana, Isaac Z. 150
Capsali, Eliyahu 293
Carletti, Carlo 246
Carmi, Ted 130, 162
Carmoly, Eliakim 221
Charles, Robert 61
Chazan, Robert 143

Chiarelli, Giuseppe 246
Chodorow, Stanley 25
Cochelin, Isabelle 35
Cohen, J. Joseph 104
Cohen, Kathleen 239
Cohen, Naftali 233
Colafemmina, Cesare 99, 126, 135, 244, 246–247, 276
Colon, Yosef ben Shelomo 193
Colorni, Vittore 247, 276, 279, 281
Cooper, Kate 21
Cooper, S. 189
Cooperman, Bernard D. 247

Dalman, Gustav 66
Dan, Joseph 175, 179, 182
Darnton, Robert 3, 174
David, Abraham 125
Davidson, Audrey B. 17
Davidson, Israel 80, 126
Day, John 177
Demsky, A. 189
Dinter, Peter 35
Dölger, Franz-Joseph 73
Dronke, Peter 140
Dutton, Paul Edward 34

Edbury, P. W. 62
Edwards, Graham R. 37
Effros, Bonnie 22
Eisenstein, Yehuda D. 67, 69, 307
Ekelund, Robert B. 17
Elbogen, Ismar 44, 46, 67–68, 75, 217
Elfenbein, Israel 132
Eliav-Feldon, Miri 167, 188
Elizur, Shulamit 129, 131
Emanuel, Simcha 81
Emanuel, Y. S. 324
Evans, Austin P. 36

Fagan, Teresa L. 37, 174
Fano, Avraham da 275–277
Faraji, Rabbi Ya'aqov 292
Fearotin, M. 75
Feintuch, Israel Z. 106
Feldman, Emanuel 103
Feuer, Avrohom C. 160
Fine, Steven 86
Finucane, Ronald C. 173
Fleischer, Ezra 101–102, 155, 168
Fraenkel, Avraham 101, 155, 163
Fraenkel, C. 48
Franz, Adolf 75
Freehof, Salomon B. 46
Frei, Judith 75
Freimann, Aron 217, 312
Freimann, E. 47
Freimann, Jacob 181, 191
Freistedt, Emil 32, 73
Friedberg, Albert 172
Friend, Robert 171
Fuchs, Uzi 204

Gafni, Isaiah M. 4, 8, 143, 163
Gaguin, Shem Tov 72
Galliano, Joseph Shalom 138
Gardiner, Eileen 34
Garvin, Barbara 135, 247
Gayle Mayor, Alisa 47
Geary, Patrick 34
Geffen, R. M. 66
Gennep, Arnold van 133–134, 192
Ginzburg, Carlo 174
Glaber, Radulfus/Raoul/Rudolfi 36
Glick, Shmuel 4, 65
Goff, Matthew 47
Gold, Avie 160
Goldbacher, Alois 24
Goldberg, Sylvie-Anne 12
Goldberg, David J. 172
Goldberg, Dov 150
Goldin, Simha xi, 149–150, 155
Goldschmidt, Daniel 80, 85, 104, 127, 130
Goldstein, David 289
Goodman, Martin 101, 105
Gordon, Bruce 19
Green, Deborah 23
Green, William Scott 46
Gross, Abraham xvi, 38, 148, 155 ff., 159, 169
Gross, H. 318
Gross, Rabbi Dr. 150
Gross, William ix, 354
Grossman, Avraham 4, 163, 195, 216
Güdemann, Moritz 66, 191, 193
Guggenheim, Yaacov 76
Gurevich, Aaron 173

Guttmann, Julius 173, 177
Gy, P.-M. 73

Habermann, Abraham Meir 59–60, 200
Hacker, Joseph 8, 143, 306
Haddad, Yvonne Y. 171
Hagenmeyer, Heinrich 59, 61
Halevi, Yehuda 314, 316, 349
Halevi, Mordekhai 292
Halkin, Abraham 175
Hamon, Aharon 320
Hamon, Av 319–320
Hamon, Moshe 320
Hamon, Shelomo 298, 307, 310, 319, 339–340
Hamon, Shemuel 318, 320
Hamon, Yehuda 296, 357–358
Hamon, Yiṣḥaq 303
Hamon, Yosef 318, 320
Hanagid, Shemuel 307, 340
Harris, Jay M. 169
Harshav, Benjamin 130, 209
Hartman, David 175
Harvey, Steven 172
Hary, Benjamin 172
Haverkamp, Alfred 165
Haverkamp, Eva 51, 53–55, 58, 60–62, 165, 206
Hazan, Ephraim 100
Hébert, Robert F. 17
Heiming, Odilo 75
Heinemann, Joseph 44, 65, 123
Heinrich, Georg 60
Hen, Y. 167, 188
Hendrix, Julian Montgomery 35
Hering, H. 74
Herman, Marc 172
Hershler, M. 192
Herzog, M. 74
Hezser, Catherine 67
Hill, John Hugh 58–59
Hill, Laurita 58–59
Hill, Rosalind 57
Hoffer, Avraham 66–67
Hollender, Elisabeth 101
Hölzle, G. 74
Howlett, Jana 173
Hrushovski, Benjamin 130, 226
Hübscher, Jacob 65, 68
Hüttenmeister, Nathanja xvii, 40, 47, 213 ff.
Hurwitz, Simon H. 105
Huyghebaert, Nicholas 33
Hyman, Arthur 171

Ignatzi, H.-J. 72
Iogna-Prat, Dominique 36–37
Isserles, Moshe 7, 69, 71, 77

Jacobs, Louis 72
Jacobson, B. S. 46
Jacobson, W. S. 72
Japhet, Sara 175
Jent, Zalman 146–147, 153
Joel, B. I. 80
Jones, A. Christopher 35
Jones, Horace Leonard 22

Kaczynski, Reiner 72
Kahana, Maoz 210
Kallir, Ele'azar 100
Kamin, Sarah 175
Kanarfogel, Ephraim 171, 174–176
Karpinski, Peter 72–73
Kendall, Keith H. 25
Keshales, H. 292
Kessler, Edward 172
Khrisula, Lady 295
Klein, Isaac 66
Klein, M. 193
Kohler, Kaufmann 66
Kraemer, David 80
Krochmalnik, Daniel 105
Kurrein, Adolf 66
Kushelewsky, Rela 70
Kuyt, Annelies 66

Lacerenza, Giancarlo 99
Lamm, Maurice 4, 66
Lampronti, Yiṣḥaq ben Shmuel 72
Landshuth, Leser M. 105
Langer, Ruth xv, 40, 47, 79 ff., 103, 107, 133
Lappin, E. 76
Lavender Fagan, Teresa 37
Lawee, Eric 175
Lehmann, Marcus 215, 221
Lehmann, Oscar 221

Lehnardt, Andreas xiv, 39, 46–47, 80–81, 105, 122, 165, 213 ff.
Lehnardt, Peter Sh. xv, 40, 47, 84, 87, 90, 99, 105 ff.
Lehrn, Abraham 70
Lemaître, Jean-Loup 33
Lentze, H. 74
Lerner, Myron B. 70
Levi, Sali 213–215
Lewin, B. M. 47, 81
Lexer, M. 66
Lieberman, Saul 51–52, 99, 135
Lifshitz, Joseph Isaac xvi, 38, 46, 141 ff.
Linder, Anna 275–276
Liss, Hanna 105
Little, Lester K. 37
Luria, Yiṣḥaq ben Shelomo 5, 70–71
Luzzatto, Samuel David 104, 237

Maimon, A. 76
Maimonides, Moses 12, 47–49, 81, 171–175, 313–314
Maino, G. 275
Malachi, Zvi 131
Malkiel, David xviii, 13, 40, 225 ff.
Malter, Henry 172
Mancinelli, Fabrizio 23
Mandelbaum, B. 205
Marcus, Ivan G. 187
Margaliot, Reuven 68
Marshall, Peter 19
Masterman, M. R. E. 18
McLaughlin, Megan 32
McMullen, Ramsay 21
Menashe ben Yisrael 70–71
Merk, Karl J. 73, 75
Meshullam ben Moshe ben Itiel 220
Migne, Jacques-Paul 60
Millgram, Abraham E. 67
Mintz, Moshe ben Yiṣḥaq 69, 193
Mirsky, Aharon 100, 130
Moellin (Molin/Mulin), Ya'aqov ben Moshe xiv, 68, 71, 142, 147, 182, 210
Mortari, A. 250, 253
Müller, Christiane E. 5
Müller, Karl 74
Müller, Karlheinz 199–200, 204
Munk, Reinier 104

Necker, Gerold 66
Neel, Carol 34
Negev, A. 44
Neusner, Jacob 173
Noble, F. X. Thomas 24
Nulman, Macy 132

Oberman, Heiko A. 188
Obermeyer, Jacob 66, 68
Oexle, O. G. 74
Ohler, Norbert 74
Oppenheimer, Steven 67, 77
Otranto, Giorgio 246

Paone, Michele 246
Paxton, Frederick S. xiii–xiv, 3, 17 ff., 43 ff.
Pendergast, Carol Stamatis 199
Pennington, Kenneth 25
Perani, Mauro ix, xviii, 40, 47, 241 ff.
Petrucci, Armando 239
Petuchowski, Jakob J. 44–46, 77
Pfeiffer, F. 74
Picard, Jean-Charles 36
Poeck, Dietrich 36
Pool, D. de Sola 46, 65, 71
Poso, Regina 247
Press, J. 71

Rabinowitz, L. I. 67
Rado, P. 75
Ranum, Patricia M. 3, 26
Rapp, Ernst Ludwig 214–215, 220, 222
Ravitzky, Aviezer 4, 8, 143, 163
Rawcliffe, C. 193
Rebillard, Éric 20–24, 27–30
Reichman, Ronen 105
Reif, Stefan C. xiv, 37, 43 ff.
Reimer, David J. 177
Reiner, Avraham (Rami) xvii, 10, 40, 47, 199 ff.
Reynolds, Andrew 32
Röcke, Werner 74
Roman, Aharon 299–300, 307, 311–312, 348, 350–352
Roman, Mazal Ṭov bat Teshuva 297, 303
Roman, Mevorakh ben Moshe 298
Roman, Shmuel 291
Romano, Elia 292
Romano, Yosef 292

Rosenfeld, Abraham 160
Rosenzweig, Franz 173
Róth, Avraham Zvi (Ernst) 220
Rousseau, Philip 21
Routier-Pucci, Jeanine 23
Rozen, Minna ix, xix, 41, 47, 289 ff.
Ruh, Kurt 74
Ruland, Ludwig 73

Safrai, Shmuel 103
Salfeld, Siegmund 165, 189, 201, 215, 221
Salomo ben Isaak (Rashi) 80, 82, 105, 132, 149, 152, 216, 221, 351
Sapir, Anna Abulafia 62
Saruq, Menaḥem Ben 132
Satz, Yiṣḥaq 68, 210
Schäfer, Peter 77
Schechter, Solomon 105
Scheindlin, Raymond P. 5, 45
Schiff, Abraham A. 183
Schirmann, Haim (Jefim) 44, 132, 228
Schmelzer, Menahem xi, 100
Schmid, K. 73
Schmidtke, Sabine 171
Schmitt, Jean-Claude 37, 39, 173, 180
Schwarzfuchs, Simon 143, 200, 206
Scodel, Joshua 239
Scribner, R. W. 187–188
Seidel, Katrin 77
Shelomo ben Yiṣḥaq, see Salomo ben Isaak (Rashi)
Shepkaru, Shmuel xiv, 8, 38, 51ff.
Shim'on bar Isaak 101
Shneurson, Barukh 152
Silver, S. L. 67
Silverman, David W. 173, 177
Simonsohn, Shlomo 99, 135, 279, 281, 294
Sirat, Colette 104, 245
Skvarics, Helga 75
Smail, R. C. 62
Smith, Jane I. 171
Smith, Julia M. H. 24
Sokoloff, Michael 103, 126
Soloveitchik, Haim 150
Somerville, Robert 57
Spano, Giovanni 248
Spath, Sigrid 35
Sperber, Daniel 106, 157
Sperka, J. S. 66
Spiro, Jack D. 103
Spitzer, Shlomo Y. 68–69, 142, 145–146, 182, 195
Stevenson, J. 23
Sullivan, Michael 239
Symons, Thomas 35
Sysling, Harry 103

Tabory, Joseph 189
Tasca, C. 248
Ta-Shma, Israel Moses 46, 65, 101, 105–106
Tassis, Carlo de 275–277
Tedeschi, Anne 174
Tedeschi, John 174
Telsner, David 70
Tollison, Robert D. 17
Toynbee, J. M. C. 22
Trachtenberg, Joshua 179
Tracy, J. D. 188
Trani, Yesh'aya di 105, 125
Trapnell Rawlings, Elizabeth 23
Trèves, Simha 231
Trèves, Yoḥanan ben Yosef 104
Tudebode, Peter 58

Urbach, Ephraim E. 166, 173

Valdez del Alamo, Elizabeth 199
Valenci, Lucette 169
Verbke, W. 74
Verhaege, Frans 32
Vest, Bernd Andreas 221
Vezin, J. 34
Volpe, Francesco 247
Vovelle, Michel 239

Wachtel, David 155
Wakefield, Walter L. 36
Weaver, Helen 3, 26, 239
Weinreich, Uriel 66
Wiener, M. 290
Wiesemann, Falk 3, 215
Wigoder, Geoffrey 47
Wistinetzki, Judah 181
Wollasch, Joachim 33, 73
Wright, Alexandra 172

Yaari, A. 46, 50, 195
Yahalom, Joseph 100, 103, 126
Yiṣḥaq of Tyrnau 69

Index of Subjects

Abraham 40–41, 54–56, 58–60, 136, 139, 178, 205–8, 234
afterlife, eschatology, garden of Eden, world to come 3, 4, 6, 9–11, 17, 19, 27, 32, 34–35, 37–38, 51–62, 71, 74, 76, 78, 88, 168, 171–74, 180, 185, 200, 206–7, 210, 232, 236, 239, 306, 311
'amida 52, 123
angel(s), demons 8, 9, 36, 45, 56, 58–59, 89, 136, 138, 140, 143, 152, 171–85, 191, 242, 288, 304, 358
aron ha-qodesh see holy ark (*aron ha-qodesh*)
Arabic 99, 130, 132, 228, 312–16
art, iconography 23, 40, 140, 144, 180, 206, 241, 251–52, 270, 278, 311, 317, 355
Ashkenazi(m) 4–5, 10, 37–40, 44, 46, 53, 59–62, 65, 67, 70–72, 130–32, 140, 142–44, 148, 150–51, 154–57, 163, 165–66, 168, 171, 174–76, 178–80, 182, 184, 187, 189–91, 193–94, 204–10, 213, 216, 221, 223, 238, 241, 265–66, 269, 271–72, 281

Babylonia(n) 4–5, 47, 80–81, 99–101
bankers 251, 271–72, 274–76, 280, 284, 287
Benedictine 18–19, 33, 36
Bible 4, 7, 9, 12, 34, 38, 40, 49–52, 54–55, 57–58, 79, 82, 87–88, 93, 122–23, 130, 132–33, 138, 156, 171, 173–74, 176–78, 180, 190, 207–8, 220, 225–26, 231–32, 236–37, 248, 255, 259, 263–65, 303–5, 308, 314, 340
birkat ha-mazon, Grace after Meals 56, 81, 102
birkat ha-avelim 81, 84
birth, child-bearing, pregnancy 21, 24, 41, 162–63, 191, 193, 208–9, 243, 251, 292, 299, 306–7, 350
Black Death 38–40, 167, 187–89, 194, 201–3, 209
blessing, benediction 49, 52, 56, 74, 79, 80, 86, 88, 123, 145–46, 209–11, 216
burial, funeral, interment 7, 12–13, 22–25, 28, 31–32, 37, 39, 44, 47, 49, 50, 60, 65–66, 80–85, 88, 93, 97, 100, 102–4, 122–24, 126–28, 131–35, 137, 139–40, 161–62, 174–75, 183, 187, 189, 190–95, 201, 203, 213, 215, 243, 261, 264–65, 274–75, 278, 290–94, 297, 303, 309, 320–21, 332, 340, 347, 353, 358
burial society/ies 12–13, 39, 243, 264
Byzantine/um 99–100, 127–28, 139–40

cemeteries 6–7, 11–12, 15, 17, 22–23, 25–26, 32–33, 38–40, 43, 47–48, 81, 83–84, 93–94, 124, 127–28, 132, 162, 183, 199–203, 209, 213–17, 222–23, 225, 238, 241, 243–244, 248–54, 257, 259–61, 266, 268–70, 273–74, 276, 278–83, 286, 289–94, 297–301, 308–10, 312, 321–22, 328–29, 331, 333–35, 339, 342, 344, 346, 348, 351, 353, 357
charitable giving 25, 36, 45–46, 50, 89, 151–52
child/ren 20, 54, 89, 128, 132, 158–60, 171, 178, 182–84, 188, 203, 205, 305, 307–8, 334
child-bearing *see* birth, child-bearing, pregnancy
childlessness 298, 306
Christian/ity 4, 17–41, 43–49, 57–62, 65–78, 88, 90, 100, 131, 143–45, 148, 154, 157, 160, 167, 171, 174, 180–82, 184, 187, 191, 193–94, 206–10, 243, 251–52, 274–76, 278, 286, 289, 313–14, 322
circumcision 102, 131, 184, 191, 251
commemoration, memorialization 19, 24–25, 32–33, 35–39, 46, 48, 65, 68, 72–73, 77, 135, 142–47, 149–50, 152–54, 155–58, 161–62, 165–9, 189, 200–1, 205, 213–15, 220, 222, 229–31, 232, 234–35, 259, 274, 286
conjuration(s) 175, 182–83
conversion 31, 40, 54, 59–61, 143, 148, 150, 205–8, 314

Crusade(r)s 3, 38, 51–53, 57–62, 72, 122, 142–43, 154–56, 162, 165, 167, 200–1, 209, 213, 217, 220

demons *see* angels, demons
dirge (*qina*) 81, 84, 103, 122, 126–28, 132, 340, 158–59, 163, 342
Divine justice *see* theodicy, reward and punishment, divine justice
Divine mercy 21, 40, 88–89, 134, 149–50, 154, 156
Divine names 175, 183
drowning 308, 312, 349, 353

England 202
epitaph, epitaph poem 17, 40–41, 43, 126, 135, 137, 139, 204, 206–8, 211, 225–91, 300, 303–313, 322, 329, 336, 339, 342–44, 353
eschatology *see* afterlife, eschatology, garden of Eden, world to come
ethics *see* moral/ity, ethics
expulsion *see* persecution, expulsion, humiliation

family 9, 13, 19, 26, 34, 37, 47, 83–84, 127–28, 150, 166, 179, 189–92, 207–8, 251, 256, 260, 286, 290, 297, 300, 303, 314
fast/ing 39, 67, 69–70, 73, 93, 146, 157, 175
folklore 187
forefathers, fathers *see* patriarchs, forefathers, fathers
France 45, 82, 85–88, 91, 93, 100, 188–89, 202, 269
funeral *see* burial, funeral, interment

garden of Eden *see* afterlife, world to come, garden of Eden, heaven
Gehinnom 10
genealogy 160, 225, 251
Genizah texts 50, 81, 126–27, 129
Geonim 4, 44, 46–49, 80–83
German 66, 70–71, 74–76, 99, 130, 140, 142, 155–56, 194–95, 200, 213–14, 225–27, 269
ghosts, revenants 38–39, 171–84, 191
Grace after Meals *see birkat ha-mazon*
grave 8, 11–12, 15, 17, 22, 31, 38–39, 40, 43, 51–52, 57, 61, 83–84, 93, 124, 126, 134, 136, 139, 161, 171, 173, 178–84, 189–90, 192–93, 202–3, 215, 217, 233, 235, 240, 264, 292, 297–300, 308, 320, 322, 328, 342–43, 347
gravestones *see* tombstones, gravestones
Greek 22, 27, 29, 127–28, 272, 315, 358

haggada 140
halakha (Jewish law) and *minhag* 4, 5–7, 14, 44, 46, 48–49, 65–73, 76–77, 80–86, 90, 102, 105–7, 132, 138, 140, 142, 144–46, 151–53, 156–57, 168, 173, 177, 181–84, 187–89, 191–94, 210–11, 221, 278, 280, 320
Hebrew language 41, 48, 53, 99, 101, 128, 130, 134, 194–95, 232, 252, 265, 271, 286, 308, 313, 315, 322
historiography 155–56, 160
Ḥol Ha-Mo'ed (intermediate days of a festival) 82, 132, 192, 347
holidays, festivals, high holy days (*yamim noraim*) 6, 7, 46, 80, 82–83, 88, 90, 101, 131–32, 145, 152–53, 157, 204
holy ark (*aron ha-qodesh*) 175–76
Holy City *see* Jerusalem, Holy City
Holy Land *see* Israel, Holy Land, Palestine
humiliation *see* persecution, expulsion, humiliation
iconography *see* art, iconography
illumination 140, 180, 232, 310–11, 341, 354–55
impurity *see* purity/impurity
interment *see* burial, funeral, interment
Islam/Muslim 4–5, 27, 37, 41, 48, 57–58, 61, 77, 148, 171, 230, 310, 317, 322, 335
Israel, Holy Land, Palestine 4–5, 14, 29, 40, 47, 51–52, 61–62, 71, 81, 99–101, 143, 195, 204, 252, 304, 323–334
Isaac 58–59, 89, 124, 136, 139
Italian language 235, 238, 248, 271, 273, 294, 315
Italian rite 71, 81, 84, 99–140
Italy 5, 12, 29, 35, 40, 68, 87, 90, 146, 221, 225–29, 237, 239–90, 293, 315, 317, 322

Jacob 58–59, 136, 139, 304, 334
Jerusalem, Holy City 28, 51, 61–62, 157, 194–95, 216–17, 223, 288, 292, 305–6, 310, 316, 320–21
Jesus 18, 29–30, 60–62

kabbala, mystic/ism 4, 8, 40, 46–48, 69–71, 76–77, 139, 176, 189, 237, 256, 268, 279–82, 306, 311, 354
kindling of lights 66–67, 77, 309

Latin 22, 29, 57, 60–62, 99, 103, 207–8, 220, 222, 245, 272, 275–77, 313–15
law *see halakha* (Jewish law) and *minhag*
liturgy *see* prayers and liturgy

magic 48, 138, 176, 183, 193
maḥzor 85, 92, 105–7, 125
marble 273–76, 280, 285, 308–11, 329, 331, 333, 335, 339, 342, 346, 348, 351, 353
marriage, wedding 24, 41, 58, 95, 102, 131, 137, 145, 159, 181, 189–91, 193, 205, 222, 225, 243, 251, 291–92, 297, 299–300, 304–8, 312, 317–18, 322, 329, 342
martyrs, victims 8, 24, 38–39, 46–47, 53–60, 62, 79, 89, 124–25, 144–47, 149–65, 167–69, 191, 200–1, 206, 210–11, 216, 220, 223
medicine *see* physicians, medicine
Memorbuch 155, 160, 165, 168–69, 215
memorialization *see* commemoration
menstruation 190, 194
messiah, messianic age 51, 55–56, 71, 137, 144, 148, 172–73, 237, 350
midrash 35, 54–58, 101, 149, 190, 204–6, 303–4, 307, 334, 355
mihrab 309–10, 331, 335, 339
minhag see halakha and *minhag*
minyan 6, 13, 183
miṣwa/ot 131
moral/ity, ethics 4, 14, 24, 32, 46, 150, 225, 233, 239, 256
mourning, *shiva‘* 5–7, 40, 45, 49, 65–66, 68–69, 73, 76–77, 80–85, 89–90, 124, 127–28, 132–34, 157–58, 160, 162, 178, 210, 233, 290, 303, 305–6, 309–10, 313, 322, 342, 350
Muslim *see* Islam
mystic/ism *see* kabbala, mystic/ism

Napoleon 260, 265, 278, 280
Ninth of Av 142, 147, 153, 157–58
North Africa 195, 274

Oriental rites 71

palaeography 104, 200–1, 203–4, 265
Palestine *see* Israel, Holy Land, Palestine
Paternoster 74–75
Patriarchs, forefathers, fathers 49, 56, 58, 124, 136, 139, 145, 151–53, 205, 207, 213, 220, 234, 303, 322
persecution, expulsion, humiliation 21, 29, 72, 76, 79, 85, 122, 125, 143–44, 155–57, 160–61, 163–67, 169, 188, 213, 220, 222–23, 243, 248, 269, 274, 276–77, 291, 293, 312, 318
peshaṭ 174
philosophy 4, 7, 12, 46, 172–73, 177, 189, 260, 312–13, 315
physicians, medicine 296, 307, 314, 317–20, 323
plague 72, 188–89, 294, 330
poetry, *piyyuṭim* 4–5, 38, 40–41, 59, 81–82, 86–87, 99–105, 122–33, 140, 143, 146–47, 156–169, 171, 199, 220–21, 225–39, 252–53, 255, 259–61, 263–65, 278, 280, 285–86, 291, 300, 303–8, 311–13, 315–17, 336, 340, 345, 347, 349
Poland 5, 85, 105–6
polemic 59, 67, 138, 143–44, 147, 150, 160, 182, 189, 313
prayers and liturgy 5, 7–8, 12, 17, 19, 30, 32–38, 41, 43–50, 52, 57, 65, 67, 71–75, 77, 80–88, 90, 93–94, 97, 100, 102–7, 122–23, 125, 131–32, 134, 138, 140–69, 204, 209, 211, 232, 239, 243, 310–11, 335, 337, 339, 354–55
pregnancy *see* birth, child-bearing, pregnancy
Provence 188–90, 228
purity/impurity 6, 12, 21, 38–39, 47, 54, 73, 178, 194, 200

qaddish 6, 39, 46, 65–78, 80–85, 122, 128, 132, 135, 139–40, 211

qedusha 102
qina *see* dirge

rabbis 4, 6, 9, 12, 39, 43, 45–49, 51–52, 56–57, 65–72, 79–83, 86–88
revenants *see* ghosts, revenants
revenge 142, 144, 148, 156–57, 168, 209, 211
reward and punishment *see* theodicy, reward and punishment
Rhineland 39, 54, 72, 83, 85–86, 142–44,
rites de passage 13, 106, 133–34, 139, 192
Roman rite 73, 100, 104–7, 125, 127–28, 134
Romaniote rite 85, 317
Rome 23, 28, 105, 137, 140, 233, 241, 244, 270, 289–94, 312, 322
Rosh Ha-Shana 130, 204–5

Sabbath 7, 68, 70, 82, 101, 131, 142, 145–47, 153, 157, 264, 349
saints 17, 31–33, 36, 39, 55, 58, 72, 184
Sarah, Rebecca and Leah 136, 139
scent of the body 180
scholars 21, 26, 37, 43–44, 66, 103, 125, 144, 155, 157, 161, 163, 172–75, 189, 200, 208, 241, 251–53, 312–13, 316
secularization 102, 168–69, 273
Sefardi(m) 40, 70–71, 82–83, 85–90, 175, 189, 231, 241, 243, 265, 267–69, 271, 274, 279, 300, 303, 305, 307, 312–13, 318, 322, 340
seliḥa 124, 156–58, 164–66
Shavu'ot (Pentecost) 142, 145–47, 153, 157
Shekhina (Divine presence) 53, 236
shema' 79, 123
shiva' *see* mourning, *shiva'*
shrouds 11, 180, 303, 332
siddur 80, 85, 94–95, 97, 145, 150, 165, 311
Sivlonot 189, 193
sin 21, 26–29, 31, 39, 71, 124, 151, 161, 181, 305
soul 8–13, 19–21, 32, 34–36, 39, 43, 45, 52–54, 57, 59–60, 68, 71, 74–75, 87, 132, 134, 136–38, 145, 159, 166, 168, 172, 176–80, 183–84, 205, 208, 210, 232–34, 236, 255, 259, 285, 305–7, 330, 332, 336, 340, 343, 345, 347, 350, 353, 358
Spain 5, 12, 39, 82, 84–86, 131, 175, 230, 269, 291, 312–14, 318, 322
suffering 10, 18, 35–36, 60, 157, 305, 345
suicide 32, 38, 40, 150, 164
Sukkot (Tabernacles) 192, 347
synagogue 6–7, 48, 51, 81, 84, 100, 102, 156, 160, 168, 175, 223, 225, 276–77, 319

ṭalit 187, 194
Talmud 12, 14–15, 40, 43, 45, 47, 49–50, 52, 54–56, 58, 80, 101, 105, 149, 172–73, 177, 179, 190, 204, 220
testaments *see* wills, testaments
theology 18, 21, 26, 39, 44–45, 53, 59, 61–62, 73–74, 88, 90, 140, 142–44, 147–48, 161, 180, 215, 225, 260, 313
theodicy, reward and punishment, divine justice 6, 8, 10, 19, 34, 39, 51, 53–55, 57–60, 62, 71, 88–90, 132, 144, 157, 161, 168, 176, 179–81, 305
tombstones, gravestones 10, 40–41, 190–205, 208–11, 213–17, 219–23, 225, 227–28, 237–38, 243, 248–49, 252, 254, 256, 260–61, 264, 268, 270–78, 280, 287–89, 290–94, 297–98, 300, 303–5, 307–12, 316, 320, 322, 324, 327–29, 331, 333, 335, 339, 342–44, 346, 348, 351, 353, 357–58
Torah, Torah scroll, study of Torah 10, 15, 40, 46, 48, 51, 56, 65, 79, 83, 127, 132, 136–38, 145–46, 151, 153, 157, 175, 191, 194, 207, 234, 270, 306, 317, 320
Turkey, Turkish 243, 274, 291, 296, 313, 315, 328, 334, 338, 341, 352, 355

Volksfrömmigkeit 74–77

wealth (riches) 10, 19, 20, 24, 32, 34–35, 234, 251, 255, 264, 271, 274–76, 280, 286, 296, 303, 310, 314–15, 320, 322
wedding see marriage, wedding
wills, testaments 14, 75, 103, 188–91
witch/craft 182, 191
women 32–34, 43, 50, 54, 60, 128, 137–38, 157, 160, 162–64, 178, 181–84, 187–95, 202–5, 208–9, 216, 221, 223, 297, 304–5, 307–8, 311, 322, 329, 336, 340, 347, 349–50, 352–53, 358

world to come *see* afterlife, world to come

yahrzeit 6, 39, 65–73, 75–77
Yemen 128, 195
yizkor, *hazkarat neshamot* 7, 46, 66, 168–69
Yom Kippur (Day of Atonement) 6–7, 101–2, 146, 151–52, 157

zemirot 101

www.ingramcontent.com/pod-product-compliance
Lightning Source LLC
Chambersburg PA
CBHW071810230426
43670CB00013B/2413
* 9 7 8 3 1 1 0 5 5 2 1 6 4 *